THE
YOGA-SYSTEM OF PATANJALI

THE
YOGA-SYSTEM OF PATANJALI

Or the Ancient Hindu Doctrine of Concentration of Mind

EMBRACING

THE MNEMONIC RULES, CALLED YOGA-SUTRAS, OF PATANJALI

AND

THE COMMENT, CALLED YOGA-BHASHYA, ATTRIBUTED TO VEDA-VYASA

AND

THE EXPLANATION, CALLED TATTVA-VAICARADI, OF VACHASPATI-MICRA

TRANSLATED FROM THE ORIGINAL SANSKRIT

BY

JAMES HAUGHTON WOODS

GYAN

Published by

Gyan Publishing House
5, Ansari Road
Daryaganj, New Delhi-110002
Phone: 011-47034999, 9811692060
E-mail: books@gyanbooks.com

Distribution Network
gyanbooks.com
India, USA, Canada, UK, Australia

ISBN: 978-93-6208-778-2 (HB)
First Published, 1914

2nd Impression 2024

Printed at: Gyan Press, Delhi.

THE YOGA-SYSTEM OF PATANJALI
Translator: JAMES HAUGHTON WOODS

THE YOGA-SYSTEM OF PATAÑJALI

Or the Ancient Hindu Doctrine of Concentration of Mind

EMBRACING

THE MNEMONIC RULES, CALLED YOGA-SŪTRAS, OF PATAÑJALI

AND

THE COMMENT, CALLED YOGA-BHĀSHYA, ATTRIBUTED TO VEDA-VYĀSA

AND

THE EXPLANATION, CALLED TATTVA-VĀIÇĀRADĪ, OF VĀCHASPATI-MIÇRA

TRANSLATED FROM THE ORIGINAL SANSKRIT

BY

JAMES HAUGHTON WOODS

PROFESSOR OF PHILOSOPHY IN HARVARD UNIVERSITY

CAMBRIDGE, MASSACHUSETTS

The Harvard University Press

1927

CONTENTS

PREFACE

1. Reasons for taking up the work.—It is not without misgiving that one ventures to render into English the texts of an intricate system which have never, with the exception of the sūtras, been translated in Europe or America. But the historical importance of those texts, as forming a bridge between the philosophy of ancient India and the fully developed Indian Buddhism and the religious thought of to-day in Eastern Asia, emboldens one to the attempt. For this system, together with the Nyāya and Vāiçeṣika systems, when grafted upon the simple practical exhortations of primitive Buddhism, serves as an introduction to the logical and metaphysical masterpieces of the Mahāyāna.

2. Difficulties of comprehending the work.—Even after a dozen readings the import of some paragraphs is not quite clear, such for example as the first half of the Bhāṣya on iii. 14. Still more intractable are the single technical terms, even if the general significance of the word, superficially analysed, is clear. This irreducible residuum is unavoidable so long as one cannot feel at home in that type of emotional thinking which culminates in a supersensuous object of aesthetic contemplation.

3. Difficulties of style.—The Bhāṣya and, still more, the Tattva-vāiçāradī are masterpieces of the philosophical style. They are far from being a loosely collected body of glosses. Their excessively abbreviated and disconnected order of words is intentional. The Mīmāṅsā discussed first the meaning of words (*padārtha*); then in a distinct section the meaning of the sentences (*vākyārtha*); and finally and most fully the implication (*bhāvārtha*) of the sentences as a whole. Wherever the sentence-form is lacking, I have introduced in brackets the words needed to make a declarative clause. Much more obscurity remains in the *bhāvārtha* section of the Bhāṣya. For here many extraneous technical terms are surreptitiously introduced under the guise of exegesis. Thus polemic with an opponent whose name is suppressed

b [H.O.S. 17]

creeps into the argument. The allusions are suggestive, but obviously elusive. The passage at iii. 14 might be quite simple if we had before us the text which it criticizes.

4. Translation of technical terms.—A system whose subtleties are not those of Western philosophers suffers disastrously when its characteristic concepts are compelled to masquerade under assumed names, fit enough for our linguistic habits, but threadbare even for us by reason of frequent transpositions. Each time that *Puruṣa* is rendered by the word "soul", every psychologist and metaphysician is betrayed. No equivalent is found in our vocabulary. The rendering "Self" is less likely to cause misunderstanding. Similarly, and in accordance with the painstaking distinctions made at the end of ii. 5, it is most important to remember that the term *a-vidyā*, although negative in form, stands for an idea which is not negative, but positive. Bearing in mind the express instructions of the text, I have adopted "undifferentiated-consciousness" as the translation of *avidyā*. Another word, which Professor Garbe discussed more than twenty years ago (in his translation of the Sāṁkhya-pravacana-bhāṣya, S. 70, Anm. 1), is *guṇa*. I prefer to translate this term by "aspect" rather than by "constituent", because, in addition to the meanings "quality" and "substance", it often seems to have the semantic value of "subordinate" as correlated to *pradhāna*. Three other words *sattva* and *rajas* and *tamas* seem untranslatable, unless one is content with half-meaningless etymological parallels. In another case I have weakly consented to use "Elevation" as equivalent to *prasaṁkhyāna*; the original word denotes the culmination of a series of concentrations; the result is the merging of the Self in the object of contemplation.

5. Punctuation.—**1.** Quotations from the Sūtras are enclosed in single angular quotation-marks (‹ ›). **2.** Quotations from the Bhāṣya are enclosed in double angular quotation-marks (« »). **3.** Quotations from authoritative texts are enclosed in ordinary double quotation-marks (" "). **4.** Objections and questions by opponents, and quotations from unauthoritative texts, are enclosed in ordinary single quotation-marks (' '). Hyphens have been used to indicate the resolution of compound words. A half-parenthesis on its side is used to show that two vowels are printed in violation of the rules of euphonic combination (Lanman's Sanskrit Reader, p. 289).

6. Texts and Manuscripts.—The text of the sūtras of the Yoga system, like that of the sūtras of all the other five systems, except perhaps the Vāiçeṣika, is well preserved; and there is an abundance of excellent printed editions. The most accessible and the most carefully elaborated of these books is the one published in the Ānandāçrama Series and edited by Kāçīnātha Shāstrī Āgāçe. Variants from twelve manuscripts, mostly southern, are printed at the foot of each page; and Bhojadeva's Vrtti is appended; also the text of the sūtras by itself and an index thereto. Another edition, in the Bombay Sanskrit Series, by Rājarām Shāstrī Bodas, is also an excellent piece of work. I have, however, made use of the edition by Svāmi Bālarāma (Calcutta, Saṁvat 1947, A.D. 1890; reprinted[1] in Benares A.D. 1908) because it is based on northern manuscripts and because of the valuable notes in the editor's *ṭippaṇa*. Of manuscripts, I have collated, with the kind permission of the Mahārāja, during a charming week's visit at Jammu just below the glistening snows above the Pir Panjal, two of the oldest manuscripts in the library of the Raghunāth Temple. In Stein's Catalogue these are numbered 4375 and 4388 and the former is dated Saṁvat 1666. Two other manuscripts were lent me, one by the courtesy of the most learned Gañgādhara Shāstrī, the other the very carefully written Bikāner manuscript, sent to me by the generosity of the Bikāner government, which proved to be extremely valuable for disputed readings in the Tattva-vāiçāradī. This latter manuscript seemed to be about a hundred and fifty years old and is described in Rājendralāla Mitra's Catalogue of Sanskrit Manuscripts in the Library of His Highness the Mahārāja of Bikāner (Calcutta, 1880) under the number 569. An old Shāradā manuscript, which, by the kind mediation of Mukundarām Shāstrī of Shrīnagar, was put into my hands, proved, upon critical examination, to have been so badly corrupted as, on the whole, not to be worth recording.

7. Acknowledgements.—At the end of one's task comes the compensation of looking back to old scenes, and to the friends and helpers who have watched the progress of the book. First of all I remember the delightful

[1] In the reprint, the pagination is unchanged, but the lines vary a little. Hence there are some small apparent inaccuracies in the references. The reprint may be had from Harrassowitz in Leipzig; it is catalogued there as *Pātanjala-darçanasya yoga-tattva*.

visit on the island of Föhr, where, besides the long friendly walks upon the sands, I enjoyed the inestimable opportunity of reciting and reading the Yoga-sūtras with Professor Deussen. The next winter, at Benares, Mr. Arthur Venis opened the doors of the Sanskrit College to me and with the utmost generosity smoothed my way through my first winter in India and initiated me into the methods of many controversial sūtras. Since my return he has always been ready to assist, and I thank him for illuminating for me the perplexing debate on the *sphoṭa* in iii. 17. Besides all this I am most grateful to him for an introduction to the lamented Shrīman Mukunda Shāstrī Adkar, a scholar who has put the wealth of the ancient tradition and his own ripe scholarship at my disposal for many years.

To many other scholars in Benares and in Kashmir and in Poona I wish to express my thanks, especially to Dr. Shripad Krishna Belvalkar and to Mr. V. V. Sovani. To Professor Arthur W. Ryder, of the University of California, I am also much indebted. Furthermore, my thanks are due to Colonel George A. Jacob of the Bombay Staff Corps for his courtesy in searching after quotations, and to Dr. Frederick W. Thomas of the India Office Library for similar favours too many to enumerate or to repay.

My deepest insight into this system and into what little I know of the philosophy of India I owe to Professor Hermann Jacobi of Bonn. Each visit to the little city on the Rhine adds to my debt of gratitude to him and reveals to me the beauty of the scholar's life.

On my return from each visit to India I laid the work in its several stages before Professor Lanman, my teacher in my student days and now my colleague. To him I owe the revision of the manuscript for the press and a comparison of most of the translation, either in manuscript or in proof, with the original. His rigorous criticism has detected many oversights which strike a fresh pair of eyes more quickly than those of the author. For his ready and ungrudging help through many years of intimate friendship my hearty thanks.

JAMES HAUGHTON WOODS.

Harvard University,
July, 1914.

INTRODUCTION

1. Authorship of the Yoga-sūtras.—Identity of Patañjali, author of the sūtras, and of Patañjali, author of the Mahābhāṣya, not yet proved. The opinion in India and in the West that the author of the Yoga-sūtras is also the author of the great grammatical comment upon Pāṇini has not been traced definitely any farther back than to the tenth century. The Yoga-bhāṣya (about A.D. 650 to 850) makes no statement as to the authorship of the Yoga-sūtras, unless the benedictory verse at the beginning be regarded as valid proof that Patañjali wrote the sūtras. Still less is there any statement in the Yoga-sūtras about the author of the Mahābhāṣya. And conversely there is no reference in the Mahābhāṣya to the author of the Yoga-sūtras. On the other hand, there is ground for believing that the author of the Comment on Yoga-sūtra iii. 44 may have had the author of the Mahābhāṣya in mind when he quotes a certain formula and ascribes it to Patañjali. This is the only mention of Patañjali in the whole Comment. The formula is *Ayutasiddha‿avayava-bheda‿anugataḥ samūho dravyam*; and although it is ascribed to Patañjali (*iti Patañjaliḥ*), it has not been found in the Mahābhāṣya. Nevertheless the Yoga-bhāṣya does here seem to contain an allusion, more or less direct, to the theory of the unity of the parts of concrete substances as set forth in the Mahābhāṣya. But the allusion is not direct enough to serve by itself as basis for the assertion that the Yoga-bhāṣya assumes the identity of the two Patañjalis. In other words, it does not justify us in assigning to the tradition of their identity a date as ancient as that of the Yoga-bhāṣya (eighth century). The allusion is, however, significant enough not to be lost out of mind, pending the search for other items of cumulative evidence looking in the same direction.

2. Tradition of identity of two Patañjalis not earlier than tenth century.—So far as I know, the oldest text implying that the Patañjali who wrote the sūtras is the same as the Patañjali who wrote the Mahābhāṣya, is stanza 5 of the introduction to Bhojadeva's comment on the Yoga-sūtras, his Rājamārtaṇḍa. This I would render as follows:

> Victory be to the luminous words of that illustrious sovereign, [Bhoja] Raṇa-rañgamalla, who by creating his Grammar, by writing his comment on the Patañjalan [treatise, the Yoga-sūtras], and by producing [a work] on medicine called Rājamṛgāñka, has—like Patañjali—removed defilement from our speech and minds and bodies.

Bhoja's Grammar, his comment called Rājamārtaṇḍa, and his medical treatise are all extant. The stanza must mean that Patañjali and Bhoja both maintained a standard of correct speech, Patañjali by his Mahābhāṣya and Bhoja by his Grammar; and that both made our minds clear of error, Patañjali by his Yoga-sūtras and Bhoja by his comment upon them; and that both made our bodies clear of impurities, Patañjali by his medical treatise and Bhoja by his Rājamṛgāñka.

This certainly implies that the writer of this stanza identified Patañjali of the Yoga-sūtras with Patañjali of the Mahābhāṣya. If the writer of the stanza of the introduction is the same as the Bhojadeva who wrote the Rājamārtaṇḍa, we may note that he is called Raṇarañgamalla here, Mahārājādhirāja in the colophon in Mitra's edition, and Lord of Dhārā or Dhāreçvara in the colophon in the edition of Āgāçe. There were a number of Bhojadevas; but whichever of them the author of the Rājamārtaṇḍa may be, no one of them is earlier than the tenth century of our era.

The tradition of the triple activity of Patañjali as a writer on Yoga and grammar and medicine is reinforced as follows:

Yogena cittasya, padena vācaṁ
malaṁ, çarīrasya tu vāidyakena
yo 'pākarot, taṁ pravaraṁ munīnāṁ
Patañjaliṁ prāñjalir ānato 'smi.

This is cited in Çivarāma's commentary on the Vāsavadattā (ed. Bibl. Ind., p. 239), which Aufrecht assigns to the eighteenth century. The stanza occurs also in some MSS. just before the opening words of the Mahābhāṣya (Kielhorn's ed., vol. I, p. 503)—that is, not under circumstances giving any clue to its date. We may add that an eighteenth-century work, the Patañjalicarita (v. 25, ed. of Kāvyamālā, vol. 51), vouches for Patañjali's authorship in the fields of Yoga and medicine in the following *gīti* stanza:

Sūtrāṇi yogaçāstre
vāidyakaçāstre ca vārttikāni tataḥ
kṛtvā Patañjalimuniḥ
pracarayām āsa jagad idaṁ trātum.

As to the precise medical work of which Patañjali was the author or with which he had to do, all three stanzas leave us uninformed. Not so the following stanza from the introduction to the commentary on Caraka, composed by Cakrapāṇi, who (according to Jolly's book on Medicine in Bühler's Grundriss, p. 25) wrote about 1060:

Pātañjala-Mahābhāṣya-Carakapratisaṁskṛtāiḥ
mano-vāk-kāyadoṣāṇāṁ hantre 'hipataye namaḥ.

This agrees in sense with the other stanzas, and in addition informs us that Patañjali's medical work consisted in a revision (*pratisaṁskṛta*) of the great compendium of Caraka.

Accordingly, the Bhoja-stanza appears to be the oldest external evidence thus far at hand for the tradition as to the identity of the two Patañjalis, and this tradition is not older than the tenth century, a thousand years and more after Patañjali the author of the Mahābhāṣya.

3. The identification of the two Patañjalis not confirmed by a comparison of philosophical concepts.—Inconsistent use of terminology and conflicting definitions of concepts in the case of a single writer of two books are frequently explained by the fact that quite distinct subjects are discussed in the different works. In other cases the subject under discussion is the same and such an explanation of the inconsistency does not hold. An instance of the latter is the discussion of the nature of substance (*dravya*) in the Yoga-system and in the Mahābhāṣya. In the commentary on Yoga-sūtra iii. 44 we have the following definition, "A substance is a collection of which the different component parts do not exist separately (*ayutasiddha‿avayava-bheda‿anugataḥ samūho dravyam iti Patañjaliḥ*)," and the definition is attributed to Patañjali as being consistent with his sūtras. This quotation is of the most technical kind and is in the same style as the Nyāya-sūtras. A similar use of language, for instance, is found in Nyāya-sūtra ii. 1. 32 (Vizianagaram edition, p. 798). On the other hand this phrase is not to be found in the Mahābhāṣya, which however does repeatedly analyse the concept of substance. And, what is more important, nothing so precise as the formula attributed (iii. 44) to Patañjali is found in the Yoga-sūtras themselves. Yet substance is partially defined in Yoga-sūtra iii. 14, "A substance (*dharmin*) conforms itself to quiescent and uprisen and indeterminable external-aspects (*dharma*)." In this terminology *dharmin* and *dharma* of the Yoga-sūtra are substitutions for *dravya* and *guṇa* of the Mahābhāṣya. In neither case is the description of substance discriminating. Yet such as it is, the difference is very slight. In the Mahābhāṣya it is substance, we are told, which makes the difference in weight between iron and cotton of the same bulk and dimension (Mahābhāṣya, Kielhorn's edition, vol. II, p. 366[19]); and it is that which causes the difference between penetrability and impenetrability. Or again it is that which does not cease to be, even when a succession of properties appears within it (vol. II, p. 366[23]). Of what kind then is this form of being (*tattva*)? The answer is that when the various reds and other properties of a myrobalan fruit, for instance, successively appear within it, we have the right to call it a substance. In short a substance is a concretion of properties (*guṇa-saṁdravo dravyam* *iti*, Kielhorn, vol. II, p. 366[26]); or, as it is put elsewhere, it is a collection of properties (*guṇa-samudāya*) such that the various states (*bhāva*) depend upon it (II. 200[14]). This collection is loosely paraphrased as being a group (*saṁgha*) or mass (*samūha*, II. 356[6]).

In order, however, to make the comparison of the *dharmin* of the Yoga-sūtras with the *dravya* of the Mahābhāṣya, we must assume that the interpretation of the Yoga-sūtras, as given in the Comment, correctly represents the concept in the mind of the author of the sūtras. There might well have been a series of redactions of the works of Patañjali, as of those of Caraka. The later interpretation, such as the formula in the Comment on iii. 44, might give us the original thought in more technical form. If this be so, we find a great similarity in the discussion of the relation of whole and parts in the two works. In the Comment on the Yoga-sūtra iii. 44 a collection (*samūha*) is of two kinds: 1. that in which the parts have lost their distinctness, for example, 'a tree', 'a herd', 'a grove'; 2. that in which the parts are distinctly described, for example, 'gods and human beings.' The second class has two subdivisions: 2[a]. one in which the distinctness of parts is emphasized, for example, 'a grove of mangoes'; 2[b]. one in which the distinctness is not emphasized, for example, 'a mango-grove.' From another point of view a group is twofold: 1. a group whereof the parts can exist separately, for example, 'a grove', wherein the trees exist separately from the aggregate whole; 2. a group whereof the parts cannot exist separately, for example, 'a tree' or 'an atom'. The question now arises, To which of these kinds of groups does a substance belong? A substance (*dravya*) is an aggregate of generic and particular qualities (*sāmanya-viçeṣa-samudāya*). This is the definition of substance from the point of view of its relation to its qualities. Furthermore, the substance is a group of the second subdivision of the second kind; it is 'a collection of which the different parts do not exist separately'. This then is the resultant definition of substance according to the traditional interpretation of the Sūtras.

What now is the relation of whole and parts in the Mahābhāṣya, with especial reference to the substance and its qualities? A collection (*samudāya*) is loosely paraphrased as being a group (*saṁgha*) or mass (*samūha*, Kielhorn, vol. II, p. 356[6]). It is, etymologically at least, a concretion of properties (*guṇa-saṁdrāva* II. 366[26]). It is a collection of parts; the characteristics of the parts determine the characteristics of the whole (III. 3[14]; *avayavāir arthavadbhiḥ samudāyā apy arthavanto bhavanti* I. 217[16]; I. 30[26-27]; *avayave kṛtaṁ liṅgaṁ samudāyasya viçeṣakaṁ bhavati* I. 289[2f]; and I. 377[11]). All these cases would belong to the first subdivision of the second kind of group, whereof the parts can exist separately.

Yet a collection (*samudāya*) is not merely an assemblage of parts, but is a unity performing functions which the parts by themselves cannot perform, for example, the blanket, the rope, the chariot, as compared with the threads, the fibres, the chariot-parts, I. 220[16–23]. All these cases would belong to the second subdivision of the second kind of group, wherein the parts cannot exist separately (*ayutasiddhāvayava*). Such then are the different groups (*samudāya*).

With regard to the substance (*dravya*), its relation to its qualities (*guṇa*) is analogous to the relation of the parts to the group, I. 220, vārt. 11.

Just as a collection (*samudāya*) is characterized by its parts (*avayavātmaka*) III. 3[14], so the substance (*dravya*) is characterized by its qualities (*guṇātmaka*) or is a collection of qualities (*guṇasamudāya*) II. 200[13]. This last formula is given tentatively as a not quite final conclusion; yet the definition is not rejected. And elsewhere, I. 411[15], II. 356[17], II. 415[13], and especially II. 366[14–26], it is accepted as a working definition. Some qualities like sound, touch, colour, and taste belong to all substances; they at least are present I. 246[ff], II. 198[5ff]. Nothing, however, is said about a generic-form being required to constitute a substance (*dravya*). At the most it is true that when one asserts the reality of a species (*ākṛti*) one does not deny the reality of the substance (*dravya*); and conversely. For each person who makes the assertion, the reality of both is asserted. Either the species or the substance may be dominant in anything, and the other subordinate. It is only a matter of the relative emphasis in the use of words. But the word substance is used for mass of particular qualities; it is not a concretion of species and qualities, but is contrasted with species. Accordingly even if we admit that the formula ascribed to Patañjali in the Comment on iii. 13 is the correct rendering of the thought in the mind of Patañjali, the author of the Yoga-sūtra, it is not true that Patañjali, the author of the Mahābhāṣya, when speaking of a substance (*dravya*) means what is contained in this formula. And there is nothing here to indicate that the tradition which identifies the two Patañjalis must be correct.

4. Date of the Yoga-sūtras between A.D. 300 and A.D. 500.—If Patañjali, the author of the Mahābhāṣya, is not the author of the Yoga-sūtras, when were they written? The polemic in the Yoga-sūtras themselves against the *nirālambana* school of Buddhists gives the answer. Very probably in the two Yoga-sūtras iii. 14 and 15 and certainly in iv. 14 to 21 this school is attacked. The idealism of the *Vijñāna-vāda* is attacked in iv. 15, 16, and 17. We cannot, it is true, maintain that the *Vijñāna-vāda* here attacked by the Sūtra must be the idealism of Vasubandhu. But the probability that the idealism is Vasubandhu's is great. And the earlier limit would then be the fourth century. There surely were idealists before him, just as there were pre-Patañjalan philosophers of yoga. Yet we have the great authority of Vācaspatimiçra to support the obvious probability that the school of *Vijñānavādins* is here combated by Patañjali. He accepts the interpretation of the Comment which introduces a *Vijñānavādinaṁ Vāināçikam* (p. 292[17], Calc. ed.) as being intended by the author of the Sūtra. It is true that the Sūtra itself obviously does not make explicit references to this or any other school. Still the fact remains that the Sūtra is attacking some idealist; that the Comment explicitly states the idealist's position; and that Vācaspatimiçra identifies the idealist as being a *Vijñānavādin*. Elsewhere Vācaspatimiçra contrasts this school with other Buddhist schools. And the possibility that he is referring to some *Vijñāna-vāda* other than Vasubandhu's is remote. If this be so, it becomes clearer why Nāgārjuna (a little before A.D. 200), the great expounder of the *Çūnya-vāda*, does not, so far as we have discovered in the portion of the Mūlamadhyamika-kārikās thus far published (fasc. I–V), mention Patañjali. Yet from the Chinese translations of Nāgārjuna it is clear that he was familiar with the philosophical yoga. For example in the Chinese translation,[1] made in A.D. 472, of Nāgārjuna's Upāyakāuçalyahṛdaya-çāstra (Nanjio, No. 1257), eight schools of philosophers and logicians are enumerated: 1. Fire-worshippers, 2. Mīmāṅsakas, 3. Vāiçeṣikas, 4. Sāṁkhya, 5. Yoga, 6. Nirgranthas, 7. Monists, 8. Pluralists. There was then a philosophical school of Yoga about A.D. 200.[2] Patañjali was not unknown to Buddhist writers. But there is nothing to indicate that Nāgārjuna is referring to Patañjali, the philosopher, who would then have preceded both *nirālambana* schools. More probably, we may suppose, he refers to some one of the authorities on Yoga, such as Jāigīṣavya or Pañcaçikha who are quoted in the Yoga-bhāṣya.

With regard to the later limit, a reference, if historically sound, would make it certain that Patañjali lived before A.D. 400. In the Mahāvaṅsa, chap. 37, vs. 167 (Turnour, p. 250; compare Dines Andersen, Pāli Reader, I, p. 113, st. 3), we have the words

> *Vihāram ekam āgamma rattiṁ Pātañjalī-mataṁ*
> *parivatteti.*

The verse refers to Buddhaghosa, who lived in the first half of the fifth

[1] I am indebted to the Rev. Kentoku Hori of Tokyo for this reference.

[2] Professor Jacobi has proved the existence of a philosophical Yoga system, resting upon logical inferences and not upon intuitive processes, as early as 300 B.C. (SB. der königl. preuss. Ak. der Wiss., 13. Juli 1911).

century. But unfortunately the Mahāvaṅsa proper, the work of Mahānāma, ends, according to the judgement of Professor Geiger, at chapter 37, verse 50, at which point also the ṭīkā stops. The quotation therefore belongs to the Cūlavaṅsa. And if, as Professor Geiger concludes, the work of Mahānāma is to be placed in the first quarter of the sixth century, the verse in question comes later, and probably later to such a degree that its value as evidence is almost nothing. If this be so, one can easily explain how it is that Buddhaghosa in the whole Visuddhimagga and in the Atthasālinī makes no allusion to Patañjali.

Much more conclusive is the fact that Umāsvāti in his Tattvārthādhigama-sūtra ii. 52 refers to Yoga-sūtra iii. 22. There can be little doubt of the reference since Umāsvāti's Bhāṣya repeats (Bib. Ind. ed. p. 53^{13} and 65^{3}) two of the illustrations given in the Yoga-bhāṣya, of the fire set in the dry grass and of the cloth rolled up into a ball. Other references (Tattvārthādhigama-sūtra xii. 5 and 6 and ix. 44–46) are quite as likely allusions to ancient Jain formulae as to Patañjali. By how much Umāsvāti's date precedes that of his commentator, Siddhasena, cannot be said until the complete text of Siddhasena is published. The date for Siddhasena is set by Professor Jacobi (ZDMG. 60. 289, Leipzig, 1906, reprint p. 3, Eine Jaina-Dogmatik) at the middle or end of the sixth century. Umāsvāti precedes him; and Patañjali the philosopher would not be later than A.D. 500 and might be much earlier.

On the other hand I should guess that he is not much earlier. Because, for one reason, as Professor Stcherbatskoi reports, Dignāga (about A.D. 550 or earlier) seems to know nothing of him. And secondly because it is improbable that the Yoga-bhāṣya was composed very much later.

Other confirmatory evidence, somewhat later but more certain, would be the reference to Yoga-sūtra i. 33 in Māgha's Çiçupālavadha iv. 55. Professor Hultzsch has kindly pointed out another reference at xiv. 62 of Māgha's poem. In respect of the date of Māgha, Professor Jacobi concluded (WZKM. vol. III, p. 121 ff.) that Māgha lived about the middle of the sixth century. But Mr. Gaurishankar Ojha's discovery of the Vasantgaḍh inscription dated Vikrama 682 adds new and most convincing evidence. Professor Kielhorn (Göttinger Nachrichten, philol.-histor. Klasse, 1906, Heft 2, p. 146) is of the opinion that Māgha, the grandson of a minister of the King Varmalāta, must be placed at about the second half of the seventh century.

Still later, Gāuḍapāda (about A.D. 700), in his comment on the Sāṁkhya-Kārikā 23, quotes Yoga-sūtra ii. 30 and 32 and names Patañjali as the author.

The conclusion would be then that Patañjali's sūtras were written at some time in the fourth or fifth century of our era.

5. Date of the Yoga-bhāṣya between A.D. 650 and A.D. 850.—Of this the limits are easier to fix. Three pieces of evidence help us to determine the earliest limit.

A. The Comment could not in any case be much earlier than A.D. 350. For (at the end of iii. 53 or 52) it quotes Vārṣagaṇya in the words

mūrti-vyavadhi-jāti-bhedābhāvān nāsti mūlapṛthaktvam iti Vārṣagaṇyaḥ.

And again (iv. 13) the Comment quotes from a *çāstrānuçāsanam* as follows:

Guṇānāṁ paramaṁ rūpaṁ na dṛṣṭipatham ṛcchati
yat tu dṛṣṭipathaṁ prāptaṁ tan māyeva sutucchakam.

Fortunately Vācaspatimiçra offers us the information that this is an exposition of the teaching of the Shaṣṭi-tantra. And furthermore, in the Bhāmatī on Vedānta-sūtra ii. 1. 2. 3 (Nirṇayasāgara edition, 1904, p. 352, line 7 of the Bhāmatī), we are told that it is Vārṣagaṇya, the founder of the Yoga system, who said these words (*ata eva yoga-çāstraṁ vyutpādayitā āha sma Bhagavān Vārṣagaṇyaḥ* "*guṇānāṁ paramam . . .*").

Thus the Comment contains two quotations from Vārṣagaṇya. There is little reason to doubt that Vārṣagaṇya was an older contemporary of Vasubandhu. Professor Takakusu[1] by a combination of dates centering about the Chinese translation of Paramārtha's Life of Vasubandhu estimated that Vasubandhu lived from about A.D. 420 till 500. Professor Sylvain Lévi (Asañga, vol. II, pp. 1 and 2) accepted the result of these discussions. But Professor Wogihara[2] had conjectured that the date of Vasubandhu must be set back. An elaborate confirmation of his suggestion is now offered by Monsieur Noël Peri,[3] who places the death of Vasubandhu at A.D. 350; and by Mr. B. Shiiwo,[4] who estimates that Vasubandhu's life was from A.D. 270 to 350. This is a return to the fourth century, the date for Vasubandhu which Bühler[5] favoured. Accordingly the Bhāṣya must in any case be later than A.D. 350.

B. Another kind of evidence which helps us to determine yet more closely the earliest limit is the fact that the decimal system is used by way of

[1] Bulletin de l'École Française d'Extrême-Orient, 1904, tome IV, pp. 48 and 56; and JRAS. Jan. 1905, pp. 16-18 of the reprint.

[2] Asañga's Bodhisattvabhūmi, Leipzig, 1908, p. 14.

[3] "A propos de la date de Vasubandhu" (Bulletin de l'École Française d'Extrême Orient, tome XI, 1911, p. 339).

[4] "Doctor Takakusu and Monsieur Peri on the date of Vasubandhu" in the Tetsugaku Zasshi, vol. 27, Nov.-Dec., 1912. I am indebted to Mr. K. Yabuki for this.

[5] "Die indischen Inschriften und das Alter der indischen Kunst-Poesie," in Sitzungsberichte der Kaiserl. Akad. der Wiss., Wien, 1890, p. 79 f.

illustration in the Comment on iii. 13. The oldest epigraphic[1] instance of the use of the decimal system is in the Gurjara inscription of A.D. 595. With one obscure and doubtful exception, there is no literary evidence of the use of the decimal system before Varāhamihira, who lived in the sixth century. If we consider this kind of evidence alone, it is improbable that the Comment precedes the year A.D. 500; it is probably later.

C. There is evidence which determines that the earliest limit of the Comment is still later, as late as the seventh century. In the stanza iv. 55 of the Çiçupālavadha by Māgha (circa A.D. 650), not only Yoga-sūtra i. 33 is referred to, but also the words of the *avatāraṇa* in the Comment. In the Comment the *parikarma* of the *citta* is enjoined. This is an uncommon term. Even if *citta-parikamma* might be found in Buddhist books, the fact that it here immediately precedes the quotation from sūtra i. 33, makes it almost certain that such a mixture of terminology is impossible. In fact the stanza is full of specific yoga-terms in each line to such an extent that reference to any other system, much less to some heretical book, is quite excluded. The point is then that the words *citta-parikarma* together with the first word of the sūtra have been wrought into the metre of the poem as one word. The poet, as we saw, probably lived in the second half of the seventh century. If this is trustworthy evidence, the Comment cannot be earlier than A.D. 650.

D. The later limit is set by the date of Vācaspatimiçra's Nyāya Index, A.D. 841—see below, page xxiii.

Accordingly the date of the Bhāṣya would be somewhere between about A.D. 650 and about A.D. 850.

6. Date of Vācaspatimiçra's Tattva-vāiçāradī about A.D. 850.—In the verse at the close of his Bhāmatī-nibandha, Vācaspatimiçra gives the names of his works, seven in number:

> *Yan Nyāyakaṇikā-Tattvasamīkṣā-Tattvabindubhiḥ* ।
> *Yan Nyāya-Sāṁkhya-Yogānāṁ, Vedāntānāṁ nibandhanāiḥ* ॥
> *Samacāiṣaṁ mahat puṇyaṁ, tat phalaṁ puṣkalaṁ mayā* ।
> *Samarpitam; athāitena prīyatāṁ Parameçvaraḥ* ॥.

The *Nyāya-vārttika-tātparya-ṭīkā* is on the Nyāya system; the *Tattva-*

[1] See p. 78, of Bühler's Palaeographie, in his Grundriss. In his Notes on Indian Mathematics (Journal of the Asiatic Society of Bengal, July 1907, vol. III, number 7, p. 482, note 5), Mr. G. R. Kaye gives a list of epigraphical instances of the notation in which "place-value" is utilized. Most of these he thinks are worthless as evidence for the introduction of the decimal system. The same conclusion is reached in a later article (JRAS. July 1910, p. 749).

kāumudī is on the Sāṁkhya system; the *Tattva-vāiçāradī* is on the Yoga; the *Nyāya-kaṇikā*, a gloss on the *Vidhi-viveka*, is on the Mīmāṅsā; the *Tattva-bindu* is on Bhaṭṭa's exposition of the Mīmāṅsā; the *Tattva-samīkṣā* and the *Bhāmatī* are both on the Vedānta.

In the same verse at the end of the Bhāmatī he speaks of himself as living under King Nṛga:

tasmin mahīpe mahanīyakīrtāu Çrīman-Nṛge 'kāri mayā nibandhaḥ.

Unfortunately there is (as Professor Lüders informs me) no epigraphical record of this king and we cannot say when or where he lived. Vācaspatimiçra was a native of Mithilā,[1] the northern part of Tirhūt, and the latter part of his name would indicate, as Fitz-Edward Hall has pointed out, that he was a native of Gangetic Hindustan.

In the introduction to his edition of the Kusumāñjali (Calcutta, 1864, p. x), Professor Cowell thinks that Vācaspatimiçra lived in the tenth century. Barth (Bull. des Rel. de l'Inde, 1893, p. 271) would set him at the end of the eleventh or beginning of the twelfth century. Professor Macdonell (Hist. of Sansk. Lit., p. 393) places him soon after A.D. 1100.

These judgements rest, more or less, upon the opinion that the Rāja-vārttika, quoted by Vācaspatimiçra in his Sāṁkhya-tattva-kāumudī on Kārikā 72, was composed by, or for, Bhoja Rāja, called Raṇaraṅga Malla, King of Dhārā (1018-1060). This opinion accords with the assertion of Pandit Kāçīnātha Çāstrī Aṣṭaputra of Benares College, who assured Dr. Fitz-Edward Hall that a manuscript of the Rāja-vārttika had been in his possession several years (Hall's edition of the Sāṁkhya-pravacana-bhāṣya, 1856, p. 33). But the visible basis for this assertion that the Rāja in question is Bhoja is not now at hand.

Similarly, Professor Pathak in his article on Dharmakīrti and Shankarācārya (see Journal of the Bombay Branch RAS., vol. XXVIII, no. 48, 1891, p. 89, and also the table in the same Journal, p. 235, no. 49, note 74) is content to rest his conclusions as to the date of Vācaspatimiçra upon the fact that Çrībhāratī, the pupil of Bodhāraṇya, in his edition of the Sāṁkhya-tattva-kāumudī (Benares, Jāinaprabhākara Press, 1889, p. 182), prints, in a note at the end, the word Bhoja before the word Rāja-vārttika. Thus it would appear that this vārttika is by Bhojarāja and that Vācaspatimiçra, who quotes it, must be later than Bhojarāja, that is, later than the tenth century. But we are not at all sure from other manuscript evidence that the word Bhoja should be read before the word Rāja-vārttika, and the date of this Rāja-vārttika is therefore undetermined.

[1] See the beginning of the Nyāyasutroddhāraḥ by Vācaspatimiçra *Çrīvācaspatimiçreṇa Mithileçvarasūriṇā* (Haraprasād Çāstrī, Notices of Sanskrit MSS., Second Series, vol. II, p. 98).

By way of contrast we now have the direct statement of Vācaspatimiçra that he finished his Nyāyasūcīnibandha in the year 898. For on the first page of this appendix to the Nyāya-vārttika, as given in the edition of the Nyāya-vārttika in the Bibliotheca Indica, 1907, he says that he is about to compose an index for the Nyāya-sūtras

Çrīvācaspatimiçreṇa mayā sūcī vidhāsyate.

And in the colophon he says that he made the work for the delight of the intelligent in the year 898.

Nyāyasūcīnibandho 'sāv akāri sudhiyāṁ mude
Çrīvācaspatimiçreṇa vasv-aṅka-vasu-vatsare.

It remains to determine whether this year belongs to the era of Vikramāditya or of Çālivāhana. In the introduction to his edition of Six Buddhist Nyāya Tracts (Bibl. Ind., 1910), Mahāmahopādhyāya Haraprasād Shāstrī gives the date as belonging to the second era, to Çaka 898. He says (p. iii) that the author of the Apohasiddhi "takes a good deal of pains in elaborately refuting the theory of Vācaspatimiçra", and that he does "not quote or refute Udayana, whose date is Çaka 905 = A.D. 983". In his Notices of Sanskrit Manuscripts, second series, vol. II, p. xix, this distinguished scholar had come to the same conclusion with regard to the era to which this date of Vācaspatimiçra should be assigned. This conclusion seemed doubtful to Mr. Nilmani Chakravarti, M.A., in his valuable Chronology of Indian Authors, a supplement to Miss Duff's Chronology of India (Journal of the Asiatic Society of Bengal, vol. 3, 1907, p. 205). And one cannot refrain from thinking that the other era is presumably more likely for a Northern writer; and that more especially a great difficulty is created if only seven years are supposed to separate Vācaspatimiçra and Udayana. The difference between the two philosophers is of such a kind that one must assume a much longer interval between their writings. And furthermore, would it not be an extraordinary coincidence that the author of the Apohasiddhi should be so minutely familiar with the work of Vācaspatimiçra, and yet not have the dimmest sense of the existence of Udayana, the light of a new dawn in the world of Nyāya? Accordingly, the date of Vācaspati's Nyāya-index would appear to be *Saṁvat* 898 = A.D. 841; and the dates of his six other works, including the Tattva-vāiçāradī, may be presumed to be not many years earlier or later. We are therefore safe in making the statement that the date of the Tattva-vāiçāradī is not far from the middle of the ninth century, or approximately A.D. 850.

ANALYTICAL SUMMARY OF THE YOGA-SUTRAS

BOOK FIRST—CONCENTRATION

BOOK SECOND—MEANS OF ATTAINMENT

BOOK THIRD—SUPERNORMAL POWERS

BOOK FOURTH—ISOLATION

TRANSLATION OF THE YOGA-SUTRAS WITHOUT THE COMMENT OR THE EXPLANATION

BEING THE SŪTRAS TRANSLATED IN GROUPS, TOGETHER WITH GROUP-HEADINGS ADDED BY THE TRANSLATOR

BOOK FIRST—CONCENTRATION

Goal of Concentration

i. 1–4. Yoga is the concentration which restricts the fluctuations. Freed from them, the Self attains to self-expression.

i. 1 Now the exposition of yoga [is to be made]. i. 2 Yoga is the restriction of the fluctuations of mind-stuff. i. 3 Then the Seer [that is, the Self] abides in himself. i. 4 At other times it [the Self] takes the same form as the fluctuations [of mind-stuff].

Forms of the mind-stuff

i. 5–11. The fluctuations are all exposed to attack from the hindrances and are five in number: 1. sources-of-valid-ideas; 2. misconceptions; 3. predicate-relations; 4. sleep; 5. memory.

i. 5 The fluctuations are of five kinds and are hindered or unhindered. i. 6 Sources-of-valid-ideas and misconceptions and predicate-relations and sleep and memory. i. 7 Sources-of-valid-ideas are perception and inference and verbal-communication. i. 8 Misconception is an erroneous idea not based on that form [in respect of which the misconception is entertained]. i. 9 The predicate-relation (*vikalpa*) is without any [corresponding perceptible] object and follows as a result of perception or of words. i. 10 Sleep is a fluctuation of [mind-stuff] supported by the cause of the [transient] negation [of the waking and the dreaming fluctuations]. i. 11 Memory is not-adding-surreptitiously to a once experienced object.

Methods of restricting fluctuations

i. 12–16. An orientation of the whole life with reference to one idea; an emotional transformation corresponding to this focused state.

i. 12 The restriction of them is by [means] of practice and passionlessness. i. 13 Practice is [repeated] exertion to the end that [the mind-stuff] shall have permanence in this [restricted state]. i. 14 But this [practice] becomes confirmed when it has been cultivated for a long time and uninterruptedly and with earnest attention. i. 15 Passionlessness is the consciousness of being master on the part of one who has rid himself of thirst for either seen or revealed objects. i. 16 This [passionlessness] is highest when discernment of the Self results in thirstlessness for qualities [and not merely for objects].

Kinds of concentration

i. 17–18. Four kinds of conscious concentration, and the concentration of subliminal-impressions alone.

i. 17 [Concentration becomes] conscious [of its object] by assuming forms either of deliberation [upon coarse objects] or of reflection upon subtile objects or of joy or of the feeling-of-personality. i. 18 The other [concentration which is not conscious of objects] consists of subliminal-impressions only [after objects have merged], and follows upon that practice which effects the cessation [of fluctuations].

Degrees of approach to concentration

i. 19–23. The worldly approach; the spiritual approach; the combinations of methods and intensities; and the devotion to the highest Self.

i. 19 [Concentration not conscious of objects] caused by worldly [means] is the one to which the discarnate attain and to which those [whose bodies] are resolved into primary-matter attain. i. 20 [Concentration not conscious of objects,] which follows upon belief [and] energy [and] mindfulness [and] concentration [and] insight, is that to which the others [the yogins] attain. i. 21 For the keenly intense, [concentration] is near. i. 22 Because [this keenness] is gentle or moderate or keen, there is a [concentration] superior even to this [near kind]. i. 23 Or [concentration] is attained by devotion to the Içvara.

Analysis of the highest Self

i. 24–28. Unique quality of the highest Self; proof of His existence; His temporal priority; His symbolical realization.

i. 24 Untouched by hindrances or karmas or fruition or by latent-deposits, the Içvara is a special kind of Self. i. 25 In this [Içvara] the germ of the omniscient is at its utmost excellence. i. 26 Teacher of the Primal [Sages] also, forasmuch as [with Him] there is no limitation by time. i. 27 The word-expressing Him is the Mystic-syllable. i. 28 Repetition of it and reflection upon its meaning [should be made].

Obstacles to the calming of the mind-stuff

i. 29-34. The inner sense is exposed to distractions which may be overcome by focusing the mind; by the cultivation of sentiments; one may also practise breathings.

i. 29 Thereafter comes the right-knowledge of him who thinks in an inverse way, and the removal of obstacles. i. 30 Sickness and languor and doubt and heedlessness and worldliness and erroneous perception and failure to attain any stage [of concentration] and instability in the state [when attained]—these distractions of the mind-stuff are the obstacles. i. 31 Pain and despondency and unsteadiness of the body and inspiration and expiration are the accompaniments of the distractions. i. 32 To check them [let there be] practice upon a single entity. i. 33 By the cultivation of friendliness towards happiness, and compassion towards pain, and joy towards merit, and indifference towards demerit. i. 34 Or [the yogin attains the undisturbed calm of the mind-stuff] by expulsion and retention of breath.

Attainment of Stability

i. 35-39. Suitable objects for fixed-attention and contemplation.

i. 35 Or [he gains stability when] a sense-activity arises connected with an object [and] bringing the central-organ into a relation of stability. i. 36 Or an undistressed [and] luminous [sense-activity when arisen brings the central-organ into a relation of stability]. i. 37 Or the mind-stuff [reaches the stable state] by having as its object [a mind-stuff] freed from passion. i. 38 Or [the mind-stuff reaches the stable state] by having as the supporting-object a perception in dream or in sleep. i. 39 Or [the mind-stuff reaches the stable state] by contemplation upon any such an object as is desired.

Mastery and concentration

i. 40-47. Classification of concentration with reference to different single objects or absence of objects, or to the mental act, or to a fusion of object and knower.

i. 40 His mastery extends from the smallest atom to the greatest magnitude. i. 41 [The mind-stuff] from which, as from a precious gem, fluctuations have dwindled away, reaches the balanced-state, which, in the case of the knower or of the process-of-knowing or of the object-to-be-known, is in the state of resting upon [one] of these [three] and in the state of being tinged by [one] of these [three]. i. 42 Of [these balanced-states] the state-balanced with deliberation is confused by reason of predicate-relations between words and intended-objects and ideas. i. 43 When the memory is quite purified, [that balanced-state]—which is, as it were, empty of itself and which brightens [into conscious knowledge] as the intended-object and nothing more—is super-deliberative. i. 44 By this same [balanced-state] the reflective and the super-reflective [balanced-states] are also explained. i. 45 The subtile object also terminates in unresoluble-primary-matter (*aliñga*). i. 46 These same [balanced-states] are the seeded concentration. i. 47 When there is the clearness of the super-reflective [balanced-state, the yogin gains] internal undisturbed calm.

Normative insight

i. 48–51. After-effects of concentrated insight efface after-effects of concentration upon objects.

i. 48 In this [concentrated mind-stuff] the insight is truth-bearing. i. 49 Has another object than the insight resulting from things heard or from inferences, inasmuch as its intended-object is a particular. i. 50 The subliminal-impression produced by this [super-reflective balanced-state] is hostile to other subliminal-impressions. i. 51 When this [subliminal-impression] also is restricted, since all is restricted, [the yogin gains] seedless concentration.

BOOK SECOND—MEANS OF ATTAINMENT

Devices for weakening hindrances

ii. 1–11. Aids serviceable to the beginner who is on the path to concentration.

ii. 1 Self-castigation and study and devotion to the Içvara are the Yoga of action. ii. 2 For the cultivation of concentration and for the attenuation of the hindrances. ii. 3 Undifferentiated-consciousness (*avidyā*) and the feeling-of-personality and passion and aversion and the will-to-live are the five hindrances. ii. 4 Undifferentiated-consciousness is the field for the others whether they be dormant or attenuated or intercepted or sustained. ii. 5 The recognition of the permanent, of the pure, of pleasure, and of a self in what is impermanent, impure, pain, and not-self is undifferentiated-consciousness (*avidyā*). ii. 6 When the power of seeing and the power by which one sees have the appearance of being a single self, [this is] the feeling-of-personality. ii. 7 Passion is that which dwells upon pleasure. ii. 8 Aversion is that which dwells upon pain. ii. 9 The will-to-live sweeping on [by the force of] its own nature exists in this form even in the wise. ii. 10

These [hindrances when they have become subtile] are to be escaped by the inverse-propagation. ii. 11 The fluctuations of these should be escaped by means of contemplation.

Karma

ii. 12–14. Origin of karma in hindrances; result of karma in state-of-existence, length of life, and pleasure or pain.

ii. 12 The latent-deposit of karma has its root in the hindrances and may be felt in a birth seen or in a birth unseen. ii. 13 So long as the root exists, there will be fruition from it [that is] birth [and] length-of-life [and] kind-of-experience. ii. 14 These [fruitions] have joy or extreme anguish as results in accordance with the quality of their causes whether merit or demerit.

All is pain

ii. 15. Present and future and past correlations with objects result unavoidably in pain.

ii. 15 As being the pains which are mutations and anxieties and subliminal-impressions, and by reason of the opposition of the fluctuations of the aspects (*guṇa*),—to the discriminating all is nothing but pain.

There is an escape

ii. 16. Only yogins are sensitive to future pain. This may be avoided in that it has not expressed itself in actual suffering.

ii. 16 That which is to be escaped is pain yet to come.

Cause of pain

ii. 17–24. The Seer-sight relation implies 1. complexes of potential stresses between aspects (*guṇa*) and between sense-organs and elements, 2. the power of the Seer who is undefiled by aspects, 3. the actual correlation until the purpose of the Seer, which is to differentiate consciousness, is completed.

ii. 17 The correlation of the Seer and the object-of-sight is the cause of that which is to be escaped. ii. 18 With a disposition to brightness and to activity and to inertia, and with the elements and the organs as its essence, and with its purpose the experience and the liberation [of the Self],—this is the object-of-sight. ii. 19 The particularized and the unparticularized [forms] and the resoluble only [into primary matter] and irresoluble-primary-matter—are the divisions of the aspects (*guṇa*). ii. 20 The Seer who is nothing but [the power of seeing], although undefiled (*çuddha*), looks upon the presented idea. ii. 21 The object-of-sight is only for the sake of it [the Self]. ii. 22 Though it has ceased [to be seen] in the case of one whose purpose is accomplished, it has not ceased to be, since it is common to others [besides himself]. ii. 23 The reason for the apperception of what the power of the property and of what the power of the proprietor are, is correlation. ii. 24 The reason for this [correlation] is undifferentiated-consciousness (*avidyā*).

The escape

ii. 25. Positive state of Isolation follows the ending of the correlation.

ii. 25 Since this [non-sight] does not exist, there is no correlation. This is the escape, the Isolation of the Seer.

Means of escape

ii. 26–27. The act of discrimination leading up to the act of insight.

ii. 26 The means of attaining escape is unwavering discriminative discernment. ii. 27 For him [there is] insight sevenfold and advancing in stages to the highest.

Eight aids to yoga

ii. 28–29. To purify the aspects and to intensify intuitive thinking there are five indirect aids and three direct aids.

ii. 28 After the aids to yoga have been followed up, when the impurity has dwindled, there is an enlightenment of perception reaching up to the discriminative discernment. ii. 29 Abstentions and observances and postures and regulations-of-the-breath and withdrawal-of-the-senses and fixed-attention and contemplation and concentration.

First indirect aid: i. Five abstentions

ii. 30–31. The elements and degrees of morality in the form of prohibitions.

ii. 30 Abstinence from injury and from falsehood and from theft and from incontinence and from acceptance of gifts are the abstentions. ii. 31 When they are unqualified by species or place or time or exigency and when [covering] all [these] classes—there is the Great Course-of-conduct.

Second indirect aid: ii. Five observances

ii. 32. Advances in morality in the form of voluntary action.

ii. 32 Cleanliness and contentment and self-castigation and study and devotion to the Içvara are the observances.

Results of the abstentions and observances

ii. 33–45. Persistent inhibitions of certain kinds reorganize an increase of activity of the opposite kind.

ii. 33 If there be inhibition by perverse-considerations, there should be cultivation of the opposites. ii. 34 Since perverse-considerations such as injuries, whether done or caused to be done or approved, whether ensuing upon greed or anger or infatuation, whether mild or moderate or vehement, find their unending consequences in pain and lack of thinking, there should be the cultivation of their opposites. ii. 35 As soon as he is grounded in abstinence from injury, his presence begets a suspension of enmity. ii. 36 As soon as he is grounded in abstinence from falsehood, actions and consequences depend upon him. ii. 37 As soon as he is grounded in abstinence from theft, all jewels approach him. ii. 38 As soon as he is grounded in abstinence from incontinence, he acquires energy. ii. 39 As soon as he is established in abstinence from acceptance of gifts, a thorough illumination upon the conditions of birth. ii. 40 As a result of cleanliness there is disgust at one's own body and no intercourse with others. ii. 41 Purity of *sattva* and gentleness and singleness-of-intent and subjugation of the senses and fitness for the sight of the self. ii. 42 As a result of contentment there is an acquisition of superlative pleasure. ii. 43 Perfection in the body and in the organs after impurity has dwindled as a result of self-castigation. ii. 44 As a result of study there is communion with the chosen deity. ii. 45 Perfection of concentration as a result of devotion to the Içvara.

Third indirect aid: iii. Postures

ii. 46–48. Bodily conditions favourable to concentration.

ii. 46 Stable-and-easy posture. ii. 47 By relaxation of effort or by a [mental] state-of-balance with reference to Ananta. ii. 48 Thereafter he is unassailed by extremes.

Fourth indirect aid: iv. Restraint of the breath

ii. 49–52. Calming of affective states is favourable to concentration.

ii. 49 When there is [stability of posture], the restraint of breath, a cutting off of the flow of inspiration and expiration, follows. ii. 50 [This is] external or internal or suppressed in fluctuation and is regulated by place and time and number and is protracted and subtile. ii. 51 The fourth [restraint of the breath] transcends the external and the internal object. ii. 52 As a result of this the covering of the light dwindles away.

Fifth indirect aid: v. Withdrawal of the sense-organs

ii. 53–55. The span of attention is confined to an inner object.

ii. 53 For fixed-attentions also the central organ becomes fit. ii. 54 The withdrawal of the senses is as it were the imitation of the mind-stuff as it is in itself on the part of the organs by disjoining themselves from their object. ii. 55 As a result of this [withdrawal] there is a complete mastery of the organs.

BOOK THIRD—SUPERNORMAL POWERS

First direct aid: vi. Fixed-attention

iii. 1. The knower focuses the process of knowing upon the object to be known.

iii. 1 Binding the mind-stuff to a place is fixed-attention.

Second direct aid: vii. Contemplation

iii. 2. A two-term relation between the process of knowing and the object to be known.

iii. 2 Focusedness of the presented idea upon that [place] is contemplation.

Third direct aid: viii. Concentration

iii. 3. A fusion of the knower and the process of knowing with the object to be known.

iii. 3 This same [contemplation], shining forth [in consciousness] as the intended object and nothing more, and, as it were, emptied of itself, is concentration.

Transition to seedless concentration

iii. 4–10. The direct aids in combination result in insight and restricted subliminal-impressions and the calm flow of the mind-stuff.

iii. 4 The three in one are constraint. iii. 5 As a result of mastering this constraint, there follows the shining forth of insight. iii. 6 Its application is by stages. iii. 7 The three are direct aids in comparison with the previous [five]. iii. 8 Even these [three] are indirect aids to seedless [concentration]. iii. 9 When there is a becoming invisible of the subliminal-impression of emergence and a becoming visible of the subliminal-impression of restriction, the mutation of restriction is inseparably connected with mind-stuff in its period of restriction. iii. 10 This [mind-stuff] flows peacefully by reason of the subliminal-impression.

Mutations of substances

iii. 11–15. In the focused state the concentration holds two time-forms within the span of attention. Mutations are in fixed orders of subliminal-impressions in the restricted state.

iii. 11 The mutation of concentration is the dwindling of dispersiveness and the uprisal of singleness-of-intent belonging to the mind-stuff. iii. 12 Then again when the quiescent and the uprisen presented-ideas are similar [in respect of having a single object], the mind-stuff has a mutation single-in-intent. iii. 13 Thus with regard to elements and to organs, mutations of external-aspect and of time-variation and of intensity have been enumerated. iii. 14 A substance conforms itself to quiescent and uprisen and indeterminable external-aspects. iii. 15 The order of the sequence is the reason for the order of the mutations.

Application of constraints to different orders of mutations

iii. 16–52. Given a single mutation of external-aspect or time-form or intensity, the whole sequence comes under control of the concentrated insight.

iii. 16 As a result of constraint upon the three mutations [there follows] the knowledge of the past and the future. iii. 17 Word and intended-object and presented-idea are confused because they are erroneously identified with each other. By constraint upon the distinctions between them [there arises the intuitive] knowledge of the cries of all living beings. iii. 18 As a result of direct perception of subliminal-impressions there is [intuitive] knowledge of previous births. iii. 19 [As a result of constraint] upon a presented-idea [there arises intuitive] knowledge of the mind-stuff of another. iii. 20 But [the intuitive knowledge of the mind-stuff of another] does not have that [idea] together with that upon which it depends [as its object], since that [upon which it depends] is not-in-the-field [of consciousness]. iii. 21 As a result of constraint upon the [outer] form of the body, when its power to be known is stopped, then as a consequence of the disjunction of the light and of the eye there follows indiscernibility [of the yogin's body]. iii. 22 Advancing and not-advancing is karma; as a result of constraint upon this [two-fold karma] or from the signs of death [there arises an intuitive] knowledge of the latter end. iii. 23 [As a result of constraint] upon friendliness and other [sentiments there arise] powers [of friendliness]. iii. 24 [As a result of constraint] upon powers [there arise] powers like those of an elephant. iii. 25 As a result of casting the light of a sense-activity [there arises the intuitive] knowledge of the subtile and the concealed and the obscure. iii. 26 As a result of constraint upon the sun [there arises the intuitive] knowledge of the cosmic-spaces. iii. 27 [As a result of constraint] upon the moon [there arises the intuitive] knowledge of the arrangement of the stars. iii. 28 [As a result of constraint] upon the pole-star [there arises the intuitive] knowledge of their movements. iii. 29 [As a result of constraint] upon the wheel of the navel [there arises the intuitive] knowledge of the arrangement of the body. iii. 30 [As a result of constraint] upon the well of the throat [there follows] the cessation of hunger and thirst. iii. 31 [As a result of constraint] upon the tortoise-tube [there follows] motionlessness of the mind-stuff. iii. 32 [As a result of constraint] upon the radiance in the head [there follows] the sight of the Siddhas. iii. 33 Or as a result of vividness the yogin discerns all. iii. 34 [As a result of constraint] upon the heart [there arises] a consciousness of the mind-stuff. iii. 35 Experience is a presented-idea which fails to distinguish the *sattva* and the Self, which are absolutely uncommingled [in the presented-idea]. Since the *sattva* exists as object for another, the [intuitive] knowledge of the Self arises as the result of constraint upon that which exists for its own sake. iii. 36 As a result of this [constraint upon that which exists for its own sake], there arise vividness and the organ-of-[supernal]-hearing and the organ-of-[supernal]-touch and the organ-of-[supernal]-sight and the organ-of-[supernal]-taste and the organ-of-[supernal]-smell. iii. 37 In concentration these [supernal activities] are obstacles; in the emergent state they are perfections (*siddhi*). iii. 38 As a result of slackening the causes of bondage and as a result of the knowledge of the procedure [of the mind-stuff], the mind-stuff penetrates into the body of another. iii. 39 As a result of mastering the *Udāna* there is no adhesion to water or mud or thorns or similar objects, and [at death] the upward flight. iii. 40 As a result of mastering the *Samāna* [there arises] a radiance. iii. 41 As a result of constraint upon the relation between the organ-of-hearing and the air, [there arises] the supernal-organ-of-hearing. iii. 42 Either as a result of constraint upon the relation between the body and the air, or as a result of the balanced-state of lightness, such as that of cotton-fibre, there follows the passing through air. iii. 43 An outwardly unadjusted fluctuation is the Great Discarnate; as a result of this the dwindling of the covering to the brightness. iii. 44 As a result of constraint upon the coarse and the essential-attribute and the subtile and the inherence and purposiveness, there is a mastery of the elements. iii. 45 As a result of this, atomization and the other [perfections] come about, [there is] perfection of body; and there is no obstruction by the properties of these [elements]. iii. 46 Beauty and grace and power and compactness of the thunderbolt,—[this is] perfection of body. iii. 47 As a result of constraint upon the process-of-knowing and the essential-attribute and the feeling-of-personality and the inherence and the purposiveness, [there follows] the subjugation of the organs. iii. 48 As a result of this [there follows] speed [great as that] of the central-organ, action of the instruments [of knowledge] disjunct [from the body], and the subjugation of the primary-cause. iii. 49 He who has only the full discernment into the difference between the *sattva* and the Self is one who has authority over all states-of-existence and is one who knows all. iii. 50 As a result of passionlessness even with regard to these [perfections] there follows, after the dwindling of the seeds of the defects, Isolation. iii. 51 In case of invitations from those-in-high-places, these should arouse no attachment or pride, for undesired consequences recur. iii. 52 As a result of constraint upon moments and their sequence [there arises the intuitive] knowledge proceeding from discrimination.

Culmination of concentration

iii. 53–55. The particular which is indiscernible in respect of class or term or point-in-space is intuitively discerned; the widest span of objectivity is also discerned. This is the attainment of Isolation.

iii. 53 As a result of this there arises the deeper-knowledge of two equivalent things which cannot be distinctly qualified in species or characteristic-mark or point-of-space. iii. 54 The [intuitive] knowledge proceeding from discrimination is a deliverer, has all things as its object, and has all times for its object, and is an [inclusive whole] without sequence. iii. 55 When the purity of the *sattva* and of the Self are equal there is Isolation.

BOOK FOURTH—ISOLATION

Substances and subconsciousness

iv. 1–13. Correspondence between imperceptible forms of substance and latent-impressions of concentrated states.

iv. 1 Perfections proceed from birth or from drugs or from spells or from self-castigation or from concentration. iv. 2 The mutation into another birth is the result of the filling in of the evolving-cause. iv. 3 The efficient cause gives no impulse to the evolving-causes but [the mutation] follows when the barrier [to the evolving-cause] is cut, as happens with the peasant. iv. 4 Created mind-stuffs may result from the sense-of-personality and from this alone. iv. 5 While there is a variety of actions, the mind-stuff which impels the many is one. iv. 6 Of these [five perfections] that which proceeds from contemplation leaves no latent-deposit. iv. 7 The yogin's karma is neither-white-nor-black; [the karma] of others is of three kinds. iv. 8 As a result of this there follows the manifestation of those subconscious-impressions only which correspond to the fruition of their [kārma]. iv. 9 There is an uninterrupted-causal-relation [of subconscious-impressions], although remote in species and point-of-space and moment-of-time, by reason of the correspondence between memory and subliminal-impressions. iv. 10 Furthermore the [subconscious-impressions] have no beginning [that we can set in time], since desire is permanent. iv. 11 Since [subconscious-impressions] are associated with cause and motive and mental-substrate and stimulus, if these cease to be, then those [subconscious-impressions] cease to be. iv. 12 Past and future as such exist; [therefore subconscious-impressions do not cease to be]. For the different time-forms belong to the external-aspects. iv. 13 These [external-aspects with the three time-forms] are phenomenalized [individuals] or subtile [generic-forms] and their essence is the aspects (*guṇa*).

Polemic against Idealism

iv. 14–23. Knowledge of the stream of consciousness is impossible unless it be a permanent order as contrasted with a succession of transient appearances.

iv. 14 The that-ness of a thing is due to a singleness of mutation.

iv. 15. Because, while the [physical] thing remains the same, the mind-stuffs are different, [therefore the two are upon] distinct levels-of-existence. iv. 16 And a thing is not dependent upon a single mind-stuff, [for then in certain cases] it could not be proved [by that mind-stuff], [and] then what would it be? iv. 17 A thing is known or not known by virtue of its affecting [or not affecting] the mind-stuff. iv. 18 Unintermittently the Master of that [mind-stuff] knows the fluctuations of mind-stuff [and thus] the Self undergoes-no-mutations. iv. 19 It does not illumine itself, since it is an object-for-sight. iv. 20 And there cannot be a cognition of both [thinking-substance and thing] at the same time. iv. 21 If [one mind-stuff] were the object-for-sight for another, there would be an infinite regress from one thinking-substance to another thinking-substance as well as confusion of memory. iv. 22 The Intellect (*citi*) which unites not [with objects] is conscious of its own thinking-substance when [the mind-stuff] takes the form of that [thinking-substance by reflecting it]. iv. 23 Mind-stuff affected by the Seer and by the object-for-sight [leads to the perception of] all intended-objects.

Complete Self-realization of the Self

iv. 24–34. All hindrances subside; all acts of the Self are spontaneous and free; absence of limitations which thwart one who wishes to attain the ultimate ideal of his own nature.

iv. 24 This [mind-stuff], although diversified by countless subconscious-impressions, exists for the sake of another, because its nature is to produce [things as] combinations. iv. 25 For him who sees the distinction, pondering upon his own states-of-being ceases. iv. 26 Then the mind-stuff is borne down to discrimination, onward towards Isolation. iv. 27 In the intervals of this [mind-stuff] there are other presented-ideas [coming] from subliminal-impressions. iv. 28 The escape from these [subliminal-impressions] is described as being like [the escape from] the hindrances. iv. 29 For one who is not usurious even in respect of Elevation, there follows in every case as a result of discriminative discernment the concentration [called] Rain-cloud of [knowable] things. iv. 30 Then follows the cessation of the hindrances and of karma. iv. 31 Then, because of the endlessness of knowledge from which all obscuring defilements have passed away, what is yet to be known amounts to little. iv. 32 When as a result of this the aspects (*guṇa*) have fulfilled their purpose, they attain to the limit of the sequence of mutations. iv. 33 The positive correlate to the moment, recognized as such at the final limit of the mutation, is a sequence. iv. 34 Isolation is the inverse generation of the aspects, no longer provided with a purpose by the Self, or it is the Energy of Intellect grounded in itself.

BOOK FIRST

CONCENTRATION

1 [H.O.S. 17]

NOTICE TO THE READER

Patañjali's **Mnemonic Rules** or Yoga-sūtras are divided into four books as follows:

Book 1. Concentration or Samādhi, with 51 rules or sūtras,— pages 1 to 100;
Book 2. Means of attainment or Sādhana, with 55 sūtras,— pages 101 to 200;
Book 3. Supernormal powers or Vibhūti, with 55 sūtras,— pages 201 to 296;
Book 4. Isolation or Kāivalya, with 34 sūtras,— pages 297 to 348.

In all, there are 195 rules. Their extreme brevity is apparent when they are printed continuously, as at the end of the Ānanda◡āçrama edition, where the entire text of the rules occupies only between four and five pages.

The **Comment** or Bhāṣya, usually after a brief introductory paragraph or phrase (called *avatāraṇa*), takes up the rules, one by one, and gives first the text and then the meaning thereof.

Vācaspatimiçra's **Explanation** is of course in the first instance an explanation of the Comment; but since the Comment comprehends also the Rules, it is in fact an explanation of both Rules and Comment. In the body of this volume, the Explanation is not put all together by itself, but is made to keep pace with the Comment, rule by rule.

Meaning of the Differences of Type

The translation of the Rules is set in pica type of full-faced **Clarendon** style;
The translation of the Comment is set in pica type of Roman style;
The translation of the Explanation is set in long primer type of Roman style.

Single angles (like these ⟨⟩) indicate that the words which they enclose are taken from the particular Rule or Yoga-sūtra under discussion.

Double angles (like these «») indicate that the words which they enclose are taken from the Comment or Yoga-bhāṣya.

Double quotation marks (" ") indicate that the words which they enclose are taken from some authoritative text.

Single quotation marks (' ') indicate that the words which they enclose are the objections or questions of an opponent, or are a quotation from some unauthoritative text.

A half-parenthesis on its side (◡) is used between two vowels to show that they are printed in violation of the rules of euphonic combination.

BOOK FIRST

CONCENTRATION

May he, who, having abandoned his primal form, exercises his power to show kindness to the world in many ways—he with the beautiful hood and many mouths, possessed of deadly poison and yet abolishing the mass of hindrances—he the source of all knowledge, and whose girdle of attendant snakes produces continual pleasure,—may he, the divine Lord [1] of Serpents, protect you, with his white stainless body—he, the giver of concentration (*yoga*), and himself concentrated in concentration.

1. Now the exposition of yoga [is to be made].

The expression ‹now› indicates that a distinct topic [2] commences here. The authoritative book which expounds yoga is to be understood as commenced. [To give a provisional definition:] yoga is concentration; but this is a quality of the mind-stuff (*citta*) which belongs to all the stages. The stages of the mind-stuff are these: the restless (*kṣipta*), the infatuated (*mūḍha*), the distracted (*vikṣipta*), the single-in-intent (*ekāgra*), and the restricted (*niruddha*). Of these [stages the first two have nothing to do with yoga and even] in the distracted state of the mind [its] concentration is [at times] overpowered by [opposite] distractions and [consequently] it cannot properly be called yoga. But that [state] which, when the mind is single-in-intent, fully illumines a distinct and real object and causes the hindrances (*kleça*) to dwindle, slackens the bonds of karma, and sets before it as a goal the restriction [of all

[1] See Liñga Purāṇa, I., lxiii. 22-37.

[2] There are six kinds of sūtras according to the Mīmāṅsā: the definition (*saṁjñā*), the key to interpretation (*paribhāṣā*), the statement of a general rule (*vidhi*), the restrictive rule (*niyama*), an original statement (*adhikāra*), an analogical application (*atideça*). The word *atha* may introduce a topic (*adhikāra-artha*), or give the purport (*prastāva-artha*), or state the subject-matter of the discussion (*ārambha-artha*). This is discussed in Çloka-vārttika i. 1. 22-24.

fluctuations], is called the yoga in which there is consciousness of an object (*samprajñāta*). This [conscious yoga], however, is accompanied by deliberation [upon coarse objects], by reflection [upon subtile objects], by joy, by the feeling-of-personality (*asmitā*). This we shall set forth later. But when there is restriction of all the fluctuations (*vṛtti*) [of the mind-stuff], there is the concentration in which there is no consciousness [of an object].

I prostrate myself before him who is the cause of the world's origination, before Vṛṣaketu, who—although for him fruition and other results of karma proceeding from the hindrances have ceased—is yet kindly [to the world he has made]. Prostrating myself before Patañjali the sage, I proceed to set forth a brief, clear, and significant explanation of the Comment by Vedavyāsa.

For here the Exalted Patañjali—wishing to announce in brief the import of the book which he is about to begin that he may thus assist the procedure of men of understanding and that he may, more especially, make the hearer easily comprehend—composed this sūtra: **1. Now the exposition of yoga [is to be made].** Of this [sūtra] the first portion, the word ‹now›, he [the author of the Comment] discusses in the phrase «The expression ‹now› indicates that a distinct topic commences here.» [The word ‹now› is used] as in [the sūtra] "Now[1] this is the Jyotis". It does not imply that it is to be preceded [by conditions as in the first Brahma-sūtra]. Now by the word ‹exposition› he means the authoritative book in the sense that it is that whereby a thing is expounded. Moreover the book may enter upon its activity when preceded not only by calm[2] and the other [five conditions required by the Brahma-sūtra]; but it must be preceded also by [Patañjali's] desire to announce [his] truth. [Calm], on the contrary, would follow when once there had been a desire to know and when the knowledge [had entered into action]. As it is written [BAU. iv. 4. 23 or 28], "After that, calm and subdued and retired and resigned and concentrated let him behold himself in the Self only." Although it would be possible [for the book to enter into action] immediately after advantage had been taken of such things as students' questions or performances of austerities or elixirs of life, [still these are] not mentioned. The reason for this is that these things would be of no use either to the student's knowledge or to [his] feeling inclined (*pravṛtti*) [for it]. [What then would be advantageous? The book's authoritativeness.] If the book be authoritative, then, even if there are no [questions or austerities or elixirs], the exposition of yoga is to be accepted; but if not authoritative, then, even if [there be questions and all the other conditions, still]

[1] These words are from the Tāṇḍya-Mahābr. xix. 11. 1 (Biblioth. Ind.). The *jyotis* is a chant by the *udgātar* in the Agniṣṭoma directly after the filtering of the soma. See Caland and Henry: L'Agniṣṭoma, I, p. 166. And compare Çāstra Dīpikā (Benares edition), p. 230[20].

[2] See Vedānta Sāra 4 and 14 and 17.

the book is to be rejected. Thus it is [by insisting upon the authoritativeness of the book] that [Patañjali] refuses to say that [the book may begin] immediately after his understanding the truth and his desire to announce. But if it be agreed that [the word ⟨now⟩ indicates] that a distinct topic commences, then when once yoga has been mentioned as the topic of the book the student easily understands the announcement of the import of the book as a whole and is started into action.—Now every one knows from Çruti and Smṛti and the Epics and the Purāṇas that concentration is the cause of final-bliss [and that yoga is authoritative]. Some one might ask, 'If the word ⟨now⟩ indicates that a distinct topic commences in all those works to which it is attached, then, if this is so, would not such an announcement[1] as, "Now therefore the inquiry into Brahma [is to be made]" also be included?' To prevent this mistake [the commentator] uses the word «here.» [Again], some one cites the Yogiyājñavalkyasmṛti, "Hiraṇyagarbha and no other of ancient days is he who gave utterance (*vaktā*) to yoga" and asks how it can be said that Patañjali gives utterance to the authoritative book on yoga. In reply the author of the sūtra says ⟨the exposition⟩: exposition in the sense of expounding something previously expounded. When then the word ⟨now⟩ signifies that here a distinct topic commences, then the point of the statement is quite consistent.—Accordingly he says, «The authoritative work which expounds yoga . . . as commenced». Here an objector interrupts, 'The topic which is commenced here is not the authoritative work, but yoga in so far as it is taught.' In reply to which, he says «is to be understood.» True, we are beginning yoga in so far as it is taught. But the instrument which is to teach this [yoga] is the authoritative work which deals with the same. Moreover the teacher's activity has to do more immediately with the instrument than with the thing he works upon. Accordingly, with emphasis upon the activity of the author (*kartṛ*), we are to understand that the authoritative work which deals with yoga is commenced. But the topic commenced is that yoga only which is limited in its activity by an authoritative work. This is the real point.—And one must suppose that the hearing of the word ⟨now⟩, which means that a distinct topic has commenced, suggests—like the sight of a water-jar[2] carried [on a girl's shoulder at early morning]—another meaning, [namely,] it serves as an auspicious beginning.—Doubt as to the actual thing [yoga] is occasioned by doubt as to the meaning of the word [yoga]. This [doubt] he removes by stating that [«yoga» in the phrase] «yoga is concentration» is etymologically derived from the stem *yuj-a* [Dhātupāṭha iv. 68] in the sense of concentration and not from the stem *yuj-i* [vii. 7] in the sense of conjunction.

Another objection is raised, 'The yoga which is to be described is a whole, and concentration is a part of it; and a mere part is not the whole.' The reply is

[1] Brahma-sūtra i. 1. 1.

[2] This is in the list of auspicious objects to which one makes a circumambulation (*pradakṣiṇa*), Viṣṇu-smṛti lxiii. 29.

in the words «But this.» The word *ca* has the sense of «but» and distinguishes the whole from the part.—«Which belongs to all the stages» refers to the stages or states which are to be described: Madhumatī [iii. 54], Madhupratīkā [iii. 48], Viçokā [i. 36], Saṁskāraçeṣā [iii. 9]. These belong to the mind-stuff. In all these [stages] is found that yoga the [more] special mark of which is the restriction of the mind-stuff. But concentration is a part [of this] and has not this as its special mark. And the words «yoga is concentration» are a statement for etymological purposes only, in so far as one is not dwelling upon the difference between the whole and the part. But [when he is referring to] the practical purpose of what he calls «yoga,» [he says] it is the restriction of the fluctuations of mind-stuff: this is the stricter sense of the term. To those [Vaiçeṣikas] who hold the view that fluctuations are sensations inherent in the soul and that therefore the restriction of them would also involve the soul (*ātman*) in which they inhere,—to these in rebuttal he says, «a quality of the mind-stuff.»—The term ‹mind-stuff› (*citta*) he uses as a partial expression for the inner-organ [1] (*antaḥkaraṇa*), the thinking-substance (*buddhi*). The point is that the Absolutely-eternal Energy of Intellect (*citi-çakti*), [since it is] immutable, cannot have sensations as its properties; but the thinking-substance may have them.—An objector says, 'This may be so. But if yoga belongs to all its stages,—why then! Sir, [since you concede that] the restless and the infatuated and the distracted states also are stages of mind-stuff, and [since] there would be among these states, reciprocally at least, also a restriction of fluctuations,—then ‹yoga› would have to include these states also (*tatrāpi*).' In replying to this difficulty he makes clear which stages are to be included and which not included [in yoga] by the words beginning with ‹the restless.› i. The restless incessantly thrown by force of *rajas* upon this or that object is excessively unstable; ii. the infatuated because of a preponderance of *tamas* is filled with the fluctuation of sleep; iii. the distracted differs from the restless in that, although prevailingly unstable, it is occasionally stable, this prevailing instability being either natural or generated by diseases and languor and other obstacles later [i. 30] to be described; iv. the single-in-intent is the focused; v. the restricted mind-stuff is that in which all the fluctuations are restricted and in which nothing remains but subliminal-impressions (*saṁskāra*). In spite of the fact that certain fluctuations of the restless and the infatuated, [the first two] of these [five stages], are restricted each by the others, still, since these two are not even indirectly causes of final bliss and since they contend against it, they are so far removed from [the possibility of] being called yoga that he has not expressly denied that these two are yoga. But in the case of the distracted [state], since occasionally it has stability when directed towards a real object, he denies that it can be yoga in the words «Of these stages.» When the mind is distracted, the concentration which is the occasional stability of the mind-stuff

[1] Compare Çaṁkara Bhāṣya on ii. 4. 6 (Nirṇayasāgara edition, p. 711[11]).

when directed to a real object, cannot properly be called yoga. Why [cannot this be called yoga]? Because it has come under the adverse influence of distraction, which is the opposite of this [yoga]. When fallen into the hands (*antargata*) of a troop of opponents, it is hard for a thing to be even what it is and it is still harder for it to produce effects. Just as any one can see that a seed which has fallen into the fire and stayed there three or four moments has not power, even if sown, of sprouting: this is the real meaning. If then concentration which has come under the adverse influence of distraction be not yoga, what then is yoga? To this he makes answer, «But that [state] which, when the mind is single-in-intent.» By the word «real» (*bhūta*) he excludes [any] imaginary [object]. Since sleep, a fluctuation of mind-stuff, is also single-in-intent with regard to *tamas*,—a real (*bhūta*) object, the peculiar (*sva*) [aspect of a substance[1]] upon which it [sleep] depends (*ālambana*),—so he says «distinct» (*sad*); which means is clear (*çobhana*), in which the *sattva* [aspect] becomes evident in a very high degree. But that thing is not clear in which the *tamas* is in preponderance, inasmuch as it, [the *tamas*,] is the cause of hindrances. Now the perception of a thing either by verbal communication [*āgama*] or by inference may, we grant, be luminous (*dyotanaṁ bhavad api*); still, in so far as it is mediately known, it does not destroy undifferentiated-consciousness (*avidyā*) which we directly experience. For in such [illusions as the sight of] two moons or a defective sense of orientation, [verbal communications or inferences] do not destroy undifferentiated-consciousness. Accordingly he uses the word «fully» (*pra*), because it means luminous to the full extent (*pra-karṣam*) and because it alludes to immediate perception [in the case of yoga]. The feeling-of-personality (*asmitā*) and the other hindrances have their root in undifferentiated-consciousness (*avidyā*). Furthermore, since knowledge (*vidyā*) destroys undifferentiated-consciousness (*avidyā*); and since, when knowledge emerges, the hindrances [arising] from undifferentiated-consciousness and so on are destroyed, inasmuch as they are contrary the one to the other, and inasmuch as [then] the cause [of the hindrances] would be destroyed; therefore he says «and causes [the hindrances] to dwindle.» This, then, is the reason why [yoga] slackens the bonds which consist of karma.—And in this passage by a figurative use of the cause for the effect he employs the word «karma», whereas subtile-influences (*apūrva*) are intended.—The word «slackens» means brings [them] down from their operation. For later [ii. 13] he says, "So long as the root exists, [there will be] fruition from it." And finally it «sets before it as a goal the restriction [of all fluctuations].»—Moreover since this [yoga] conscious of objects is four-fold, he employs the words [beginning] «This [conscious yoga].» He describes [the yoga] not conscious of objects with the words «all the fluctuations.» [In other words,] we know (*kila*) that sources-of-valid-ideas and other fluctuations (*pramāṇādivṛtti*) made of *rajas* and *tamas* are

[1] 'Aspect of a substance' is *dharma* (see iii. 13) or *pariṇāma*.

restricted in [yoga] conscious [of objects] while fluctuations of *sattva* are retained; but that in [yoga] not conscious [of an object] all fluctuations whatsoever are restricted. Therefore [the final result] is established (*siddham*) that «belonging to all stages» means occurring in all these [four] stages, Madhumatī and so on, which [four] are [all] included in these two stages [of the conscious and the unconscious yoga].

The intent of the following sūtra is to state the distinguishing characteristic of this [yoga].

2. Yoga is the restriction of the fluctuations of mind-stuff.

By the non-use of the word 'all' [before ‹the fluctuations›], [the yoga which is] conscious [of objects] is also included under the denomination of yoga. Now mind-stuff has three aspects (*guṇa*), as appears from the fact that it has a disposition to vividness (*prakhyā*), to activity (*pravṛtti*), and to inertia (*sthiti*). For the mind-stuff's [aspect] *sattva*, which is vividness, when commingled with *rajas* and *tamas*, acquires a fondness for supremacy and for objects-of-sense; while the very same [constituent-aspect, *sattva*,] when pervaded with *tamas*, tends towards demerit and non-perception and passionateness and towards a failure of [its own rightful] supremacy; [and] the very same [*sattva*],—when the covering of error has dwindled away,—illumined now in its totality (*sarvatas*), but faintly pervaded by *rajas*, tends towards merit and knowledge and passionlessness and [its own rightful] supremacy; [and] the very same [*sattva*],—the stains of the last vestige of *rajas* once removed,—grounded in itself and being nothing but the discernment (*khyāti*) of the difference between the *sattva* and the Self (*puruṣa*), tends towards the Contemplation of the Rain-cloud of [knowable] Things. The designation given by contemplators (*dhyāyin*) to this [kind of mind-stuff] is the highest Elevation (*prasaṁkhyāna*). For the Energy of Intellect (*citi-çakti*) is immutable and does not unite [with objects]; it has objects shown to it and is undefiled [by constituent-aspects] and is unending. Whereas this discriminate discernment (*viveka-khyāti*), whose essence is *sattva*, is [therefore] contrary to this [Energy of Intellect and is therefore to be rejected]. Hence the mind-stuff being disgusted with this [discriminative discernment] restricts even this Insight. When it has reached this state, [the mind-stuff], [after the restriction of the fluctuations,] passes over to subliminal impressions (*saṁskāra*). This is the [so-called] seedless concentration. In this state nothing becomes an object of consciousness: such is concentration not conscious [of objects]. Accordingly the yoga [which we have defined as] the restriction of the fluctuations of the mind-stuff is two-fold.

He introduces the second sūtra with the words «the distinguishing characteristic of this.» The words «of this» refer to the two kinds of yoga mentioned in the previous sūtra. **2. Yoga is the restriction of the fluctuations of mind-stuff.** Yoga is that particular state of mind-stuff in which sources-of-valid-ideas and the other fluctuations are restricted. The objection is made that this cannot be the distinguishing characteristic [of yoga] since yoga conscious [of objects] would be excluded. For in this [conscious yoga], [those] fluctuations of mind-stuff which have the *sattva*-aspect are not restricted. The reply is «by the non-use of the word 'all'.» If yoga had been said to be the restriction of all the fluctuations of mind-stuff, [yoga] conscious [of objects] would not have been included. But [if the objection be made that this includes too much since there is restriction of *sattva* in the first three states, the reply is,] the restriction of the fluctuations of mind-stuff which are hostile to the latent-deposit (*āçaya-paripanthin*) of karma from the hindrances [i. e. the restriction, as thus qualified] includes this [yoga] also. [And this is so] because there is a restriction of those mind-stuff's fluctuations which have the *rajas* and *tamas* aspect in this [conscious yoga] also, and because this (*tad*) [hostility to the hindrances] is (*bhāvāt*) a part of that (*tasya*) [restriction]. But why is this mind-stuff, which is a single thing, in connexion with [its own] restless and other stages? And since some one might be in doubt why the fluctuations of mind-stuff which is in such [a three-fold] state should be restricted, he now makes clear first of all the reason for [the mind-stuff's] connexion with [these] states. «Now mind-stuff» [is in this threefold state] since the aspect *sattva* has a disposition to vividness [and] since the aspect *rajas* has a disposition to activity [and] since the aspect *tamas* has a disposition to inertia. The use of the word «vividness» is the use of a part for the whole (*upalakṣaṇa*). It alludes also to other kinds of *sattva*, to serenity and lightness and joy (*prīti*); and «activity» alludes to [the other] kinds of *rajas*, to pain and grief. Inertia is a property of the *tamas*-fluctuation and is opposed to activity. The use of the word «inertia» is a partial expression for heaviness and covering and dejection and similar states. What he means to say is this: the mind-stuff, although a single thing, has, inasmuch as it is made up of three aspects and inasmuch as the aspects are not in equilibrium, a multitude of mutations (*pariṇāma*) arising from a multitude of reciprocal antagonisms; and thus may consistently have many states. He shows that the restless and other stages of the mind-stuff have according to circumstances a variety of subordinate states. «For . . . which is vividness.» Mind-stuff's *sattva* is *sattva* in its form as a mutation of mind-stuff; [and] this [mind-stuff's *sattva*] in its form as vividness is thus shown to be a preponderance of *sattva* in the mind-stuff. In this mind-stuff when *rajas* and *tamas* are somewhat less than the *sattva*, and when they two are equal each to the other, then (*tadā*) [that mind-stuff] is that thing thus described [in the Comment] which acquires a fondness for supremacy and for objects-of-sense, sound and so on. Although the mind-stuff under the predominance of *sattva* desires to meditate upon reality (*tattva*), still, when the reality is concealed by *tamas*, it thinks that such supremacies as atomization (*aṇiman*) are the reality and desires to meditate upon them (*tad*). It meditates a moment, and then, caught by *rajas*, although obtaining no permanence [in its meditation] on them, it gains nothing except a fondness for these things. But its natural inclination towards sound and so on [the objects of sense] is quite well known. Accordingly in this way the mind-stuff is said to be distracted.—While describing the restless mind-stuff, he alludes also to the infatuated: «the very same . . . with *tamas*.» Now when *tamas* suppresses *rajas* and extends itself, then, since *rajas* has become incapable of removing the *tamas* which covers the mind-stuff's *sattva*, the mind-stuff covered with *tamas* tends towards demerit and other [forms of ignorance]. «Non-perception» is declared to be misconceived perception [i. 8], and also to be sleep-perception [i. 10] which is supported (*ālambana*) by a cause (*pratyaya*) of a [transient] negation. And from this [word] comes the suggestion (*sūcitā*) of the infatuated state also. A «failure of its [own rightful] supremacy» is an obstruction to one's will in every direction. Thus it is that mind-stuff becomes pervaded with demerit and the other [forms of ignorance]. But when this same substance (*sattva*) of the mind-stuff comes to have its *sattva*[-quality] manifest [and] its cover of *tamas* removed [and] is accompanied by *rajas*, then it tends, as he says, towards merit and perception and passionless and [rightful] supremacy, as he says in the phrase «dwindled away.» That [substance of the mind-stuff] is referred to, the covering, that is, the *tamas* [-quality], that is, the infatuation of which has almost entirely (*prakarṣeṇa*) dwindled. For the same reason «it is illumined in its totality»: in substances-as-effects (*viçeṣa*) and substances-as-causes (*aviçeṣa*) and in the *liñga* and the *liñgin* [see ii. 19] and the Self. Still it has not the capacity for merit and [rightful] supremacy since it lacks activity. With regard to this he says «pervaded by *rajas* only.» In other words when *rajas* is the active agent, merit and the rest do persist. Accordingly for the two middle classes of yogins,[1] the

[1] See below, iii. 51, and cf. Kern's 'Lotus', SBE. xxi. 387.

Madhubhūmika and the Prajñājyotis who have attained to concentration conscious [of an object], the substance (*sattva*) of the mind-stuff is included.—He now describes the state of the mind-stuff of the fourth class of contemplators, the Atikrāntabhāvanīya, with the words «the same.» Since the stain of the last vestige of *rajas* is removed, the mind-stuff is grounded in itself. Now the gold of the substance (*sattva*) of the thinking-substance (*buddhi*),—when once the stain of the *rajas* and *tamas* is purified by the joining [of the upper and lower parts] of the crucible (*puṭa-pāka*), which are practice and passionlessness, and when it has withdrawn [see ii. 54] the organs which are concerned with objects-of-sense, and is grounded in itself,—has still a further function to perform (*para kārya*), namely, the discriminative discernment [referring to the *sattva* and the Self], which performs its function in so far as its task (*adhikāra*) is unfinished. With this in mind he says «the mind-stuff.» The mind-stuff which is nothing else than the discriminative discernment referring to the *sattva* and the Self tends towards the Contemplation [called] the Rain-cloud of [knowable] Things. The Rain-cloud of [knowable] Things will also be described [iv. 29]. He tells what is perfectly clear to yogins with regard to this [state] in the words, «this . . . is the highest.» The mind-stuff which is nothing else than the discernment of the difference between the *sattva* and the Self and which lasts until the Rain-cloud of [knowable] Things, is designated by contemplators as the highest Elevation. And if one does not wish to make the distinction between the substance and its property, [this Elevation] may be regarded as having the same office as the mind-stuff [: the mind-stuff itself is the Elevation.]—In order to introduce the Concentration of Restriction as the ground for rejecting the discernment of the difference and as the ground for accepting the Energy of Intellect, he shows the excellence of the Energy of Intellect and the inferior value of the discriminative insight by the phrase «the Energy of Intellect» and the following words.—Impurity has as its essence pleasure and pain and infatuation. For even pleasure and infatuation give pain to the man of discrimination [ii. 15]; therefore, like pain, they too are to be escaped. Moreover exceptional beauty also comes to an end and so gives pain. Accordingly, that too the man of discrimination can only reject. Since this same impurity and this coming to an end do not occur in the Energy of Intellect [which is] the Self, it is said to be «undefiled and unending.» An objection is made, 'How can this (*iyaṁ*) [Energy of Intellect] be free from defilement, if, in being aware of things which have as their essence pleasure and pain and infatuation, it assumes their form? and how can it be unending if it accepts and rejects their forms?' In reply it is said «it has objects shown to it.» It [the Energy of Intellect] is that to which the various objects are shown. That [objection] would be sound, if, like the thinking-substance (*buddhi*), the Energy of Intellect assumed the form of objects; but it is the thinking-substance only which, because it undergoes mutations (*pariṇatā sati*) in the form of the objects, shows the object to the Energy of Intellect, which [latter however] does not take their form. And when this happens, the Self is then said to become aware [of the objects]. The objector asks, 'How can the Energy of Intellect unless it strike upon the thinking-substance which has taken the form of some object, know [that] object? or, if it do strike upon [that] object, how is it that it does not undergo a change into the form of that [object]?' To this he replies «does not unite [with objects].» Union is contagion; not any of this is in Intellect: this is his meaning. If any one asks why there is no [union] of this [Intellect with objects], the reply is, it «is immutable.» Mutation, which has the three-fold character [see iii. 13] of external aspect (*dharma*) and time-variation (*lakṣaṇa*) and intensity (*avasthā*), does not appertain to the [Energy of] Intellect also (*api*) [as it does to the mind-stuff] in any such way that (*yena*), by passing into a mutation in the form of an action, the Energy of Intellect should mutate in correspondence with the thinking-substance. That it, [this Energy,] even if it does not unite [with objects], can [nevertheless] be conscious of objects, he will now show to be possible. This [much] is established, that the Energy of Thought is unsullied by [the aspects (*guṇa*)]. But it has been said that the discriminative discernment, since it has as its essence the substance of the thinking-substance is not unsullied. It is «[therefore] contrary to this» Energy of Intellect. And since even the discriminative discernment is to be rejected, then how can you make mention of the other fluctuations which abound in defects: this is the real meaning. Thence, [that is,] for this reason, the introduction of the Concentration of Restriction is fitting. And so he says, «Hence . . . with this.» The meaning is that he restricts even the discriminative discernment by the higher passionlessness which, surely, is nothing more than the complete calming of the perceptions.—Now, what kind of a mind-stuff would that be that has all its fluctuations restricted? In reply he says «[When it has reached] this state.» He speaks of that [mind-stuff] the state of which has restriction.—He tells what restriction itself is: «This is the [so-called] seedless.» The latent-deposit (*āçaya*) of karma, which corresponds with the hindrances—birth and length-of-life and kind-of-enjoyment [ii. 13],—is the seed. That which is exempt from this is «seedless.» For this same [seedless concentration], he indicates the proper technical term which is current among yogins when he says «In this state nothing.» He sums up with the words «the yoga [which we have defined as] the restriction of the fluctuations of the mind-stuff is two-fold.»

The mind being in this [unconscious] state, what will then be the condition of the Self? For it is the essence (*ātman*) [of the Self to receive] knowledge (*bodha*) [reflected upon it] by the thinking-substance (*buddhi*), [as this in its turn receives the impression of external objects, and in this case] there is a [total] absence of objects [in the thinking-substance].

3. Then the Seer [that is, the Self,] abides in himself.

At that time the Energy of Intellect is grounded in its own self, as [it is] when in the state of Isolation. But when the mind-stuff is in its emergent state, [the Energy of Intellect], although really the same, [does] not [seem] so.

To introduce now the next sūtra, he raises the question beginning «The mind being in this [unconscious] state . . .» The question has the force of an objection: 'Now this Self, whose essence is [that it receives] the knowledge (*bodha*) [reflected upon it] by the thinking-substance which is mutated into the form of one [object] after another, is always undergoing an experience, [but there is] no [experience] when [the Self] is deprived of the knowledge from the thinking-substance. For the very nature of this Self is the knowledge (*bodha*) thrown upon the thinking-substance precisely as shining is [the nature] of the sun. Moreover this [knowledge of the thinking-substance] does not occur in that kind of mind which consists of subliminal-impressions (*saṁskāra*) only. And further a thing cannot exist without its own nature. If this is so, then why does not the Self know that thinking-substance also which consists of subliminal-impressions only?' To this he replies «there is a [total] absence of objects.» The thinking-substance as such (*buddhi-mātra*) is not the object of the Self, but (*api tu*) only in so far as it fulfils the purposes of the Self [iv. 32]. Now the two purposes of the Self are discriminative insight and the enjoyment of objects; and these do not exist in the restricted state [of the mind-stuff]. Thus the [total] absence of objects is established. The rebuttal is [also] given in the sūtra: **3. Then the Seer [that is, the Self] abides in himself.** The words ‹in himself› mean that the peaceful and the cruel and the infatuated nature falsely attributed [to the Self] has ceased. For the Self's Intelligence (*cāitanya*) is himself (*svarūpa*), [and is] not conditioned; while the knowledge of the thinking-substance has the various forms peaceful and other. And so it is subject to conditions just as the crystal which is in its own nature absolutely transparently white [is subject to conditions]: the redness of the [crystal] is its condition of being near the China-rose. And when a condition ceases, there is no cessation of the thing conditioned; since this would prove too much. This is the real point. And although [the Seer] in himself (*svarūpataḥ*) cannot [actually] be divided,[1] still when-he [the author of the Comment] -supposes-a-predicate-relation (*vikalpya*) [between the *draṣṭṛ* and his *svarūpa*], the words ‹in himself› (*svarūpe*) are put in the locative case. This same meaning is made clear by the author of the Comment when he says «grounded in its own self.» «At that time» means in the state of restriction [and] not in the state of emergence. [The objection is made,] 'This may be true. But if while in the state of emergence the Energy of Intellect is not

[1] Literally, although the essential-attribute (*svarūpa*) cannot be divided [from the Self].

grounded in itself and while in the state of restriction is grounded [in itself], then it would enter into mutation; or else if in [the state of] emergence it [remains] grounded in itself, [then there would be] no difference between emergence and restriction.' In reply to this he says «But when the mind-stuff is in its emergent state.» Never does the Energy of Intellect, [in that it is] absolutely eternal, deviate from itself. Accordingly, as [it is] in restriction, just so [is it] in emergence also. Assuredly, mother-of-pearl as such (*svarūpa*) does not suffer increase or decrease of being, no matter whether the perception (*jñāna*) which refers to it (*gocara*) be the source of a valid idea (*pramāṇa*) or [the source of] a misconception. The observer however, although the thing is really the same, is under the illusion that it is not so (*atathātvena*). Compared with the concentration of restriction, even [the concentration that is] conscious [of an object] is nothing more than emergence.

How in that case [is it that the Energy of Intellect does not seem the same in the emergent state]? [The answer is,] Since objects[1] are shown to it.

4. At other times it [the Self] takes the same form as the fluctuations [of mind-stuff].

In the emergent state [of the subliminal-impressions], the Self has fluctuations which are not distinguished from fluctuations of the mind-stuff; and so we have a sūtra [of Pañcaçikha[2]], "There is only one appearance [for both],—that appearance is knowledge." The mind-stuff is like a magnet; and, as an object suitable to be seen [by the Self as Witness], it gives its aid [to the Self] by the mere fact of being near it, and thus the relation between it and the Self is that between property (*svam*) and proprietor (*svāmin*). Hence the reason why the Self experiences (*bodha*) the fluctuations of the mind-stuff is its beginning-less correlation [with the thinking-substance].

To introduce the next sūtra, he inquires «How in that case?» If [the Energy of Intellect], though really the same, [does] not [seem to be] so, in what kind of a way in that case does it assume an appearance? such is the meaning. He supplies the words «Since objects are shown to it» which give the reason, and [then] rehearses the sūtra. **4. At other times it takes the same form as the fluctuations [of mind-stuff].** ‹At other times› means «in the emergent

[1] Compare Viṣṇu Pur. i. 14. 35.

[2] See Garbe: Pañcaçikha und seine Fragmente in Festgruss an Roth, Stuttgart, 1893, p. 75.

state ;» ‹the fluctuations [of mind-stuff]› are the tranquil and the cruel and the infatuated ; «not distinguished» means not different. These [three] are those [fluctuations] which the Self has.—‹The same form :› in these words the word 'same' is synonymous with 'one'. What he means to say is this: when, by reason of nearness to each other, the difference between [the colour] of the China-rose and of the crystal [vase], or analogously, between the thinking-substance and the Self, does not come to consciousness (*a-bheda-grahe*), then the individual by wrongly attributing the fluctuations of the thinking-substance to the Self, recognizes [wrongly] that he is tranquil or pained or infatuated. Likewise, wrongly supposing that his face when reflected upon the dirty surface of a mirror is itself dirty, [the individual] bemoans himself at the thought that he is dirty. Although[1] the fluctuation of the thinking-substance, like the perception of sounds or other [perceptible] things, is also wrongly attributed to the Self, and although in so far as it is primary-substance it should be experienced as being unintelligent, nevertheless by transferring the quality of the Self to the thinking-substance, [the fluctuation of the thinking-substance] appears as if it were a fluctuation of the Self, as if it were an experience [of the Self]. And so although the Soul (*ātman*) has no misconceptions, it seems to have misconceptions; although not an experiencer, it seems to be an experiencer; although it lacks the discriminative discernment, it seems to be provided with it, [and] it shines forth by the discriminative discernment.[2] And this will be set forth in detail in this [sūtra] [iv. 22], "The intellect (*citi*) which unites not [with objects] is conscious of its own thinking-substance when [the mind-stuff] takes its form [by reflecting it];" and in this [iii. 35], "Experience is undistinguished from a presented-idea on the part of the *sattva*-aspect and of the Self, each absolutely uncommingled [in the presented idea]." And this has been established in another system also [the Sāṁkhya]. Accordingly with the words «and so» he introduces (*āha*) the sūtra of Pañcaçikha the *ācārya*, "There is only one appearance [for both],—that appearance is knowledge." The question is raised, 'How is there one appearance? considering that you say that the fluctuation of the thinking-substance—occupied on the one hand with the different kinds of things, and occupied on the other hand with insight, and perceptible as being unintelligent in so far as it is primary-substance—is appearance; and [considering that you at the same time say that] the Self's intelligence (*cāitanya*), which is different from this and which is the perception, is [also] appearance.'

1 Literally: Although yet another Self-wrong-attribution possesses a fluctuation of the thinking-substance like the perception of sounds and so on, and although . . .

2 Reading *iva vivekakhyātyā*. Or: it seems to be provided with it up to discriminative discernment [*that is*, so long as there is no discriminative discernment: reading *iva ā vivekakhyātyāḥ*]. Or: it seems to be provided with it during the time of non-discriminative discernment [reading *iva a-vivekakhyātyām*].

To this he replies [in the words of Pañcaçikha] «that appearance is knowledge.» When he says «only one», he says it with reference to ordinary (*lāukika*) knowledge, [which is] a fluctuation subject to origination and dissolution.[1] But knowledge (*khyāti*) is not intelligence (*cāitanya*), [which latter is] the very nature of the Self. On the contrary that [i.e. intelligence] is concerned not with an ordinary perception (*lokapratyakṣa*), but rather with verbal-communication and inference. Consequently after [the author of the Comment] has shown that undifferentiated-consciousness (*avidyā*) is the original cause [of making wrong attributions] in the emergent state, he suggests that this [consciousness] is the cause of the contact [of the Self with the thinking-substance], and also that the relation between property and proprietor is the cause of experience. He makes this [series of assertions] consistent by saying «the mind-stuff.» Mind-stuff is the property of its proprietor, the Self: this is the connexion [of the statements]. The objection is made that that-by-which-one-is-intelligent (*cetana*), [namely,] the agent that is Master of the mind-stuff, accepts aid (*upakāra*) afforded by the mind-stuff, whereas it is impossible that he [the Master of the mind-stuff should accept] aid afforded by this [mind-stuff]. The reason for this is that there is no correlation [of the Self] with this [mind-stuff], since [the Self] cannot be aided [by it]. But on the other hand (*ca*) if it be the case (*-tve*) that there is a connexion with this [mind-stuff] or that aid is accepted from it, one would have to admit that [the Self] enters into mutation. In reply to this objection he says «like a magnet; and, as an object suitable to be seen [by the Self as Witness], it gives its aid [to the Self] by the mere fact of being near it.» The mind-stuff is not in connexion with the Self, but is near it. [This] nearness, moreover, does not result from a correlation either spatially or temporally of the Self with it [the mind-stuff]. But the distinguishing characteristic [of this nearness] is [that the Self stands to the mind-stuff in a relation of] pre-established harmony (*yogyatā*). Moreover the Self has the capacity for being the experiencer [while] the mind-stuff has the capacity for being experienced. Accordingly [mind-stuff] is described «as an object suitable to be seen.» In other words it is described as an object-for-experience when it enters into mutations which have the forms of various kinds of things (*çabdādi*). Although experience is a fluctuation in the form of sounds and of other [perceptible] things and is an external aspect (*dharma*: see iii. 13) of the mind-stuff, still it [experience] belongs to the Self, because the Self ‹takes the same form as the fluctuations:› [that is, because they result from the false supposition of an identity between mind-stuff and intelligence (*cāitanya*): this is what is

[1] The original, *udaya-vyaya-dharmiṇī*, may be a reminiscence of one of the most famous of all Buddhist gāthās,

aniccā vata saṅkhārā
uppāda-vaya-dhammino,

Dīgha-nikāya, ii. 157, ed. PTS. But Vācaspati seems to understand it more pregnantly here as 'subject to rising into and passing out of consciousness'.

meant. Therefore although there is no correlation with the mind-stuff, still it is established that the Self accepts aid afforded by it, and that it does not enter into mutation. A question is raised, 'The relation of property and proprietor is [we grant] the reason for experience and is subject to the conditions of undifferentiated-consciousness. But subject to what conditions is undifferentiated-consciousness? Not subject to conditions (as everybody admits) no effect is produced. As they say, "Is there any commencement of undifferentiated-consciousness for him [that is, man] as in the case of sleep and so on?"' While apparently summing up, he [in fact] removes this doubt with the words «Hence the reason why . . . experiences the fluctuations of the mind-stuff.» The reason for the [Self's] awareness of the mind-stuff's fluctuations in the form of tranquil and cruel and infatuated forms is the [above-mentioned] correlation, which is without beginning since it is under the conditions of undifferentiated-consciousness which is without beginning. And the serial-order (*santāna*) of undifferentiated-consciousness and of the subconscious-impressions (*vāsanā*) is, like the serial-order of seed and sprout, without beginning.

Moreover these—for there are many such found in the mind-stuff—must be restricted.

5. The fluctuations are of five kinds and are hindered or unhindered.

The hindered (*kliṣṭa*) are those which are caused by the hindrances (*kleça*) [undifferentiated-consciousness, &c.: see ii. 3] and are the field for growth of the accumulation of the latent-deposits of karma; the unhindered have discriminative discernment as their object and thus obstruct the task (*adhikāra*) of the aspects (*guṇa*). These are still unhindered even when they occur in the stream of the hindered. For even in the midst of the hindered [fluctuations] they are unhindered; while in the midst of the unhindered [they are] hindered. Corresponding subliminal-impressions are produced by nought else than [these] fluctuations, and fluctuations [are made] by subliminal-impressions. In this wise, the wheel of fluctuations and subliminal-impressions ceaselessly rolls[1] on [until the highest concentration is attained]. Operating in this wise, this mind-stuff, having finished its task, abides in its own likeness, or [rather] becomes resolved [into primary substance].—These, either hindered or unhindered, are the five-fold fluctuations.

[1] Compare iv. 11, p. 288[3] (Calc. ed.).

Let this be granted. Still a man is qualified for that in which he has capacity. Furthermore the restriction of fluctuations is impossible unless one has an idea of the fluctuations. And yet no one even in a thousand years could count them. Numberless as they are, how [then] can they be restricted? In reply to this difficulty he introduces the sūtra whose purpose is to teach us their number and their nature with the words «Moreover these—for there are many such found in the mind-stuff—must be restricted:» **5. The fluctuations are of five kinds and are hindered or unhindered.** The fluctuations form a single whole. Of this [whole] there are five parts, and of them the first is the source-of-a-valid-idea. Accordingly, there is a fluctuation which has the parts of this [whole], [namely] five-fold, [that is] of five parts. And since these fluctuations are many, inasmuch as there are different mind-stuffs belonging to Chāitra and to Māitra and to other people, the use of the plural is consistent. What he wishes to say is this: Whether Chāitra or Māitra or any one else—of all these without exception, the fluctuations are of exactly five kinds [and there are] no more [fluctuations]. And the word «mind-stuff,» which has a collective sense (*jātyabhiprāya*), is a singular, but is to be taken as [a plural,] mind-stuffs. He shows that there are differences of a subordinate kind which are serviceable in the pursuit [of yoga] in the words ‹hindered or unhindered.› By the help of the unhindered [fluctuations], the hindered should be restricted; and the former, [should be restricted] by the higher passionlessness. He gives the explanation of this in the words «caused by the hindrances;» in other words the fluctuations have the feeling-of-personality and the other hindrances as their cause of action. Another interpretation would be that, for a person whose chief end is to fulfil the purposes of the Self, those fluctuations which consist of *rajas* and *tamas* act as hindrances in so far they cause hindrance. «Hindrance» is in the sense [Pāṇ. v. 2. 127] of having something hindered [as its effect]. This [hindrance] belongs to those [fluctuations] and therefore they are called hindered.—Since the action of those [hindered] fluctuations tends towards an increase of hindrance, it is they which are the field for growth of the accumulation of the latent-deposits of karma. For this observer [namely, the thinking-substance whose chief end is to fulfil the purposes of the Self] decides definitely (*ava-sāya*) by sources-of-valid-ideas and in other ways what the [intended] object is and becomes attached to it or averse to it and [then] accumulates latent-deposits of karma. Thus, hindered fluctuations become the soil for the propagation of the accumulated merit and demerit. He explains the unhindered [fluctuations] by saying that they «have discriminative discernment as their object.» When the *sattva* of the thinking-substance is cleansed of *rajas* and *tamas* and flows calmly onwards, the clearing of the insight (*prajñā*) is the [discriminative] discernment. By [thus speaking of] that which has [discernment as its] object he partially describes that discrimination (*viveka*), between *sattva* and the Self, which is the object of this [insight]. Accordingly, since [the unhindered] have as their object the discrimination of [the difference between] the *sattva* and the Self, for this very reason they obstruct the task of the aspects (*guṇa*). Now the aspects have the task to develop products. Since moreover this [development] lasts until the end of discriminative discernment, and since when the aspects have accomplished their task (*adhikāra*) [these unhindered fluctuations] restrict their authority (*adhikāra*), for this reason sources-of-valid-ideas and the other fluctuations are these unhindered ones. [The objection is made :] 'This may be true. But all living creatures have hindered fluctuations only, since there is nothing born that is free from desire. Furthermore, unhindered fluctuations cannot exist in the stream of hindered fluctuations. And even if those [unhindered fluctuations] could exist, they could not produce effects since they have fallen into the midst of obstructors. For this reason restriction of the hindered by the unhindered and of these latter by the higher passionlessness is nothing more than a wish.' In reply to that objection he says «in the stream of the hindered.» Practice and passionlessness are produced by devoting oneself steadily to verbal communications and to inferences and to the instruction of teachers. «In the midst of the hindered» [means] among [them]. That they occur there means that they are in themselves quite unhindered although they occur in the stream of the hindered. Surely a Brahman, although he reside at Çālagrāma which is crowded with hundreds of Kirātas, is not [on that account] a Kirāta. This is an example of what is meant by [occurring] in the midst of the unhindered. And in so far as they are found among the hindered, the unhindered, without being suppressed by the hindered, do after all, as gradually their own subliminal-impressions come to fruition, suppress the hindered. «Corresponding» means that unhindered subliminal-impressions [are produced] by unhindered fluctuations. This is that wheel of fluctuations and subliminal-impressions which ceaselessly rolls on until the concentration of restriction [is attained]. Operating in this wise, the mind-stuff reaches the state of restriction and, coming [then] to consist of nothing but subliminal-impressions, abides in its own likeness (*ātmakalpena*): this is the superficial view. Or else—and this is the stricter view—it becomes resolved into primary substance.—He joins together the meaning of sūtras [5 and 6] by the word «These.»—The word «five-fold» [literally, five times] is an expression of the sense merely ; but it is not a literal rendering of the force (*vṛtti*) of the termination (*çabda*), because it is not taught [by Pāṇini, at v. 2. 42] that the termination *taya* (*tayap*) has the meaning of 'kinds'.

6. Sources-of-valid-ideas and misconceptions and predicate-relations and sleep and memory.

These [five] he announces by their technical names. **6. Sources-of-valid-ideas and misconceptions and predicate-relations and sleep and memory.** [The compound] is analysed according to the order of words in the enumeration [of the sūtra]. The compound is a copulative (*cārthe dvaṁdvaḥ*, Pāṇini ii. 2. 29) in the sense of mutual conjunction.—Just as once more in the statement [ii. 5], "The recognition of the permanent, of the pure, of pleasure, and of a self in what is impermanent, impure, pain, and non-self,—is undifferentiated-consciousness," such illusions as the loss of the sense of orientation or as the fire-brand [whirled about so as to be seen as a] circle, are not expressly excluded,—so here also, even in the mentioning of the sources-of-valid-ideas and the rest, since doubt as to the real existence of other fluctuations would not [otherwise] be excluded, in order to exclude them [these others], the words 'of five kinds' should be added. Thus it becomes clear that fluctuations are just so many and no more.

7. Sources-of-valid-ideas are perception and inference and verbal-communication. i. Perception is that source-of-valid-ideas [which arises as a modification of the inner-organ] when the mind-stuff has been affected by some external thing through the channel of the sense-organs. This fluctuation is directly related to that [object], but, whereas the intended-object (*artha*) consists of a genus[1] and of a particular, it [the fluctuation] is chiefly concerned with the ascertainment of the particular [the genus being subordinate in perception to the particular]. The result [of perception] is an illumination by the Self (*pāuruṣeya*) of a fluctuation which belongs to the mind-stuff, [an illumination which is] undistinguished (*a-viçiṣṭa*), [that is, one in which the Self does not distinguish itself from the thinking-substance], [as] we shall explain in detail hereafter [ii. 17] in the passage[2] beginning "Self is conscious-by-reflection of the thinking-substance." ii. Inference is [that] fluctuation [of the mind-stuff] which refers (*-viṣayā*) to that (*tat-*) relation (*sambandha*) which is present in things belonging to the same class as the subject-of-the-illation (*anumeya*) and absent from things belonging to classes different [from that of the subject-of-the-illation]; and it is chiefly concerned with the ascertainment of the genus. Thus, for instance, the moon and stars possess motion, because, like [any man, for instance,] Chāitra, they get from one place to another; and because [negatively] the Vindhya [mountain-range] does not get [from one place to another, it] does not possess motion. iii. A thing which has been seen or inferred by a trustworthy person is men-

[1] Compare ii. 14, p. 214[1]; iii. 44, p. 257[1] (Calc. ed.).
[2] Compare also i. 29; ii. 20; iv. 19.

tioned by word in order that his knowledge [thereof] may pass over to some other person. The fluctuation [in the mind-stuff] of the hearer which arises from that word and which relates to the object-intended by that [word] (*tad-artha-viṣayā*) is a verbal-communication. That verbal-communication is said to waver, the utterer of which declares an incredible thing, not a thing which he himself has seen or inferred; but if the original utterer has himself seen or inferred the thing, [then the verbal-communication] would be unwavering.

Among these [five], [of one, that is,] the fluctuation which is the source-of-valid-ideas, he gives (*āha*) [what may pass as the naturally expected] general distinguishing characteristic (*lakṣaṇa*), by analysing [that one into three and saying]: 7. The sources-of-valid-ideas are perception and inference and verbal-communication. A valid-idea (*pramā*) is an illumination of a thing[1] not already presented and is caused by the operation of the Self. The instrument for this is the source-of-the-valid-idea (*pramāṇa*). And the mention [of the sources-of-valid-ideas] analytically [is] for the purpose of definitely excluding either a less or a greater number.

i. Of these [three] he gives first the distinguishing-characteristic of perception, since it is the root of all the [other] sources-of-valid-ideas, in the words beginning «of the sense-organs.» By using the words «intended-object» he rejects [the doctrine of *māyā* according to which the object is] a false attribution. With the words «directly related to that,» in so far as [the fluctuation] has an external field-of-action, he renounces [the Buddhist doctrine which conceives] the field-of-action as having the form of mental-objects [literally, form of knowledge]. With the words «affected by some external thing» he shows what the relation is between something to be externally known and [the object] in the form of a sensation which is found in the mind-stuff. With the words «through the channel of the sense-organs» he tells the reason for the affect of this [external thing] upon the [mind-stuff which is] separated[2] [from it by the sense-organ in question].—The object is the genus and nothing more: thus some maintain. Particulars only: thus others. Members of yet other schools [say that the object is something that has] the genus and the particular as its properties. To reject these [points of view] he says that [the object] «consists of a genus and of a particular.» The object does not have these two as its properties; but it consists of these two [by a relation of identity]. This will again be the topic of discussion in that passage [iii. 13] where it is said "since we do not maintain an absolute unity." With the words

[1] Literally, Of a that-ness not yet presented to consciousness. That is, something recognized as existent but of unknown quality.

[2] *Vyavahita*: compare Sāṁkhya Kārikā 7.

«chiefly concerned with the ascertainment of the particular» he distinguishes that which relates to perception from that which relates to inference and to verbal-communication. In other words, although the genus itself does shine forth [into consciousness] in perception, still it is subordinated to the particular. This would also be a partial characterization of direct experience (*sākṣātkāra*). And so even the discriminative-discernment receives its characteristic mark.—With the words «The result [of perception] is an illumination by the Self of a fluctuation which belongs to the mind-stuff» he denies that there is any contradiction in the result. An objector asks how an illumination which is found in the Self can be the result of a fluctuation situated in the mind-stuff? For surely when an axe[1] is busy with a khadira-tree, it is not chopping on a palāça-tree. In reply [Vyāsa] says «undistinguished.» For the illumination whose seat is in the Self is not produced, but is the result when the intelligence (*cāitanya*) is reflected in the mirror of the thinking-substance and assumes the form of that [thinking-substance] in so far as the fluctuation of the thinking-substance has the form of the object. And this [intelligence] in this [assumed] condition is undistinguished from the thinking-substance and has its being in the thinking-substance. Moreover since the fluctuation has its being in the thinking-substance there is ground for the relation of the source-of-the-valid-idea to the result in the fact that [both] have the same locus [namely, in the thinking-substance]. And this he says «we shall explain» in the passage " Self is conscious-by-reflection."

ii. After perception [and before verbal-communication], because [in the first place] verbal-communication depends upon inference, in so far as it obtains its validity[2] from a knowledge of the connective-power-of-words (*sambandha*) resulting from an inference with regard to a cognition (*buddhi*) on the part of the hearer which [inference] is based on actions and so on, and [in the second place] because [in this sūtra] the inferred is followed-in-enumeration by verbal-communication,—[therefore] he gives the characteristic marks of inference, before [he gives those of] verbal-communication, in the words «subject-of-the-illation.» A subject-of-illation is a subject (*dharmin*) distinguished by attributes (*dharma*) which we wish to know. Things belonging to the same class with it [the subject-of-illation], [are] objects similar to the genus which is an attribute of the major-term (*sādhya*), [that is, objects that are] similar instances (*sapakṣa*). «Which is present» in these [things belonging to the same class],—with these words he excludes [both] contrariety[3] and lack of community as between an attribute of the middle-term (*sādhana-dharma*) [and the attributes of the major].[3] Things belonging to different classes are dissimilar instances, and they are other than the similar instances, [that is,] contrary to them and containing the negation of them. «Absent» from these [things belonging to a different class].

[1] See G. A. Jacob: A Handful of Popular Maxims, part 1, 2nd edition, 1907, p. 32.

[2] *Samutthatayā: sāmarthyaṁ gṛhṇāti*, Bālarāma.

[3] See Athalye and Bodas, Tarka-saṁgraha, § 54, p. 306, and § 53, p. 302.

Accordingly (*tad*) by this he rules out over-inclusive (*sādhāraṇa*) non-coextensiveness (*anāikāntikatva*). Things-are-brought-into-relation—such is the use of the word «relation», a syllogistic-mark (*liṅga*). Thus describing the minor premiss (*pakṣa-dharmatā*) he avoids the fallacious-reasoning (*asiddhatā*) [of the *svarūpa* type[1]].—«Refers to that» [means] having [necessary] con-nection with that, because of the etymology[2] of the word «refers» (*vi-ṣaya*) based on this [statement of Dhātu-pāṭha, v. 2, that] "the root *si* means -nect."—With the words «the ascertainment of the genus» he distinguishes [the object of an inference] from the object of a perception. Inference arises on condition that there be an awareness of a relation [between two terms]. In so far as, in the case of particulars, one does not apprehend relations, it is only the genus which, as affording an easy apprehension of relations, comes into the discussion. For this he gives an example in the passage beginning «Thus, for instance.» The word *ca* [after the word Vindhya] carries with it a reason.—Because the Vindhya [range] has no motion, therefore it does not get [from one place to another]. Hence, as there is an absence of motion[3] (*gati-nivṛttāu*), there is an absence of getting [from one place to another]. [And conversely,] because they do get from one place to another, the moon and stars, like Chāitra, do have motion. Thus [the point] is established.

iii. Of the fluctuation which is a verbal-communication he gives the distinguishing characteristic in the words «a trustworthy person» [and so on]. Insight and compassionateness and dexterity-of-the-sense-organs combine into trustworthiness. A man whose ways are governed by that is a trustworthy one. He is the one by whom the object is seen or inferred. Unless there be a heard word, there is no receiving [of the seen or inferred object on the part of another person], because, in so far as this [word] is rooted in something seen or inferred, it is only by these two that its meaning becomes complete. «His knowledge [thereof] passing over» [to some other person] means that in the mind-stuff of the hearer there arises [into consciousness] knowledge similar to knowledge found in the mind-stuff of the trustworthy person. To effect this [passing], «a thing is mentioned» [that is,] is made known, as a means to obtain what is good for the hearer and to avoid what is bad [for him]. The rest is easy. The verbal-communication «the utterer of which declares an incredible thing»—for example, 'These identical ten pomegranates are going to be six cakes[4],'—«not a thing which he himself has seen or inferred»—for example, 'A shrine let him worship who desireth heaven,'—that verbal-communication «wavers.»

An objector says, 'If that be so, then the verbal-communication even of such persons as Manu would waver, [and thus they would not be supreme authorities,] for even they [declared] things which they themselves had not seen or inferred.'

[1] See Athalye, p. 310.

[2] According to this, *viṣaya* ought to mean 'dis-nection'. In fact it means 'sphere of action' from root *viṣ* 'act'.

[3] See Dhātu-pāṭha, i. 975, *ṣṭhā gati-nivṛttāu*, 'to stand still means not to move'.

[4] This is an allusion to Patañjali's Mahābhāṣya on i. 2. 45 (Kielhorn i. 217[13]). Cakes (*apūpa*) are made with ghee: see Sāyaṇa on RV. x. 45. 9.

In reply he says «but if the original utterer.» For in case of such persons (*tatra*), the original utterer was the Īçvara, who had himself seen or inferred the things. For instance, it is said [at Manu ii. 7], "Whatever law has been ordained for any person by Manu, every such [law had been already] laid down in the Veda. That, surely, contains within itself all knowledge." This is the meaning.

8. Misconception is an erroneous idea (*jñāna*) **not based on that form [in respect of which the misconception is entertained].**

Why is it not a source-of-a-valid-idea? Because it is inhibited by the source-of-a-valid-idea, for the reason that the source-of-a-valid-idea has as its object a positive fact. In such cases there is evidently an inhibition of the source-of-the-invalid-idea by the source-of-the-valid-idea, as for instance the [erroneous] visual-perception of two moons is inhibited by the actual (*sad-viṣaya*) visual-perception of one moon. This [fluctuation, namely, misconception] proves to be that [well-known] five-jointed undifferentiated-consciousness [the joints of which are enumerated at ii. 3 in the words]: "Undifferentiated-consciousness and the feeling-of-personality and passion and hatred and the will-to-live are the hindrances." These same [are known] by peculiar technical [1] designations: Obscurity and Infatuation and Extreme Infatuation and Darkness and Blind-Darkness. These will be discussed in connexion with the subject of the defilements of the mind-stuff.

8. Misconception is an erroneous idea not based on that form [in respect of which the misconception is entertained]. The word ‹Misconception› indicates the thing to be characterized; the words ‹erroneous idea› and so on [give] the distinguishing characteristic. A form which appears [in consciousness] as an idea (*jñāna*) is un-based on that form, [or, to put it as does the sūtra,] ‹not based on that form›. As, [to give another example in which the negation applies to the action [2] and not to the object,] 'One who eats not the funeral-feast.' Accordingly doubt also would be included [in the definition of misconception]. But there is a distinction to this extent: in this case [the case of doubt] the failure to be based [on the true form] is overridden by a [clear] perception (*jñāna*); but [in the other case], such as [the vision] of two moons, [the misconception is over-

[1] Compare Viṣṇu Pur. i. 5. 5.

[2] A case of prasajya-pratiṣedha. The negation applies to *pratiṣṭhā* and not to *rūpa*. Compare Patañjali: Mahābhāṣya, Kielhorn's edition, i, p. 215, last line; 221[11]; 319[12]; 341[5].

ridden] by the perception of the inhibition [of the one idea by the other idea]. An objector says, 'If this be granted, the predicate-relation (*vikalpa*), in that it is not based on the true form, would also upon consideration prove to be a misconception.' In reply to this he says «an erroneous perception.» For these words describe an inhibition familiar in common experience to everybody.[1] Now this [inhibition] occurs in misconception; but not in the predicate-relation, forasmuch as the business-of-life [is done] by this [predicate-relation], and because, on the other hand, only the learned kind of persons when they might be engaged in reflection would have in this matter any idea of an inhibition.—[The author of the Comment] puts forward the objection «Why is it not a source-of-a-valid-idea?» The point is that a previous [perception] should not be inhibited by a later [perception] which has incurred contradiction; on the contrary the later [perception should be inhibited] by just that previous [perception] which occurred first and has not incurred contradiction. He gives the rebuttal in the words «Because . . . by the source-of-a-valid-idea.» For this rule [of the Mīmāṅsā] applies (*evam*) when a later [perception] arises in dependence upon a previous. But in this present case two perceptions, each from its particular cause, in entire independence of each other, spring up. Accordingly the later [perception] does not attain to a rise [into consciousness] unless it has destroyed the earlier [perception]; and in fact its rise [into consciousness] has its being in the removal of that [previous perception] by inhibition. But it is not true that the rise [into consciousness] of a previous [perception] has its being in an inhibition of the later, for the reason that, at that time [the time of the earlier perception], this [later perception] does not yet exist. Hence the fact that [one perception] has not incurred contradiction is the reason why [another perception] is to be inhibited; and [hence also] the fact that [a perception] has incurred contradiction [is the reason] why it should act as inhibitor. Consequently it is established that the source-of-a-valid-idea, because its object is a positive fact, can inhibit the source-of-an-invalid-idea. An example is given in the words «In such cases . . . . . by the source-of-the-valid-idea.» In order that it may be rejected, he shows the worthlessness of this [source-of-invalid-ideas, i.e., of undifferentiated-consciousness] in the words «This . . . that . . five.» So, undifferentiated-consciousness as a genus [exists] in five special-forms [literally, in five joints], namely, undifferentiated-consciousness, sense-of-personality, and so on. The mental-process (*buddhi*) which [recognizes: compare ii. 5] the self in eight forms which are not the self, that is, in the undeveloped [primary substance] and in the Great [thinking-substance] and in the substance of personality and in the five subtile-elements (*tanmātra*),—is undifferentiated-consciousness, the [so-called] Obscurity. Similarly the mental-process which [recognizes] welfare (*çreyas*) in forms where no welfare is, in atomization (*aṇiman*: technical, see iii. 45) and the rest of the eight supremacies of yogins, is eight-fold, the [so-called] Infatuation. [This is] worse than the pre-

[1] On the form sārvajanīna see Pāṇ. iv. 4. 99, Siddhānta Kāumudī, § 1651, or Whitney's Grammar, 1223 d.

ceding. And this is called the sense-of-personality (*asmitā*). In this way, after one has obtained eight-fold supremacy by yoga and after becoming perfected (*siddha*), the resolution (*ātmikā pratipattiḥ*) to enjoy the ten objects which are seen [in the world] (*dṛṣṭa-*) and taught [in the *çāstra*] (*anuçrāvika*: see i. 15) is [called] Extreme Infatuation; this is desire. In case atomization and the other supremacies do not come-into-play (*an-utpattāu*), because while working on in this way with this same intention he is impeded by something or other, [then,] while he is bound down by this [impediment,] there arises, from the failure to enjoy the objects seen [in the world] and taught [in the *çāstra*], anger towards the impediment. This is the so-called Darkness; this is hatred. In like manner, if he have success with the [supernatural] qualities, atomization and so on, and if he dwell in thought close to the objects seen [in the world] and taught [in the *çāstra*], [then] the fear that all this will perish at the end of the mundane period is the will-to-live, the [so-called] Blind-Darkness. It hath been said [Sāṁkhya-kārikā[1] xlviii] "There are eight different kinds of Obscurity and of Infatuation. Extreme Infatuation is of ten kinds. Darkness is eighteen-fold; likewise Blind-Darkness."

---

9. The predicate-relation (*vikalpa*) **is without any [corresponding perceptible] object and follows as a result of perceptions or of words.**

This [predicate-relation] does not amount to a source-of-valid-ideas, nor does it amount to a misconception. In spite of the fact that there is no [corresponding perceptible] object, [nevertheless,] because there is dependence upon the authority of perceptions or of words, something is evidently said [literally, there appears something-said (*vyavahāra*) which possesses a dependence]. Thus for instance, when it is said [by some philosophers] that 'The true nature of the Self is intelligence (*cāitanya*)', then in this case [of absence of perceptible object] we may well ask—since the Self is itself nothing but intelligence—what thing is in the attributive relation to what [other] thing? For (*ca*)[2] the expressive-force (*vṛtti*) [of language] lies in the attributive-relation, as for instance 'Chāitra's cow'. [The cow is distinguished as being Chāitra's, who is something different from her.] Likewise [there is expressive-force when the subject and the predicate are identical, when for instance] the Self is said to be the unchanging [Absolute and thus is characterized] by the negation of some quality which is found in some [percep-

[1] Compare (the unedited) Çiva-sūtras ii. 13. [2] For *ca* meaning 'for', see p. 28[13], above.

tible] thing.[1] [Or when there is a connexion between a positive and a negative, when for instance] it is said, The arrow comes to a standstill [or] will come to a standstill [or] has come to a standstill. The bare meaning of the verbal-root [*sthā*, 'stand still': compare page 23] is understood to be 'not to move'. [In this case also there is expressive-force in the attributive relation even in the absence of any factor or *kāraka.*] So too [there is expressive-force] in the sentence 'The Self is something which has the property that it does not come into existence.' All that is meant is that there is an absence of the property of coming into existence; not [any negative] property inherent in the Self. Therefore this property [which is a negation so far as perceptible objects are concerned] is predicated and as such it is something-that-is-thought (*vyavahāra*).

9. The predicate-relation (*vikalpa*) is without any [corresponding perceptible] object and follows as a result of perceptions or of words.

The objection is made that, if the predicate-relation follows as a result of perceptions or of words, then one would have to admit that it is included under [that] source-of-valid-ideas [which is termed] verbal-communication, or [on the other hand], if the predicate-relation has no [corresponding perceptible] object, it ought to be a misconception. In reply to this he says «This [predicate-relation] does not.» This is not included among sources-of-valid-ideas nor among misconceptions. Why not? Because he says «object.» With the words «In spite of the fact that there is no [corresponding perceptible] object,» he denies that [the predicate-relation] is included among sources-of-valid-ideas. And with the words «because there is dependence upon the authority of perceptions or of words,» [he denies] that it is included among misconceptions. What he means to say is that a man in some cases falsely attributes diversity to things that are identical, and again in other cases identity to things that are diverse. Therefore since identity and diversity are non-existent as perceptible objects, the portrayal (*ābhāsa*) of these two is a predicate-relation [and] not the source-of-a-valid-idea. Nor yet would it be a misconception, because it is not in contradiction with the fact that something is said. He gives an illustration which is well established in the systems (*çāstra*) in the words «Thus for instance.» What subject (*viçeṣya*) is in the attributive-relation (*vyapadiçyate*), that is, is defined (*viçeṣyate*) by what [other] thing? For when there is identity, there is no relation of subject and predicate. Because [for instance] a cow cannot be defined as a cow; but by something different [from herself], by Chaitra. To this he replies by the phrase «For the expressive-force [of language] lies in the attributive-relation.» The relation between that to which the attribute is

[1] Literally 'possessing negated perceptible-object-qualities'.

to be applied and that which furnishes the attribute is the attributive-relation, that is to say, the relation-of-predicate-and-subject. In this [lies] the expressive-force (*vṛtti*) of the sentence «as for instance Chaitra's cow.» He adds another example found nowhere but in the books of the systems (*çāstriya*), «Likewise [there is expressive-force].» [A negated quality found in some perceptible thing would be, for instance,] motion, a quality belonging to some such [perceptible] thing as earth [and this quality as belonging to the Self] is negated. Who would that one [thus characterized] be? «The Self is said to be the unchanging [Absolute].» Surely it cannot be urged in a Sāṁkhya system that there is a certain quality in perceptible-objects called non-existence and that the Self could be defined by this.—Sometimes there is found a reading 'Qualities of a perceptible thing are negated'. The meaning of this would be that negated [qualities] are those concomitant with negation; qualities of [perceptible] objects cannot be concomitant with this [negation], because [in them] there cannot be a connexion between an existent and a non-existent. While on the other hand in this way [by the predicate-relation] there is distinct-knowledge.—In the words «The arrow is coming to a standstill» he gives an example from everyday life. Now just as when we say 'he cooks' or 'he chops', we mean that the accumulated moments of an action in serial order and characterized by a unity in the result are distinctly known, so it is also quite as truly a serial order to which he refers when he says «comes to a standstill.» When he says «will come to a standstill, has come to a standstill,»—then some objector may say, 'If we grant [that the action of coming to a standstill is] like that of cooking, then the arrow could have as its attribute an action, namely, stopping still,[1] which is in a serial order and is over-and-above (*bhinna*) the arrow itself.' To this he replies, [that stopping still is not a series of actions, but that] «The bare meaning[2] of the verbal-root is understood to be 'not to move'.» To begin with (*tāvat*), not-to-move is a mental-structure (*kalpita*); then too (*api*) the existence-in-positive-form (*bhāvarūpatva*) of this [non-moving (reading *tasyā api*)] [is a mental-structure]; [and] then too a serial order in this [existence-in-positive-form] [is again a mental-structure]—if that's what you mean (*iti*), whew! what a string of mental-structures!—such is the intention [of the Comment.]—[On the other hand,] a non-existent is conceived (*gamyate*) as in relation with all the Selves, [although not with perceptible-objects,] not only (*ca*) as if it were an existent, but also (*ca*) as if it were inherent (*anugata*)—[provided it be] a mental-structure.[3] But a [non-existent is] not any kind of a property [existentially] distinct from the Self. By way of another illustration, he says, «So too . . . .

[1] The words *sthāsyati*, *sthita* and so forth explain the succession implied in the word *tiṣṭhati*.

[2] Compare Patañjali: Mahābhāṣya on Pāṇini i. 3. 2, vārt. 11 (Kielhorn i. 258[18 f]).

[3] The Self (*puruṣa*) can be defined in terms of assertion, but no less also in terms of negation, and both may be equally inherent in the concept of the Self, as when we say 'Not coming into existence is a property of the Self', or 'The Self is un-changing'.

the property that it does not come into existence.»—Many thinkers [of the Mīmāṅsā and Nyāya schools] have advanced the assertion that there is no fluctuation [called] predicate-relation other than the source-of-valid-ideas or the misconception. To enlighten them, is, as we may suppose, the purpose of this abundance of illustration.

10. Sleep is a fluctuation [of mind-stuff] supported by the cause (*pratyaya*, that is *tamas*) of the [transient] negation [of the waking and the dreaming fluctuations].[1]

And this [fluctuation] by [the operation of] connecting-memory becomes, upon awakening, a special kind of presented-idea (*pratyaya*). How is it that one can reflect: 'I have slept well, my mind is calm, it makes my understanding clear; I have slept poorly, my mind is dull, it wanders unsteadfast; I have slept in deep stupor, my limbs are heavy, my mind remains unrefreshed (*klānta*) and languid and as it were stolen [from my grasp]?' [The answer is:] the man [just after] awakening would of course not have this connecting-memory, had there not been [during sleep, some] experience of [this form] of a cause (*pratyaya*, that is *tamas*); nor would he have the memories based upon it and corresponding with it [at the time of waking]. Therefore sleep is a particular kind of presented-idea (*pratyaya*); and in concentration it also, like any other presented-idea, must be restricted.

10. Sleep is a fluctuation [of mind-stuff] supported by the cause of the [transient] negation [of the waking and the dreaming fluctuations].[1]

For, the word 'fluctuation' given-in-the-topical [sūtra i. 5] is made-the-subject-of-an-assertion [here]. Because, with regard to sources-of-valid-ideas and misconceptions and predicate-relations and memories being fluctuations, there is no disagreement among investigators,—therefore this word is-made-the-subject-of-an-assertion (*anūdyate*) [namely, that one of the fluctuations is sleep,] in order that this particular [fluctuation] may be mentioned. But as to whether sleep is a fluctuation or not, there is disagreement among investigators. Accordingly it must be expressly said that it is a fluctuation. And the fact that the matter-in-hand [namely, that one of the fluctuations is sleep] is made-the-subject[2]-of-an-assertion cannot serve as an express statement [to the effect that sleep is a fluctuation].

[1] The point here is that sleep is a positive experience and not, as some Vedāntins, Udayana, for instance, would teach, the absence of a fluctuation. It is therefore of sufficient importance to require an explicit assertion.

[2] Compare Jacobi: Ānandavardhana's Dhvanyāloka, p. 28, note 1.

Consequently the word fluctuation is used [here] again. That fluctuation is called sleep the object or support of which is a cause (*pratyaya*), that is, a cause (*kāraṇa*),—the *tamas* which covers over the substance (*sattva*) of the thinking-substance,—of the [transient] negation of the fluctuations of waking or of dreams. For the substance of the thinking-substance has three aspects; and when *tamas*, the coverer of all the organs, preponderates over *sattva* and *rajas* and becomes manifest (*āvis*), then, because there is no mutation of the thinking-substance into the form of an object, the Self, aware of a thinking-substance which consists of intensified *tamas*, is in deep sleep and inwardly conscious. Thus it is explained.

[An objection:] why not consider sleep to be merely an absence of fluctuations, as in the case of restricted isolation (*kāivalya*)? He answers «This.» And this [fluctuation] by [the operation of] connecting-memory, that is, a remembrance which can be made the basis of an argument (*sopapattika*), is a special kind of presented-idea. How [is the argument? He replies]: When *tamas* is manifest in company with *sattva*, then the connecting-memory of a man just arisen from sleep is of such a kind that he reflects «I have slept well, my mind is calm, it makes my understanding clear;» clarifies it, in other words. But when *tamas* is manifest in company with *rajas*, then the connecting-memory is of such a kind that he reflects (*āha*) «I have slept poorly,» in other words, my mind is dull and unfit for work. Why? Since it wanders unsteadfast. [The author of the Comment] describes the connecting-memory, of a man [just] awakened, with reference to a sleep in which *tamas*, preponderating altogether over *rajas* and *sattva*, comes-quite-to-the-fore (*samullāse*), in the words «I have slept in deep stupor, my limbs are heavy, my mind remains unrefreshed and languid and as it were stolen [from my grasp].»—In the words «. . . of course not have this . . .,» he gives a negative instance of the middle-term (*hetu*), [that is, experience,] in order to show that the major-term (*sādhya*) [that is, memories] does not exist. «Awakening» means just after awakening. «[Had there not been during sleep, some] experience of [this form] of a cause» means [had there not been] an experience of the cause of the [transient] negation of the fluctuation. «Based upon it» is said with reference to the time of waking. An objection is made that sources-of-valid-ideas and other fluctuations have their locus in the emergent mind-stuff and must be restricted because they are enemies to concentration; but that sleep, since it amounts to a fluctuation single-in-intent, is in no wise a foe to concentration. To this he replies with the words «And in concentration.» Sleep, to be sure, does amount to [a fluctuation] single-in-intent; but, because of its quality of *tamas*, it is a foe to concentration-with-seed and to seedless-[concentration], [that is, concentration without subliminal-impressions]. And therefore it also must be restricted: this is the meaning.

11. Memory (*smṛti*) is not-adding-surreptitiously (*asampramoṣa*) to a once experienced object.

Does the mind-stuff remember the presented-idea or does it [remember] the object? The presented-idea, if affected by the object-known (*grāhya*), shines-forth-in-consciousness (*nirbhāsa*) in a form[1] of both kinds, both of the object-known and of the process-of-knowing (*grahaṇa*), and gives a start to the corresponding subliminal-impression. This subliminal-impression [of these two kinds changes into] its phenomenal [form[2]] by the operation of the conditions-which-phenomenalize (*vyañjaka*) it (*sva*) [that is to say, the subliminal-impression], and brings forth [in its turn] a memory which [also] consists of the object known and of the process-of-knowing. With regard to these two (*tatra*),—in the case of the idea (*buddhi*), the form of the process-of-knowing is predominant; and in the case of memory, the form of the object-known is predominant. The latter [that is, memory] is of two kinds, in that the-things-to-be-remembered are imagined (*bhāvita*) or not imagined. In a dream the-things-to-be-remembered are imagined, whereas in waking the-things-to-be-remembered are not imagined. All memories arise out of an experience either of sources-of-valid-

[1] The object as such is not directly perceived, but only its form (*ākāra*) as reproduced in the thinking-substance (*buddhi-sattva*), which in its turn reflects the image cast upon it by the Self.

[2] Literally, "possessing a manifestation of the manifester of itself." (1) The word *sva* denotes some mutation or time-form or intensity [iii. 13] yet to be phenomenalized. Anger or fear would serve as an example. (2) The word *vyañjaka* denotes the conditions which transform the unphenomenalized-form into a phenomenon. The approach of the tiger would be a concrete example. (3) The word *añjana*, that is *prakāçana* or *āvirbhāvaka*, is the presented-idea of the tiger. The discussion is not with regard to things in themselves, but to their phenomenal forms. A phenomenalized-form (*vyakti*) is in Vācaspatimiçra's terminology equivalent to a fluctuation (*vṛtti*). And this phenomenalized-form is further conceived to be any change in a substance (*dharmin*) which realizes some purpose (*arthakriyākāritva*). When we so regard a substance that we see it doing anything which interests us, we call it a thing, in other words, a mutation (*pariṇāma*) or a phenomenalized-form (*vyakti*). Consequently things do not arise and pass out of existence, as Buddhists would contend; but our conscious experience temporarily isolates successive phenomenal aspects of permanent substances. In fine, all phenomena are latent or implicit in the substance and become fluctuating or explicit under certain determined conditions.

ideas or of misconceptions or of predicate-relations or of sleep or of memory. And all these fluctuations have as their being pleasure and pain and infatuation; and pleasure and pain and infatuation are to be explained among the hindrances [ii. 3-9]: "Desire is that which dwells upon pleasure" [ii. 7]; "Aversion is that which dwells upon pain" [ii. 8]; while undifferentiated-consciousness is the same as infatuation. All these fluctuations must be restricted. Because it is [only] upon their restriction that there ensues concentration whether conscious or not conscious [of objects].[1]

11. Memory (*smṛti*) is not-adding-surreptitiously (*asampramoṣa*) to a once experienced object.

This not-adding-surreptitiously-to, which is the same as not stealing for, an object once experienced by means of sources-of-valid-ideas and other fluctuations is memory. For in the case of knowledge produced by nothing but a subliminal-impression, the object which appeared in that experience which was the cause of the subliminal-impression, is the own peculiar [object of that knowledge]. But the appropriation of any object in addition to that [own peculiar object] is a surreptitious addition, that is, a stealing [from other experiences]. Why [is there any stealing at all]? Because there is similarity [between the subliminal-impression and other experiences].—Since this word «surreptitious adding» (*sam-pra-moṣa*) is etymologically derived[2] from the root *muṣ* 'to steal'. What he means to say is this: all sources-of-valid-ideas and other fluctuations give access (*adhi-gam*), either by the generic or the special form, to a hitherto inaccessible object. But memory does not go beyond the limits of a previous experience. It corresponds with that [previous experience] or corresponds with less than that, but it does not correspond to [any experience] in addition to that. This fact distinguishes memory from other fluctuations.—He puts forth for discussion the problem «Does [the mind-stuff remember] the presented-idea?» Because experience (*anubhava*) directs itself towards the object-known, [therefore] the subliminal-impression resulting from it (*taj-ja*), [that is, from experience,] since it has no [present] experience of its own, makes us remember only the object-known: this is one view of the case. [Another view is that the subliminal-impression makes us remember] only the experience [of knowing], for the reason that [subliminal-impressions] are derived solely from experience. After putting forth this problem, [the author of the Comment,] by way of bringing the two views into consistency, decides that remembrance must be of both kinds. In so far as it directs itself towards the object-known, [the subliminal-impression] is affected by the object-known. But, strictly speaking, it makes-to-shine-forth-in-consciousness, [that is,] it illumines, not only the object-known but also

[1] Compare the definition of memory as a 'keeping *or* maintenance of a sensation', at Philebus 34 A σωτηρία αἰσθήσεως.

[2] Dhātu pāṭha i. 707.

the process-of-knowing, that is, the form of both kinds, the nature of the two. This [subliminal-impression] is thus described as one which has the manifestation (*añjana*) or form (*ākāra*) of the manifester (*vyañjaka*) or cause (*kāraṇa*) of itself, in other words, which has the form of the cause of itself. [The subliminal-impression produces a memory corresponding to the cause of that impression, that is, to the experience (*anubhava*).] Another interpretation would be that [this subliminal-impression is one] which has the manifestation (*añjana*) or the bringing-to-the-point-of-fruition (*phalābhimukhikaraṇa*) of the manifester (*vyañjaka*) or suggestive-stimulus (*udbodhaka*). An objection is made: 'If, in so far as both refer to the cause [that is, to experience], there is a similarity between the idea (*buddhi*) and the remembrance, then what difference is there between them?' In reply to this he says «With regard to these two . . . the process-of-knowing.» i. [Perception:] the process-of-knowing (*grahaṇa*) is an apprehending (*upādāna*). And there cannot be an apprehending of that which is [already] known. Accordingly an idea (*buddhi*) is said to be an illumination (*bodhana*) of that which has not been already got at (*adhigata*) by this [process-of-knowing]. This [idea] is that in which the configuration (*ākāra*) or form (*rūpa*) of the process-of-knowing is the predominant or principal [element]. Though the relation between the idea and the process-of-knowing is one of identity, [still][1] by predicating [the one of the other] the relation may be treated here as if it were that of principal and subordinate. ii. [Memory:] that whose predominant or primary [element] is the configuration of the object-known. This same predominance of the object-known in the configuration of the object-known lies in the fact that the object-intended (*artha*) has already been made the object of one of the other [four] fluctuations. Accordingly memory is declared to be concerned with objects which have already been made the object of one of the other fluctuations: this is precisely what is meant by not adding surreptitiously [to the once experienced object]. It might be urged that there is even in memory a surreptitious addition. For in a dream one's parents and others deceased who have been experienced in one time and place are brought [by memory] into relation with another time and place not previously experienced. The reply is «The latter [that is, memory] is of two kinds:» that [memory] by which imagined or mentally-constructed things are to be remembered; [that memory by which] not imagined, that is, not mentally-constructed [or] real things [are to be remembered]. This [memory of imagined things] is not [really] memory, but is misconception; because it agrees with the characteristic-mark [i. 8] of this [misconception]. But it is called memory in so far as it resembles memory, just as that which resembles a source-of-valid-ideas is called a source-of-valid-ideas. This is his point.—But why is memory placed at the end [of i. 6]? To this he replies «All memories.» Experience (*anubhava*) means getting to [an object]. Memory is a fluctuation preceded by a getting to [an object]. [Not until] after this [getting to an object]

[1] Literally, 'a relation of principal and subordinate is here (*ayam*) predicated.'

do memories associate themselves [with the subliminal-impression and with the experience]. The objection is made that a reasonable person should restrict those objects only which hinder[1] a man. Moreover the hindrances [affect him] thus; but fluctuations do not. Why then should these [fluctuations] be restricted? In reply he says «And all these.» [The rest is] easy.

Now what means are there for the restriction of these [fluctuations]?

12. The restriction of them is by [means of] practice and passionlessness.

The so-called river of mind-stuff, whose flow is in both directions, flows towards good and flows towards evil. Now when it is borne onward to Isolation [*kāivalya*], downward towards discrimination, then it is flowing unto good; when it is borne onward to the whirlpool-of-existence, downward towards non-discrimination, then it is flowing unto evil. In these cases the stream towards objects is dammed by passionlessness, and the stream towards discrimination has its flood-gate opened by practice in discriminatory knowledge. Thus it appears that the restriction of the mind-stuff is dependent [for its accomplishment upon means] of both kinds, [practice and passionlessness].

With the word «now» he asks what is the means for restriction. He gives the answer in the [following] sūtra: **12. The restriction of them is by [means of] practice and passionlessness.** If the restriction is to be effected, then both [these] distinct activities, practice and passionlessness, must operate together, but not either one or the other separately.[2] Accordingly he says «The river of mind-stuff.» The words «borne onward to» [connote] a continuous connexion; «downward towards» [suggest] depth or bottomlessness.

13. Practice (*abhyāsa*) is [repeated] exertion to the end that [the mind-stuff] shall have permanence in this [restricted state].

Permanence is the condition of the unfluctuating mind-stuff when it flows on in undisturbed calm. Practice is an effort (*prayatna*) with this end in view,—a [consequent] energy, a persevering

[1] Read *kliçnanti*.

[2] Literally, There is [= must be] a piling-up-together (*samuccaya*) [= simultaneous action] of practice and passionlessness, with the distinction that there be [two] subordinate activities, but not an alternative [action].

struggle,—the pursuit (*anuṣṭhāna*) of the course-of-action-requisite thereto with a desire of effectuating this [permanence].

Of these [two], he characterizes practice by telling what it is (*svarūpa*) and what its purpose is, [and does so in the words] **13. Practice is [repeated] exertion to the end that [the mind-stuff] shall have permanence in this [restricted state].** This he discusses in the words «of the . . mind-stuff.» The word «unfluctuating» means without fluctuations of *rajas* and *tamas*. Its flowing on in undisturbed calm is stainlessness, is the flowing on of the fluctuations of *sattva*; it is singleness-of-intent; it is permanence. It is with this end in view [that there is practice]. In the words ‹shall have permanence› there is [a pregnant use of] the locative case expressive of the reason [for the action] as in the phrase "He kills the leopard for the sake of the skin." He makes the word «effort» clear by a pair of synonyms «a [consequent] energy, a persevering struggle.» That this [effort] starts from a specific volition (*icchā*) he declares in the words «with a desire of effectuating this.» The word «this» refers to permanence. In the words «the course-of-action-requisite thereto» he describes the goal of the effort. The [eight] means-of-attaining [this] permanence are the [three] inner means (*aṅga*) and the [five] outer means, of which [eight] the first [two] are the abstentions and the observances [ii. 30 and 32]. The sense is that the functional-activity of the agent is occupied with the means [of the action], and not with the result.

---

14. But this [practice] becomes confirmed when it has been cultivated for a long time and uninterruptedly and with earnest attention.

[Practice,] when it has been cultivated for a long time, cultivated without interruption, and carried out with self-castigation and with continence and with knowledge and with faith,—in a word, with earnest attention,—becomes confirmed. In other words it is not likely to have its object suddenly overpowered by an emergent subliminal-impression.

An objection is made that practice is obstructed by emergent subliminal-impressions, which are the foes of practice [from time] without beginning. How does [practice] conduce to permanence? In reply he says, **14. But this [practice] becomes confirmed when it has been cultivated for a long time and uninterruptedly and with earnest attention.** This same practice becomes a confirmed state only when (*san*) provided with [these] three qualifications. And its goal, namely permanence, is not suddenly overrun by emergent subliminal-impressions. But if, even after having done practice of this kind, a man should fail to persevere, then in the course of time he might be overrun [reading *abhibhūyeta*]. Therefore one must not fail to persevere.

15. Passionlessness is the consciousness of being master on the part of one who has rid himself of thirst for either seen or revealed objects.

The mind-stuff (*citta*),—if it be rid of thirst for objects that are seen, such as women, or food and drink, or power,—if it be rid of thirst for the objects revealed [in the Vedas], such as the attainment of heaven or of the discarnate state or of resolution into primary matter,—if, even when in contact with objects either supernormal or not, it be, by virtue of Elevation (*prasaṁkhyāna*), aware of the inadequateness of objects,—[then the mind-stuff] will have a consciousness of being master, [a consciousness] which is essentially the absence of immediate-experience[1] (*ābhoga*) [and] has nothing to be rejected or received, [and that consciousness is] passionlessness.

He describes passionlessness. **15. Passionlessness is the consciousness of being master on the part of one who has rid himself of thirst for either seen or revealed objects.** He describes this riddance from thirst for seen objects whether animate or inanimate in the words beginning with «women.» «Power» is sovereignty. Revelation is Veda; «revealed» is that which is known from this [revelation], heaven for instance. Thirstlessness even for these things is specified in the words beginning «heaven.» «Discarnate» means without carnate body. «The discarnate state» is the state of those who are resolved into their organs. But there are others deeming themselves to be nothing but primary-matter, persons who worship primary-matter, who are resolved into primary-matter, which of course has its task [still unfulfilled in so far as primary-matter is for them an object of desire]: the state of these is «resolution into primary-matter.» A man rids himself of a thirst which is directed to the attainment of this. Now one who is rid of thirst for a revealed object is said to be rid of a thirst which is directed to the attainment of heaven or the like. It might be objected: 'If passionlessness is riddance from thirst and nothing more,—why! then this [riddance from thirst] exists even if you don't get to your objects. And for that reason (*iti*) [that riddance from thirst] would [also] be passionlessness.' The reply to this is in the words «supernormal or not.» Passionlessness is not merely riddance from thirst. But it is [the consciousness of being master] on the part of the mind-stuff, and is

[1] This word *anābhoga* occurs in Asaṅga's Mahāyāna-Sūtrālaṁkāra (1907), p. 8[19]. In his translation (1911) on page 8, note 7, Sylvain Lévi discusses this word and states that it apparently is lacking in classical Sanskrit. The fact that it occurs here is another indication of the intimate relation between Patañjali and the Mahāyāna. Haribhadra Sūri uses it at Yoga-bindu, vs. 91 and elsewhere.

essentially the absence of immediate-experience of objects whether supernal or not, even when in contact with them. This same [consciousness] he makes more clear by saying «[has nothing] to be rejected.» The words «has nothing to be rejected or received» mean free from flaw of attachment. This idea, [a state of] indifference, is the «consciousness of being master.» But whence comes this idea? In reply he says «by virtue of Elevation.» Objects are encompassed by the three kinds of pain. That is their inadequateness. By meditation upon that, [results] a direct perception of it, [and that is] Elevation. By virtue of that. 1. The Consciousness of Endeavour (*yatamāna-saṁjñā*); 2. The Consciousness of Discrimination; 3. The Consciousness of a Single Sense; 4. The Consciousness of Being Master: these are the four consciousnesses, according to those who know the tradition. 1. Such things as desires are of course taints found in the mind-stuff. By these the senses (*indriya*) are turned each toward its particular object. So, in order that the senses may not turn toward this or that particular object, there is a beginning, an effort [made] to bring these taints to maturity [and thus to cast them off]: this is the Consciousness of Endeavour. 2. When this beginning is made, some taints have matured and others are maturing or are about to mature. In this [situation,] the ascertainment of the matured by [a process of] discriminating [them] from those about to mature is the Consciousness of Discrimination. 3. Inasmuch as the senses are [now] incapable of turning [toward objects], the matured [taints] persist in the central-organ[1] as a faint [barren] desire: the Consciousness of a Single Sense. 4. The faint [barren] desire also is destroyed and there is indifference to objects, whether supernal or not, even when they are close at hand: this idea (*buddhi*), higher than the other three [forms of consciousness], is the Consciousness of Being Master. And inasmuch as the [three] preceding ones have their purpose fulfilled by this same [fourth form of consciousness], therefore these are not separately mentioned. Thus all is quite cleared up.

16. This [passionlessness] is highest when discernment of the Self results in thirstlessness for qualities [and not merely for objects].

[One yogin becomes] passionless on knowing the inadequateness of [all] objects, seen or revealed. Through practice in the vision of the Self, [another yogin,] because his thinking-substance is satiated with a perfect discrimination, resulting from the purity of this [vision], [between the qualities (*guṇa*) and the Self], [becomes]

[1] The central-organ (*manas*) is counted as the eleventh sense-organ and is the Single Sense here referred to.

passionless with regard to [all] qualities whether perceptible or not-perceptible. Thus passionlessness is of two kinds. Of these [two], the latter is nothing but an undisturbed calm of perception [untouched by any objects whatsoever]. And at the rising of this [state, the yogin] on whom this insight has dawned, thus reflects within himself, 'That which was to be attained (*prāpaṇīya*) has been attained; the hindrances which should have dwindled have dwindled; the close-interlocked succession of existences-in-the-world, which—so long as it is not cut asunder—involves death after life and life after death, has been cut.' It is just this uttermost limit of knowledge that is passionlessness. For it is with this that Isolation, as they term it, is inseparably connected.

After describing the lower passionlessness he tells of the higher: **16. This [passionlessness] is highest when discernment of the Self results in thirstlessness for qualities [and not merely for objects].** Lower passionlessness serves as a cause of higher passionlessness. He points out the means to this [higher passionlessness] in the words «passionless on seeing the inadequateness of [all] objects, whether seen or revealed.» By this [statement] the lower passionlessness has been set forth. «Practice in the vision of the Self» is the practice in that vision of the Self who has become accessible through verbal-communications and inference and the instruction of teachers. [This practice] is a constantly reiterated performance—through this. Purity of this vision is a focusedness upon *sattva* in so far as *rajas* and *tamas* have been rejected. Resulting from this [purity] is that perfect discrimination between the qualities and the Self—to the effect that the Self is pure and exists from time-without-beginning, whereas the qualities [in respect of which it is not contaminated] are the opposite of this—by which [discrimination] the thinking-substance of the yogin is satiated (*ā-pyāyita*). It is to such a yogin that reference is made. Now these same words (*anena*) describe the concentration called the Rain-cloud of [knowable] Things [iv. 29]. A yogin of such a kind as this is altogether passionless with regard to qualities (*guṇa*), whether their properties be developed or undeveloped,—that is to say, even to the extent that he is passionless with regard to the discernment of the difference between *sattva* and the Self, [for to this discernment] qualities are essential.—«Thus» that is, therefore, passionlessness is of two kinds. The first is when the substance (*sattva*) of the mind-stuff has [all] its *tamas* washed away by the excess of its *sattva*, and when the mind-stuff's *sattva*[1] is in contagion with a tiny stain of *rajas*. This [passionlessness,]

[1] This use of *sattva* is an intentional ambiguity. *Sattva* is not only the 'substance' (of the mind-stuff), but is also *sattva* (as a *guṇa*), which in the higher stages of attainment preponderates in the *citta* (Sāṁkhya-sāra, iii, near beg.).

moreover, is common to those also whose wishes have been fulfilled (*tauṣṭika*).[1] For they also have by virtue of the same [discrimination] been merged in primary matter. In this same sense it has been said [Sāṁkhya-kārikā 45] "From discrimination results resolution into primary-matter." Among these, that is, of these two [kinds of passionlessness] the latter is nothing but an undisturbed calm of perception. The use of the words «nothing but» indicates that this [passionlessness] is without any object. For it is the mind-stuff's substance (*sattva*) of precisely such a kind as this that is untouched by the stain of even a particle of *rajas*. This is the substrate for that [kind of passionlessness]. For this very reason it is called the undisturbed calm of perception. Because the substance (*sattva*) of the mind-stuff, although by nature undisturbed, [sometimes] experiences defilement from contact with *rajas* and *tamas*. But when all defilement by *rajas* and *tamas* is washed away by a stream of the undefiled water of passionlessness and practice, it [the substance of the mind-stuff] becomes absolutely undisturbedly calm and becomes so that nothing more is left of it than an undisturbed calm of perception. He shows its qualities so that we may be inclined to receive it. He says «at the rising of this.» The meaning is: When this [state] arises, then the yogin—on whom this insight has dawned; in other words, when there is this particular insight [that is, the undisturbed calm,]—has present insight [that is, the Rain-cloud of knowable Things]. «That which was to be found» that is, Isolation, has been found. In this sense he will say [iv. 30] "Even while living the wise man becomes liberated." The reason would be that what is nothing but subliminal-impression has its root [in undifferentiated-consciousness] cut: this is the point. How is it that [Isolation] has been found? Since all the hindrances which should have dwindled,—undifferentiated-consciousness and the [four] others together with subconscious-impressions (*vāsanā*),—have dwindled. It is urged as an objection that there is a mass of merit and of demerit; there is the succession of existences-in-the-world, the unbroken sequence of birth and death for [all] living creatures. How then can there be Isolation? In reply to this he says «has been cut.»—That [succession] the joints of which show no connexion is close-interlocked. These sections of the whole (*samūhin*) multitude (*samūha*) of merits and demerits, which are the parts, are close-interlocked. For nothing alive is ever free from connexion with bondage to birth and death. This is that same succession of existences-in-the-world. When hindrances dwindle, it is cut. To this same effect he will say [ii. 12] "The latent-deposit of karma has its root in the hindrances," [and ii. 13] "So long as the root exists there will be fruition from it." Some one might ask 'Without the full maturity of the Elevation (*prasaṁkhyāna*) and the restriction of the Rain-cloud of [knowable Things], what is this undisturbed calm of perception?' To this he replies «uttermost limit of knowledge.» Higher passionlessness is only one kind of the Rain-cloud of

[1] Cp. Sāṁkhya-kārikā 50.

[knowable] Things; nothing but that. To this same effect he will say [iv. 29] "For one who takes no interest even in Elevation there always follows, as a result of discriminative discernment, the concentration [called] the Rain-cloud of [knowable] Things," and [iv. 31] "Then, because of the endlessness of perception from which all defilements and coverings have passed away, the knowable amounts to little." For this reason Isolation is inseparably connected with it [and] is an essential characteristic (*avinābhāvin*) of it.

Now when the fluctuations of mind-stuff have been restricted by these two means, how are we to describe the [ensuing] concentration conscious [of an object]?

17. [Concentration becomes] conscious [of its object] by assuming forms either of deliberation [upon coarse objects] or of reflection [upon subtile objects] or of joy or of the sense-of-personality.

Deliberation (*vitarka*) is the mind-stuff's coarse direct-experience (*ābhoga*) when directed to its supporting [object]. Reflection (*vicāra*) is the subtile [direct-experience]. Joy is happiness. The sense-of-personality is a feeling (*saṁvid*) which pertains to one self [wherein the Self and the personality are one]. Of these [four] the first, [that is, deliberation] which has [all] the four associated together is concentration deliberating [upon coarse objects]. The second, [that is, reflection,] which has deliberation subtracted [from it] is [concentration] reflecting [upon subtile objects]. The third, [that is, joy,] which has reflection subtracted from it, is [concentration] with [the feeling] of joy. The fourth, [that is, the sense-of-personality,] which has this [joy] subtracted from it, is [concentration] which is the sense-of-personality and nothing more. All these kinds of concentrations have an object upon which they rest.

After having mentioned the means (*upāya*), in order that he may state what-may-be-obtained-by-these-means (*upeya*) in all its variations, he asks «Now . . . by these two means?» **17. [Concentration becomes] conscious [of its object] by assuming forms either of deliberation [upon coarse objects] or of reflection [upon subtile objects] or of joy or of the sense-of-personality.** Since [concentration] not conscious [of an object] is preceded by [concentration] conscious [of an object], he describes first concentration [conscious] of an object. The generic-nature of [concentration] conscious [of an object] is to be learned from its association with the forms of deliberation and of reflection and of joy and of the sense-of-personality as they are in themselves. He explains deliberation by the words «the mind-stuff's.» The direct-experience (*ābhoga*) [of an object] is an insight (*prajñā*) with a direct-perception (*sākṣātkāra*) of the thing itself. And this is coarse because the object is coarse. For just as an archer, when he is a beginner, pierces first only a coarse, and afterwards a subtile target, so the yogin, when a beginner, has direct experience merely of some coarse object of contemplation made of the five [material] elements, [for example] four-armed [Vishnu], and afterwards a subtile [object]. Likewise the subtile direct-experience, when directed to its supporting [object], is a reflection upon an object which is either the unresoluble-primary-matter (*aliṅga*) or the resoluble-matter (*liṅga*) or the five *tanmātra* which are the subtile elements, the causes of the coarse [elements].—Having thus described the object to be known, he describes the object which is the process-of-knowing with the word «joy.» Happiness is the mind-stuff's direct-experience when directed towards a sense-organ as a coarse[1] supporting object. Sense-organs, as every one knows, arise from the personality-substance (*ahaṁkāra*), in so far as they have a disposition to illumine because of the predominance of the *sattva* [quality]. And because the *sattva* [gives] pleasure, these sense-organs also [give] pleasure. Thus direct-experience when directed to them is happiness.—With the words «a feeling which pertains to one self» he tells of the concentration which has the knower as its object (*grahītṛviṣaya*). Organs-of-sense are produced out of the sense-of-personality. Consequently the sense-of-personality is their subtile form. Moreover this [sense-of-personality] together with the [Self as] known becomes the idea (*buddhi*), that is, the feeling which pertains to one self. And because the knower becomes included in this [feeling], one may say that there is a [concentration] conscious of the knower as its object.—He gives another subordinate difference between [these] four in the words «of these [four] the first.» The effect adjusts itself to the cause, not the cause to the effect. Hence this coarse direct-experience becomes associated [by inherence] with coarse [objects] and with subtile [objects], with sense-organs and with the feeling-of-personality, which are four kinds of causes. Furthermore, the other [first three direct-experiences, inasmuch] as they have three or two or one cause, assume a triple or double or single form. The words «All these» distinguish [concentration conscious of an object] from [concentration] not conscious [of an object].

Now by what means is that concentration produced which is not conscious of any object? or what is its nature?

18. The other [concentration which is not conscious of objects] consists of subliminal-impressions only [after

[1] The word *sthūla* is used here in the sense of product as contrasted with *sūkṣma* in the sense of cause: cp. iii. 44.

objects have merged], and follows upon that practice which effects the cessation [of fluctuations].

The concentration which is not conscious [of objects] is that restriction of the mind-stuff in which only subliminal-impressions are left and in which all fluctuations have come to rest. The higher passionlessness is a means for effecting this. For practice when directed towards any supporting-object is not capable of serving as an instrument to this [concentration not conscious of an object]. So the supporting-object [for this concentration] is [the Rain-cloud of knowable things][1] which effects this cessation [of fluctuations] and has no [perceptible] object. For (*ca*) [in this concentration] there is no object-intended. Mind-stuff, when engaged in the practice of this [imperceptible object], seems as if it were itself non-existent and without any supporting-object. Thus [arises] that concentration [called] seedless, [without sensational stimulus], which is not conscious of objects.

To introduce [the topic of] [concentration] not conscious [of objects] which comes next in order, he asks «Now?» **18. The other [concentration which is not conscious of objects] consists of subliminal-impressions only [after objects have merged], and follows upon that practice which effects the cessation [of fluctuations].** The first[2] clause [‹follows upon› to ‹fluctuations›] relates to the means; and the last two[2] words [from ‹the other› to ‹merged›] relate to the thing itself. The middle words [from ‹consists› to ‹only›] are discussed in the words «all fluctuations.» He discusses the first[2] clause in the phrase «The higher . . . . this.» The cessation is the non-existence of fluctuations. That which effects this [passionlessness] is the cause [of it]. The practice of it is the repeated pursuit of this [cause]. [The concentration] is that which follows upon this same pursuit. If it should be asked why lower passionlessness is not the cause of restriction, the reply is in the words «when directed towards any supporting-object.» A cause ought to be homogeneous with its effect, not heterogeneous. And, because it is directed towards a supporting-object, lower passionlessness is heterogeneous from its effect, which is concentration [not conscious of objects], [and] not directed towards a supporting-object. This is the ground for the statement that it [restriction] arises from the undisturbed calm of perception which is not directed towards a supporting-object. For when all the defilements of *rajas* and *tamas* have fallen away from the *sattva*, it is the concentration of the Rain-cloud of [knowable]

[1] Literally, [the Rain-cloud] is-made-the-supporting-object.

[2] The words *first* and *two* apply to the original, not to the translation.

things which is produced; its activity continues quite transcendent to any object; it has no end; it beholds the taints in objects; and because it altogether rejects all objects, it remains grounded in itself and so is not directed to any supporting-object; [and thus] it may consistently be the cause of the concentration wherein subliminal-impressions only are left and which is not directed to any supporting-object because of the homogeneity [between the restriction and the concentration not conscious of objects]: this is his meaning. Coming to be directed to a supporting-object (*ālambana*) is coming into dependence upon [an object] (*āçrayaṇa*). It «seems as if it were itself non-existent» because it does not perform its functions as a fluctuation. It is «seedless,» that is, not directed to any supporting-object. Another interpretation might be [that «seedless»] is that from which the seed, namely, the latent-deposit of the karma from the hindrances, has passed away.

This same concentration is, as every one knows, of two kinds. It is produced either by [spiritual] means [i. 20] or by worldly [means]. Of these two, that produced by [spiritual] means is the one to which yogins [who are on the way to Isolation] attain. **19. [Concentration not conscious of objects] caused by worldly [means] is the one to which the discarnate attain and to which those [whose bodies] are resolved into primary-matter attain.** The discarnate, that is, the gods, attain to the [concentration not conscious of objects which is] caused by worldly [means]. For in so far as their mind-stuff uses only their own subliminal-impressions they experience a *quasi*-state of Isolation, and [then] pass beyond [the period during which] the fruit corresponding to their own subliminal-impressions ripens [for their enjoyment]. [But at the end of this period they must return to the world.] Likewise those whose bodies are resolved into primary-matter experience a *quasi*-state of Isolation, during which the mind (*cetas*), with its task still undone, is resolved into primary-matter. But this lasts only till the mind-stuff, under the pressure of its [unfulfilled] task, returns [to the world].

In order to show what is to be accepted and what rejected he points out with the words «This same . . . as every one knows» a subsidiary distinction [to be found] in the concentration of restriction. The word «this» means the concentration of restriction; it is «of two kinds. It is produced either by [spiritual] means [i. 20] or by worldly [means].» He refers to that concentration of restriction produced [or] caused by faith and other [means] as will be described [i. 20]. The world[1] (*bhava*) is undifferentiated-consciousness (*avidyā*). It is called the world because living beings are born [or] grow (*bhavanti*) in it. Those whose wishes have been fulfilled (*tāuṣṭika*), who have attained to passionlessness, find the self (*ātman*) in the not-self, either in the elements or the sense-organs, which are evolved-effects (*vikāra*), or in evolving-causes (*prakṛti*), which are undeveloped [primary-matter], or in the personality-substance or in the five fine-substances (*tanmātra*).—The [concentration] produced by worldly [means] is that concentration of restriction produced [or] caused by the world. Of these two [concentrations] that produced by [spiritual] means is for yogins who are on the way to liberation. By specially mentioning [the fact that spiritual means are for yogins], he denies that the other [means] have any relation with persons who are merely desirous of liberation [that is, who are not yogins]. To whom then do the worldly [means] appertain? He replies to this with the sūtra. **19. [Concentration not conscious of objects] caused by worldly [means] is the one to which the discarnate attain and to which those [whose bodies] are resolved into primary-matter attain.** In other words [this concentration] is attained by both the discarnate and by those [whose bodies] are resolved into primary-matter. This he discusses in the words «The discarnate, that is, the gods.» By serving one or the other of the organs or elements they have become identified with them. And inner-organs are permeated by subconscious-impressions from these [organs or elements]. After the body falls to pieces they are resolved into organs or into the elements. Their central-organs (*manas*) contain nothing left but subliminal-impressions. And they are stripped of the outer six-sheathed body.[2] [Thus they may be termed] discarnate. For in so far as their mind-stuff uses only their own subliminal-impressions, they experience a *quasi*-state of Isolation. Being discarnate they attain [to this]. And the similarity [of this state] with Isolation is in the absence of fluctuations. Its dissimilarity is in the presence of subliminal-impressions with their task [unfulfilled]. In some [manuscripts] there is the reading 'by the enjoyment of nothing but subliminal-impressions'. The meaning of this would be 'that of which the enjoyment is nothing but subliminal-impressions'. The meaning is that there are no fluctuations of mind-stuff. When they have reached their

[1] Vijñāna Bhikṣu objects to this interpretation and interprets the compound (*bhava-pratyaya*) as that which has birth (*janma*) as its cause. But he seems to assume that the discussion is in respect of the classification of two kinds of unconscious concentration. Whereas it would appear that the classification is of the two kinds of restriction of fluctuations. That restriction which is temporary and which leads again to fluctuations is called *bhava-pratyaya*; that which follows upon belief (*çraddhā*) as the result of higher passionlessness is *upāya-pratyaya*. This latter is fit for persons aiming at liberation. The former is a pseudo-yoga and is to be rejected.

[2] See Mokṣa-dharma, MBh. xii. 305. 5 f. = 11332-3.

limit, they pass beyond or go beyond [the period during which] the fruit corresponding to the subliminal-impressions ripens. Yet once again they enter the round-of-rebirth. And so it has been declared in the Vāyu[-purāṇa], "Ten periods of Manu the devotees of sense-organs remain here below; a full hundred, the worshippers of elements."[1] Similarly those [whose bodies] have been resolved into primary-matter,—in so far as they have become identified with one or the other of the five fine-substances or the personality-substance or the Great [thinking-substance] or the undeveloped [primary-matter] by serving [one or the other] of these,—have their inner-organs permeated by subliminal-impressions from one or the other of these. After the body falls to pieces they are resolved into one or the other [of these] from the undeveloped [primary-matter] downwards. The words «with its task still undone» mean that its purpose is unfulfilled. For that mind would have its purpose fulfilled, if it could also generate the discernment of the difference. The mind, however, which has not generated the discernment of the difference has not fulfilled its purpose and its task is still undone. Thus, as he says, they experience a *quasi*-state of Isolation, during which the mind (*cetas*), with its task still undone, is resolved into primary-matter. «But this lasts only till the mind-stuff, under the pressure of its [unfulfilled] task, returns [to the world].» Even after it has been reduced to a state of uniformity with primary-matter, it reaches the limit [of its time] and yet once again appears, that is, it becomes discriminated from this [primary-matter]. Precisely so after the rains are passed, a frog's[2] body, after having been reduced to an earthy state, when sprinkled with water from the cloud, experiences yet once again the state of being a frog's body. And in this same sense it has been said in the Vāyu[-purāṇa], "But those who-identify-themselves-with-illusions-of-personality (*ābhimānika*), remain a thousand [periods of Manu]; those who identify themselves with the thinking-substance, ten thousand, and from them fevers [of desire] have passed away; those who meditate upon undeveloped [primary-matter], remain for a full hundred thousand; but after attaining to the Self, who is out of relation with qualities, there is no tale of time."[1] Thus inasmuch as this [state which is resolved into primary-matter] leads to a recurrence of births, its worthlessness (*heyatva*) has been established.

---

20. [Concentration not conscious of objects,] which follows upon belief [and] energy [and] mindfulness [and] concentration [and] insight,[3] is that to which the others [the yogins] attain.

[1] Not yet traced in either edition.

[2] In the corresponding passages i. 27, p. 64[27]; ii. 17, p. 140[12] (Calc. ed.), we find 'plant' for 'frog'.

[3] These five, saddhā, viriya, sati, samādhi, paññā, Buddha says that he too, as well as Āḷāra Kālāma, inculcates: Majjhima Nikāya, i. p. 164. Cf. 'The Balance of Powers,' Visuddhi Magga, book 4, p. 111 of 1st Rangoon ed.

[That concentration not conscious of objects, which is] caused by [spiritual] means is that to which yogins attain. Belief is the mental approval [of concentration]; for, like a good mother,[1] it protects the yogin. For him [thus] believing and setting discrimination [before him] as his goal there is the further (*upa*) attainment of energy. For him who has reached the further attainment of energy mindfulness is at hand. And when mindfulness is at hand the mind-stuff is self-possessed and becomes concentrated. When his mind-stuff has become concentrated he gains as his portion the discrimination of insight, by which he perceives things as they really are. Through the practice of these means and through passionlessness directed to this end there [finally] arises that concentration which is not conscious [of any object].

But for yogins he describes a series of means for the attainment of concentration. **20. [Concentration not conscious of objects,] which follows upon belief [and] energy [and] mindfulness [and] concentration [and] insight, is that to which the others [the yogins] attain.** It might be objected that those who reflect upon sense-organs might also be just the persons to have belief. To this he replies in the words «Belief is the mental approval [of concentration].» This [approval], moreover, has as its object a reality which is quite accessible by verbal-communication or by inference or by the instruction of teachers. For it is this mental approval, [which is itself] an extreme delight [and] a great volition, [that is called] belief. Those who are under the illusion that the self is in such things as sense-organs, have not an extreme delight. Because it is a disapproval [of concentration which they feel]; the reason [for this disapproval is that] it has its origin in downright infatuation. This is the meaning.— Why does he speak of just this [particular] belief [in concentration not conscious of objects]? He replies, «for, like a good mother, it protects the yogin» from calamities which follow upon a deviation from the way. This is a particular kind of volition and it generates an exertion directed towards the object desired. So he says «For him [thus] believing.» The exposition for the words «for him» is in the words «setting discrimination [before him] as his goal.» [For such a man] «there is the further (*upa*) attainment of energy.» «Mindfulness» is contemplation (*dhyāna*). «Self-possessed» is undistracted. «Becomes concentrated» means having (*yukta*) the concentration of the [eight] aids to yoga. And by mentioning the concentration which is inseparably connected with the abstentions (*yama*) [ii. 30] and with the observances (*niyama*) [ii. 32], the abstentions and the observances and the other [six aids] are hinted at.

[1] Compare Metta Sutta in Sutta Nipāta, i. 8[7], p. 26, Fausböll's ed.

In this same way [concentration] conscious [of objects] arises for one who is endowed with all the aids to yoga. Therefore he says «when his mind-stuff has become concentrated.» Discrimination of insight, the exceptional quality (*prakarṣa*) [of mind-stuff], is attained. In the words «through practice of these means» he states that concentration not conscious [of an object] follows after conscious [concentration]. After reaching the stages in this same concentration, one after another, and as a result of passionlessness for the various objects, concentration not conscious [of an object] arises. Now this is the occasion for Isolation. For the insight into the difference between the *sattva* and the Self is followed by restriction which causes the mind-stuff to cease from working at its task, since now, inasmuch as all its duties are done, its purpose is fulfilled.

Now these yogins are of nine kinds, as being respectively followers of the gentle and the moderate and the vehement method; that is to say, the follower of the gentle method, the follower of the moderate method, and the follower of the vehement method. Among these, the follower of the gentle method is also of three kinds: with gentle intensity, with moderate intensity, and with keen intensity. Likewise the follower of the moderate method [is found with the three intensities]. Likewise the follower of the vehement method [is found with the three intensities]. Now, among those who follow the vehement method,

21. For the keenly intense, [concentration] is near.

[For them] there is gaining of concentration and the result of concentration.

Some one raises the objection that if belief and the other qualities are means for [attaining] yoga, then all [the yogins] without distinction would possess concentration and its results. Whereas it is observed that in some cases there is perfection (*siddhi*); in other cases the absence of perfection; in some cases perfection after a delay; in other cases perfection after still more delay; [and] in other cases quickly. In reply to this objection he says «Now these yogins are of nine kinds.» Those are called [followers of gentle or moderate or vehement methods], in whose case, through the force of subliminal-impressions and the invisible-influences (*adṛṣṭa*) of previous births, the methods, that is, belief and the other [means], become gentle or moderate or vehement. «Intensity» is passionlessness. And its gentle or moderate or vehement character is due to the force of previous subconscious-impressions and invisible-influences. Among these [yogins,] he describes those who are of such a kind that perfection is [for them] very quick, in the sūtra **21. For the keenly intense, [concentration] is near.** This is the statement of the sūtra; the comment completes the phrase. The result of concentration conscious [of an object] is [concentration] not conscious [of an object]; and [the result] of this is Isolation.

---

22. Because [this keenness] is gentle or moderate or keen, there is a [concentration] superior (*viçeṣa*) even to this [near kind].

In that there is a gently keen and a moderately keen and a vehemently keen, there is a superior even to this [concentration]. Because there is a superior to this [near kind], the attainment of concentration and the result of concentration is near to him who follows the vehement method and is of mildly keen intensity; still more near to him who is of moderately keen intensity; and most near to him who is of vehemently keen intensity.

22. Because [this keenness] is gentle or moderate or keen, there is a [concentration] superior (*viçeṣa*) even to this [near kind]. This is explained by the Comment which is explained if you simply read it aloud.

Is [the attainment] of concentration most near as a result of this last [method] only, or is there some other method also for its attainment, or not?

23. Or[1] [concentration] is attained by devotion to the Içvara.

By devotion,[2] by a special kind of adoration, the Içvara inclines [to him] and favours him merely because of [this yogin's] profound-desire. Also as a result of the profound-desire for Him, the yogin becomes most near to the attainment of concentration and to [Isolation] the result [of concentration].

In order to bring forward another sūtra he puts forth a topic for consideration in the words «Is . . . . as a result of this last [method] only.» The phrase «or not» is the remover of a doubt. **23. Or [concentration] is attained by**

[1] As distinguishing from the conscious concentration of i. 17, and from the not conscious or 'other' of i. 18.

[2] Compare ii. 1, and see Bhag. Gītā xi. 55, and also SBE. xlviii, p. 284.

devotion to the Içvara. He discusses the words «By devotion.» By devotion [that is] by a special kind of adoration either mental or verbal or bodily. «He inclines», that is, He is brought near [to him] and favours him. «Profound-desire» is a wish for some thing yet to come, to the effect that this thing coveted by him may be his. By this means only and not by any other functional-activity. The rest is easy.

But it is now asked who is this [being] that we have called the Içvara, as distinct from the primary-substance and the Self?

24. Untouched by hindrances or karmas or fruition or by latent-deposits the Içvara is a special kind of Self.

The ‹hindrances› are undifferentiated-consciousness and the rest [ii. 3]. The ‹karmas› are good (*kuçala*) or evil. The ‹fruition› is the consequences which these [evolve]. The ‹latent-deposits› (*āçaya*) are subconscious-impressions (*vāsanā*) corresponding to these [fruitions]. These [hindrances and karmas and fruitions and latent-deposits], although they are found in the central-organ (*manas*), are attributed to the Self. For it is he that is said to be the experiencer of the results of these [in the central-organ]. Just as the victory or defeat which depends upon the combatants is attributed to [their] lord (*svāmin*). For, the Içvara is a special kind of Self who is untouched by this [kind of] experience.

Then there are those who have obtained Isolation; and those who are in Isolation (*kevalin*) are many.[1] Now these by severing the three instruments of bondage[2] have obtained Isolation; and the Içvara's relation to this [Isolation] belongs neither to the past nor to the future, [but is eternal]. Thus it is not with Him as with the [ordinary] liberated [Self] that there has been expressly made known a terminus a quo of bondage (*pūrvā bandhakoṭi*). Nor is it with Him, as it is with one [whose body] is resolved into primary-matter, that there is a terminus ad quem, when bondage

[1] According to Sāṁkhya-sūtra i. 91–92 the Içvara should be classed as one of these.

[2] The three *bandhana* would be 1. *prakṛti*, 2. *vikāra*, 3. *dakṣiṇā*. Compare Sāṁ. Tat. Kāum. xliv. The three *vipāka* are *jāti*, *āyus*, and *bhoga* (ii. 13). These three are also the *upasarga* (Vācaspati-miçra, i. 29, Calcutta edition, p. 66[14]).

might recur. But He is at all times whatsoever liberated and at all times whatsoever the Içvara.

But it might be asked, 'That universally admitted eternal superiority (*utkarṣa*) of the Içvara which results from his assuming a *sattva* of perfect (*prakṛṣṭa*) quality—has that any proof [to authorize it], or is it without proof?' [The reply is, His] sacred-books (*çāstra*) are its proof. [But then] again [it may be asked], what proof have the sacred-books? [The reply is] they have their proof in the perfect quality of [His] *sattva*. Inasmuch as both [the sacred-books and the superiority] reside in the Içvara's *sattva*, there is a never-beginning relation between the two. From these [sacred-books, therefore] this proves to be true that He is at all times whatsoever liberated and at all times whatsoever the Içvara. Now this His pre-eminence (*āiçvarya*) is altogether without anything equal to it or excelling it. For, to begin with, it cannot be excelled by any other pre-eminence, because whatever might [seem] to excel it would itself prove to be that very [pre-eminence we are in quest of]. Therefore that is the Içvara wherein we reach this uttermost limit of pre-eminence. Nor again is there any pre-eminence equal to His. [Why not?] Because when one thing is simultaneously desired by two equals, the one saying 'let this be new' and the other saying 'let this be old', if the one wins his way, the other fails in his wish and so becomes inferior. And two equals cannot obtain the same desired thing simultaneously, since that would be a contradiction of terms. Therefore [we maintain that,] in whomsoever there is a pre-eminence that is neither equalled nor excelled, he is the Içvara, and He is, as we said, a special kind of Self.

He anticipates the objection that 'the universe (*viçva*) is pervaded by animate and inanimate [beings] only and by nothing else. Consequently if the Içvara be inanimate, then He is primary-substance (*pradhāna*), since what is evolved from primary-substance also falls within primary-substance. And by this hypothesis he could not be made inclined since he is inanimate. Or on the other hand, if he be animate, still,—since the Energy of Intellect is indifferent (*āudāsīnya*) and since in so far as it is not in the round-of-rebirths it has no feeling-of-personality or other [hindrance],—how can the Energy of Intellect be inclined, [or] how can profound-desire [have anything to do with Energy of Intellect]?'

In alluding to this he says «But now . . . . primary-substance.» He gives the reply to this objection in the following sûtra. **24. Untouched by hindrances or karmas or fruition or by latent-deposits the Içvara is a special kind of Self.** «The ‹hindrances› are undifferentiated-consciousness and the rest», for it is these that, by the stroke of various kinds of misery, hinder a man within the round-of-rebirth. «Good (*kuçala*) or evil» are merit and demerit; and by a figurative expression they are called karma, because they proceed from karma. «Fruition» is birth and length-of-life and the [kind of] experience [ii. 13]. «Corresponding to these :» the subconscious-impressions corresponding to the fruitions. These subconscious-impressions are called latent-deposits because they lie in the ground of the mind-stuff. For, until [that particular] karma, [that is, some demerit], which precipitates (*nirvartaka*)[1] the birth [of an individual] as a young elephant, makes manifest an impression (*bhāvanā*) [latent in his mind-stuff] which is characterized by a previously (*prāg*) [existing] and potential kind of experience [proper to] a young elephant,—for so long [that karma] is not capable of [producing] the experience proper to a young elephant. Therefore it proves to be true that the impression which produces the experience (*anubhava*) of being born as a young elephant corresponds to the fruition as a young elephant. It might be said: 'Such things as hindrances, inasmuch as they are properties of the thinking-substance, can by no means whatsoever touch the Self. Accordingly merely by mentioning the word ‹Self› the absence of any trace of these [hindrances] is established. Consequently what need is there of the words ‹hindrances or karmas› and the rest?' In reply to this he says «These.» These [hindrances and karmas and fruitions and latent-impressions] although they reside in the central-organ (*manas*) are attributed to the Self who is in the round-of-rebirths. Why? «For it is he that is said to be the experiencer of the results of these [in the central-organ].» That is to say, he is the thinker (*cetayitṛ*). Consequently the Içvara, because he is a Self, comes into relation with these. For this reason, [because these are only attributed to the Self], it is consistent to make a denial of this [relation]. This he does in the word «who.» For the Içvara is a special kind of Self who is untouched by this [kind] of experience, namely, that also found in the thinking-substance and common to the Selves in general.—It is ‹a special kind› in that it is specialized [and] discriminated from [all] other Selves. Desirous of pointing out what is not to be included in the words ‹a special kind› he first raises a counter-objection (*paricodana*) and then rebuts it in the words «Now these . . . have obtained Isolation.» 1. There is the bondage to primary-matter in the case of those [whose bodies] are resolved into primary-matter. 2. There is [the bondage] to evolved-matter in the case of the discarnate. 3. There is the bondage to

[1] This word is glossed in the Rahasyam by the word *janaka*. And the word 'young elephant' *karabha* is said to mean an elephant which eats grass and twigs (*kaṭakāṣṭhāçī hastīti*).

sacrificial gifts in the case of those who partake in the experience of objects supernal or not supernal. These are those three well-known «instruments of bondage.» For, those whose central-organs are [subliminally] refined (*saṁskṛta*) by impressions from primary-matter, attain to resolution into primary-matter only after the body has broken up. For the others [the liberated Selves] the terminus a quo is expressly made known; accordingly the terminus ad quem alone is mentioned [as applying to those whose bodies are resolved into primary-matter, although the terminus a quo also applies to them]. But in this case [of the Içvara] both the terminus a quo and the later terminus are denied. Having stated the case in brief he now gives the details in the words «But He is at all times whatsoever liberated and He is at all times whatsoever the Içvara.» He possesses pre-eminence in richness of knowledge and of action and of power. With reference to this he asks «That universally admitted . . . which.» Perception and action are impossible in the case of the Energy of Intellect which does not enter into mutations. In case this be admitted and if it be said that therefore a substrate must be supposed to be made up of pure *sattva* without *rajas* and *tamas*, then the Içvara who is at all times whatsoever liberated cannot be in the relation of proprietor to his property towards an effulgence (*utkarṣa*) of the *sattva* in a mind-stuff which depends upon undifferentiated-consciousness. In reply to this he says «from his assuming a *sattva* of perfect (*prakṛṣṭa*) quality.» In the case of the Içvara there does not exist as in the case of the ordinary man a relation, caused by undifferentiated-consciousness, of proprietor to his property, with the *sattva* of the mind-stuff. But [the relation is that] expressed by the resolve, 'By the teaching of knowledge and right-living (*dharma*) I will lift up beings, encompassed by the three anguishes, from the great sea of the state after death (*pretya*).' And this [knowledge and right-living] cannot be taught unless there be an abundance of excellence in the adequacy of [His] knowledge[1] and of [His] activity. And there cannot be this [abundance of excellence] unless a *sattva* be assumed which has been purified from stains by the removal of *rajas* and *tamas*. With this resolve the Exalted One reflects, and assumes a *sattva* of perfect quality. Although He is untouched by undifferentiated-consciousness, it appears as if He were under the illusion of identifying Himself with undifferentiated-consciousness and as if He were ignorant of the real nature of undifferentiated-consciousness. But He does not deal with undifferentiated-consciousness as if it were undifferentiated-consciousness as such. The actor who takes the rôle of Rāma and represents the different kinds of behaviour [belonging to the character] is not of course confused [as to his real personal identity]. For he knows that this [rôle] is only a deliberately assumed form and not his [form] in reality. An objector might say, 'This may be so. It may be true that the Exalted One must assume *sattva* in order to uplift [the world]. On the other hand His desire to lift it up is based on His assumption of

[1] Compare Çvetāçvat. Up. vi. 8.

this [*sattva*]; and inasmuch as this [desire] is also derived from primary-matter [the fallacy of] mutual interdependence results.' In reply to this he says «Eternal.» This [objection] might be true, if this were the very first creation. But the succession of creations and contractions [of worlds] is from time-without-beginning. And when the period of the desire for contraction has come to a full end, then the Exalted One, while in the act of contemplating within Himself, 'I must assume a *sattva* of perfect quality,' contracts the world. At that time the *sattva* of the Içvara's mind-stuff becomes subconsciously-impressed by the contemplation. And although the Içvara's mind-stuff be tending towards a homogeneity with primary-matter, still,—when the period of the great mundane-dissolution has come to a full end, under the pressure of the subconscious-impression of the contemplation,—it enters into a mutation of precisely the same kind as a state of *sattva*. In precisely the same way Chāitra contemplates 'To-morrow I must get up just at day-break'; and then after having slept gets up at that very time because of the subliminal-impression resulting from his contemplation. Consequently since [the worlds] are from time-without-beginning, and in so far as the Içvara's contemplation and His assumption of the *sattva* are eternal, there is no [logical fallacy] of interdependence. Nor can it be urged [1] that the *sattva* of the Içvara's mind-stuff does not pass out [of the phenomenal state] into homogeneity with primary-matter. For that which [by reason of its subconscious-impression] never becomes homogeneous with primary-matter is not secondary-matter (*prādhānika*). And again it is not the Energy of Intellect, because it is non-perceptive (*ajña*). This being the meaning, one might assume another [kind of] thing which could not be proven by any source-of-valid-ideas. This too would be a quite groundless [assumption].—Because there is no other [kind of] thing distinct from primary-matter and the Self, has this kind of universally admitted and eternal superiority of the Içvara any proof [to authorize it, and] is it based on any source-of-valid-ideas, or is it without proof [and] not based on any source-of-valid-ideas? The answer is in the phrase «sacred-books (*çāstra*) are its proof.» The sacred books are the Revealed-Word (*çruti*) and the Tradition (*smṛti*) and the Epics and Purāṇas.—He brings forward an objection in the words «what proof have the sacred-books?» For sacred books presuppose that there is inference and perception. And no one can perceive or infer the perfection of the Içvara's *sattva*. Again, there is no ground for saying that the sacred books have their source in a perception by the Içvara. For even if we imagine [Him saying that he perceives the sacred books], He would then be speaking to publish abroad His own pre-eminence. [This is inconceivable since no one could imagine that the Içvara would boast.] Such is the [objector's] meaning. In rebuttal he says «they have their proof in the perfect quality of His *sattva*.» This is what he intends [to say]. Incantations (*mantra*) and the Medical Vedas are composed by the Içvara. In these [two] cases their authori-

[1] Cp. Comment iii. 13.

tativeness is granted by reason of their adequacy in action. [This adequacy] is undoubted because there is no failure to effect purposes. [The authoritativeness is granted. He shows that it is not based upon experimental evidence.] And in the case of the different herbs and of the particular combinations of one [herb] with another, and in the case of the incantations in so far as single syllables are connected or excluded, no one who uses only profane methods of proof, could, even in a thousand lives, make the connexions and exclusions.—Furthermore there is no ground for asserting that connexions and exclusions [of the proper herbs or syllables] are a result of verbal-communication (*āgama*) and that verbal-communication is a result of these [connexions and exclusions] on the ground that the succession of these two [1. verbal-communication, 2. connexions and exclusions] forms a series from time-without-beginning. The reason for this is that the succession of these two is severed at the time of a great mundane dissolution. Neither [is there ground for saying that] there is no method of proving that there is this [great mundane dissolution]. For he will set forth in detail [iii. 13] that the world is an evolved-form of primary-substance and is identical [with it in substance]. There is evidently a heterogeneous mutation [e.g. curds] of the [original] homogeneous mutation [e.g. milk]. Analogously, milk or sugar-juice or similar substances assume various forms such as curds or treacle [and so forth]. And it is evident that the heterogeneous mutation presupposes the homogeneous mutation. So in the point at issue, the primary-substance can also have heterogeneous mutations by assuming such forms as the Great [thinking-substance] and the personality-substance; occasionally also it can have a homogeneous mutation. And its homogeneous mutation is the state of equipoise [of the primary-substance]. This, moreover, is the great mundane dissolution. [There is therefore a great mundane dissolution.] [To revert to the argument that the authoritativeness of the sacred books is not experimentally to be found.] Accordingly, the Exalted One is first of all the composer of the Incantations and of the Medical Vedas. Hence it must be acknowledged that, in so far as the obscuration due to the stains of *rajas* and of *tamas* has been removed, the substance of [His] thinking-substance illumines everywhere.

To resume the argument (*tathā ca*). Because He was aiming to give instruction in [worldly] happiness and in [eternal] bliss [incapable of test by experience here], the Vedas as a whole were composed by the Içvara and must also be supposed to have their source only in the perfect quality of His thinking-substance. And in the superiority of the substance (*sattva*) there is no possibility of error or deceit, which have their origin in *rajas* and *tamas*. This [then] is established that sacred books have their proof in the perfect quality of His *sattva*.—[A further objection.] 'This may be so. But then if the sacred books make known the perfection in so far as they are the effect of the perfection, there would be an inference from effect to cause[1] (*çeṣavat*). But that would not give us a verbal

[1] See Nyāya Bhāṣya xviii. 4.

communication (*āgama*).' Replying to this he says «Inasmuch as both.» The sacred books do not make known a relation of cause and effect, but do make known the correspondence[1] from time without beginning between the word-expressing-a-meaning (*vācaka*) and the thing-expressed (*vācya*). For the perfection has its existence in the substance of the Içvara's thinking-substance; and the sacred books, in that they give expression to this [thinking-substance], also have their existence in it. In summing up he says «From these.» From these sacred books, which give expression to the perfection of the substance of the Içvara's thinking-substance, this proves to be true, [that is] is known,—since the object (*viṣaya*) [the sacred books] is the distinguishing-characteristic of that-to-which-the-object-refers (*viṣayin*) [the Içvara],—that «He is at all times whatsoever liberated and at all times whatsoever the Içvara.»—Having thus distinguished [Him] from any other Self, he distinguishes [Him] from any other Içvara also by saying «Now this His.» He describes its being altogether without anything excelling it, in the words «For to begin with.» Why is this? The reply is «whatever . . . very.» For what reason is this pre-eminence altogether free from everything that might excel it? He replies «Therefore . . . that wherein.» In other words, as applied to those who have not reached the uttermost limit, the term pre-eminence is [only] a figurative expression.—He describes the state of freedom from anything equal to it by saying «Nor again . . . equal to His.» Wish is unhindered volition; by failure in this a man becomes inferior. Or if there be no inferiority, then it would be that both fail in their wishes. For no effect would occur, or if it did occur, the effect [of the two wishes] simultaneously would be perceived to have the logical mark (*samāliñgita*) of two contradictory qualities. Alluding to this he says «And two.» If however the intentions [of the two] are not contradictory and if the pre-eminent quality (*içvaratva*) is attached to each, then what need of any others? Because then [the intention] could be accomplished by a single pre-eminent (*içanā*) alone. On the other hand, if [all] work together, no one would be the Içvara; but there would be a parliament. Furthermore it is not fitting that those who are fit for uninterrupted pre-eminence [should rule] by turns. And besides this would be a more difficult supposition. Since this is evident, all is cleared up.

Furthermore,

25. In this [Içvara] the germ of the omniscient is at its utmost excellence.

This our process-of-knowing (*grahaṇa*) the supersensuous, whether in the past or future or present, whether separately or collectively,—[this process,] whether it be small or great, is the germ

[1] This would constitute an *āgama*.

of the omniscient. He, verily, in whom this germ as it increases progressively reaches its utmost excellence is the omniscient. It is possible for the germ of the omniscient to reach this [uttermost] limit, for it admits of degrees of excellence, as in the case of any ascending scale. He in whom the limit of thinking is reached is the omniscient and He is a special kind of Self. [If you object that this argument would prove the omniscience of Buddha or of Jina, there would be this reply.] An inference exhausts (*upakṣaya*) its force in bringing a general proposition to a conclusion,[1] but is powerless to prove a particular instance. Therefore the ascertainment of the [Omniscient] one's special name is [not a matter of inference, but is rather] to be sought out in the verbal-communication, [which excludes the supposed cases, since their tradition is false]. Although He is above all feelings of self-gratification, yet [to this Içvara] the gratification of living beings is a sufficient motive. He may be conceived as resolving, 'By instruction in knowledge and in right-living, at the dissolution of the mundane period and at the great dissolution, I will lift up human beings, who are whirled in the vortex of existence.' And likewise it hath been said,[2] "The First Knower, assuming a created mind-stuff through compassion, the Exalted, the Supreme Sage, unto Āsuri who desired to know, declared this doctrine."

After having mentioned the sacred books as a means of proving [His] power of action and of knowledge, he shows that inference is a means of proving [His] power of knowledge. This is stated in the words «Furthermore.» **25. In this [Içvara] the germ of the omniscient is at its utmost excellence.** He discusses [the sūtra] in the words «This our.» In proportion to the degree to which the *tamas* which covers the *sattva* of the thinking-substance has been removed, this our process-of-knowing supersensuous things, past and future and present, which occur separately as well as collectively,—[this] process may be qualified as being either small or great. This is the germ [or] cause of the omniscient. Some one knows a very little of the past or of the other times, another

[1] Compare *sāmānyenopasaṁhāraḥ*, p. 100, line 4, Calcutta ed. of this work.

[2] By Pañcaçikha in the first fragment as collected by Garbe in his article on Pañcaçikha und seine Fragmente (in Festgruss an Roth, Stuttgart, 1893), p. 77. This fragment is also discussed by Fitz Edward Hall in his edition of the Sāṁkhya-Pravachana-Bhāshya, 1856, Preface pp. 10 and 17. See also Garuḍa Purāṇa i. 18.

much, another still more. Thus with regard to objects to be known there is a [relative] smallness or greatness of the knowing-process. He, verily, in whom this [germ] as it increases progressively has come to a stop because of its excellence,—he is said to be the omniscient. In this wise only the object of proof is described; now he gives the means of proof in the words «It is possible.» In the words «It is possible for the germ of the omniscient to reach this [uttermost] limit» there is a statement of the major term. The limit is the reaching of the utmost excellence; it is that state higher than which there is no excellence. Accordingly it should not be urged that this is establishing what is already established. For [this higher than which there is no excellence, is established] only so far as it is a terminal-point. [For,] the middle term (*hetu*), as he gives it, is «for it admits of degrees of excellence.» Whatever admits of degrees of excellence, all that is [capable of reaching] the utmost excellence. Similarly in the case of the *kuvalaya* berry and the *āmalaka* fruit and the *bilva* fruit there is a size that admits of degrees. And in the soul (*ātman*) [there is a magnitude which has reached its] utmost excellence. Thus he shows that there is a concomitance [of terms].—And when he says «as in the case of any ascending scale,» it is not relevant to object that there is a discrepancy in so far as the properties [of a substance], such as its magnitude, [form an ascending scale but do not reach utmost excellence]. For in the case of the whole, its magnitude does of course not excel the magnitude of the parts. But whatever magnitudes there are, each functioning by itself, from the smallest atom up to the final whole, may be so arranged that one may assert a progressive increase of magnitudes. But, because it is not finished as contrasted with the object to be thought, in so far as it has [successively] one or two or a multitude of objects, thinking may with reason be said to admit of degrees of excellence. Thus there is no discrepancy. He brings the discussion to a close in the words «He in whom the limit.»—It might be objected that there are many authors of sacred books (*tīrthakara*), Buddha and Arhata and Kapila the Sage and many others. Why, by this line of inference, may they not be counted as omniscient? In reply he says «a general proposition.» Whence then can we be informed of his particular qualities? The reply is «the [Omniscient] one's.» The point is that the pseudo-sacred-words composed by Buddha or by the others are not a Sacred Word (*āgama*). For they give instruction in the way of soullessness and of momentariness, both of which are contradicted by all sources-of-valid-ideas. The reason for this is that they are deceitful. A Sacred Word has as its distinguishing-characteristic the Revealed-Word (*çruti*) and the Tradition (*smṛti*) and the Epics and Purāṇas. The Sacred Word (*ā-gama*) is that from which the [spiritual] means for [worldly] happiness and [final] bliss come to (*ā-gam*) or strike upon the thinking-substance. From this [Sacred Word] comes information as to [the Içvara's] particular qualities, such as His name—any particular name, for example Çiva or the Içvara—which are firmly established in the Revealed Word and in the other books. Under the word 'such as' (*ādi*) are included the sexpartite nature and the ten eternal principles, as described in the Vāyu Purāṇa [xii. 32],[1] "Omniscience and Contentment and Limitless Knowledge and Freedom and Ever-unthwarted Energy and Infinite Energy—these, the experts in the sacred ordinances tell us, are the six parts of the all-pervasive Maheçvara." Likewise "Knowledge and Passionlessness and Pre-eminence and Self-control and Truth and Patience and Perseverance and Creative Energy and Right Knowledge of Self and Competency to Rule [the Universe]—these ten eternal principles abide eternally in Çaṁkara." It is objected, 'This may be so. But inasmuch as the Exalted One, who is eternally free and who has attained to the utmost excellence of passionlessness, cannot cherish craving merely for his own self; and inasmuch as, if he be compassionate, he should create, to the end that every one should be intent upon happiness, for the reason that we cannot explain the production of a world of living beings in which pain predominates; and inasmuch as, if he have no motive, we cannot explain his act [of creation] as being that of a being of understanding,—therefore, even if he be endowed with the power of action, the world cannot be the result of his action.' In reply to this he says «Although He is above all feelings of self-gratification.» The gratification of beings in whom is the breath of life is [for Him a sufficient] motive. Now it is clear that the mind-stuff ceases from the production of its [two kinds of] effects: the outer experience of the various kinds of things and [secondly] the discriminative discernment. Then it is that the Self enters into its Isolation. Accordingly as a means to motivate this [Isolation] the compassionate [Içvara] describes the discriminative discernment. Accordingly, although the Içvara with the help of merit and demerit makes living creatures feel pleasure and pain, for the reason that the mind-stuff has its task yet to fulfil,—still he is not incompassionate.—He tells of the way by which he makes known the discriminative discernment as a [spiritual] means in the words «By instruction in knowledge and in right-living.» Both in knowledge and in right-living; by instruction in both of these. By the combination of knowledge and of right-living as a result of reaching full maturity of discriminative discernment. «At the dissolution of the mundane period,» that is, at the end of a Day of Brahma[2], at which time the world with the exception of the Heaven of Truth (*satya-loka*), vanishes. «At the great dissolution,» at which time there is the destruction of Brahma together with the Heaven of Truth. «Whirled in the vortex of existence» that is,[3] those merged in the [primary] cause; and therefore partaking of the pain of that [cause] up to the time of death. The words «dissolution of the mundane period» is an expression of a part for the whole; for at other times also [the Içvara may be conceived as] resolving «I will lift up human beings.» In other words human beings by attaining to Isolation are lifted up. It might be objected that this

[1] Anandāçrama ed., p. 43[1-2].

[2] See Viṣṇu Purāṇa vi. 3.

[3] The words "that is . . . resolving" are not in the Bikāner MS. and may be a gloss.

instruction in knowledge and right-living by one whose motive is compassion is also well known to the followers of Kapila. In reply to this he says «And likewise it hath been said.» In this sense it hath been said by Pañcaçikha the Master (*ācārya*). «The First Knower» is Kapila. The statement of Pañcaçikha the Master with regard to the First Knower applies to the First Teacher in the succession [of teacher and disciple] to which he belonged ; and [this First Teacher] was the First Liberated. But it does not apply to the Supreme Teacher who is free from time-without-beginning. Of those who were the First Liberated and of those [other] knowers who were at other times liberated, Kapila is for us the First Knower [and the First] Liberated. And it is he that is the teacher, [but not from time without beginning]. For it is revealed that even Kapila attained to knowledge, by the favour of Maheçvara only, just as soon as he was born. He whom we call Kapila is accepted as being the [fifth] incarnation of Vishnu. [It might be objected that] Hiraṇyagarbha is the Self-existent [and thus he would be the First Knower]. [For] it is revealed in the Veda[1] [that he was the First-born and] that he also acquired Sāṁkhya and Yoga. [The reply would be that] this same Içvara, the First Knower, the Self-existent[2] Vishnu [is] Kapila. "But [He is] the Içvara of those descended from the Self-existent." This is the point.

This same [Içvara is]—

26. Teacher of the Primal [Sages] also, forasmuch as [with Him] there is no limitation by time.

No-one-doubts-that the Primal Sages are limited by time ; [but] He to whom time does not apply, in so far as it might be a limiting object, is the Teacher even of the Primal Sages. As He is perfected (*siddha*) in that mode-of-existence (*gati*) which is perfection at the commencement of the present creation, so He is to be recognized [as being in this mode of perfection] at the beginning of past creations also.

He now states the distinction between the Içvara and such beings as Brahma by saying «This same [Içvara].» These words «This same [Içvara]» form the transition to the sūtra. **26. Teacher of the Primal [Sages] also, forasmuch as [with Him] there is no limitation by time.** He explains the sūtra in the words «No-one-doubts-that the Primal.» Time, however, a period of a hundred years or some other period, does not apply, [that is] has no reference [to Him] in

[1] Çvet. Up. iii. 4, iv. 12, vi. 18.

[2] If the reading be *na sva°*, the meaning would be that although the Self-existent is the First Knower, still in this passage the term 'First Knower' applies to Kapila and not to the Self-existent.

so far as it might be a limiting object, [that is] limiting motive. The mode-of-existence of perfection is the attainment of perfection. This is to be recognized as coming from the Sacred-Word. Such is the inner meaning.

27. The word-expressing Him is the Mystic-syllable (*praṇava*).

The Içvara is the object-expressed by the mystic syllable. Is the expressiveness of this [Syllable] the work of [ordinary] usage (*saṁketa*), or is it permanent [and self-manifesting] like [the relation of] the light to the lamp? The relation of this thing-to-be-expressed to the expressive-word is fixed. But the usage [as determined] by the Içvara declares this its fixed meaning. Thus the [actual] relation of father and son is permanent, but the verbal statement that that man is this man's father is suggested [to the mind] by usage. And the usage with regard to the relation between expressive-words and things-expressed is made by [the Içvara] to serve with a distinct reference to the power of expression which they had in former creations also. The authoritative sages maintain that the relation between a word and an intended-object is eternal is so far as the consensus (*sampratipatti*) [of successive generations of speakers] is eternal.

In this same series [of sūtras] the Exalted Içvara has been made known. Now in order to make known the devotion [paid] to Him he tells of the word-expressive of Him. **27. The word-expressing Him is the Mystic-syllable** (*praṇava*). He begins the explanation with the words «. . . the object-expressed.» On this point he clears up [the topic] by setting forth for consideration the opinion of others. [This he begins] by asking «Is the expressiveness.» «Expressiveness» is ability to give information. For to others[1] it seems as if the relation between word and intended-meaning is natural. [And] if this object-intended is to be recognized as having an essence of such a kind when it comes by usage from this word, then, whenever that [natural] relation does not exist, that [object-intended] will not be manifested even by hundreds of usages. For when a water-jar, which is capable of being made manifest by a lamp, is not [there], then even with thousands of lamps it cannot be made manifest. On the other hand, the word young-elephant (*karabha*), made by

[1] He refers to the Vāiyākaraṇas, such as, for example, Patañjali in Mahābhāṣya (Kielhorn's edition), vol. i, p. 6[ff].

usage to denote an elephant (*vāraṇa*) evidently gives information with regard to an elephant. As a result of this, one might say that expressiveness is made by usage only. After reflection [as to whether the relation is accidental or eternal] he determines what the author's opinion is by saying «is fixed.» The import would be this. All words are capable of naming intended-objects of all kinds of forms. Thus the natural relation of them [i. e. of words] to intended-objects of all kinds of forms is most surely fixed. The usage, however, [as determined] by the Içvara is both a manifester [of this natural relation] and a limitation. And this [relation] has a word expressing it when the usage [as determined] by the Içvara [is followed]; [but the relation suffers] corruption when the usage [as determined] by the Içvara is not [followed]. This is the distinction. It is this that he states in the phrase «But the usage [as determined] by the Içvara.» He gives an example when he says «Thus.» It is objected, 'A word is a product of the primary-cause; at the time of the great dissolution it tends towards the primary causal state; and its [expressive] power would also be resolved [into primary matter]. Then it would not be possible that the usage [as determined] by the Great Içvara (*māheçvara*) should revive the expressive power [of such a word] only as had been deprived of its expressive [power] after having been changed successively into [the different evolved forms of primary matter] beginning with the Great [thinking-substance].' In reply to this he says «in former creations.» Although the word together with its expressive power passes into the primary causal state of equipoise, when it appears again it does appear endowed with the [expressive] power of that [word]. Similarly a plant [*udbhijja*], utterly reduced to an earthly condition after the rains have [ceased] to fall, [becomes as it was before] when sprinkled vigorously with the stream of water let fall from the clouds. Therefore the Exalted One makes the usage conform to the previous relation [of the word to the intended object]. Accordingly, in so far as the consensus [of previous creations, which is the same as] the series of similar modes-of-expression (*vyavahāra*), is eternal, the authoritative sages (*āgamika*) maintain[1] that this relation is not absolutely eternal. But their point is that it is impossible without the help of the Sacred Word to assert that the usage was exactly of the same kind in other creations also.

Now, by the yogin who has recognized the power of the word to express the thing,

28. Repetition of it and reflection upon its meaning [should be made].

The repetition of the Mystic Syllable, and reflection upon the Içvara who is signified by the Mystic Syllable. Then in the case

[1] See Patañjali, Mahābhāṣya (Kielhorn), vol. i, p. 6^{14} and 7^{21}.

of this yogin who thus repeats the Mystic Syllable and reflects upon its meaning, mind-stuff attains to singleness-of-intent. And so it hath been said,[1]

> "Through study let him practise yoga;
> Through yoga let him meditate on study.
> By perfectness in study and in yoga
> Supreme Soul shines forth clearly."

Having designated the Mystic Syllable he tells of the contemplation. **28. Repetition of it and reflection upon its meaning [should be made].** He explains [the sūtra] by saying «Of the Mystic Syllable.» Reflection is an absorption in the mind again and again. What follows from this? He replies by saying «the Mystic Syllable.» He attains to singleness-of-intent [and his] mind-stuff comes to rest in the One Exalted. In illustration of this he introduces a stanza from Vyāsa (*vāiyāsikī gāthā*) by saying «And so.» The Içvara then gratifies him by conferring upon him concentration and the fruit of concentration.

What else comes to him?

29. Thereafter comes the right-knowledge of him who thinks in an inverse way, and the removal of obstacles. Whatever obstacles there be, disease and the rest, all these are removed by devotion to the Içvara, and [the yogin] comes to a sight of his own real self. He has the right knowledge which sees that as the Içvara is a Self and is undefiled and undisturbed [by hindrances] and isolated and exempt from accidents, so he also is a Self conscious [by reflection] of its thinking-substance.

What in addition comes to him? **29. Thereafter comes the right-knowledge of him who thinks in an inverse way, and the removal of obstacles.** One is inverted who knows in an opposite way [to the ordinary person whose mind-stuff flows out and becomes modified by objects]. One who thinks in that way thinks inversely; [in other words] the [ordinary] man [still] under the conditions of undifferentiated-consciousness (*avidyāvant*). In such wise [the author] demarks [such a one] from the Içvara who is free from undifferentiated-consciousness (*vidyāvant*), and who is endowed with eternal superiority of the *sattva*. Right-knowledge comes to the kind of thinking which is under the conditions of undifferentiated-consciousness and which is inverted. A perception of himself as he is in his own self comes to him.—‹Obstacles› and ‹the removal› of them are

[1] Compare Viṣṇ. Pur. vi. 7. 33 f.; Nāradīya Pur. xlvii. 12-14.

to be described [ii. 32]. The words «Whatever . . .» give the exposition of these [latter words]. The word «own» [refers to his] soul (*ātman*), that is, his self. The word «self» (*rūpa*) excludes all qualities attributed [to him] by undifferentiated-consciousness. One might well say that devotion to the Içvara has the Içvara as its object; how then can it apparently give a direct perception, a thinking in the inverse way [upon one's own real self]? For this would prove too much. In reply to this he says «as the Içvara.» «Undefiled:» not subject to origination or dissolution in so far as He is absolutely unchanged. «Undisturbed» means free from hindrances. «Isolated» means beyond the scope of merit and demerit [and] consequently «exempt from accidents.» «Accidents» are birth and length of life and kind of experience [ii. 13].—Since a homogeneity implies a certain degree of difference, he shows the difference between [Selves in general] and the Içvara by saying «conscious [by reflection] of its thinking-substance.» In such wise the word ‹inverse› has been described.—In the case of two objects which are totally irrelevant to each other, prolonged meditation on either one unfits one for a direct perception of the other. Whereas prolonged meditation upon one object proves to be of service for the direct perception of another similar to it. Similarly the study of one book proves to be of service for the acquisition of knowledge of another book similar to it. As for (*tu*) immediate-perception (*pratyāsatti*), it is the cause of direct perception with regard to one's own self, but not with regard to another self. [Thus by meditating upon the Içvara, we learn about our own selves.] Thus the argument is cleared up.

But what are these obstacles? Those which distract the mind-stuff. But what are these [that are distractive] and (*vā*) how many are they? [He replies.]

30. Sickness and languor and doubt and heedlessness and listlessness and worldliness (*avirati*) and erroneous perception and failure to attain any stage [of concentration] and instability in the state [when attained]—these distractions of the mind-stuff are the obstacles.

There are nine obstacles, the distractions of the mind-stuff. These appear together with the fluctuations of the mind-stuff. And they are not found where the aforesaid fluctuations of mind-stuff are not. Sickness is a disorder in the humours [of the body] or in the secretions or in the organs. Languor is a lack of activity in the mind-stuff. Doubt is a kind of thinking which touches both alternatives [of a dilemma], so that one thinks 'This might be so; might not be so.' Heedlessness is a lack of reflection upon the means of attaining concentration. Listlessness is a lack of effort due to heaviness of body or of mind-stuff. Worldliness is greed of the mind-stuff; and its essence lies in addiction to objects of sense. Erroneous perception is the thinking of misconceptions. Failure to attain any stage is not attaining any stage of concentration. Instability in the state [when attained] is the failure of the mind-stuff to remain in the stage attained. If the concentrated stage of development had been reached, [the mind-stuff] would, of course, have remained in it.—Thus it is that these distractions are called the nine blemishes of yoga [and] the nine foes of yoga [and] the obstacles of yoga.

He asks a question by saying «what.» He gives the answer in general in the words «Those which.» With regard to their kinds and their number he asks «But what.» He gives the answer by the sūtra beginning with the word **30. Sickness.** Obstacles are nine. These are fluctuations of mind-stuff and obstructive to yoga and opposed to yoga. Distractions of the mind-stuff are, of course, so-called because sickness and the other [obstacles] distract [or] divert the mind-stuff from yoga. He gives the reason for their being foes to yoga by saying «These . . . together with.» First, in the case of doubt and of erroneous perception, they are foes to the restriction of fluctuations from the mere fact that they are fluctuations. And of those that are not fluctuations, such as sickness and the rest,—these too are foes to it because they associate with fluctuations. He explains the things intended, by the words beginning with «Sickness.» The humours (*dhātu*), wind and bile and phlegm, are so-called because they sustain (*dhāraṇa*) the body. A secretion is a special kind of mutation of nourishment eaten or drunk. The organs are the senses (*indriya*). A disorder in them is a state of defect or excess. A lack of activity is an incapacity for action. Doubt is a kind of thinking which touches both[1] alternatives [of a dilemma]. Although there is no difference between doubt and error (*viparyāsa*) in so far as both do not remain in the proper form of that [in respect to which they are entertained], still,—by emphasizing the subsidiary difference, that is, the touching or not touching of the two alternatives [of the dilemma], the distinction in this case [of doubt] is made clear. A lack of reflection is a lack of action. This is about the same as saying that it is a lack of effort with regard to this thing. Heaviness of the body is the result of phlegm; heaviness of the mind-stuff is the result of *tamas*. Greed is thirst. The stages of concentration are the Madhumatī and the other [three]. If after reaching a given stage [the yogin] should deem himself sufficiently well off with only so much [progress], there would be a breach in the concentration; and as a result of this there would be a retro-

[1] Compare Nyāya-sūtra i. 1. 23.

gression even from that stage. An effort should therefore be made in such a way that when [the yogin] has reached concentration, [the mind-stuff] should be stable there.

31. Pain and despondency and unsteadiness of the body and inspiration and expiration are the accompaniments of the distractions.

Pain proceeding from self [and] pain proceeding from living creatures and pain proceeding from the gods. Pain is that by which living beings are stricken down and for the destruction of which they struggle. Despondency is agitation of mind due to an impediment [to the fulfilment] of a desire. Unsteadiness of the body is that which makes it unsteady [and] makes it tremble. Inspiration is breathing which sips in the air which is outside. Expiration is that which makes abdominal[1] air flow outwards. These are the accompaniments of the distractions. These occur in one whose mind-stuff is distracted. These do not occur in one whose mind-stuff is concentrated.

Not only the nine obstacles but also pain and the other accompaniments of these [obstacles] occur to this [yogin]. So [Vyāsa] recites the sūtra beginning with the word **31. Pain.** Pain is that which is to be felt as unpleasant. [Pain] proceeding from self is bodily by virtue of sickness, or mental by virtue of such things as passion. [Pain] proceeding from living creatures is such as is generated by tigers. [Pain] proceeding from the gods is such as is generated by the baleful influence of planets. And this pain, inasmuch as living beings in general would feel[2] it to be unpleasant, is to be rejected. Accordingly he says «by which . . . stricken down.» The breathing which without volitional action sips in the air which is outside [and] drinks it [or] makes it enter,—this inspiration is opposed to emission (*recaka*), which is accessory to concentration. The breathing also, which without volitional action makes abdominal air flow outwards [and] expels it,—this expiration[3] is opposed to inhalation (*pūraka*), which is an accessory to concentration.

Furthermore these distractions, the foes of concentration, are to

[1] Only one MS. has *koṣṭhyam*. Yet as Bālarāma points out, the rule as given in Pāṇini v. 1. 6 (see Siddhānta Kāumudī, third Nirṇaya Sāgara edition, 1904, p. 265[3]) would require that the *vṛddhi* should not take place when the termination *yat* is affixed to a stem signifying a member of the body.

[2] See Tarka-saṁgraha, § 67.

[3] *Recaka* and *pūraka* are volitional (ii. 51).

be restricted by the same[1] practice and passionlessness. Of these [two], in summing up, he describes the object to which the practice [applies].

32. To check them [let there be] practice upon a single entity. To check them let [the yogin] practise his mind-stuff by making it rest upon a single entity. But one whose mind-stuff is nothing more than an idea limited to one object after another, and is momentary (*kṣaṇika*),—of this [Buddhist] the mind-stuff as a whole is surely not single-in-intent and it is surely not distracted. But if this [mind-stuff when single-in-intent] is withdrawn from all [objects] and concentrated upon one [entity], then it may be said to be single-in-intent [and] hence not limited to one object after another. If, on the other hand,—[in the opinion] of him who maintains that the mind-stuff becomes single-in-intent as a stream of similar ideas,—singleness-in-intent be a property of the mind-stuff [conceived] as a stream, then the mind-stuff [conceived as] a stream could not be a single thing, because [as he insists] it changes from moment to moment. If however [it be maintained[2] that] singleness-of-intent is a property of an idea only in so far as it forms a part of the stream, then—whether it consist in a stream of similar ideas or in a stream of dissimilar ideas—it is all of it in nowise other than single-in-intent, inasmuch as it is limited to one object after another, and the fact that mind-stuff is distracted is unexplained. Therefore it may be said that mind-stuff is a single thing [and] has many intended objects [and] is stable.

Furthermore if ideas accidentally related and different in nature were produced by a single mind-stuff, then what a situation! One idea would be the remembrancer of a thing seen by another idea; and one idea would be later the experiencer of the latent-impression of karma accumulated by another idea. Even if this could in some way be harmonized[3] (*samādhīya*), it would surpass [in falsity] the maxim of the Cowdung[4] as a milky preparation.

[1] See i. 12.

[2] As, for example, by Dharmakīrti.

[3] This same word also has the meaning of 'concentrated'.

[4] See Colonel Jacob's Handful of Popular Maxims, Part 1, 2nd ed., p. 25. Compare Sarvadarçana-saṁgraha (Anandāçrama ed.), p. 15[1].

Moreover if the mind-stuff is to be [one idea after] another, then [the Buddhist who holds this opinion] denies the experience of his own self. How does the idea 'I' in such expressions as 'I am touching what I have seen' and 'I am seeing what I have touched' inhere in one common (*abheda*) substrate-of-ideas, if all the ideas have nothing in common? How could the idea 'I am this undivided self'—which has a single idea ['I'] as its object and which persists in absolutely different mind-stuffs—become hypostasized (*āçrayet*) in one generic substrate-of-ideas? The idea 'I am this undivided self' is knowable in one's own experience. Moreover the authority of a perception is not overthrown by [that of] any other source-of-valid-ideas. Whereas any other source-of-valid-ideas comes into use only by virtue of a perception. Consequently the mind-stuff is one [and] has many objects and is stable.

He introduces a sūtra which summarizes the meaning which he has been stating. This he does by saying «Furthermore these.» Furthermore [that is] after the meaning which he has been stating. The connexion [of the sentences] is that he sums up by reciting this sūtra. The reason why [the distractions] must be restricted is told in the words «the foes of concentration.» Although the words beginning 'By devotion to the Içvara' [i. 23] refer to practice only, still in this case passionlessness must be deemed to be a co-operator with this [practice]. Accordingly he says «by the same two.» By the same two already characterized, by practice and by passionlessness, [distractions are] to be restricted. The words «of these» [mean] of these two, namely, practice and passionlessness; the words «the practice», that which is to be described next. **32. To check them [let there be] practice upon a single entity.** A single entity, that is, the Içvara. For [He] is the subject-matter [of the discussion].—According to the Destructionists the mind-stuff as a whole is single-in-intent, [that is] is not in any degree whatsoever distracted. Consequently their teachings and their actions subservient to their teachings are meaningless, as he says in the words «But one whose.» [He refers to one] in whose opinion [the mind-stuff] is directed to one object after another whether to one [at a time] or to more than one [at a time]. Limited [in time], that is, present (*samutpanna*) only so long as the intended-object is vivid (*ābhāsa*), [and] ending just there [and] not going elsewhere. 'Why not first take the foremost intended-object and afterwards take the next object?' In reply he says «and is momentary.» Inasmuch as a moment is indivisible, it cannot have [within itself] the relation of before and after. In our system, however, since mind-stuff is not momentary; and since it can be stable with regard to its object, whether this be one or many; and since at each moment, in so far as one object is taken and another left,—[mind-stuff can be] distracted. Consequently, by removing the mutations of distraction, singleness-of-intent may be imposed [upon the mind-stuff]. That the teaching and the doing of this is not futile, is stated in the words «But if.» He sums up by saying «hence not.» He sets up for refutation a Destructionist (*vāināçika*) by the words «on the other hand . . . who.» The meaning is that there shall be no attempt to impose singleness-of-intent upon a mind-stuff that is single and momentary. But in the case of a mind-stuff in serial order that is from time without beginning and that is not momentary, distraction will be removed and singleness-in-intent will be imposed. He takes up these two alternatives and shows the faults [of the one] by saying «of him.» In his system, if singleness-of-intent is to be the property of the mind-stuff conceived as a stream or of a serial-order of mind-stuff, then the stream of mind-stuff is not a unit and is not persistent in the presented-ideas as they successively arise. Why [is this so]? Because in your system whatever is at all is all of it momentary, and there is nothing not momentary: this is the point. He takes up the other alternative in the words «If however.» A presented-idea which is a portion of [this whole] subjective (*sāṁvṛta*) stream might be real. For this reason the singleness-of-intent with reference to this presented-idea would be a property [belonging to a portion of the stream] [and] to be obtained by an effort. He shows the fault [in this alternative] by saying «all of it.» Accordingly in so far as it has the form of real being, it is—since it [must] be limited to one object after another [and] because it therefore arises during the vividness (*ābhāsa*) of the object-intended by this (*yat*) [presented-idea] and because it is finished during this [moment of vividness]—single-in-intent only. And thus the fact that mind-stuff is distracted remains unexplained. While it is to remove this [distraction] that singleness-in-intent is imposed. He sums up by saying «Therefore.» Hence also mind-stuff is one and has many objects and is stable as he explains by saying «Furthermore if.» For just as Chāitra cannot be he who remembers the book read by Māitra and just as Chāitra cannot be the enjoyer of the fruit of the latent-impressions of karma, heaped up by Māitra, with which he has had no connexion, whether meritorious or bad, so likewise something seen by one presented-idea cannot be remembered by another presented-idea; nor can the fruit of a latent-deposit of karma heaped up by one presented-idea be experienced by another idea. [The Destructionist might reply that his doctrine of momentariness] does not prove too much, provided we add the qualification 'if there be a relation of cause and effect'. For in such cases as the funeral-sacrifice (*çrāddha*) and the *vāiçvānarī* sacrifice (*iṣṭi*) [at the birth of a son] we find that the fruition [of the sacrifice] passes [in the one case] to the father and mother and [in the other case] to the son, whereas none [of the three] is the actual agent[1] [in the sacrifice]. Or [again] in such cases[2] as that of the [bitter]

[1] In the *çrāddha* the son sacrifices for the benefit of the father; in the *vāiçvānarī*, the father for the son. For the latter see Tāittirīya Ar. ii. 6. A discussion of the two sacrifices is found in the Bhāṣya on Jāimini-sūtra iv. 3. 38.

[2] This seems to refer to Kumārila's refutation of the Buddhists in Çlokavārttika,

mango-seeds that have been nourished with sweet juices [we see] that the fruition by an indirect process must become sweet. [Thus the effort of one momentary idea could find its result in another idea single-in-intent and indirectly related to it through a serial-order.] In reply to this he says «Even if this could in some way be harmonized.» The connexion of thought is this. What shall we say is the difference between ideas resident in one serial-order and different[1] ideas resident in another serial-order, so that—when [something] has been experienced or[2] when [some] latent-impression of karma has been heaped up by an idea resident in one serial-order—[another] idea belonging to the same serial-order should be the one to remember or to enjoy it and not an idea belonging to a different serial-order? For this that we call a serial-order is not such a [materially] real thing that it could [as such] distinguish the unit-in-the-serial-order (*santānin*) from [ideas] resident in other serial-orders. Furthermore an imaginary distinction cannot consistently exert activity. Surely the Brahman-boy cannot cook with fire that he imagines to be present. Moreover the relation of cause and effect is also nothing that is [materially] real [in this case of the two ideas, one of which appears in a series after the other has disappeared]. Because it is impossible that there should be in the present time a substrate for two things which are not co-existent, just as there cannot be [a substrate] for two things [separate in space] like the left horn and the other horn which do however coexist [in time]. For the past and the future cannot function as the present by being-partially-in-relation-and-partially-out-of-relation[3] (*vyāsañj*) [since momentariness is by hypothesis assumed]. Consequently ideas are not under the limiting-conditions either of a serial-order or of a causal relation which is a part of their being; [and], because they are real, they cannot, in so far as there are no reciprocal contacts, be distinguished from other ideas whether resident in the same serial-order or in other serial-orders. This same line-of-reasoning is continued by an allusion to the cow-dung and the milk; cow-dung is milk, because it is a product of the cow, like milk, which both sides admit [to be a product of the cow]. [The Buddhist argument] «surpasses» this [in falsity] because it is superior [in falsity] even to this [line-of-reasoning] in so far as it has the false appearance of being a line-of-reasoning.—And this [system of ours] cannot be charged [with the fault of] destroying[4] what has been accomplished and accepting what has not been accomplished. For [we hold that] it is mind-stuff that is the agent of actions;

pp. 262 and 267 (Chowkambha ed.). Compare De la Vallée Poussin's Le Bouddhisme, 1902, page 63, notes 177 and 178.

[1] Reading *bhinnapratyayānām* with the Bombay Sanskrit Series edition and with the Bikāner MS.

[2] This word is omitted by the two texts just mentioned and *ca* is inserted before *karmāçayasya*.

[3] That which is in several simultaneously and is not completely in any one. See Nyāyakoça s. v. *vyāsaṅga* and contrast it with its opposite *ekaparyāptatva*.

[4] See Bhāskarodaya (Nirṇ. Sāg. ed.), p. 49[3]. The charge by the Buddhist is that the Yoga system assumes a common substance for the thinking-substance as causal agent and for the Self as experiencer. Whereas the Yoga system itself denies such a common substrate.

it is this [mind-stuff] that is connected with the pleasures and the pains generated by these actions. For the mind-stuff when changed [by receiving] the image (*chāyā*) of the intelligence experiences pleasures and pains. Hence the supposition that experience in the Self is because of the assumption (*graha*) of an identity of the mind-stuff and the Self. Such is the very nature itself of these [mental pleasures and pains], which originate in dependence upon their own causes,[1] that they themselves remember and experience later the consequence, while others[2] do not [remember]. And the very-natures [of these mental pleasures and pains] ought not to be an injunction (*niyoga*) so that one says 'Let this be so' or 'Let this not be so', nor should it be a question (*paryanuyoga*) so that one asks 'Why is this not so?'—To him who will not be satisfied with what has already been said he speaks with the words «Moreover . . . his own self.» The idea 'I' is bound up with the mind-stuff which is not distinguished [from the idea] and is the substrate of experiences and of memories of experiences that have qualities of originating and of ceasing, however varied they may be. How can [this idea] be attached to ideas that are absolutely distinguished from itself? It might be objected that—inasmuch (*a*) as there is a distinction between the two causes 1. the process-of-knowing [in direct perception] and 2. memory, and inasmuch (*b*) as there is a coherence (*saṁsarga*) of the two contradictory qualities of immediate-perceptibility and of mediate-perceptibility—the so-called recognition [that this was that] (*pratyabhijñāna*) is not a single idea such that there could be a unity of the mind-stuff which contains these [contradictory] ideas. For this reason he says «in one's own experience.» The objector might reply that '1. the distinction between the two causes and 2. the coherence between two contradictory causes have been mentioned as inhibiting this [one's own experience].' In reply to this he says «Moreover . . . of a perception . . . not.» The totalities-of-causes (*sāmagrī*) do not remain distinct,—on one condition only, that they are reduced-to-terms (*anusāra*) of perception. And [that the totalities-of-causes do not remain distinct] is not contradicted by the fact that the qualities are immediate-perceptibility and mediate-perceptibility,—this is shown to be consistent in the Nyāyakaṇikā. And the action of objects-intended by a [mind-stuff] that is not momentary is shown to be consistent in the Nyāyakaṇikā[3] and in the Brahmatattvasamīkṣā. Thus all is made clear.

Of which [stable mind stuff] this purification[4] is enjoined by the system. By what means is this?

[1] Compare Çāṁkarabhāṣya ii. 2. 21 (Nirṇ. Sāg. ed., 1904, p. 457, last line).

[2] It is the agent himself that has the experience of the consequences.

[3] Both these books are in Vācaspatimiçra's own list of his works which he gives at the close of the Bhāmatī-vyākhyā; the first is a gloss on the Mīmāṅsā book called Vidhiviveka, the second is a gloss on the Vedānta work called Brahma-siddhi. The first has been published in Benares by E. J. Lazarus, first in the Pandit (1907) and later as a separate volume.

[4] See pp. 80[1] and 84[10] (Calc. ed.).

33. By the cultivation of friendliness towards happiness and compassion towards pain and joy towards merit and indifference towards demerit [the yogin should attain] the undisturbed calm of the mind-stuff.

Of these[1] [four] he should cultivate friendliness towards all living beings that have reached the experience of happiness; compassion towards those in pain; joy towards those whose character is meritorious; indifference towards those whose character is demeritorious. When he thus cultivates [friendliness and the rest] the white[2] quality [of karma] comes into being [within him]. And then the mind-stuff becomes calm; and when calm it becomes single-in-intent and reaches the stable state.

Because one whose central-organ is unpurified and full of such [feelings] as jealousy cannot successfully (*saṁpatti*) effect concentration and the means of concentration, he proceeds to set forth the means of [securing] undisturbed calm of the mind, which are hostile to such [feelings] as jealousy. This he does by saying «Of which [stable mind-stuff] this.» In other words, of which stable mind-stuff this is the purification. The sūtra begins with the words **33 . . . friendliness and compassion** and ends with the words **undisturbed calm . . . .** When towards those who are happy the mind-stuff[3] cultivates friendliness, that is, cordiality[4], [then] the taint of envy ceases. When towards those who are in pain [the mind-stuff] cultivates compassion, that is, a desire to destroy pain in another as if it were his own, [then] the taint of a desire to injure others ceases from the mind.[5] When towards living-creatures whose disposition is meritorious the mind cultivates joy,[5] that is, gladness, [then] the taint of jealousy ceases. When towards those whose disposition is demeritorious, the mind cultivates indifference, that is, neutrality, [then] the taint of wrath ceases. And then, after the qualities (*dharma*) made of *rajas* and of *tamas* have ceased, the white quality made of *sattva* comes into being. One may say that he becomes endowed with a superiority of *sattva*. When there can-properly-be-said-to-be (*pakṣa*) a restriction of the fluctuations, his mind-stuff,

[1] These form the chapter on the Brahma vihāras in the Visuddhi-Magga.

[2] Compare the statements in iv. 7 on white and black karma; and in ii. 13 on the rise of white karma.

[3] This construction is a good instance of ἀπὸ κοινοῦ (*kākākṣi*).

[4] This form (*sāuhārdam*) does not seem to accord with the examples given in Siddhānta kāumudī on vi. 3. 52 (Nirṇ. Sāg. ed., 1904, p. 207[2]).

[5] Medhātithi on Manu, in a characteristically Schopenhaurian frame of mind, informs us that friendliness is the absence of aversion (*dveṣābhāva*) and not an attachment to one's friends. For that would be bondage. Similarly joy is the cessation of grief but not positive gladness. Because that would be the result of passion. See Bālarāma's note † p. 77 (Calc. ed.). I have not traced the passage to Medhātithi-bhaṭṭa.

because its true nature is undisturbed calm, becomes undisturbedly calm. And when undisturbedly calm, by means which are to be stated,[1] it becomes single-in-intent and gains the stable state. But if there be no cultivation of friendliness and the other [feelings] these means are not adequate for stability.

34. Or [he gains stability] by expulsion and retention of breath.

Expulsion is the ejection of the abdominal air through the apertures of the nose by a special kind of effort. Retention is restraint of the breath.—‹Or› by these two he should attain to a stability of the central-organ.

He now states these means of [obtaining] stability.

34. Or [he gains stability] by expulsion and retention of breath.

The word ‹Or› signifies that there is a choice with regard to other means [now] to be stated, but not with regard to cultivation of friendliness and of the [other] feelings; because [the alternatives now mentioned] are in addition to that [cultivation]. He explains the expulsion by saying «of the abdominal.» By a special kind of effort, described in books of Yoga, by means of which the abdominal wind is gradually emitted through the apertures of the nose. He explains retention by saying «Retention is restraint of the breath.» It is the restraint of that portion of the abdominal wind that is emitted breath; it is the keeping of it outside; it is, on the other hand, not allowing it to enter suddenly. By these two, the expulsion and retention of wind, his body becomes light and his central organ gains the stable state. In this [sūtra] we have to supply (*ākṛṣ*) the word 'stability' from the phrase 'comes into a relation of stability' found in the next sūtra; and this is to be connected with the words 'should attain' as is understood from the context (*artha*).

---

35. Or [he gains stability when] a sense-activity (*pravṛtti*) **arises connected with an object [and] bringing the central-organ into a relation of stability.**

The consciousness of supernormal (*divya*) odour in one who attends fixedly to the tip of his nose is sense activity with odour [as object]; on the tip of the tongue, the consciousness of supernormal taste; on the palate, supernormal colour; on the middle of the tongue, the consciousness of touch; on the root of the tongue, the consciousness of sound. These sense-activities when arisen bring the mind-stuff into a relation of stability [and] dispel doubt and become a way of approach to concentrated insight.[2] Thus sense-activity

[1] Book ii. 1 ff.

[2] Compare i. 20.

with regard to the moon or the sun or planets or gems or [the rays of] a lamp or similar objects, when it arises, should be regarded as being connected with an object. For although the true nature of things as they really are [1] becomes accessible by means of the various sciences and by inferences and by the instruction of masters,—since these [means] are adequate to inform us of the things as they are,—still, so long as any part whatsoever has not become consciously knowable by the appropriate organ, the whole seems mediately-perceived. And the thinking-substance is not made to arise firmly with regard to such subtile intended-objects as Release. Therefore [if] only for the sake of reinforcing books and inferences and the instruction of masters, some one particular thing must necessarily be made an object of perception. Then after a portion of the intended-object as taught by these [three means] has been made the object of perception, the whole, even unto such an exceeding subtile object as Release, is thoroughly believed. For precisely this purpose the purification [2] of the mind-stuff is enjoined. If there are fluctuations unrestrained [as contrasted with this portion], then, when the Consciousness of being Master with regard to these has been produced, [the mind-stuff] would be adequate to effect a perception of these various intended-objects. And this done, [the yogin] will without hindrance acquire belief [and] energy [and] mindfulness [and] concentration [i. 20].

He tells of another means for stability. **35. Or [he gains stability when] a sense-activity (*pravṛtti*) arises connected with an object [and] bringing the central-organ into a relation of stability.** He explains by saying «in one who attends fixedly to the tip of his nose.» In one performing fixed-attentions [and] contemplations [and] concentrations there arises, as a result of success in these, that direct-perception which is a supernormal consciousness of odours. Similarly [what is said] is applicable to the other sense-activities also. And this is to be believed on the strength of the authoritative-word [3] and not from probable-reasonings (*upapattitas*). An objection, 'This may be

[1] This word *yathābhūta* is thought by Mrs. Rhys Davids to be 'specifically and uniquely Gotamic'. (C. A. F. Rhys Davids: Seeing Things as they Really are, in Buddhism, vol. i, no. 3, p. 382, March, 1904.) The fact that it occurs here is another proof of the intimate connexion between the Yoga system of philosophy and Buddhism.

[2] See also above, p. 70 end, or text, p. 77[1] (Calc. ed.).

[3] Compare Māitri Up. vi. 20.

so. But of what use is this kind of fluctuations which are of no service as regards Isolation?' In reply he says «These.» These fluctuations, when once arisen, in a very short time bring the mind-stuff into a relation of stability with the object whether it be the Içvara or the discriminative discernment. Another objection, 'How could a fluctuation in relation to one object bring [the mind-stuff] into a relation of stability with another object?' In reply to this he says «dispel doubt.» It dispels [that is] it removes. Consequently [it becomes a way of approach] «to concentrated insight.» By the word «Thus» he shows by analogy that other fluctuations also, which are taught in the revealed word, can be made objects. If it be objected, 'Whence can there be a doubt with regard to matters made known by the revealed word and by other [authorities],' he replies with the words «For although.» For Yoga is based upon belief. And when a portion of the intended-objects taught is made the object of perception, contemplation and the other [states] which are based upon this [belief], follow for him without obstruction.

---

36. Or an undistressed [and] luminous [sense-activity when arisen brings the central-organ into a relation of stability].

The words 'sense-activity when arisen brings the central-organ into a relation of stability' are supplied from [sūtra 35]. This is that consciousness of the thinking-substance which occurs when [the yogin] fixes his attention upon the Lotus of the Heart. For 1. the *sattva* of the thinking-substance becomes resplendent and [all-pervasive] like the air (*ākāça*). By skill in keeping [his central-organ] stable in this [Lotus], this sense-activity, because resplendent as the sun or the moon or planets or gems, becomes transformed in appearance. Thus 2. his mind-stuff comes to a state of balance with regard to the feeling-of-personality and becomes waveless like the Great Sea [and] peaceful [and] infinite [and] the feeling-of-personality and nought beside. With regard to which it has been said[1] "Pondering upon this self which is a mere atom, one is conscious in the same way as when one is conscious to the extent that one says 'I am'." This undistressed sense-activity is of two kinds: 1. in connexion with an object, and 2. the feeling-of-personality and nought beside; [and] is called luminous. By means of which the mind-stuff of the yogin gains the stable state.

[1] Garbe (Festgruss an Roth, p. 78) from this fragment infers a doctrine of the atomic nature of the self. Might it not however refer to a particular state only of the self?

36. Or an undistressed [and] luminous [sense-activity when arisen brings the central-organ into a relation of stability]. Without distress means freed from pain. Luminous means something having lumination. Luminous in the form of [casting] radiance «upon the Lotus of the Heart.» That lotus eight-petalled which is situated with head downwards between the abdomen and the thorax, he should turn, by the force of an emissive restraint of breath, head upwards and fix the mind-stuff attentively upon it. In the middle of this [lotus] is the circle of the sun [and] the letter A [1] [and] the locus of the waking-state. Above it is the circle of the moon [and] the letter U [and] the locus of sleep. Above this is the circle of fire [and] the letter M [and] the locus of deep-sleep. Above which is the highest, whose essence is the air [and] the prolonged nasal (*brahma-nāda*) [and] the locus of the fourth [*turīya*] state [and] a half-measure. [All this] the knowers of Brahma relate. In this [Lotus], that is, in the pericarp [of the lotus], is the tube (*nāḍī*) of Brahma, with upturned face, and reaching to the circle of the sun and the other [circles]. And upward from this there extends the tube called Sushumnā.[2] This passes through the outer circles also beginning with that of the sun. Now this [tube] is the locus of the mind-stuff. And by fixing attention upon this [tube] the yogin acquires in addition the consciousness of mind-stuff. After showing the consistency [of his statement] he indicates what the appearance of the consciousness of the thinking-substance is by saying «For 1. the *sattva* of the thinking-substance.» The words «like the air (*ākāça*)» describe its pervasive character. It takes various forms, it is transformed into the appearance [that is] into the form of the splendours of such [bodies] as the sun. And here thinking-substance (*buddhi*) is understood to be the central-organ (*manas*) and not the Great Principle (*mahat-tattva*). Moreover, placed in the Sushumnā and produced from the personality-substance which is itself evolved [3] [from *sattva*], it has an abundance of *sattva*; for this reason its luminosity is emphasized. Furthermore, in so far as it is concerned with various objects, its pervasiveness is also established. Having shown the state of balance (*samāpatti*) with regard to the central-organ, an effect of the feeling-of-personality, he describes what the state-of-balance is in itself with regard to the feeling-of-personality by saying «Thus . . . comes to a state of balance.» «Peaceful» [that is] that from which the waves of *rajas* and *tamas* have passed away. «Infinite» is all-pervading. «The feeling-of-personality and nought beside» is a form in which the splendours of various kinds do not reoccur. He makes his own opinion accord with another authoritative-work (*āgama*) by saying «With regard to which.» With regard to which this has been said by Pañcaçikha. It is called an atom because it is hard of access [to knowledge]. The self has the personality-substance as its basis. Pondering [that is] reflecting [upon it], one knows in the same way as when one knows 'I am'. An objector says, 'This may be true that the luminous [sense-activity]

[1] See Māṇḍ. Up. 9. [2] So MSS., not *suṣumṇā*. [3] See Sāṁ. Kār. xxv.

assumes various forms of splendour, but how can the luminous [sense-activity] assume the form of the feeling-of-personality and nought beside?' In reply to this he says «This . . . is of two kinds.» The point is that the sense-of-personality is itself, when cleansed from the defilement of *rajas* and *tamas*, lumination. He states also the consequences of the two-fold luminous [sense-activity] by saying «By means of which.»

37. Or the mind-stuff [reaches the stable state] by having as its object [a mind-stuff] freed from passion. Or influenced by having as the supporting-object a mind-stuff freed from passion,[1] the yogin's mind-stuff reaches the stable state.

37. Or the mind-stuff [reaches the stable state] by having as its object [a mind-stuff] freed from passion. Those freed from passion are Kṛṣṇadvāipāyana[2] and certain others. Mind-stuff is affected by having as the supporting-object the mind-stuff of these.

38. Or [the mind-stuff reaches the stable state] by having as the supporting-object a perception in dream or in sleep. Or, assuming that form which has as its supporting-object either a perception in dream or in sleep, the yogin's mind-stuff reaches the stable state.

38. Or [the mind-stuff reaches the stable state] by having as the supporting-object a perception in dream or in sleep. For when in his dream he adores the Exalted Maheçvara's image which abides within a sequestered forest and seems as if it were sculptured out of the moon's orb; [and] its members and limbs are soft as lotus stems; it is made of precious moonstone-gems and festooned with garlands of exceeding fragrant jasmine and Mālatī flowers; it captivates the heart.—When in the very [act of adoration] he awakens with mind in undisturbed calm; then, reflecting upon that same [image] which had become the object supporting the perception in his dream, while his central-organ is identical in form with that [object], his mind-stuff reaches a stable state in that very [condition].—And sleep in this case is to be understood as having the quality of *sattva*. Of which sleep, when he wakes, he has the connecting-memory 'I slept well'. For in this sleep his central-organ has become single-in-intent. And to this extent only [that is, in a sleep tainted only in so far as it refers to some *sattva* aspect of a thing], the knowers of Brahma

[1] For an illuminating instance, see Hopkins, Yoga-technique (1901), Journal Am. Oriental Soc., vol. xxii, pt. 2, p. 356-7.

[2] See Çaṁkara Bhāṣya Nirn. Sāg. ed. p. 782[10]. Compare Telang, Journal of the Bombay Br. RAS., vol. xvi (1885), p. 196.

tell us that the form of Brahma is in a state of deep sleep.—Moreover, since perception severed from the object to be perceived cannot come within the range [of the sense-organs], he brings that object also which is to be perceived within the range [of the sense-organs].

39. Or [the mind-stuff reaches the stable state] by contemplation upon any such an object as is desired.

Let [the yogin] contemplate whatever object he desires. Having reached stability there, the mind-stuff reaches the stable state elsewhere also.

39. **Or [the mind-stuff reaches the stable state] by contemplation upon any such an object as is desired.** Why say more? Whatsoever [object] is desired, [let him contemplate] just that, whichsoever particular deity it be.

40. His mastery extends from the smallest atom to the greatest magnitude.

The mind-stuff entering into a subtile thing reaches a stable state which extends to the smallest atom; entering a coarse thing it reaches a stable state which extends to the greatest magnitude. This freedom from obstruction of his, while advancing in this way to both of these kinds of limits, is complete mastery. So the yogin's mind-stuff filled full of mastery needs not again the purification perfected by practice.

But how is the becoming one's self (*ātmībhāva*) to be understood as being a stable state? In reply he says, **40. His mastery extends from the smallest atom to the greatest magnitude.** He explains by saying «into a subtile thing.» Summarizing the meaning given above he tells the meaning of the word ‹mastery› by the words «both of these kinds.» He tells of the secondary results of mastery by saying «So . . . of mastery.»

Now when the mind has reached stability, what is the balanced-state (*samāpatti*) as such (*svarūpa*) and (*vā*) as directed to an object? This is told [in the sūtra].

41. [The mind-stuff] from which, as from a precious gem, fluctuations have dwindled away, is, with reference either to

the knower or to the process-of-knowing or to the object-to-be-known, in the state of resting upon [one] of these [three] and in the state of being tinged by [one] of these [three], and [thus] is in the balanced-state.

The meaning of the words ‹from which . . . . fluctuations have dwindled away› refers [to the mind-stuff] of which the presented-ideas have come to rest. He takes as the example the words ‹as from a precious gem.›[1] Just as a crystal is tinged by the various colours of the different things next to which it lies and appears as having the form of the coloured (*rūpa*) thing-next-to-which-it-lies (*upāçraya*), so the mind-stuff is influenced by referring to the object-to-be-known and comes into a state-of-balance with the object-to-be-known and appears as having the form of the object-to-be-known as it is in itself. Influenced by a subtile element it comes into a state-of-balance with the subtile element and seems to be the subtile element itself. Likewise, influenced by referring to a coarse [element] it comes into a state-of-balance with a coarse form and seems to have a coarse form. Similarly, influenced by particular things of the world it comes into a state-of-balance with the particular thing of the world and seems to have the form of the world. An analogous situation would be found to exist also with reference to the processes-of-knowing, [that is] in the organs of sense. Influenced by referring to a process-of-knowing it comes into a state-of-balance with the process-of-knowing and appears as having the form of the process-of-knowing as it is in itself. Similarly, influenced by referring to the Self as knower it comes into a state-of-balance with the Self as knower and appears as having the form of the Self as knower. Similarly, influenced by referring to a liberated Self it comes into a state-of-balance with the liberated Self and appears as having the form of the liberated Self. Thus it is that the mind, which is like a precious gem, in the state of resting upon [one] of these, upon the knower or upon a process-of-knowing or upon the object-to-be-known [that is] upon the Self or a sense-organ or an element, [and which is] in a state of being tinged by [one of] these, [that is] while resting upon [one of] these,

[1] Compare Çākuntala, First prose speech after ii. 7 (Pischel, p. 125[12]).

changes into their form—this [mind] is said to be in the balanced-state.

Thus the means for stability of the mind-stuff have been stated. The mastery of that mind-stuff which has reached stability has also been shown. Now a question is asked, 'When the mind has reached stability, what object has [concentration] conscious [of an object] and what is [concentration] itself?' This he asks by saying «Now.» Referring to this he introduces the next sūtra by saying «This is told.» He recites the sūtra **41. [The mind-stuff] .... as from a precious gem .... the balanced-state.** He explains this by the words «dwindled away.» The mind-stuff from which such fluctuations as sources-of-valid-ideas, when they are of *rajas* or of *tamas*, have dwindled away as a result of practice and of passionlessness. The explanation of this is «of which the presented-ideas have come to rest.» In this manner it is stated that the *sattva* of the mind-stuff, which is naturally pure, is not overpowered by the *rajas* and the *tamas*. He makes the example clear by saying «Just as.» —«The thing next to which it lies» is the limiting condition, such as the hibiscus flower.—«Influenced by» means changed into its likeness. It appears as if marked by the form of the red or blue or other colour which is peculiar to the thing next to which it lies. He applies [the illustration] to the thing illustrated by saying «so .... the object-to-be-known.» It is influenced by, [that is] it penetrates into, the object-to-be-known to which it refers. In this way he distinguishes the object-to-be-known from the knower and from the process-of-knowing. [The mind-stuff] covers over its own peculiar form as inner organ and comes into a state of balance with the object-to-be-known; or it might be said that it seems to change into an objective state of being known. As a result of this it appears as having the form of the object-to-be-known as it is in itself. Influence (*uparāga*) comes only from an object-to-be-known. [This] he subdivides into subtile and into coarse [forms] by saying «a subtile element.» The particular things of the world are evidently those with an animate nature, for instance, cows; and those with an inanimate nature, for instance, water-jars. In accordance with this it has been shown that there are two concentrations: that accompanied by deliberation [upon coarse objects]; and that accompanied by reflection [upon subtile objects]. When he says «An analogous situation .... also with reference to the processes-of-knowing, [that is] in the organs of sense» he means that sense-organs are processes of knowing in that by them intended-objects are known. He makes the same clear by saying «referring to a process of knowing.» Since the process of knowing is itself that to which it refers, it is influenced, [that is] permeated, by this. It covers over its own peculiar form as inner organ and seems to be changed[1] into a process of knowing, as if it were an outer organ. Having described in this way [the concentration] accompanied by joy, he tells of that

[1] The cosmological analogue is found in iii. 26, p. 240, last line (Calc. ed.).

accompanied by the feeling-of-personality by saying «Similarly . . . the Self as knower.» Because the Self as Knower is the locus of the feeling of personality: this is the point. Since there is no distinction between Selves, released Selves, like Çuka[1] and Prahlāda, as objects of concentration, must be included as being described by the words «Similarly . . . released.» Coming to a close he explains the words ‹resting upon [one] of these [three] and in the state of being tinged by [one] of these three› by saying «Thus it is that.» The mind-stuff's *sattva* freed from the defilement of the *rajas* and *tamas* [aspects], by virtue of the purification by contemplation, rests upon [that is] fixedly attends to one of these, either the knower or the process-of-knowing or the object-to-be-known. This state of being tinged by [one] of these [three], [that is] taking the form of [one] of them, is called the balanced-state, in other words, Yoga with the distinguishing-characteristic of being conscious [of an object].—And here the order of words in the sūtra ‹knower or process-of-knowing or object-to-be-known› need not be heeded since it runs counter[2] to the order of objects-intended [as given in experience]. Similarly, in the Comment also, the clearing [of the statement with regard to the concentration upon] the subtile elements as being the first [in the order of statements] is not to be respected. Thus all becomes satisfactory.

---

42. Of these[3] [balanced-states] the state-balanced with deliberation is confused by reason of predicate-relations between words and intended-objects and ideas.

For example, although the word[4] 'cow' and the intended-object 'cow' and the idea 'cow' are things distinct from each other, one finds that in the process-of-knowing they are undistinguished. When these are distinguished from each other, the properties of words are of one kind, the properties of objects-intended are of another kind, [and] the properties of thoughts are of another kind. Thus the levels-of-existence (*panthan*) are distinct. If now a yogin has come into a state of balance with one of these [objects in

[1] The Vedānta books place Çuka in the succession between Vyāsa and Gāuḍapāda.

[2] See the discussion by Jacobi: the Dates of the Philosophical Sūtras, JAOS., vol. xxxi (1911), p. 26.

[3] Rājendra Lāla Mitra apparently omits this word from the sūtra in his edition of Bhojarāja's Rājamārtaṇḍa (1883).

[4] Compare Patañjali: Mahābhāṣya, vol. i, p. 1[6] (Kielhorn's edition), and the elaborate discussion in Vācaspatimiçra's Tattvabindu in which he contrasts two different theories of the Vāiyākaraṇas (Bhartṛhari in his Vākyapadīya and Vātsyāyana) with three schools of Mīmāṅsakas (1. followers of Upavarṣa, such as Çaṁkara, 2. Prabhākara, 3. Kumārila).

the predicate-relation], and if such an intended-object as 'cow' strikes upon his concentrated insight, and if it comes to him permeated with predicate-relations between words and intended-objects and ideas, then that confused balanced-state is said to be ‹with deliberation.›

The balanced-state in general has been described. By classification into sub-divisions there are four kinds of it: deliberative and super-deliberative, reflective and super-reflective. Of these [four] he describes the state-balanced in deliberation [upon a coarse object] in the sūtra beginning with the words **42. Of these** and ending with the words **balanced-state** . . . ‹Of these› [that is] from among these balanced-states it is the state balanced in deliberation that is to be understood. Of what kind is this [balanced-state]? Although in reality diverse, words and intended-objects and ideas have predicate-relations because the words and the other [two] are attributed the one to the other. And the predicate-relation represents the diversity that there is in one thing and the identity that there is in diverse things. Consequently [the balanced-state] is confused or mixed with predicate-relations between words and intended-objects and ideas. When he says «For example . . . the word 'cow'» it is evident that there is a predicate-relation which identifies the word with the intended-object and the idea, both of which have been appropriated by the [word] 'cow'. When he says «the intended-object 'cow'» it is evident that there is a predicate-relation which identifies the intended-object with the word and the idea, both of which have been appropriated by the [intended-object] 'cow'. When he says «the idea 'cow'» it is evident that there is a predicate-relation which identifies the idea with the word and the intended-object, both of which have been appropriated by the [idea] 'cow'. Thus in ordinary life it is evident that, although word and intended-object and idea are distinct, in the process of knowing they are not distinguished. If in the process of knowing they are not distinguished, why then should there be any distinction? In reply to this he says «When these are distinguished.» When in accordance with methods of agreement and difference they are distinguished by experts, then 1. properties of words are of one kind [that is] a word which is nothing but a mutation of sound has such properties as high [pitch], 2. [properties] of an intended-object are of another kind [that is] such properties as insensibility and [definite] shape, 3. properties of an idea are of another kind [that is] illumination and no [definite] shape. Therefore the level (*panthan*) of their existences is distinct [that is] the way which leads to the various things themselves. When it is said that a yogin has come into a state of balance with one of these intended-objects, such as a cow, then the lower perception of the yogin has been described.—The rest is easy.

When however the memory is purified from [remembrances of] the conventional-use (*saṁketa*) of words and when the concentrated insight is free from predicate-relations [in the form] of ideas either of inferences or of something that has been heard, the intended object remains as it is in itself and nothing more, and is specifically characterized as having just that form which it has in itself and as nothing more. And this is the super-deliberative balanced-state. This is the higher perception. And this is the germ of inference and of anything that has been heard. From it inference and anything heard have their being. Moreover this knowledge (*darçana*) is not accompanied by an idea either of an inference or of anything that has been heard. Therefore the yogin's knowledge derived from super-deliberative concentration is not confused by any other source of a valid idea. He illustrates the distinguishing characteristic of the super-deliberative concentration by the sūtra.

43. When the memory is quite purified, [that balanced-state]—which is, as it were, empty of itself and which brightens [into conscious knowledge] as the intended object and nothing more—is super-deliberative.

That insight which, when the memory is quite purified from predicate-relations [in the form] of ideas either of inferences or of anything that has been heard, and from the conventional usage of words, is influenced by the thing in itself (*svarūpa*) which is to be known; and which, after as it were in its form of insight throwing off itself, the essence of which is a process of knowing, becomes the thing-intended (*padārtha*) and nothing more; [and becomes] as it were changed into the thing in itself which is to be known,—this is the super-deliberative balanced-state. And as such it has [just] been explained. For to this [balanced-state] the world [so far as it is visible], whether [it be an animate object] such as a cow or whether [it be an inanimate object] such as a water-jar, is 1. the formation of a single mental-act (*buddhi*), 2. its essence is an intended-object, 3. [and] its essence is that it is a special kind of conglomeration of atoms. And this particular kind of arrangement[1] [which constitutes the object] is an apparent-form (*dharma*)

[1] For this word *saṁsthāna* see pp. 170[15], 205[10], 216[12], 272[7] (Calc. ed.).

common to the subtile elements [which compose it] and it is inferred [as being a whole] from its phenomenalized effects[1]; it is self-dependent and presents itself by [changing] into its phenomenal[2] form by the operation of the conditions-which-phenomenalize it (*sva*); and it disappears when another apparent-form arises in consciousness. This same apparent-form is called a whole (*avayavin*). And it is this that is one[3] and great or very small and tangible and that in which actions occur and impermanent. By this [kind of] wholes the business-of-life is carried on. But one to whom such a particular conglomeration is not [perceptibly] real—since by an indefinite-first-impression[4] (*avikalpa*) a subtile cause is imperceptible—for him, since there is no whole, nearly everything, in accordance with the statement that an erroneous idea is not based upon the form [i. 8] of that [in respect of which the idea is entertained], is reduced to erroneous ideas. And then what would be a complete idea, seeing that there are no objects to which it would refer? For whatever is perceived, all that is a bit influenced by its nature of being a whole-having-parts. Therefore a whole exists which becomes changed by receiving what is called sizes and the like. This is the object of the super-deliberative balanced-state.

In order to show the connexion of the sūtra he explains first super-deliberative [concentration] by saying «When however.» — Purification is removal. For certainly inference and verbal-communication begin to function when occasioned by memories of the conventional use of words. And this conventional-usage has its essence in the false attribution to each other of the word and the intended object and the idea 'cow'. And as a result of this the two predicate-relations in the form of an idea either of an inference or of a verbal-communication arise. So when occasioned by one of these, concentrated insight still has deliberation [upon some coarse object]. But when the mind,—in so far as it is absorbed in the intended object and nothing more and is zealous for the intended object and for nothing more,—reaches by practice upon this [intended object] a state of inseparable fusion [with this object], [then] the memory of conventional-usages

[1] The atom carries within itself the miniature of its effects.

[2] The expression *sva-vyañjaka-añjana* also occurs at pp. 37[3], 112[2], 207[6], and 282[1] (Calc. ed.).

[3] The relation of whole and part is discussed in Nyāya-sūtra ii. 1. 36 and iv. 2. 14 ff., and also in Udayana's Atma-Tattva-Viveka.

[4] All the MSS. including the Bikāner and Gañgādhara Shāstri's MSS. omit this word.

is thrown off. And when these are thrown off, predicate-relations in the form of an idea either of an inference or of anything heard, which two are rooted in memory, are thrown off. Then in the concentrated insight, freed from these predicate-relations, the intended object remains as it is in itself and nothing more; and becomes accurately characterized as having just that form which it has in itself and as nothing more, and as not having any form of predicated-relation. This is the super-deliberative balanced-state. This is the higher perception of the yogin, since in it there is not even a trace of false attribution. An objection might be raised, 'This may be so. But yogins, having known the that-ness of the intended object, make it consistent [with other knowledge] and teach it. And (*vā*) how can this intended object be taught by verbal communication or be made consistent by inference which is intended for another, both of which cases not referring to that [object which is intended in the higher perception]? Accordingly verbal-communication and inference [must] refer to that [higher object]. And since these two are predicate-relations, the higher perception is also nothing but a predicate-relation.' In reply to this he says «And this . . . anything heard.» For if this [knowledge], like that with deliberation, were accompanied by inference or by anything that had been heard, that is, if it had been tainted by either of these, then it would be confused. But it is only the germ of these two. For from it inference and anything that has been heard have their being. And it is not the rule that whatever is a cause of an effect has the same object as itself as its effect. For because the idea of smoke is the cause of the idea of fire, it does not therefore have this [fire] for its object. Consequently [the yogins] having known [the thatness of the intended object] by a perception free of predicate-relations[1], teach it and make it consistent through the medium of predicate-relations. He sums up by saying «Therefore,» and shows the connexion with the sūtra which is to be explained by using the word «super-deliberative.» The sūtra begins with the words **43. When the memory is quite purified.** The purification[2] is the removal of the memory which follows (*tasmād*) upon the predicate-relation which is nothing but the idea of the inference and of anything that has been heard and of the conventional-usage of words. When this occurs (*tasyām*). And in this case the purification from the memory of conventional-usages is the cause (*hetu*), and the purification from the memory of ideas, such as, of anything that has been

[1] A favourite verse to illustrate the gradual advance from the first dim impression to an assertion in distinct predicate form is Māgha's verse in Çiçupālavadha i. 3. First a ball of light; then a body; then a person is seen; finally one says "It is Narada!" as one beholds him falling from the sky.

[2] This purification seems to be a relaxation of attention which has been given to a too closely limited field. Our deepest convictions may speak to us in dissociative processes wherein any fixed succession of apperceptive acts has ceased. The purification lies in a distribution of attention so that it regards a whole and disregards the successive parts.

heard, is the effect (*hetumant*).—And the word «inference» is to be understood as expressing the object[1] of the action [as expressing that which is inferred, and not that from which an inference is drawn]; it is a word denoting the thing to be inferred.—The word «as it were» (*iva*) in the clause «as it were . . . itself» (*svam iva*) is out of its right position and should be construed after the words «throwing off.» — He rejects the theory[2] that there is [in this state] a diversity of objects by saying «to this . . . a single.» It is 1. the formation of a single mental-act, in the sense that it forms[3] or brings forth a single mental-act. Consequently since it is [single], the atoms, in that they are many, are not the objects of the super-deliberative [balanced-state]. What he has wished to say is this: Assuming that they are fit [to be the object of the balanced-state], still, in that they are very subtile, and because they are collected into a manifold [each unit of which has its own subtile idea], they are not fit to be the object of a presented idea which brightens [into a conscious knowledge] of the unity of the single intended-object which has magnitude [*mahattva* as contrasted with *aṇu*]. An objection, 'Granted that the atoms are real[4] existences, then the [so-called] coarseness would be [only] a subjective (*sāṁvṛta*) property of that which shines clearly [in consciousness].' In reply to this[5] he says «2. its essence is an intended object.» The point is that when once a coarse object [as a whole] has been established in experience, it cannot, unless there be something inhibitory, be denied.—To those [Vāiçeṣika] who think that [animate things] like cows and [inanimate things] like water-jars are produced[6] by binary and other atoms in gradations, he says «3. conglomeration of atoms.» A conglomeration of atoms is a mutation in gross form and this [form of] mutation differentiates[7] it from other [coarse] mutations. That of which this [differentiated] mutation is the essence[8], in other words, the-thing-itself (*svarūpa*), is that which is called [«a conglomeration of atoms»]. [Animate] things such as cows possess an [animate] seat-of-experience.[9] And such [inanimate] things as water-jars are [merely inanimate] objects [of this balanced-state]. And both of these same two kinds of objects are also seen (*lokyate*); and so [each] may be called the world (*loka*) [so far as it is visible to this balanced-state]. It might be objected that this [conglomeration, which is a gross form of mutation] might

[1] Pāṇ. iii. 3. 113.

[2] The theory of the Sarvāstivādin. See Sarvadarçanasaṁgraha (Anand. ed.), p. 7, l. 9.

[3] This would be the theory of the Vāibhāṣika school, which asserts the perception of outer objects. See Sarvadarçanasaṁgraha (Anand. ed.), p. 7[9].

[4] Compare Dharmakīrti's Nyāyabinduṭīkā (Peterson's ed.), p. 16[20], (Tscherbatskoi's ed. Bibl. Buddhica), p. 13[21], also the ṭippaṇī, p. 37.

[5] This would be the doctrine of the Yogācāra School.

[6] See on the whole subject Jacobi's illuminating article on the 'Atomic Theory' in Hastings's Dict. of Religion and Ethics, and especially p. 201[a], line 10.

[7] Compare Vāiçeṣika-sūtra vii. i. 9 and Çaṁkara on ii. 2. 12.

[8] As contrasted with a special kind of conglomeration (*pracaya-viçeṣa*).

[9] This seat-of-experience is, according to the Pātañjala Rahasyam, the body.

be either different from the subtile elements or not different [from them]. 1. If it be different from them, how can it be the [common] substrate of them and how can it be the form (*ākāra*) [which gives them oneness]? For a water-jar is a different thing from a piece-of-cloth and cannot be the substrate [of the properties of the piece-of-cloth] nor can it be that which gives the form [of oneness] to this piece-of-cloth. 2. If, on the other hand, it [the object, so far as visible, which is a conglomeration of atoms] be not different [from its subtile elements], then it would be, like them, subtile and not common [to the whole group]. The point is this: any such thing as a water-jar is not absolutely different from the atoms, neither is it absolutely identical [with them]. In case it were different, as a horse and a cow are different, the relation [between them] of substance to its properties could not be consistently explained. In case it were identical, [so that the atoms were] like the substance, then this [substance] could not be consistently explained. Consequently it is in some respects different and in some respects identical. And so it must be, if all is to be consistently explained. By putting the words «subtile elements» in the genitive case, he indicates that there is in some respects a difference; and by the words «it is self-dependent», that there is an identity. [It is inferred] by its phenomenalized effects: phenomenalized in the sense that its [effect] is experienced; and phenomenalized in the sense that it [serves] the business-of-life. [And] it is proven by inference to any one who takes the opposite view. And in so far as it is identical with its cause, we may consistently say that it has the form of its cause. Accordingly he says «by [changing] into its phenomenal form by the operation of the conditions-which-phenomenalize it.»—'Is this apparent-form (*dharma*), which is identical with it, permanent?' He gives a negative answer in the words «when another apparent-form.» Another apparent-form [that is,] as a potsherd [is another apparent-form of a water-jar broken in pieces]. —That this whole has a form not-to-be-found (*vyāvṛttam*) in the atoms he shows by saying «This same.» For it has properties, which give it a specific-character, such as the holding of honey or of water, which actions are other than actions which could be accomplished by atoms.[1] [The whole is known] not only by [perceptual] experience, but also by the business-of-life since the conduct of men depends upon these [wholes]. This he states in the words «and by this.» A [Buddhist] objection, 'This may be true. If there were nothing to contradict, experience might establish [by the help of inferences] that [the mutation in its gross form] is a whole-having-parts. But (*ca*) there is a contradiction. [For in the line of reasoning,]—(*a*) All that exists is without parts, (*β*) like thought (*vijñāna*), and (*γ*) such things as cows and water-jars exist,—we have a natural [and valid] middle-term[2] [that is, existence]. [But the point is made that there

[1] The system insists that not even the subtile (*sūkṣma*) is perceptible to the *avikalpita* type of thinking.

[2] This is a term of the "Eastern school" of Logicians, equivalent in their usage to an unconditioned middle term, which

is no existence in coarse form.] For existence is subsumed (*vyāpta*) under absence of contradictory qualities.[1] And connexion with contradictory qualities, which is contradictory with it [that is, existence], being found to exist in a thing-having-parts, excludes existence also, since in such a case something contrary to the subsumer [which is, absence of contradictory qualities] has been found. And so [to revert to the original point] there is in the whole a connexion with contradictory qualities, for example, belonging to that place and not belonging to that place, being covered and not being covered, being red and not red, moving and not moving. [Accordingly wholes in gross form do not exist.]' In reply to this he says «But one to whom.» The intention [of what was first asserted] is this. [The whole in gross form is now said to be given in experience and to be an action realizing a purpose.] The existence which is given as the middle-term (*hetu*) must either be given by experience and be such as even a ploughman[2] with dusty feet can understand, or it must be other than what is given by experience. Of these two the latter is not a middle-term since it is not given in experience, [that is, it must itself be established as existing in the middle-term]. But water-jars and such things have an existence given in experience, namely, activity realizing a purpose. [This form] is not other than its gross [form]. This [form given by experience and realizing a purpose] is the middle-term, [that is, existence], and by removing [the existence of] coarseness [as thus defined, this middle-term] destroys itself. In reply to this [the Buddhist] says, 'Existence is not [a permanent] coarseness, but is the negation of non-existence. And coarseness is negative non-coarseness. Moreover negativations differ according to the variations of the things negatived. So even when there is no coarseness, there is no destruction of existence.' [The reply to this would be:] By reason of variations in the negativations we may admit that there is a variation in the objects of the determination (*avasāya*). But would you, Sir, be good enough to say what the object is of the source-of-the-valid-idea which is not a first faint impression (*vikalpa*), and which is the necessary-condition (*pūrvaka*) for the determinations? For if you say that the atoms of colour which arise continuously, and the minute that-ness of which is unknown, [are the object], the reply is, Very well. These are intermingled[3] with the atoms of odour and taste and touch and are [therefore] not continuous. Therefore if it be unaware of the

would not be a *hetvābhāsa*, but a valid (*sad*) term. The later term would be *sad-anumāna*. See Nyāya-Koça, s. v. Such terminology points to the Eastern country as the home of Vācaspatimiçra. Compare for this kind of logical language Dharmakīrti's Nyāya-bindu-ṭīkā (Peterson's ed.), p. 104.

[1] See Nyāya-bindu-ṭīkā ii. 2 (Peterson's ed.), p. 106[7].

[2] Compare Patañjali: Mahābhāṣya on i. 1. 23 (Kielhorn i. 81[4]).

[3] One does not see merely the colour series. For this is intersected by the taste and smell and touch series. On the other hand the continuum of colour is not an illusion as the Vedāntin, Udayana for example, would say (Atma-Tattva-Viveka, Jībānanda's ed., Calc., 1873, p. 83[1]). The Yoga system explains these series as the mutations of a substance.

intermediate [atoms], this indefinite-first-impression, based upon the atoms, like the presented-idea of a forest as single and as dense [although it too is full of intermediate spaces,] would be false. Accordingly the indefinite-first-impressions proceeding from this [other first faint impression] are not even mediately in relation with a [perceptible] object. Thus how could one succeed in establishing that there are no parts in existences which are determined by these [indefinite-first-impressions]? Therefore if one desires to hold to the validity of perceptions which are definite-later-impressions, the existence of that very coarseness which is being experienced by this [perception] must be admitted, [even] if one does not assent to that which is to be determined by [perception which is] definite-and-later-impression. To proceed: if existence inhibits this [kind of perception], it would inhibit itself. That the atoms are exceedingly subtile and that they become the objects of experience through the medium of other kinds of atoms—to acknowledge this is self-destructive. Having this in view he says «One to whom this particular conglomeration which is not [perceptibly] real» [is the object of a perception which is a definite-and-later-impression], one, that is, who says that the subtile atoms should therefore be objects of perceptions which are definite-and-later-impressions—to him he replies «since by an indefinite-first-impression a subtile cause is imperceptible.» For the reason that for him there is no whole, everything,—according to the characterization given [i. 8] that "an erroneous idea is not based on that form [in respect of which it is entertained],"—is reduced to erroneous idea, all that which rests upon coarseness and all that which rests upon the existence which is the locus of this [coarseness].—It might be objected that even so [and finally] knowledge is not erroneous in regard to one's self, because this does not appear as a whole having parts. In reply to this he says «Nearly.» The objector might reply 'What even if it be so?' In reply to this he says «And then.» If such an idea as that of existence be erroneous, then such an idea, caused by existence or something of the kind as this that there are no wholes having parts, would also be erroneous. Because its object also, in so far as it is something to be determined, is certainly nothing coarse[1] [and this latter is] not concerned with definite-and-later-impressions. And this [object] does not exist. Such is the meaning of the argument. And if it be asked why there is no object, he replies with the word «whatever.» And the [apparent] contradiction must be removed in accordance with the explanation (*upapatti*) previously given based on identity in difference and on manifoldness in mutations. Then all would be satisfactory.

---

44. By this same [balanced-state] the reflective and the super-reflective [balanced-states] are explained as having subtile objects.

[1] One suspects that the reading might be *sthūlam*.

Of these [two], that is called the reflective (*savicāra*) balanced-state which refers to subtile elements the apparent forms of which have been manifested and which are characterized by an experience of place and time and cause. In this case also a subtile element capable of being apperceived by one idea and particularized by uprisen (*udita*) apparent-forms serves as that upon which the concentrated insight rests. But that balanced-state which in all ways and by all means refers to such [subtile elements] as are free from characterization by apparent-forms whether quiescent (*çānta*) or uprisen (*udita*) or indeterminable (*avyapadeçya*) and which yet corresponds to all apparent-forms and is the essence of all apparent-forms is called super-reflective (*nirvicāra*). Since the subtile element is of this kind, it becomes, in this very form, that on which the concentrated insight rests and it influences the insight itself. When moreover the insight becomes, as it were, emptied of itself and becomes the intended object and nothing more, then it is called super-reflective. Of these [four] the deliberative and the super-deliberative have as object[1] something great; while the reflective and the super-reflective have a subtile object. Thus by this same super-deliberative [balanced-state] the destruction of predicate-relations of both[2] kinds has been explained.

44. By this same [balanced-state] the reflective and the super-reflective [balanced-states] are explained as having subtile objects. Those [whose apparent-forms have been manifested] are those by which the apparent-forms of such things as water-jars have been manifested, in other words, those that have included the apparent-forms of such things as water-jars. «Place» [for instance] above or below or at one side. «Time» [for instance] the present. «Cause» [for instance] the atom of earth is produced by the five fine elements among which the fine element of odour predominates. Likewise the atom of water [is produced] from the four fine elements among which the fine element of taste predominates. Likewise the atom of fire [is produced] from the three fine elements, excluding the fine element of odour and of taste, and among which the fine element of colour predominates. Likewise the atom of wind [is produced] from the [two] fine elements beginning with odour, and of which [two] the

[1] Vijñāna Bhikṣu glosses *mahad-vastu* with the words 'coarse' (*sthūla*) and 'modification only' (*kevalavikṛti*). This is the use of the word in iii. 44.

[2] The two kinds must be the super-deliberative and the super-reflective; and not, as Vijñāna Bhikṣu says, the reflective and the super-reflective. This would be a gross inconsistency. For the reflective kind has predicate relations.

fine element of touch predominates. Likewise [the atom] of air from the fine element sound alone.—This is the cause in the case of the subtile elements. These [subtile elements] are experienced when they have a place and a time and a cause. An idea (*buddhi*) which is capable of being particularized does not follow unless it be particularized by [such] an experience. An objector might ask, 'What similarity is there between [the balanced-state] with deliberation and [that] with reflection?' In reply to this he says «In this case also.» For the atom of earth which consists of the conglomeration of the five fine elements may be apperceived by a single idea. Similarly the atom of water and the other atoms [too] which have as their essences four or three or two or one fine element may be apperceived by a single idea.—«Uprisen» means a present apparent-form; [the element]' would be particularized by that. And finally with regard to this [uprisen apparent-form], it is pointed out that there is an interpenetration of the predicate-relations of verbal-communications and of inferences by the memory of the conventional-use [of words]. For when something coarse is the object of perception, the atoms do not appear. But [they do appear objectively] as the result of verbal-communications and of inferences. Thus it is consistent that this [balanced-state] should be confused.—He describes the super-reflective [balanced-state] in the words «But that which.» «In all ways» means in all forms [of phenomenalization], such as blue and yellow. The termination[1] *-tas* [Pāṇ. iv. 3. 13] in the word «*sarvatas*» is used [as equivalent] to all inflected case-endings. In other words it means «by all means» [that is] by experiences of place and of time and of cause. By this statement it is shown that the atoms as such are not particularized by time. Neither are they [particularized by time] mediately through apparent-forms which have their origin in these [atoms]. It is this that he describes in the word «quiescent.» «Quiescent» are past. «Uprisen» are present. «Indeterminable» are future apparent-forms. [Atoms] are not characterized by these. Not being characterized by apparent-forms, is it quite right to say that atoms are unrelated to them? In reply to this he says «correspond to all apparent-forms.»—With[2] which kind of a relation do these atoms correspond to apparent-forms? In reply to this he says «are the essence of all apparent-forms.» In other words, the apparent-forms are different from the atoms in some respects and in other respects not different.—But why has this balanced-state this kind of an object? In reply to this he says «Since . . . of this character.» In other words, having an apperception of the that-ness of a perceptible object, it does not become active with regard to that which has not this that-ness.—Having stated the object of this [balanced-state], he tells what it is itself by saying «Moreover the insight.» Bringing the [four] together, he

[1] The termination *tasi* is the same as *tasil* (Pāṇ. v. 3. 7).

[2] Rāghavānanda Yati in his Pātañjala Rahasyam thinks that some words have been lost at this point from the Tattva Vāiçāradī of Vācaspati-miçra.

describes the object as being serviceable to distinguish what they are themselves by saying «Of these.» He sums up with the word «Thus.» «Of both kinds» means both its own [super-deliberative] and also super-reflective forms.

45. The subtile object likewise terminates in unresoluble-primary-matter (*aliñga*).

In the case of the earthen atom the fine element of odour, [which is the cause of the atom of earth,] is the subtile object of the [reflective and super-reflective] balanced-states ; in the case of the watery atom the fine element of taste [is the subtile object] ; in case of the fiery atom the fine element of colour ; in case of the windy atom the fine element of touch ; in case of the aerial atom the fine element of sound. The personality-substance which is the cause of these [elements is also the subtile object of this balanced-state]. Resoluble-primary-matter-as-such (*liñgamātra*) [which is the cause] of this [personality-substance] also is the subtile object [of the balanced-state]. Unresoluble-primary-matter [which is the cause] of this [resoluble-primary-matter-as-such] also is the subtile object [of the balanced-state]. And beyond the unresoluble-primary-matter there is nothing subtile. If the objection be raised that the Self is subtile, the reply is that this is true. The subtilty of the Self in relation to the resoluble-primary-matter [thinking-substance] is, however, not that of the unresoluble-primary-matter to the resoluble-primary-matter. For the Self is not the material cause (*anvayin*) of resoluble-primary-matter, but the instrumental cause (*hetu*).

Accordingly it is explained that subtilty reaches its utmost degree in the primary-substance.

Does the balanced-state, which has a thing-to-be-known as its object, end in the subtile element only ? No. But, 45. The subtile object likewise terminates in unresoluble-primary-matter (*aliñga*). That state of the fine element of odour which is in relation to the earthen atom is the subtile object of the balanced-state. Similarly in the later cases also the connexion is to be made. The resoluble-primary-matter-as-such (*liñga-mātra*) is the Great Principle [that is, the thinking-substance (*buddhi*)]. For it goes to dissolution (*laya*) in the primary-substance. Unresoluble-primary-matter is primary-substance. For it does not dissolve into anything. This is the meaning. He says that subtilty terminates

in unresoluble-primary-matter in the words «And beyond the unresoluble-primary-matter there is nothing subtile.» He raises a doubt by saying «If the objection be raised.» That is to say, the Self also is subtile not the unresoluble primary-substance alone. He rebuts [this objection] by saying «true.» In other words, in so far as it is a material cause there is in the unresoluble-primary-substance subtilty, but not in the other [that is, the Self]. In this case, since the purpose of the Self is the instrumental cause of the Great Principle and of the personality-substance and of the others, the Self is also, like unresoluble-primary-matter, a cause. Having in mind the question as to how subtilty, characterized in this way, is to be understood as regards the unresoluble, he asks «however.» He gives the answer in the words «not that of the resoluble-primary-matter.» True, [the Self is] a cause, but not a material cause. For the Self is not, like the primary-substance, a cause of these [states], in so far as being the Great or the other [states] it enters into mutations. This is the meaning. He sums up in the words «Accordingly it is explained that subtilty reaches its utmost degree in the primary-substance.»

46. These same [balanced-states] are the seeded concentration.

These four balanced-states have external [perceptible] things as their seed. Therefore the concentration is seeded. Of these four the deliberative and the super-deliberative refer to a coarse intended-object, the reflective and super-reflective to a subtile intended-object. Thus in four kinds, one after another, concentration has been enumerated.

And in the four balanced-states the object of which is a thing-to-be-known he says that [concentration] conscious [of an object may occur]. **46. These same [balanced-states] are the seeded concentration.** The word *eva* is out of place and should be understood after ‹seeded.› As a result of this, the four balanced-states, the object of which is the thing-to-be-known, are limited in so far as they are seeded. The seeded state, however, is not limited [to the thing-to-be-known], since, even in the case of the balanced-state the object of which is the knower or the process-of-knowing, it persists, not being negated by the distinction into predicate-relations and unpredicated-relations [with reference to the thing-to-be-known]. So with regard to the thing-to-be-known there are four balanced-states and four in respect of the knower and the process-of-knowing: thus there are eight[1] of these [concentrations]. The Comment is explained by a [mere] reading.

[1] The Bikāner MS. and the Bombay San. Ser. text read *siddhā* in place of *te*.

47. When there is the clearness of the super-reflective [balanced-state, the yogin gains] internal undisturbed calm. When freed from obscuration by impurity, the *sattva* of the thinking-substance, the essence of which is light, has a pellucid steady flow not overwhelmed by the *rajas* and *tamas*. This is the clearness. When this clearness arises in the super-reflective balanced-state, then the yogin gains the internal undisturbed calm, [that is to say] the vision by the flash (*sphuṭa*) of insight which does not pass successively through the serial order [of the usual processes of experience] and which has as its intended-object the thing as it really is. And in this sense it has been said,[1] "As the man who has climbed the crag sees those upon the plain below (*bhūmiṣṭha*), so the man of insight who has risen to the undisturbed calm of insight, himself escaped from pain, beholds all creatures in their pain."

Of the four balanced-states which have as their object the thing-to-be-known, excellence belongs to the super-reflective [balanced-state]. [This] he describes in the sūtra 47. **When there is the clearness of the super-reflective [balanced-state, the yogin gains] internal undisturbed calm.** He describes the meaning of the word ‹clearness› by [the words beginning with] «impurity.» Impurity is an accretion of *rajas* and *tamas*. And it is the defilement which has the distinguishing-characteristic of obscuration. [Clearness] is freed from this. «The essence of which is light» means naturally light. For this reason the *sattva* of the thinking-substance is not overwhelmed. An objection is made, 'This may be true. But if the balanced-state has as its object the thing-to-be-known, how could the undisturbed calm have itself as its object?' To this he replies with the words «has as its intended-object the thing as it really is.» In other words, it does not have the self as its object but as its substrate[2] (*ādhāra*). «Does not pass successively through the serial order» means that it is simultaneous. On this very point he cites the teaching of the Supreme Sage (*pāramārṣīṁ gāthām*) with the words «And in this sense.» Seeing that he is above all by virtue of the perfection of his perceptive vision,[3] he knows that the creatures are «in their pain», encompassed by the three kinds of pain.

[1] Compare MBh. xii. 17. 20; 151.11; Dhammapada 28. Compare also Bacon's Essay on Truth, "No pleasure is comparable to the standing upon the vantage-ground of truth (a hill not to be commanded and where the air is always clear and serene) and to see the errors and wanderings and mists and tempests, in the world below."

[2] This is explained in the Pātañjala Rahasyam thus, 'There is a doubt as to there being a relation of cause and effect in things which are in different places (*vyadhikaraṇatve kāryakāraṇatā nāstīty āçañkya*).'

[3] Compare p. 62[1] and Sūtra ii. 15.

48. In this [calm] the insight is truth-bearing.

In one whose mind-stuff is concentrated, the insight[1] which arises in this [calm] receives the technical name of ‹truth-bearing.› And this is a [term] whose meaning is intelligible of itself: [this insight] bears truth[2] and nothing else; in it there is not even a trace of misconception. And in this sense it has been said, "By the Sacred Word [and] by inference and by eagerness for practice in contemplation, in three ways he promotes his insight and gains the highest yoga."

With regard to this same point he gives the consensus of yogins by telling of the term current among yogins which itself expresses the intended-object. **48. In this [calm] the insight is truth-bearing.** The Comment is easy. By the expression «Sacred Word» is meant the hearing (*çravaṇa*) prescribed by the Vedas; by the expression «inference» is meant consideration (*manana*). Contemplation is reflection. Practice in this is following it up one time after another. Eagerness for this is close attention [to it]. So in this way absorption (*nididhyāsana*) is described.

But this [insight]—

49. Has an object other than the insight resulting from things heard or from inferences inasmuch as its intended-object is a particular.

‹A thing heard› is knowledge derived from verbal-communication. This deals with generic objects. For a particular cannot be connoted by a verbal-communication. Why [not]? Because a word does not have its conventional-usage established by the particular. Similarly inference deals with generic objects only. [For instance, compare i. 7], we say, where there is getting [to a place], there is motion; and where there is no getting [to a place], there is no motion. And by an inference we get a conclusion in generic [terms only]. Therefore no particular can be the object of verbal-communication or of inference. And of this subtile and hidden and remote[3] thing there is no knowledge by ordinary perception. Furthermore we cannot assert that this particular has no validity and does not exist. Therefore this particular as object, whether it belong to a subtile element or to the Self, is apper-

[1] See iii. 51. [2] Pātañjala Rahasyam gives the gloss: *ātma-tattvam*.

[3] Compare Sāṁkh. Kār. vii.

ceptible by the concentrated insight only. Consequently this insight has an object other than [the object of] the insight resulting from a thing heard or from inference, inasmuch as its intended-object is a particular.

The objection is made, 'This may be true. But the super-reflective [balanced-state] which is produced by perfection of impressions whose objects[1] refer to that which is known by verbal-communication or by inference can refer (*gocarayet*) only to the objects of verbal-communication and of inference. For surely a subliminal impression derived from the experience of one object is not able to produce knowledge with regard to another. For that would be an unwarranted assumption. Therefore if the super-reflective [balanced-state] is truth-bearing, verbal communications and inferences must also be assumed to be this [that is, truth-bearing].' In reply to this he says **49. Has an object other than the insight resulting from things heard or from inferences inasmuch as its intended-object is a particular.** For the *sattva* of the thinking-substance is naturally bright; although it has the power of seeing all intended-objects, it becomes obscured by *tamas*; only when by *rajas* it is set-free-to-stream-forth, then only does it know [the object]. But when by practice and passionlessness the defilement of *rajas* and *tamas* is cast off and it shines forth spotlessly clear, then passing beyond the limits of all measures (*māna*) and of all things measurable (*meya*) and having endless brightness—what then, pray, can there be that is not within its scope? He explains [the sūtra] in the words «A thing heard is knowledge derived from verbal-communication. This deals with generic objects.» Why? «For a particular cannot be connoted by a verbal-communication.» For what reason? Because a word does not have its conventional usage established by a particular, since [the word] is an infinite and since it has a too-wide-pervasion (*vyabhicāra*). For we do not perceive the relation of word and thing expressed in connexion with any particular instance of this [word]. And furthermore the sense of the sentence cannot be such a particular. Even in case of an inference which depends for its origin upon the knowledge of the relation between the syllogistic-mark (*liñga*) and the subject-of-the-proposition (*liñgin*), the same procedure holds good, as he says «Similarly inference.» In the expression «where there is no getting to a place» the words «where» and «there» should by logical conversion be made to indicate the pervaded and the pervader. Therefore here by an inference we get a conclusion in generic [terms only]. He sums up with the word «Therefore.» It might be admitted that then we have ordinary perception irrespective of a knowledge of the relation [between the word and the thing-expressed] and that this [perception] does not deal with generic objects only. In reply to this he says, «And of this . . . no.» It may not be admitted that ordinary perception depends upon a knowledge of the relation [of word and thing-expressed]; but it must be admitted that it depends upon

[1] The sequence is, first an *anubhava*, next a *saṁskāra*, and then a *smṛti*.

the senses. And with this [higher insight] the senses have no pre-established harmony. This is the meaning. It is objected that if the individual is not within the scope of verbal-communications and inferences and perceptions, then it does not exist. For there is no source-of-valid-ideas for [it]. In reply to this he says «Furthermore . . . not.» For a source-of-valid-ideas is not [necessarily] a pervader nor a cause of the object-of-knowledge (*prameya*) to the extent that, if that [source-of-valid-ideas] should cease, the [object-of-knowledge] would cease to be. For surely, when the moon is a slender crescent (*kalāvant*), those who accept sources-of-valid-ideas do not doubt the real existence of the deer[1] which is situated in the other part [of the moon's surface not then visible]. «Therefore,» for this reason it «is apperceptible by the concentrated insight only.» And here the atoms and the selves which are subjected to [this] discussion are endowed with a particularity peculiar to themselves, because, being substances, they are distinct from each other. Whatever things, being substances, are distinct from each other, these are endowed with particularity peculiar to themselves, like a cripple or a man with a shaven head. According to this inference, and to the verbal-communication which is devoted to teaching what the truth-bearing insight is, [the peculiar individuality of this insight has been defined]. Although the individual is described, still in the absence of such a description doubt might arise, because it has been obtained by a line-of-reasoning; yet in so far as it is not far[2] or remote, this *sattva* is brought, with some difficulty, within the scope of verbal-communication or of inference. But they do not [make evident the existence of the particular] by as direct an experience as words of connexion, for instance, through their application of gender and number, [bring] the meaning of the word 'and' [within the scope of verbal-communication or of inference]. Therefore it is established that [this insight] has an object other than the insights resulting from things heard or from inferences.

When the yogin has gained concentrated insight, the subliminal-impression made by the insight is reproduced again and again.

50. The subliminal-impression produced by this [super-reflective balanced-state] is hostile to other subliminal-impressions.

The subliminal-impression arising from concentrated insight inhibits the latent-impression from the emergent subliminal-impression. After emergent subliminal-impressions have been repressed,

[1] Compare Subhāṣitaratnabhāṇḍāgāram (Nir. Sāg. fourth ed.), p. 318, no. 162, s.v. *aṅkaṁ ke 'pi*. See also Kuvalayānanda Kārikā (Nir. Sāg. ed.), p. 27[4].

[2] According to Pātañjala Rahasyam the meaning of 'not far' is that from which there results a generic idea (*sāmānyato bodhayataḥ*); and of 'remote', that from which there results no particular idea *viçeṣato na bodhayata iti*.

the presented-ideas arising from them do not occur. When presented-ideas are restricted, concentration follows after. Then concentrated insight; after that, subliminal-impressions made from insight; thus latent-impressions from subliminal-impressions are reproduced again and again. Thus first comes insight and then [follow] subliminal-impressions. How is it that this excess of subliminal-impressions will not provide the mind-stuff with a task? [The answer is:] these subliminal-impressions made by the insight do not provide the mind-stuff with a task since they cause the dwindling of the hindrances. For they cause the mind-stuff to cease from its work. For the movement of the mind-stuff terminates at [the time of] discernment (*khyāti*).

'Let this be granted. Let the [concentration] conscious [of an object] have a reality as its object by the practice of the aforesaid means. But this concentrated insight may be obstructed by beginningless emergent subliminal-impressions in so far as it is closely enveloped [by them], like minute flashes [of light] from a lamp in the eddy of a whirling wind.' To remove this doubt he introduces the next sūtra with the words «concentrated insight.» He recites the sūtra 50. **The subliminal-impression produced by this [super-reflective balanced-state] is hostile to other subliminal-impressions.** The word ‹this› refers to the super-reflective balanced-state. The word ‹other› describes the emergence. It is the nature of thoughts to incline[1] to intended-objects as they really are. This instability continues unsteady only so long as it does not reach the reality [literally, that-ness]. After reaching that and because it has taken a stable position there, [this] idea from the subliminal-impression does most certainly inhibit the series of ideas from subliminal-impressions which refer to what is not reality, even although [this series] is beginningless and rolls on as the wheel[2] of the series of [fluctuations and] subliminal-impressions. And in this sense outsiders[3] also say, "There is no inhibition of the unviolated essence of a thing-as-it-really-is by contradictions even although these latter be from time without beginning. For it is the nature of the mind to incline to things as they are." The objector would say, 'This may be true. We may admit that, as a result of concentrated insight, there is a restriction of a subliminal-impression produced during the emergent state. Still there exists uninjured (*avikala*) an excess of subliminal-impressions which is produced by concentration and which causes the generation of the concentrated insight. So the fact that the mind-stuff has a task still remains.'—With this in mind, he raises an objection, «How is it that

[1] Compare Sāṁkh. Tatt. Kāu. lxiv.

[2] Compare i. 5, p. 20[2] (Calc. ed.).

[3] Either Jains or Buddhists. The quotation is found in Vācaspatimiçra's Bhāmatī (Jībān. ed.), p. 60[27].

this,» which he removes with the words «these . . . do not.» For the work of the mind-stuff is of two kinds, the enjoyment of sounds and other [perceptible] things (*çabdādi*) and discriminative discernment. With regard to these two [kinds of work], the mind-stuff, when it has latent-impressions of karma from the hindrances, proceeds to the enjoyment of sounds and other [perceptible] things ; but for the mind, all of whose latent-impressions of karma from the hindrances have been uprooted by subliminal-impressions arising in insight, and whose state is that its task is nearly ended, the only work that remains is discriminative discernment. Accordingly subliminal-impressions from concentration are not the reasons why the mind-stuff has enjoyment as its task. On the contrary they are hostile to that. They cause the mind-stuff to cease from its work ; they make it incapable [of that work] which has the character of enjoyment. This is the meaning. Why? «For the movement of the mind-stuff terminates at [the time of] discernment.» Since in order to enjoy, the mind-stuff moves until it experiences discriminative discernment. But when discriminative discernment has come to pass, hindrances cease and it has no longer the task of enjoyment. Consequently the complete quiescence of the task of enjoyment is the purpose for which subliminal-impressions from insight exist. It is this that has been stated here.

What further does he gain?

51. When this [subliminal-impression] also is restricted, since all is restricted, [the yogin gains] seedless concentration.

This [seedless concentration] is counter not only to concentrated insight but is opposed even to subliminal-impressions made in insight. Why? Because the subliminal-impression produced by restriction inhibits the subliminal-impressions produced by concentration. The existence of subliminal-impressions made by the mind-stuff in restriction may be inferred from the experience of the lapse of time during which there is stability (*sthiti*) of the restriction. Together with the subliminal-impressions which arise out of the emergent and restricted concentrations and which are conducive to Isolation, the mind-stuff resolves itself into its own permanent primary-matter. Therefore these subliminal-impressions are counter to the mind-stuff's task and are not causes of its stability. Consequently, its task ended, together with the subliminal-impressions which are conducive to Isolation, the mind-stuff ceases [from its task]. When it ceases, the Self abides in himself and is therefore called pure and liberated.

He asks, «What further?» What does he also gain? [Since] the mind-stuff contains subliminal-impressions [produced] in insight, it has, as before, in so far as it is capable of generating a stream of insight, a task [to fulfil]. Thus to remove the task something else is also still required. This is the meaning. He gives the answer in the sūtra 51. **When this [subliminal-impression] also is restricted, since all is restricted, [the yogin gains] seedless concentration.** The higher passionlessness,[1] which has as its distinguishing characteristic the undisturbed calm of perception, by an increase in subliminal-impressions restricts even those subliminal-impressions made by insight and not merely the insight [itself]. This is the meaning of the word «even.» Since the whole stream of subliminal-impressions as it rises [into consciousness] is restricted, [then,] inasmuch as there is no cause, no effect can be produced. This same is seedless concentration. He explains [the sūtra] in the words «This [seedless concentration].» «This» is seedless concentration arising out of higher passionlessness, which is counter to concentrated insight, and which with the help of itself as cause[2] becomes not only counter to concentrated insight, but also contradictory to subliminal-impressions made by insight. It might be objected that, 'A distinct-idea (*vijñāna*) produced by passionlessness would, since a distinct-idea is real, inhibit what is insight and nothing more. But how does it inhibit a subliminal-impression which is different in kind from a distinct-idea? For evidently a man even when awake has a memory of the object seen in [his] dream. [Therefore subliminal-impressions are not inhibited].' With this in mind he asks, «Why?» He gives the answer in the words «produced by restriction.» Restriction is that by which insight is restricted. It is the higher passionlessness. Produced from this it is [called] a subliminal-impression produced by restriction. Only by the subliminal-impression produced by the higher passionlessness when it has been cultivated for a long time and uninterruptedly and with earnest attention, and not by a distinct-idea, are the subliminal-impressions of insight inhibited. This is the meaning.—The objector continues, 'This may be so. But what is the source-of-valid-ideas for the existence of subliminal-impressions produced by restriction? It might be either perceived directly, or inferred from memory, its effect. And when all the [mind-stuff's] fluctuations are restricted, the yogin has no perception nor yet memory, forasmuch as, in so far as he has destroyed all fluctuations whatsoever, it is impossible for him to produce a memory.' In reply to this he says, «in restriction.» The stability of the restriction is the restricted state of the mind-stuff.—[The existence of subliminal-impressions is proved] by an experience of the lapse of time in [periods of] eight-and-forty minutes (*muhūrta*) or half-a-watch or a whole watch, or a day and night and so forth. What he means to say is this: according to the degree of the perfection in passionlessness and in practice, perfection of restriction is experienced by the yogin. And the moments of the higher passionlessness, in so far as they are

[1] Pātañjala Rahasyam identifies this with *dharma-megha*.

[2] As explained in i. 18.

not related to each other in a fixed sequence, are not capable, in so far as they last for various periods of time, of producing the full excellence of restriction. So the point is that we must admit that there is a permanent accumulation of subliminal-impressions produced by the accumulations of the various moments of passionlessness. The objector says, 'Subliminal impressions from insight may perish, but why should the subliminal-impression from restriction perish with them; or if it does not perish, [then the mind-stuff would still] have its task [to perform].' In reply to this he says, «out of the emergent.» [This is the analysis of the compound :] conscious [concentration] has (*tasya*) both emergence and the concentration of emergence which restricts this [emergence]. The subliminal-impressions arising out of these two are the subliminal-impressions which are conducive to Isolation. [And these are the same as] those produced by restriction. The subliminal-impressions of emergent insight are resolved into mind-stuff. Thus the mind-stuff contains subliminal-impressions of emergent insight. But the subliminal-impression from restriction lies (*āste*) just uprisen in the mind-stuff. Although [this] subliminal-impression is [uprisen], the mind-stuff has no task [to fulfil]. For the mind-stuff has its task [to fulfil] when it is bringing to pass the two purposes of the Self, the experience of sounds and other [perceptible things] and the discriminative discernment. Such are the two purposes of the Self. But when nothing is left but subliminal-impressions [of restriction],—now that the Self is not assimilated-by-reflection[1] (*pratisaṁvedin*) to the thinking-substance,—this is not one of the purposes of the Self. On the other hand, in the case of the discarnate and of those [whose bodies] are resolved-into-primary-matter, the mind-stuff,—not only in so far as it is conducive to restriction, but also in so far as it is pervaded (*vāsita*) with hindrances,—still has its task [to fulfil]. With this in mind he says «Consequently.» The rest is easy.

The announcement (*uddeça*) and the definition (*nirdeça*) of Yoga, the characteristic-mark of the fluctuations which exist for the sake of this [Yoga], the means of Yoga and its subdivisions,—[these] have been sketched in this Book.

Of Patañjali's Yoga-treatise entitled Exposition of Sāṁkhya (*Sāṁkhya-pravacana*), the First Book, on Concentration.

Of the Explanation of the Comment on Patañjali's-Treatise, which Explanation is entitled Clarification of Entities (*Tattva-Vaiçāradī*) and was composed by the Venerable Vācaspatimiçra, the First Book, on Concentration, is finished.

[1] Compare pp. 22[1]; 66[3]; 138[9]; 152[2]; and 305[9] (Calcutta ed.).

BOOK SECOND

MEANS OF ATTAINMENT

BOOK SECOND

MEANS OF ATTAINMENT

It has been stated what the yoga is of one whose mind is concentrated. [This sūtra] gives the start to the problem [which considers] how even one whose mind-stuff is emergent may be concentrated (*yukta*) in concentration (*yoga*).

1. Self-castigation and study and devotion to the Içvara are the Yoga of action.

Yoga is not perfected in him who is not self-castigated. Impurity —which is variegated with subconscious-impressions (*vāsanā*), from time without beginning, coming from the hindrances and from karma, —and into which [the meshes of] the net of objects have [therefore] found entrance, is not reduced (*sam̐bhedam āpadyate*) except by ‹self-castigation.› This is the use[1] of self-castigation. And this [kind of self-castigation], not being inhibitory to the undisturbed calm of the mind-stuff, is therefore deemed [by great sages] to be worthy of his (*anena*, the yogin's) earnest attention. ‹Recitation› is the repetition[2] of purifying formulae such as the Mystic Syllable (*praṇava*) or the study of books on Liberation. ‹Devotion to the Içvara› is the offering[3] up of all actions to the Supreme Teacher or the renunciation of the fruit of [all] these [actions].

If it be objected that the First Book described yoga with its means [and] with its subordinate divisions [and] with its results, and that no reason remains why a Second Book should be begun, he replies in the words «has been stated.» For in the First Book practice and passionlessness were described as means to yoga. And since these two, for one whose [mind-stuff] is emergent, do not instantly come into being, he stands in need of the means taught in the Second Book in order to purify the *sattva*. For by these he quite purifies the *sattva* and performs the protective ordinances and daily

[1] Similarly i. 41, p. 85[8] (Calc. ed.).

[2] See ii. 44 and compare Liñga Pur. viii. 39.

[3] Contrast this with i. 23 and see also Liñga Pur. viii. 40.

cultivates practice and passionlessness. The state of being concentrated is the state of being undistracted.—How could even a man whose mind-stuff is emergent be, because concentrated (*yukta*) by the means which are to be taught, a yogin? This is the meaning. From among those observances which are to be described, having made a selection [of some] as being rather more serviceable to the beginner, the author of the sūtras first of all teaches [what] the yoga of action [is]. **1. Self-castigation and study and devotion to the Içvara are the Yoga of action.** Action which is itself yoga is the yoga of action since it is a means-of-effecting yoga. Therefore, in the Viṣṇu Purāṇa, in the dialogue between Khāṇḍikya and Keçidhvaja, starting with the passage,[1] 'At first the yogin who is [just] beginning to apply himself is called a novice (*yoga-yuj*),' self-castigation and recitation and the like are set forth. With the words «in him who is not self-castigated» he shows by a negative instance that self-castigation is a means. By the words «from time without beginning» he shows that self-castigation has a subsidiary function which is serviceable as a means[2] [of attaining yoga]. Variegated by reason of the subconscious-impressions, from time without beginning, coming from hindrances and from karma, [and] therefore that in which [the meshes of] the net of objects have found entrance, that is, inserted themselves, impurity, which is the excess of *rajas* and *tamas*, is not thoroughly reduced without self-castigation. Reduction is the thorough thinning out of that which was closely woven.—The objection is raised: 'Even if we have recourse to self-castigation, still—in so far as it causes disorders of the humours—it is hostile to yoga; how then is it a means [to attain] this [yoga]?' In reply to this he says, «And this[3] [kind].» Self-castigation should be performed only so long as it does not bring on a disorder[4] of the humours. This is the meaning. «Such as the Mystic Syllable» that is, such as, the Hymn to the Puruṣa [RV. x. 90] or the Rudra-maṇḍala[5] or a Brāhmaṇa or the like from the Vedas, or the Brahma-pārāyaṇa[6] from the Purāṇas.—Içvara, that is, the Supreme Teacher, the Exalted,—to him. With regard to Whom this[7] hath been said, "Whatever I do, whether auspicious or inauspicious, whether intentionally or unintentionally, all that is committed unto Thee. Moved by Thee I do [it all]."—Renunciation of the fruit of [all] these [actions] is doing the actions without attachment to the fruit [thereof]. And with regard to this it hath been said,[8] "You are concerned with actions only and never with fruits. Do not be one whose motive is the fruit of actions. Nor let your attachment be to inaction."

VP. vi. 7. 33. See also Nāradīya Pur. xlvii.
Literally, is serviceable by being a means, *upāyatā-upayoginam*.
As opposed, for instance, to VP. ii. 11.
Compare i. 30, p. 67[1] (Calc. ed.).
This seems to refer to the Çatarudriya-homamantras, Tāittirīya-saṁhitā iv. 5, Vājasaneyi-saṁhitā xvi, Kāṭhaka xvii.
[6] Refers perhaps to Viṣṇu Purāṇa i. 15.
[7] Vijñāna Bhikṣu calls this *smṛti*.
[8] Bhagavad Gītā ii. 47.

Now this yoga of action is—

2. For the cultivation of concentration and for the attenuation of the hindrances.

For when the yoga of action is given earnest attention, it cultivates concentration; attenuates the hindrances to an extreme degree; [and] will make the hindrances, when they are extremely attenuated, disqualified for propagation, like seeds burned by the fire of Elevation (*prasaṁkhyāna*). But the subtile insight, which is the discriminative discernment between the *sattva* and the Self, untouched by the hindrances because they are so much attenuated, with its task finished, will be ready for inverse-propagation[1] (*pratiprasava*).

In order to mention the purpose of this [yoga of action] he introduces the sūtra with the words «For the.» **2. For the cultivation[2] of concentration and for the attenuation of the hindrances.** It is objected that if the yoga of action alone is able to attenuate the hindrances, then there is no need of Elevation. To this he replies with the words «the extremely attenuated.» The yoga of action operates only for the extreme attenuation, but not for the sterilization of the hindrances, but Elevation [operates] for the sterilization of those [hindrances]. The words «like burned seeds» indicate that the burned seeds of winter rice [and the hindrances] are of the same kind in so far as both are sterile. The objector says, 'This may be true. But if Elevation alone can disqualify the hindrances from propagation, then there is no need for their attenuation.' In reply to this he says, «of these.» For if the hindrances are not attenuated, the discriminative discernment between the *sattva* and the Self, submerged (*grasta*) by mighty foes, is incapable even of uprising, still less of sterilizing them. But when the hindrances are quite thinned out and impotent, [the discernment], although in opposition to them, does, with the aid of passionlessness and of practice, finally arise. And when the discernment which is nothing more than the [sense] of the difference between the *sattva* and the Self is finally arisen, it is un-touched by them,—that is, not overwhelmed by them,—for just so long as it is not touched [by them]. «The subtile insight» is so-called, because its object is subtile inasmuch as its object is beyond the range of the senses. «Will be ready for inverse-propagation,» that is, for resolution. Why? Because its task is finished. [In other words,] that is said to be of this kind by which, acting as a cause, the task of giving starts to the effects of the aspects (*guṇa*) has been finished.

---

[1] Compare ii. 2, p. 107[6]; ii. 10, p. 120[1]; ii. 27, p. 167[1]; iii. 50, p. 265[1]; iv. 34, p. 319[2] (Calc. ed.).

[2] Deussen's excellent rendering of this word is *Verinnerlichung*.

Now what are these[1] hindrances and (*vā*) how many are they?

3. Undifferentiated-consciousness (*avidyā*) **and the feeling-of-personality and passion and aversion and the will-to-live are the five[2] hindrances.**

This means that the so-called hindrances are five misconceptions [i. 8]. These when flowing out make the authority (*adhikāra*) of the aspects (*guṇa*) more rigid; make a mutation more stable; swell the stream of effects and causes; and, becoming interdependent upon one another for aid, bring forth the fruition of karma.

He raises a question by saying «Now» and replies [to it] by the sūtra upon «Undifferentiated-consciousness.» **3. Undifferentiated-consciousness** (*avidyā*) **and the feeling-of-personality and passion and aversion and the will-to-live are the five hindrances.** He explains the word «hindrances» by the words «five misconceptions.» Undifferentiated-consciousness, to begin with, is nothing but misconception. The feeling-of-personality and the others also have undifferentiated-consciousness as their material cause, [and] since they cannot exist without it, [they too] are misconceptions. And hence when undifferentiated-consciousness is destroyed, there would follow the destruction of them also. He mentions the reason why they should be destroyed, in that they are the cause of the round-of-rebirths. This he states in the word «These.» When flowing out [that is] moving[3] continuously forth, «make the authority of the aspects more rigid,» that is, more powerful; [and] in consequence «make a mutation [more] stable.» For in successive forms as unphenomenalized [primary matter] and as the Great [thinking-substance] and as the personality-substance, they swell, that is, they intensify, the stream of cause and effect. He shows for what purpose they do all this in the words «one another.» The [three] fruitions of karma, distinguished [ii. 13] as being birth and length of life and kind of experience, have their purpose (*artha*) in the Self. That [purpose] those hindrances bring to pass, that is, accomplish. Do they accomplish this singly? He says, 'No.' But «upon one another for aid,» that is, the hindrances [aided] by the karmas, and the karmas [aided] by the hindrances.

4. Undifferentiated-consciousness (*avidyā*) **is the field for the others whether they be dormant or attenuated or intercepted or sustained.**

Of these [five], undifferentiated-consciousness is the field [or] propagative soil. The others are feeling-of-personality and the rest

[1] Many MSS. omit *te*. [2] Many MSS. omit *pañcā*.

[3] Compare ii. 4, p. 110[8]; iii. 13, p. 207[9].

[of the five hindrances]. In four kinds of forms, the dormant and the attenuated and the intercepted and the sustained.—1. Of these [four], what is the dormant state? It is the tendency [of the hindrances] which remain merely potential in the mind towards the condition of seed. The awakening of that [dormant hindrance] is the coming face-to-face with the [particular] object [which makes that dormant hindrance manifest]. But for one who has [reached] Elevation (*prasaṁkhyāna*), and whose hindrances have become burned seed, there is not that [awakening of the hindrances] even when he is brought face-to-face with the object [which manifests them]. For out of what can burned seed germinate? For this reason the fortunate (*kuçala*) man whose hindrances have dwindled away is said to be in his last [1] body (*caramadeha*). In him only the burned state of the seeds, the fifth stage of the hindrances [is found], and not in other [persons]. So although the hindrances are existent, the vitality (*sāmarthya*) of the seed is said to be already burned. Accordingly, even when the object is face-to-face, there is no awakening of these [hindrances]. Thus dormancy and the failure of the burned seed to propagate have been described.—2. Attenuation is now described. The hindrances, when overpowered (*upahata*) by the cultivation of their opposites,[2] become attenuated.—3. When this is the case, [the other hindrances] intercept [the attenuated hindrances] repeatedly, and move forth actively again in this or that [unattenuated] form (*ātmanā*). In that case [3] they are called intercepted. How is this? Since [for instance] when one is in love, no anger is felt, inasmuch as, when one is in love, anger does not actively move forth; and love, when felt in one direction, is by no means unfelt towards another object. When Chāitra is known to be in love with one woman, it is not assumed that he is out of love for other women. Rather, his love finds its fluctuation fixed in this direction, in other directions its fluctuation is yet to come. For this [third fluctuation] is for the moment both dormant and attenuated and intercepted.—4. That fluctuation which is fixed upon an object is sustained (*udāra*). No one of all

[1] See VP. v. 10. 7 and Bh. Gītā viii. 26.

[2] See ii. 33.

[3] When they form a succession of *tanu* and *atanu*.

these [four] passes beyond the limits of the hindrances [and therefore all four are to be rejected]. If this is so (*tarhi*), what is this hindrance that is intercepted [or] dormant [or] attenuated or sustained? The answer-is-now-given (*ucyate*). It is exactly true [that all hindrances are forms of undifferentiated-consciousness]. But only when these [hindrances] are particularized, do they become intercepted and so on. For just as these stages cease when their opposites are cultivated, so they become manifest (*abhivyakta*) when [changed] into the phenomenal-form (*añjana*) by the operation of their phenomenalizing-conditions (*vyañjaka*). So all those hindrances without exception are varieties of undifferentiated-consciousness. Why is this? Since it is undifferentiated-consciousness and nothing else that pervades[1] all [hindrances]. Whatever [perceptible] object is given a form by the undifferentiated-consciousness, it is that [object] which is permeated[2] by the hindrances. Whenever there is a misconceived idea, they become apperceived; and when undifferentiated-consciousness dwindles, they too dwindle away.

He shows that hindrances are to be rejected in that they have their root in undifferentiated-consciousness. **4. Undifferentiated-consciousness** (*avidyā*) **is the field for the others whether they be dormant or attenuated or intercepted or sustained.** When he asks «1. Of these [four], what is the dormant state?» his intention is to say that there is no proof for the real existence of hindrances, if they are not performing their peculiar purposeful activity. He tells the answer in the words «in the mind.» The hindrances may not indeed perform their purposeful activity, but in the case of the discarnate and of those [whose bodies] are resolved into primary matter, they assume the form of seed and exist merely potentially, as curds exist in milk. For other than discriminative insight there is nothing to cause the sterility of these [hindrances]. Hence the discarnate and those [whose bodies] are resolved into primary matter, who have not obtained discriminate discernment, have their hindrances dormant, until such time as [these hindrances] reach the time of their limitation. But when they reach that, since the hindrances revert once more, they come face-to-face with the various objects [of sense]. Thus these [hindrances] are those of which the basis is merely potential. In this way their potential rising [into consciousness] is described. By the words «tendency . . . towards the condition

[1] Bālarāma says, "'Undifferentiated-consciousness is inseparably-connected with hindrances' (*kleçeṣu avidyānvīya*).

[2] Bālarāma explains the word *anuçerate* by saying 'become inherent in' (*anugatā bhavanti*).

of seed» their potentiality of action is indicated. To meet the question why, in the case even of one who has discriminative discernment, hindrances are not dormant, he says, «for one who has [reached] Elevation.» «In his last body,» in other words, in his case no other body will be produced with reference to which [this] body of his could be called prior. «Not in other persons,» in other words, not in the discarnate and similar cases. An objection is raised, 'Since there is no total destruction of any existing thing, what, we ask, becomes of the force of the magical powers of this kind of yoga? Are not the hindrances awakened when face-to-face with objects?' In reply to this, he says, «existent.» Although the hindrances are existent, still in their state as seeds they are burned by the fire of Elevation (*prasaṁkhyāna*). This is the meaning.—2. The opposite of the hindrances is the yoga of action; by the cultivation, by the following up, of this, the hindrances become overpowered, that is, attenuated. Or we may say that thinking-focused-to-a-point (*saṁyag-jñāna*) is the opposite of undifferentiated-consciousness; that the knowing of distinctions is [the opposite] of the feeling-of-personality; that the detached attitude (*mādhyasthya*) is [the opposite] of passion and aversion; [and] that the cessation of the thought of continuance is [the opposite] of the will-to-live.—3. He describes the interception with the words «When this is the case.» Either because overcome by any one of the hindrances which moves actively forth, or because resorting excessively to objects, they intercept repeatedly and move actively forth in one form or another, that is, come into appearance (*āvirbhavanti*), either as the result of using aphrodisiacs and the like or as the result of the weakness of [the other hindrances] which overcome it. By the repetition he signifies the reiteration of the interruption and of the moving actively forth. Thus the difference [of this] from the aforesaid dormant [hindrance] has been described. When love moves actively forth, anger which is different in kind is overpowered; or again love itself set upon one object overpowers, though like in kind, another love which is set upon a different object. This he states by the word «love.»—The fluctuation which is yet to come is to be understood as having a three-fold course according to circumstances. With this in mind he says, «For this.» The pronoun ['this'] refers only to the hindrance from the fluctuation which is yet to come; it does not refer to Chāitra's love, just because that [love] is intercepted.—4. He describes the sustained [hindrance] in the words «upon an object.» If some one suggests as an objection that the sustained [hindrance], since it hinders men, might be [properly] called a hindrance, but that the others do not hinder [and so can] by no means be called hindrances, he says in reply «all these [four].» They do not pass beyond the limits of the hindrances, that is, beyond the limits of the thing expressed by the word hindrance, when they become changed into the sustained state. Therefore they too are to be rejected. This is the point.—Presupposing the unity of the hindrances[1] he raises an objection in the words

[1] Literally, Presupposing a unity in so far as the quality of being a hindrance goes.

«If this is so, what.» He rebuts it by showing that although they are of the same kind in so far as they are hindrances, they are particular because of the different previously described states. This he does in the words «The answer-is-now-given. It is true.» The objector says,[1] 'This may be true. The hindrances may result from undifferentiated-consciousness; still why should they cease when undifferentiated-consciousness ceases? For surely no one would suppose that a piece of cloth ceases to be, when the weaver ceases to be.' In reply to this he says «all these . . . without exception.» The distinctions[2] are only apparently distinctions, that is to say, they do not exist separably from this [undifferentiated-consciousness]. He asks a question in the words «Why is this?» He gives the reply in the words «all [hindrances].» This same point is made clear by the word «whatever.» «Is given a form» [that is] is falsely attributed. The rest is easy.

'In the case of those who have been resolved into entities, the hindrances are dormant; for yogins, attenuated; and in case of those attached to objects, hindrances are intercepted or sustained.' This is the summarizing-stanza.[3]

At this point undifferentiated-consciousness itself is described.

5. The recognition of the permanent, of the pure, of pleasure, and of a self in what is impermanent, impure, pain, and not-self is undifferentiated-consciousness.

1. It is the recognition of the permanent[4] in an impermanent effect, for example, that the earth should be perpetual, that the sky with the moon and stars should be perpetual, that celestial beings are deathless.—2. Likewise in the impure and highly repulsive[5] body there has been the recognition of purity. And it

[1] Namely, in reply to the hedgings which in the Comment follow «It is true».

[2] Compare Kāv. Prak. Ullāsa iii. and the verse quoted in the comment on Appayadīkṣita's Kuvalayānandakārikā p. 11[1] (Nirṇaya Sāg. ed., 1903):
Gaganaṁ gaganākāraṁ
sāgaraḥ sāgaropamaḥ
Rāmarāvaṇayor yuddhaṁ
rāmarāvaṇayor iva.

[3] Discussed in Patañjali's Mahābhāṣya (Kielhorn's ed.), p. 6[12]. The application is only general here.

[4] The parallel between this and the discussion in Āryadeva's Catuḥçataka is very striking. The concept of *avidyā* is fundamental in the Mahāyāna. Āryadeva is said to be the pupil of Nāgārjuna; consequently he wrote a couple of centuries before Patañjali. We are indebted for this important discovery to Mahāmahopādhyāya Haraprasād Shāstrī (Notes on the newly-found Manuscript Chatuḥsatika by Aryadeva, Journal Asiatic Society of Bengal, New Series, vol. vii, no. 7, 1911, p. 431).

[5] Compare Māitrī Up. iii. 4.

has been said, "Because of its [first] abode [and] because of its origin [and] because of its sustenance [and] because of its exudations [and] because of its decease and because it needs [constant] cleaning, the learned recognize that the body is impure." Here the recognition of the pure in the impure is evident. If we say, 'This girl, beautiful as the sickle of the new moon, her limbs formed of honey and nectar, her eyes large as the petals of the blue lotus, seeming to refresh the living world with her coquettish glances, so that we think that she has issued forth from the moon,'—then what could be the connexion of this [body] with that (*kena*) [to which it is compared]? Just so[1] it is that there is a misconceived idea of the pure in the impure. In this way, [by showing the recognition of the pure in the impure, one sees that there is] the [misconceived] idea of merit where there is only demerit and of the useful where there is only the useless.—3. Similarly [Patañjali] will describe[2] the recognition of pleasure in pain in the words, "By reason of the pains of mutations and of anguish and of subliminal-impressions and by reason of the opposition of fluctuations of the aspects (*guṇa*)—to the discriminating all is nothing but pain." Undifferentiated-consciousness is the recognition that there is pleasure in this [pain].—4. Likewise the recognition of a self in the not-self, either in external aids[3] whether animate or inanimate, or in the body as the seat of outer experience, or in the central-organ which aids the Self,—this is the recognition of a self in the not-self. In this sense it has been said of this, "He who counts any existing thing, whether phenomenalized or unphenomenalized [primary matter], as himself; or who rejoices in the success of these (*tasya*) [things], deeming it his own success, or who grieves at the ill-success of these [things], deeming it his own ill-success,—these (*sa*) are all unenlightened." It is this four-fold undifferentiated-consciousness which becomes the root of that unbroken-series (*santāna*) of hindrances and of latent-impressions of karma together with its fruition. And this undifferentiated-consciousness (*a-vidyā*), pre-

[1] Compare the tale in Henry Warren's Buddhism in Translations, p. 297.

[2] See ii. 15.

[3] Bālarāma says 'Such as sons or cattle or servants or beds or seats, which are not the self'.

cisely as in the case of a foe (*a-mitra*) or of a trackless forest (*a-goṣpada*), is to be conceived as a really existing object (*vastusa-tattva*). Just as a foe (*amitra*) is not a negative friend [and] not something amounting to a friend, but the opposite of this [friend], a rival,—so too a trackless forest[1] (*a-goṣpada*) is not [a place] not-visited-by-cows (*goṣpada-abhāva*), nor again is it merely a [quantity of] land which has a cow's foot as its measure, but, on the contrary, it is nothing less than a definite place, a different thing, other than these two [and the opposite of a cow's footprint]. Precisely so, undifferentiated-consciousness is not a source-of-valid-ideas nor the negation of a source-of-valid-ideas, but another kind of thinking the reverse of knowledge.

5. The recognition of the permanent, of the pure, of pleasure, and of a self in what is impermanent, impure, pain, and not-self is undifferentiated-consciousness. 1. The word «effect» is a qualification which serves [to indicate] the impermanence. Some indeed, deeming the elements permanent and longing to attain to the form of these, pay devotion even to these. Thus deeming the moon and sun and stars and heavenly regions permanent, in order to attain these, they pay devotion to the Paths [that is, the Way of the Fathers and the Way of the Gods] which begin with the Smoke. Similarly deeming the celestial beings, that is, the gods, to be deathless, they drink soma in order to reach their condition. For it is written [RV. viii. 48. 3], "We have drunk the soma; we have become deathless." It is this recognition of the permanent in the impermanent that is undifferentiated-consciousness. 2. «Likewise in the impure and highly repulsive body»—when the sentence is only half-finished he recites a stanza (*gāthā*) from Vyāsa[2] to show the repulsiveness of the body. The words are «Because of its [first] abode.» The abode is the mother's womb polluted by such things as urine; the seed is the mother's blood and the father's semen. The sustenance is formation into juices of the food eaten and drunk; for by it the body is held together. Exudation is sweat. And death defiles the body of even a scholarly man. Inasmuch as a bath is required after his [dead body] is touched.—An objector might say, 'If the body is impure, there is no use in cleansing it with earth and with water.' To this he replies «because it needs [constant] cleaning.» Although the body is naturally impure, purification must be applied [to it], just as women produce fragrance [by applying] ointments

[1] This illustration occurs in Siddhānta Kāumudī, § 1060, on Pāṇ. vi. 1. 145. The word has the two meanings given in the Comment: 1. 'Not-visited' (*asevite*); thus *goṣpadāny* = *araṇyāni*; 2. 'Measure' *pramāṇe*; thus *goṣpada-mātram* = *kṣetram*.

[2] Patañjali discusses the word *Vāiyāsikīḥ* in the first vārttika on iv. 1. 97.

to the body. He completes the half-finished statement by saying «Here . . . in the impure.» The meaning is that it is impure on the grounds stated before. He describes the recognition of purity [in the impure] by the words «the new.» «Coquettish» is that which is playful as the result of an erotic-mood. What could be the connexion of the highly repulsive body, by a highly remote (*mandatama*) similarity, with such a thing as the sickle of the new moon?—«In this way,» by showing the recognition of purity in the impure body of a woman. «Where there is only demerit» as in the case of murder (*hiṅsā*), there is [the discovery of] an idea of merit in things which liberate from the round-of-rebirths. Similarly in case of a thing that is useless, such as money, because of the amount of pains [required] for getting it and keeping it, it is explained that there is [a discovery of] the idea of the useful [in the useless]. All these in that they are abhorrent are impure.—3. «Similarly . . . in pain.» Easy.—4. «Likewise . . . in the not-self.» Easy.—It was Pañcaçikha[1] who spoke of this in this way.—The "phenomenalized" [primary-matter] is the animate, such as sons or wives or cattle; the "unphenomenalized" is the inanimate, such as beds or seats or food.—«These (*sa*) are all unenlightened» [that is] stupid.—It is called four-fold (*catuṣpadā*) because it has four parts (*pada*), four places [where it becomes phenomenalized]. It might be objected, 'There is also another kind of undifferentiated-consciousness which has as its object such [states] as loss[2] of the sense of orientation or as [the sight] of the firebrand [whirled about so as to be seen as a] circle. Undifferentiated-consciousness has [therefore] an indefinite number of parts. Why then say that it is four-fold?' In reply to this he says, «the root . . . of that.» There may also be of course other undifferentiated-consciousnesses, but the undifferentiated-consciousness which is the seed of the round-of-rebirths has only four parts.

An objector says, 'Undifferentiated-consciousness (*a-vidyā*) might be a negative determinative[3] compound (*nañ-samāsa*). In which case, 1. the first member (*a-*) might be determinative (*pradhāna*), as for example, without-flies (*a-makṣika*); or 2. the final member might be determinative, as for example, not a-king's officer (*a-rājapuruṣa*); or 3. [the compound] might have a third thing as determinative, as for example, a flyless place (*amakṣika deça*). This being the situation, if we suppose 1. that the first member is determinative, then undifferentiated consciousness (*a-vidyā*) would be understood as a negation whereto an affirmative is expected[4] (*prasajjya-pratiṣedha*). And this [kind of a negation] could not be the cause of such things as the hindrances. Or if we

[1] This is the fifth fragment according to Garbe: Festgruss an Roth, 1893, p. 78. See also Garbe's Introduction to his translation of the Sāṁkhya-Tattva-Kāumudī, p. 7.

[2] Compare i. 6, p. 21[5] (Calc. ed.).

[3] Pāṇ. ii. 2. 6.

[4] A negative connected with a verbal stem. See Patañjali: Mahābhāṣya (Kielhorn's ed.) i. 215, last line; 221[11]; 319[12]; 341[6]; iii. 35, last line. See also the discussion in Apodeva: Mīmāṅsā-nyāya-prakāça (1906), p. 109. There is also a chapter on this in Vāiyākaraṇa Bhūṣaṇa.

suppose 2. that the final member is to be the determinative, then it is undifferentiated-consciousness that is to be particularized by the negation of something. And this [kind of] undifferentiated-consciousness would be destructive of such things as the hindrances and not the seed of them [because it would be a consciousness of the absence of something]. For it cannot be that the [member] subordinate (*guṇa*) to the determinative (*pradhāna*) [member of the compound] should break down that determinate. Therefore in order to make sure that it does not break down the determinative, something irregular, [that is, the absence of something] must be supposed, on the other hand, to be found in the subordinate [member of the compound]. Accordingly, in order that undifferentiated-consciousness as such should not be broken down, another meaning must be given to the negative or [another] negative must be supplied. Or if we suppose, on the other hand, 3. that another thing be the determinative [to the compound], we should have to say that [undifferentiated-consciousness] is a state-of-mind (*buddhi*) in which knowledge (*vidyā*) does not exist. And that could not be the seed of such things as the hindrances merely in so far as it is the absence of knowledge. For then a similar-state-of-things would also have to be admitted in the case of that [form of undifferentiated-consciousness] which is attained in the restriction when preceded by discriminative discernment, [since here too there is absence of knowledge]. Accordingly in all [these three] ways [it has been shown] that undifferentiated-consciousness is not the root of such things as the hindrances.' In reply to this he says, «And this . . . has.» «A really existing object» is the state of existence of a real object, that is, really existing objectivity. So in this way [it is evident] that undifferentiated-consciousness is neither 1. a negation-whereto-an-affirmative-is-expected (*prasajya-pratiṣedha*); nor again 2. nothing but [a defective kind of] knowledge; nor even 3. is it a state-of-mind characterized as being the absence of this, [that is, knowledge]; but 4. undifferentiated-consciousness is described as being misconceived thinking, the opposite of knowledge (*vidyā*). For the relation of word and thing is determined by conforming to the [usage of the] world. And because [according to the usage] of the world even a [compound] whose final member is determinative and which is a negative compound and which suppresses (*upamardaka*) the thing to be described by the last word [of the compound] is now and then found in a sense contrary to this [final member as determinative] and [at the same time] suggested by this [final member],—there is [therefore] in this case also an expressive-meaning (*vṛtti*) in the sense of being contrary to this [knowledge]. —He analyses the example «Just as a foe (*a-mitra*) is not.» [A foe] is not «a negative friend» nor again «. . . amounting to a friend.» Supply[1] at this point [in the text] 'Some other thing, but «the approach of this, a rival.»' «So too a trackless forest» is not a negative cow's[2] footprint, nor again is it merely a [quantity of] land which has a cow's foot as its measure; but, on

[1] It would appear that Vācaspatimiçra did not read the words *kiṁ tu . . . sapatnaḥ*.

[2] See the discussion s. v. *goṣpadam* in Çabda-Kalpa-Druma.

the contrary, nothing less than a spacious place, the opposite [in extent] of a cow's foot and other than the two negative *a-goṣpada* [that is, 1. without footprints-of-the-cow, and 2. not-a-cow's footprint would form together the first nogative cow's footprint; and 8. land covered by a cow's footprint would form the second negative cow's footprint], in fact, a different thing [altogether, the trackless forest]. He applies this to the matter in hand which he is illustrating, with the words «Precisely so.»

---

6. When the power of seeing and the power by which one sees have the appearance (*iva*) of being a single-self, [this is] the feeling-of-personality.

The Self is the power of seeing; the thinking-substance is the power by which one sees. The hindrance called the feeling-of-personality is a change by which these two appear to become a single essence (*svarūpa*). When there is any kind of failure to distinguish him who has the power of the enjoyer from that which has the power of being enjoyed, which are as distinct as possible and as unconfused as possible, enjoyment is ready at hand. But when each has recovered its own essence, there is Isolation.—How is it that [at that time there could be anything] that could be called enjoyment? In this sense it has been said,[1] "He who should fail to see that the Self is other than the thinking-substance, distinct in nature and in character and in consciousness and in other respects, would make the mistake of putting his own thinking-substance in the place of that [Self]."

Having said that undifferentiated-consciousness (*avidyā*) is the cause, he says that the feeling-of-personality is the effect, which [in its turn] is supreme (*variṣṭhā*) over passion and the other [hindrances]. **6. When the power of seeing and the power by which one sees have the appearance of being a single-self, [this is] the feeling-of-personality.** The seeing and that by which one sees are precisely the two powers of the two, the self and the not-self. That undifferentiated-consciousness (*avidyā*) which is characterized as being the perception of a self in what is the not-self, and which has the appearance of being a single intended-object, but which, in the strict sense, is not a single self,—this [*avidyā*] is the feeling-of-personality. Instead of saying 'of seeing and of that by which one sees', he uses the words ‹power of› in order to indicate the relation between them, that is, the capacity to be an enjoyer and to be objects to be enjoyed.—He elaborates the sūtra by saying «The Self.»—It might be asked, 'Why, since

[1] This is the sixth fragment of Pañcaçikha according to Garbe. Compare Bh. Gītā vi. 41.

they are perceived as identical, should they not be identical and why should [the appearance of] unity hinder the Self?' In reply he says «he who has the power of the enjoyer . . . that which has the power of being enjoyed.» He who has the power of the enjoyer is the Self; that which has the power of being enjoyed is the thinking-substance. These two are as distinct as possible. If it be asked, 'Whence comes this distinction?' the reply is, «as unconfused as possible.» Immutability and other [qualities] are the properties of the Self; mutability and other [qualities] are the properties of the thinking-substance. Thus there is no confusion. Thus by these words it is asserted that the identity, although presented-as-an-idea, is not in-the-strict-sense-real.—The words «failure to distinguish» state the fact that hindrances exist. After having given an affirmative [line of reasoning], he states a negative [line of reasoning] in the words «its own essence.» The recovery is the discriminative discernment. That another also holds this same opinion he says in the words «In this sense it has been said» by Pañcaçikha that «the thinking-substance.»—«In nature» means in its own self, which is, at all times whatsoever, pure [of aspects (*guṇa*)]; «in character» means in its detachment; «in consciousness» means in its intelligence (*cāitanya*); whereas the thinking-subject is impure and not detached and inanimate (*jaḍa*). Undifferentiated-consciousness (*avidyā*) is the mental state with regard to these two [to the effect that they are one] self. «The mistake» is a subliminal-impression generated by a previous undifferentiated-consciousness; or else it is the *tamas* [quality], because undifferentiated-consciousness is *tamas*.

7. Passion is that which dwells[1] upon pleasure.

That greed [or] thirst [or] desire, on the part of one acquainted with pleasure, ensuing upon a recollection of pleasure, for either the pleasure or for the means of attaining it, is passion.

When one feels the discrimination, such states as passion cease. So the feeling-of-personality brought to pass by undifferentiated-consciousness (*avidyā*) is the root (*nidāna*) of such states as passion. Accordingly, directly after the feeling-of-personality he gives the distinguishing-characteristic of passion and of the rest [of the hindrances]. **7. Passion is that which dwells upon pleasure.** Since memory [of pleasure] is impossible in the case of one unacquainted with pleasure, the text says «acquainted with pleasure.» Passion for a recollected pleasure ensues «upon a recollection of pleasure.» But while a pleasure is in experience there is no need of recollection. Since, however, the means for attaining pleasure are either remembered or perceived, the passion must ensue upon a recollection of pleasure. And even when the means of attaining pleasure are

[1] See the gloss *sukham anuçete viṣayīkaroti* (Maṇiprabhā). Compare i. 11, p. 38[6] (Calc. ed.). See also Vācaspati's gloss (*anukurvanti*), p. 281[17] (Calc. ed.), and the last words of the Bhāṣya on iv. 28 with Bālarāma's note.

perceived, it is only after remembering that one of this same kind is the source of pleasure that he infers that this one is a source of pleasure in so far as it is of the same kind. After this follows the desire. He explains the words ‹dwells upon› by the word «That.»

8. Aversion[1] is that which dwells upon pain.

That repulsion [or] wrath [or] anger, on the part of one acquainted with pain, ensuing upon a recollection of pain, for either the pain or for the means of attaining it, is aversion.

8. Aversion is that which dwells upon pain. The words «acquainted with pain» are to be explained as [in the] previous [sūtra]. He explains the words ‹dwells upon› by the word «that.» Repulsion in the sense that it repels. The same he elaborates by synonyms, [for instance,] «wrath.»

9. The will-to-live (*abhiniveça*) **sweeping on [by the force of] its own nature[2] exists in this form even in the wise.**

In all living beings this craving for one's self ceaselessly rises, 'May I not cease to live! May I live!' This craving for one's self does not arise except in one in whom the experience of death resides. And from [the existence] of this [hope] the experience of other births is made clear. And this is that well-known hindrance [called] the will-to-live. This [fear of death], inconceivable as a result of either perception or inference or verbal-communication, sweeping on [by the force of] its own nature, as a vision of extermination, forces the inference that the pangs of death have already been experienced in previous births. And just as it is evident that this fear is to be found in the unspeakably stupid, so also even in the wise, who have some understanding of the prior limit [of human lives], [that is, the round-of-rebirths,] and of their final

[1] Professor Deussen quotes most appositely Spinoza, Ethica iii. 13, Scholion, *Amor nihil aliud est, quam laetitia concomitante idea causae externae; et odium nihil aliud, quam tristitia concomitante idea causae externae.*

[2] See Ruyyaka: Alaṁkārasarvasva (Kāvyamālā 35), p. 55[4], interprets the word as meaning merely *eo ipso* or by its own nature. Compare Rāmānanda Yati in Maṇiprabhā (Benares Sanskrit Series), 1903, p. 30[7], *vāsanā-āsaṅgaḥ svarasaḥ.*

limit [that is, Isolation]. Why is this? Because this subconscious-impression, the result of the fear of death, is alike in both fortunate and unfortunate.

9. The will-to-live sweeping on [by the force of] its own nature exists in this form even in the wise. He discusses the meaning of the term «will-to-live» in the words «all living beings.» «This craving for one's self» is the longing for one's self expressed in the words «May I not cease to live,» that is, 'May I not become non-existent,' [and also expressed] in the words «May I live (*bhūyāsam*)» [that is] 'May I be alive (*jīvyāsam*).' The longing for one's self is not possible unless the living creature have had residing in himself an experience of death. It is he only that has this craving for himself, [that is] the will-to-live, the fear of death. In the course of the discussion (*prasañgatas*) he refers by the words, «And from [the existence] of this» to a heterodox-person (*nāstika*) who denies that there is another birth. From the fact that the present body is being held together, it follows that there is an experience of a previous birth. In other words, a birth is a conjunction[1] [of the soul] with a body and sense-organs and feelings which are different from those of any previous [conjunction] and are characterized by the [definite location] in the collection. This [birth] is experienced [or] attained. And it is this [experience or attainment] that is made clear. How is this? In reply he says «And this is that well-known will-to-live.» Breaking off the sentence in the middle he tells of its hindering character in the word «hindrance.» This [will-to-live] is called a hindrance because it hinders, [that is] pains, living-creatures with unkindly actions and the like. He finishes what he had begun to say by the words «sweeping on by its own nature.» It has a disposition to sweep on by virtue of its own nature in the form of subconscious-impressions. But this disposition is not accidental. Even in the case of a worm just born [that is] full of pain and low in intelligence [this disposition] is not accidental. He tells the reason for this in the words «as a result of perception.» This fear of death, being inconceivable, that is, not acquired in this present (*pratyudita*) birth as a result of perception or inference or verbal-communication, it must be inferred that the pangs of death have been experienced in a previous birth. This is the point at issue. For even a child just born trembles at the sight of a murderous thing. And from this peculiar quivering [the child] infers the nearness (*pratyāsatti*) to himself of the experience of death and is found to be afraid of it. Thus we see that fear results from pain or from whatever leads to pain. Moreover in this birth he has not experienced or inferred or heard of death. So we gather that he has known only in a previous [birth] the pains [of death] or that which leads to the pain. And from this a memory of himself as he was in that condition persists. This moreover does not occur unless there be subliminal-impressions. Furthermore this subliminal-impression [cannot occur] without experience and the experience does not belong to this life. Therefore the only

[1] See Çaṁkara on Brahma-sūtra ii. 2. 23 with Ānandagiri's gloss.

remaining alternative is [a subliminal-impression] from a pre-existent birth. Thus there was a connexion with a previous birth.—The word ‹so (*tathā*)› requires a correlative «just as.» Thus by supplying the word «just as» from the sense of the sentence, he shows, in the words «just as . . . this,» how the meaning of the sentence would be.—«In the unspeakably stupid» means in the most sluggish intelligences.—He shows [what the kind of] learning is by saying «some understanding of the prior and of the final limits [of human lives].» The limit is the end. Now the prior limit of man is the round-of-rebirths; the latter is Isolation. He by whom this has been understood from things heard or from inferences is called [one who has understanding of the prior and of the final limits].—This well-known fear exists [and] has become established in the case of the worm and of the wise man. It might be objected that in the case of the unwise fear-of-death is conceivable, but not in the case of the wise man, since [in him] it has been eradicated by knowledge. Or else if the fear-of-death has not been eradicated, it would be eternally present. With this in view he asks «Why is this?» The answer is «Because . . . it is alike.» He does not refer to the wise man who has conscious [concentration], but to him who discriminates upon the basis of things heard and of inference. This is the point.

10. These [hindrances] [when they have become] subtile are to be escaped by the inverse-propagation.[1]

These five hindrances when they have become like burned seeds, after the mind which has predominated over the deeds of the yogin is resolved [into primary matter], come with it to rest.

Thus the hindrances have been characterized, and of those which should be escaped, four states, the dormant and the attenuated and the intercepted and the sustained, have been shown. But 'why is not the fifth state, which is subtile, mentioned by the author of the sūtras, inasmuch as it is in the state of burned seed?' To this he replies, **10. These [hindrances] [when they have become] subtile are to be escaped by the inverse-propagation.** It is that of course which is within the scope of the exertions of man which has been described; but the subtile is not within the scope of a man's exertions that he might escape (*hāna*) [it]. It may, however, be escaped ‹by the inverse-propagation› [that is] by a reduction of the mind-stuff, which is an effect and which is characterized by the feeling-of-personality, to the state of its own cause, [the thinking-substance]. He explains [the sūtra] by the word «These.» Easy.

[1] Compare ii. 2, p. 107[6] (Calc. ed.), and the passages given above, at p. 105.

But of permanent hindrances consigned to the condition of seeds—
11. The fluctuations of these should be escaped by means of contemplation.
Those fluctuations of the hindrances which are coarse, after having been attenuated by the yoga of action, should be escaped by the Elevated (*prasaṁkhyāna*) contemplation until subtilized [and] made like burned seeds. And just as a spot of coarse matter upon pieces of cloth is first shaken off and afterwards the spot of fine matter is removed with an effort and by [some appropriate] means, so coarse fluctuations are those whose opposition to hindrances is very slight, but the subtile fluctuations are those whose opposition[1] is very great.

'Now when the hindrances have been attenuated by the yoga of action, by directing his exertions towards what, does a man accomplish the rejection [of these hindrances]?' In reply to this he says «But of permanent hindrances consigned to the condition of seeds.» By these words he distinguishes them from those that have been sterilized (*vandhya*). He recites the sūtra. **11. The fluctuations of these should be escaped by means of contemplation.** He discusses [the sūtra] in the words «of the hindrances.» Now when attenuated by the yoga of action these also may be eradicated—themselves and their effects—by reducing them to the condition of [their own] causes. [This is the] inverse propagation. Thus the coarse fluctuations have been explained. When a man's exertion is [still] within the scope of the Elevation, [the author] states what the limit is in the words [beginning] «until.» He elaborates the expression «subtilized» by saying «burned.» On this same point he gives a simile in the words «And just as . . . upon pieces of cloth.» With an effort, such as by washing it [and] by some means, such as an alkaline (*kṣāra*) mixture. The likeness between the simile and the thing to which it is compared lies merely in the fact that there is a coarseness and a subtilty, but not in the [fact that they are both] removable by an effort. For this [removal] is impossible in the case of hindrances which are to be escaped by the process of inverse propagation.—Those whose opposition is very slight, which have been described, are such as have [slight] causes of destruction. Those whose opposition is very great are such as have [great] causes of destruction. And next below[2] the inverse propagation as a means of attaining the destruction

[1] Some MSS. read *pratipakṣeti.* If correct, a case of double *saṅdhi.* Corrected in the Benares revision of the Calcutta edition.

[2] Coarse stains are removed by shaking; minute stains by washing; more minute by alkali. Hindrances which are sustained are attenuated by yoga of action; the attenuated are reduced to burned seed by Elevation; the burned seed is destroyed by inverse propagation.

of the hindrances would be the Elevation (*prasaṁkhyāna*). In view of this inferiority the Elevation has been called very slight.

12. The latent-deposit of karma has its root in the hindrances and may be felt in a birth seen or in a birth unseen.

In this case we have a latent-deposit of the karma of merit and of demerit propagated [1] from lust [or] from greed [or] from infatuation [or] from anger. And this may be felt either in a birth seen or may be felt in a birth not seen. Of these, that [latent-deposit of karma] which, in so far as there is keen intensity, proceeds from sacrificial formulae [and] from self-castigation [and] from concentration, and which is perfected by worship of the Içvara [or] of a deity [or] of a sage or magnanimous [2] beings, has instantly its fruition as a latent-deposit of meritorious karma. Thus [for instance] when, in so far as the hindrance is keen, contempt is shown again and again to those who have sought protection in terror and in sickness and in wretchedness, or again to those magnanimous beings who castigate themselves, this [contempt] also has fruition [3] as a latent-impression of evil karma. Just as the youth Nandīçvara passed out of the human form and was transformed into a divinity, so also Nahuṣa, Prince of the Gods, passed out from his proper mutation and was transformed into the condition of a brute.[4] Among these [latent-deposits] there is, in the case of those who dwell in the underworlds, no latent-deposit of karma which might be felt in a birth seen [in this life]; and in the case of those hindrances which have dwindled, there is no latent-deposit of karma which might be felt in a birth unseen [that is, in another life].

'This may be true. Hindrances [are hindrances] because they hinder [and because] they are the causes of birth and of length-of-life and of kind-of-experience; and the latent impressions of karma are of this kind (*tathā*). But undifferentiated-consciousness (*avidyā*) and the other [hindrances do not hinder

[1] A better reading is *prabhava*.

[2] If *mahānubhāva* were a title of respect, it would precede the other members of the compound according to Pāṇ. ii. 2. 30 and Siddhānta Kāum. (Nir. Sāg. ed.), 1904, p. 155[6].

[3] See Liṅga Pur. viii. 43. 7–53.

[4] See MBh. v. 17.

and are not such causes]. How then can undifferentiated-consciousness and the rest be called hindrances?' In reply to this he says **12. The latent-deposit of karma has its root in the hindrances and may be felt in a birth seen or in a birth unseen.** That for whose production and causal activity a hindrance is the root,—that [is the latent-deposit of karma]. What he means to say is this. The latent-deposit of karma which is the cause of birth and of length-of-life and of kind-of-experience has its root in undifferentiated-consciousness. So undifferentiated-consciousness and the rest are also the causes of them. — He explains the sūtra with the words «In this case.» That in which all Selves in the round-of-rebirths are latent (*āçerate*) is[1] a latent-deposit (*āçaya*). The latent-deposits of karma are merit and demerit. Merit which is the cause of heaven and similar states occurs when, as a result of some desire, there is an inclination for a work which is desirable. Similarly there is demerit in such cases as when from avarice another is robbed of his money. Likewise there is nothing but demerit in such cases as when from infatuation the idea of merit directs itself to killing or something of the kind which is demerit. But there is no merit which comes from infatuation. Merit does, however, come from anger, as for instance, the case of Dhruva[2] from anger at the slight [put upon him] by his father [Uttānapāda]. For as a result of the meritorious latent-deposits of karma which were performed in the desire to surpass his father, he obtained a position above the dwellers in regions of the sky. Demerit, however, due to anger and resulting in the murder of Brahmans is well enough known to every one. He describes the double character of this [latent-deposit] by saying «And this may be felt in a birth seen.» He describes this that may be felt in a birth seen by saying «in so far as there is keen intensity.» In their respective order he gives examples in the words «Just as Nandīçvara.» The dwellers in the underworlds are those who make latent-deposits of karma as a result of which certain underworlds, such as the Cooking Pot,[3] are reached. These have no latent-deposits to be felt in a birth seen [in this life] For no human body nor any kind of mutation of it can endure such torment (*vedanā*) as is to be endured by them and uninterruptedly for thousands of years. The rest is easy.

13. So long as the root exists, there will be fruition from it [that is] birth [and] length-of-life [and] kind-of-experience.

While the hindrances exist, the latent-deposit of karma starts the fruition, but not so the cut root of the hindrances. Just as the

[1] This sentence is omitted in the Bikāner MS. It might well be a gloss.

[2] VP. i. 11. 24 with the context.

[3] Manu xii. 76; Bhāg. Pur. v. 25. 13; compare Jātaka, vol. iii, p. 43, no. 314.

grains of rice, when encased within the chaff, as seeds in an unburned condition, are fit for propagation, but neither the winnowed chaff nor seed in the burned condition is so [fit], similarly the latent-deposits of karma, when encased within hindrances, are propagative of fruition, but neither the winnowed hindrances nor seed in the condition of having been burned by the Elevation (*prasaṁkhyāna*) [is propagative]. And this fruition is of three kinds, birth and length-of-life and kind-of-experience. In regard to these [three,] this is under discussion, whether 1. one karma is the cause of one birth, or whether 2. one karma gives the impulse to more than one birth. There is a second discussion as to whether 3. more than one karma projects more than one birth, or whether 4. more than one karma projects one birth. Now it is not true 1. that one karma is the cause of one birth. Why so? Because if the karma remaining over, accumulated from time-without-beginning and innumerable, and [the karma] of the present, should not have in their results an order limited [in its time], discouragement would be inflicted upon everybody. And this is prohibited. Neither 2. is one karma the cause of more than one birth. Why is this? Because if, while there were more than one karma, only one karma at a time were to be the cause of more than one birth, a lack of time for fruition would be inflicted upon the remaining karmas. And that too would be prohibited. Neither 3. is more than one karma the cause of more than one birth. Why is this? Since it is impossible that more than this one birth should occur simultaneously, it must be supposed that they occur successively. This, likewise, would involve the same difficulty as in the last [case]. The result is then 4. the diverse accumulation of latent-deposits of karma, whether of merit or of demerit, made between birth and the end of life, remains in a relation of subordinate [parts] and a dominant [part]. This is made manifest at the ending of life after growing compact by one single impulse (*ekapraghaṭṭakena*). After accomplishing death, it assumes a rigid form and causes a single birth only. And this birth receives its length from that same karma. And again in that same length-of-life from that same karma it attains to its kind-of-experience. This latent-deposit of karma since it is the source of the birth and the length-of-life and the kind-of-experience, is said to have a three-fold fruition. Consequently [this] latent-deposit of karma is said to have [its limit in] one existence. On the other hand [a latent-deposit of karma] which is to be felt in [this] seen birth is said, since it is the cause of the kind-of-enjoyment only, to originate a single [kind of] fruition [and not a single existence]. Or, when it is the source of the length-of-the-life and the kind-of-enjoyment, it is said to originate two fruitions, as for instance in the case of Nandīçvara or of Nahuṣa. But this mind-stuff like a fish-net made in different shapes on all sides and having, from time without beginning, a form-fixed (*sam̐mūrchita*) by subconscious impressions, which are like knots, caused by the experience of the fruition of the karma from the hindrances, is spread abroad. Therefore these subconscious-impressions are said to be preceded by more than one existence. It is this particular latent-deposit of karma, however, which is said to have [its limit] in one existence. Those subliminal-impressions which produce memory[1] are said to be subconscious-impressions (*vāsanā*) and these are said to subsist from time-without-beginning. But that latent-deposit of karma which has [its limit] in a single existence has both a fruition limited [in time] and a fruition which is without limit [of time]. Of these two [orders], the limitation [in time] (*niyama*), [in so far as it has its limit in one existence], belongs only to the fruition which is to be felt in a birth of [this] seen [life] and which is limited [in time]; whereas the fruition which is not to be felt in [this] seen [life] and which is without limit [of time] does not [have the limit in time which has its limit in a single existence]. Why so? Because that fruition which is not to be felt in [this] seen [life] and which is without limit [of time] has three kinds of outcome[2] (*gati*): Either 1. it is annihilated (*nāça*) when this [latter] fruition is finished and become unfruitful; or 2. it is cast away (*āvāpa-gamana*) into the dominant karma; or 3. it may continue for a long time, subjected to the dominant karma which has a fruition limited [in time]. Of these [three], 1. the annihilation of [the karma] which is finished and become unfruitful is like the annihilation in this present

[1] See iii. 18, p. 230[a] (Calc. ed.).

[2] Consult Çabda-Kalpa-Druma, p. 846[a].

world of the dark karma when once the bright karma has dawned. With regard to which this has been said, "Verily indeed karmas should be known to be by twos and twos. A single mass made of merit destroys [the dark and the dark-bright] evil[1] [mass]. Wish thou then to do well-done deeds. Right here to thee the wise make karma known."—2. Casting away into the dominant karma: with reference to which it has been said[2], "Should there be a very slight admixture of guilt in the sacrifice, it is either to be removed or to be overlooked. [Therefore this admixture is] not enough to remove the good-fortune [won by merit]. Why [not]? Because in my case there is much other good-fortune. Where then this [admixture of guilt] is cast away [into the dominant karma], even in heaven it will make only a slight reduction [of merit]."—3. When he said, 'it may continue for a long time subjected to the dominant karma which has a fruition limited [in time],' how was this? [The answer is], because, in the case of the karma the fruition of which is not to be felt in [this] seen [life] and which is limited [in time], death is said to be the appropriate cause of the manifestation. Not so, however, in the case [of the karma] the fruition of which is not to be felt in [this] seen [life] and which is without limit [of time]. On the contrary, [in this latter case], karma the fruition of which is not to be felt in [this] seen [life] and which is not limited [in time], either is annihilated or is cast away or is quiescent (*upāsīta*) in subjection [to the dominant karma] for a long time until the appropriate manifesting-conditions of the cause of the karma bring it close to its fruition. But since of this very fruition [of karma] the place or the time or the cause is none of them determinable, therefore it is that the ways of karma are [known as] mysterious and not easily discernible. Moreover, since the general rule is not broken down, even if there be exceptions,

[1] The genitive is object of *apahanti* according to the Vārttika, which refers to Pāṇini ii. 3. 56. Vācaspatimiçra makes *kṛṣṇa-kṛṣṇaçukle* an accusative object of *apahanti*. In this case *pāpakasya* would mean belonging to a sinful man (see p. 129[32] below).

[2] See the careful discussion of this fragment of Pañcaçikha in Garbe's translation of the Sāṁkhya Tattva Kāumudī, 1892, p. 538, note 2. Compare also Çāṇḍilya-sūtra xc (1861) and Cowell's translation (1878), p. 96.

therefore the latent-deposit of karma having [its limit in] a single existence [must] be acknowledged.

[The objector says,] 'Let this be granted. Since the latent-deposit of karma is based upon undifferentiated-consciousness (*avidyā*), there may result, after the production of knowledge (*vidyā*), a destruction of undifferentiated-consciousness, and so there might not be any subsequent latent-deposit of karma. Still the latent-deposits of karma, done previously and accumulated by the succession from time without beginning of innumerable births, being unsettled in their period of development, it would be impossible by realizing the effects to cause [these latent-deposits] to dwindle in so far as they might be experienced. Because of this it would be impossible to cut off the round-of-rebirths.' To this he replies with the sūtra 13. **So long as the root exists, there will be fruition from it [that is] birth [and] length-of-life [and] kind-of-experience.** What he means to say is this. The result of the latent-deposit of karma is pleasure and pain, and, in so far as both birth and length-of-life have the same purpose [as the latent-deposit] and are the necessary consequence of it, [these two] are also propagated [by the latent deposit]. Moreover pleasure and pain are attached to passion and aversion. And the latter are the necessary conditions [for pleasure and pain], since pleasure and pain are not possible in the absence of these [that is, passion and aversion]. Furthermore it is impossible to say that that wherein a man is pleased or disgusted is not to him, as the case may be, either a pleasure or a pain. So this soil of the self sprinkled with the water of the hindrances becomes a field propagating the fruits of karma. Thus it is true that the hindrances co-operate with the latent-deposit of karma for producing also the after-effects of the fruits. So when the hindrances are quite cut off, [the latent-deposits] are deprived of this [aid] also. Therefore, although the latent-deposits are endless and their period of ripening is unsettled, still, when in their condition as seeds, they are burned by Elevation (*prasaṁkhyāna*), they cannot be in a position to bear fruit. The sense expressed is made clear by the Comment in the words, «While . . . exist.» With regard to this same point he gives a simile «Just as . . . the chaff.» Although they have their chaff, their condition as seed is burned by heat (*sveda*) and in other ways. He applies the simile to the point-to-be-illustrated by saying, «similarly.» If it be objected that the hindrances cannot be removed, because no [really] existing things are removed, he replies in the words, «nor seed in the condition of having been burned by the Elevation.» He shows the threefold character of the fruition in the words, «And this.» Fruition is that which is brought to fruition or brought to perfection by karmas. The first point-under-discussion [1. and 2.] deems the unity of karma to be fixed and considers whether births are one or more than one. The second [3. and 4.], however, deems the manifoldness to be fixed and considers whether births are one or more than one. Thus there are four alternatives (*vikalpa*). Of these he refutes the first with the words «Now it is not true 1. that one karma is the cause of one birth.» He asks, «Why so?» He gives the answer by saying, «from time-without-beginning.» If the karma accumulated by each birth, one after another, in time without beginning, and therefore innumerable, which remains over after the karma which has been made to dwindle in each life, one after another, has been deducted, the world would feel discouragement. And this is prohibited. What he means to say is this. Since the dwindling of karma is broken-by-intervals (*virala*), and since [karma] is produced in abundance, the latent-deposits pressing one against the other and springing up incessantly, in breathless haste, towards their own fruition,— [for this reason] even a very clever man could not determine the order of the results. Thus discouragement as regards the following up of meritorious [acts] would be inflicted [upon everybody].—He rejects the second alternative in the words «Neither 2. is one karma the cause of more than one birth.» He asks, «Why is this?» He gives the answer by saying, «of more than one birth.» If a single karma only belonging to (*āhita*) more than one birth is the cause of a fruition which characterizes more than one birth, then a lack of time would be inflicted upon the remaining karmas. And that too would be prohibited. Thus in so far as karma would be fruitless, there would be the likelihood that it would not be followed up. And if there would be discouragement on the ground that there is no order of fruition limited [in time] (*niyata*), in case one karma is to be uprooted in one life, how much more there would be in case one karma must be uprooted during more than one life. For then, since there is no chance, [one would infer] that there would be no time [in the future] for the fruition of the present karma [and thus again discouragement would follow].—He refutes the third alternative with the words, «Neither 3. is more than one karma the cause of more than one birth.» He gives the reason for this in the word, «this.» Since for those who are not yogins it is impossible that more than this one birth should occur simultaneously, it must be supposed to occur successively. For if a thousand karmas could simultaneously generate a thousand births, there would be—since a thousand karmas would have dwindled away—time for the fruition of the remainder and an order of results limited [in time]. But there is no such simultaneity of births.—Having thus rejected the three propositions, he accepts as the result of the process of elimination 4. the proposition which remains, to the effect that more than one karma is the cause of one birth, as he says in the words, «The result is . . . birth.» The compound «between-birth-and-the-end-of-life» means in the interval [that is] between the two, both birth and the end-of-life.—[This accumulation is] diverse because it gives forth results diversified by pleasures and pains. That is dominant which will give its result with absolute intensity and immediately. Whereas that is subordinate which [gives its result] after a delay. The «ending-of-life» is death. «Made manifest» by it means being brought into the presence of that which tends to produce its effects.—By one single impulse means simultaneously. Growing compact or rolled[1] together into one lump in relation to the effect to be produced [that is] the next birth, it produces one birth only and not more than one birth. And this birth is the human or some other state. «And this birth receives its length-of-life from that same karma» [would mean that] its life is limited by various periods of time. «And again in that same length-of-life from that same karma it attains to its kind-of-experience» [would mean that] a direct experience of pleasure and of pain is attained. Thus this latent-deposit of karma since it is the source of the birth and of the length-of-life and of the kind-of-experience is said to have a threefold fruition. He sums up the main statement in the words, «Consequently [this] latent-deposit of karma is said to have [its limit in] one existence.»—Having one existence is one existence. [This] compound is in accordance [with Pāṇini's sūtra ii. 1. 49] beginning with the words, "A temporal antecedent, *eka*, &c." The termination [-ika] is in the sense of possession (*matvarthīya*).[2] Thus the meaning [of the compound] is 'one who has one existence'. Elsewhere the reading is (*āikabhavika*). In this case the *ḍhak* termination [-ika] in the sense of 'existing in' is added to the word 'one-existence'. Then the meaning would be that its existing is limited to one birth. Thus having announced his main statement, namely, that [this] karma which [has its limit] in one existence has a three-fold fruition, he now distinguishes the three different kinds of fruition which belong to the karma that is to be felt in [this] seen birth and that is a part of this-present-world (*āihika*). By the word «seen» he refers, of course, to Nandīçvara whose length-of-life in a human birth was cut off at eight years. [Here] was a particular kind of merit produced by a vehement method of keen intensity. This merit had two fruitions in that it was the source of the length-of-life and of the kind-of-experience. But in the case of Nahuṣa, since the length of his life had been determined by a karma which led him to the attainment of Indra's position, there was a particular kind of demerit, leading only to a kind-of-enjoyment, by reason of the contrary [karma] coming from his striking[3] Agastya with his heel. An objector asks, 'Have the subconscious-impressions from the hindrances, like a latent-deposit of karma, their [limit] in one existence? And [if] the subconscious-impressions of the experiences of the fruition of the karma are favourable to [the pointing out of] the kind-of-experience, then a human being reduced to the body of a beast would not experience (*bhuñjīta*) what is proper to his species.' In reply to this he says «the karma from the hindrances.» Having a fixed form (*saṁmūrchita*) means rolled together into one lump. He describes the subconscious-impression as such in order to distinguish it from

[1] Vijñāna Bhikṣu glosses the word *saṁmūrchita* by *pravṛddhavega* (p. 106[5]) and by *upacitam* or *puṣṭam* (p. 107[3] Benares ed.).

[2] Pāṇini v. 2. 115.

[3] This story is given in its setting by Jacobi in his article on Agastya (Hastings: Cycl. of Rel. and Ethics, I, p. 181[a], line 10).

right-action (*dharma*) and from wrong-action by saying «subliminal-impressions which.»—In order to state certain exceptions to the general proposition [that the latent-deposit of karma] has [its limit in] a single existence he prepares the ground by saying «But that . . . which.» By the word «But» he shows that there is a distinction from the subconscious-impressions. The limitation [in time] of having [a limit in] a single existence is that which belongs only to the fruition which is to be felt in a birth of [this] seen [life] and which has a limit [in time]; whereas the fruition which is not to be felt in [this] seen [life] does not [have the limit in time which has its limit in a single existence].—Of what kind then is fruition which is not limited in time? He asks the reason in the words «Why so?» He tells the reason in the words «Because that.» First he gives one outcome (*gati*) in the words «is finished;» the second, in the words «dominant;» the third, in the words «has a limit [in time.]» Of these three he analyses 1. the first by saying «Of these [three] . . . is finished.» Other than the karmas of the mendicant (*saṁnyāsin*), which are neither bright nor dark, there are only three karmas, the dark and the bright-dark and the bright. Now in this world a latent-deposit of bright karma, to be obtained by self-castigation and by recitation and by other means, when once uprisen [in the mind,] is the annihilator of dark [karma] which has not yet given its fruit. And because there is no distinction [between the dark and the dark-bright] we must suppose [that it is the annihilator] of the many-coloured [that is, the dark-bright karma] by reason of the conjunction [of this last] with the dark part. With reference to the same the Exalted [Vyāsa] cites the Sacred Word when he says, «With regard to which this.» Verily indeed karmas [should be known to be] «by twos and twos,» that is, the dark and the dark-bright. [These the mass made of merit] destroys. Such is the construction [of the sentence]. By repeating the word «twos» he indicates that there is a very great number. In reply to the question, 'Belonging to whom' he says, «belonging to a sinful.» In other words, belonging to a sinful man. What is it that destroys? To this he replies, «A single mass made of merit.» Because a collection includes the units-of-the-collection (*samūhin*). Thus the bright latent-deposit of karma is described as the third. What he means to say is this. This bright latent-deposit of karma, which is to be obtained by methods which are free from injury to others, is of such a kind, we may say, that although it is single, it destroys dark and dark-bright latent-deposits of karma, which are absolutely opposed, even when they are in great numbers.—The word «then (*tat*)» means therefore.—The word «Wish thou» is middle because Vedic. The rest is easy. And so we see (*atra*) that the power in the uprising of the bright karma is so indescribably great that it alone makes the others cease to be. But one could not say that they cease because of the pain resulting from recitations and other [right actions]. For a wrong-action (*adharma*) does not have, as its opposite, pain in general, but only that particular kind of pain which is the effect of itself [that is, the wrong-action]. Now the pain resulting from recitations and other [right actions] is not their effect. [And if this pain resulting from recitations and other right actions] is supposed to be the effect of this [wrong-action], then it is needless to make [special] prescriptions of recitations and other right actions, because then these [recitations and right actions] could be produced (*utpatti*) merely by the help of those [wrong-actions]. And if [this wrong-action] should not produce (*anutpatti*) [the pain which results from recitations and other right actions], then the Cooking Pot [Hell] and other [pains] are [specially] prescribed,—[because the wrong-action must result in something—and] because, if [Hells and other pains] be not [specially] prescribed, these [Hells] would never be produced at all.[1]

Thus all is four-square.—He analyses 2. the second outcome in the word «dominant.» In the dominant karma, as for instance in the Jyotiṣṭoma and similar [sacrifices], that which is accessory (*añga*) [karma] to this, namely the killing of the animal, is cast away [into the dominant karma]. For there are two effects of killing and of the other [acts]: 1. since it is prescribed [by the tradition] in so far as it is accessory to the dominant [karma], it assists; 2. since killing is forbidden by the rule "Let no living being be killed", it is needless. We see then that [killing], because it is performed as accessory to the dominant [karma] and not as being the dominant, ought not immediately [*drāg*] and independently of the dominant [karma] to generate its own fruition, a useless result, but that it remains rendering assistance to the dominant [karma], the fruition of which has already commenced. And while rendering assistance to the dominant karma it remains, with reference to its own effect, as seed only, and is cast away into the dominant karma. «With reference to which it has been said» by Pañcaçikha. The slight admixture of the invisible-influence (*apūrva*), which is the dominant [karma] resulting from the Jyotiṣṭoma and other [sacrifices], with the invisible-influence resulting from the killing of the animal and similar [acts] and producing what is not desired (*anartha*),—[this admixture] may be removed. For, by doing a certain amount of penance it may be removed. Or should a man heedlessly not have gone through the penance, [the slight admixture of guilt] comes to fruition at the time of the fruition of the dominant karma. In spite of all this, whatever undesired result be generated by this [accessory invisible-influence] may be overlooked. For the fortunate (*kuçala*), plunging deep into the great pool of the nectar of pleasure brought near by the gathering together of merit, overlook a slight spark of

[1] Since however Hells are produced without any special prescription (*vidhāna*), it follows as a general rule that the consequences of wrong-actions require no special prescription. But in the case of recitations and other right-actions there is the special prescription. Therefore right-actions and the pain resulting from right-actions cannot be the consequences of wrong-actions. Not being such a consequence, the pain from right-action cannot annihilate wrong-action.

the fire of pain brought about by a very little evil. Hence [the slight admixture] is not enough or adequate to remove or to cause to dwindle good-fortune or great merit. He asks «Why [not]?» The answer is «the good-fortune.» For in the case of me, the meritorious, much other good-fortune exists, the fruition of dominant karma, beginning with the initiatory rites and ending with the donations. Where then this admixture is very slight, it will make even in heaven, the result of it, a slight commingling of pain, that is, a slight reduction from the heaven which, [although] its beginning is gained by mixed merit, is [in itself] quite untouched by pain.—He analyses 3. the third outcome in the words, «limited [in time].» The predominance here is conceived as being extremely powerful but not as having accessories. And it is powerful in so far as its fruition is without limit [of time], because there is no opportunity [for its fruition] at any one time. But in the case of [the dominant karma] the fruition of which is without limit [of time] there is a weakness, because there is an opportunity [for its fruition] at some other time. The continuance for a long time is only in the condition of seed, but not as [actively] helping the dominant [karma] because this latter is independent. It is objected, 'It has been stated that the latent-deposit of karma is by the ending-of-life made manifest at one point of time only. Whereas now you say that it continues a long time. How then is the latter [statement] not in opposition to the previous [statement]?' With this in mind he asks, «how was this?» He answers in the words, «not . . . in [this] seen [life].» The singular number denotes a class. He determines the outcome of that which is different from this by the words, «On the contrary . . . not . . . in [this] seen [life].» The rest is easy.

14. These [fruitions] have joy or extreme anguish as results in accordance with the quality of their causes whether merit or demerit.

‹These› [that is] birth and length-of-life and kind-of-experience. Those with merit as cause have pleasure as result; those with demerit as cause have pain as result. And just as the nature of this pain is counteractive, so for the yogin, even at the moment of pleasure in an object, there is nothing but counteractive pain.

It has been stated that karma is rooted in hindrances and that fruitions are rooted in karma. Now the question is, 'of what are the fruitions the root, since you say that these are to be renounced?' In reply to this he says, **14. These [fruitions] have joy or extreme anguish as results in accordance with the**

quality of their causes whether merit or demerit. He explains the sūtra in the words, «‹These› [that is] birth and length-of-life and kind-of-experience.» Although birth and length-of-life, since they precede joy and extreme anguish, do have the latter as their results,—whereas the kind-of-experience follows the rise [in consciousness] of joy and extreme anguish and in fact has its essence in the [direct] experience (*anubhava*) of them,—still in so far as being [directly] experienced is the same as a kind-of-experience (*bhoga*), we may suppose that [joy and extreme anguish] are results of the kind-of-experience only so far as they are the objects of the kind-of-experience. It is objected, 'The birth and length-of-life and kind-of-experience, which are the results of extreme anguish, are things to be rejected (*heya*), since they are felt to be counteractive. But why should those [fruitions] which have merit as cause be renounced? they have pleasure as their result since they are felt to be co-active (*anukūla*). Nor can their co-activity, which may be felt by every one, be gainsaid by even a thousand verbal communications and inferences. Moreover neither joy nor extreme anguish can exist without the other. For while joy is being received, extreme anguish, since it cannot be driven off, may also fall to one's lot, because the two have separate causes and because they have separate forms.' In reply to this he says, «And just as . . . this.» Although ordinary individuals, at the time when there is pleasure in objects, are not conscious of them as counteractive, still yogins are conscious of this [counteractiveness].

How can this be accounted for?

15. As being the pains which are mutations and anxieties and subliminal-impressions, and by reason of the opposition[1] **of the fluctuations of the aspects (*guṇa*),—to the discriminating all is nothing but pain.**

1. For every one this experience of pleasure is permeated with passion and is dependent upon animate and inanimate instruments. In this case we have a latent-deposit of karma arising from passion. Likewise also [a man] hates the instruments of pain and becomes infatuated [by the instruments of infatuation]. Thus there is also a latent-deposit made by aversion and by infatuation. And in this sense it has been said, "Enjoyment is impossible unless one has killed some living creature." Therefore there is also the latent-deposit of karma, effected by killing, belonging to the body. Thus it has been said, "Undifferentiated-consciousness (*avidyā*)

[1] This sūtra seems to have influenced Umāsvāti: Tattvārthādhigama-sūtra vii. 6.

is pleasure in an object of sense[1]." That which is the subsidence of the organs because of their satiation with enjoyments is pleasure; after there has been a craving, the failure to subside is pain. And by the application of the organs to enjoyments one cannot make one's self free from thirst [for enjoyment]. Why is this? Since passions increase because-of (*anu*) application to enjoyments, and the skill of the organs also increases. Therefore application to the enjoyment of pleasure is not a way of approach [to freedom from thirst for objects]. Surely one aiming at pleasure and permeated by objects is sunk in the deep bog of pain, like the man who, while in fear of the scorpion's poison[2] is bitten by the poisonous snake. This is the so-called painfulness of mutation; it is counteractive; even in a condition of pleasure it hinders the yogin himself.—2. Now what is the painfulness of anxiousness? Every one has the experience of anxiousness; it is permeated by aversion and is dependent upon animate and inanimate instruments. Here we have a latent-deposit of karma arising from aversion. And [a man] yearning for the instruments of pleasure, throbs in the body and in [the organs of] speech and in the central-organ (*manas*). Since it then aids or (*ca*) thwarts others by aiding them or by injuring them, it amasses right-actions and wrong-actions. This latent-deposit of karma is the result of greed and of infatuation. For this reason it is called the painfulness of anxiousness.—3. But what is the painfulness of subliminal-impressions? There is a latent-deposit of subliminal-impressions of pleasure arising from the experience of pleasure; and there is a latent-deposit of subliminal-impressions of pain arising from the experience of pain. Thus analogously (*evam*), while the fruition from the karmas is under experience, there is on the other hand an accumulation of a latent-deposit of karma. Thus this stream of pain from time-without-beginning, spreading wider and wider, agitates even the yogin because its essence is counteractive. Why is this? It is because a wise man is like an eyeball. Just

[1] Perhaps an allusion to the phrase ***sukhakhyātir avidyā*** (ii. 5, Calc. ed. 114[1]).

[2] Colonel Jacob (Second Handful of Popular Maxims, 2nd ed., 1909, p. 76) points out that Vācaspati uses this ***nyāya*** again in the Tātparyaṭīkā (1898), p. 53[13].

as a fine thread of wool fallen upon the eyeball by its touch gives pain, but not so when it falls upon other parts of the body, so these pains [from subliminal-impressions] hinder the yogin only, who is like an eyeball, but not any other perceiver. But upon the other, [not a yogin],—who casts off the pain received time after time which has been brought upon him by his own karma,—and who receives the pain cast off time after time,—and who is as it were permeated through and through from all sides with fluctuating mind-stuff complicated from time-without-beginning with its subconscious-impressions,—and who under [the influence of] undifferentiated-consciousness (*avidyā*) conforms [himself] to the 'I-substance' and to the 'Of me-substance' with regard to those very things which are to be rejected,—upon him, born again and again, the triple anguishes from both kinds of causes, both inner and outer, sweep down. This being so, the yogin, having seen himself and the whole multitude of creatures borne away by this stream of pain from time-without-beginning, seeks refuge in the focused-insight (*saṁyag-darçana*), the cause of the dwindling of all pain.—‹And by reason of the opposition of the fluctuations of the aspects (*guṇa*),—to the discriminating all is nothing but pain.› The aspects (*guṇa*) of the thinking-substance in the form of brightness and of activity and of inertia, having become interdependent by aid given each to the other, give rise to a presented-idea either tranquil or cruel or infatuated, [either one or the other] of just these three aspects. "And because the changes (*vṛtta*) of the aspects (*guṇa*) are unstable, the mind-stuff is in rapid mutation." Thus we have been told.[1] "The [outer] forms [when developed to] a high degree and the [inner] fluctuations [when developed to] a high degree oppose each other; but the generic forms co-operate with [these when developed to] a high degree." Thus since these aspects (*guṇa*) have presented-ideas of pleasure and of pain and of infatuation obtained by reliance of one [aspect] upon another, each (*sarve*) [of them] has the form of each of [the others]. But the distinction between them is due to their being either in a subordinate (*guṇa*) or in a dominant state. Therefore ‹to the discrimi-

[1] By Pañcaçikha. Compare iii. 9 and 13, pp. 199[3] and 204[4]; iv. 15, p. 298[3] (Calc. ed.).

nating all is nothing but pain.› So the seed out of which this huge aggregate of pain grows forth is undifferentiated-consciousness (*avidyā*). And the reason for the failure-of-growth (*abhāva*) in this [*avidyā*] is the focused-insight.—Just as a system of medicine has four divisions, [on] Disease [and on] Cause of Disease [and on] Health [and on] Remedy, so this system also has four divisions, [on] the Round-of-Rebirth [and on] the Cause of the Round-of-Rebirth [and on] Release [and on] the Way to Release. Of these [four], the Round-of-Rebirth with its mass of pains is that which is to be escaped; the conjunction of the primary-cause and of the Self is the cause of this which is to be escaped (*heya*); the final destruction of the correlation is the escape (*hāna*); the means of escape is focused-insight. In this [focused-insight] he who escapes—as he is in himself—can neither be accepted nor rejected (*heya*). For if there be a rejection (*hāna*), that would involve the doctrine of the extermination of him [who escapes]. And [1] if there be an acceptance [that would involve] the doctrine [that he has] a cause. And [1] by denying both [the rejection and the acceptance], we have the doctrine [that the Seer as he is in himself is] eternal. This is the focused-insight.

In order to account for this he introduces the sūtra after first asking the question, «How can this be accounted for?» The sūtra begins with the word **15. . . . mutation** and ends with the word **discriminating . . .** [The compound in the sūtra is analysed,] mutation and anxiety and subliminal-impression—these themselves are the pains—it is by these . . . He describes the painfulness of the pleasure in objects of sense in so far as mutations are painful by saying, «For every one this.» Pleasure is surely impossible unless it be permeated by passion. For one cannot possibly say that one finds no happiness in a thing and at the same time take pleasure in it. Moreover, since pleasure leads to action and action causes a latent-deposit of merit and demerit, there is also a latent-deposit of karma produced by passion, because a thing which does not exist cannot be produced. Under these circumstances (*tadā*), a man experiencing pleasure and feeling attachment to it, feels aversion towards the instruments of pain with an aversion that is in an intercepted state. Furthermore, being unable to prevent these [instruments of pain] he becomes infatuated. Thus there is also a latent-deposit of karma made by aversion and by infatuation. And there is nothing contradictory in making infatuation, whose other name is misconception, the cause of a latent-deposit of the karma of infatuation also. If it be asked,

[1] Omitted in most MSS.

How can a man in love feel aversion or infatuation, since, when he is in love, aversion and infatuation are not evidently existent, he replies, «And in this sense it has been said» by us when explaining [ii. 4] hindrances with intercepted states. In this way merit and demerit have been shown as produced by sense-activities of speech and mind. Because a mental volition produced by passion, so that one wills, 'this must be done,' is also not to be distinguished from the verbal form [of the volition] in so far as it is equally desired. As they say, 'A volition with desire does not go beyond intended-objects which can be expressed by words.' He also shows a latent-deposit of karma belonging to the body in the words, «"Impossible . . . unless one has killed"». Hence authors of the Law Books say [Manu iii. 68, Viṣṇu lix. 19], "Five kinds-of-slaughter are open to the householder." The objector says, 'This may be true. Yet it is not fitting that a yogin should reject pleasure in objects-of-sense which can be felt by anybody. For that would be running counter to experience.' In reply to this he says, «it has been said, "Undifferentiated-consciousness (*avidyā*) is pleasure in an object-of-sense"» by [us when] showing [ii. 5] that undifferentiated-consciousness is characterized by four kinds of misconceived ideas. The ancient sages (*vṛddha*) do not pay heed to anything merely at the first impression. There is of course, merely at the first impression (*āpātatas*), an experience which any one can feel of pleasure which follows even after eating food mixed with sweet poison; but after a lapse of time there is no pleasure. And as such it has been shown by The Exalted [Içvara in the Gītā xviii. 38], "After there has been contact of the sense-organs with objects, that pleasure which is at the beginning like nectar and in the course of time like poison is known to be full of *rajas*." He raises a doubt by saying, «which . . . with enjoyments.» The objector says, 'We do not accede to the statement that pleasure is the joy in objects. On the contrary, when men are not satiated and when their minds are afflicted with yearnings for one object after another, it is the very thirst itself that is the great pain. And this [thirst] does not subside unless enjoyment follow. Furthermore the full subsidence of this [thirst] is not permeated with passion and similar [states of mind]. Thus it cannot be said that this subsidence has the painfulness of mutation.' This is the point.—«Because of their satiation» means: Because the thirst [for enjoyment] has dwindled, there is a subsidence of the organs, in other words, there is no activity [of the organs] with regard to objects-of-sense. He makes this same clear by a negative instance in the words «arising from a craving.» He rebuts an objection with the words «And . . . by the organs . . . not.» The word «because of (*anu*)» is used in the sense of cause. It is true that the dwindling of thirst [for objects] is the flawless[1] pleasure. But application to enjoyment is not the cause of this [dwindling of thirst]; but it is the cause of the thirst which is just the opposite of this [dwindling of thirst]. Just as they say,[2] "Lust by the enjoyment of

[1] Without the flaw of *rāga*.

[2] See Manu ii. 94; Viṣṇu Purāṇa iv. 10. 9; Nāradīya Purāṇa xxxiii. 38; Liñga Purāṇa lxvii. 17.

lusts never subsides; just as by the butter-oblation the flames flare up yet once again."—The rest is without obscurity.—2. He asks a question with regard to the painfulness of anxiety in the words, «Now what?» The answer is «every one.» As everybody knows what it is, he does not make a detailed statement of it as such. And the detailed statement is analogous to that of the painfulness of mutation.—3. He asks about the painfulness of subliminal-impressions by saying «what?» He gives the answer in the words «the experience of pleasure.» For an experience of pleasure gives rise to a subliminal impression and this to a memory of pleasure; and this to a passion; and this to movements of the central-organ and of the body and of [the organ of] speech; and this [gives rise] to merit and demerit; from these [comes] the experience of fruition; from this a subconscious-impression. Thus there is a beginningless [chain]. Here the connexion should be understood in this way. There is a memory of pleasure and of pain according to the variation in the degree of the subliminal-impressions of pleasure and of pain; and from this comes passion and aversion; from these two come karma; from the karmas, fruition. Streaming on in this way the stream of pain hinders the yogin only, but not the other perceiver, [that is] any ordinary person, as he says in the words «Thus this . . . from-time-without-beginning.» But the triple anguishes sweep down upon the other. This is the construction [of the sentence].—In so far as the two anguishes, that from the gods and that from the elements, are [each] external, their unity is emphasized.—Since it is a fluctuation in the mind-stuff, undifferentiated-consciousness (*avidyā*) is said to be «fluctuating mind-stuff.» Under [the influence of] this, «with regard to those very things which are to be rejected» [that is] with regard to the thinking-substance and the organs and the body and so on [as the 'I',] and with regard to wife and children [as the 'of me'], «he conforms [himself] to the 'I-substance' and to the 'Of-me-substance.'» This being the case, there is no other refuge for him than the focused-insight. So he says «This being so.» This being so, he has mentioned the extrinsic (*āupādhika*) painfulness of the pleasure in objects as a result of mutation and of subliminal-impressions and of contact with anxiousness. He [now] indicates the intrinsic [painfulness] by saying «‹And by reason of the opposition of the aspects (*guṇa*).›» He explains [this part of the sūtra] by saying «brightness.» Brightness and activity and inertia are the forms, in so far as they are forms of the thinking-substance, which enter into mutation. The aspects (*guṇa*) are *sattva* and *rajas* and *tamas* [and they] are interdependent upon each other. They give rise to either 1. a tranquil (its essence is pleasure), or 2. a cruel (its essence is pain), or finally (*eva*) 3. an infatuated (its essence is dejection) presented-idea of [these] three aspects, although its form is an experience of pleasure. And not even this mutation of this [thinking-substance] having such a presented-idea as its form is fixed. Because of this he says «"And because the changes of the aspects (*guṇa*) are unstable, the mind-stuff is in rapid mutation."» It is objected, '[There is] one presented-idea; how can it at one time make known tranquillity and cruelty and infatuation, which are opposed to each other?' In reply to this he says, «"The [outer] forms [when developed to] a high degree and the [inner] fluctuations [when developed to] a high degree oppose each other."» The «forms» are the eight states[1] (*bhāva*) beginning with right-action. The «fluctuations» are pleasure and so on. So in this case wrong-action, since it is in such a condition [of high development], is opposed by right-action when it is in process of fruition. Similarly with knowledge [and] with passionlessness [and] with power [as well as] with pleasure and so on their corresponding contraries are in opposition. But the generic[2] forms, which are not actively moving forth, since they do not oppose [those which are developed] to a high degree, co-operate with those which are actively moving forth.—The objector says, 'We know [all] this. Yet how can pleasure in objects have an intrinsic painfulness?' In reply to this he says, «Thus since these.» Because the material cause [of both] is not different and because their essence is the material cause, there is also no difference in the material effects (*upādeya*). 'So then is this identity absolute? If so, the difference [between the two terms] in the attributive relations of the thinking-substance would not be possible.' In reply to this he says, «in a subordinate or in a dominant.» In relation to the generic element (*ātman*) there is subordination; in relation to the element [which is developed] to a high degree there is dominance. So both extrinsically and intrinsically (*svabhāvatas*) ‹to the discriminating all is nothing but pain.› Consequently by men of insight pain should be escaped (*heya*). And it cannot be escaped unless its cause (*nidāna*) be escaped. Moreover it cannot be escaped unless its cause be thoroughly understood. So he shows what its radical cause is in the words, «So . . . of this.» That seed out of which the aggregate of pain grows forth [or] arises. He shows the reason for the extermination of this growth in the words «And . . . in this.» Now he shows that this system which has entered upon its activity for the sake of showing favour [i. 1] to all is similar to another system of the same kind by saying, «Just as.» [A system described as being of four divisions] is one of which there are the four divisions, that is, four compactly arranged parts.—It is objected, 'Why is there not a contradiction when you said that pain is to be escaped and when you [now] describe the round-of-rebirth as something to be escaped?' In reply to this he says «Of these [four], ... with its mass of pains.» That, by doing which undifferentiated-consciousness (*avidyā*) makes the round-of-rebirth, [that constitutes] its special form of activity which is the cause of the round-of-rebirths. This he describes in the words, «of the primary cause and of the Self.» He tells what liberation is in the words, «of the correlation.» He tells what the means of liberation are in the words, «the means of escape.» Some[3] there are who regard the extermination of him-who-escapes (*hātṛ*)—as he is in himself—to be liberation.

[1] Right-action, knowledge, passionlessness, power, and their opposites. See Sāṁkhya Kār. xl.

[2] The unspecialized forms. See iii. 44.

[3] The Yogācāra school of Buddhists.

In this sense they say, "Like the blowing-out (*nirvāṇa*) of a lamp is the deliverance of this anguished[1] (*tāpin*) [mind]." Others[2] again teach that, as a result of the extermination of the hindrances with their subconscious impressions, purified mental-states (*vijñāna*) are produced; and that this itself is liberation. In reply to these he says, «In this [focused-insight].» In this case he first finds fault with the escape by saying, «For if there be an escape . . . for him.» Since no rational man ever exerts himself to exterminate himself. It is objected, 'We see some persons, all of whose pleasures are uprooted by intense disease and who drag about their bodies, as it were, laden with pain, striving to exterminate themselves.' True, he says in reply, there are a few such. But not of this kind are men living in [the ordinary] round-of-rebirth. [For] their lot is to enjoy diverse and strange and celestial delights. Even those [others], however, are evidently desirous of liberation. Accordingly we should not concede that liberation is the extermination of him who escapes—as he is in himself—since that would involve what is not one of the aims of man. The objector says, 'Very well then, let us say that he who escapes—as he is in himself—is something that may be accepted.' In reply to this he says, «And if there be an acceptance . . . the doctrine [that he has] a cause.» For if there be an acceptance [of him], then, because he would be impermanent in so far as he is an effect, he might also fall even from [his] state of liberation. For liberation is deathlessness. And [we could] not [say] that an uninterrupted succession of purified mental-states is deathless. Because the uninterrupted series, over and above the members-of-the-series (*saṁtānin*), not being anything [perceptibly] real, does not exist; and because the members-in-the-series are not permanent. Therefore we should strive to have such a theory as [would teach that the Self as he is in himself is] eternal. For this being so, liberation (*apavarga*) might be [one of] the aims of men. So he says, «And by denying both.» Consequently, liberation is nothing but [the Seer] abiding in himself [i. 3]. Precisely this is the right point of view.

This same system is set forth in its four divisions.

16. That which is to be escaped is pain yet to come.

Pain past, that is, transferred beyond experience, cannot properly be called (*pakṣe vartate*) a thing to be escaped. And present pain in its own moment [of existence] has attained experience; so it cannot at the next moment be so changed that it can be escaped. Consequently only that pain which is yet to come is that which hinders the yogin only, who is like an eye-ball,[3] but [this does] not [hinder] any other perceiver. Only this pain becomes so changed that it may be escaped.

1 The Bikāner MS. reads *cetasa iti*. *Tāpin* appears to be correct instead of *tāyin*.

2 The Mādhyamika school of Buddhists.

3 Compare ii. 15, p. 134[9] (Calc. ed.).

«This same system is set forth in its four divisions.» 16. That which is to be escaped is pain yet to come. The words «yet to come» exclude the past and the present. He makes this consistent by saying «pain past.» If it be objected that present pain now in experience is not to be transferred beyond experience, he replies «And present.» Easy.

Therefore the cause of this same thing that is described as something to be escaped is once more specified.

17. The correlation of the Seer and the object-of-sight is the cause of that which is to be escaped.

The Seer is the Self conscious by reflection of the thinking-substance. Objects-of-sight are all external-aspects (*dharma*) which have struck upon the *sattva* of the thinking-substance. So this same object-of-sight giving its aid, like a magnet,[1] by the mere fact of being near, becomes, by reason of its being an object-of-sight, the property of the Self, its proprietor, whose nature is seeing. It becomes changed into an object upon which experience operates,—in so far it has the nature of another. Having acquired [this new] being, although self-dependent, [it becomes] by serving one-not-itself,[2] dependent on one-not-itself. The correlation of these two, the power of seeing and the power by which one sees, is from time-without-beginning and is effected for [two] purposes. [This correlation is] the cause of that which is to be escaped, in other words, the cause of pain. And in this sense it has also been said, "By avoidance of the cause of correlation with this [thinking-substance] the antidote for pain would be absolute." Why [would this be so]? Because we know the antidote to prevent the cause of pain. For example, we know that the liability-to-scratches inheres in the sole of the foot, the power to scratch inheres in the thorn, the prevention [of scratching] is either by not stepping with the foot upon the thorn or by stepping [upon it when the sole of the foot] is covered by a foot-protector. Whoever understands these three [scratch and cause and prevention] has begun the antidote therefor and is not exposed to the pain from scratches.

[1] Compare i. 4, p. 17[1]; ii. 18, p. 143[3]; iv. 17, 300[7] (Calc. ed.).
[2] Compare iv. 24.

Why [is this]? Because of his power to apperceive the three-fold character [of the case]. And to resume the argument (*atrāpi*), the *sattva*, the castigated, comes under the ownership of *rajas*, the castigator. Why [so]? Since it stands in a passive relation to the activity of the castigator. The act of castigation affects the *sattva* as a passive object, but does not affect the immutable and inactive Soul (*kṣetrajña*). [Why inactive?] Since it has objects shown to it. But if the *sattva* be under castigation, the Self, it appears, conforming itself to the form of this [*sattva*] is itself castigated along with [the *sattva*].

That which is to be escaped has been described. Its cause (*nidāna*) is [now] described 17. **The correlation of the Seer and the object-of-sight is the cause of that which is to be escaped.** He tells of the Seer himself in the words «The Seer . . . conscious by reflection of the thinking-substance.» The intelligence (*citi*) belonging to the Self (*Puṁs*), although it is detached, becomes conscious by reflection of the thinking-substance, and this consists in the thinking-substance being imaged (*chāyā*) [in the intelligence]. It is objected that 'even if this be so, [the Self] could see the thinking-substance only, but could not see the various things (*çabdādi*) which are absolutely shut off [from it]'. To this he replies, «Objects-of-sight . . . the (*sattva*) of the thinking-substance.» When by the channel of the senses the thinking-substance enters into mutations having the forms of various things and when it is an object-of-sight, the various things, the external-aspects, are also objects-of-sight. It is objected, 'In so far as the thinking-substance has assumed the form of these [things], it may have the form of the various things. But if, in the case of the Self, his relation to the thinking-substance be assumed, he would be mutable. Yet if there be no relation between them, how can the various things, although present in the (*sattva*) of the thinking-substance, be objects-of-sight? For surely an object-of-sight not in relation with the Seer cannot be called an object-of-sight.' To this he replies, «this same object-of-sight.» All this has been given in detail by us in Book First, where we showed [i. 7, p. 22] that the *sattva* of the thinking-substance, although not in combination with intelligence (*cāitanya*), in so far as it is absolutely clear, still, in so far as it contains the image (*bimba*) of the intelligence, seems to come into a balanced state [with the intelligence] and [so] experiences the various things. Hence also the Seer, enjoying within himself the pleasures and other [experiences] offered by the *sattva* of the thinking-substance which has entered into mutation in the form of the various things, becomes the proprietor. And the *sattva* of the thinking-substance [having mutations] of such a kind becomes his property. So this same *sattva* of the thinking-substance, containing the forms of the various things, becomes the object-of-sight; and being like a magnet, it becomes the property of the Self whose nature is seeing and who is the proprietor.

Why [is this]? He says, «the experience.» Because [the *sattva* of the thinking-substance] is changed into an object upon which experience operates. The «experience» is the enjoyment on the part of the Self; the «operation» is the activity; the «object» is the condition of being enjoyed; because it is «changed into» this, it becomes the property [of the Self].—The objection is made, 'How can the *sattva* of the thinking-substance, which is luminous in itself, be the object of an experience?' In reply to this he says, «in so far as it has the nature of another.» For if the *sattva* of the thinking-substance were really like the intelligence (*caitanya*), it would be luminous in itself. But it has acquired [this new] being, it is property (*sva*), it is other than intelligence (*caitanya*), and inert in nature. Therefore it is the object of the experience on the part of this [intelligence]. It is objected, 'One thing is dependent upon another thing, when in some way or other it exerts itself for the sake of the other. Whereas the *sattva* of the thinking-substance does not in any way exert itself for the Self which is detached [from it]. And how can [the thinking-substance] be dependent on this [intelligence]? And this being so, it cannot be an object upon which [the Self] operates.' In reply to this he says, «although self-dependent.» «By serving the purpose of one-not-itself,» by serving the purpose of the Self, it becomes «dependent on one-not-itself,» dependent upon the Self. The objector says, 'This relation between the power of seeing and the power by which one sees must be either natural or accidental. If it be natural, since the two terms of the relation are permanent, the relation is one that cannot be exterminated; and this being so, the round-of-rebirth would be permanent. But if it be accidental, then in so far as hindrances and karma and its subconscious-impressions are fluctuations of the inner-organ, the former exist only so long as the inner-organ exists, and if at the same time (*ca*) the inner-organ is to have these as its cause, there would be the fault of mutual interdependence; and [you could not explain this fault away by bringing in a series without beginning,] because it is impossible that there should be anything from time-without-beginning at the beginning of the creation, for then the round-of-rebirth would not be produced at all. On which point it has been said, "Even in the opinion of those who think that the Self is not an agent, how can the aspects (*guṇa*) bring about the very first activity? For then karma does not yet exist. Neither is there then an erroneous idea nor passion nor hatred nor similar [hindrances]. For all these are fluctuations of the central-organ and the central-organ has not been produced at that time."' This doubt he removes by the words, «The correlation of these two, the power of seeing and the power by which one sees, is from time-without-beginning and is effected for [two] purposes.» It is true that the relation is not natural, but accidental. But it is not to be supposed that it has a beginning. For in so far as it is the result of a cause (*nimitta*) which is from time-without-beginning, it itself is also from time-without-beginning. Furthermore the uninterrupted succession of hindrances and karma and subconscious-impressions of these is from time-without-beginning.

And although at the time of [each] reversal of creation [this succession] has been reduced to the state of equipoise (*sāmya*) in the primary cause, still at the beginning of a creation it becomes again as before, just as some kinds of plants[1] (*udbhijja*), reduced at the end of the rains to a state of earth, when the rains [return], assume again their proper form. More than once this has been made known previously. In so far as it brings it to growth, undifferentiated-consciousness is the cause of the correlation; in so far as it is the reason for [its] stability, the purpose of the Self is the cause. For this [conjunction] is stable by virtue of this [purpose of the Self]. It is this that is stated in the words, «effected for [two] purposes.» «And in this sense it has also been said» by Pañcaçikha.[2] «By conjunction with this» means by conjunction with the thinking-substance. This same is the cause of pain. By the avoidance of this [conjunction] this antidote for pain would be absolute. So what is implied is (*arthāt*) that pain results from a failure to avoid it. In connexion with this same point he states an extremely well-known simile in the words, «For example.» «A foot-protector» is a sandal. An objector says, 'Let this be granted. But if it be said that correlation with the aspects (*guṇa*) is the cause of the castigation, then we must say that the aspects (*guṇa*) are castigators. And since the action of castigating does not remain within the agent, as is the case in such an [intransitive] act as being, we must expect some other thing to be castigated. And the Self is not the passive object of this [act] as being something to be castigated, for in so far as he is immutable, it is not fitting that he should be such as to [reap] the consequences which come from actions. Therefore we come to the result that the act of castigating, which is concomitant with the thing castigated, ceases when [the thing castigated] also ceases, just as there is absence of smoke when fire is lacking.' So he says, «And to resume the argument . . . . the castigator.» It is the aspects (*guṇa*) only that are in the relation of castigated and castigator. Of these [three], *sattva*, because it is soft like the sole of the foot, is the object to be castigated. Whereas *rajas*, inasmuch as it is keen, is the castigator. This is the point. He asks, «Why [so]?» That is to say, why is *sattva* alone, and not the Self, the object to be castigated? He gives the answer in the words, «the *sattva* as a passive[3] object.» 'Is not then the Self castigated at all? If so, let it be the inanimate *sattva* that receives the castigation. What does it matter to us?' In reply to this he says, «Since it has objects shown to it. But if the *sattva* be under castigation, the Self, it appears, conforming itself to the form of this [*sattva*] is itself castigated along with [the *sattva*].» The cause of its being castigated along with it is that objects are shown to it and this has been explained previously [i. 4].

---

[1] The frog's body (*maṇḍūka-deha*) is used as the simile in i. 19, p. 51^{10} (Calc. ed.).

[2] This is the seventh in Garbe's collection of Pañcaçikha's fragments, Festgruss an Roth, p. 79.

[3]

1.	kartar	kaṇṭaka	rajas	tāpaka
2.	kriyā	bheda	abhibhava	tāpa
3.	karma	pādatala	sattva	tapya
4.	upāya	pādatrāṇa	viveka	parihāra

He tells what the object-of-sight itself is.

18. With a disposition to brightness and to activity and to inertia, and with the elements and the organs as its essence, and with its purpose the experience and the liberation [of the Self],—[this is] the object-of-sight.

The *sattva* has the disposition to brightness; the *rajas* has the disposition to activity; the *tamas* has the disposition to inertia. These aspects (*guṇa*) with the [three] separate parts influencing each other,—with external-aspects (*dharma*) in conjunction or in separation,—with limitations[1]-in-extent (*mūrti*) brought about by basing them upon an interdependence of one upon another,—with separate powers, although in subservience to each other, still unconfused,—with conformations (*anupātin*) according to various disparate and comparate powers,—with their presence manifested at the time when they become dominant,—with their existence, although subordinate to the dominant [aspects] yet from their functional-activity (*vyāpara*) inferred as included in the dominant,—with their faculties employed as effective for the purposes of the Self,—with their aid given, like that of a magnet, from the mere fact of being near,—following without any external cause after a fluctuation of any one of themselves—these aspects (*guṇa*) are denoted by the word primary-cause. And this is called ‹the object-of-sight.› This same object-of-sight enters into mutation as elements and as organs,—as elements such as earth and the others in coarse[2] and in subtile [form]. It enters likewise into mutation as organs such as the organ-of-hearing (*çrotra*). But it is not without an impelling force. On the contrary, it acts only by accepting an impelling force. For the object-of-sight exists for the sake of the experience and the liberation of the Self. Of these [two], experience is the ascertainment of things with desirable qualities and of things with undesirable qualities so long as this [ascertainment] does not divide [the Self from the thinking-substance]. Liberation is the ascertainment[3] of the

[1] Compare iii. 44, p. 254[2] (Calc. ed.).

[2] This refers forward to the important and peculiar definitions of coarse and subtile in iii. 44. See the illuminating words of Bālarāma in notes 1 and 2 of p. 144 (Calc. ed.).

[3] Compare *draṣṭuḥ svarūpopalabdhiḥ so 'pavargaḥ*, ii. 23, p. 157[4] (Calc. ed.).

enjoyer himself. Thus there is no other process-of-knowing in addition to these two. And in this sense it has been said,[1] "But he who in the three aspects (*guṇa*) which are agents and in the Self which is not an agent,—but which is of the same kind in some respects and of a different kind in other respects,—sees all the produced states presented to the fourth, the witness of their action—he has no suspicion that there is another kind of knowledge [the pure intelligence]." 'How is it that these two, experience and liberation, made by the thinking-substance and existing in the thinking-substance only, are attributed to the Self?' Just as a victory or a defeat on the part of actual fighters[2] is ascribed to their commander, for he as we know is the experiencer of the result, so bondage and release, existing in the thinking-substance only, are ascribed to the Self. For he as we know has the experience of the results of these. Bondage is of the thinking-substance only and is the failure to attain the purposes of the Self. Release is the termination of the purpose of the Self. Thus it is that processes-of-knowing and processes-of-retention and comprehensions-of-particulars[3] (*ūha*) and removals-of-faults (*apoha*) and real-knowledge and the will-to-live, [all] existing in the thinking-substance, are assumed to exist in the Self. For he as we know has the experience of the results of these.

He explains the object-of-sight by the sūtra beginning with the word **18. . . . brightness** and ending with the words **object-of-sight.** Brightness is a portion of the *sattva*; it is influenced by dejection which is a quality of *tamas* or by pain which is a quality of *rajas*. Similarly it must be understood in the case of the quality of *rajas* and the rest. It is this that is stated in the words «with the [three] separate parts influencing each other.» «With external-aspects (*dharma*) in conjunction or in separation» with [or from] the Self. As it is written [Çvet. Up. iv. 5], "One male goat [i.e., the unborn soul] has pleasure in leaping upon the one female goat [i.e. primary matter] which is

[1] This is Garbe's eighth fragment of Pañcaçikha. It is introduced to support the statement that experience consists in determining the nature of the *guṇas* which have been identified with the Self. Although the three *guṇas* are active agents, the indiscriminating man looks upon all things as the deeds of the Self, who never acts, who is different in nature from the *guṇas*, and who merely witnesses their changes. He does not suspect the existence of an intelligence which is an insight discriminated from the *guṇas*.

[2] Compare i. 24, p. 55[2] (Calc. ed.).

[3] See Nyāya-sūtra i. 1. 40.

red and white and black and which brings forth many offspring like herself; while another male goat deserts her after having enjoyed her."—Limitations-in-extent, such as earth, are those which have been brought about by basing them upon interdependence of one upon another. The objector says, 'This may be true. When a quiescent idea is to be produced by *sattva*, since *rajas* and *tamas* also, in so far as they are accessory to *sattva*, are the causes of this [idea], there is a power in them. If this be so (*iti*), and whenever *rajas* or *tamas* might be principal, then always a quiescent idea might arise, not a cruel nor an infatuated one, just as in the case when *sattva* was dominant.' In reply to this he says, «with separate powers, although in subservience to each other, still unconfused.» Let it be granted, when a quiescent idea is to be produced, that *rajas* and *tamas* are in an accessory relation, still their powers are not commingled. For the fact that their powers are not commingled may be inferred from the fact that there is no commingling of effects. Whereas effects of the quiescent and cruel and infatuated forms are seen to move actively forth in so far as their form is uncommingled. Thus it is established that the powers are unconfused. The objector says, 'Suppose this be granted. If the powers are unconfused, then the aspects (*guṇa*) cannot be supposed to work harmoniously together. Evidently things whose powers are different never have effects that are produced by a harmonious working together. Threads, for instance, and lumps of earth and dry grasses do not work harmoniously together and produce a jar.' In reply to this he says, «with conformations according to various disparate and comparate powers.» Although the power of serving as material cause is in [a thing which is] comparate [with its effect], and not elsewhere, and although the power of serving as co-operative [cause may be] in disparate things, still when it is a water-jar that is to be generated, it is not in the power of the dry grasses to serve even as co-operative [causes], and this being so, these [grasses] do not work harmoniously with threads. This is the point. —[He analyses the compound.] Those are referred to whose character it is to conform to certain kinds of powers with regard to possible disparates and comparates.—«At the time when they become dominant.» When a super-normal body is to be generated, the *sattva* is dominant and the *rajas* and *tamas* are accessory. Similarly when a human body is to be generated, the *rajas* is dominant and the *sattva* and *tamas* accessory. Likewise when an animal body is to be generated, the *tamas* is dominant and the *sattva* and *rajas* are accessory. Thus these aspects (*guṇa*) have their presence manifested at the time when they become dominant. In other words, they contribute to the effect in proportion as they become reintensified. And the word «dominant» is to be taken as the abstract form of dominance[1] (*bhāvapradhāna*).

[1] He wishes to exclude the other meaning of *pradhāna*, that is, primary cause. Just as 'one and two' have an abstract and a particular sense, so also this word has the sense of 'dominant' and of 'primary cause'. See Pāṇ. iii. 4. 69.

Just as [in the phrase of Pāṇini's sūtra i. 4. 22,] "The dual and singular are used in case of two and one", [the words two and one are] in this case to be understood as twoness and oneness; in other cases [such as of measurable numbers], they are to be understood as two and as one.—An objector says, 'At that time [of dominance], it is possible to say that the dominant exists in so far as it is in its intense form. But is there any source-of-valid-ideas [to prove] the real existence of its accessories which are not in the intense form?' In reply to this he says, «although subordinate.» Although not intensified, still, because they have no discrimination [to recognize that they are themselves inanimate], and [yet] because they do work harmoniously together,—from the mere fact of their functional-activity in so far as there is co-operation, —their existence is inferred as being included in the primary cause. The objector says, 'We may grant that the aspects (*guṇa*) have faculties and work harmoniously together, but why do they perform this [co-operation]? For surely just because one says there is a faculty, one generates no [actual] effect on the ground that there may not be any cessation in the production of effects.' In reply to this he says, «employed as effective for the purposes of the Self.» After this [purpose has been effected], when all the purposes of the Self have been ended, the aspects [afterwards] cease and produce no effects. This is what he means to say. If it be asked, 'How can a thing which does not aid the Self, use impelling force as being a purpose of the Self,' he replies «aid given merely by being near.» It is objected that 'the impeller of the aspects is a cause characterized only as being merit and demerit; but can [these aspects be made to produce effects] when impelled by the purpose of the Self?' In reply to this objection he says, «without any external cause.»—[He explains the phrase.] «The rest» [of the aspects], even «without any external-cause (*pratyaya*)» [or] efficient-cause (*nimitta*) such as merit, «following the fluctuation of any one of them,» either of *sattva* or of *rajas* or of *tamas*, as dominant and as being active towards the production of its own effect. In which sense he will say later [iv. 3], "The efficient-cause gives no impulse, but [the mutation] follows when the barrier to the evolving-causes is cut, just as in the case of the peasant."—The construction of the sentence is, these aspects (*guṇa*) are denoted by the word primary-cause (*pradhāna*). According to its derivation [the word *pradhāna*] is that by which the universe is produced (*pradhīyate*) or put forth.[1] This is said to be the object-of-sight. —Having mentioned the nature of the aspects (*guṇa*) he describes the effect of this disposition in the words, «this same.» In order to establish the doctrine of the pre-existent effect (*satkāryavāda*), he says that a thing enters into mutation as a form of that thing, whichever it may be, that is its essence. He makes clear that its essence is elements and organs by the words beginning, «as an element.» To the words, ‹with its purpose the experience and

[1] Compare ii. 23, p. 159[8] (Calc. ed.).

the liberation,› which are a part of the sūtra, he gives an introduction by saying «not without an impelling-force.» He elaborates the word ‹experience› by saying «of these [two].» For pleasure and pain belong to the thinking-substance as such in so far as it has three aspects (*guṇa*). Because this thinking-substance enters into mutation as being of such a kind [as one that has three aspects]. There is said to be experience in so far as there is an ascertainment [of the things] as belonging to [these] qualities.[1] Accordingly he says, «so long as undivided.» And this has been made known by us more than once.—He elaborates the word ‹liberation› by saying «of the enjoyer.» Liberation is that by which one is liberated [literally, wrenched off]. He states that there is no other impelling-force [than these two] by saying «in addition to these two.»—«And in this sense it has been said» by Pañcaçikha in the words «" But he who ".» An objection is raised, 'As matters of [perceptible] reality, experience and liberation are made by the thinking-substance. How are they attributed to the Self who is neither their cause nor their locus?' In reply to this he says, «These two.» And that the Self is enjoyer has been explained and will be stated later [iii. 34]. But in the strict sense it is as the text says, «Bondage is of the thinking-substance only and is the failure to attain the purposes of the Self.» «Thus» means in the way that experience and liberation are mentioned as being related to the Self. [So] processes-of-knowing and the rest are also to be understood as being related to the Self. Of these, «the process-of-knowing» is the thinking of the intended-object as it is in itself; the process-of-retention is memory with regard to this [object]; «comprehension-of-particulars (*ūha*)» is the maintaining (*ūhana*) of the particulars belonging to a thing; «removal-of-faults (*apoha*)» is the removal for statable reasons (*yukti*) of particulars when falsely attributed; it is by these two only, by comprehension-of-particulars and by removal-of-faults, that the given thing is determined, that is, that there is real knowledge; and will-to-live is rejection or acceptation preceded by this determination of the reality.

This sūtra is begun with the intent of determining the various forms of the aspects (*guṇa*), the objects-of-sight.

19. The particularized and the unparticularized [forms] and the resoluble only [into primary matter] and irresoluble[2]-primary-matter—are the divisions of the aspects (*guṇa*).

Of these [four], the elements air and wind and fire and water and earth are the particularized [forms] of the unparticularized fine

[1] The Vārttika says *iṣṭāniṣṭaguṇāḥ* are *sukhaduḥkhātmakāḥ*. This illustrates the closeness of the term *guṇa* as the three 'aspects' to the common use of the term as 'quality'.

[2] Compare i. 45.

elements (*tanmātra*) sound and touch and colour and taste and smell. Similarly the organs of the thinking-substance are ear and skin and eye and tongue and nose, and the organs of action, voice and hands and feet and organ-of-excretion and organ-of-generation. And as the eleventh the central-organ which has all kinds of things as its intended object. These are the particularized [forms] of the unparticularized [personality-substance] which is characterized as having the feeling of personality. This is the sixteen-fold mutation of the aspects (*guṇa*). The unparticularized [forms] are six, namely, the fine element of sound and the fine element of touch and the fine element of colour and the fine element of taste and the fine element of smell. Thus, as we know, sound and the rest with one or two or three or four or five distinguishing-characteristics are five unparticularized [forms]. And the sixth is that of which we can only say that it is the feeling-of-personality. These are the six unparticularized forms of the Great thinking-substance of whose being we can only say that it exists. That which is prior to the unparticularized [forms] is that of which we can only say that it is resoluble [primary-matter], the Great Substance (*mahat-tattva*). Remaining in this Great Being (*ātman*) of which all that we can say is that it exists, these [six] unparticularized [forms] experience the limit of development. And reversing the process of creation they remain in that same Great Being of which all that we can say is that it exists, and revert to that which has neither existence nor non-existence, from which both existence and non-existence have been removed, from which non-existence has been removed, to the unphenomenalized and unresoluble primary-cause. This [Great Being of which all that we can say is that it exists], is the [first] mutation of these aspects. And that [Being] which has neither existence nor non-existence is the mutation [of these aspects] which is unresoluble [primary cause]. So the purpose of the Self is not the reason for the unresoluble state. Since the fact that the Self has a purpose is not known (*bhavati*) at the beginning as the cause of the state unresoluble [into primary matter], therefore the fact that the Self has a purpose is not a cause [1] of this [state].

[1] See i. 45, p. 96[6] (Calc. ed.).

And since that state is not effected by the purpose of the Self, it is called permanent. But at the beginning of the three states that are particularized, the fact that the Self has a purpose is known to be the cause. And this purpose is known to act as purpose and as efficient cause. Hence this state is called impermanent. But the aspects, which conform themselves to all kinds of external-aspects (*dharma*), neither cease to be nor come into being, but appear as if they had the properties of coming into existence and of passing out of existence by reason of the [individual] phenomenalized forms, past and yet to come, going and coming, inseparably connected with the aspects. As for example we say, 'Devadatta is poor'. Why? 'Because his cows are dying.' Since his poverty is due to the dying of his cows and not to his loss of himself, the parallel (*samādhi*) [to the going and coming of the phenomenalized forms as affecting the aspects (*guṇa*)] applies (*sama*).—That of which we can only say that it is resoluble [into primary matter] is next [in development] to that which is irresoluble [into primary matter]. Formed therein it becomes distinguished from it [as its effect], since the order [of the development of the mutations] is not transgressed. Likewise the six unparticularized [forms] formed in that of which we can only say that it is resoluble [into primary matter] become distinguished [from it]. Because the order of mutations is fixed. Similarly the elements and organs formed in these unparticularized [forms] become distinguished [from them], as has been already described. There is no other entity (*tattva*) beyond the particularized [forms]. So there is no mutation into any other entity beyond the particularized [forms]. But their mutation into external-aspect and time-variation and intensity are to be explained [iii. 13] later.

«This sūtra is begun with the intent of determining the various forms of the aspects (*guṇa*), the objects-of-sight.» The sūtra begins with the words 19. The particularized and ends with the words divisions . . . He mentions the particularized [forms] which are the evolved-matter (*vikāra*) of the unparticularized [forms] which [latter] are without the serene and cruel and infatuated characteristics—[the evolved forms], but not the [forms] evolving[1] other entities (*tattva*). He describes the [forms] belonging to these [entities] in the words,

[1] See the discussion by Vācaspati in Sāṁkhya Tattva-Kāum. on Kār. iii.

«Of these [four], . . . air.» The order of explanatory-statement follows exactly the order of production. The organs of intelligence (*buddhi*) are particularized [forms] of the [personality-substance (*ahaṁkāra*)] which is characterized as having the feeling-of-personality, and which has *sattva* as its dominant [aspect]. But the organs of action [are particularized forms of the personality-substance] which has *rajas* as its dominant [aspect]. Whereas the central-organ (*manas*), the essence of which is of both kinds, must be supposed to be the [particularized form of the personality-substance] which has both kinds [that is, *rajas* and *sattva*] as its dominant [aspects]. And [there is an inference] on this point, that the five fine elements have the thinking-substance as their cause, because they are unparticularized [forms], like the feeling-of-personality. Moreover, being an unparticularized form is [the same as] being the cause of evolved matter; and both in the fine elements and in the feeling-of-personality there is nothing particularized.—After grouping them together he enumerates the particularized [forms] in the words, «This . . . of the aspects.» He numbers the unparticularized [forms] also with the word «six.» He groups them together and sums them up with the word «namely.» Now the prior is particularized by the subsequent. So smell itself [together with the subsequent four] has five[1] characteristics; taste itself [together with the subsequent three] has four characteristics; colour itself [together with the subsequent two] has three characteristics; touch itself [with the subsequent sound] has two characteristics; sound has the characteristic of sound only. 'But of what are these six unparticularized [forms] the effect?' In reply to this he says «These . . . . of which we can only say that it exists.» The existent (*sat*) is that which is capable of actions fulfilling a purpose; having existence (*sattā*) is the abstract form of this. The Great Substance is that which is made of this. In other words, whatever action fulfilling a purpose there be, whether its characteristic be enjoyment [of various things] from sound downwards, or whether its characteristic be the discernment of the difference between the *sattva* and the Self, it is all of it comprehended in the Great Thinking-substance. By saying «of whose being» he shows what it really is and denies that it is nothing at all (*tuccha*). This is equivalent to saying that this first mutation of primary matter is a real thing, and not an appearance (*vivartta*). That which is prior to these, [that is] distant in time as compared with the unparticularized [forms] which are near in time, is that of which we can only say that it is resoluble [primary-matter], the Great Substance (*mahat-tattva*). Remaining in this Great Being of which all that we can say is that it exists, these six unparticularized [forms],—since it is established that the effect pre-exists [in its cause],—experience [or] reach the limit of development. On the other hand, of these non-particularized which have particularized [forms] there are also the mutations of external-aspect (*dharma*) and of time-variation and of intensity. It is this that is the limit of development, that is, the limit of mutation of these particu-

[1] See Garbe: Sāṁkhya Philosophie, p. 236, note 3.

larized [forms]. Having thus mentioned the order of growth he describes the order of dissolution in the words, «reversing the process of creation.» «Reversing the process of creation» [means] becoming resolved (*pralīyamāna*) [into primary-matter]. In other words particularized forms are resolved into their own form, that is, become non-particularized. And they remain [or] are dissolved (*nilīya*) in that same Great Being of which all that we can say is that it exists. And then even with the Great [Being], these unparticularized [forms] revert to unphenomenalized [primary-matter], called unresoluble because in none (*a*) else are they resolved (*lī*). This same [unphenomenalized primary matter] is qualified by the words, «which has neither existence nor non-existence.» Existence is that which is capable of acts fulfilling a purpose of the Self. Non-existence is worthlessness (*tucchatā*) as regards the purpose of the Self. That is so-described [as having neither existence nor non-existence] which is beyond-the-range of both existence and non-existence. What he means to say is this. The state when *sattva* and *rajas* and *tamas* are in equipoise is never of use in fulfilling a purpose of the Self. And so it is not existent. Neither does it have a worthless kind of existence like the sky-lotus. Therefore it is also not non-existent. The objector says, 'This may be so. Still in the unphenomenalized state there are the Great [Thinking-substance] and the other [entities] in so far as these are identical with this [unphenomenalized state]. For there is no utter annihilation of the existent, or if utterly annihilated it cannot be made to grow again. For because one cannot make the non-existent grow, the Great [Thinking-substance] and the other [entities] would really exist [in the unphenomenalized state] and therefore might function as acts fulfilling the purpose of the Self [and so the unphenomenalized state might be said to exist]. Then how could you say that it has no existence?' In reply to this he says, «from which both existence and non-existence have been removed.» [The non-existent] is a cause which [exists] beyond any existing effect. Although in the causal state the effect does exist as potential being (*çaktyātmanā*), still in so far as it does not fulfil its peculiar purpose it is said to be non-existent. This cause does not however have an effect [worthless for the purpose of the Self] like a hare's horns. Accordingly he says «from which non-existence has been removed.» [A cause which exists] beyond an effect that is non-existent or worthless [with regard to the purpose of the Self]. For if that were so, the effect would not be produced from this [cause] any more than the sky-lotus [would be produced from this cause]. This is the point. He brings the [topic of the] reversal of creation which has been described to a close in the words, «This . . . of these.» The word «This» points back to that which has been stated just prior to that which immediately precedes. The states beginning with that of which we can only say that it is resoluble [into primary matter], since they are effected by a purpose of the Self, are not permanent. Whereas the state which is unresoluble [into primary matter], since it is not effected by a purpose of the Self, is permanent. He gives the reason for this in the words, «of the state unresoluble into primary matter.» But why is the purpose of the Self not a reason? In reply to this he says, «not . . . of the state unresoluble.» By using the object (*viṣaya*) [the purpose of the Self] in place of that which contains the object (*viṣayin*) [the unresoluble state], he partially describes the knowledge [in the Self of this state]. What he means to say is this. For this being so, it should be known that the purpose of the Self acts as a cause in the state unresoluble [into primary matter], provided the state unresoluble [into primary matter] could produce (*nirvartayeta*) the enjoyment of objects or the discernment of the difference between the *sattva* and the Self, [either of which is] a purpose of the Self. When however these two are produced, there can be no longer a state of equipoise. Therefore this [unresoluble state] is not known as a cause of the fact that the Self has a purpose. Thus the fact that the Self has a purpose is not the reason for this [unresoluble state]. He concludes with the words, «that . . . not.» The word *iti* is used in the sense of therefore.—He describes the impermanent state in the words «of the three.» In other words, that of which we can only say that it is unresoluble, the unparticularized, and the particularized. Having shown what the divisions are, he tells what the aspects are in the words, «But the aspects.» He gives a simile in the words, «Just as Devadatta.» In case the increase or decrease of the cows, which are absolutely distinct from Devadatta, is the reason for Devadatta's increase or decrease, how much more [in the parallel case] of the growth or decline of the [individual] phenomalized [forms], which are not different in some respects and different in other respects from the aspects (*guṇa*). An objector asks, 'Is then the order of production not fixed?' No. As he says in the words, «that of which we can only say that it is resoluble.» For surely the seeds of the Nyagrodha tree do not in a single day shoot forth the Nyagrodha tree, with its dense mass of green leaves, which has absorbed in its branches and twigs a multitude of the fierce rays of the sun; but gradually, through contact with earth and water and warmth, they produce in succession sprout and leaves and stalks and stems and the rest. So here also an order[1] [of production] must be accepted in that it is established by reasoning and by verbal-communication.—How are the elements and organs formed from unparticularized [forms]? In reply to this he says, «as has been already described» [by us] when explaining the first part of this very sūtra. And if it be asked why, in the case of the particularized [forms], there is no mutation into any other entity, he replies «no . . . the particularized [forms].» So is it true then that the particularized [forms] actually enter into no mutations? And if that were so, would not one have to say that they are permanent? In reply to this he says, «But their.»

[1] For example, the Sāṁkhya-sūtra i. 62, and Sāṁkhya-kārikā xxii.

The object-of-sight has been explained. Now this sūtra is introduced with the intent of determining what the Seer as such is.

20. The Seer, who is nothing but [the power of] seeing, although undefiled (*çuddha*), looks upon the presented-idea.

‹Who is nothing but [the power of] seeing› means who is nothing but the power of seeing untouched by any qualifications. This Self becomes conscious-by-reflection (*pratisaṁvedin*) of the thinking-substance. He is not homogeneous with the thinking-substance nor utterly heterogeneous. Why [do we say that the Self] is not even heterogeneous [to the thinking-substance]? Because the thinking-substance is something that enters into mutations,[1] inasmuch as an object is known or not known [according as the thinking-substance has or has not changed into the form of that thing]. And the fact that an [external] object, for instance, a cow or a water-jar, is sometimes known and sometimes not known, proves that the thinking-substance is something which enters into mutations. Whereas the fact that, in the case of the Self, its object is always known, proves that the Self does not enter into mutations. Why [do we say this]? Because it surely is not possible for the thinking-substance to be an object to the Self, and at the same time be something now comprehended and something again not comprehended [by the Self]. Hence it is proved that the Self always knows its object. And from this it follows that the Self does not enter into mutations. Moreover the thinking-substance exists for the sake of another, since it acts by combining[2] causes. Whereas the Self exists for its own sake. Thus [continuing the argument], the thinking-substance is a complex of the three aspects, because it determines[3] each thing (*sarva-artha*) [as consisting of one or another of the three aspects, that is, as pleasurable or as painful or as indifferent]. And since it consists of the three aspects (*guṇa*), it is inanimate. The Self, on the other hand, is that which later beholds the aspects [by being reflected in them]. Hence it is not homogeneous with [the

[1] Compare ii. 15, p. 135[11]; ii. 18, p. 152[3]; iii. 35, p. 244[7]; iv. 17, p. 301[1]; iv. 22, p. 306[4]; iv. 33, p. 316 (Calc. ed.).

[2] Compare Mṛcchakaṭika, act 10, verse 59 and YS. iv. 24.

[3] The concept *adhyavasāya* is defined in the comments on Sāṁkhya-kārikā xxiii.

thinking-substance]. '[Very well] then, suppose the Self to be heterogeneous [to the thinking-substance].' [Still], it is not utterly heterogeneous. Why [do we say this]? Because though pure[1] in itself, the Self beholds the presented-ideas, that is to say, it beholds that [mutation of matter which the thinking-substance undergoes when it takes the form of an object, and] which is a presented-idea of thinking-substance (*bāuddha*). Looking [thus] upon this [change in the thinking-substance] the Self seems to be it [the thinking-substance], although it really is not it [the thinking-substance]. And in this sense it has been said,[2] "For the power of the enjoyer enters not into mutation nor unites [with objects]. Seeming to unite with a thing in mutation [the thinking-substance], it conforms itself to the fluctuation [which that thinking-substance undergoes]. And it is commonly termed a fluctuation of the thinking-substance in so far as it resembles (*anukāramātratayā*) a fluctuation of thinking-substance that has come under the influence (*upagraha*) of intelligence (*cāitanya*)."

«The object-of-sight has been explained. Now this sūtra is introduced with the intent of determining what the Seer as such is.» **20. The Seer, who is nothing but [the power of] seeing, although undefiled (*çuddha*), looks upon the presented-idea.** He explains [the sūtra] by the words «nothing but [the power of] seeing.» The qualifications are the properties. «Untouched» by these in this way shows the import of the words «nothing but.» An objector says, 'This may be true. If the power of seeing is without all qualifications, then [the various things] from sound downwards would not be known. For the object-of-sight cannot be something out of contact with the seeing.' In reply to this he says, «This Self.» The union (*saṁkrānti*) of the reflection of the Self with the mirror of the thinking-substance is itself the Self's consciousness by reflection in the thinking-substance. And so the [various things] from sound downwards become connected with the thinking-substance which has been changed into the likeness (*chāyā*) of the power of sight. In other words, [they become] objects-of-sight. The objector says, 'This may be true. Still why is not the unity, even in the strict sense, of the thinking-substance and of the Self to be accepted? What is the use of changing it into the likeness of this [Self]?' In reply to this he says, «It is not homogeneous with the thinking-substance.» 'In this case it would be difficult for it to change into the likeness [of the Seer].' In reply to this he says, «nor

[1] That is to say, unspecialized.

[2] This is Pañcaçikha's ninth fragment. It is quoted again in iv. 22.

utterly heterogeneous.» Of these [two], he rejects the homogeneity in the words, «not even homogeneous.» The reason [for this] he asks by saying «why?» For the heterogeneity he gives a reason which itself contains a reason, in the words, «known or not known.» Because the thinking-substance enters into mutations, it is heterogeneous. When, as we know, this [thinking-substance] changes into the form of [the various things from] sound downwards, then the object, having the distinguishing characteristics of [the various things from] sound downwards, becomes known to this [thinking-substance]; but when not so changed into the form of these [things], the object does not become known to it. And so only occasionally it assumes the forms of these [things] and enters into mutations. And the argument is [of this kind]: The thinking-substance enters into mutations; since objects are [sometimes] known and [sometimes] not known by it; just as the organ of hearing and other organs [are sometimes active and sometimes not]. And the Self proves to be of different properties to this, because the middle term [that is, always-known] is contrary to this, as he says, «always known.» The objector says, 'This may be so. But if the Self always has its object known, then he could not be isolated.' With this in mind, he asks, «Why [do we say this]?» He gives the answer in the words, «Because surely . . . not . . . for the thinking-substance.» In the state of restriction the thinking-substance may exist and at the same time there may be no process of apperception [by the Self]. Therefore in order to indicate the contradiction, it is said, «an object to the Self.» So the first «and» (*buddhiç ca*) has an accumulative force and makes the thinking-substance an object; but the two remaining «ands» (*viṣayaç ca* and *'grahītā ca*) are to make the contradiction clear. The argument, however, is this. The Self enters not into mutation; because objects are always known to it in the conscious and emergent states [1]; whatever enters into mutation does not always have its objects known; just as the organ of hearing or other [organs]. This is a negative instance of the middle term [*sadā-jñātaviṣayatvāt*]. He gives another [instance] of difference in properties in the words, «Moreover . . . for the sake of another.» For the thinking-substance, in so far as it fulfils the purpose of the Self by combining with hindrances and karma and subconscious-impressions and with objects and organs, is for the sake of another. The argument, moreover, is this: The thinking-substance is for the sake of another; because it acts by combining causes [2]; like a bed or a seat or an ointment. But the Self is not like that, as he says «the Self exists for its own sake.» Everything serves the purpose of the Self, but the Self serves no other. This is the point. He gives yet another [instance] of difference in properties in the words, «Thus . . . each thing.» The thinking-substance determines all things as being serene or cruel or infatuated when it mutates into their forms. And these [three] are mutations of the *sattva* and *rajas* and *tamas* aspects. Thus

[1] This excludes the state unconscious of objects.

[2] Compare Sāṁkhya-kārikā xvii.

it is established that the thinking-substance is a complex of the three aspects. And again the Self is not like that, as he says, «The Self, on the other hand, later beholds the aspects.» It beholds them in that it is reflected in them, but it does not become mutated into their form. He brings the discussion to a close with the word, «Hence.» «[Very well] then, suppose . . . heterogeneous.» [But] it is not utterly heterogeneous [to the thinking-substance]. Why [do we say this]? Because though pure in itself, it looks upon the presented-ideas. And that this is so, is [also] stated in these [words i. 4], "At other times it takes the same form as the fluctuations [of mind-stuff]." And in this sense it has been said by Pañcaçikha «"For the power of the enjoyer enters not into mutation."» [The power,] in other words, the self (*ātman*). And therefore it does not unite with the thinking-substance. «Seeming to unite» with the thinking-substance which is in mutation, «it conforms itself to the fluctuation» which that thinking-substance [undergoes]. An objector asks, 'If it does not unite, how is it that it seems to unite, or how does it conform itself [to the thinking-substance] without [assuming] a fluctuation [of its own]?' To this he replies with the words, «And it.» That thing has come under the influence of intelligence whose form has been affected (*uparakta*) [by intelligence]. What he means to say is this. Although the moon does not unite with the clear water, still it seems to unite [with it] in so far as its reflection unites [with the water]. Similarly in this case also, although the power of intellect (*citi*) does not unite [with the thinking-substance], still it seems to unite since its reflection has united [with it]. Thus the power of intellect, changed into the essence of the thinking-substance, conforms itself to the fluctuation which the thinking-substance undergoes. In this way the word «beholding» has been explained. It beholds it in the sense that it sees [itself] as resembling it.

21. The being (*ātman*) of the object-of-sight is only for the sake of it [the Self].

Since the object-of-sight is changed in so far as it becomes the object of the action of the Self who is so much (*rūpa*) seeing (*dṛçi*), ‹the being (*ātman*) of the object-of-sight,› that is to say, the object-of-sight itself (*svarūpa*) exists only for the sake of the Self. But inasmuch as it is itself only so long as it has acquired its being as having the form of another, it is no [longer] seen by the Self when once it has accomplished the purpose of the Self, [of giving the Self] experience and liberation. So by escaping from itself it attains cessation; but it does not utterly cease to be.

Having stated what the Seer and the object-of-sight are, he says that the object-of-sight serves the purpose of the Self. [And this purpose is] based upon the relation characterized as being that of proprietor and property. **21. The being (*ātman*) of the object-of-sight is only for the sake of it [the Self].** He explains [the sūtra] in the words, «who is so much (*rūpa*) seeing (*dṛçi*).» Since the object-of-sight has become the object-of-action (*karma-rūpatā*), [that is] has been changed into the object-of-experience by the experiencer [that is] the Self who is so much seeing,—therefore the being of the object-of-sight must be only for the sake of the Seer, but not for the sake of the object-of-sight. The objector asks, 'How can the being [*ātma* in *dṛçyātma*] be for the sake of this [*ātma* in *tadātma*] [that is, the Self]?' In reply to this he says, «is itself.» What he means to say is this: The object-of-experience is the object-of-sight as having pleasure or pain. And pleasure and pain being co-agents or counter-agents persist as such (*tattvena*) only for this purpose [of acting with or against the Self]. For the [various things] from sound downwards as objects-of-sense are co-agents or counter-agents [for the Self] only because they are identical [with pleasure and pain]. And it cannot be said that they exist to be co-active or to be counter-active to themselves. For that would be a contradiction of a fluctuation with itself. Therefore by a process of elimination it is the power of intellect (*citi*) only for which they are co-active or counter-active. Consequently the object-of-sight is for this [Self] and not for the object-of-sight [itself]. And therefore the ‹object-of-sight is only for the sake of it [the Self],› not for the sake of the object-of-sight. Because (*yat*) it is itself as long as the purpose of the Self continues. And when the purpose of the Self is complete it is also completed. Accordingly he says, «But . . . it . . itself.» But the object-of-sight itself is inert (*jaḍa*), yet it has acquired its being [that is] it is experienced as having the form of another [that is] the form of the soul (*ātman*) [that is] the intelligence (*cāitanya*). When experience and liberation have been accomplished it is no [longer] seen by the Self. [This was] the kind-of-experience,[1] the perception (*anubhava*) of sound and the other [perceptible] things. Liberation is the perception (*anubhava*) of the difference between *sattva* and the Self. Both these two kinds [of things, experience and liberation,] belong to the Self only who, by reason of the fact that the likeness of the Self becomes changed by the inert thinking-substance, [does know them both]. And so when experience and liberation have been accomplished for the Self, [the subservience of] the object-of-sight to the purpose of the Self is finished. Hence it is said, «when once it has accomplished the purpose of the Self.» Meanwhile he raises an objection in the words, «by escaping from itself.» He rebuts [this] with the words, «but it does not utterly cease to be.»

[1] Vijñāna Bhikṣu expands this definition and emphasizes the fact that experience is a fluctuation of the mind (*sukhaduḥkhātmakaçabdādivṛttiḥ*).

Why [does it not utterly cease to be]?

22. Though it has ceased [to be seen] in the case of one whose purpose is accomplished, it has not ceased to be, since it is common to others [besides himself].

Although the object-of-sight has ceased in so far as one Self whose purpose has been accomplished is concerned, it has not ceased to be, because it is common to others besides him. Although it has ceased so far as one fortunate man is concerned, [still] it has not ceased in the case of unfortunate men, since their purpose has not been fulfilled. So for these persons it becomes the object-of-the-action of seeing and receives its form of being as having the form of another. And therefore since the power of seeing and the power by which one sees are permanent, the conjunction [of the two] is said to be from time-without-beginning. And in this sense it has been said, "The substances being in correlation from time without beginning, the external-aspects in general are also in correlation from time without beginning."

An objector says, 'If [the object-of-sight] is absolutely inapperceptible, how is it that it does not cease to be?' With this in mind he asks, «Why [is this]?» In the sūtra he tells the answer beginning with the words **22 . . . whose purpose is accomplished** and ending with the words **since it is common to others [besides himself]**. A Self whose purpose has been accomplished is of such a kind. For him the object-of-sight although it has ceased [to be seen], has not ceased [to be]. Why? Since it is common to all Selves fortunate or unfortunate. He explains [the sūtra] in the words, «one whose purpose has been accomplished.» Cessation is the absence of that by which one sees. But the object-of-sight has not ceased to be, since it is common to other Selves. Hence the nature (*rūpa*) of the being (*ātman*) who is higher than the object-of-sight is intelligence (*cāitanya*). So (*tena*) here we have that [being] which is made known in the Sacred Word and the Sacred Tradition and in the Epics and Purāṇas, the unphenomenalized, the whole-without-parts, the one, the independent, all-pervasive, permanent, [and] capable of producing-all-effects. Although [the object-for-sight] is not seen by the fortunate man, since for him its effect has been accomplished, it is not, however, something not seen by the unfortunate man. For because colour is not seen by the blind man, it does not become non-existent, since it is seen by the man who has eyes. For the Self is not, like the primary cause, only one. Because its plurality is established[1] in so far as there is the orderly arrangement of births and deaths, pleasures and

[1] Compare Sāṁkhya-sūtra i. 149.

pains, later kind-of-experience and release and round-of-existence; and because the passages of the Sacred Word which teach the unity [of the Self] and which contradict the other sources-of-valid-ideas, can somehow be made consistent, as partial statements, by supposing that there is no division[1] in place or in time; and because the fact that primary matter is one and the Selves many is expressly taught by the Sacred Word[2] itself, "One male goat [the unborn Soul] has pleasure in leaping upon the one female goat [primary matter] which is red and white and black and which brings forth many offspring like herself, while another male goat deserts her after having enjoyed her." And the meaning of this same Sacred Word is said over again by this sūtra. Although the object-for-sight has ceased [to be seen], still so far as another Self is concerned it has not ceased to be. Therefore, since the power of seeing and the power by which one sees are permanent, their correlation is said to be from time-without-beginning. He states that those who have the tradition[3] (*āgamin*) concur with this teaching, as he says, «And in this sense it has been said.» Since the correlation of substances, in other words, of the aspects (*guṇa*), with the souls is from time without beginning, [so] in the case of the mere external aspects (*guṇa*), such as the Great [thinking-substance], there is a correlation from time without beginning. The correlation of the Great [Thinking-substance] and of the rest, one by one, although from time without beginning, is not permanent. Still it is permanent when we regard the Great [thinking-substance] and the rest as a whole, since [these external aspects] are common to the other Selves. Accordingly he says «the external-aspects in general.» The words «in general» (*mātra*) point out the comprehensive character [of the compound]. Hence what follows is this: Although the correlation of one Great thinking-substance has become changed so that it is past, still the correlation of one Self[4] with another Great [thinking-substance] is not past. So [the correlation is] said to be permanent.

The intent of this sūtra is to describe what the correlation itself is.

23. The reason for the apperception of what the power of the property and of what the power of the proprietor are is correlation.

The Self as proprietor becomes correlated for the purpose of sight

[1] The Pātañjala Rahasyam says that the unity of all souls is only figurative. All Selves are permanent and all-pervasive. The unity is that of a collection, like that of a forest or of an army, in so far as no division is made in time or in place.

[2] Çvet. Up. iv. 5.

[3] The attribution of this quotation to Pañcaçikha rests upon the authority of Vijñāna Bhikṣu.

[4] Reading *puruṣāntareṇa* with the Bikāner MS.

with the object-for-sight as property. That apperception of the object-for-sight which results from this correlation is experience. Whereas the apperception of what the Seer is, is liberation. Since the correlation lasts until sight is effected, sight is said to be the cause of discorrelation. Since sight and non-sight are opposite to each other, non-sight is said to be the instrumental cause of correlation. Sight in this [system] is not the cause of release ; but the absence of bondage results from the absence of non-sight. This is release. Where there is sight, non-sight, which is the cause of bondage, ceases [to be felt]. Thus the perception which is sight is said to be the cause of isolation. And what is this so-called non-sight ? 1. Is it the authority (*adhikāra*) of the aspects (*guṇa*) [over the Self] ? 2. Or is it the case that, when in [the equipoised state of] the primary-cause, the mind-stuff, by which the objects are shown to the proprietor in his capacity as Seer, fails to produce [effects], there is non-sight,[1] although the property, the object-for-sight, exists ? 3. Or is it that the aspects (*guṇa*) possess the intended-objects [in potential form] ? 4. Or is undifferentiated-consciousness (*avidyā*), which, together with its own mind-stuff, has been restricted, the seed for the production of its peculiar mind-stuff ? 5. Or is it the manifestation of subliminal-impressions in motion (*gati*) after the subliminal-impressions in equilibrium (*sthiti*) have dwindled away ? Of which [theory] this has been said,[2] "The primary cause if it existed, on the one hand, in equilibrium (*sthiti*) only, would be a non-primary cause, because it would not cause any evolved effect. Similarly, if on the other hand it existed in motion (*gati*) only, it would be a non-primary cause, because the evolved effects would be permanent. And since it does act[3] in both ways [equilibrium and motion] it is ordinarily termed primary substance ; not otherwise. Also with regard to other supposed causes the same reasoning [applies]." 6. According to some non-sight is nothing but the power by which one sees, as the Sacred Word says, "The primary cause acts with the intent of displaying itself." The Self capable of illuminating all illuminable

[1] Compare iv. 34.

[2] Udāsīna Bālarāma attributes this to Pañcaçikha.

[3] Reading *vṛtti*.

things does not, before the primary cause acts, see. [On the other hand], the object-for-sight capable of making all kinds of effects is not then [without the Self] seen. 7. According to others non-sight is a property of both kinds also. From this point of view, this sight, although independent of the object-for-sight, requires a presented-idea [that is, the reflection] of the Self; and so is a property of the object-for-sight. Similarly sight, although not independent of the Self, still requires a presented idea in the object-for-sight; and appears as if it were actually a property of the Self. 8. Certain others assert that non-sight is only the perception [of things only] by sight. These are the alternatives found in the books on this [topic of the nature of non-sight]. These many alternatives deal with a common subject-matter, the correlation of all the Selves with the aspects (*guṇa*).

Thus the serving the purpose [of the Self] as the cause of correlation has been stated. And as incidental [to this] the cause of the permanence of the primary cause and the cause of the permanence of the correlation in general have been stated. With the intent to describe what correlation itself is, in other words, its special particular [nature], the sūtra has come into being. **23. The reason for the apperception of what the power of the property and of what the power of the proprietor are is correlation.** Because the object-for-sight is for his sake, therefore the Self, accepting the aid rendered by this [object], becomes its proprietor. And the object-for-sight becomes his property. And the correlation of these two which has had a merely potential arrangement is the reason for the apperception of what the two are in themselves. This same is made clear in the commentary in the words «The Self.» The Self as proprietor merely by [his] pre-established harmony becomes correlated with the object-for-sight as his property for the sake of sight. The rest is easy. An objector says, 'This may be true. Liberation may be said to be the apperception of what the Seer himself may be, [that is, it may be] that by which he is liberated. And moreover release is not the effect of means. Should this be so, it would cease being what could be rightly called release.' In reply to this he says, «until sight is effected.» Until sight is effected there is a correlation of a particular Self with a particular thinking-substance. Thus sight is said to be the cause of discorrelation. 'But how does correlation last until sight is effected?' In reply to this he says, «non-sight.» Non-sight, undifferentiated-consciousness (*avidyā*), is said to be the instrumental cause of correlation. He makes clear the meaning of what he said before by saying, «in this [system]... not.» The objector says, 'Sight may quite remove non-sight, its opposite. But how can it remove bondage?' In reply to this he says, «is sight.» Release has been stated [i. 3] to be the self's (*ātman*) abiding in his own form as discriminated from the thinking-substance and other [substances]. And the means for effecting this is not only sight, but the removal of non-sight. This is the meaning. — In order to obtain a particular kind of non-sight as the special reason for the correlation he puts forth the following alternatives with respect to non-sight in the words, «And what is this.» 1. Assuming that [non-sight] is some positive thing (*paryudāsa*)[1] [not sight] he asks, «1. Is it the authority of the aspects (*guṇa*) [over the Self]?» Authority is the competency to initiate effects. For it is as the result of this that the correlation, which is the reason for the round-of-existence, is produced.—2. Assuming that [non-sight] is a negation where there is a possibility of an affirmation (*prasajya-pratiṣedha*),[2] he puts forth a second alternative with the word, «2. Or.» [Non-sight] is the failure, by the mind-stuff which shows objects-of-sense [to the Self], to produce either the [various things] from sound downwards or the [discrimination of] the difference between *sattva* and the Self. It is this that is made clear by the words, «the property.» The object-for-sight is [both] the various things from sound downwards and the difference between *sattva* and the Self. The primary cause is in motion only so long as it has not completed the two-fold sight. But when both kinds of sight have been accomplished, it desists [from being further in motion].—3. On the assumption that [non-sight] is some positive thing [not sight], he puts forth the third alternative, «3. Or is it that the aspects (*guṇa*) possess the intended-objects [in potential form]?» For if the doctrine of pre-existent causes (*satkārya*) is established, experience and liberation are also yet to come in so far as they are [at present] indeterminable. This is the meaning.—4. Assuming that [non-sight] is some positive thing [not sight], he puts forth the fourth alternative and asks «4. Or is undifferentiated-consciousness (*avidyā*)...?» At the time of the reversal of creation, it is restricted together with its peculiar mind-stuff [that is to say] it is reduced to the state of equipoise in the primary cause, the seed for the production of its peculiar mind-stuff. To this extent (*tena*) a subconscious-impression of undifferentiated-consciousness is other than sight and is precisely what is called non-sight.—5. Assuming that [non-sight] is some positive thing [not sight], he puts forth the fifth alternative and asks, «5. Is it... in equilibrium?» When the subliminal-impressions in equilibrium, [that is] existing in the primary cause, and flowing on in a succession of mutations in the equipoised [state of the primary cause], have dwindled away, there is a start given to evolved-effects (*vikāra*), such as the Great [thinking-substance] and the rest,—this is motion (*gati*). The reason for this [start given] is a subliminal-impression of the primary cause, the subliminal-impression in motion. The manifestation of it is its readiness to produce effects. He says that another theory admits the real existence of subliminal-impressions of both

[1] Compare Patañjali: Mahābhāṣya (Kielhorn's ed.) i. 93^{8}; 101^{8}; 167^{9}; 183^{7}; 216^{1}; 319^{13}; 334^{4}; 341^{5}; ii. 338^{8}; 343^{5f}; iii. 35^{6}; and elsewhere.

[2] Compare p. 24, note 2; and p. 113, note 4.

kinds in the words, «Of which [theory] this has been said» by those who deny the absoluteness of either one. Primary cause (*pra-dhāna*) is that by which the totality of evolved effects is put forth (*pra-dhīyate*) or produced.[1] If this primary cause always remained in equilibrium and never in motion, then because it would not cause any evolved effect, it would not put forth anything, and would not be a primary cause (*pra-dhāna*). Or if it always remained in motion and never in equilibrium, then he says, «Similarly . . . in motion.» Elsewhere the reading is 'for the purpose of equilibrium, for the purpose of motion'; the dative is here purposive and we must supply (*draṣṭavyaḥ*) 'only' (*eva*) after it. If it did not act for the purpose of equilibrium, no evolved effect would ever cease to be. And this being so, if a thing (*bhāva*) exists and does not cease to be, it could not rise [again]. Thus there would be a cessation of evolution of effects altogether. And there would likewise be nothing put forth in this case and [thus] it would be a non-primary cause. Therefore its activity must be of both kinds, in equilibrium and in motion, [and] it is ordinarily termed primary substance; «not otherwise,» as when for instance the absoluteness [of either] might be assumed. This reasoning or argument applies not only to the primary cause, but also to other supposed causes, to the higher Brahman or to its illusion (*māyā*) or to atoms or to other [causes]. For these also if they existed in equilibrium only, would not be causes, since they do not cause evolved effects; and if existing in motion only, would not be causes, since the evolved effects would be permanent.—6. Assuming that [non-sight] is some positive thing [not sight], he puts forth a sixth alternative in the words, «nothing but the power by which one sees.» Just as in the vow of Prajāpati [Manu iv. 37], "One should not look upon the rising sun," a mental resolution [in positive form] closely related to not looking is understood, so in this case also [of non-sight], when there is a negation of sight, a power closely related to it and based upon it is described. And this [power] in order to give birth to sight characterized by experience and so forth brings about the pre-established harmony of the Seer with the object-for-sight. On the same point he recites a [passage from] the Sacred Word, «The primary cause.» The objector says, 'This may be true. But the Sacred Word says that the primary cause acts with the intent of displaying itself; yet it does not say that it acts as the result[2] of the power by which one sees.' In reply to this he says, «capable of illuminating all illuminable things.» Because before the primary substance acts, mere displaying of itself is not capacity as an impelling force for action. For there is no ground for this [activity] in the absence of capacity to act as impelling force. Therefore in accordance with the Sacred Word it is said that capacity is the impelling force for action.—The sixth alternative is based upon the assumption that the power by which one sees is in the primary cause.—7. The seventh alternative makes this same power reside in both kinds [the primary cause and the Self], as he says, «Non-sight . . . of both

[1] Compare ii. 18, p. 144[9] (Calc. ed.). [2] Reading *çakteḥ*, p. 160[6] (Calc. ed.).

kinds also.» Some say that non-sight belongs to both kinds, both to the Self and to the object-for-sight and that it is a power [or] a property of sight. An objector says, 'This may be true. We may grant this with regard to the object-for-sight, because it is the repository of all powers; but we could not grant it with regard to the Seer, because the power of perception does not reside (*ādhāra*) in him, for the reason that perception does not have the relation to him of part to whole (*samavāya*). Should that be so, he would be subject to mutation.' To this he replies, «From this point of view, this.» That non-sight might be included in the object-for-sight might be conceded, still, since the object-for-sight is unintelligent (*jaḍa*), seeing, which is an effect of a power residing in this [object-for-sight], would also be unintelligent (*jaḍa*). So sight cannot be thought as a property of this [object-for-sight], for an unintelligent [thing] has not illumination in itself. Hence sight becomes, [that is] is known as, a property of this [object-for-sight] only as based upon the presented-idea of the Seer, the self (*ātman*), that is, upon a change into the likeness of the intelligence (*cāitanya*). Because that which-has-to-do-with-the-object (*viṣayin*) [that is, the power of seeing] is partially expressed by the object [that is, the object-for-sight]. The objector says, 'Even so, this perception becomes a property of the object-for-sight, but not a property of the Self.' To this he replies, «Similarly . . . of the Self.» It is true that it is not independent of the Self, still it does appear to become a property of the Self as based upon the presented-idea [that is] the likeness of the intelligence (*cāitanya*) in the *sattva* of the thinking-substance of the object-for-sight, but it is not actually a property of the Self. What he means to say is this. In so far as there is no difference between intelligence and the thinking-substance, the external-aspects (*dharma*) of the thinking-substance distinctly appear (*cakāsati*) as if they were external-aspects of intelligence, in so far as they receive the image of intelligence.—8. He describes the eighth alternative in the words, «non-sight is only the perception.» Only perception of the [various things] from sound downwards is non-sight; but not the perception of the difference between *sattva* and the Self. So some say. Just as the eye, although the source-of-a-valid-idea for colour, is not the source-of-a-valid-idea for taste and the other [sensations]. What follows is this: The perceptions of the [various things], of sounds and so on, have the forms of pleasure and other [forms] and imply the correlation of the Seer and the object-for-sight, in so far as it is necessary for the sake of their perfection.—Having thus put forth alternatives, and in order to accept the fourth alternative, he points-out-the-flaws in the other [seven] alternatives mentioned in the Sāṁkhya system, on the ground that they would lead to an absence of diversity in experience, since [non-sight according to the other theories] is common to all the Selves. So he says, «These . . . are found in the books.»

But when there is a correlation of an individual consciousness with its own thinking-substance,

24. The reason for this [correlation] is undifferentiated-consciousness (*avidyā*).

In other words, [undifferentiated-consciousness] is a subconscious-impression (*vāsanā*) from erroneous thinking. The thinking-substance pervaded (*vāsita*) by subconscious-impressions from erroneous thinking does not attain to the discernment of the Self, which is the goal of its actions, [and] returns again with its task yet unfulfilled. But that [thinking-substance] which terminates in the discernment of the Self attains the goal of its actions, and, its task done, and its non-sight repressed, does not, since the cause of its bondage no longer exists, return again. Some [heterodox] person ridicules this [teaching of Isolation] with the anecdote[1] of the impotent man, 'He is told by his simple-minded wife, "O impotent, my wedded lord, my sister has a child; for what reason have not I?" He says to her, "When I am dead, I will beget thee a son."' Similarly, [the objector continues,] since this thinking [of the discernment], even while existing, does not make a repression of mind-stuff, what expectation is there that it will in the future make it cease to be? On this point one who is almost a master (*ācāryadeçīya*) says, "Is release anything but the cessation of the thinking-substance? When there is no cause of non-sight the thinking-substance ceases. And this non-sight which is the cause of bondage ceases when there is sight." Then release is nothing but the cessation of the thinking-substance. Why then is there this confusion of ideas of his[2] that is so much out of place?

In order to fix upon the fourth alternative he introduces the sūtra with the words, «But when there is a correlation of an individual consciousness with its own thinking-substance.» Individual (*praty-añc*) in the sense that it turns

[1] See Jacob, Maxims, II. 28, 2d ed.

[2] Two interpretations seem justified. 1. The whole passage to the end of the comment on this sūtra would be the statement of the *ācāryadeçīya*. And *asya* would refer to the nāstika. 2. The last two sentences would be that of the author of the comment and *asya* would refer to the *ācāryadeçīya*. The difference between these two would be that the latter teaches that release is only a cessation of mutations, whereas the comment teaches that release is resolution of the thinking-substance (*buddher vilaya*) into the primary cause.

(*añcati*) [or] gets back (*prati*) [or] in the opposite direction (*pratīpam*). A special correlation of each single Self with each single thinking-substance is the reason for the diversity between [individuals]. He recites the sūtra **24. The reason for this [correlation] is undifferentiated-consciousness** (*avidyā*). An objector says, 'Undifferentiated-consciousness is erroneous thinking. And the reason for this is the correlation of the Self with its own thinking-substance, just [as correlation is the reason] for experience and for liberation. For unless correlated with a thinking-substance, undifferentiated-consciousness (*avidyā*) does not arise. How then is undifferentiated-consciousness the reason for a particular kind of correlation?' In reply to this he says, «a subconscious-impression from erroneous thinking.» From undifferentiated-consciousness (*avidyā*), even when belonging to another creation and restricted together with its own mind-stuff, a subconscious-impression exists in the primary-cause. And the primary-cause pervaded with the subconscious-impression from this [undifferentiated-consciousness] sends forth the same kind of a thinking-substance for the sake of correlation with one Self or another. Similarly in successive previous creations. And since [the series] is from time without beginning, there is no flaw in the argument. For this very reason the Self at the time of [mundane] dissolution is not released, as he says, «erroneous thinking.» When [the thinking-substance] reaches the goal of its actions [that is] the discernment of the Self, then since there is no subconscious-impression from erroneous thinking, which is the cause of bondage, the thinking-substance does not return again, as he says, «But that.» Some heterodox person makes fun of this teaching with regard to Isolation by [telling] the anecdote of the impotent man. He tells the anecdote of the impotent man by the words, «simple-minded.» The word «reason (*artha*)» in the expression «for what reason» signifies a ground, because a motive is also a ground. He draws the analogy with the anecdote of the impotent man in the words, «Similarly since this.» 'This existing perception of the discernment of the difference between the aspects (*guṇa*) and the Self does not cause a repression of the mind-stuff; what expectation is there that the mind-stuff, when it together with its subliminal-impressions is restricted by virtue of the higher passionlessness, will cease to be? The point is that a thing has an effect when it exists; and not, when it does not exist.' With regard to this he gives a rebuttal by means of an opinion which partially [agrees], «On this point one who is almost a master.» One who is little short[1] of a master. A master, moreover, has his characteristic given in the declaration of the Vāyu,[2] "One who not only collects (*ācinoti*) the meaning of the books, but also makes the people steadfast in good conduct, and observes (*ācarate*) good conduct himself, he is a master (*ācārya*)." Release is nothing but the repression of the thinking-substance which has entered into mutations in the form of experience and of

[1] See Pāṇini v. 3. 67.

[2] See Vāyu Purāṇa lxix. 2; and Liṅga Purāṇa x. 15-16.

discriminative discernment. But there is no repression of the thinking-substance as such. This [repression], moreover, takes place only after the [thinking-substance] is established in the discriminative discernment which lasts up to the Rain-cloud of [Knowable] Things *(dharma-megha)*. Even though the thinking-substance abides as itself and nothing less, [still it does exist elsewhere]. He makes this clear by the words, «non-sight.» There is a repression of the thinking-substance when there is no non-sight [which is] the cause of bondage. And this non-sight [which is] the cause of bondage ceases as a result of sight. But as for the repression of sight, [that] is to be effected by the higher passionlessness. The point is, although the thinking-substance abides in itself and nothing less, there is release. Having cleared up the opinion which partially [agrees], he states his own opinion in the words, «Then release is nothing but the cessation of the thinking-substance.» An objector asks, 'Have you not already[1] said that, when seeing is repressed, there results soon after a repression of the mind-stuff itself. How then can [this repression] be the result of sight?' In reply to this he says, «Why then is there this confusion of ideas of his that is so much out of place?» The meaning is this. If we were to admit[2] that sight is the direct cause of the repression of the mindstuff, then we should be subject to this rebuke. But we take our stand upon the view that discriminative sight reaches its limit of perfection when the mind-stuff is repressed and when it is subservient to the abiding of the Self in his own form, according to its degree of perfection in the cultivation of restricted concentration. How then should we be subject to this rebuke?

The pain which is to be escaped and the cause of pain, the so-called correlation, together with their reasons, have been described. Next the higher escape (*hāna*) is to be described.

25. Since this [non-sight] does not exist, there is no correlation. This is the escape, the Isolation of the Seer.

Since this non-sight does not exist, there is no correlation of the thinking-substance and of the Self, in other words, a complete ending of bondage. This is the escape, the Isolation of the Seer, the unmixed state of the Self; in other words, the state in which [the Self] is not again correlated with aspects (*guṇa*). Upon the repression of the cause of pain there follows the ending of pain, the escape. Then the Self is said to be grounded[3] in his own self.

Having thus spoken of two divisions, with the intent to describe the third division, he introduces the sūtra with the words, «The pain which is to be

[1] See p. 162[3] (Calc. ed.).

[2] Reading °*kurvīmahi*, with the Bikāner MS. and the Ānandāçrama ed. (96[17]).

[3] Compare i. 3.

escaped.» 25. Since this [non-sight] does not exist, there is no correlation. This is the escape, the Isolation of the Seer. He explains the sūtra in the word, «this.» For even in the great mundane dissolution there is no correlation. For this reason he uses the word «complete.» The words «the ending of pain, the escape» show that this is a fulfilment of the purposes of the Self. The rest has nothing obscure.

Now what is the means of attaining escape?

26. The means of attaining escape is unwavering discriminative discernment.

Discriminative discernment[1] of the presented-idea of the difference between *sattva* and the Self. But this discernment wavers when erroneous perception is not repressed. When erroneous perception, reduced to the condition of burned seed, fails to reproduce itself (*vandhya-prasava*), then the flow of the presented-ideas of discrimination—belonging to the *sattva*, which is cleansed from *rajas* belonging to the hindrances, and which continues in the higher clearness [and] in the higher consciousness of being master—becomes stainless. This unwavering discriminative discernment is the means (*upāya*) of escape. After this, erroneous perception tends to become reduced to the condition of burned seed. And its failure to reproduce itself is the Path (*mārga*) to Release, the way-of-approach (*upāya*) to escape.

Wishing to denominate the fourth division as having the distinguishing-characteristic of the means of escape, he introduces the sūtra with the word «Now.» **26. The means of attaining escape is unwavering discriminative discernment.** Even by verbal communication and by inference there is discriminative discernment. This [kind of discriminative discernment] does not, however, repress emergence or the subliminal impressions from emergence, because these two latter follow a man who has both [the verbal-communication and the inference]. Accordingly in order to repress this [emergence] he says, «unwavering.» Wavering is erroneous perception; [unwavering] is free from that. What he means to say is this. He obtains discrimination by perception derived from something heard; and he makes this logically tenable (*vyavasthāpya*) [by ideas] derived from reasonings. The discriminative discernment, which in concentration has reached the utmost perfection of cultivation for a long time, uninterruptedly, and with earnest

[1] Discussed in Sāṁkhya Tattva Kāumudī on Kār. 51.

attention, [and which] has direct perception and has uprooted erroneous perceptions together with their subconscious impressions, [and which is thus] unwavering,—this is the means of escape. The rest of the comment is easy.

27. For him [there is] insight seven-fold and advancing in stages to the highest.

The words ‹for him› refer[1] to him[2] in whom discernment is re-uprisen. The word ‹seven-fold› means that the insight of the discriminating [yogin], after the removal of the defilements from the covering of impurity, when no other kind of presented-idea is generated in the mind-stuff, has just seven forms, as follows. 1. The thing to be escaped has been thought out; nor need [the yogin] think it out again. 2. The reasons for the thing to be escaped have dwindled away; nor need they dwindle away again. 3. The escape is directly perceived[3] by the concentration of restriction; [nor need anything beyond this be discovered]. 4. The means of escape in the form of discriminative discernment has been cultivated; [nor need anything beyond this be cultivated]. So this is the four-fold final release (*vimukti*), belonging to insight, which may be effected. But the final release of the mind-stuff is three-fold [as follows]. 5. The authority of the thinking-substance is ended. 6. The aspects (*guṇa*), like rocks fallen from the top of the mountain peak, without support, of their own accord, incline towards dissolution and come with this [thinking-substance] to rest. And when these [aspects] are quite dissolved, they do not cause growth again, because there is no impelling-cause. 7. In this stage the Self has passed out of relation with the aspects (*guṇa*), and, enlightened by himself and nothing more,

[1] See Nyāya-Koça, s.v. *pratyāmnāya* ख.

[2] The Vārttika insists that ‹for him› is rather ‹for it,› and that it refers to the means of escape. It denies that the reference is to the Self since there is no mention of the Self in the previous sūtra. Bālarāma replies that the Comment expressly wishes to avoid reference to the means of escape in the previous sūtra and that it says that ‹for him› means «him in whom discernment is re-uprisen.» This explanation is corroborated by the use of the words *vivekino bhavati*.

[3] See i. 3 and compare iii. 16, p. 218[4]; iii. 18-19, pp. 230[6] and 231[15]; iii. 26, p. 241[4]; iii. 51, p. 266[4]; and iii. 52, p. 269[8] (Calc. ed.).

is stainless and isolated.—The Self beholding this seven-fold insight advancing in stages to the highest is denominated fortunate (*kuçala*). Even when there is also the inverted generation of the mind-stuff the Self is said to be released [and] fortunate, because he has passed beyond the aspects (*guṇa*).

He describes the goal as such which belongs to discriminative discernment in the sūtra **27. For him [there is] insight seven-fold and advancing in stages to the highest.** He explains [the sūtra] by saying «‹for him.›» «In whom discernment is re-uprisen», that is to say, the yogin in whom discernment is present. The word «refer» means allude. One whose mind-stuff has reached the goal of discriminative discernment, since the defilement of impurity, which is the covering of mind-stuff, has been taken off, and because no other presented-idea arises, that is to say, no presented-idea belonging to emergence of *tamas* or of *rajas*,—in him there is the insight of just the seven forms which belong to the discriminating. There are different discernments according to the different objects.—The compound [advancing in stages to the highest] means those stages [or] states the end of which is perfection. Complete perfection [1] is that higher than which there is nothing. That insight [or] discriminative discernment [is advancing by stages] whose stages are advancing. These seven kinds of stages he takes up beginning with the word «as follows.» Of these [seven], from among the four stages which may be completed by a man's effort, he takes up the first with the words, «1. The thing to be escaped has been thought out.» Whatever is an effect of the primary-cause, all that is surely nothing but pain by reason of the pains due to mutations, to anxiety, and to subliminal impressions, and by reason of the opposition of the fluctuations,—and is therefore to be escaped. This has been thought out.—He shows what the advancement to the highest is in the words «nor need he think it out again.»—2. He describes the second in the words «dwindled away.» He tells what the advancement to the highest is by saying «nor . . . again.» —3. He describes the third in the words «directly perceived.» Even in the state conscious [of objects] I have discovered by perception the escape which I am to perfect in the concentration of restriction. We need to supply the words, 'nor need anything beyond this be discovered.'—4. He describes the fourth by saying «cultivated.» The cultivated is the perfected means of escape belonging to discriminative discernment. We need to supply the words, 'nor need anything beyond this be cultivated.' This the four-fold final release [or] completion may be effected. And in so far as it may be effected, it is shown to be included within the efforts [of a man]. Elsewhere the reading is *kāryavimukti*. This would be the final release of insight with respect to effects.—He describes the final release [2] of the mind-stuff which is not to be

[1] This word (*samprakarṣa*) does not occur elsewhere in the Comment nor elsewhere in Vācaspati's Explanation.

[2] Compare SBE. xxi. p. 31 (Lotus).

accomplished by effort, but which is to be accomplished subsequent to that which is to be attained by effort by saying «But the final release of the mind-stuff is three-fold.»—5. He describes the first [of these last three] in the words «5. The authority[1] of the thinking-substance is ended.» In other words, the two tasks (*kārya*) of experience and liberation have been done. —6. He describes the second [of these last three] in the words «The aspects.» —He shows what the advancement to the highest is in the words «And . . . they do not.»—7. He describes the third [of these last three] in the words «In this stage.» In this stage, even while alive, the Self is called fortunate [and] released, since [this] is his last body. Accordingly he says, «this.» He says that [the yogin] is not released in a figurative[2] sense [as merely being free from his last body] in the words, «inverted generation.» Even when his mind-stuff is resolved into the primary cause, he is said to be released and fortunate,[3] because he has passed beyond[4] the aspects (*guṇa*).

When discriminative discernment is perfected there is the means of escape. And there is no perfection without the means [of attaining it]. So this [topic of the means] is begun.

28. After the aids to yoga have been followed up, when the impurity has dwindled, there is an enlightenment of perception reaching up to the discriminative discernment.

The aids to yoga are the eight which are about to be enumerated. As the result of following them up there is a dwindling or cessation of the five-sectioned [ii. 3] misconception. Upon the dwindling of this follows the manifestation of focused thinking. And in proportion as the means [of attaining discriminative discernment are followed up], so the impurity is reduced to a state of attenuation. And in proportion as it dwindles, the enlightenment of perception also, in accordance with the degree of dwindling, increases. Now this same increase experiences a perfection reaching up to discrimi-

[1] Compare ii. 10, p. 120[2]; ii. 24, p. 162[2]; iii. 55, p. 274[6]. The phrase *carita-artha* occurs iii. 50, p. 265[2] (Calc. ed.).

[2] Compare *āupacārikam āiçvaryam* i. 24, p. 59[2] (Calc. ed.); and for definition of *āupacārikam* iii. 55, p. 274[5] (Calc. ed.). See also for use of word iv. 10, p. 286[6].

[3] Fortunate because he is free from attachment to the consequences of his own actions which are the cause [of bondage]. Because of this he is not bound. (*hetuṣu karmasu phalasañgarahitatvān na baddho bhavatīti kuçalatā.*)—This is the suggestion of the Pātañjala Rahasyam. For other instances see i. 24, p. 54[7]; ii. 9, p. 119[4]; iv. 30, p. 314[2] (Calc. ed.).

[4] Compare Bh. Gītā xiv. 20.

native discernment [or] up to the perception [ii. 26] which distinguishes between the aspects (*guṇa*) as such and the Self. The following up of the aids to yoga is the cause of discorrelation (*viyoga*) with impurity, just as an axe [is the cause of the disjunction (*viyoga*) of a tree] which is to be cut [from its root]. Now [the eight aids] are the cause of attaining discriminative discernment, just as right-living (*dharma*) is [the cause of getting] to happiness; in other ways it is not a cause.—Furthermore how many of these causes, according to the system, are there? Just nine, he[1] says, as follows, "Cause is nine-fold, rise [into consciousness] and permanence and manifestation and modification and presentation and attainment and disjunction and transformation and sustentation." Of these [nine], 1. The cause of rise [into consciousness], [is for instance] the central-organ [as the cause] of a mental-process (*vijñāna*); 2. the cause of permanence: [for instance] the fact that the Self has purposes [is the cause of the permanence] of the central-organ, just as food [is the cause of the permanence] of the body; 3. the cause of manifestation [is for instance] the shining [of the Self upon a fluctuation as the cause of the manifestation] of colour, just as the perception of colour [which is in the fluctuation, is the cause which manifests the shining of the Self]; 4. the cause of modification [is for instance] another object-of-sense [which modifies] the central-organ, just as fire [is a cause which modifies] food to be cooked; 5. the cause of presentation: [for instance] the thought of smoke [is the cause of the presentation] of the thought of fire; 6. the cause of attaining: [for instance] the following up of the aids to yoga [is the cause of attaining] discriminative discernment; 7. the cause of disjunction [is for instance] the same [following up as the cause which disjoins the Self] from impurity; 8. the cause of transformation is for instance the goldsmith [as the cause which transforms] the gold. Similarly if a single presented idea of a woman has the quality of infatuation, undifferentiated-consciousness (*avidyā*) [is the transforming cause]; if it has the quality of painfulness, hatred [is the transforming cause]; if it has the quality of pleasurability, passion

[1] Apparently this is a *saṁgrahaçloka*. Vijñāna Bhikṣu says *kārikoktāni nava kāraṇāni*.

[is the transforming cause]; if it has the quality of the detached attitude,[1] the recognition of the reality [is the transforming cause]; 9. the cause of sustentation [is for instance] the body [as the cause which sustains] the sense-organs, and these [organs as the cause sustaining] this [body], [and again] the great elements [as the sustaining cause] of bodies, and these [elements] reciprocally of all [elements], since human and animal and supernormal bodies depend upon each other.—So much then for the nine causes. And these so far as possible are also to be applied to other things. But as for the following up of the aids to yoga, it comes into play as cause in two ways only, [as the cause of disjunction and as the cause of attainment].

So much for the four divisions which have been described. Since discriminative discernment, the means of escape, which falls within these [four], cannot be perfected before [one follows up the means], as in the process of milking a cow: and since what is not perfected cannot be a means [to something else], he proceeds to describe the means for its perfection in the words, «When . . . perfected.» At this point the way by which the means-of-attainment, which are about to be mentioned, serve as a means for discriminative discernment is shown by the sūtra which begins with the word **28. . . . yoga** and ends with the word **discernment.** For the aids to yoga, according to circumstances, by seen or unseen[2] methods, cause the impurity to dwindle away. That misconception has five sections must be understood as a partial statement, since merit and demerit, in so far as they are causes of birth and of length-of-life and of kind-of-enjoyment, are also impure. The rest is easy. Since we find that causality is multiform, what kind of causality belongs to the following up of the aids to yoga? In reply to this he says, ‹After the aids to yoga have been followed up›. Since it disjoins the *sattva* of the thinking-substance from impurity it is the cause of disjunction from impurity. He gives a simile in the words, «just as an axe.» An axe disjoins the tree to be cut from its root. The *sattva* of the thinking-substance, when disjoined from impurity, causes one to attain to discriminative discernment. Just as merit is [the cause of attaining] pleasure, so the following up of the aids to yoga is the cause of attaining discriminative discernment. And [it is a cause] in no other form. So he says, «Now . . . discriminative insight.» Having heard the denial in the words «in other ways . . . not,» he asks, «Furthermore how many of these?» The answer is, «Just nine.» He shows what these are by a memorial verse (*kārikā*), «as follows, " . . . rise [into consciousness]."» He gives an illustration

[1] Read the tale in H. C. Warren: Buddhism in Translations, p. 298.

[2] A visible means would be *çāuca*; an invisible means would be *svādhyāya*.

of this in the words, «Of these [nine], 1. The cause of rise [into consciousness].» 1. The central organ is the cause of the origin of a mental process because it brings out a mental process from an indeterminable stage to the present stage. 2. The cause of permanence [is for instance] the fact that the Self has purposes. The central organ rising [into consciousness] out of the feeling-of-personality lasts only so long as the two-fold purpose of the Self is not fully accomplished. When the two kinds of purposes of the Self are accomplished it passes out of permanence. Therefore the fact that the Self has purposes is the cause of the permanence of the central organ which has risen [into consciousness] out of its own cause. He gives a simile in the words, «just as food is of the body.» 3. The efficient cause of perceptive thinking, the preparation (*saṁskriyā*) of an object either of itself or by a sense-organ, is manifestation. The cause of this manifestation [is for instance] the shining [of the Self upon a fluctuation as the cause of the manifestation] of colour. 4. The cause of modification [is for instance] another object-of-sense [which modifies] the central organ. For just so Mṛkaṇḍu, whose central organ had become concentrated, heard the fifth[1] note ripening upon the lute, and lifted up his eyes and beheld the heavenly-nymph Umlocā[2] in the perfection of beauty and loveliness, so that he lapsed from concentration, and his central organ became attached to her. He gives an instance bearing upon the same point in the words «just as fire.» For just as fire is the cause of the modification of a thing to be cooked, like rice, in such manner that a thing whose arrangement of parts was compressed becomes loosely conjoined in parts. 5. An object which is definitely existing is the cause of presentation [just as] the thought of smoke [is the cause of the presentation] of the idea of fire. What he means to say is this. The thought (*jñāna*) is that which is thought; and the thought of fire is fire and it is thought [that is, it is a descriptive compound].[3] 6. The cause of attainment. The natural action of effects belonging to causes which are independent is [what he means by] attainment. Occasionally there is an exception to this [action of the effects, which is the] non-attainment. Just so waters whose nature it is to flow down a slope (*nimna*) are held back by a dam. Similarly also in this case, the *sattva* of the thinking-substance, which is disposed to pleasure and brightness, is by its own nature the producer of pleasure and of discriminative discernment. This is attainment. Sometimes this [attainment], because it is held back, by reason of demerit or of *tamas*, does not follow. When by reason of merit or of following up the aids to yoga this [holding-back] is removed, then as a reason merely of the nature of the fluctuations of the thinking-substance's *sattva* when not held back by this [demerit or *tamas*], and in so far as it [this *sattva*] is the producer of this [pleasure and discernment], [this *sattva*] attains [them],

[1] See Raghuvaṅça ix. 26 and 47; Karpūramañjarī i. 16[a] (HOS. vol. 4, p. 228). The seventh note of the lute resembles the cooing of the koïl.

[2] Compare MBh. i. 4821 = i. 123. 64.

[3] The compound is not a genitive dependent (*ṣaṣṭhītatpuruṣa*), but rather a descriptive (*karmadhāraya*).

as[1] he will [iv. 3] say, "The efficient cause gives no impulse, but [the mutation] follows when the barrier to the evolving causes is cut, just as in the case of the peasant." Thus there is said to be a cause of attainment only with reference to the effect characterized as discriminative discernment. 7. In respect to anything subsidiary [to discriminative discernment] the same thing would be a cause of disjunction. So he says, «7. the cause of disjunction.» 8. He describes the cause of transformation in the words «the goldsmith . . . the gold.» In so far as the emphasis is upon the difference with respect to the gold, which is both different and not different from the bracelets and ear-rings and anklets, and in so far as the emphasis is upon the absence of difference [in the gold], which is not different from the bracelets and other things, there is a cause which transforms [the gold] from the bracelet [into something else]. And the goldsmith, who made the bracelet, in so far as he transforms the gold, which is [now] identical with the ear-ring, becomes the cause of transformation. Although fire [given as an example of 5. modification] is a cause of transformation with respect to the thing to be cooked, still since the difference between the substance[2] and the property, the rice-grains and the lump of rice, is not emphasized, therefore even though the properties come and go, still the substance persists. It is not possible therefore to say that [the fire] is a cause of transformation. For this reason it was said that the fire is a cause of modification. And accordingly there is no cross-division. Moreover it should not be supposed that the cause of transformation in the case of the substance is merely a difference in the arrangement of parts. For this would be inconsistent with the words «the goldsmith.» Having made clear what the cause of outer transformation is, he illustrates the inner [cause] in the words «Similarly if a single.» «Undifferentiated-consciousness (*avidyā*),» that is, such a thought as 'This girl is to be loved'. The very same presented idea of a woman becomes, in the case of Chāitra, in consequence of his complete infatuation, infatuated, that is to say, dejected. For he says to himself, 'Alas! that jewel of a woman has come into the hands of that lucky Maitra, not into the hands of me, bereft (*hīna*) of luck.' Similarly the rival wives' hatred of her is the cause of the painfulness of the idea of [this] woman. And again the passion of her husband Māitra for her is [the cause] of the quality of pleasurability in this same idea of the woman. The recognition of the reality, that the body of the woman is a congeries of skin and flesh and fat and bones and marrow, and is impure because of its [first] abode[3] [and] because of its origin and the rest, becomes, in the case of the discriminating, the cause of the detached attitude [that is to say] passionlessness. 9. The cause of sustentation is that which sustains the body and organs. And in the case of the body it is the organs. For the five breaths, beginning with the vital air, are functions

[1] Compare ii. 18, p. 144[2] (Calc. ed.).
[2] Compare Patañjali: Mahābhāṣya, vol. I, p. 7 middle (Kielhorn's ed.).
[3] Compare ii. 5, p. 111[1].

of the organs in general. For if they were not, the body would fall. Similarly in the case of the parts of the body, the flesh and the other [parts], there is the reciprocal relation of sustained and sustainer. Likewise the great elements, that is, the earth and the other [elements]; and these [elements] are in the reciprocal relation [of sustained and sustainer] in the case of bodies dwelling in the worlds of human beings or of Varuṇa or of the Sun or of the Wind (*gandhavaha*) or of the Moon. Thus in the case of earth, which has the qualities (*guṇa*) of odour and taste and colour and touch and sound, there are five great elements standing in the reciprocal relation of sustained and sustainer; in the case of water there are four; in the case of fire three; in the case of wind two. Furthermore animal and human and divine [bodies] stand in a relation of sustained and sustainer. Some one asks, 'How can this [reciprocal relation of sustained and sustainer] be so, if the bodies are not in the relation of holder and held?' He replies, «since human . . . depend upon each other.» For the human body is sustained by the use of the bodies of tame animals and of birds and of wild animals and of plants. Similarly bodies like the tigers [are sustained] by the use of the human bodies and those of tame and wild animals and of others. And again in the same way the body of the tame animal and of the bird and of the wild animal [is sustained] by the use of plants and similar things. Likewise the divine body [is sustained] by the use of sacrifices, of goats and deer and the flesh of grouse and ghee and baked-rice-cakes[1] and branches of mango (*sahakāra*) and handfuls-of-darbha grass (*prastara*), offered by human beings. In the same way the deity also sustains human beings and the rest by granting boons and showers. Thus the dependence is reciprocal. This is the meaning.—The rest is easy.

In this [sūtra] the aids to yoga are determined.

29. Abstentions and observances and postures and regulations-of-the-breath and withdrawal-of-the-senses and fixed attention and contemplation and concentration are the eight aids.

The following up of these must be performed in succession. And what they are we shall describe.

Now with the intent of excluding either a larger or a smaller number he determines what are the aids to yoga by saying «In this [sūtra] the aids to yoga are determined.» The sūtra begins with the word **29. Abstentions** and ends with the word **aids.** Practice and passionlessness and belief and energy and the rest [i. 20], both by reason of their own selves and in so far as they are indispensable, are also properly to be included among these same.

[1] Their use is described in Āpastamba-Yajña-Paribhāṣā-Sūtra xcix and cxxix (SBE., vol. xxx), and their preparation in Çatapatha-Brāhmaṇa i. 2. 2. 1 f. And again in Manu vi. 11 and vii. 21.

Of these [eight]—

30. Abstinence[1] from injury and from falsehood and from theft and from incontinence and from acceptance of gifts are the abstentions.

Of these [five] abstinence from injury means the abstinence from malice towards all living creatures in every way and at all times. And the other abstentions and observances are rooted in it. In so far as their aim is the perfection of it, they are taught in order to teach it. And in this sense[2] it has been said, "Surely this sam brahman in proportion as he desires to take upon himself many courses-of-action,[3] in this proportion refraining from heedlessly giving injury, fulfils [the abstention of] abstinence from injury in order to give it the full character of its spotlessness." Abstinence-from-falsehood (*satya*) means speech and mind such as correspond to the object-intended; and speech and mind corresponding to what is seen or inferred or heard.[4] If speech is spoken in order that one's own knowledge may pass to some one else, it should not be deceitful or mistaken or barren of information; [then it would be abstinence from falsehood]. It should be used for the service of all; not for the ruin of creatures. And even when used thus, should it be only for the ruin of creatures, it would not be an abstinence from falsehood; it would be nothing less than wrong. In so far as there would be a false kind of merit [and] a resemblance of merit, it would become the worst of evils. Therefore let [the yogin] consider [first] what is good[5] for all creatures and [then] speak with abstinence-from-falsehood.—Theft[6] is the unauthorized (*açāstrapūrvaka*) appropriation of things-of-value from another. While abstinence-from-theft, when free from coveting, is the refusal to do this.—Continence is control of the hidden organ of generation.—Abstinence-from-acceptance-of-gifts is abstinence-from-appropriating objects, because one sees the disadvantages in acquir-

1 This sūtra and the following are quoted in Gāuḍapāda's Bhāṣya on Sāṁkhya-kārikā xxiii.

2 Similar plans of life in Bhāg. Pur. xi, second half.

3 JAOS. Proceedings, xi. 229.

4 Compare Liñga Purāṇa viii. 13.

5 The principle would seem to be that a speech which does not harm any one and which does some good, although untrue, must be regarded as true. See Manu iv. 138 and viii. 138.

6 Compare Liñga Purāṇa viii. 15.

ing them or keeping them or losing them or in being attached to them or in harming them. These then are the abstentions.

Having announced the aids [to yoga] of which the first are the abstentions and the observances, he introduces a sūtra which specifies the abstentions by saying «of these [eight].» The sūtra begins with the words 30. Abstinence from injury and ends with the word abstentions. He describes the aid to yoga [called] abstinence from injury by saying, «in every way.» He praises such abstinence-from-injury with the words, «And the other.» «Rooted in it» would mean that, even if these are performed without observing abstinence from injury, they are as if they had not been performed, since they are quite fruitless. This is the meaning. The following up of them has nothing as its aim but the perfection of this [abstinence-from-killing]. 'If abstinence-from-killing has the others rooted in it, how can it be that they aim at the perfection of the abstinence-from-injury?' To this he replies, «in order to teach it.» «Perfection» [in other words] the rise into consciousness of a thought. An objector asks, 'This may be true. But if the others exist for the sake of knowing abstinence from injury, what need of them, since this thought comes from the other source?' In reply he says, «its spotlessness.» If the others were not followed up, abstinence-from-injury would be defiled by falsehood and other [vices]. With reference to this same point he tells of a concurrent opinion of those-who-have-the-tradition (*agamika*) in the words, «And in this sense it has been said.» Easy.—He gives the distinguishing characteristic of abstinence-from-falsehood in the words, «speech and mind such as correspond to the object-intended.» The word such (*yathā*) raises an expectation which is fulfilled by the words «corresponding to what is seen.» He brings this into connexion with the correlated word «corresponding-to (*tathā*)» in the expression «speech and mind corresponding to.» [This should be,] whenever there is a desire to say [something]. [If spoken] otherwise [than as seen], it is not abstinence-from-falsehood. This is stated with an explanation in the words «to some other person.» In order that knowledge thereof may pass to some one else, speech is spoken [or] uttered to produce knowledge similar to one's own knowledge. If it is not deceitful [or] the cause of deceit, [it is abstinence-from-falsehood]. Just as when Droṇa the Master [MBh. vii. chap. 190] asked Yudhiṣṭhira [the king] with regard to the death of his own son Açvatthāman, 'Venerable sir (*āyuṣman*), thou who art rich in truth, has Açvatthāman been slain?' And he having in mind the elephant who had the corresponding name said, 'It is true, Açvatthāman is slain.' This is an answer which does not make Yudhiṣṭhira's own knowledge pass to [the other person]. For his own knowledge derived from the sense-organ[1] had as its object the slaying of the elephant and this [knowledge] was not passed [to Droṇa]. But quite another knowledge, that of the slaying of the latter's son, was formed [in Droṇa's mind].—«Or mistaken» means due to a mistake, either

[1] **Reading *indriya-janmā* with the Bikāner MS. and the Bombay and Poona editions.**

at the time when one desires to say something, or at the time of determining what the object-to-be-perceived is.—«Barren of information» is barren as regards information, as for instance an outlandish tongue is barren of information to Aryans; or it might be purposeless, as for instance speech the utterance of which is not meant to be uttered. For in this [latter case], although one's own knowledge does pass to the other person, still it is exactly the opposite of making [knowledge] pass [to another], because it was not purposed.[1] An abstinence-from-falsehood even when it has these distinguishing characteristics, if it results in injury to another, would be a false kind of abstinence-from-falsehood, but would not be abstinence-from-falsehood, as he says in the words, «If it.» For example, one who practises austerities in abstinence-from-falsehood, when asked by robbers which way the rich merchant had gone, told the way the rich merchant had gone. «It should be used,» that is, uttered. The rest is easy.—Since an [explanatory] negative idea depends on that of the positive he explains the distinguishing characteristic of theft by saying, «Theft is the unauthorized.» Here the generic idea is characterized by a qualification. This is the meaning. Since verbal and bodily operations are preceded by mental operations, it is the operation of mind, because it is dominant, that is mentioned in the words, «free from coveting.»—He tells what continence is in the word «hidden.» For even if his organ of generation is held in control, still if he become attached at the sight of a woman or upon [hearing] her talk or upon touching her limbs which are the seats of Kandarpa, he has no continence. So to exclude this case he says, «the hidden organ.» Other organs also that are very ardent for this [woman] are to be watched.—He tells what abstinence-from-acceptance-of-gifts is by saying, «objects.» He mentions the disadvantage due to attachment to these [objects] in the words [ii. 15], "Since passions increase because of application to enjoyments, and the skill of the organs also increases." The disadvantage which is characteristic of injury is also expressed by the words,[2] "Enjoyment is impossible unless one has harmed some living creatures." Although obtained without effort, objects if unauthorized have disadvantages when one acquires them, since the acquisition of such things is censured. And even authorized objects, when acquired, are evidently disadvantageous, in that they must be kept and so on. Therefore abstinence-from-acceptance-of-gifts is the refusal to appropriate them.

Now as for these [five abstentions]—

31. When they are unqualified by species or place or time or exigency and when [covering] all [these] classes—[under these circumstances exists] the Great Course-of-conduct.

Of these [five], abstinence-from-injury is qualified in respect of species as follows, a catcher of fish does injury to fishes only and

[1] Mṛcchak. (Nirṇ. Sāg. edition), p. 238⁸. [2] Compare ii. 15, p. 132⁸ (Calc. ed.).

to nothing else.—The same is qualified in respect of place, as when one says, 'I will not slay in a holy place.'—The same is qualified in respect of time, as when one says, 'I will not slay on the fourteenth day [of the lunar fortnight] nor on a day of good omen. —The same, in the case of one who refrains from [these] three is qualified in respect of exigency, as when one says, 'For the sake of gods and brahmans and not otherwise I will slay.' Likewise also in the case of the warrior who says, 'In battle only [I will do] injury, and nowhere else.' Abstinence-from-injury and the other [abstinences] unqualified by these species or times or places or exigencies must be kept when [covering] no less than all [these] cases. ‹In all [these] classes› means with regard to all [these] objects. Without exceptions in no less than all [these] classes—this is what is meant by speaking of the Great Course-of-conduct[1] when [covering] all [these] stages.

«Now as for these.» The sūtra begins with the words **31 . . . by species** and ends with the words **Great Course-of-conduct**. ‹When [covering] all [these] classes› means of those which are found in all [these] stages which are characterized as being species and the other [three stages]. The words «Abstinence-from-injury and the other [abstinences]» mean that the definition [of the Great Course-of-conduct] must be asserted in the case of the other abstentions also. The Comment is easy.

32. Cleanliness and contentment and self-castigation and study and devotion to the Içvara are the observances.

Of these [five], cleanliness is produced by earth or by water or the like, and by the consumption and other [requirements] with regard to pure sacrificial food. This is outer. Inner [cleanliness] is the washing away of the blemishes of the mind-stuff.—[To practise] contentment means not to covet more than the means at hand.—Self-castigation is the bearing of extremes, hunger and thirst, cold and heat, standing and sitting, stock-stillness and formal stillness, and, according to usage, courses-of-conduct such as mortifications (*kṛcchra*)[2] and lunar fasts[3] and rigid penances.[4]—Study is the

[1] Compare Manu xii. 1-6.
[2] Manu xi. 106, &c.
[3] Manu vi. 20, &c.
[4] Manu xi. 213, &c.

recital of books that treat of release or the repetition of the syllable of adoration (*praṇava*).—Devotion to the Içvara[1] is the offering up of all actions to the Supreme Teacher. "He who rests in himself, for whom the network of perverse-considerations (*vitarka*) has been destroyed, whether resting upon a bed or on a seat, or wandering upon a road, would behold the destruction of the seed of the round-of-rebirths, would be permanently released, would participate in deathless delights." With regard to which this has been said, [i. 29], "Thereafter comes the right knowledge of him who thinks in an inverse way, and the removal of obstacles."

He expounds cleanliness and the other observances. The sūtra begins with the word **32. Cleanliness** and ends with the word **observances.** He explains [the sūtra] by saying «cleanliness.» The words «or the like» are meant to include cow-dung and such things. Pure sacrificial food is the barley [mixed with] cow's urine and the rest [eaten at the Çrāvaṇī festival]. There is a consumption and other [requirements] with regard to this [food]. «The other requirements» are meant to cover regulation of the dimensions and of the number of these morsels. Instead of saying 'produced by the consumption and other requirements with regard to pure sacrificial food' he says «and by the consumption and other [requirements] with regard to pure sacrificial food.» For in the effect the cause is supposed figuratively to exist.—The «stains of the mind-stuff» such as arrogance and pride and jealousy; the removal of this is cleanliness of the central-organ.—«Contentment» is the desire to take no more than is necessary for the general maintenance of life, because it follows the renunciation[2] of what had been before one's own property. This is its distinction [from abstinence-from-acceptance-of-gifts].—«Stock-stillness» is the absence of any indication of one's intention even by signs; «formal stillness» is merely refraining from speech.—In the phrase «for whom the network of perverse-considerations has been destroyed» the words «perverse-considerations» will be [later ii. 33] described. And doubts and misconceptions should be added [as parts of the network]. To this extent his intention is said to be pure.—These abstentions and observances are also described in the Vishṇu Purāṇa [vi. 7. 36-37],[3] "Wishing to reduce the mind to its proper state he should resort to abstinence from incontinence and from injury and from falsehood and from theft and from acceptance-of-gifts. A man whose self is curbed should practise study and cleanliness and contentment and self-castigation. He should also make his mind incline towards the higher Brahman. These abstentions together with

[1] Compare ii. 1, p. 106[6] (Calc. ed.). [2] Illustrated in Chānd. Up. i. 10. 1-11.
[3] See also Nāradīya Purāṇa xlvii. 12-14.

the observances are declared to be five each. They give a special result when they are approached with a desire [for some special thing], and in the case of persons free from all desires they yield final release."

As for these abstentions and observances,

33. If there be inhibition by perverse-considerations (*vitarka*), **there should be cultivation of the opposites.**

Whenever [in the mind] of this brahman [practising the abstentions and observances] injuries and similar [faults] arise as perverse-considerations, such as for instance, 'I will kill him who hurts me; I will also lie; I will also appropriate his money; and I will commit adultery with his wife; and I will also make myself master of his property.' Thus inhibited by the blazing fever of perverse-considerations, let him cultivate the opposites of these. Let him ponder, 'Baked upon the pitiless coals of the round-of-rebirths, I take my refuge in the rules (*dharma*) for yoga by giving protection[1] to every living creature. I myself after ridding myself of perverse-considerations am betaking myself to them once more, like a dog. As a dog to his vomit, even so I betake myself to that of which I had rid myself.' Other similar [inhibitions of perverse-considerations] should be applied in the other sūtras also [upon the aids to yoga].

Since "good things[2] are full of difficulties", he introduces a sūtra whose object is to give advice which will prevent the possibility of exceptions to these [abstentions and observances]. So he says, «As for these abstentions and observances.» The sūtra, 33. If there be inhibition by perverse-considerations, there should be cultivation of the opposites. In the Comment upon perverse-considerations there is nothing at all that seems obscure.

34. Since perverse-considerations such as injuries, whether done or caused to be done or approved, whether ensuing upon greed or anger or infatuation, whether mild or moderate or vehement, find their unending consequences in pain and in lack of thinking, there should be the cultivation of their opposites.

[1] This phrase occurs in Manu viii. 303.

[2] Compare *aho vighnavatyaḥ prārthitārtha-siddhayaḥ*, Çākuntala, Act iii, near end; and χαλεπὰ τὰ καλά Repub. 435 C, 497 D.

Of these [considerations], first of all, injury, since it is done or caused to be done or approved, is three-fold. Moreover, each of these is three-fold, in so far as there is greed [such as] desire for the meat or for the skin, or in so far as there is anger as when a man thinks he has been 'hurt by that man', or in so far as there is infatuation as when a man thinks [that what he is doing] 'will be merit for me'. Again, since greed and anger and infatuation are three-fold as being mild and moderate and vehement, there are thus seven-and-twenty varieties of injuries. Yet again, since [these are] gentle and moderate and extreme [these are] three-fold as follows, gently mild and moderately mild and keenly mild; similarly, gently moderate and moderately moderate and keenly moderate; likewise, gently keen and moderately keen and vehemently keen. Thus injury is of one-and-eighty varieties. It is, however, innumerable because of the varieties due to specifications (*niyama*) and to options (*vikalpa*) and to aggregations (*samuccaya*), due to the fact that the varieties[1] of those-who-breathe-the-breath-of-life are innumerable. In the same manner [the classification] is to be applied to falsehood and to the other [crimes]. Now since these perverse considerations have endless consequences in pain and in lack of thinking, one should cultivate their opposites. [In other words], there is a cultivation of those things the endless consequences of which are pain and a lack of thinking.—And to continue, he who commits an injury first of all reduces the strength of the victim, then causes him pain by falling upon him with a knife or something of the kind, [and] afterwards even deprives him of life. When once he has taken away [the victim's] strength, his own animate or inanimate aids[2] begin to have their strength dwindle away. As a result of causing pain, he himself experiences pain in hells and in [the bodies of] animals and of departed spirits and in other [forms]. As a result of uprooting [the victim] from life, he himself continues from moment to moment at the very point of departure from life. And even while wishing for death he

[1] Rāghavānanda in the Patañjala-Rahasyam attributes this quotation to Pakṣilasvāmin. It is found in Vātsyāyana's Bhāṣya (Vizian. ed. p. 1[7]); and quoted, with a change in the order of words, by the Udyotakāra in the Nyāya-Vārttika (Bibl. Ind. p. 9[10]).

[2] See Vācaspati on ii. 15, p. 114[6] (Calc. ed.).

pants laboriously since the fruition[1] of pain is to be felt in a fruition which has[2] a limit [in time]. Furthermore, even if [the effects of] injury could be somehow done away[3] by merit, even then, if he obtained happiness, it would be [on condition that] his length-of-life be short.—In the same way, so far as possible, [the classification] is to be applied to lying and to the other [violations of the abstentions]. Thus pondering on that same [painful consequence] of perverse considerations, which is inevitable (*anugata*) and undesired, the yogin should not devote his central organ to perverse considerations. As a result of the cultivation of the opposites, the perverse considerations become things that may be escaped.

With the intent to describe what the cultivation of the opposites is, he states the different natures and kinds and causes and properties and results of the contrary-considerations, as well as the objects for the meditation on the opposites in the sūtra which begins with the words **34. . . . perverse-considerations** and ends with the words **cultivation of their opposites.** He explains [the sūtra] with the words, «Of these . . . injury.» Because the varieties of those-who-breathe-the-breath-of-life are innumerable, specifications and options and aggregations are possible with regard to injuries and the other [crimes]. In this situation, because there is a preponderance of *tamas*, as a result of wrong living, a lack of thinking also arises characterized by the four kinds of misconception [ii. 5]. So it is that these perverse-considerations also result in lack of thinking [as well as arise out of undifferentiated-consciousness]. For the cultivation of their opposites is precisely [the thought of] the endless consequences in pain and in lack of thinking. By virtue of this there is a revulsion from these. This same cultivation of the opposites he makes clear by the words, «of the victim.» The victim is some tame animal. «Strength» is the energy which is the cause of the functional activity of the body. [This] he first reduces by tying him to a sacrificial post. For in this way the animal loses his spirit. The rest is very clear.

When [the perverse considerations] become for this [yogin] unsuitable for generation, then the power caused by this fact becomes indicative of the yogin's perfection. For example,

[1] The word *vipāka* is omitted in the Bikāner and the two Kāshmīr and several other good MSS.

[2] Compare the discussion in ii. 13, especially p. 127 (Calc. ed.).

[3] The better reading is *avāpagata*. In this case, the injury would not be independent fruit since it would be cast away as a portion of the sacrifice.

35. As soon as he is grounded in abstinence from injury, his presence begets a suspension of enmity.

[This] occurs on the part of all living creatures.[1]

The abstentions and observances have been described, and the escape from the exceptions to these, the perverse considerations, as a result of the cultivation of the opposites has been described. Now he makes clear the signs indicative of thorough knowledge of perfection in these various abstentions and observances which results from practice in these [latter]. By a thorough knowledge of which signs [the yogin] accomplishes what is to be done in each particular case and acts with reference to what is yet to be done, as he says, «When . . . for this [yogin].» **35. As soon as he is grounded in abstinence from injury, his presence begets a suspension of enmity.** Even [enemies] whose hostility is everlasting[2] like horse and buffalo, mouse and cat, snake and mongoos, in the presence of the Exalted [yogin] who is grounded in abstinence from injury, conform themselves to his mind-stuff and renounce altogether their hostility.

36. As soon as he is grounded in abstinence from falsehood, actions and consequences depend upon him.

If [the yogin] says to a man (*iti*), 'Be[3] thou right-living,' the man becomes right-living. If he expresses the wish (*iti*) 'Attain thou heaven,' the man attains heaven. What he says (*vāk*) comes true.

35. As soon as he is grounded in abstinence from falsehood, actions and consequences have their residence [in him]. Actions mean right-living and wrong-living; and consequences of these are such things as heaven and hell. Dependence upon the sense that these same depend upon him. Having dependence upon him is the abstract state of this [dependence]. Since such a thing happens in the case of the Exalted One's speech, [the Comment] says that actions depend upon him by saying «right-living.» He says that consequences depend upon him by saying «heaven.» «Comes true» signifies that it is not prevented.

37. As soon as he is grounded in abstinence from theft, all jewels approach him.

From all directions jewels approach to be his.

37. As soon as he is grounded in abstinence from theft, all jewels approach him. Easily understood.

[1] Compare Raghuvança ii. 55, xiii. 50, xiv. 79 and Kirāta iii. 2.

[2] See Pāṇini ii. 4. 9 with the illustrations from the Kāçikāvṛtti and the Siddhānta-kāumudī. Compare also Bāṇa's Kādambarī p. 93[8] (Parab's ed.) and Çākuntala (Nir. Sāg. ed.) p. 23, two lines up.

[3] Whitney: Grammar 924.

38. As soon as he is grounded in abstinence from incontinence, he acquires energy.

By the acquisition of which the yogin increases [his] unhindered[1] qualities. And when he is perfected he is able to transfer [his] thinking to [his] pupils.

38. As soon as he is grounded in abstinence from incontinence, he acquires energy. Energy [that is] power. By the acquisition of which he increases [or] accumulates qualities, such as minuteness, which are unhindered [that is] which have not been hindered. And when perfected he is endowed with the eight perfections of which the first is [called] *tāra*[2] and also by other names such as Reasoning (*ūha*). He is able to transfer his thinking which relates to the aids to yoga to his pupils [or] disciples.

39. As soon as he is established in abstinence-from-acceptance-of-gifts, a thorough illumination upon the conditions of birth—

—Becomes his. 'Who was I? How was I? Or what [can] this birth be? Or how [can] this [birth] be? Or what shall we become? Or how shall we become?' Such a desire to know his own condition in former and later and intermediate times becomes of itself fulfilled[3] for him. These when he is established in the abstentions are the perfections.

39. As soon as he is established in abstinence-from-acceptance-of-gifts, a thorough illumination upon the conditions of birth. Birth is [coming into] relation with a body and with sense-organs and the rest which are particularized as belonging to some class [of beings]. There is a thorough illumination, a direct perception of the conditions [of birth] [or] of what kinds [of birth]. That is to say, a thorough knowledge of a quiescent or uprisen or indeterminable birth together with its form [of experience]. He desires to know the past in the words, «'Who was I?'» He desires to know the different details as to origin and persistence of this same [birth] in the words, «'How was I?'» He desires to know what the present birth itself is in the words, «'Or what?'» Is the body made directly of elements, or is it nothing but an aggregation of elements, or is it other than these? Here also the words 'Or how' might be supplied.[4] Elsewhere this is the actual reading. He desires to know the future in the words, «'Or what shall we become?'» Here again the words 'Or how' are [to be] supplied.[4] «Such . . . for him.» The former [time] is past time;

[1] See Manu xii. 28. [2] Sāṁkhya-kārikā li. [3] The Vārt. says *viçiṣṭā bhavati*.
[4] In the text of Vācaspati *kathaṁ vā* apparently was lacking.

the later is future; the intermediate is the present. The existence of the self in these is a relation with a body and the rest. There is a desire to know this and from desire comes knowledge according to the maxim, "He who desires anything, does that same thing."

We will speak with regard to observances.

40. As a result of cleanliness there is disgust at one's own body and no intercourse with others.

As soon as there is disgust with his own body, he has begun cleanliness. Seeing the offensiveness of the body,[1] he is no longer attached to the body and becomes an ascetic (*yati*). Moreover there is no intercourse with others. Perceiving the true nature of the body, desirous of escaping[2] even his own body, even after he has washed it with earth and water and other [substances], not seeing any purity in the body, how could he have intercourse with the bodies of others absolutely unhallowed as they are?

40. As a result of cleanliness, there is disgust at one's own body and no intercourse with others. By this [sūtra] it is told what is indicative of perfection in outer cleanliness.

Furthermore [as other results],

41. Purity of *sattva* and gentleness and singleness-of-intent and subjugation of the senses and fitness for the sight of the self—

The word 'arise' completes the sentence. As a result of cleanliness there is purity of *sattva*; therefrom [it acquires] gentleness; from this [it acquires] singleness-of-intent; therefrom [it acquires] subjugation of the senses; and from this fitness for the sight of the self is acquired by the *sattva* of the thinking-substance. So to this [last] there is access, as a result of his being established in cleanliness.

He tells what is indicative of inner perfection by saying «Furthermore.» **41. Purity of *sattva* and gentleness and singleness-of-intent and subjugation of the senses and fitness for the sight of the self.** When the defilements of

[1] Compare ii. 5, p. 113[3] (Calc. ed.). [2] See Liñga Pur. viii. 32-33.

mind-stuff are washed away, the mind-stuff comes-forth-to-sight undefiled. And as a result of freedom from defilement there is gentleness [or] transparency of *sattva.* In the transparent [*sattva*] there is singleness-of-intent. Therefrom, by the subdual of the central-organ, there results the subdual of the sense-organs which are dependent on the central-organ. After that the *sattva* of the thinking-substance becomes fit for the sight of the self.

42. As a result of contentment there is an acquisition of superlative pleasure.

And in this sense it has been said,[1] "What constitutes the pleasure of love in this world and what the supreme pleasure of heaven are both not to be compared with the sixteenth part of the pleasure of dwindled craving (*tṛṣṇā*)."

42. As a result of contentment there is an acquisition of superlative pleasure. Superlative is that beyond which nothing more excellent exists. As was said by Yayāti[2] when he conferred youth upon his [father] Puru, "The wise man, casting entirely away that craving which is hard for the strong-willed to cast off and which even in the aged ages not, is filled quite full with pleasure and nothing else." This same he shows by the words beginning «What constitutes the pleasure of love.»

43. Perfection in the body and in the organs after impurity has dwindled as a result of self-castigation.

Self-castigation in the very act of completing itself destroys the defilement from the covering of impurity. As a result of the removal of the defilement of the covering of this [impurity] there is perfection of the body, such as atomization [iii. 45]; likewise perfection of the organs, such as hearing and seeing at a distance [that is, telepathy].

He tells what is indicative of perfection of self-castigation. **43. Perfection in the body and in the organs after impurity has dwindled as a result of self-castigation.** Whatever covering has the characteristics of impurity, has the qualities and so on which are effects of the *tamas.* «Such as atomization» would be greatness or lightness or getting [to any place]. Easy.

[1] MBh. Çāntiparvan 174. 46 and Vāyu Pur. xciii. 101 and Liñga Pur. lxvii. 23. Compare Bhartṛhari Vāir. Çat. 49 and Dhvanyāloka, p. 176 (Kāvyamālā ed.).

[2] Viṣṇu Pur. iv. 10. 12 and Vāyu Pur. xciii. 99 and Liñga Pur. lxvii. 20. Compare also MBh. i. 89-91 = 3577 ff.

44. As a result of study there is communion with the chosen deity.

Gods and sages and perfected men come within the range of vision of [the yogin] who has the disposition to study; and are helpful to his work.

He tells what is indicative of perfection in study. **44. As a result of study there is communion with the chosen deity.** Easy.

45. Perfection of concentration as a result of devotion to the Içvara.

One whose whole nature is surrendered [1] to the Içvara has perfection of concentration. By which [concentration] he knows as the thing really is (*avitatham*) all that he desires to know, in other places and in other bodies and in other times. Thereafter his insight sees into things as they are (*yathābhūtam*).

45. Perfection of concentration . . . of devotion to the Içvara. And it should not be urged that if, only as a result of devotion to the Içvara, concentration conscious [of objects] has its perfection, there is no need of the seven [other] aids. Because these [seven] by subsidiary activity, both seen and unseen, are of service to the perfection of devotion to the Içvara, and at the same time to perfection of concentration conscious [of objects]. Just as by a separation of correlations [2] curds fulfil the purposes of the sacrifice and also fulfil the purposes of men. Thus if this is so, [one should not say] that fixed-attention and contemplation and concentration are not the immediate [3] aids [to yoga]. Because it is clear that these [three] (*asya*) are immediate aids, in so far as for the perfection of [concentration] conscious [of an object] these [three] have the same object as [concentration] conscious [of an object], whereas the other aids [which have the Içvara as object] have an object which is not this. For the devotion to the Içvara has also the Içvara as its object, and has not as its object that which is to be consciously known. Accordingly this is a mediate aid. Thus all is cleared up.—The words «sees into» are intended to show the etymology of the word «insight.»

[1] See ii. 1.

[2] See Jāimini Mīmāṅsā-sūtra iv. 3. 5. 2.

[3] Bālarāma defines *antarañga* by the words 'whatever happens immediately next to a thing is the *antarañga* of it'. Thus devotion to the Içvara is the last cause of the effect (*antarañgasādhana*) of concentration conscious of an object.

The abstentions and observances together with their perfections have been described. We have the following to say of the postures [1] and the other [aids to yoga]. In this [sūtra, it is said]—

46. Stable-and-easy posture.

For example, the lotus-posture and the hero-posture and the decent-posture and the mystic-diagram and the staff-posture and [the posture] with the rest and the bedstead, the seated curlew and the seated elephant and the seated camel, the even arrangement, the stable-and-easy—also called, as-is-easiest—and others of the same kind.

He introduces the next sūtra with the words «The abstentions and observances have been described. We have the following to say of the postures and the other [aids to yoga].» In this [sūtra, it is said] **46. Stable-and-easy posture.** Stable means motionless. That posture which is easy, which brings ease is the one intended by the sūtra. The word *āsana* means either that whereon a man sits [that is, a seat] or the manner in which he sits [that is, a posture]. The lotus-posture is well known.[2]—A man settled down (*sthitasya*) rests one foot on the ground and the other is placed over the partially contracted knee, —this is hero-posture.—Bringing the soles of his feet near to each other close to the scrotum, he should make a hollow of his hands and place them over it in the shape of a tortoise,—this is the decent-posture.—Inserting the contracted left foot into the space between the right shin and thigh and inserting the contracted right foot into the space between the left shin and thigh,—that is the mystic diagram.—Sitting down with the great-toes placed together and with ankles placed together and stretching out upon the ground shins and thighs and feet placed together, let him practise the staff-posture.—Because there is a use of the yogic table[3] (*yoga-paṭṭaka*), this is [the posture] with the rest.—Lying down with the arms stretched around the knees is the bedstead.—The curlew and the other seats may be understood by actually seeing a curlew and the other animals seated. — The two feet are contracted and pressed against each other at the heels and at the tips of

[1] Liṅga Pur. viii. 87–90.

[2] An illustration of this by a native hand is given in Richard Schmidt's Fakire und Fakirthum, to face p. 12; hero-posture faces p. 28; decent-posture faces p. 16, but diverges from this description in its details; mystic-diagram faces p. 24. The order of the illustrations does not correspond to the order of this book, and there is a vast number of fantastic and repellent additions.

[3] Bālarāma says that this yogic table is a special kind of support for the arms of a yogin who is about to practise concentration. It is made of wood and is well known among *uddāsin* by the name of 'changan'.

the feet,—this is the even arrangement.—That arrangement in which one finds entire (*sidhyati*) stability and ease,—this is the posture that is stable-and-easy. This is the one from among these [postures] which is approved by the Exalted Author of the sūtras. An elaboration of this is given in the words, «as-is-easiest.»

47. By relaxation of effort or by a [mental] state-of-balance with reference to Ananta—

—[A posture] results. With these words the sentence is completed. When efforts cease the posture is completed, so that there is no agitation of the body. Or the mind-stuff comes into a balanced-state with reference to Ananta[1] and produces the posture.

Having stated what the postures are, he tells what are the means of attaining them. **47. By relaxation of effort or by a [mental] state-of-balance with reference to Ananta.** A natural effort sustaining the body is not the cause of this kind of posture which is to be taught as an aid to yoga. For if its cause were such, the preaching of it would be purposeless in that it could be naturally perfected. Therefore this natural effort does not accomplish this kind of posture which is to be taught and is contrary [to it]. For in so far as this [natural posture] is the cause of an arbitrarily chosen posture it is the destroyer of the specific kind of posture. Consequently a man, practising the specific posture as taught, should resort to an effort which consists in the relaxation of the natural effort. Otherwise the posture taught cannot be accomplished.—«Or . . . with Ananta,» the Chief of Serpents, who upholds the globe of the earth upon his thousand very steadfast hoods,—[with him] the mind-stuff comes into a balanced state and produces the posture.

48. Thereafter he is unassailed by extremes.

As a result of mastering the postures he is not overcome by the extremes, by cold and heat and by the other [extremes].

He tells what is indicative of complete mastery of postures by saying **48. Thereafter he is unassailed by extremes.** The Comment explains itself by a mere reading. Posture is also described in the Vishṇu Purāṇa [vi. 7. 89], "Having assumed a posture so as to possess the excellences of the decent-posture and the other [postures]."

[1] Compare Bh. Gītā x. 28. Ananta is Vāsuki, the Lord of Serpents. See also MBh. i. 35. 5 ff.

49. When there is this [stability of posture], the restraint of breath cutting off the flow of inspiration and expiration [follows].

After the mastery[1] of posture [follows the restraint of the breath]. Inspiration is the sipping in of the outer wind; expiration is the expulsion of the abdominal wind. Restraint of the breath is the cutting off of the flow of these two, the absence of both kinds.

After describing [postures], he shows that these precede restraint of the breath and tells the distinguishing characteristic of this [restraint of the breath]. **49. When there is this [stability of posture], the restraint of breath cutting off the flow of inspiration and expiration [follows].** In the case of emission (*recaka*) and inhalation (*pūraka*) and suspension (*kumbhaka*), the words «the cutting off of the flow of inspiration and expiration» give the general characteristic of restraint of the breath. To explain: when in inhalation the outer wind sipped in is held inside, there is a break in the flow of inspiration and expiration; again when in emission the abdominal wind forced out is held outside, there is also a break in the flow of inspiration and expiration. Similarly in the case of suspension also. This same is said by the Comment in the words «After the subjugation of posture.»

But this [restraint of breath] is,

50. External or internal or suppressed in fluctuation and is regulated[2] in place and time and number and is protracted and subtile.

It is external in case there is no flow [of breath] after expiration; it is internal in case there is no flow [of breath] after inspiration; it is the third [or] suppressed in fluctuation in case there is no [flow] of either kind [neither of expiration nor inspiration], as the result of a single effort [to suppress both], just as water dropped upon a very-hot stone shrivels up wherever it falls, so both at once cease to be. And each of these three is regulated in space; [each] deals with a certain amount of space. [Each] is regulated in time; in other words, defined by a limitation to a certain number of moments. [Each] is regulated in number; the first rising up [of the vital current from the navel to the palate is measured] by so

[1] Many MSS. omit this word *jaye* and read *saty āsane*.

[2] The Vārttika says *paridṛsto nirṇīto niyamito*.

many inspirations and expirations. In the same manner, the second rising up of the checked [vital current] is measured by so many inspirations and expirations. Likewise the third. Similarly it is gentle [in method]; similarly it is moderate; similarly it is keen. Thus it is regulated by number. So then, practised in these ways, [it becomes] protracted and subtile.

He introduces the sūtra which gives the characteristics of the three particular restraints of the breath by saying, «But this.» The sūtra begins with the word **50. External** and ends with the word **subtile.** The words «in fluctuation» are connected with each [of the three]. He refers to emission (*recaka*) when he says «In case . . . expiration.» He refers to inhalation (*pūraka*) when he says «In case . . . inspiration.» He refers to suspension (*kumbhaka*) when he says «the third.» This same he makes clear when he says «in case . . . of either kind.» When by only one effort of retention there results an absence of both inspiration and expiration, and when there is not, as before, an effort to prolong a long stream of efforts of emission; but, on the other hand, just as water thrown upon a very-hot stone dries altogether and shrivels up wherever it falls, so this wind, whose nature it is to flow, when its action is restricted by a mighty effort of retention, becomes subtilized and remains in the body. [Suspension] does not inhale and so is not inhalation; does not emit and so is not emission. The words «deals with a certain amount of space» means as measured by a span, [the space between the outstretched tips of the thumb and the forefinger], by a *vitasti* [from the extended thumb to the tip of the little finger], or by a hand. And it is inferred as being external [in so far as it causes] motion in a blade of grass or a piece of cotton in a windless spot. Similarly if internal, it begins at the sole of the foot and extends to the head. And it is inferred by [an internal] touch light as that of an ant [moving on the body]. A moment is one quarter of the time required for the act of winking. [The wind] is defined by the limitation of a certain number of these [moments]. An instant (*mātrā*) is the time limited by snapping thumb and forefinger after having three times rubbed one's own knee-pan with the hand. The first rising up (*udghāta*) measured by thirty-six such instants is called slow. The same [*udghāta*] when doubled is moderate. The same tripled, called the third, is keen. This same restraint of the breath he describes as being regulated by number in the words «by number.» The time for snapping thumb and forefinger as described is equal to the time defined by the action of inhalation and exhalation of a man in good health.[1] The rising up[2] which has been made the object of the action of the first rising-up is conquered [and] mastered [and] checked. It is intended [by these measures of

[1] The meaning of the word *svastha* might also be 'at ease' or 'motionless'.

[2] See Kūrma Pur. ii. 11. This process is elaborated at length in most of the later books of decadent yoga. Compare also Vāyu Pur. v. 79–81.

instants to indicate] the time of a certain number of moments. [And this time is equal to] a certain number of inspirations and expirations. Thus there is a slight difference [between the two kinds of measures, between the *mātrā* and the inspirations and expirations]. This same [restraint of breath] when practised day by day, [increasing gradually] by a day [at a time] or by a fortnight or by a month becomes, in so far as it is made to cover an increasing number of places or of times, protracted. And in so far as it is reached by a concentration of the most extreme delicacy it is said to be subtile, but not in so far as it is weak.

51. The fourth [restraint of the breath] transcends the external and the internal object.

The external object regulated in place and time and number is transcended; the internal object regulated in the same way is transcended; in both kinds of cases [restraint] is protracted and subtile. Following after these there is no flow of either kind. This is the fourth restraint of breath. Now the third restraint of breath is without regard to objects, has no flow [of breath], is begun once only, is regulated in place and time and number, and is protracted and subtile. But the fourth,[1] because, in consequence of its mastery of the stages in order, it has made out the objects of both expiration and inspiration, after transcending both [external and internal objects], is without flow and is the ‹fourth› restraint of breath. This is the distinction.

Thus the three particular restraints of breath have been characterized. The fourth he characterizes with the words **51. The fourth [restraint of the breath] transcends the external and the internal object.** [The Comment] explains [the sūtra] in the words «place and time and number.» Transcended means cast down because its form has been mastered by practice. It is also protracted and subtile. Similarly, «Following after these» means the restraint of breath which has external and internal objects and which follows after knowledge of place and time and number. The fourth does not, like the third, arise by a single effort and instantly. But while in practice and after having reached the various stages according as it succeeds in one stage after another it proceeds as he says «in consequence of its mastery of the stages.» It is objected, 'In the repressed fluctuation also there is no flow of either. What then is [its] distinction from this [fourth]?' In reply he says, «the third.» The third does not follow after any regard paid to [objects] and is completed by a single effort.

[1] See Liñga Pur. viii. 111.

But the fourth is preceded by the regard paid to objects and has to be completed by many efforts. This is the distinction. The object of these two, the inhalation and the emission, is not considered; but this [object] is regarded in respect of place and time and number. This is the meaning.

52. As a result of this the covering of the light dwindles away.

In the case of the yogin who is practising restraints of breath, the karma capable of covering discriminative thinking dwindles away. What this is they tell in the words, "Having covered the *sattva* which is disposed to light with delusion (*indrajāla*) made of infatuation, [undifferentiated-consciousness] assigns the same [obscured form] to deeds which are not to be done." Therefore by practising restraint of breath his karma which covers the light, together with its bondage to the round-of-rebirth, becomes powerless. And from moment to moment it dwindles away. And in this sense it has been said, "There is no self-castigation higher than restraint of breath; from it comes purity from defilement and the clear shining of thought."

He describes the subsidiary purpose [served by] restraint of breath. **52. As a result of this the covering of the light dwindles away.** The covering is that by which the *sattva* of the thinking-substance is covered, in other words, hindrances and evil. He explains [the sūtra] in the words «restraints of breath.» Thinking (*jñāna*) is that by which anything is thought. It is the light of the *sattva* of the thinking-substance. Discriminative thinking is the thinking of discrimination. For this [hindrance], since it covers discriminative thinking, is called the coverer (*āvaraṇīya*) according [to the sūtra of Pāṇini iii. 4. 68 which says that] *bhavya* and *geya* and *pravacanīya* and similar forms have been shown to be used as exceptional forms in the sense of agent, just as for instance the words *kopanīya* and *rañjanīya*. So here also the affix of the future passive participle is used to denote the agent. The word «karma» connotes the merit which results from it and the hindrance which is the cause of it. On this same point he states that there is a concurrence of opinion with those who have the tradition (*āgamin*) in the words «What this is they tell.» Extreme infatuation is passion. Undifferentiated-consciousness (*avidyā*) too, which is inseparable from it, is also to be understood by this word. A deed «not to be done» is wrong-living. An objector asks, 'If restraint of the breath causes evil to dwindle, what need is there of self-castigation?' In reply to this he says «becomes powerless.» It does not dwindle away entirely. Therefore to make it dwindle away altogether self-castigation is needed. On this point also he states that there is a concurrence of opinion with those who have the tradition (*āgamin*) by saying «And in this

sense it has been said.» Manu also [vi. 72] says, "By restraints of breath one should burn up defects." And that restraint of breath is also an aid to yoga is also stated[1] by the Vishṇu Purāṇa [vi. 7. 40–1], "But restraint of breath which masters by practice the wind called breath is to be recognized as being seeded and as seedless. When the two winds, breath (*prāṇa*) and out-breath (*apāna*) have overcome each other, that is two-fold. The third is the result of a subdual of these two."

Furthermore,

53. For fixed attentions also the central organ becomes fit.

Merely in consequence of practice in restraint of breath [the central organ becomes fit for fixed attentions] in accordance with the statement [i. 34], "Or [he gains stability] by expulsion and retention of breath."

Furthermore, 53. For fixed attentions also the central organ becomes fit. For restraint of breath steadies the central organ and makes it fit for fixed attentions.

Now what is the withdrawal of the senses?

54. The withdrawal of the senses is as it were the imitation of the mind-stuff itself on the part of the organs by disjoining themselves from their objects.

When there is no conjunction with their own objects, the organs in imitation of the mind-stuff, as it is in itself, become, as it were, restricted. When the mind-stuff is restricted, like the mind-stuff they become restricted; and do not, like the subjugation of the senses, require any further aid. Just as when the king-bee[2] flies up, the bees fly up after him; and when he settles down, they settle down after him. So when the mind-stuff is restricted, the organs are restricted. This then is the withdrawal of the senses.

The [yogin] being refined in this way by means of abstentions and other [aids], begins, for the sake [of attaining] constraint, the withdrawal of the senses. In order to introduce the sūtra giving its distinguishing characteristic he asks the question, «Now?» The sūtra begins with the word 54. . . . themselves and ends with the words withdrawal of the senses. The mind-stuff also is not in contact with the [various kinds of things], sounds and so forth,

[1] Compare Nāradīya Pur. xlvii. 16–17.

[2] Compare Praçna Up. ii. 4. Repeated below iii. 38. This is what we call queen-bee.

which bring about infatuation and attachment and anger. And because it is not in contact with them, the eye and the other organs are not in contact. This is what is called the imitation of the mind-stuff by the senses. Because, as the mind-stuff settles down upon an entity, the organs of this [mind-stuff] cannot be said to imitate the mind, since their object is always external,—therefore he says «in imitation . . . as it were.» [In the compound beginning] with the word «their own (*sva*)» he shows by the locative case [in the word *abhāve*] that the reason why the mind-stuff is imitated is because of the property common [to the mind-stuff and to the organs], namely, the disjunction from their own objects of sense. He elaborates [the meaning of] the imitation by saying «when the mind-stuff is restricted.» The similarity is that the effort which causes the restriction of both is similar. Here he gives a simile [1] by saying «Just as when the king-bee.» He applies [the simile] to the thing illustrated by saying «So.» On this point also [he quotes] a sentence from the Vishṇu Purāṇa [2] [vi. 7. 43], "A man skilled in yoga, having restrained the organs attached to [the various things], sound and so forth, should make them imitate the mind-stuff, in that he is intent upon the withdrawal of the senses." And the motive for this is shown in the same place [vi. 7. 44], "In the case of men who have become motionless, the result of that [withdrawal] is perfect mastery of the organs. A yogin with unmastered [organs] cannot accomplish yoga."

55. As a result of this [withdrawal] there is complete mastery of the organs.

There are some who think 1. that the mastery of the organs is a lack of desire for the various things sounds and so forth. Longing (*vyasana*) is attachment in the sense that it puts him a long way from (*vy-asyati*) a good. 2. [Others think that] unforbidden experience is legitimate. 3. Others, that there may be conjunction [of the organs] with the [various things] sounds and so forth as one desires. 4. Others think that there is a subjugation of the senses when there is no passion or aversion after the thinking of the various things is without pleasure or pain. 5. Jāigīṣavya thinks that it is refusal to perceive [the various things beginning with sound] as a result of the mind-stuff's singleness-of-intent. And as a result of this, when [the yogin's] mind-stuff is restricted, the organs are restricted, [and] there is not as in the case of the subjugation of the other organs, any further need of

[1] Compare iii. 38. [2] See also Nāradīya Pur. lxvii. 19–20.

means performed with effort. But this mastery which is this singleness-of-intent is the complete [mastery].

The sūtra is explanatory of this [mastery]. **55. As a result of this [withdrawal] there is complete mastery of the organs.** An objector asks, 'Are there other and incomplete masteries in comparison with which this may be called complete?' Undoubtedly, [he says in reply]. He shows what these are in the words «the various things beginning with sound.» He elaborates the same by saying «desire.» Desire is passion, attachment. According to what derivation? It is that which rejects him [or] throws him away from a good. When there is none of this, there is absence of desire, in other words, mastery. 2. He describes yet another [incomplete] mastery in the words «unforbidden.» That devotion to things which is not forbidden by the Sacred Word and other [authorities], and the absence of sense activity with regard to those things which are forbidden by these. Such is legitimate because it does not depart from the law. 3. He describes yet another [incomplete] mastery in the words «contact [of the senses] with the [various things] beginning with sound.» Contact of the organs with the [various things], sounds and so forth, as one desires. The meaning is that with regard to matters of enjoyment he is independent and not dependent on enjoyment. 4. He describes yet another [incomplete] mastery in the words, «no passion and no hatred.» Some say that it is a thinking without pleasure or pain, of the [various things], sounds and so forth, by a detached observer. 5. He describes that mastery which is approved by the author of the sūtras and is also approved by the Supreme Sage, as he says, «as a result of the mind-stuff's singleness-of-intent.» Jāigīṣavya says that when the mind-stuff together with the organs is single-in-intent, there is no sense-activity with regard to [various things] beginning with sound. The [commentator] says that this is the complete mastery in the words, «But . . . the complete.» The word «but» distinguishes it from other masteries. For the other masteries, in so far as they are in contact with the poisonous snake[1] (*āçīviṣa*) of objects-of-sense (*viṣaya*), do not escape the possibility of contact with the poison of the hindrances. For even a man who knows the lore of poisons and who is a perfect master of serpents does not take a serpent on his lap and quietly go to sleep. This mastery, on the other hand, from which all intermixture with objects has been removed, since [in it] there is no distrust, is called complete, as he says, «not as in the case of the subjugation of the other organs.» Although, in the case of consciousness of endeavour [ii. 15], when one organ is subdued there is still need of another effort to conquer the other organs, yet, when the mind-stuff is restricted, there is no such need of further exertion in order to restrict the other senses. This is the meaning.

[1] 'One in which poison is lying' according to the Gaṇa on Pāṇini vi. 3. 109.

Here in this Book he has taught the yoga of action and the hindrances to karma and the fruitions of karma; the painfulness of these [karmas] and also the [four] divisions: a group of five subjects appertaining to yoga.

Of Patañjali's [Yoga-treatise] the Second Book, entitled Specification of the Means of Attainment.

Of the Explanation of the Comment on Patañjali's [Yoga-treatise], whose Explanation is entitled Clarification of the Entities (*Tattva-Vāiçāradī*), and which was composed by the Venerable Vācaspatimiçra, the Second Book, called Specification of the Means of Attainment, is finished.

BOOK THIRD

SUPERNORMAL POWERS

BOOK THIRD

SUPERNORMAL POWERS

The five indirect aids [to yoga] have been described. Fixed attention [1] is [now] to be described.

1. Binding the mind-stuff to a place is fixed-attention.

Binding of the mind-stuff, only in so far as it is a fluctuation, to the navel or to the heart-lotus or to the light within the head or to the tip of the nose or to the tip of the tongue or to other [2] places of the same kind or to an external object,—this is fixed-attention.

The First and Second Books described Concentration and the means thereto. In the Third Book the supernormal powers are to be described which are reasons for propagation of belief and which are favourable to this [concentration and its means]. These supernormal powers are to be accomplished by constraints (*saṁyama*). And constraint is the combination of fixed-attention and of contemplation and of concentration. So inasmuch as these [three] are the means of accomplishing the supernormal powers, we have here a mention of these three, in order to make known the particular quality of each as being direct aids to yoga and as contrasted with the five which are indirect aids. And with regard to these [three], fixed-attention and contemplation and concentration are in the relation of cause to effect, and the serial order [3] [of causes and effects] is specified. Therefore this order is followed in the order of the statements. Accordingly, fixed-attention is the first to be characterized. So he says **1. Binding the mind-stuff to a place is fixed-attention.** He describes a place belonging to one's self by the words «to the navel.» By the words «other places of the same kind» we must understand the palate and so forth. The binding is a relation. He describes an external place by the words «or to an external.» And with an external object the mind-stuff as such cannot have a relation. So it is said, «only in so far as it is a fluctuation,» in other words, only so far as it is a perception. On this point also there is a Purāṇa,[4] "Having mastered his breath by restraint of breath and his organs by with-

[1] See also ii. 29 and 53.

[2] Compare Māitrī Upan. vi. 20 and Garuḍa Pur. ccxxvi. 21.

[3] Compare Patañjali: Mahābhāṣya I. 225[8]; I. 356 (Kielhorn's ed.) and frequently.

[4] Vishṇu Pur. vi. 7. 45 and Nāradīya Pur. lxvii. 21.

drawal of the senses, he should make a localization of the mind-stuff upon some auspicious support." Auspicious supports are external, Hiraṇyagarbha and Vāsava and Prajāpati and so forth. And this has also been said,[1] "The incarnate form of the Exalted One leaves one without desire for any [other] support. This should be understood to be fixed-attention, when the mind-stuff is fixed upon this form. And what this incarnate form of Hari, on which one should ponder, let that be heard by thee, O Ruler of Men. Fixed-attention is not possible without something on which to fix it. His face is calm, his eye like the lovely lotus petal, his cheek is beautiful, the expanse of his broad forehead is resplendent [with the light of thought], the charming ornament of the ear-ring is placed under the lobes of his ears which are equal in size, his neck is [marked with three lines] like a shell of the sea, his great broad chest is marked with the Çrīvatsa, his belly has a deep navel and broken folds, he has eight long arms or, as Vishṇu, four arms, his thighs and legs are evenly placed, his excellent[2] lotus feet [are arranged] as a mystic diagram. He is like Brahma with a stainless yellow garment, and is adorned with a diadem and with charming armlets and bracelets; he has Çārn̄ga [Vishṇu's bow] and the discus and the mace and the sword and the conch and the rosary—upon him, Vishṇu, let the yogin ponder; and, lost in him, concentrate his own mind until, O King, the fixed-attention becomes firmly fixed upon him only. While performing this or while doing, as he wills, some other action wherein his mind does not wander, he should then deem this [fixed-attention] to be perfected."

2. Focusedness of the presented idea upon that place is contemplation.

The focusedness of the presented idea upon the object to be contemplated[3] in that place, in other words, the stream [of presented ideas] of like quality unaffected by any other presented idea.

He characterizes the contemplation which is to be effected by fixed-attention. **2. Focusedness of the presented idea upon that place is contemplation.** Focusedness is singleness-of-intent. The Comment is easy. On this point also there is a Purāṇa,[4] "An uninterrupted succession of presented-ideas single-in-intent upon His form without desire for anything else, that, O King, is contemplation. It is brought about by the first six aids [to yoga]."

3. This same [contemplation], shining forth [in consciousness] as the intended object and nothing more, and, as it were, emptied of itself, is concentration.

When the contemplation only shines forth [in consciousness] in the

[1] Vishṇu Pur. vi. 7. 77-85 and Nāradīya Pur. lxvii. 54-62.

[2] Reading *vara*, not *kara*.

[3] See Garuḍa Pur. ccxxxv. 28. 29.

[4] Vishṇu Pur. vi. 7. 89.

form of the object-to-be-contemplated and [so] is, as it were, empty of itself, in so far as it becomes identical with the presented-idea as such, then, by fusing [itself] with the nature of the object-to-be-contemplated, it is said to be concentration.

He gives the characteristic of concentration which is to be attained by concentration [in the sūtra] **3. This same [contemplation] . . . . concentration.** He explains [the sūtra] in the words, «the contemplation only.» The words «shines forth [in consciousness] in the form of the object-to-be-contemplated» signify that it shines forth in the form of the object-to-be-contemplated and not in the form of the contemplation. That is why he says, «empty.» An objector asks, 'If it be empty, how could the object-to-be-contemplated appear?' In reply he says, «as it were.» He gives the reason for the same in the words, «by fusing [itself] with the nature of the object-to-be-contemplated.» On this point also there is a Purāṇa,[1] "The knowing of this same [Vishṇu] as he is when free from two-termed-relations (*kalpanā*) is a completion of the contemplation by the central-organ,—this is termed concentration." A two-termed-relation (*kalpanā*) is a distinction between the contemplation and the object-to-be-contemplated. Concentration is free from this. This is the meaning. Keçidhvaja after having described to Khāṇḍikya the eight aids to yoga, sums them up by saying,[2] "The soul (*kṣetrajña*) has the means. Thinking is the means. It is inanimate. When [thinking] has completed its task of release, it has done what it had to do and ceases."

These same three, fixed-attention and contemplation and concentration, in one are constraint.

4. The three in one are constraint.

When having a single object the three means are called constraint. So the technical term [now laid down] in this system for these three is constraint.

These three, fixed-attention and contemplation and concentration, are used in many places [as one]. It would be laboured to enunciate [each time] their respective technical terms. So for brevity's sake he introduces a sūtra which [lays down] a technical term (*paribhāṣa-sūtra*) by saying «These same.» **4. The three in one are constraint.** He explains [the sūtra] by saying «When having a single object.» He removes a doubt as to whether [these three] are the [naturally] expressed meaning [of the word constraint] by saying «for these three.» The system (*tantra*) is that authoritative-book (*çāstra*) by which yoga is systematized or expounded. «In this system» means in

[1] Vishṇu Pur. vi. 7. 90 and Nāradīya Pur. lxvii. 67.
[2] Vishṇu Pur. vi. 7. 92 and Nāradīya Pur. lxvii. 69.

what belongs to this [system]. And the passages [where the word] constraint [is used] are such as [iii. 16], "As a result of constraint upon the three mutations."

5. As a result of mastering this constraint, there follows the shining forth of insight.

As a result of mastering this constraint there follows the shining forth of concentrated insight.[1] Just in proportion as constraint enters the stable state, in that proportion the concentrated insight becomes clear.

He mentions the result of success in constraint, for which the means-of-attainment is practice, by saying, **5. As a result of mastering this constraint, there follows the shining forth of insight.** The shining forth of insight is due to the fact that it remains in the clear stream of [the yogin who is] not overcome by other ideas. The Comment is easy.

6. Its application is by stages.

The application[2] of it, that is, the constraint is to that stage which is next the stage already mastered. For by overleaping the next stage without having first mastered the lower stage, [the yogin] does not gain constraint in the highest[3] stages. If he did not [gain that constraint], how could he gain the shining forth of insight? Again, the constraint of one who by the grace of the Içvara has gained a higher stage does not apply to such things as the mind-stuff's thinking[4] in other persons who are on the lower stages. Why is this? Since the purpose of this has been obtained from elsewhere. Yoga is itself the only spiritual guide [which can show] that this stage is next to that stage. How is this? Because it has been said to be thus,

By yoga, yoga must be known,
Yoga increaseth yoga's store.
He who for yoga care hath shown
In yoga rests for evermore.

[1] See also i. 35, p. 80[4]; i. 42, p. 88[2]; i. 44, p. 94[8]; i. 49–51, pp. 100[7], 101[2,5], 102[2], 103[3]; iv. 23, p. 308[6]. In this system *prajñā* is psychological rather than ethical.

[2] A good illustration is found in Bhāg. Pur. ii. 2, in which Viṣṇu is adored from his feet up to his smile.

[3] Compare ii. 27.

[4] See iii. 19.

But when applied, in what cases can this constraint have these results? In reply he says, **6. Its application is by stages.** The author of the Comment particularizes [the meaning of the word] stage by saying, «of it.» Its application is to that state as yet unmastered which is next to the stage [already] mastered. When the reflective concentration, whose object is coarse, is mastered by constraint, the [next] application of constraint is to super-reflective concentration which has not yet been mastered. When this too is mastered, the application [of the restraint] is to deliberative [concentration]. Similarly, [when this is mastered], the application is to super-deliberative [concentration]. Hence in the Purāṇa,[1] when the balanced-state the object of which is coarse is perfected, then there is later introduced that concentration the object of which is subtile, in that the various weapons and ornaments are removed: "Then the wise man should ponder upon the serene form of the Exalted One, without its conch-shell and mace and discus and Çārnga, but having its string of beads. When the fixed-attention has become stable upon this form, then he should keep in mind the form without the ornaments, especially the diadem and the armlets. The wise man should make the god to have only one limb and [should think] 'I am he'. Then after that he should devote himself to thought of 'I'." But why after having mastered a lower stage does he master a higher stage? [And] why is there not a reverse process? In reply to this he says, «without having first subjugated the lower stage, [the yogin] does not.» For a man proceeding to the Ganges from Çilāhrada does not reach the Ganges unless he first get to the Meghavana. «Again of one who by the grace of the Içvara has gained a higher stage»—why does he say this? Because the purpose of this, the success in the higher stage which comes next, has been obtained from elsewhere, that is, from the devotion to the Içvara. For when an act has its action finished, then a means-of-attaining, which does not produce anything in particular, falls outside the function of [what can be called] a means. The objector says, 'This may be true. It is known in a general way (*āgamataḥ*) what the different subordinated stages are. But how is there a knowledge of which comes after the other?' In reply to this he says, «this stage.» Yoga which has been previously mastered is the reason for proceeding to the thinking of the yoga which comes after. This passage is to be understood by supposing that a state is equivalent to [a yoga which] contains a state.

---

7. The three are direct aids in comparison with the previous [five].

The same three, fixed-attention and contemplation and concentration, are direct aids to conscious concentration in comparison with the previous means, the five[2] beginning with the abstentions.

[1] Vishṇu Pur. vi. 7. 86-88 and Nāradīya Pur. lxvii. 63-65.

[2] Reading *yamādibhyaḥ pañcabhyaḥ*.

But why is constraint applied in various places, and not the other five aids to yoga, although all without distinction are aids to yoga? In reply he says, **7. The three are direct aids in comparison with the previous [five].** These three means-of-attainment, inasmuch as their object is the same as [the object of the yoga] to be accomplished, are direct aids. But abstentions and the other [four] are not so. They are therefore indirect aids. These three means-of-attainment are direct aids only with reference to [yoga] conscious [of objects], but not to [yoga] not conscious [of an object]. For since [yoga] not conscious [of an object] is seedless [and has no object], it does not have the same object as these [three]. And since after these have been restricted for a long time, [unconscious yoga] arises subsequent to the higher passionlessness consisting in the undisturbed calm of perception, another name of which is the higher limit of conscious [yoga]. So he says, «The same three.»

8. Even these [three] are indirect aids to seedless [concentration].

Even these, the three direct means-of-attainment, are indirect aids to seedless yoga. Why is this? Since this latter occurs even when these are absent.

8. Even these [three] are indirect aids to seedless [concentration]. Hence that which determines the relation of direct aid to this is sameness of objects and not a mere sequence. For this [sequence] in so far as it might exist in the case of devotion to the Içvara, which is an indirect aid, would make the application [of direct aid] too wide (*vyabhicāra*). If this is established, even this over-wideness of the characterization which would include mere sequence could not apply to this [constraint]. Therefore it is still less probable that [this] constraint would be a direct aid to [concentration] not conscious [of an object]. To show that this is so it is said, «Since this latter occurs even when these are absent.»

Now since during the restricted moments of the mind-stuff the changes of the aspects (*guṇa*) are unstable,[1] of what sort at those times is the mutation of the mind-stuff?

9. When there is a becoming invisible of the subliminal-impression of emergence[2] and a becoming visible of the

[1] This again is apparently a portion of the fragment of Pañcaçikha quoted in ii. 15 (p. 135[11] of the Calcutta text), to be placed before fragment 11 of Garbe. The phrase is also found at ii. 15, p. 135[11]; iii. 13, p. 204[3]; iv. 15, p. 298[1]. Compare for use of word *vṛtta* in the sense of 'behaviour' ii. 33, p. 177[4] (Calc. ed.).

[2] Reading *abhibhavaprādurbhāvāu*.

subliminal-impression of restriction, the mutation of restriction is inseparably connected with mind-stuff in its period of restriction.

The subliminal-impressions of emergence are external-aspects (*dharma*) of mind-stuff; since they do not consist of presented-ideas they are not restricted when presented-ideas are restricted. The subliminal-impressions of restriction are also external-aspects of mind-stuff. ‹When these two [states of mind-stuff] become visible or become invisible,› [that is when] the subliminal-impressions of emergence are withdrawing and the subliminal-impressions of restriction are being brought into place. The period of restriction is inseparably connected with the mind-stuff. Accordingly the mutation of restriction is this periodicalteration of subliminal-impressions of a single mind-stuff, because then the mind-stuff has nothing but subliminal-impressions, as has been explained [i. 18] with reference to the concentration of restriction.

With the intent to give information here about the three mutations which are to be made use of in the sūtra [iii. 16], "As a result of constraint upon the three mutations," he asks, incidentally to the topic of seedless [concentration], «Now ?» In the case of emergence and of yoga conscious [of objects], since there is an experience of an accumulation of various very clear mutations, there has been no introduction of the question. But in the case of restriction the mutation is not experienced. Furthermore it cannot be said that because it is not experienced it does not exist. For inasmuch as mind-stuff is made up of three aspects (*guṇa*), and since also the changes of the aspects are unstable, an absence of mutation even for a moment is impossible. The answer to the question is the sūtra **9. . . . emergence . . . . mutation of restriction . . . .** In comparison with concentration unconscious [of any object] conscious concentration is emergence. Restriction is that which restricts. It is the undisturbed calm[1] of perception [and it is also] the higher passionlessness. There is a becoming visible and a becoming invisible of these two subliminal impressions of emergence and the subliminal impression of restriction, that is to say, the becoming invisible of the subliminal-impression of emergence and the becoming visible of the subliminal-impression of restriction. The mind-stuff which is the substance in the period of restriction, that is, on the occasion of restriction, is inseparably connected with

[1] This does not refer to *samādhi* in general, but only to the concentrated insight (*prajñā*) described in i. 47–48, which is without influence from objects and is an undisturbed succession of clarified *saṁskāra*. See also i. 18, p. 47[6]; ii. 27, p. 166[3] (Calc. ed.); also i. 51 and the sūtras iii. 9–15.

both of these states. For the mind-stuff as substance, whether in the conscious or unconscious state, does not differ in itself in so far as subliminal impressions become visible or become invisible [within it]. An objector says, 'Just as later hindrances based upon undifferentiated-consciousness *(avidyā)* cease when undifferentiated-consciousness ceases, and consequently there is no need of further special effort to repress them, so the subliminal-impressions based upon ideas of emergence may cease at the very moment of the cessation of the emergence. And therefore for the repression of them there should be no need of the subliminal-impressions of restriction.' With this in view he says, «The subliminal-impressions of emergence.» The cessation of a cause in general is not a reason for the cessation of the effect. So that even if the weaver cease to be, there need be no cessation of the cloth. But with the cessation of that cause which is constitutive of the nature of the effect, there is a cessation of the effect. Now the other hindrances have been said to consist of undifferentiated-consciousness *(avidyā)*. So with the cessation of that undifferentiated-consciousness it is right that these [hindrances] should cease. But the subliminal-impressions whose essence is presented-ideas are not such. For even if the idea be restricted for a long time, we observe a connecting recollection at the present time. Therefore even if the presented-ideas are repressed *(nivṛtti)*, still an accumulation of subliminal-impressions of restriction must be resorted to in order to repress these [subliminal-impressions from presented-ideas]. This is the meaning. The rest is easy.

10. This[1] [mind-stuff] flows peacefully by reason of the subliminal-impression.

By reason of the subliminal-impression of restriction, the peaceful flow of the mind-stuff requires dexterity in the application of the subliminal-impressions of restriction. When these[2] subliminal-impressions become weak, the subliminal-impression which has external aspects of restriction is overwhelmed by the subliminal-impression which has external aspects of emergence.

But if there be an overwhelming *(abhibhava)* of the emergent subliminal-impressions in all respects, of what sort is the mutation with a powerful subliminal-impression of restriction? In reply to this he says, **10. This [mind-stuff] flows peacefully by reason of the subliminal-impression.** Calm flowing is a flowing of a succession of restrictions only undefiled by the subliminal impressions of emergence. Why is dexterity of subliminal impressions needed, but not ordinary subliminal-impressions? In answer to this he says, «When these

[1] The sūtra is an instance of *dharma-pariṇāma*, as explained in the Comment on iii. 13.

[2] In the text as received, *tat* refers to *nirodha*. If the variant *nābhibhūyate* be accepted, *tat* must refer, as Vācaspati points out, to *vyutthāna*.

subliminal-impressions become weak.» The word «these (*tat*)» refers back to restriction. But those who have the reading 'are not overwhelmed' would refer by the word «these (*tad-ā*)» to emergence.

11. The[1] mutation of concentration is the dwindling of dispersiveness and the uprisal of singleness-of-intent belonging to the mind-stuff.

Dispersiveness[2] is an external-aspect of the mind-stuff. Singleness-of-intent is an external-aspect of the mind-stuff. The dwindling of dispersiveness means that it disappears; the uprisal of singleness-of-intent means that it becomes apparent. The mind-stuff is inseparably connected with both of these as the substance [in which they inhere]. This same mind-stuff being inseparably connected with these two external-aspects which belong to itself,—the passing away [of the distributiveness] and the coming forth [of the singleness-of-intent],—becomes concentrated. This is the mutation of concentration

He shows what the state of the mind-stuff is in the mutation of concentration conscious [of objects]. 11. . . . **dispersiveness** . . . . **mutation of concentration.** Dispersiveness is distractedness. Being existent[3] it does not (*san na*) cease to be. Dwindling is disappearing. Because a non-existent does not arise [in consciousness], an uprisal is a becoming apparent. The mind-stuff which is inseparably connected with the passing away of dispersiveness and the coming forth of singleness-of-intent, which are its external-aspects—the dispersiveness having the passing away and the singleness-of-intent having the coming forth—this mind-stuff is concentrating itself, that is, is becoming qualified as having a concentration which is to be attained in successive steps.

12. Then[4] again when the quiescent and the uprisen presented ideas are similar[5] [in respect of having a single object], the mind-stuff has a mutation single-in-intent.

The quiescent is a previous presented idea of one whose mind-stuff is concentrated; the uprisen is a later presented-idea of the same

[1] The sūtra is an instance of *lakṣaṇa-pariṇāma*, as explained in iii. 13.

[2] See iv. 23.

[3] If the reading be *sā na*, the translation would be simpler, 'It does not cease to be.'

[4] According to the scheme of iii. 13 this would appear to be an instance of *avasthā-pariṇāma*.

[5] The Maṇiprabhā explains the word 'alike' (*tulya*) by adding *ekaviṣayatvena*.

kind as this [previous presented-idea]. But the mind-stuff of concentration is likewise inseparably connected with both. This is so until the breaking down of the concentration. This same mutation of singleness-in-intent belongs to the mind-stuff in which it resides (*dharmiṇaḥ*).

12. Then . . . a mutation . . . Then again, that is, when the serial order of the states of concentration is completed, the quiescent and the uprisen [that is] the past and the present are similar-presented-ideas, that is, similar and presented-ideas. But the similarity is a result of the singleness-in-intent. The words «of one whose mind-stuff is concentrated» indicate that the concentration is completed. The words «This is so» mean that it is single-in-intent. He tells what the limit of this is by saying «until the breaking down of the concentration» [that is] until there is a falling [of the concentration].

13. Thus, with regard to elements and to organs, mutations of external-aspect and of time-variation and of intensity have been enumerated.

‹Thus,› by the already (iii. 9) described mutations of mind-stuff in external-aspect and in time-variation and in intensity. The mutation of external-aspect in elements and organs, the mutation of time-variation and the mutation of intensity are to be understood as having been described. Of these [three] the mutation of external-aspect takes place in the substance and is the becoming invisible of the external aspect of emergence and the becoming visible of the external aspect of restriction. And the mutation of time-variation is the restriction having the three time-variations, [that is,] connected with the three time-forms (*adhvan*). This [restriction], one may say, puts aside the first time-form whose time-variation is yet to come, and passes into the present time-variation, without however passing out of its state as external-aspect. But in this [condition] it becomes manifest as being what it is. This is its second time-form. And it is not completely severed from past or from future time-variations.—Likewise emergence has the three time-variations; it is connected with the three time-forms. Having put aside the present time-variation it passes over into the past time-variation, without however passing out of its state as external-aspect. This is its third time-form.

And it is not completely severed from the future and the present time-variations. In the same manner, emergence, completing itself again [as a phenomenalized form], having put aside the future time-variation, and not having passed out of its state as external-aspect, passes into the present time-variation. In which [time], since this [emergence] manifests itself as it is, it obtains its functional activity. This is the second time-form of this [emergence]. And it is not completely released from past and future time-variations. —In the same way it continues, now restriction, now emergence.— Similarly the mutation of intensity [is described]. In it, during the moments of restriction, the subliminal-impressions of restriction become powerful and the subliminal-impressions of emergence become weak. This then is the external-aspects' mutation of intensity. In these cases the substance has a mutation in its external-aspects; the external-aspects have mutation in time-variations; and the time-variations also have mutation in intensities. Consequently the changes of the aspects (*guṇa*) do not remain, even for a moment, devoid of mutations of external-aspect and of time-variation and of intensity. For (*ca*) the changes of the aspects (*guṇa*) are unstable.[1] And we say [hereafter in this sūtra] that it is of the very nature of the aspects to cause activity.—Thus we have to understand the three-fold mutation [of external-aspect and of time-variation and of intensity] in the case of elements and organs, because there is the distinction between the substance and the external-aspects. But in the strict sense there is but a single mutation. For the external-aspect is nothing more than the substance itself. Since it is merely an evolved form of the substance amplified in the form of an external-aspect. In such cases there is within the substance an alteration of the condition of the present external-aspect with regard to past and future and present time-forms. There is no alteration of the matter. Just as by dividing a plate of gold there is an alteration of its condition, in so far as it is altered; [but] there is no alteration of the gold. An opponent objects as follows, 'A substance is nothing over and above the

[1] Once more this appears to be quoted from fragment 11 of Pañcaçikha in its completer form. Compare above, p. 184, note, and p. 208, note.

external-aspects [which as properties depend upon it]. For [a substance] cannot pass beyond its [own] previous existence. If, again, [substance] were a something present in all its external-aspects, but different from them, then it would come to be known[1] (*viparivarteta*) as a something itself absolutely unchanged, although connected[2] with a series of changes [in the external-aspects].' But this, [he replies, involves] no weakness [in our position]. [And] why [not]? Because we do not maintain an absolute[3] unity. [The fact is that all] this world passes out of the state of a phenomenalized [individual] form.[4] And this we say because [we are bound to] deny that [the world] is permanent [in the sense of not entering into mutations]. Again [the world of things] continues to exist even after it has passed out [of phenomenalized individual existence]. For [we are obliged] to deny its annihilation. On being refunded [into its primary cause by the dissolution of the coarse elements,] it [the world takes on] a subtile form. And by reason of this subtile form it becomes unapperceived. An external-aspect[5] in the mutation of time-variation exists really in [all three] time-forms. [It is said to be] past [that is] having the past time-variation, though not completely severed from future and present time-variations. [So too it is said to be] future [that is] having the future time-variation, though not completely severed from present and past time-variations. [So also it is said to be] present [that is] having a present time-variation, though not completely severed from past and future time-variations. Take the case of a man enamoured of one particular woman—he has not thereby lost his sexual feeling for the rest of women-folk. Here the difficulty is

[1] Compare *abhidhāna-çakti-parivṛtta* iii. 17, p. 228[1] (Calc. ed.).

[2] The word *viparivarteta* implies a series of changes in some subordinate and additional thing, or some added property in the unchanged thing. Compare *parivartanam* in Sarva-darçana-saṁgraha (Anandāçrama Sanskrit Series), page 8, line 8 from below.

[3] This word is discussed in Patañjali: Mahābhāṣya I. 180[3], 207[10], 266[23] (Kielhorn).

[4] This *vyakti* is the condition of the thing when so changed as to be manifest to our consciousness, that is, when we can observe the effects it brings about.

[5] In the Yoga system the *dharma* is real; in the Vedānta it is unreal (*vivarta*). The *dharma* is constantly changing into another thing; but involves the concept of permanence.

brought forward by others 'that since all three time-variations are [thus said to be] connected with everything that is in the mutation of time-variation, it must follow (*prāpnoti*) that the time-forms are confounded.' We meet this objection thus (*tasya parihāra*). What is termed the common nature of things as external-aspects cannot be brought into existence [at our pleasure]. The common nature [as external aspect] exists [independently] and therefore in regard to it the distinctions of time-variations must be maintained. Thus it must not be said that the common nature of this or that thing exists only in the present time. Because if this were so, the mind-stuff could never become subject to passion [for a certain object]. For anger [against some other object being by supposition now present in the mind-stuff], desire would not move actively forth. Moreover it is not possible for the three time-variations to belong simultaneously to one and the same [individual] phenomenalized form. But what is possible is the presentation (*bhāva*) in successive times of its phenomenal [1] [form] by the operation of the conditions-which-phenomenalize (*vyañjaka*) it. Thus it has been said,[2] "The [outer] forms [when developed to] a high degree and the [inner] fluctuations [when developed to] a high degree oppose each other; but the generic forms co-operate with [these when developed to] a high degree." Hence [time-variations] are not confounded. To take an example. When we say absolutely (*eva*) that passion for a certain thing has shown itself, [we do not mean] that at that time [passion] for another object is non-existent; [but we mean that passion for another object] continues to be present [in the mind-stuff] though in a generic [unphenomenalized] form. Hence it [the passion] for that [other object] exists at that time (*tadā tatra tasya bhāva*). A similar [explanation can be given] in the case of time-variation [also]. The three time-forms do not belong to the substance but to the external-aspects. These [external-aspects] have a time-variation or do not have a time-variation. And as entering into various intensities are known by different names [which imply] an alteration of intensity but not of matter. Thus

[1] Compare i. 11, p. 37[3] (Calc. ed.).
[2] Compare ii. 15, p. 136[1] (Calc. ed.) and the parallels given there.

the same stroke is termed one[1] in the unit-place and ten in the ten's place and a hundred in the hundred's place. So too the same woman is called a mother and a daughter and a sister. Some persons have objected 'that in the case of a thing which mutates in intensity [the substance of the thing] must logically be held to be (*prasaṅga*) absolutely permanent. How is this? On the ground that it is functional activity[2] of the thing which determines the [special] time-form of the thing. Thus a thing is said to be a future thing when it is not exerting its own activity, and a present thing when it is thus active, and a past thing when it has ceased from activity. Hence, say these persons, it follows that substance and external-aspect and time-variation and intensity are all absolutely permanent.' But that [alleged] weakness, [we say], does not exist [in our position]; for we hold that although a substrate (*guṇin*) is permanent, its aspects (*guṇa*) suffer a variety of antagonisms. Just as any arrangement of parts, (*saṁsthāna*) [which are coarse elements,] is only an external-aspect of the imperishable subtile elements, sound and the rest, and has a beginning and an end, so the resoluble [into primary matter] is only an external-aspect of the imperishable aspects (*guṇa*), the *sattva* and the others, and has a beginning and an end, and to it [and to the rest] the term evolved-form (*vikāra*) is applied. The following serves as an illustration. 1. The substance clay passes from its external-aspect in the form of a round lump of clay into another external-aspect. And thus as an external-aspect enters into mutation in the form of a water-jar. 2. The water-jar-form putting aside its future time-variation assumes its present time-variation; here is the mutation as time-variation. 3. The water-jar is every moment undergoing oldness and newness [in its parts] and thus passes through mutations of intensity. Thus the substance also has another external-aspect, which is, the intensity; and the external-

[1] Contrary to Mr. G. R. Kaye's opinion the following passages show that the place-system of decimals was known as early as the sixth century A.D. See Āryabhaṭa (born 476 A.D.) in his Āryabhaṭīya (ed. Kern, 1874), p. x and 3[4,5]; Varāha Mihira (born 505 near Ujjain) in his Pañcasiddhāntikā (ed. Thibaut, 1889), p. xxx.

[2] The point is that the thing is neither produced nor destroyed, but is its activity.

aspect has also another time-variation, which is, the intensity. There is therefore only one [kind of a] mutation of matter, though variously described [by us]. The same explanation is applicable to other things[1] also. The mutations of external-aspect and of time-variation and of intensity [as here described] do not transcend the substance[2] as such. Hence there is only one kind of a mutation which includes all those varieties we have described.[3] What then is a mutation? It is the rise of another external-aspect in a permanent matter after an earlier external-aspect has been repressed.

As being relevant to the discussion and as being useful to further discussion he gives the divisions of the mutations of elements and of organs in the sūtra 13. Thus . . . enumerated. He explains [the sūtra] by saying «Thus.» An objector asks, 'It is only the mind-stuff that has been described as being in mutation, not its various kinds, the mutation of external-aspect and of time-variation and of intensity. So how can this [that has been said] be extended by analogy[4] to these latter?' In reply to this he says, «of emergence and of restriction.» Although the words external-aspect and time-variation and intensity have not been previously mentioned, it is not however true that the mutations of external-aspect and of time-variation and of intensity have not been described. This is the point in brief.—To continue. The mutation of external-aspect has been described in the words of this sūtra [iii. 9], "subliminal-impression of emergence . . . subliminal-impression of restriction." And in showing this mutation of external-aspect, he has at the same time indicated the mutation of time-variation, which has its locus in the external-aspect, as he says in the words, «the mutation of time-variation.» A time-variation (*lakṣaṇa*) is that by which a kind of time is characterized. For, characterized by this, a thing is distinguished from other things with other times connected with them. The expression, «the restriction having three time-variations» has its explanation in the words «connected with the three time-forms.» The word «time-form» is an expression for time. «This [restriction], one may say, puts aside the first time-form whose time-variation is yet to come.» Does it then go beyond its state as an external-aspect possessing a time-form? No, he says. «Without however passing out of its state as external-aspect.» That very mutation which was yet to come is now present; but the restriction [which was yet to come]

[1] This would apply to the whole κόσμος.

[2] The mutations do not differ from the substance, but are the conditions for the self-identity of the substance.

[3] For the reason that all change depends upon the *dharmin* which remains unchanged amid change.

[4] The words *atideça*, *anudeça*, and *ādeça* are discussed in Patañjali's Mahābhāṣya on i. 1. 56, vārt. 1, p. 133 foot (Kielhorn's ed.).

does not [now] cease to be a restriction. This is the meaning.—Now comes his explanation of the present in the words «in which condition it becomes manifest as being what it is» in other words, in its nature[1] as producing certain effects peculiar to it. «A manifestation» is a moving actively forth. This is its second time-form as compared to its first time-form which was yet to come. An objector says, 'This may be so. But if one has reached the present after having put aside the future time-form, and after having put aside this [present] he is to reach the past, then Sir, there would be a creation and destruction of [these] time-forms. And this is not a desired result. For nothing is made to grow out of a non-existent, nor is an existent ever destroyed.' In reply to this he says «And it is not.» The meaning is that he is not disconnected from the future and the past time-forms, inasmuch as they persist in their generic form. Having shown that the future restriction has a present time-variation, he shows that the present emergence has a past, its third form, by saying, «In the same way, emergence.» So then is the restriction alone future, and is the emergence not [future]? No. As he says, «In the same manner, now emergence.» So there is a re-existence as regards the generic form of emergence, but not as regards the [individual] phenomenalized form. For the past does not exist again.—Manifestation of itself, as it is, is the same as the fact that that which is able to produce effects becomes visible. This mutation of time-variation, as described, recurs again and again in things of this kind, as he says, «In the same way . . now.»—He describes the mutation of intensity, which has only been pointed out by the mutation of external-aspect, by saying, «Similarly, . . . intensity.» In the case of external-aspects, the time-form of which is present, the intensity is equivalent to the presence or absence of power. And the mutation is the gradation of this [intensity] from moment to moment. He concludes this discussion by the words «In these cases.» He specifies the various mutations as having a variety of relations[2] in accordance[3] with the teaching of the system, as he says «In these cases the substance.» Then is this mutation of the aspects (*guṇa*) occasional? The reply is, No. As he says «Consequently.» But why is this mutation perpetual? In reply he says «For (*ca*) . . . unstable.» The word «For (*ca*)» is in the sense of cause. The «changes» are the behaviour (*pracāra*). Why is it just so? In reply he says «that which constitutes the aspects (*guṇa*).» «Is said to be» later in this same [sūtra].—So this three-fold mutation of mind-stuff also is expounded by the author of the sutras with regard to elements and organs as he says «Thus.» This three-fold mutation is the result of the distinction between substance and external-aspects; it is based upon the distinction between the substance and the external-aspects. So we have (*tatra*) a mutation

[1] The thing is what it is (τόδε τι) because the mutation is fulfilling a purpose. This is the essence of any individual form.

[2] A *saṁbandha* is a relation; a *saṁbandhin* is a thing in relation.

[3] Referring to the Pañcaçikha's *calaṁ ca guṇavṛttam*, which is not, however, here expressly attributed to him. Compare p. 213, note 1.

such as a cow or a water-jar as an external-aspect of the substances earth and other elements. And the external-aspects have mutations of time-variation such as past and future and present. Again the cow or other [animal] changed into its present time-variation has mutations of intensity, such as childhood and boyhood and youth and old age. And the water-jar or other [thing] has its mutation of intensity, such as newness or oldness.—Similarly organs, which are substances, have external aspects, which are the seeing of blue or of other colours. The external aspect has the present and the other time-variations. The time-variation which has the seeing of a jewel or some other [thing] has a mutation of intensity, such as the clearness or lack of clearness [of the seeing]. This mutation, thus described, of elements and of organs, is to be understood as being based upon the distinction between the substance and its external-aspects and time-variations and intensities. But as referring to the lack of distinction between them, it is mentioned when he says «But in the strict sense.» The word «but» differentiates this from the view that they are distinct. The absolute reality of this [mutation] is asserted, but [the absolute reality] of the other [three-fold] mutation is not denied. Why? «For the external-aspect is nothing more than the substance itself.» An objector says, 'If the external-aspect is merely an evolved form of the substance, how then should the idea prevail in the world that there is no confusion in the case of these [three] mutations?' In reply to this he says, «in the form of an external-aspect.» The word «external-aspect» is here equivalent to external-aspect and to time-variation and to intensity. It is the substance that enters into evolved-forms through the medium of these. So the [evolved-form] is one and is also not confused with [another]. Because [the external-aspects] the medium of this [substance], although not distinct from the substance, are not confused with each other. An objector says, 'If the external-aspects are not distinct from the substance, and if the time-forms of the substance are distinct, then since the external-aspects are not different from the substance, the external-aspects would be like a substance.' To which he replies, «In such cases . . . of the . . . external-aspect.» The «state» means a particular arrangement-of-parts.[1] Just as a plate of gold[2] or of some other substance may receive a particular name and [be called] a necklace or a svastika, [so] there is an alteration only as [concerns the form of the ornaments], but the matter gold does not become something not gold, because there is no absolute distinction [between the substance and the external-aspect]. This is the intention of what he is about to say. He brings forward a Buddhist, who holds the doctrine of the absolute unity [of substance and of external-aspect], by saying, «An opponent objects as follows.» 'For the necklace and other things thus coming into existence are external-aspects only and are real in the strict sense. But there is no such thing called "gold", some one thing present in many external-aspects [and yet different from them]. But if it be assumed that the matter persists even in

[1] Compare i. 48, p. 90[1] (Calc. ed.) and the parallels given there.

[2] See ii. 28, p. 170[2] (Calc. ed.).

the external-aspects which are ceasing to be, then [the matter], like the Power of Intellect (*citi*), would not enter into mutations, but would continue existing absolutely unchanged. The continued existence in another form means the throwing away of its own form as consisting of mutations and the exchange of this for another, the absolutely changeless. Just as the Power of Intellect (*citi*), although the aspects divide themselves into one alteration after another, does not relapse from its own self and remains absolutely unchanged, so likewise gold, &c., would remain absolutely unchanged,—a proposition which you do not admit. So matter is something not different from its external-aspects.' This objection he refutes by saying «this, [he replies, involves] no weakness.» «Why?» «Because we do not maintain an absolute unity.» Had we to admit the absolute permanence of matter, as of the Power of Intellect[1] (*citi*), then we should have lain open to this taunt. We, however, do not take our stand upon the doctrine of absolute permanence. On the contrary, we say that all these three worlds, and not merely matter, pass out of their phenomenalized individual forms, as producing effects fulfilling a purpose. Why? «For [we are bound to] deny that [the world] is permanent,» on the ground of a source-of-valid-ideas. For if the water-jar were not to pass out of its [individual] phenomenalized form, then even though reduced to the condition of potsherds or of broken bits, it would be as before clearly apperceived as a water-jar and it would have to fulfil the purposes [of a water-jar]. [But this cannot be.] Consequently the three worlds are not permanent. 'Very well then, suppose that [the jar] does not exist permanently in so far as it is not apperceived and does not fulfil the purposes of a water-jar, because like the sky-lotus it is illusory (*tuccha*).' In reply to this he says, «even after it has passed out.» It is not absolutely illusory existence, so that it would be absolutely impermanent. Why? Because [we are obliged] to deny its annihilation, on the ground of a source-of-valid-ideas. To explain. Whatever is illusory existence, cannot be apperceived or produce effects, quite as in the case of the sky-lotus. Whereas these three worlds are from time to time apperceived and do produce effects, [and so are not absolutely illusory existences]. Similarly we should cite as illustrations proving existence (*sattvahetu*) (a) capacity for rising into consciousness, (b) materiality, (c) fitness for external-aspects and time-variations and intensities and others, [which proofs] are wanting in the case of the sky-lotus or the man's horns, which are absolutely illusory existences. Similarly [the jar] is not absolutely permanent so that it would be absolutely permanent like the Power of Intellect (*citi*), but on the contrary it is [only] in some respects permanent. And thus it is established that it enters into mutations. So we must understand that, in the states of the lump of clay and of the following states, the effects such as the water-jar, which are yet to come, have an existence. The objector says, 'This may be true. But if an effect even after it has passed out [of individual phenomenalized existence] exists, why is it not apperceived? The reply is, «On being refunded.» «Refunded» [that is] resolved into its own

[1] Reading *citiçakter*.

cause. «A subtile form» [that is] one not capable of being seen. And hence there is no apperception of it.—Having thus substantiated the mutation of external-aspect, he substantiates the mutation of time-variation also, in so far as they are inseparably connected with each other, by saying, «in the mutation of time-variation.» The meaning is that each time-variation is inseparably connected with the two others. The objector says, 'When one time-variation is in connexion, other time-variations are not perceived. How then [are these] connected with the former?' In reply he says, «Take the case of a man.» For an absence of experience does not do away with that which is established by the source-of-a-valid-idea. For the very fact that this [time-variation] has been made to rise [in consciousness], is the source-of-the-valid-idea for the real existence of these [other time-variations], because a non-existent thing, such as a man's horns, cannot be made to rise in consciousness. He sets up the objection uttered by another when he says, «Here . . . in the mutation of time-variation.» 'If when an external-aspect is present, it is at the same time past and future, then all the three time-forms would be confounded. And if the time-forms are to be in successive times, then it would follow that the production of the non-existent [becomes possible].' He meets the objection with the words, «We meet this objection thus.» For the existence of external-aspects in the present only is established by experience. From this it follows that [external-aspects are] in relation to earlier and to later time. [Why does it follow?] Because of course a non-existent does not come into being, nor is an existent annihilated, as he says, «Because if this were so, the mind-stuff could never.» For the mind-stuff at a time following after anger, is experienced as having the external-aspect of passion. And if passion did not exist at the time of anger, in so far as [passion] was [at that time] future, how then could [passion] rise into consciousness? And if it should not rise in consciousness, how could it be experienced? [The objector continues,] 'Even if this be granted, why would there not still be confusion of time-forms?' The question is [contained in the phrase,] «Moreover it is not possible.» 'What (*kim*) cause is there for not confounding [the time-forms]?' And (*ca*) is used in the sense of 'but'. The answer is given in the words, «the three.» The three time-variations cannot possibly exist simultaneously. In what? In one fluctuation of mind-stuff. But in successive times it is possible for each one of the time-variations to exist in its phenomenal [form] by the operation of the conditions which phenomenalize it [the time-variation]. Since the discussion of the time-variations depends upon the things-which-have-time-variations, therefore the time-variations, in so far as they have the form of the things-which-have-time-variations, belong to [or have the same nature as (*tad-vattā*)] these, that is, the things-which-have-time-variations. On this same point he states his concurrence of opinion with Pañcaçikha the Master by saying «it has been said.» This has been explained[1] before. He brings the discussion to a close by the word «Hence.» The time-forms are

[1] ii. 15, p. 135[11] (Calc. ed.).

not confounded in so far as external-aspects which are opposed to each other, for instance, those that have become visible and those that have become invisible, are refunded into [their own causes]. He gives an illustration in the words «To take an example.» Previously it was shown that anger must be thought to be in relation with passion. Now a passion referring to one object is shown to be in relation to a passion referring to another object. He takes up the subject referred to in the illustration by saying, «A similar [explanation] in the case of time-variation.» An objector says, 'Even when it is assumed that [the mutations] are not absolutely distinct, the distinction may yet exist. So when the external-aspect or the time-variation or the intensity alters, the substance, in that it is not distinct from them, should also alter. And it is just this that we do not accept, because it is contrary to the experience that the [permanent] substance is inseparably connected [with its own states which are impermanent].' In reply to this he says, «The three time-forms do not belong to the substance.» Because it is the external-aspects, which are distinct from it, that have the three time-forms. That it is the external-aspects which are connected with the three time-forms is made clear by the words, «These [external-aspects].» «Have a time-variation» means manifested [that is] present. «Do not have a time-variation» means unmanifested [that is] future or past. Of these [two], those-that-have-a-time-variation, when they attain to the various intensities, either to powerfulness or to weakness, are referred to as being different[1] from other intensities, but not from other matter. The word «intensity» is here used in the sense of external-aspect and of time-variation and of intensity. What he means to say is this: Now it is experience alone which determines the difference or the absence of difference between the substance and the external-aspects and the other [mutations]. Since the external-aspects and the rest are not absolutely identical with the substance, to the extent that the common nature of the external-aspect and of the other [mutations] should have the form of the substance. Nor is there absolute difference, to the extent that the common nature of external-aspects should be [as different as] horses and cows. Experience moreover although not establishing the fact that there is absolute [identity or difference], does show the substance as one[2] and as persisting in the external-aspects and other [mutations] which have the quality of coming into and of passing out of experience, and it does exclude the external-aspects from each other. [All] this is experienced by every one. So we conform ourselves to this experience. We are not at liberty to throw it away, and to dispose of the experiences of the external-aspects as we like. On this same point he gives an example from ordinary life in the words, «Thus the same stroke.» Just as the stroke, which in itself is precisely the same, in relation to the various positions is called a hundred and other names, so the substance, which in itself is precisely the same, is repeatedly given a name in accordance with the alteration of its external-aspect and its

[1] Reading *anyatvena.*

[2] Thus the *bauddha* theory p. 205[4] (Calc. ed.) is partially conceded.

time-variation and its intensity. This is the meaning. To illustrate the matter he gives another simile in the words, «So too the same woman.» At this point he raises an objection, made by an opponent, by saying, «intensity.» When there is a mutation of intensity, [that is] a mutation of external-aspect and of time-variation and of intensity, one would be involved in a fault with regard to the absolute [permanence] of the substance and of the external-aspect and of the time-variation and of the intensity. He asks, «How?» [The objector] gives the answer in the words, «On the ground that the functional-activity . . . the time-form.» For we can see that the functional-activity of that which is future in its time-form as belonging to curds is present as belonging to milk, because [the functional activity of the future] is shut off by this [functional-activity of the present]. For this reason when the external-aspect which has the time-variation (*lakṣaṇa*) of the curds, although existent in the milk, does not exert its own functional-activity, then the undertaking of the business [of the effects to be accomplished] by curdling and the other [changes], is called future. And it is called present when it is thus active; and past when it has done the business of curdling and the other [changes] and stopped. To this extent then it must follow that the substance and the external-aspects and the time-variations and the intensities, although persisting in all three times, are absolutely [permanent]. For permanence is existence at all times. And in [these] four cases, whether they exist at all times or do not exist [at all times], there is no production.[1] This much only is the time-variation (*lakṣaṇa*) of the absolutely permanent. And in the case of the Power of Intellect (*citi-çakti*) also, which is absolutely permanent, there is no other special feature. This is the point. He meets the objection in the words «But that [alleged] weakness does not exist.» There is no weakness there. Why? Because although the substrate (*guṇin*) is permanent, the aspects (*guṇa*) suffer antagonisms,[2] the one of [the aspects] being capable of being overcome and the others of overcoming. This is their variety. What he means to say is this: Although there is existence at all times in the case of all four, still, in so far as there is a variety in the antagonisms of the aspects (*guṇa*), in that the various evolved-forms of which this [variety] consists become visible or invisible, and in so far as they enter into mutations, there is no absolute [permanence]. Whereas in the case of the Power of Intellect (*citi-çakti*) there is no becoming visible or becoming invisible of evolved-forms which belong to itself. Thus [this] is absolutely permanent. As they say,[3] "The learned call that permanent the nature of which does not perish." That this variety of antagonisms is the cause of the variety of the evolved forms in the case of both the evolving-substance and the evolved-substance is shown by the words, «Just as.» Just

[1] If it is to exist at all times, then, like the *citiçakti*, it could not be produced. Or if it is not to exist at any time, then, like the horns of a man, it could not be produced. This is Bālarāma's gloss.

[2] This word *vimarda* occurs once only in the Bhāṣya. But Vācaspati uses it four times besides this, i. 2, p. 11^{3}; iii. 13, pp. 209^{16}, $210^{3, 6}$ (Calc. ed.).

[3] Compare MBh. xii. 318. 102 (= 11826).

as the arrangement of parts,[1] as distinguished (*lakṣaṇa*) by being a mutation of earth and of other [coarse elements], is itself merely an external aspect and has a beginning and an end, in that it becomes invisible,—[so] «sound and the rest,» the subtile elements sound and touch and colour and taste and smell, are not perishable as compared with their own products, and do not, like them, become invisible. He shows how this is in the case of the evolving-matter by the words, «so the resoluble.» «To it the term evolved-form (*vikāra*) is applied.» But the Power of Thought (*citi-çakti*) is not subject to this kind of evolution of form. This is the point.—Having thus taken up by way of illustration both the evolved-matter and the evolving-cause, which are well enough known to thinking persons, he takes up in the case of the evolved-matter only, which is well enough known to the popular [mind], the variety of the antagonisms of the aspects (*guṇa*) which leads to variety in the mutations of external-aspect and of time-variation and of intensity, by saying, «The following serves as an illustration.» There is no necessity that the mutation of intensity should belong to time-variations only. For all [three], external-aspect and time-variation and intensity, are expressed by the word 'intensity'. Therefore the one [kind of] mutation is intensity which is common to all. Accordingly he says, «Thus the substance only.» He gives the distinguishing-characteristic of the mutation which includes [all] by saying, «in a permanent.» The word 'external-aspect' is an expression for external-aspect and for time-variation and for intensity, in so far as it is that in which they inhere.

Among these [mutations],

14. A substance conforms itself to quiescent and uprisen and indeterminable external-aspects.

An external aspect[2] is [to speak precisely] only a power of the substance as limited by its pre-established harmony[3] [with regard to effects]. And it is known as an actual existence, of which the existence is inferred by the kind of effect which it generates, as

[1] Vācaspati uses *saṁsthāna* as the equivalent to *saṁniveça* iii. 26, p. 238[7], and iv. 13, p. 291[6]. It is applied only to collections of *mahābhūta*; and is sometimes not different from external form (*mūrti*), iii. 53, p. 272[1], and iii. 13, p. 210[8]; or again, the parts of grains, iii. 13, p. 205[4], iii. 15, p. 216[3]; or the parts of words, iii. 17, p. 222[12]; or of the limbs of birds, ii. 46, p. 185[10]. See also ii. 28, p. 170[11], and iii. 26, p. 239[8] (Calc. ed.).

[2] The same entity, regarded from the side of permanence, is a mutation (*pariṇāma*); from the side of change is an external aspect.

[3] The word *yogyatā* is used in the sūtra ii. 53. The word *yogyatva* is in the sūtra ii. 41 and in the Bhāṣya, p. 182[11] (Calc. ed.). Vācaspati uses it five times: ii. 6, p. 116[5]; ii. 23, p. 157[6]; ii. 32, p. 176[10]; iii. 14, p. 211[10-12].

one or another [form] of the single [substance]. Of these [forms] that is called present, if it be that the external-aspect is passing through [the state] of its peculiar functional-activity. This is different from the other external-aspects both the quiescent and the indeterminable [states]. But when it has rejoined its general [or latent] form, then how could that external-aspect be distinguished from any other, since it is then of the very nature of the substance itself? There are, as every one knows, three of these external-aspects within the substance, the quiescent and the uprisen and the indeterminable. Of these the quiescent are those that have come to rest by finishing their functional-activity. The uprisen are those in active function; and these [uprisen] are immediately-contiguous (*samanantara*) to the future time-variation. While the past come after the present. Why do not the present come after the past? Because there is no relation of antecedent and consequent [between them]. The relation of antecedent and consequent in the case of the future and the present [1] is not the same as [this relation] in the case of the past [2] [and of the present]. Therefore there is [no later external-aspect] immediately contiguous to the past. Consequently the future only is immediately contiguous [as being antecedent] to the present.—Now the indeterminable [external-aspects], what are they? Everything containing the essence of everything. Upon which it has been said, "That which in the various forms [3] of taste and other [subtile elements] contains the mutations of [the coarse elements of] water and of earth is found in plants; likewise [that which is mutable] in plants is found in animals, and of animals in plants." In this sense, in so far as the common nature is not destroyed, we use the term 'everything contains the essence of everything.' Still, because of connexion with place and time and form [4] and cause, the external-aspects do not of course manifest themselves at the same time.[5] That which passes through a

[1] The Vārttika says that this is *prāgabhāva*.

[2] In this case there is *prāgdhvaṅsa*.

[3] Compare Vācaspati's quotation iv. 13, p. 291[6] from the Vāyu Pur.; and also Yogavāsiṣṭa, Utpattiprakaraṇa 78.

[4] The word *rūpa* is used for colour and form; the word *ākāra* for form when a discrimination is made. The contrast between the two is similar to the Cartesian use of 'clear' and 'distinct.'

[5] The Bikāner MS. and the text of Bodas (Bom. Sanskrit Ser.), p. 134[8], both read *upabandhāt*.

succession of these external-aspects, whether manifested or unmanifested, and which has as its essence the generic form and the particular,[1] and which is present-in-all-but-different-from-them[2] (*anvayin*),—that is a substance. But the [Yogācāra] who holds that this world is nothing but external-aspects without [a substance] present-in-all-but-different-from-them,—for him there would be no experience. Why would this be so? [The reply is,] how could one consciousness of a subject-of-experience (*bhokṛtvena*) be held responsible for a deed done by another consciousness? And there would also be no memory of this [consciousness]. For there is no such thing as recollection by one consciousness of something seen by another [consciousness]. And it is the substance permanently present-in-all-but-different-from-them which, upon the recognition of a thing is recognized as participating in the alteration of the external-aspect. Consequently it is not true that [this world] is nothing more than external-aspects without [a substance] present-in-all-but-different-from-them.

He gives the distinguishing-characteristic of this substance to which the threefold mutation belongs by the sūtra. **14. Among these [mutations] a substance conforms itself to quiescent and uprisen and indeterminable external-aspects.** A substance (*dharmin*) is a thing that has external-aspects (*dharma*). And because, unless one knows the external-aspects, one cannot know the substance, he makes known what the external-aspect is in the word «pre-established-harmony.» «The substance» means a material object such as clay. «Only a power» [that is] the power of producing the dust and the lump of clay and the water-jar. This is the external-aspect,[3] in so far as these are contained in this [substance] in an unphenomenalized state. This is the point. An objector says, 'In so far as these exist therein in an unphenomenalized state they may become visible from within it, but how can the capacity to fetch water [in the jar] and similar [purposeful acts], which could not have been got out of their cause [the clay], be obtained by them [that is, the finished products]?' In reply to this he says, «as limited by its pre-established-harmony.» The power to produce the water-jar is defined as being pre-established-harmony for things which fetch water. Hence the power to fetch water and the other [purposeful] acts are also obtained by the water-jars and other things from their own cause only. Thus [the capacity to fetch water] is not accidental [with

[1] Compare i. 7, p. 21[4], and iii. 44, p. 257[2] (Calc. ed.).

[2] See also i. 45, p. 96[4]; iii. 13, p. 205[6]; iii. 44, p. 257[6] (Calc. ed.).

[3] Reading *dharmaḥ*.

regard to the substance]. This is the point.—There is another interpretation. One might be asked, 'What are substances?' The reply is, «of the substance as limited by its pre-established-harmony.» One might be asked, 'What is an external-aspect?' The reply is, «An external-aspect is only a power.[1]» The meaning is that an external-aspect is only a pre-established-harmony belonging to these [substances]. Hence it is proven that the thing which has this [external-aspect] is the substance. Thus it becomes clear.—He describes the source-of-the-valid-idea [which proves] the real existence of these [external. aspects] in the words, «And it . . . is inferred by the kind of effect which it generates.» Of the single substance in one or another form as dust or as a lump of clay or as a water-jar. This is the meaning. And it differs because there are evidently different effects. This is another way of putting it (*iti yāvat*). It is observed [or] apperceived. With regard to these [external-aspects] he describes the difference between the lump of clay, which strikes upon [the thinking substance of] experience and is present, and the quiescent state of the clay as dust, and the indeterminable state of the clay as water-jar by saying «Of these [forms] that is called present.» If there be no difference, then the dust and the water-jar would have their functional-activity co-extensive with that of the lump of clay. This is the point. But in the case of the unphenomenalized lump of clay, the establishment of the difference, as stated above, is impossible. [This] he says in the words, «But when.» What [then] is this [difference]? By establishment of what difference will there be a differentiation? Having thus mentioned that there is [this] establishment of a difference between the external-aspects, he analyses this difference in the words, «There are, as every one knows.» The word «uprisen» means present. He now deduces the priority and the sequence of the time-forms in the words, «And these.» A question is raised in the words, «Why does not?» 'For what reason does not the present come after the past?' This is the meaning. The reason is, «There is no relation of antecedent and consequent [between them].» By speaking of the object [that is, absence of antecedence and consequence] he indicates that which contains as its object [the absence of antecedence and consequence], that is to say, the non-apperception [of this object]. He shows what this same non-apperception is, in so far as its properties are opposite to those of apperception, in the words, «in the case of the future and the present.» He brings the discussion to a close with the word, «Consequently.» Consequently (*tat*) means for this reason. The future only is immediately contiguous as being antecedent to the present; but the past is not. The present is immediately contiguous to the past as being antecedent to it; but the indeterminable is not. Therefore it is established that the youngest of the time-forms is the past. An objector says, "This may be true. The uprisen and the past may be surmised

[1] Compare the passage at the end of the Explanation of iii. 15, "Power also is a subtile state of effects that are intensified. It is an external-aspect of the mind and it is inferred only by the experience of its coarse effects."

to be those external-aspects which are in experience and those which have been experienced. But external-states which are indeterminable cannot, in so far as they are indeterminable, be surmised." With this in mind he asks, «Now . . . ?» What are the indeterminables? In what things do we look[1] for them? To this the answer is in the words «Everything containing the essence of everything. Upon which it has been said.» This is made consistent in the words, «. . . of water and of earth.» For, in the case of water which contains [the subtile elements of] taste and colour and touch and sound, and in the case of earth which contains odour and taste and colour and touch and sound, various forms containing the mutations are observed as perceived in the taste and other [subtile elements] which are found in the root and fruit and blossoms and foliage and in the other parts of trees and creepers and shrubs. This cannot be a mutation of earth which is not of a similar essence, or of water which is not of a like kind. For, as it has already[2] been consistently stated, there can be no production of that which does not already exist. Similarly in the case of animals, human beings and beasts tame or wild, various tastes, &c., are observed coming from mutations of plants. For these [human beings and other animals] in eating the fruits [and leaves] and so on acquire a rich variety of forms, &c. In the same way, plants are observed to have a variety of forms coming from the mutations of animals. For it is known that pomegranates become as large as coco-nuts when sprinkled with blood. He brings the discussion to a close with the words, «In this sense.» Thus everything, earth and water and all, contains all tastes and other [subtile elements]. He gives the reason for this in the words, «in so far as the common nature is not destroyed.» Because, in so far it is recognized everywhere, that-which-is-asserted (*jāti*) of the common nature of earth and of water is not destroyed. An objector says, 'If everything contains the essence of everything, then, Sir, since everything everywhere is always in every part close at hand, there would be a manifestation of all existences whatsoever at one and the same time. For an effect whose cause, lacking nothing, is close at hand, ought not long to delay.' With this in mind he says, «with place and time.» Although everything containing the essence of everything is a cause [of everything], still there has to be [a manifestation] 1. of that [particular] place which belongs to a [particular] effect [of this cause]. For instance, Kashmir is the place of the saffron-plant. Because although these [causes] exist in Pāñcāla and other countries, there is no coming actively forth[3] [of the plant]. Accordingly there is no manifestation of the saffron-plant in a place such as Pāñcāla. 2. Likewise during the hot season, since no rain moves actively forth, there is no manifestation of rice-plants. 3. Similarly a doe

[1] Reading *samīkṣāmahe.*

[2] Compare ii. 19, p. 149[6]; iii. 11, p. 201[2]; iii. 13, pp. 206[17], 207[2]; and *asato 'nupajananāt*, ii. 15, p. 132[5].

[3] The word *samudācāra* occurs once only in the Bhāṣya iii. 13, p. 207[9]. In Vācaspati it is the equivalent of *abhivyakti* and occurs ii. 4, p. 111[9]; iii. 13, p. 208[1]; iii. 14, p. 214[2f]. Bālarāma glosses the word *vidyamānatā āvirbhāva iti*, p. 214, note 3 (Calc. ed.).

does not give birth to a human being, because in her the human form does not develop. 4. In the same way, a non-meritorious person does not experience anything like pleasure, because in him no meritorious cause moves actively forth. Therefore because of connexion [or] separation by place or time or form or cause, things [that is] forms of being do not manifest themselves [1] at the same time.—Having thus given a classification to the external-aspects, he shows that the substance is present-in-all-but-different-from-them by saying, «. . which . . . of these . . .» The generic-form is the substance as such; the particular is the external-aspect. The meaning is that its essence is of both these kinds.—Having thus shown that the substance which is established by experience is present-in-all-but-different-from-them, he reminds the Annihilationist (*vāināçika*), who does not assent to this and who assents to the theory of a momentary mind-stuff made of consciousness only, of the undesired contingency previously [i. 32] mentioned, and he does so in the words, «But the [Yogācāra].» [Also in the words,] «And . . . upon the recognition of a thing.» For a thing observed by Devadatta is not recognized by Yajñadatta. Accordingly it is he who experiences that also recognizes.

15. The order of the sequence (*krama*) is the reason for the order of the mutations.

If it be possible [2] that a single substance has only a single mutation, then the order of the sequence is the cause of the order of the mutation. One finds, for example, clay in the form of dust, clay in the form of a lump, clay in the form of a water-jar, clay in the form of potsherds [and] clay in the form of small bits. It is in this sense that there is a sequence. 1. Whenever one external-aspect is immediately-contiguous to another external-aspect, it is [then in] sequence with it. The lump of [clay] falls away and the water-jar comes into existence. It is in such cases that a sequence in the mutation of external-aspects occurs. 2. There is a sequence in the mutation of time-variations. By reason of there being a future [time-variation] of the water-jar, there is a sequence [to it in the] present [time-variation]. Likewise by reason of there being a present [time-variation] of the lump [of clay], there is a sequence [to it in the]

[1] Reading with Bikāner MS. *ātmanām*.

[2] Reading *prasakte*, which represents this system. But if the reading be *prasakteḥ* (Kashmir MS. and Gaṅgādhara Shāstri's MS.), then the word would be used as indicating that this is not possible. The form would be used as equivalent to a verbal form in *-ya* according to Pāṇ. i. 4. 31 with Siddh. Kāum. (Nir. Sāg., ed. 1904), p. 144, last line.

past [time-variation]. There is no sequence for the past. Why is this? When there is a relation of antecedent and sequent there is an immediate contiguity. But this relation does not occur in the case of the past. Consequently there is a sequence for two time-variations only. 3. There is none the less a sequence in the mutations of intensity, as when the oldness of a brand-new water-jar becomes evident first on its rim[1] (*prānte*), and then manifesting itself in a sequence which conforms to the succession of moments, [finally] reaches a complete [individual] phenomenal [form]. This then is the third mutation and it is other than the external-aspect and the time-variation. These same sequences become what they are, so long as the distinction between the substance and the external-aspect holds. For the external-aspect as such also can become the substance in so far as another external-aspect is concerned. But since, strictly speaking, this same substance can be named external-aspect by virtue of attributing to it an identity with the substance, therefore this sequence shines forth in consciousness as a unit only. The external-aspects of the mind-stuff are of two kinds, those that are perceived and those that are unperceived. Of these two, the perceived have as their essence presented-ideas; those that are unperceived have as their essence real-things (*vastu*) only. These latter are moreover just seven; by inference the existence of [these external-aspects] as real things only is brought within reach. "Restriction[2] and right-living and subliminal-impressions and mutations and vitality and movement and power are external-aspects of mind-stuff excluded from sight."

15. The order of the sequence (*krama*) is the reason for the order of the mutations. [A question is stated for discussion.] 'Does one substance have only one mutation characterized (*lakṣaṇa*) by external-aspect and time-variation (*lakṣaṇa*) and intensity? Or does it have many mutations characterized by external-aspect and time-variation and intensity? Of these two which seems plausible? [The answer of the objector is,] because the substance is one, the mutation is only one. For from a cause, which as such is one, there ought not to be a diversity of effects, because that diversity would have to be the result of chance.' If this be taken so, the reply is given. As a result of the order of the sequence

[1] In making a jar the rim is moulded first.

[2] This seems to be a mnemonic verse by the author of the Comment. Compare iii. 18, p. 230[4] (Calc. ed.).

there is an order of the mutations. Both ordinary men and men of trained minds search out with their own eyes, in clay which is one, a sequential succession of mutating form of dust and lump and water-jar and potsherds and small bits. And the immediate succession between the dust and the lump is one thing; and that between the lump and the water-jar is another; and that between the water-jar and the potsherds is another; and that between the potsherds and the small bits is another. Whatever is sequent with respect to the one is antecedent with respect to the other. This same difference of sequences, since it does not correspond to a single mutation, leads one to conclude that there are different mutations. Moreover the clay, although a single substance, undergoes a succession of mutations in sequences following the sequence of contact (*samavadhāna*) with various co-operating causes which fall one after another into the sequence, and does not leave it [the succession of mutations] to chance. And as in the case of the order of the mutation of the external-aspects, so the reason for the order of the mutation of time-variations and for the order of the mutation of intensities is of the same kind as the order of the sequence. All this is made luminous in the words of the Comment, «a single substance.» On the assumption that there is an identity between the sequence and that which is in the sequence, it is said that this is its sequence, in the words, «There is none the less a sequence in the mutations of intensity.» For it is thus when rice-grains, carefully guarded in a granary by a miser, after very many years become reduced to atoms, in that the arrangement of the parts [of the grain] is likely to crumble even at a touch of the hand. Such a [condition] would not result so suddenly (*akasmāt*) in the case of brand-new rice-grains. Therefore in the sequence of successive moments this fact [that they are reduced to atoms] is seen to characterize those [grains] which have gotten into the sequence of very large and less large and large and minute and more minute and very minute. This same order in the sequence does depend upon the distinction between the substance and the external-aspects, as he says, «These same sequences.» Extended from the evolved-effect and up to resoluble [primary matter] there is this contingent relation of substance and external-aspects. Even [coarse elements] such as earth are external-aspects as compared with subtile elements, as he says, «the external-aspect also.» Because unresoluble [primary matter] is, strictly speaking, the only substance, it is usual to attribute identity to it. «By virtue of (*taddvāreṇa*)» [that is] by virtue of having a common locus the substance would itself be an external-aspect. For this very reason there would be only one mutation, that of the substance, since external-aspects and time-variations and intensities have entered into the substance itself. If this is so, it is almost equivalent to saying that the substance is far-removed from being absolutely permanent.—While discussing the mutations of the external-aspects he also states the diversity in the kinds of external-aspects of the mind-stuff by saying «of the mind-stuff.» «Perceived» means direct perceptions; «unperceived» means indirect perceptions. Of these two, those whose essence is presented-ideas are sources-of-valid-ideas and passions and the like. By the words «real things only» he refers to the non-illuminating character [of things]. An objector says, 'This may be so. But if unperceived, they surely do not exist.' In reply to this he says «by inference.» These [external aspects] are so described whose existence as real things only is brought within reach by inference. The word inference (*anu-māna*) means the proof (*māna*) which comes after (*anu*), and, as having the same nature, verbal-communication is also [included in the term]. He brings together in a memorial-verse the seven unperceived external-aspects by saying, «Restriction.» 1. The restriction of fluctuations is the unconscious stage [i. 51] of the mind-stuff. We come to a knowledge of it by verbal-communication and by inference as being a state in which subliminal-impressions alone remain. 2. The word «right-living» is meant to include merit and demerit. Elsewhere the reading is 'karma'. In this case also merit and demerit produced by this [right-living] would have to be understood. And these are known either by verbal-communication or by inference based upon a knowledge from an experience of pleasure or of pain. 3. But «subliminal-impression» is inferred from memory. 4. Likewise, since the aspects (*guṇa*) are three, the changes of the aspects of the mind-stuff are unstable, and so «mutation» from moment to moment is inferred. 5. Similarly «vitality» which is a kind of effort to sustain the breath. And since it is not known [to the mind], this external-aspect is inferred from expiration and inspiration. 6. Likewise «movement» of the mind (*cetas*) is activity, in accordance with its activity in connexion with the various senses and portions of the body, and this [activity] also is inferred from the connexion with it [that is, the mind]. 7. Similarly «power»[1] also is a subtile state of effects that are intensified. It is an external-aspect of the mind and it is inferred only by experience of its coarse effects.

From here on the field-of-operation for the constraint [reached] by the yogin who has acquired all the means for the attainment of the desired object is discussed.

16. As a result of constraint upon the three mutations [there follows] the knowledge of the past and the future.

Yogins acquire knowledge of the past and of the future as a result of constraint upon the mutations of external-aspects and of time-variations and of intensities. Fixed-attention and contemplation and concentration, three in one, has been called [iii. 4] constraint. By this [constraint] the three mutations directly experienced

[1] Compare ii. 14, p. 211[13] (Calc. ed.).

produce knowledge of the past and of the future in these [three mutations].

From this point up to the end of the [third] Book the field-of-operation for the constraint and the supernormal powers indicative of the mastery over objects will be described. Here we have first discussed as the field-of-operation for constraint, for that yogin who has appropriated to himself all the aids to yoga, just those three mutations which have been described in detail. This is in the words, 16. **As a result of constraint upon the three mutations there follows the knowledge of the past and of the future.** An objector asks, 'Direct-experience occurs only where there is constraint. How then can constraint upon the three mutations directly-experience the past and the future?' In reply to this he says, «By this [constraint].» When the three mutations are brought under direct-experience by this [constraint], those [time-variations] of the past and the future, inseparably-connected-with-the-mutations-yet-different-from-them, become the objects of [intuitive] knowledge. And the direct-experience of the three mutations itself has as its essence the direct-experience of the past and the future which are included in [the three mutations]. Thus there is no difference of objects in the two cases of the constraint and of the direct-experience.

---

17. Word and intended-object and presented-idea are confused because they are erroneously identified with each other. By constraint upon the distinctions between them [there arises the intuitive] knowledge (*jñāna*) of the cries of all living beings.

With regard to these [three,] voice has its function [in uttering] only the [sounds of] syllables. And the organ-of-hearing has as its object only that [emission of air] which has been mutated into a sound [by a contact with the eight places of articulation belonging to the vocal organ]. But it is a mental-process (*buddhi*) that grasps the word [as significant sound] by seizing[1] the letter-sounds each in turn and binding them together [into one word]. Sounds-of-syllables (*varṇa*) do not naturally[2] aid each other, for they

[1] This same point is much more elaborately discussed by Vācaspati in his Tattvabindu (Benares, 1892), on page 10 at the top, and also p. 3[b].

[2] The question is whether the sounds one by one or collectively make the prototype (*sphoṭa*) manifest. The reply seems to be that just as the full knowledge of the real jewel does not shine out clear at the first sight, but shines out in its fullness in the final idea, the resultant of several impressions,—so the sounds singly do make the prototype manifest, but do not immediately make the prototype in its perfection manifest.

cannot coexist at the same time. Not having attained-to-the-unity-of a word and not having [conveyed a definite meaning], they become audible (*āvis*) and they become inaudible (*tiras*). Hence it is said that individually [letter-sounds] lack the nature of a word. On the other hand the [sounds of the] syllables one by one may be said to have the essence of a word [1] as being filled (*pracita*) with the power to furnish expressions for everything through their association with other [sounds of] syllables which also co-operate [in this result]. And so they seem to pass into a multiplicity [2] of [word]-forms. A preceding [sound of a syllable] is mentally determined by the following and the following by the preceding to become-a-distinct-and-separate word. Thus a group of [sounds of] syllables follows in a sequence [of utterance] and is assigned by conventional usage to a [single] intended-object (*artha*). Hence though competent to indicate a great-number-of-things (*sarva*), a certain number of these [sounds of syllables], whatever that number may be, makes [but the one] object clear [to consciousness]. For example, g-o-ḥ indicate [only that] thing [known as 'cow'] with its dewlap and other specific features. Hence [also] the unity, which the mental-process makes known out of these [many sounds of syllables], determined as these are by conventional-usage by a single intended-object and seized and bound together into a fixed sequence of sounds, is the word. This unity [termed] a word is in every case the object of a single [3] mental-process and requires a single [distinct] effort [of the organs of articulation]. It is a thing not having parts, and not having a sequence [4] [of parts]. It does not consist of [sounds of] syllables. It is a thing of the mind, and is brought into its function by means of the presented-idea [which we retain] of the final syllable-sound [in a group of these sounds]. If a man wish to convey information to another, he must express himself by these same syllable-sounds to which the others must listen. This use of speech to which no beginning [can be

[1] Compare Tattva Bindu, p. 6[8] (Ben. ed.).

[2] A universe of meanings attached to one word. The concept *vāiçvarūpyam* is approached by Vācaspatimiçra in Sāṁk. Tatt. Kāum. on Kārikā xv.

[3] That is, a separate and distinct mental process.

[4] Compare Patañjali Mahābh. (Kielhorn), i. 6[18]; i. 7[3]; i. 75[9]; i. 112[24]; ii. 123[1], and elsewhere.

assigned] permeates the thinking-substance of the ordinary man with subconscious-impressions [which come from the syllable-sounds]. Thus as a result of common understanding (*sampratipatti*) [the word] is thought to be something real in itself. It is owing to our knowing what this [word] means in accordance with conventional-usage that we attempt to divide it [into sounds of syllables]. Thus we say that the seizing-in-turn-and-binding-together of this or that number of [sounds of] syllables in some such kind [of fixed sequence] is a word expressive of a single intended-object. But conventional-usage is essentially [what has been handed down] by the memory [of man]. It is a kind of erroneous identification of the word and the thing signified. So that there is a confusion of the word with the intended-object, and of the intended-object with the word. Here we see how conventional usage is a kind of erroneous identification of each with the other based upon memory. Thus it is that these [three], the word 'cow' and the intended-object 'cow' and the presented-idea 'cow', get confused, because erroneously identified with one another. But he who recognizes these three as quite distinct is the knower of all. Furthermore, every word has the power[1] to express a [complete] sentence. Thus when we utter the word 'tree', we imply that it exists. For no intended-object of a word can lack existence. Similarly no action expressed [by a verb] is possible without the means-of-attaining [the action]. And so when we utter the word 'cook-s', certain relations which are later expressly mentioned[2] are supplied to specify the meaning [by excluding other relations]. Thus we mention the man Chāitra as the agent,[3] rice as the object,[4] and fire as the means[5] of the action [expressed by the verb 'cook']. We observe also that words are so constructed as to give the meaning of the sentence; thus a 'Reader'[6] is 'one who recites Vedas'; thus if we say 'lives', we mean [that he] 'keeps the breath of life.' [And conversely] in this sentence there is a manifestation

[1] The *vākyaçakti* is discussed in the Tattva Bindu, p. 16 (Benares ed.).

[2] In accordance with Patañjali Mahābhāṣya on i. 2. 45, vārt. 4; Kielhorn, i. 218[4].

[3] Pāṇ. i. 4. 54 *kartṛ*.

[4] Pāṇ. i. 4. 49 *karma*.

[5] Pāṇ. i. 4. 42 *karaṇa*.

[6] Pāṇ. v. 2. 84.

of the meaning of words. But to determine whether a particular word denotes an action [described by a verb] or some relation [therewith, we must withdraw it from the sentence] and analyse its formation by making distinctions. Without such an [analysis] many a word such as *bhavati* or *açvaḥ* or *ajāpayaḥ*[1] would remain ambiguous, because as regards its outer form it might be analysed either as a noun or as a verb (*ākhyāta*). There is a distinction between these words and intended-objects and presented-ideas. To illustrate this [distinction]. 'The palace whitens'; here the action [of a verb] is meant. 'The white palace'; here a relation is meant, [that of the quality white with the action or process which produced it]. The word is in essence both an action [denoted by a verb] and a relation, and the termination [at the end of the word] conveys these meanings of [action and of relation]. But why is this so? Because this [process of whitening] is identified with that, [its result, the quality white]; so that in conventional-usage the presented-idea [of these objects seems to be] one and the same. But the white intended-object is that which becomes the thing upon which the word and the presented-idea depend. For this [intended-object] by reason of its own intensities passes-through-evolved-forms and does not correspond to the word nor to the mental-process [which are unchanging in themselves]. Similarly the word and similarly the presented-idea do not correspond the one with the other. The word [changes] in one way; the intended-object in another way; and the presented-idea in another way. Thus there is a distinction. And so it happens that by constraint upon this distinction a yogin attains [intuitive] knowledge of the cries of all creatures.

Here is another field-of-operation for constraint stated in sūtra 17. Word . . . knowledge . . . In this [sūtra] while his intention is to explain a word as an expression of meaning, he describes first of all the object of the functional-activity of the vocal-organ by saying «In this [sūtra].» The «voice» is the organ of voice; it is that which phenomenalizes [the sounds of the] syllables and it has eight places of articulation. As is said [in the Çikṣā 13], "There are eight places of articulation of the [sounds of the] syllables, the chest and the throat and the head and the root of the tongue and the teeth and the nose and

[1] Whitney: Grammar, 2nd ed., 1042, l.

the lips and the palate." This vocal organ has its function only in [uttering the sounds of the] syllables as they are known to ordinary sense-perception, and not as expressive of meanings. He explains the object of the functional-activity of the organ of hearing in the words «the organ-of-hearing.» The organ-of-hearing, however, has that only as its object which is mutated in the form of a particular [sound of a] syllable, which has as its essence a particular mutation of an emission-of-air (*udāna*) subjected-to-contact (*abhighātin*) with [the various places-of-articulation] belonging to the vocal organ. But its object is not a word-expressing-a-meaning. This is what he wishes-to-say (*ity artha*). He distinguishes the word-expressing-a-meaning from the [sounds of the] syllables as known to ordinary sense-perception, by saying «the word [as significant sound].» But it is the mental-process that grasps the word as expressing-meaning by seizing the letter-sounds each in turn (*anu*) and binding them together [into one word]. Having grasped the letter-sounds (*nāda*) as [the sounds of] syllables (*varṇa*) one by one as they are known in sense-perception, it binds them in turn [that is] afterwards so that they are made to change into a unity and we can say g-o-ḥ [that is to say] one word. By this [mental-process] the word is grasped. Although each of the preceding mental-processes [by stages] brings each word, [so long as it] has the form of the [sounds of] syllables, into consciousness, still the word [expressing meaning] does not clearly lie [before us]. But at the last mental-act (*vijñāna*) it becomes clear. Thus it is said «a mental-process (*buddhi*) grasps the word [as significant sound] by seizing the letter-sounds each in turn and binding them together [into one word].» To [the Mīmāṅsaka] who maintains that the [sounds of the] syllables in themselves express a meaning, in that a word cannot be discerned as one because the [sounds] are heterogeneous, he replies «the [sounds of the] syllables.» Now these [sounds of the] syllables must either 1. each singly (*pratyeka*) arouse the idea (*dhī*) having a word expressing meaning as its content, like a row of pegs[1] upon which a bag-of-netted-cords is hung; or 2. in combination (*saṁhata*) like the stones which when together hold the pot. Not, in any case, 1. the first alternative, because from the single [sound of a syllable] the sense-perception of the thing does not rise in consciousness; or because if it did proceed from a single one, the second and the third need not have been uttered. For when an action is completed, a means-of-attaining [that action] which adds nothing new cannot be counted as (*nyāyātipāta*) a means-of-attaining. Therefore 2. the second [alternative] remains. For the stones in combination can hold up the pot, because they are there at the same time. But the [sounds of the] syllables cannot be simultaneous. Accordingly, since it cannot be that aid is reciprocally given and received, they cannot by being together arouse the idea of the meaning. These [sounds of syllables] not attaining by themselves to a single special word and therefore not conveying [the meaning], become now audible (*āvis*) and now inaudible (*tiras*). Like the iron rods [of a

[1] This phrase in almost the same words occurs in Vācaspati's Tattva Bindu, p. 5[13].

tripod which co-operate to hold a vessel] they are not, as being each by itself, termed a word. If, however, the [sounds of the] syllables were to attain to a word as a unit by being [each by itself] identical with the word, then the defect mentioned before would not apply, as he says «On the other hand the [sounds of the] syllables one by one may be said to have the essence of a word.»—«Being filled with the power to furnish expressions for everything» [means] having an accumulation of a great number of powers to indicate [things]. For the letter 'g' occurs in words like *gau* and *gaṇa* and *gaura* and *naga* expressing various meanings such as, for instance, the common-nature-of-cows. Thus [this letter] has the power to express this or that [meaning]. Likewise the letter 'o' occurs in words like *somaḥ* and *çociḥ* in words denoting the Içvara as the object-intended. This is to be said *mutatis mutandis* with regard to all [the letters]. Furthermore the [sound of a] syllable such as 'g' which co-operates[1] [in one set of cases], is the very same which is associated [and] connected with [the sound of] another syllable such as 'o'. These [sounds of the] syllables which have been so described are a general condition (*bhāva*) or state. Therefore they seem to pass into a multiplicity of forms [or] a plurality. But it does not actually pass into a plurality just because of [its own peculiar] state.—The «preceding» [sound of a] syllable, the letter 'g' by association with the following letter 'o' is thus distinguished from words like *gaṇa*; and the following letter 'o' by association with the letter 'g' is distinguished from words like *çociḥ* and thus becomes determined in the mental-process which seizes each in turn and binds them together to become a distinct-and-separate word-expressive-of-the-meaning (*vācaka*) of the common-nature-of-the-cow, [to become] the word-prototype of the word 'cow'. The connexion of ideas is this. [This happens in this way] because the presented-idea of the thing cannot be effected by successive [sounds of] syllables which do not occur [in a word] in a fixed sequence. Nor, when heaven or the highest sacrificial-merit (*apūrva*) is to be brought to pass, is it proper to say that just as sacrifices such as the Āgneya[2] co-operate (*sāhitya*) by means of purifications (*saṁskāra*), so the [sounds of the] syllables [by means of subliminal-impressions (*saṁskāra*)] co-operate in the production of the mental-process of the thing. [It is not proper to say this,] because the argument breaks down when we apply the method of alternatives (*vikalpa*). Surely this subliminal-impression (*saṁskāra*) produced by the experience of [the sounds of the] syllables is either the one which generates memory, or it is the other, which is called sacrificial-merit[3] (*apūrva*) and is likened to the purification (*saṁskāra*) by the Āgneya and similar [sacrifices]. Now first of all the second

[1] Discussed at length on p. 6[14] of the Tattva Bindu (Benares ed.).

[2] Six sacrifices are performed in two groups, three without a break in the groups. Three on the first day after the full moon, the Āgneya, the Upāñçu, the Agniṣṭoma; three *yāga* on the first day after the new moon. All six have the name of *darçapūrṇamāsayāga*.

[3] Compare the discussion of the *sphoṭa* as analogous to the sacrifice in Çāstra Dīpika i. 1. 5, p. 68; i. 2. 10, p. 127. See also Tattva Bindu, p. 6[10]. On the intermixture of *apūrva* see Çāst. Dīp. ii. 1. 5, p. 200.

[of these alternatives] cannot [be admitted], because of the difficulties in the assumption. It must be assumed that this [purification] is the very same as that which follows (*pūrva*) sacrificial-merit. Whereas this [word-type] which is one cannot be produced by experiences of [sounds of] syllables in sequences. Since we should have to assume [the existence] of many subsidiary purifications (*saṁskāra*) each of the same kind [as the others]. It is this that is the difficulty. Furthermore so long as we do not know that this purification serves as a cause to make the intended-object known, it cannot be accepted as serving to produce this [meaning]. For a relation which is not known to serve the purpose of presenting the intended-object, cannot be accepted as serving [that purpose]. And, as for the subliminal-impression which is inferred from the memory which is its result, it is restricted [i. 11] to that object, namely, the experience which was its cause. And it is therefore not in a position to arouse a subliminal-impression which has something else, [namely, the presentation of the intended-object of that experience] as its object. For if this were so, any one having experienced any one object, would be able to know any [other] object. And it is not right to say that [sounds of] syllables which arise in the mirror of such a memory as takes its origin in the sum-total (*piṇḍa*) of subliminal-impressions—produced by the experience of each syllable singly—can express meaning [because the sounds of the syllables] are recognized as belonging together. For that would involve-the-conclusion that the idea of the intended object could be produced indiscriminately (*aviçeṣeṇa*), whether the [sounds of the syllables] be experienced in a sequence or out of a sequence or in reversed sequence. And it cannot be that this knowledge from memory can bring before itself (*gocarayitum*) that succession of sounds of syllables which was active in the previous experience. Hence in so far as it is not possible from the [sounds of the] syllables to have the presentation of the intended-object, it must be supposed that there is an experience[1] of the word as being single which could give rise to [the presentation of the intended-object[2]]. The same objection, moreover, does not apply with reference to the word. For the word i[illegible]omenalized by [sounds of] syllables only when single and differing acco[illegible]o the difference[3] in the effort [of articulation]. And inasmuch as the wo[illegible]are alike in so far as they are produced through the action of the like places [of articulation] by sounds which are the conditions-which-phenomenalize the various words each unlike the other, [the sounds] do make a word similar [to other words]. This word [*go*] is similar to other words which have the 'g' sound, but in other respects it is dissimilar, since their dissimilarities are different in so far as the various other [syllables] are associated [with this syllable]. Because of [this] peculiarity of this [word], although it is one, and

[1] So his position is this. The *sphoṭa* is a subliminal-impression in the *buddhi*. The *buddhi* forms the intended-object under the influence of the *sphoṭa*.

[2] The word *sva* evidently refers to the bracketed phrase.

[3] See Patañjali: Mahābhāṣya on i. 1. 9, vārt. 2, vol. i, p. 61; also on viii. 4. 48, vol. iii, p. 466 (Kielhorn).

altogether a unit (*anavayava*), still the sounds-of-the-syllables make it appear as a collection (*sāvayava*) and not as a unit. Just as a face, although it is one, with a definite colour and dimension and look, is made to appear, by [reflection in] a gem [1] or a sword-blade or a mirror, to be more than one and as having more than one colour and dimension and look. But this is not so in the strict sense. Whereas the [sounds of the] syllables are parts of the partless word and are formed of the similarities and peculiarities.

Therefore the mental-process (*buddhi*) of this [word], in the case of a particular word, supports itself upon the word-prototype (*sphoṭa*) which is undivided and partless, although it seems to be divided and seems to have parts. Therefore a part, the letter 'g', of one particular word-prototype, the word 'go' cannot cause that [namely, the partless prototype] of which it [the 'g'] is part to come forth, because of the similarity of this word-prototype with that of words like *gaura*. Therefore when made special-and-distinct by the letter 'o', it is able to cause that of which it is a part, [namely the word-prototype 'go',] to come forth. Similarly the part which is the letter 'o' is also not able, because of its similarity with words like *çociḥ*, to cause that of which it is a part, namely the word-prototype 'go', to come forth. So when made special-and-distinct by the letter 'g', it is able to cause [its own prototype] to come forth. And although [these two 'g' and 'o'] do not naturally belong together, still through [their] subliminal-impressions they do belong together. And thus it is consistent to have the relation of qualified and qualifier between them. Nor can it be said that the two subliminal-impressions have each a different object, since the experiences whose objects were the two parts, and also the two subliminal-impressions which result from the experiences, have one word as their object. The word moreover is not distinctly (*avyakta*) experienced when only part of it is experienced. Whereas it is perceived distinctly by the idea which seizes the [sounds of the] syllables in turn and binds them together,—[the idea] which is produced by the subliminal-impressions which arise from the experience of the parts. This is the difference. And we find that the first indistinct experience does produce a distinct experience by arousing subliminal-impressions in a sequence [of degrees of distinctness], just as the presented-idea that the tree when seen from a distance is green [2] (*harita*), although indistinct, leads to the distinct presented-idea of the tree. But this kind [of an idea] is impossible in an experience wherein the [sounds of the] syllables should represent intended-objects. For surely one cannot say that the [sounds of the] syllables do each singly give rise to an indistinct presented-idea of the intended-object, and ultimately to a distinct idea. For distinctness and indistinctness are restricted to cases of perceptive thinking. But [in this case] the presentation of the intended-object is to be aroused by the

[1] The illustration and discussion are given more fully in the Tattva Bindu, p. 6[2].

[2] This reading given in the analogous passage in the Tattva Bindu [p. 5[2]] by the same author seems preferable to the reading of 'elephant' (*hasti*).

syllables, and is not a perception. So if this [unperceived presentation of the intended-object] is produced by the [sounds of the] syllables, it would be produced quite clear (*sphuṭa*) or it would not be produced at all. But it could not be unclear. Whereas for the word-prototype you have to assume a clear or an unclear form in that there is a perception of it made distinct by sounds. So the case is not analogous [in that the word cannot be perceived unless the sounds be distinct, whereas the sounds can be distinctly perceived]. Thus the [sounds of the] syllables combined in the mental-process which seizes them in turn and binds them together, and which has its origin in the organ-of-hearing, —in this, together with the subliminal-impressions generated by experience of the [sounds of the] syllables, one by one, become the word-prototype of a single word. If there should be an alteration of the sequence, [then], in so far as there might not be any special-and-distinct effort [of the organ-of-voice], giving heed to the fixed order,[1] which would set in operation the special-and-distinct effort that alone can make this [word-prototype] manifest, it would follow that there would be no manifestation of it at all. In so far as the [sounds of the] syllables conform to [this] sequence and are determined by being the conventional-usage for an intended-object they display as their object a word as-it-is-usually-understood as having parts and as having its determination by conventional-usage only.—«Whatever that number might be» means two or three, three or four, five or six. Though competent to indicate a great number of things, a certain number of these [sounds of] syllables makes but the one intended-object clear [to consciousness, for example] g-o-ḥ [makes clear to consciousness only the one object known as 'cow'] having its dewlap [and other specific features]. It might then be said that the [sounds of the] syllables only, in so far as they accord with conventional-usage, have expressive power, and accordingly there is no so-called word which is a unit. In reply to this he says, «Hence . . . of these.»—«Into a fixed sequence of sounds» means a sequence caused by sounds.—«Seized and bound together» are those in whose case the sequence of sounds is of that kind.—«Which the mental-process makes known» in the sense that it is made known or becomes clear by reason of the mental-process. It has been said, in harmony with the view of persons of not very fine insight, that the 'g' and 'o' and 'ḥ' are determined by conventional-usage [as denoting the thing termed 'cow']. And this is so because, in so far as the 'g' and the other [sounds of syllables] are parts of this [word], they are identical with it and so express its meaning. But we are of opinion, that, as any one can see, it is a unity that is called a word which expresses a meaning. This he makes clear by saying «This unity.» The connexion [of ideas] is that this unity [termed] a word is by an ordinary mental-process believed [to be made of sounds of syllables]. Why should it be a unit? In reply to this he says «object of a single mental-process.» It is

[1] Precisely as there is a fixed sequence without break of the several sacrifices.

a unit since it is the object of that mental-process which is a unit in form so that one says 'g-o-ḥ' [that is] one word. He shows what it is that makes this distinct by saying «requires a single [distinct] effort.» The effort [of articulation] which makes the word r-a-s-a distinct is different in character from that which makes the word s-a-r-a distinct (*vyañjaka*). This [effort] moreover is determined by the result in the form of the manifestation of the word s-a-r-a in that[1] it begins [differently]; it has a definite succession [of sounds]; and this is the single [and distinct effort]. This it was which was required. «It is a thing without parts» because in reality it has no parts. These we only assume because of certain similarities and dissimilarities. Hence also it is «without a sequence of parts» because there it has no definite succession. An objector says, 'The [sounds of the] syllables have a definite succession, and they are parts of this [word]. How then can the word be without parts, and without a sequence of parts?' In reply to this he says «It does not consist of [sounds of] syllables.» For it does not have the [sounds of the] syllables as its parts. On the contrary the word itself, because of certain similarities and dissimilarities, is generally assumed to have the form of this or that [sound] and [so] appears in what is not its real form. For the faces as reflected in a jewel or a sword-blade or a mirror are not parts of the real face. «It is a thing of the mind» made known by the mental-process which seizes in turn and binds together [the sounds of the syllables]. «It is brought before [us]» [or] made an object by the operation (*vyāpāra*) of the presented-idea of the final [sound of the] syllable,—[by the operation, that is, of] the subliminal-impression [of the final syllable] together with the subliminal-impressions generated by the experience of [sounds of] the previous syllables. For it has already (*adhastāt*) been explained that the experience of the syllables and of the subliminal-impressions arising from them are the object of the word. The objector says, 'This may be so. But if the word-as-such (*pada-tattva*) has no parts or sequence or [sounds of] syllables, why is it not generally assumed to be of such a kind? For a bead of crystal, when overlaid with a coating of red-dye, does not, when that coating is removed, cease to be perceived as transparent and white. Therefore the [sounds of the] syllables are real [parts of the word].' In reply to this he says «to another.» If a man wish to convey information he must express himself by, he must utter, the very [sounds of the] syllables to which the hearers must listen. This use of speech, to which no beginning [can be assigned], depends upon words consisting of distinct syllables. And the subconscious-impression produced by it has also no beginning. The mental-process of the ordinary man (*loka*) is permeated [and] pervaded (*vāsita*) by this [subconscious-impression] and has to do with a word constructed of separate [sounds of] syllables. Thus as a result of usage, by the consensus of the elders, this word is thought of as something real in itself, as having reality in the strict sense. What he means to say is this: There is a certain thing, the limiting-condition, which is in correlation with the thing-

[1] Does *upakramatas* mean 'which is under consideration'?

to-be-exposed-to-limiting-conditions (*upadheya*) and which is sometimes in correlation and sometimes out of correlation with it. Such a thing is red-dye. Now when this is out of correlation, the crystal shines forth in its natural transparent and white form. And it is quite proper [that the crystal should then shine forth]. But the presented-idea of the word,—because it is not brought into [consciousness] (*anutpāda*) by anything other than the particular sound brought about by the particular effort [of articulation], and in so far as this [presented-idea] is always turbid with flaws of dissimilarity,—can generate the presented-idea [of the word] only as being in essence [sounds of] syllables. So how can there be the ordinary knowledge of a word when divested of its limiting conditions? As they[1] say, "Sounds because in themselves alike bring about false notions; that which makes these [sounds] apperceived is the cause of this false notion. And for those whose knowledge of words is made known by the means [which produce it, that is, the sounds of the syllables] there is an inevitable false notion. This results in an overthrow (*bādhā*) of [all] knowledge and would cause an unfailing confusion of [all dealings] in the world." Because the essence of a word shines out turbid with separate [sounds of] syllables, for this reason persons of not very fine insight, deeming the syllables themselves to be the word, use conventionally these very [sounds of] syllables, which have taken certain forms, with certain intended-objects, as he says «of this.» This word, although by nature (*ājānatas*) a unity, is separated on the basis of the knowledge of the conventional-usage [of this word] to suit the purposes of persons whose insight is not very fine, as if its essence were separate [sounds of] syllables. He describes this separation of the word into [sounds of] syllables by saying «this or that number.» Of this or that number [that is] neither more nor less. «In some such kind» means a particular continuous sequence. «The seizing in turn and binding together» means under the influence of a single mental-process. [This is] a word expressive of a single intended-object, such as a cow. The objector says, 'If conventional-usage is such a word expressive of a single intended-object only, then, Sir, there would be an erroneous identification of word and intended-object.' In reply to this he says «But conventional-usage.» «Essentially . . . memory» is that which in itself is memory. For conventional-usage, merely because you can say that it prevails (*kṛta*), is not sufficient to define the intended-object; but it must also be remembered. What he means to say is this. In a conventional-usage which makes no difference a difference is somehow imagined. [And therefore] the genitive case is used [to denote the distinction between the word and the thing].—When one who knows the

[1] Professor Gaṅgānāth Jhā has found a reference to these same verses in the Nyāyaratnākara, a commentary on the Çlokavārttika (Chaukhambha Sans. Series, p. 880). Herein we find them referred to as *vāiyākaraṇāir uktam*. Consequently they are not from any Mīmānsā work. Possibly they may be found in the unpublished portions of the Vākyapadīya. I have not found them in the printed fascicles.

distinction between these [three] performs constraint upon this [distinction] he becomes the knower of all,—has an [intuitive] knowledge of the cries of all living beings.—Thus having analysed that unit, the word, which is without parts, although the parts are assumed to be in the [sounds of the] syllables, he says, with the intent to analyse the sentence, which has an imaginary division into parts, but which is a unit and has no parts «Furthermore, every word has the power to express a [complete] sentence.» The connexion [of ideas] is this. A word is used to convey information to another. And the other should have precisely that information conveyed to him which the words are intended to convey. And these [words] are also capable of giving that same information which deals with acceptance or [rejection (*hāna*) or indifference (*upekṣā*)]. And they do not deal (*tadgocara*) with the meaning (*artha*) of the word only, but with the meaning of the sentence. So all words must subserve the meaning of the sentence. And accordingly the meaning of the sentence is that of these [words] also. And it is for this reason that whenever a word is used alone, it is always associated with another word, and the sense follows from that word, but not from the [first] word used alone. Why? Because by itself (*tanmātrasya*) it has no capacity. Thus it is the sentence that in all cases expresses the words; but the words do not. However, as forming parts of this [that is, the sentence], the words also have expressive power with respect to the sense of the sentence, just as with respect to the word the [sounds of the] syllables as constituting it have also expressive power. Thus then just as each single [sound of a] syllable embraces the power to express all intended-objects of words, so also each single word embraces the power to express the meaning of all sentences. This is what is expressed by the words «Furthermore, every word has the power to express a [complete] sentence. Thus when we utter the word 'tree', we imply that it exists.» The meaning is that the word 'tree' in conjunction with the implied word 'is' leads to the meaning of the sentence. Therefore as forming part of the sentence, the word 'tree' produces that meaning (*tatra vartate*). But if it be asked why the word 'is' is implied, the reply is «No intended-object can lack existence.» For the means for defining the meanings of words is popular-usage[1] (*loka*). And this popular-usage combines the meaning of the word as it is alone with the meaning 'is' and in all such cases makes the meaning of a sentence. This same [popular-usage] is the meaning of a word which cannot lack existence. Hence those[2] who know the functions of words have [this] agreement-of-usage (*vyavahāra*), "Wherever there is no other verb, 'is' in the sense of being should be used." —Having stated that a nominal-base[3] never lacks its action [expressed by a verb], he shows that any particular verb is never without a relation by saying «And so

[1] Compare Patañjali Mahābhāṣya i. 2. 1, vārt. 2 (Kielhorn's ed., vol. i, p. 217).

[2] See also for comparison Patañjali Mahābhāṣya on v. 2. 94.

[3] Discussed in Patañjali Mahābhāṣya on i. 2. 45.

when we utter.» For when we utter the word 'cook-s', all relations which are suitable for association with it are implied. For this reason there is an express statement of the special relations of this [verb], and the purpose [of this statement] is to exclude other [relations]. Thus the meaning of the sentence consists in nothing but the specializing [of the relations]. Similarly although out of all relations, a word is found to stand for the meaning of the sentence; and the sentence is still more potential in the words. So he says «We observe.» But this does not mean that words like Reader, which are complete in themselves, can present a meaning so long as they are not combined with words like 'is'. So even in the case of this word [Reader, as complete in itself], the meaning is to be assumed only in so far as it forms part of a sentence. This is the point. [An objector] says, 'This may be true. But if the words by themselves have the expressive power of the sentence, then there is no further need of the sentence, since its meaning can be ascertained from them.' In reply to this he says «[And conversely] in this sentence.» It has been said already that if there be a desire on the part of the speaker to convey information, the meaning of [his] words is not understood from the words alone, so long as these words are not brought into combination with other words. So then supposing the words to be separated from the sentence, a part of it, the relation or the verb, is to be explained by analysing [and] enumerating these [words], by allotting the shares to this word, the bases (*pratyaya*) and so on. 'But why is so much trouble taken to go through this account [of the analysis of words]?' In reply to this he says «Without such [an analysis].» Because of the similarity of noun and verb in such cases[1] as, 'A water-jar is (*bhavati*) there' and 'O Lady (*bhavati*), give an alms' and 'While Your Honour (*bhavati*) is standing'[2]; or similarly in such cases as 'Thou didst go[3] (*açvas*)' and 'The horse (*açvas*) walks'; or similarly in such cases as 'Goat's milk (*ajā-payas*) drink thou' and 'Thou didst conquer (*ajāpayas*) the foes,'—because there is a likeness [in the form] of the verb and of the noun, it is ambiguous whether the words might be analysed as nouns or as verbs. And when there is no such accounting [for the form of the word, and because] when withdrawn [from the sentence] it cannot be known [whether it is a noun or a verb], how can it be analysed as a noun or as a verb?[4] Therefore the words should be withdrawn from the sentence and analysed. But by a mere accounting [for the form of the word] there is not strictly speaking a distinction of the words [from the intended-objects and the presented-ideas]. Having thus treated the [different] kinds of words etymologically, he has the intention of telling that [in reality] there is no confusion between words and intended-objects and

[1] It would appear that Vācaspatimiçra is referring to Çloka-vārttika iv. 191.

[2] Or possibly, 'Something is standing upon Your Honour (*bhavati*).'

[3] Or 'swell', from root *çvi* or *çvā*.

[4] This whole subject is discussed with much greater elaboration in another work by Vācaspatimiçra called Tattvabindu (Benares, reprinted from the Pandit, 1893). This particular passage occurs on p. 15 of that text.

presented-ideas which had got into confusion as a result of conventional-usage [which erroneously identifies one with the other], and proceeds to say «There is a distinction between these words and intended-objects and presented-ideas.» «To illustrate this [distinction]. 'The palace whitens'; here [the word[1]] means the action [of a verb].» For here it is quite clear that this action 'grows white', which is of a kind yet to be completed and which takes place by a succession [of acts], is different from the action 'white', which is of the completed kind. And even in those cases where both the word and the intended-object are of a completed kind, there also the word is different from the intended-object, as he says «'The white palace'; here a relation is meant.» Here[2] there is no case-ending expressing relation because this is expressed [by the nominative case according to Pāṇini ii. 3. 1].—He makes the distinction between the intended-object [and the word] by saying, «in essence both an action [denoted by a verb] and a relation . . . the intended-object of which.» The meaning is that the intended-object of both these words is in essence an action [denoted by a verb] and it is in essence a relation.—He makes the distinction between the presented-idea [and the word] by saying «and the presented-idea.» The word «and» shows that the words «the intended-object of which is this [the action and relation]» are to be supplied. The word «this» is to be understood (*saṁbadhyate*) as in subordination to another word [in a possessive compound]. It is so-described as being that of which the intended-object is in essence an action [denoted by a verb] and a relation because they are understood as alike. An objector asks 'Since words and intended-objects and presented-ideas are confused, how can there be any distinction between them?' With this in mind he asks «But why is this so?» He gives the answer by saying «Because this [process] is identified with that, [its result, the quality white].» The presented-idea which identifies them is limited by conventional-usage [which erroneously identifies them with each other]. But this presented-idea has no basis in fact. The word conventional-usage is in the locative case. This shows that conventional-usage is the cause [of the presented-idea which fails to distinguish the act of whitening and the quality white]. He states what the real fact is in the words «But the white intended-object is that which.» Intensity such as newness or oldness. «Correspond» [that is] be confused. Thus by the yogin's constraint upon the distinctions [he knows] the cries of all living beings, tame and wild animals, creeping things, birds and the rest, even the unphenomenalized speech among them and the intended-objects [denoted by these cries] and the presented-ideas of them. So in this case constraint performed upon the presented-ideas of the things-expressed by the utterances of human beings is performed upon these [objects and words] also, since they are comparate. Thus

[1] Vācaspatimiçra seems to have read *çabdaḥ* in his text of the Comment. And this reading is also in the excellent MS. belonging to Gaṅgādhara Shāstrī.

[2] Compare the phrase *çveto 'çvo* in Tattva Bindu, p. 16[11].

it is established that the yogin has [intuitive] knowledge of these cries and of the objects intended by them and of the presented-idea of them.

18. As a result of direct-perception of subliminal impressions there is [intuitive] knowledge of previous births.

Those subliminal-impressions are of course of two kinds. 1. The causes of memory and of the hindrances in the form of subconscious impressions; 2. the causes of fruition in the form of right-living and wrong-living. These subliminal-impressions formed in previous births are, like mutation and movement and restriction and power and vitality and right-living, unperceived external-aspects of mind-stuff [iii. 15]. Constraint upon these is sufficient for direct-perception of subliminal-impressions. Moreover there is no direct experience of these, unless there be experience of place and time and cause. It is thus, therefore, as a result of [intuitive] knowledge of subliminal-impressions that the knowledge of previous births arises [in the mind] of the yogin. Precisely as in other cases there is also, as a result of the direct-perception of subliminal-impressions, a consciousness (*saṁvedana*) of the births of others. On this point this tale is handed down. "To the Exalted Jāigīṣavya, who as a result of direct-perception of subliminal-impressions beheld the sequence of his birth-mutations in ten great creative-periods, the knowledge born of discrimination became visible. Then to him spake the Exalted Āvaṭya who had assumed a [coarse] body [for the purposes of this speech]. 'In ten great creative-periods, forasmuch as the *sattva* of [thy] thinking-substance is unsuppressed [by *rajas* and *tamas*] in consequence of spotlessness, thou beholdest the pain caused by birth in hells and in the bodies of brutes; coming into existence over and over again among gods and human beings, which hast thou apperçeived to be more, pleasure or pain?' Jāigīṣavya[1] spake to the Exalted Āvaṭya. 'In ten great creative-periods, forasmuch as the *sattva* of [my] thinking-substance is unsuppressed [by *rajas* and *tamas*] in consequence of spotlessness, I behold the

[1] See also ii. 55, p. 192[7], and Açvaghoṣa's Buddhacarita xii. Compare Garbe: Mondschein d. Sankhya-Wahrheit, p. 35; and Garbe: Aniruddha, p. vii.

pain caused by birth in hells and in the bodies of brutes; coming into existence over and over again among gods and human beings this I trow. Whatever [pleasure] I have passed through, all[1] this is nothing but pain.' The Exalted Āvaṭya spake thus. 'Are Your Worship's mastery[2] over the primary-cause and the pleasure of bliss ineffable,—are these also to be counted as pain?' The Exalted Jāigīṣavya spake: 'This can be called the pleasure of bliss ineffable only in comparison[3] with pleasure from objects of sense; but it is nothing but pain in comparison with Isolation. Because this [bliss ineffable] is an external-aspect of the *sattva* of the thinking-substance and [so] has the three aspects (*guṇa*), and because a presented-idea of anything having the three aspects is counted as something to be thrown aside, the thread of desire [in the bliss ineffable] is of the nature of pain. But by the removal of the anguish of the pain of desire, this pleasure [of bliss ineffable] is undisturbed-calm,[4] uninhibited, favourable in the eyes of all.'"

18. As a result of direct-perception of subliminal-impressions there is [intuitive] knowledge of previous births.

For the subliminal-impressions which are produced by knowledge are the causes of memory, whereas the subliminal-impressions produced by undifferentiated-consciousness are the causes of the hindrances which begin with undifferentiated-consciousness. As to the causes of fruition. Fruition is [ii. 13] birth and length-of-life and kind-of-enjoyment. The causes of it are the kinds of right-living and wrong-living. The subliminal-impressions put together in previous births are completed by their own peculiar causes. Just as a curry (*vyañjana*) is put together (*saṁskṛta*) [by combining many undistinguished things] so it follows that it has been made. Mutation and movement and restriction and power and vitality are external-aspects of the mind-stuff. Likewise, the unperceived [subliminal-impressions] are external-aspects of the mind-stuff. Constraint upon these together with their attachments [of place and time and cause], whether they are something heard or inferred, is adequate to bring to pass direct perception of both kinds of subliminal impressions. And if it be asked how there can be direct perception of previous births, even if it be possible to have direct perception of these [subliminal-impressions in place, time and cause] through constraint, he replies «Moreover there is no . . . of place.» «Cause» is the previous body, the organs and the rest. Direct-perception of subliminal-impressions, with their adjuncts,[5]

[1] Compare ii. 15.

[2] See Aniruddha on Sāṁkhya-sūtra v. 82.

[3] Compare Aniruddha on Sāṁkhya-sūtra p. 3[5].

[4] See iv. 29, p. 313[5] (Calc. ed.).

[5] Bālarāma mentions as instances of attachments, mother and father or birth or country or city or time.

necessarily involves the direct-perception of such things as births. This is the meaning. The constraint with respect to one's own subliminal-impressions he extends by analogy to those of others also in the words «Precisely as in other cases also.» With this in view he introduces as an aid to faith the dialogue between Jaigīṣavya and Āvaṭya, who had passed through the experience, by saying «On this point this tale is handed down.» A great creative-period is a great mundane cycle. By the words «who had assumed a [coarse] body» the perfection of a created body [1] is described. Spotless is brilliant; that from which the stains of *rajas* and *tamas* have been removed. Mastery over the primary cause means power. By having this [power] and by creating movements in the primary-cause he gives to any one that kind of perfection of body or of organs which he wishes to confer upon him; and further having created his own bodies and organs by thousands he roves through air and sky and earth at will. Bliss (*santoṣa*) is the dwindling of desire and the external-aspect of undisturbed calm belonging to the *sattva* of the thinking-substance.

19. [As a result of constraint] upon a presented-idea [there arises intuitive] knowledge of the mind-stuff of another.

As a result of constraint upon a presented-idea, in consequence of the direct-perception of the presented-idea, there arises the [intuitive] knowledge of the mind-stuff of another.

19. [As a result of constraint] upon a presented-idea [there arises intuitive] knowledge of the mind-stuff of another.

«As a result of» direct-perception of the presented-idea, [that is] of mind-stuff in general of another.

20.[2] But [the intuitive knowledge of the presented-idea of another] does not have that [idea] together with that upon which it depends [as its object], since that upon which it depends is not-in-the-field [of consciousness].

The yogin knows that the presented-idea is affected. But he does not know that it is affected in dependence upon [this or] that [object]. When the presented-idea of another [person] is in dependence upon something, this [object] does not become something upon which the mind-stuff of the yogin depends. But it is the other's presented-idea only upon which the yogin's mind-stuff comes to depend.

[1] For the word *nirmāṇa* see Garbe: Festgruss an Roth, p. 78[4].

[2] This sūtra is omitted by Vijñāna Bhikṣu and consequently the numbering of the remaining sūtras of the third part of Yoga-vārttika is at fault.

32 [H.O.S. 17]

Just as the direct-perception of subliminal-impressions implies the direct-perception of previous births and of the adjuncts to these, so the direct-perception of another's mind-stuff might imply the direct-perception of that upon which that [mind-stuff] depends. To this conclusion (*prāpta*) he says **20. But [the intuitive knowledge of the presented-idea of another] does not have that [idea] together with that upon which it depends [as its object], since that upon which it depends is not-in-the-field [of consciousness].** That constraint [ii. 19] has for its object the subliminal-impressions with their adjuncts [1]; but this has as its object the other's mind-stuff and nothing more. This is what he means to say.

---

21. As a result of constraint upon the [outer] form of the body, when its power to be known is stopped, then as a consequence of the disjunction of the light and of the eye there follows indiscernibility [of the yogin's body].

As a result of constraint upon the form of the body, [the yogin] inhibits that [imperceptible] power by which [the coarse and external] is known. When its power to be known is stopped, as a consequence of the disjunction of the light [that is, of the other person, the observer] and of the eye [that is, the organ], indiscernibility of the yogin is produced. In this way it must be understood that indiscernibility to sound and to other objects of sense has also been described.

21. . . . body . . . indiscernibility.

A body has its essence in the five [coarse elements]. And as having form it comes under the eye. For as having form the body and the colour of the body pass through the experience of being the object-of-the-action of the process-of-knowing by the eye. Thus when the yogin performs a special kind of constraint upon the [external] form, then the power of being known, which belongs to the colour and which is the source of the direct-perception of a body having form, is stopped. Therefore when the power to be known is stopped, the yogin becomes indiscernible. In other words, the body of the yogin does not become the object of the thinking [coming from] the eye. The meaning is that when this is done, indiscernibility is the cause.—«In this way.» When as a result of constraint upon sound or touch or taste or smell with reference to the body the power of these [four objects of sense] to be known is stopped, and when there is no connexion between the light [that is, of the other person, the observer] and the [other's] organ-of-hearing or of touch or of taste or of smell,—then [the yogin] becomes indiscernible to these [organs]. Such, *mutatis mutandis*, is the meaning of the sūtra.

---

[1] These Bālarāma has defined in his note (5) on p. 230[5] (Calc. ed.).

22. Advancing and not-advancing is karma; as a result of constraint upon this [two-fold karma] or from the signs of death [there arises an intuitive] knowledge of the latter end. Karma having its fruition in length-of-life is of two kinds, the advancing[1] and the not-advancing. Of the two, 1. just as a wet cloth spread-out dries in a shorter time, so is advancing karma; 2. and just as the same [cloth] rolled into a ball becomes dry a long time after, so is not-advancing [karma]. 1. Advancing karma is also like fire set in dry[2] grass, which spreads on all sides with the breeze, and burns in the briefest time. 2. And just as the same fire, put bit by bit into a pile of grass, burns a long time after, so is not-advancing [karma]. This is the karma having [its limit in] a single existence and causing the length-of-life, of two kinds, the advancing and the not-advancing. As a result of constraint upon this there is [intuitive] knowledge of the latter end, of the decease.—‹Or from the signs of death [there arises an intuitive] knowledge of the latter end.› A sign-of-death[3] is of three kinds, that pertaining to self and that pertaining to [other] creatures and that pertaining to divine beings. Of these [three], a sign-of-death 1. pertaining to one's self [would occur when] one with stopped[3] ears does not hear the sound [of the vital spirits] within one's own body; or when one with closed eyes does not see the inner light. Likewise 2. a sign pertaining to other creatures [would occur when] one sees the Men of Yama, [or] when one sees unexpectedly the Fathers, the Departed. Similarly 3. [a sign] pertaining to divine beings [would occur when] one sees heaven or the Siddhas unexpectedly, or when everything is reversed. By this [sign] also he perceives that the latter end is near at hand.

22. Advancing . . . or . . . And karma having its fruition in length-of-life is of two kinds, the advancing and the not-advancing. Now that karma which has [its limit] in a single existence and which is the source of birth and of length-of-life and of kind-of-enjoyment has a fruition in length-of-life. 1. And this is ready to afford the kind-of-enjoyment without the delay of even a very

[1] This word occurs here only in the Bhāṣya and in Vācaspati.

[2] Umāsvāti's Tattvādhigama-sūtra ii. 52.

[3] Compare Mārkaṇḍeya Pur. xl. 1 ff. Liṅga Pur. xci. 1–36. Mahābhārata xii. 317–18 ff.

short time. It has afforded much of the kind-of-enjoyment and only a little of its fruit remains. Its functional-activity continues only because it is impossible for it to have its fruition suddenly in one body; therefore it delays. This is advancing [karma]. The advance is the functional-activity; the [karma] is connected with this [functional-activity]. 2. The same karma, when it affords little fruit and requires time for this, and when, engaged in affording fruit, its functional-activity is intermittent and slow, is not-advancing. This same is made clear in two similes with the words «Of these 1. just as.» On the same point for greater clearness he gives another simile in the words «2. Or just as fire.»—The final-end is the great mundane-dissolution. As compared with this, death is the latter end. As a result of constraint upon the right-living and wrong-living in that karma, [there follows intuitive] knowledge of the latter end. And as a result of this the yogin, knowing his own karma which is advancing, and having created many bodies for himself, experiences suddenly the fruit [of karma] and dies when he wills. Incidentally [the author] says «Or [the intuitive knowledge of the latter end] is the result of the signs-of-death.» Signs-of-death (*ariṣṭa*) are things which terrify such as the enemy (*ari*). The indications of death are of three kinds.—«Or when everything is reversed» [that is] even when there is no jugglery, villages and cities he deems to be heaven, and the world of only human beings to be a world of divine beings.

23. [As a result of constraint] upon friendliness and other [sentiments there arises] powers [of friendliness].

Friendliness[1] and compassion and joy are the three sentiments. As to these [three], by feeling friendliness for living beings who are in happiness he discovers the power of friendliness; by feeling compassion for those in pain he discovers the power of compassion; by feeling joy for those who are disposed to merit he discovers the power of joy. As a result of the sentiments there arises the constraint which is concentration, and from it there arise powers of unfailing energy. Indifference, however, for those disposed to evil is not one [of these practised] sentiments. And therefore there is no concentration upon it. For this reason, since it is impossible to perform constraint upon it, there is no power resulting from indifference.

23. [As a result of constraint] upon friendliness and other [sentiments there arise] powers [of friendliness].

By constraint upon friendliness and other [sentiments] he gains powers of friendliness and other powers. Of these three as a result of the sentiment

[1] See i. 33.

of friendliness there arises [in him] that kind of power by which he makes everybody happy. As a result of this he is kindly to all. Similarly through the power resulting from compassion he delivers living beings from pain and from the causes of pain. Likewise through the power of joy he imparts the detached-attitude to everybody. He states what will be of assistance in what will be said, namely, that sentiments cause concentration, as he says «As a result of the sentiments there arises the constraint which is concentration.» Although constraint is the three, fixed-attention and contemplation and concentration and not concentration alone, still since constraint follows as an effect after concentration, and since concentration is the dominant of the three, concentration is figuratively used for constraint.—Some manuscripts read 'The sentiments are concentration.' In this case we must suppose that the sentiments and concentration, as being parts of the whole which is constraint, serve as causes of the constraint. «Energy» is exertion. By its means a man who has the powers of friendliness, &c., towards persons in happiness, &c., becomes unfailing in his exertion when things are to be done for others. Indifference is the detached attitude. In this case there is no sentiment. Nor is there anything that might arise [out of it] as in the case of those who are in happiness.

24. [As a result of constraint] upon powers [there arise] powers like those of an elephant.

As a result of constraint upon the power of an elephant one has the power of an elephant. As a result of constraint upon the power of Vāinateya [the Garuḍa bird] one has the power of Vāinateya. As a result of constraint upon the power of the wind one has the power of the wind. And so forth in the same way.

24. [As a result of constraint] upon powers [there arise] powers like those of an elephant. He gains the power of that upon which [he exercises] constraint.

---

25. As a result of casting the light of a sense-activity [there arises the intuitive] knowledge of the subtile and the concealed and the obscure.

The yogin by casting the light of that sense-activity of the central organ which is called luminous [i. 36] upon an object whether subtile[1] or concealed or obscure has access to that object.

25. . . . Sense-activity . . . intuitive knowledge. Casting [his mind] with constraint upon a subtile or concealed or obscure intended-object he has access to that intended-object.

---

[1] Compare Sāṁkhya-kārikā vii.

26. As a result of constraint upon the sun [there arises the intuitive] knowledge of the cosmic-spaces (*bhuvana*).

The enumeration of these [cosmic-spaces]: there are seven worlds. Among them, 1. starting from the Avīci [nadir] and extending up to the summit of Meru is the Earth-world (*bhū-loka*); 2. beginning from the summit of Meru and going as far as the Pole-star (*dhruva*), the world of Intermediate Space diversified by planets and asterisms and stars. Beyond that is the five-fold Heaven-world (*svar-loka*): 3. the world of Mahendra, the third world; 4. the Mahar world of Prajāpati, the fourth world; the three-fold world of Brahma, that is, 5. the Jana-world and 6. the Tapas-world and 7. the Satya-world.[1]

"The world-of-Brahma in its three stages,
Below it the world-of-Prajāpati, the Great [world],
And [below it] Mahendra's [world]: [these five] are called Heaven (*svar*).
In the sky [of Intermediate-Space] are the stars; on earth, the creatures."

Thus saith the Summary-Stanza.[2] Rising in a series above Avīci there are six regions (*bhūmi*) of the Great-Hell (*mahā-naraka*), supported [respectively] by solid-matter, by water, by fire, by wind, by air, and by darkness, namely, the Mahākāla, the Ambarīṣa, the Rāurava, the Mahārāurava, the Kālasūtra, and the Andhatāmisra, wherein living creatures, having been allotted a long and grievous length-of-life, feeling the misery incurred as the result of their own karma, are born. Next, the seven lower-worlds (*pātāla*), with the names Mahātala, Rasātala, Atala, Sutala, Vitala, Talātala, and Pātāla, and as the eighth this earth[3] with its seven lands (*dvīpa*), and in the midst of it, the golden King of Mountains, Sumeru. Its peaks on the four sides are made of gems of silver, of lapis

1 Svar { Brahma { 7. Satya, 6. Tapas, 5. Jana }, 4. Mahar Prājāpatya, 3. Mahendra }
2. Antarikṣa
1. Bhū

2 Compare VP. ii. 4. 97.

3 For a very valuable collection of parallel material in the Epic see Hopkins: Mythological Aspects, JAOS, 1910.

lazuli, of crystal, and of gold. By reason [of the reflection] of the brilliant colour of the lapis lazuli, the southern quarter of the sky is the deep blue of the petal of the blue-lotus; the eastern is white; the western is translucent; the northern is like the golden amaranth. And on its southern slope is the Rose-Apple tree, from which this land is called the Land of the Rose-Apple. As the sun moves forward, day and night,[1] as it were fast bound to him,[1] revolve[2] [about Sumeru]. North of this [Sumeru] are three mountains, blue-and-white-peaked, two thousand yojanas in extent. Between these, three zones (*varṣa*), nine thousand yojanas each, called 1. Ramaṇaka, 2. Hiraṇmaya, and 3. the Northern[3] Kurus. On the south, the [mountains] of Niṣadha, of the Goldhorn, and of the Snow-crags, two thousand yojanas in extent. Between these, three zones of nine thousand [yojanas] each, called 4. the Harivarsha, 5. Kiṁpuruṣa, 6. Bhārata. On the East of Sumeru, [the countries of] 7. Bhadrāçva, bounded by the Mālyavat [mountains]; on the West, [the countries of] 8. Ketumāla, bounded by the Gandhamādana [mountains]. In the middle, the zone of 9. Ilāvṛta.—This same [Land of the Rose-Apple], a hundred thousand yojanas in extent, stretches in each direction from Sumeru for half this distance. Now the Land of the Rose-Apple, a hundred thousand yojanas in extent, is encompassed by a girdle-shaped sea of salt the double thereof. And then [there are] the lands of Çāka, Kuça, Krāuñca, Çālmala, Magadha, and Puṣkara, each double the preceding, fringed with marvellous hills, and the Seven Seas, [flat] like a pile of mustard seeds, with their waters of Sugar-cane-juice, of Spirits, of Butter, of Curds, of Cream, of Milk, and of Treacle. [These lands] encompassed by the Seven Seas and girdle-shaped and encircled by the Lokāloka Mountains [are] estimated at five hundred millions of yojanas [in extent]. This whole well-founded configuration stretches out in the midmost part of the [World] Egg. And the Egg is a minute fragment of the primary-cause, like a firefly in the sky. 1. Here, in the lower world, in

[1] Siddhānta Kāumudī on v. 4. 77 (Nir. Säg. ed., 1904, p. 208[a]).

[2] Just so Raghuvança vii. 24.

[3] Described in Rām. iv. 43 and Mahā Bh. vi. 7. 1 ff. and discussed by Jacobi in the article on the Abode of the Blest (Hastings: Cyclopaedia of Rel. and Ethics, II. 698[a]).

the sea, in these mountains, groups of gods have their abode, Asuras, Gandharvas, Kinnaras, Kimpuruṣas, Yakṣas, Rākṣasas, Bhūtas, Pretas, Piçācas, Apasmārakas, Apsarases, Brahmarākṣasas, Kūṣmāṇḍas, Vināyakas. In all the lands meritorious gods and human beings [have their abode]. Sumeru is the pleasure-ground of the thirty-[three] [gods]. In it are the pleasure-grounds, Miçravana, Nandana, Cāitraratha, and Sumānasa. Sudharmā is the gods' assembly-hall. Sudarçana is their castle. Vāijayanta is their palace. 2. The planets and asterisms and stars, fastened to the pole-star, have their courses [1] regulated by the steady impulsion of the wind, and arranged at different points above [2] Sumeru move round about it. 3. They who dwell in [the world of] Mahendra are six groups of gods, the Thirty-three, the Agniṣvāttas, the Yāmyas, the Tuṣitas, the Aparinirmita-vaça-vartins, and the Parinirmita-vaça-vartins. All [these] fulfil their desires and are endowed with atomization and the other powers. They live for a mundane period; they are goodly to behold and they delight in love. Their bodies are not caused [by parents]. Their retinue is made of incomparable and not prudish Apsarases. 4. In the Great world of Prajāpati there is a five-fold group of gods, the Kumudas, the Ṛbhus, the Pratardanas, the Añjanābhas, and the Pracitābhas. These have the mastery over the great elements; their food is contemplation; their lives are for a thousand mundane periods. 5. In the first of the worlds-of-Brahma, in the Jana [3] world, there is a four-fold group of gods, the Brahmapurohitas, the Brahmakāyikas, the Brahmamahākāyikas, and the Amaras. These have the mastery over the elements and the organs. 6. In the second [of the worlds-of-Brahma], in the Tapas-world, there is a three-fold group of gods, the Ābhāsvaras,[4] the Mahābhāsvaras, and the Satyamahābhāsvaras. These have the mastery over the elements and the

[1] They are driven by the wind, as cows are driven by the ploughman in a circle around the threshing-post. Fastened by wind-ropes to the pole-star, according to Māitri Up. i. 4. For the astronomy see Sūrya Siddhānta ii. 1; for the simile, see Çakuntalā vii. 6, and G. A. Grierson: Behar Peasant Life, § 889, with the illustration.

[2] Compare Viṣṇ. Pur. ii. 12 and Umāsvāti Tattvādhig. Sūt. iv. 14.

[3] Vijñāna Bhikṣu reads *Janar.*

[4] Reading ābhā°. The name indicates that they are self-luminous. An instructive article upon them by Professor Jacobi is found in Hastings: Cycl. of Rel. and Ethics, I. 202ᵃ.

organs and evolving-matter. Each lives twice as long as the previous [group]; their food is contemplation; their lives are chaste (*ūrdhvaretas*). Upwards there is no impediment to their thinking and in regions below there is no object obscure to their thought. 7. In the third [world] of Brahma, in the Satya-world, there are four groups of gods, the Acyutas, the Çuddhanivāsas, the Satyābhas, and the Saṁjñāsaṁjñins. By them no laying down foundations for a dwelling is made; they are grounded in themselves and placed one above the other; they have the mastery over the primary cause and live as long as there are creations. Of these [four] the Acyutas delight in deliberative contemplation; the Çuddhanivāsas delight in reflective contemplation; the Satyābhas delight in contemplation where there is nothing but joy; and the Saṁjñāsaṁjñins delight in contemplation where there is the feeling of personality and nothing more. These also remain in the three worlds.[1] These seven worlds are all without exceptions worlds of the Brahman. But the discarnate and those [whose bodies] are resolved into primary matter exist in the state of release and are not placed in the worlds. By performing constraint upon the door of the sun[2] the yogin should directly perceive [all] this. Then also upon other [objects than upon the sun]. Thus to this extent he should practise, until all this is seen.

26. As a result of constraint upon the sun [there arises the intuitive] knowledge of the cosmic-spaces (*bhuvana*).

Up to the pole-star from the summit of Meru in this world. Thus in this way from here up to the end of the Summary-Stanza (*saṁgraha-çloka*) the seven worlds[3] are briefly described. He describes them in detail in the words «Among them... above Avīci.» The word «solid-matter» means earth. [The word] «region» means a place [but not a hell]. These great hells must be understood to be accompanied by several lesser hells. These same are brought together under other names in the words, «Mahākāla.» As the sun moves forward, day and night, revolve [about Sumeru], as it were fast bound to him. The meaning is that night is in that part of it which the sun leaves; and day is in that part which the sun shines upon. He gives the extent of the whole Land of the Rose-Apple

[1] In the World-Egg. They are not released.

[2] This seems to be the entrance to the world of Brahma. Compare Māitrī Up. vi. 30 (*sūryam dvāram*) and Muṇḍaka Up. i. 2. 11 and Chāndog. Up. v. 10. 2.

[3] On this whole subject see Jacobi's article on the Abode of the Blest in Hastings: Cyclopaedia of Religion and Ethics, vol. II, p. 698a.

in the words «This same [Land of the Rose-Apple], a hundred thousand yojanas.» What kind of a hundred thousand yojanas? In reply he says «It stretches out in each direction from Sumeru for half this distance.» «For half» would be fifty thousand yojanas. «It stretches out» [amounts to] is comprehended, inasmuch as Sumeru occupies the middle of it. The Seven Seas, each like piles of mustard seeds, are each double [the preceding]. This is the connexion [of the sentence]. Just as a pile of mustard-seed is not heaped like a pile of rice-grains, nor quite [flat] like the earth, so are those seas. This is the meaning. Islands are fringed with marvellous hills, so that one could say that they seem to have fringes of marvellous hills. All this circuit of the earth, encompassed by garlands of lands and forests and mountains and cities and oceans, and encircled by the Lokāloka Mountains, extends, is comprehended, in the midst of the Egg of Brahma. «This well-founded configuration» means that it is that whose arrangement [is well-founded]. He now tells who they are that dwell there in the words «Here, in the lower-world.» He describes the arrangement of Sumeru in the words, «Sumeru is»—Thus having described the Earth-world specifically, he describes specifically the world of Intermediate Space with the words «The planets.» The «impulsion» is the functional activity.—He shows the Heaven-world in the words «They who dwell [in the world of] Mahendra.» 3. «Groups of gods» are kinds of gods. He also describes the perfection of the form of the six groups of gods by saying «All [these] fulfil their desires.» All objects yield to them even at nothing more than a desire. «Goodly to behold» [that is] to be worshipped. They delight in love [that is] are fond of sexual pleasure. Their bodies are not caused by parents, [but] quite without cause, without union of parents, they obtain a supernal body from atoms thoroughly purified[1] by peculiar merit. 4. He describes the Mahar-world in the words, «In the Great.» These have the mastery over the great elements. Whatever they like the great elements confer upon them. And the great elements remain in this or that arrangement as they desire. «Their food is contemplation» means that they are sated with contemplation merely and are nourished [thereby]. 5. He describes the Jana-world with the words «In the first.» In accordance with the order of the worlds as described «they have the mastery over the elements and the organs.» Earth and the other elements, and the organ-of-hearing and the other organs are employed just as they choose to employ them. 6. He describes, in accordance with the order already described, the second [world] of Brahma in the words «In the second.» «These have the mastery over the elements and the organs and evolving-matter.» Evolving-matter (*prakṛti*) is the five fine elements. Over these they have the mastery. For at their wish the subtile

[1] This is an allusion to the story of Dadhīci, whose body was the very essence of knowledge and of courses of austerities (Bhāg. Pur. vi. 9. 51–54). While absorbed in yoga he was unaware that Indra took his body and made it into a thunderbolt (vi. 10. 12). The thunderbolt becomes energized with the sage's austerities (*Dadhīces tapasā tejitaḥ* vi. 11. 20).

elements actually enter into mutations in the form of bodies. So say those who have the tradition. «Twice as long as the previous.» The Mahābhāsvaras have double as long a life as the Ābhāsvaras; and the Satyamahābhāsvaras have double as long a life as these latter. «Upwards.» Upwards in the Satya-world there is no impediment to their thinking. But from Avīci right up to the Tapas-world they discern all subtile and concealed or other things. This is the meaning. 7. He describes the third world of Brahma in the words «In the third.» They are so described by whom the laying down of a dwelling or house has not been made. Just because they have nothing to hold them, they are grounded in themselves. They are such as are grounded in their own bodies. They have the mastery over the primary cause; at their wish the *sattva* and *rajas* and *tamas* come into activity. «They live as long as the creation,» as it is handed down in the Sacred Word,[1] "All these having perfected their souls, together[2] with Brahma enter, when the reversal-of-creation (*pratisaṁcara*) is reached at the end of the highest [world], into the highest state." Having thus stated the common qualities of these four groups of gods, he describes their special qualities by taking them up in detail with the words, «Of these [four].» The gods called Acyuta take delight in contemplation upon coarse objects. With this they are satisfied. The gods called Çuddhanivāsa take delight in contemplation upon subtile objects. With this they are satisfied. The gods called Satyābhas take delight in contemplation upon the organs[3] as objects. With this they are satisfied. The gods called Saṁjñāsaṁjñins take delight in contemplation upon the feeling of personality and nothing more. With this they are satisfied. All these have recourse to concentration conscious [of objects]. And if it be asked why there is no mention here, among [these] worlds, of those who have given themselves to concentration not conscious [of an object], those namely who are discarnate and those [whose bodies] are resolved into primary matter, the reply is «But the discarnate and those [whose bodies] are resolved into primary matter.» For those whose thinking-substance is in fluctuation, and to whom objects are shown, carry on worldly affairs and remain in the world. But the discarnate[4] and those [whose bodies] are resolved into primary matter, although they have a task to perform, do not so remain. This is the meaning.—All this, with the exception of the Satya-world and as far [down] as to Avīci, is directly perceptible to the yogin. «Upon the door of the sun» means upon the tube called Suṣumnā. And inasmuch as, even with such an extent [of constraint], direct perception of [all] this does not occur, he says «Then.» Then also upon other [objects], that is, also upon objects other than the Suṣumnā taught by the professor of yoga, until all this world is seen. For the *sattva* of the thinking-substance is by its own nature capable of illumining the whole [world]. But when covered by the defilement

[1] Contrast with Vāyu Purāṇa ci. 85.

[2] Compare Bh. Gītā viii. 16.

[3] Compare *bahiḥkaraṇam ivāpannam iti, tad anendnandānugatam* i. 41 of Vācaspati's comment, p. 86[8] (Calc. ed.).

[4] See i. 19.

of *tamas* it illumines only that portion which is laid bare by *rajas*. It illumines the cosmic space laid bare by the constraint upon the door of the sun. But this does not apply similarly in other cases also. Since constraint upon this [cosmic space] has power to lay only so much bare. Thus all is cleared up.

27. [As a result of constraint] upon the moon [there arises the intuitive] knowledge of the arrangement of the stars.

By performing constraint upon the moon he would discern the arrangement of the stars.

28. [As a result of constraint] upon the pole-star [there arises the intuitive] knowledge of their movements.

Then by performing constraint upon the pole-star he would know the movements of the stars. By constraint upon heavenly cars, [for example, the chariot of the sun], he would discern them.

29. [As a result of constraint] upon the wheel of the navel [there arises the intuitive] knowledge of the arrangement of the body.

By performing constraint upon the wheel[1] of the navel he would discern the arrangement of the body. The humours are three, wind and bile and phlegm. The [corporeal] elements[2] (*dhātu*) are seven, skin and blood and flesh and sinew and bone and marrow and semen. Here (*eṣa*) the mention is such that the preceding element is in each case exterior to that next preceding.

30. [As a result of constraint] upon the well of the throat [there follows] the cessation of hunger and of thirst.

Below the tongue there is a cord; below that is the throat; below that the well. As a result of concentration upon that, hunger and thirst do not torment.

[1] Compare H. Walter: Haṭhayogapradīpikā, pp. xiii-xiv.

[2] Compare i. 80, p. 67[4] (Calc. ed.). By adding *prāṇa* and *ātman* the list is increased to nine.

31. [As a result of constraint] upon the tortoise-tube [there follows] motionlessness [of the mind-stuff].

Below the well there is, within the chest, a tube in shape like a tortoise. By performing constraint upon this, the yogin gains a motionless state like that of a serpent or of a guana.[1]

Whenever the yogin desires to know one thing or another, he should perform constraint upon that. Thus constraint which leads to the cessation of hunger and of thirst, and which leads to motionlessness, is taught by the words of the Sūtra and is explained by the Comment with an explanation which is a [mere matter of] reading. So it is not explained [here].

---

32. [As a result of constraint] upon the radiance in the head [there follows] the sight of the Siddhas.

Within an aperture in the skull there is a resplendent radiance.[2] As a result of constraint upon this [radiance there follows] the sight of the Siddhas roving in the spaces between the sky[3] and the earth.

32. [As a result of constraint] upon the radiance in the head [there follows] the sight of the Siddhas.

The words ‹in the head› imply the tube (*nāḍi*) called *Suṣumnā*,—‹constraint upon› that, he means.

---

33. Or as a result of vividness (*prātibha*) [the yogin discerns] all.

The so-called vividness is the deliverer[4] (*tāraka*). This is the preliminary form of the [intuitive] knowledge derived from discrimination. Just as the light at dawn [precedes] the sun. In this other way (*tena vā*) the yogin knows all[5] at the rise of the vivid [intuitive] knowledge.

33. Or as a result of vividness (*prātibha*) [the yogin discerns] all.

Vivid-light [that is] self-cogitation (*ūha*). This develops into vividness. For in the case of one who practises a constraint which leads to the Elevation (*prasaṁ-*

[1] These two animals exemplify the rigidity, and not as Vijñāna Bhikṣu says, the convoluted state of the mind-stuff. The word *godhā* is mentioned in Cowell and Gough's translation of the Sarvadarçanasaṁgraha, p. 238.

[2] Compare Mahānārāyaṇa Up. xi. 10-12.

[3] Pāṇ. iv. 2. 32.

[4] See iii. 54.

[5] See J. H. Leuba: Hallucinations of Light (Revue Philosophique, vol. 54, 1902, p. 447). And compare iii. 40.

khyāna), there results, when he attains perfection therein, an [intuitive] knowledge due to that self-asserting which is the preliminary indication (*liñga*) of the dawning of the Elevation. In this way the yogin discerns all. And this [intuitive] knowledge, since it serves to bring the Elevation near, delivers from the round-of-rebirth and so is called the 'deliverer'.

34. [As a result of constraint] upon the heart [there arises] a consciousness of the mind-stuff.

In this citadel of Brahma[1] is the house [of the mind-stuff], a tiny lotus [of the heart]—[there arises] a discernment of that. As a result of constraint upon this [there arises] a consciousness of the mind-stuff.

34. [As a result of constraint] upon the heart [there arises] a consciousness of the mind-stuff.

The word «heart» is explained in the words. «in the citadel of Brahma.» Because it is great (*bṛhat*) the self is Brahma. His «citadel», [that is] retreat. For with reference to this [citadel] he knows this,—that it is his property. The cave is a den. That same lotus with downward head is the dwelling of the central-organ. He gives the reason for this consciousness of the mind-stuff by saying «a discernment of that.» By constraint upon this he discerns the mind-stuff with its own peculiar fluctuations.

35. Experience is a presented-idea which fails to distinguish the *sattva* and the Self, which are absolutely uncommingled [in the presented-idea]. Since the *sattva* exists as object for another, the [intuitive] knowledge of the Self arises as the result of constraint upon that which exists for its own sake.

The *sattva* of the thinking-substance, with its disposition to brightness, by mastering the *rajas* and *tamas* which are equally dependent upon the *sattva*, enters into a mutation as a result of the presented-idea of the difference between the *sattva* and the Self. Therefore the Self, of which we can only say that it is Intellect (*citi*), which is other [than the aspects (*guṇa*)], and which is undefiled (*çuddha*) [by objects], is absolutely contrary in quality even to the *sattva* which is mutable. Experience is a presented-idea which fails to distinguish these two which are absolutely

[1] Chānd. Up. viii. 1. 1.

uncommingled. Because the Self has objects shown to it. This [same] presented-idea of experience is an object for sight, since the *sattva* exists for the sake of another. But as a result of constraint upon that presented-idea, which is distinguished from this [*sattva*], which is Intellect and nothing more, and which is other [than the aspects (*guṇa*)], and which belongs to the Self,—[as a result of this,] that insight whose object is the Self arises. The Self is not seen by that presented-idea of the Self whose essence is the *sattva* of the thinking-substance. It is the Self which sees the presented-idea which depends upon its own self. For in this sense it has[1] been said, "Wherewith, pray, could one discern the Discerner?"

35. . . . *Sattva* . . . [**intuitive**] **knowledge.** When, by reason of its being altogether overwhelmed by *rajas* and *tamas*, even the thinking-substance, bright in form and exceedingly clear though it is, can in its mutation as a discriminative discernment, be absolutely distinguished from intelligence, how much more so then the *rajas* and *tamas*, which are inert (*jaḍa*) by nature! With this in mind the author of the Sūtras uses the words, ‹the *sattva* and the Self.› Taking up this same point the author of the Comment also says «The *sattva* of the thinking-substance, with its disposition to brightness.» Not merely one whose disposition is to brightness, but one which has entered into a mutation in the form of discriminative discernment. Inasmuch as it is altogether undefiled [by objects] and bright, it is absolutely similar to intelligence (*cāitanya*). So there is a commingling, as he implies in the words «equal.» «Dependent upon *sattva*» means a relation without which it cannot exist. The *rajas* and *tamas* which are equally dependent upon the *sattva* are so-called [in the Comment]. Mastered means overwhelmed. He states that there is no commingling in the words «Therefore . . . even.» The word *ca* is here in the sense of 'even'. [Contrary in quality] not merely to the *rajas* and *tamas* [but even to the *sattva*]. This is the meaning. The word «mutable» indicates the quality contrary to the Self who is immutable. A presented idea which fails to distinguish, because the thinking-substance, which is serene and cruel and infatuated, takes the image of the intelligence (*cāitanya*). And so the serene and other forms are falsely attributed to the intelligence, just as the trembling of the clear water which reflects the moon is falsely attributed to the moon. He gives the reason for the experience in the words «Because the Self has objects shown to it.» This has been explained more than once.[2] If it be objected that the *sattva* of the thinking-substance might be different from

[1] Bṛhad-Āraṇ. Up. ii. 4. 14 and iv. 5. 15.

[2] For example, i. 4, p. 16; ii. 17, p. 141; and also iv. 22, p. 306 (Calc. ed.).

the Self, but that experience could not be different from the Self, he replies «This [same].» This [same] presented-idea of experience is a presented-idea of a kind of experience belonging to the *sattva*. Hence as something for the sake of another experience is an object-for-sight. For the *sattva* is for the sake of another in that it is a combination of parts. And because experience is an external-aspect of this [*sattva*], it would also be for the sake of another. Furthermore, that other for whose sake it is, would be the experiencer. His is the experience.—Or [another explanation]. For experience (*bhoga*) is passing-through (*anubhava*) pleasure or pain which are felt to be coactive or counteractive. And this [experience] cannot be coactive or counteractive to itself. Because a fluctuation cannot be opposed to itself. Therefore experience must be for the sake of something that is to be made coactive or counteractive. This experiencer is the self. Experience is an object-for-sight to him. «But . . . that presented-idea, which is distinguished from this» which is for the sake of another. These words [from the Comment] are explained by supplying the other words in the ablative case 'for the sake of another'. An objector says, 'This may be true. But if the insight has the Self for its object, then whew! Sir! the Self becomes the object-for-insight by the insight! There would surely be other insights, one after the other, and we should fall into an infinite regress!' In reply to this he says «The Self is not . . . . by that presented-idea of the Self.» The connexion-of-ideas is this. The Intellect (*citi*) illumines that which is inert (*jaḍa*), and that which is inert does not [illumine] the intellect. The idea presented to the Self has as its essence that which is not intelligent. How can this [presented-idea] illumine a being whose essence is intelligence? On the other hand, how can [the Self], whose essence is intelligence and whose brightness does not depend upon another, be properly said to illumine that which is inert? When he says «whose essence is the *sattva* of the thinking-substance» he describes the inertness in so far as there is identity with the non-intelligent form. [We say that the *sattva* of the thinking-substance] depends upon the Self to the extent that it depends on the image of the Self as entered into the *sattva* of the thinking-substance, in the same sense that a person depends upon [his] face reflected in a mirror [if he wish to see himself]. [And the *sattva* is said to depend upon the Self.] But not [as the objector said], because the *sattva* of the thinking-substance illumines the Self. It is the *sattva* of the thinking-substance which reflects the Self united with this presented-idea, and which depends upon the Intelligence (*cāitanya*) which has been mirrored (*chāyāpanna*) in it [as the intelligence] of the Self. Thus it exists for the sake of the Self. On this same point he quotes the Sacred Word by saying «For in this sense it has been said» by the Içvara «" the Discerner."» The meaning is that [He is discerned] by no one.

---

36. As a result of this [constraint upon that which exists for its own sake], there arise vividness and the organ-of-[supernal]-hearing [1] and the organ-of-[supernal]-feeling and the organ-of-[supernal]-sight and the organ-of-[supernal]-taste and the organ-of-[supernal]-smell.

As a result of vividness, there arises an [intuitive] knowledge of the subtile or concealed or remote, whether past or future. As a result of the organ-of-[supernal]-hearing, one hears supernal sounds; as a result of the organ-of-[supernal]-feeling, one has access to supernal touch; as a result of the organ-of-[supernal]-sight, one has the consciousness [2] of supernal colour; as a result of the organ-of-[supernal]-taste, one has a consciousness of supernal flavour; as a result of the organ-of-[supernal] smell,[3] one has an [intuitive] knowledge [4] of supernal fragrance. These unceasingly arise.

This restraint, moreover, upon that which exists for its own sake continues until the primary cause has fulfilled its peculiar task (*kārya*), the [intuitive] knowledge of the Self. He describes all the supernormal powers which [the yogin] receives before that [intuitive knowledge comes]. **36. As a result of this . . . there arise . . .** So then it has been asserted that the central-organ and the organ of hearing and of feeling and of sight and of taste and of smell, which have been helped by the external-aspects which arise from yoga, are in each single case in direct causal relation with the supernal sounds and so forth and with the [intuitive] knowledge of vividness (*prātibha*). The five organs, of hearing and so on, which apperceive supernal sounds and so forth have technical names such as the organ-of-[supernal]-hearing and the rest. The Comment is easy.

---

37. In concentration these [supernal activities] are obstacles; in the emergent state they are perfections (*siddhi*).

These, the vividness and so forth, arising in the yogin whose mind-stuff is concentrated, are obstacles, in that they go counter to the sight which belongs to this [concentrated mind-stuff].

[1] This word *çrāvaṇa* is from the causative stem. The Maṇiprabhā (p. 64[21], Ben. ed.) explains it as being 'the organs of knowing supernal sounds and so on' (*divyānāṁ çabda . . . ādīnāṁ grāhakāṇi*).

[2] A *saṁvid* is a perception with little direct relation to the object.

[3] Compare Hopkins, Yoga-technique, JAOS, (1901), vol. 22, p. 344[20].

[4] The word *vijñāna* is loosely used. It seems to indicate whatever comes to consciousness.

[But] arising [in the yogin] whose mind-stuff is emergent, they are perfections.

Occasionally a man, after beginning constraint upon the self as object, acquires those perfections which are subsidiary to this, and thinks because of the power (*prabhāva*) of these [perfections] that he has effected his purpose, and so might cease the constraint. So [the author] says, **37. In concentration these [supernal activities] are obstacles; in the emergent state they are perfections** (*siddhi*). For a man whose mind-stuff is emergent thinks highly of these perfections, just as a man born in misery considers even a small bit of wealth a pile of wealth. But a yogin whose mind-stuff is concentrated must avoid these [perfections] even when brought near to him. One who longs for the final goal of life, the absolute assuagement of the three-fold anguish, how could he have any affection for those perfections which go counter to [the attainment] of that [goal]? This is the meaning both of the Sūtra and of the Comment.

38. As a result of slackening the causes of bondage and as a result of the consciousness of the procedure [of the mind-stuff], the mind-stuff penetrates into the body of another.

By virtue of the latent-deposit of karma in the body, the central-organ which is changeable and unstable becomes established. This is bondage. By virtue of concentration there is a slackening of this karma which is the cause of bondage. And the consciousness of the procedure [of the mind-stuff] comes only from concentration. As a result of the dwindling of the bondage of karma, and as a result of the consciousness of the procedure of his mind-stuff, the yogin by withdrawing mind-stuff from his own body deposits it in other bodies. The organs also fly after [ii. 54] the mind-stuff thus deposited. Just [1] as, for instance, when the king-bee flies up, the bees fly up after him, so the organs follow after the mind-stuff in its penetration into the body of another.

After thus stating that power, in the form of [intuitive] knowledge extending as far as to the sight of the Self, is the result of constraint, he gives, as another result of constraint, power in the form of action. **38. . . . The causes of bondage . . . penetration.** When he says «By virtue of concentration» this means under 1. the power of the constraint whose object is the causes of bondage. The word «concentration» is used [instead of 'constraint,'] because it is predominant [in constraint].—A procedure is that by which something proceeds into

[1] Compare Praçna Up. ii. 4.

another thing. It means the tubes (*nāḍi*) [that is] the paths for the coming and going of mind-stuff. As a result 2. of constraint upon this passage there is a consciousness of it. And as a result of this [as well as of 1. the constraint upon the causes of bondage], since the causes of bondage are slackened, it [the mind-stuff] is not held back by this [yogin]. Although the mind-stuff is not held back as it soars into the upward path, it cannot without impediment pass forth from his body nor enter into the other's body. Therefore the passage for this must also be known.—The organs moreover follow the mind-stuff and settle down in their respective places in the other's body.

39. As a result of subjugating the *Udāna*, there is no adhesion to water or mud or thorns or similar objects, and [at death] the upward flight.

The fluctuation of the whole complex of organs which is distinguished by having the different vital-forces (*prāṇa*) is vitality.[1] Its activity is five-fold. *Prāṇa* has its course through the mouth and nose and its fluctuation extends as far as the heart. And *Samāna*, since it distributes equally, has its fluctuation from the navel. *Apāna*, since it leads down, has its fluctuation as far as the sole of the foot. *Udāna*, since it leads up, has its fluctuation as far as the head. *Vyāna* is pervading. Among these *Prāṇa* is predominant. As a result of subjugating the *Udāna* there is no adhesion to water or mud or thorns or similar objects; and at the time of decease there is the upward flight. This [upward flight] he attains by mastery [of the *Udāna*].

39. *Udāna* . . . and . . . the upward flight. The fluctuation of the whole complex of organs is life. The words «distinguished by having the different vital-forces (*prāṇa*)» refer to that [fluctuation] of which the different vital-forces are the distinction. The organs have two kinds [of fluctuations], an inner and an outer. The outer is distinguished by the external-sense (*ālocana*) of colour and similar sensations. The inner is life. For this is a special kind of effort and it leads to the different activities of the winds (*māruta*) which the body comprehends. This effort is common to all the organs. As they say[2] "The fluctuations common to the [inner] organs are the five winds (*vāyu*), vital-airs and so on." Because they are the distinguishing-characteristic of this [life].

[1] Defined as a struggle for life by Vācaspati *jīvanaṁ prāṇa-dhāraṇa-prayatna-bhedo 'saṁviditaç cittasya dharmaḥ* iii. 15, p. 217[8]. It is mentioned in the list iii. 18, p. 230[4] (Calc. ed.).

[2] Sāṁkhya-kārikā 29.

The action [or] function of this effort is of five kinds. 1. *Prāṇa* extends from the tip of the nose to the heart. 2. *Samāna* is one which evenly distributes as required in different places the various juices which are mutations of food eaten and drunk. And its locality extends from the heart and to the navel. 3. *Apāna* is that which leads to the carrying off of urine, faeces, foetus, &c. And its activity (*vṛtti*) is from the navel and to the sole of the foot. 4. *Udāna* is so-called because it leads up [that is] leads upwards such things as secretions. And its activity is from the tip of the nose and to the head. 5. *Vyāna* is one that pervades [the whole body].—Of these thus described *Prāṇa* is predominant, since the Sacred Word[1] declares that when that goes forth all goes forth, "Following the *Prāṇa* when it goes forth, all the vital-forces (*prāṇa*) go forth."—Having thus explained the differences between the vital-forces (*prāṇa*) with respect to activity and locality, he leads up to the meaning of the sūtra with the words «As a result of subjugating the *Udāna*.» When constraint has been performed upon the *Udāna*, [then] as a result of its subjugation, [the yogin] is not held back by water or similar objects. And at the time of decease his upward flight is by the path[2] which commences with the flame. As a result of this [constraint] he attains by mastery to this upward flight. These supernormal powers that result from constraint upon the vital-forces beginning with *Prāṇa*, if there be success in it, should be understood according to the differences in the subjugations of activities and of localities [in the body].

40. As a result of subjugating the *Samāna* [there arises] a radiance.

The yogin who has subjugated the *Samāna* by causing a pulsation of the flames, becomes radiant.[3]

40. . . . the *Samāna* . . . a radiance. There is «a pulsation,» a flaming forth of the flame in the body.

---

41. As a result of constraint upon the relation between the organ-of-hearing, and the air (*ākāça*), [there arises] the supernal organ-of-hearing.[4]

For all organs-of-hearing the air is the [physical] basis, and for all sounds. In which sense it has been said "All[5] those whose

[1] Compare Bṛhad Ar. Up. iv. 4. 3.

[2] This is the *devayāna*. See Bṛhad Ar. Up. vi. 1. 3 and 18 and Chānd. Up. iv. 15. 5-6; Chānd. Up. v. 10. 1.

[3] Compare *prabhā bhāskarasya* (iii. 13, p. 243[6], Calc. ed.).

[4] iii. 51, p. 267[1] (Calc. ed.).

[5] Reading *ekaçrutitvaṁ* with six MSS. including the *çāradā* MS. instead of *ekadeça-çrutitvaṁ*. One is tempted to surmise that there might be another reading *tulya-deçya* or *tulya-deçīya* instead of *tulyadeça*, with a meaning similar to Vācaspati's gloss *jātīya*. This is Pañcaçikha's twelfth fragment according to Garbe.

processes-of-hearing (*çravaṇa*) are in the same place have the same kind-of-hearing (*eka-çrutitvam*)."[1] And this [fact that the air is the locus of sounds] is declared to be the [first] characteristic mark of air. And the second is that it is not covered[2] [by anything more extensive]. Thus because a thing which is not-limited-in-extent (*amūrta*) is evidently not covered [by anything], it is also recognized that air is [all] pervasive. From the perception of sounds it is inferred that the organ-of-hearing exists. For in the case of a deaf man and of a man not deaf, the one perceives sound and the other not. Hence it is the organ-of-hearing only which is the field of operation for sound.—For the yogin who has performed constraint upon the relation between the organ-of-hearing and the air, the supernal[3] ear begins.

It has already been stated [iii. 36, p. 246[1-3] Calc. ed.] that as a result of constraint upon that which exists for its own sake [this would be the *mukhya*], there remains a subsidiary [perfection], the organ-of-[supernal]-hearing and other [organs]. Now the organ-of-[supernal]-hearing and other [organs] result from the constraint which has the organ-of-[supernal]-hearing and other [organs] as its sole purpose. **41. . . . Organ-of-hearing . . . organ-of-hearing.** He says that the object of the constraint is the relation between organ-of-hearing and the air in the relation of the contained to the container, in the words «For all.» All organs-of-hearing, although made of the personality-substance, have the air which is [contained in] the hollow-space of the auditory canal as its [physical] basis. The organ-of-hearing has its seat (*āyatana*) there. For if we assist or injure this [auditory canal], we find that the organ-of-hearing has been assisted or injured. [Air is] also [the physical basis] for sounds which are causes co-operating with the organ-of-hearing. When a sound is to be heard as coming from an earthen or other substance, the organ-of-hearing, which is in the hollow of the auditory canal, presupposes that there is a special sound residing in the air[4] (*nabhas*) which is its own [that is, the organ's] substance. [That this is so is] clear (*dṛṣṭam*) [from analogy]. Thus when, for instance, one wishes to have an external sense (*ālocana*) of smell, which is contained in this case in earth, by means of the organ-of-smell which is a co-operating [non-material] cause for those things which have smell and [taste] as their [specific] qualities, [we find similarly that the sense of smell

[1] The Yogavārttika, p. 237[11], also suggests this reading.

[2] The word *anāvaraṇam* in the sense of *nāvriyate anena*. In the Vārttika it is said to be 'free space' (*avakāça*).

[3] Bālarāma says that the supernality consists in a kind of hyperaesthetic perception of minute sounds, &c., which are like subtile elements (*divyatvam tanmātrādirūpasūkṣmaçabdādigrāhakatvam*).

[4] That is to say the *ākāça*.

requires such a special kind of smell in so far as it is contained in the earthen thing which contains it]. And it has already been said that the organs of smell and of taste and of touch and of sight and of hearing, although made of the personality-substance, do have the elements as their locus. For if we assist or injure the elements, we find that we have assisted or injured the organ-of-smell or some other of the organs. This same organ-of-hearing, which is made of the personality-substance, moreover resembles a piece of iron in that it is attracted by a magnet-like sound, in the mouth, produced by the mouth of the speaker, and, by a succession of its own functions (*vṛtti*), has the external sense of the word which has come to the mouth of the speaker. Hence there are sense-presentations of sounds functioning at different points of space. [And this sense-presentation], common to all living-beings, cannot in the absence of inhibition, be counted as an invalid-source-of-ideas. And in this sense there is an utterance by Pañcaçikha, "All those whose-processes-of-hearing (*çruvaṇa*) are in the same place have the same kind-of-hearing." Those persons whose processes-of-hearing are in the same place are those persons, like Chāitra, whose organs-of-hearing are of that kind. The meaning is that the processes-of-hearing of all are in the air (*ākāça*). The air, moreover, the locus of the organs-of-hearing, because it is produced from the fine-element (*tanmātra*), whose [specific] quality is sound, has sound as its specific quality.[1] By which sound as a co-operating [non-material] cause it grasps the sounds from earthen and other substances. Therefore there is for all one species of hearing (*çruti*) with regard to sound. This is the meaning. Thus then it has been shown that air is the locus of the organ-of-hearing and that it has sounds as its [specific] quality.—And this fact that there is one kind of hearing (*ekaçrutitvaṁ*) is the [first] characteristic mark of air. For this one kind of hearing is that condition which phenomenalizes sound. This very thing which is its substrate (*āçraya*) is the thing expressed by the word air. For in the absence of such a hearing there is no [individual] phenomenal sound [belonging to earthen and other substances]. Moreover such a hearing cannot be a quality (*guṇa*) of the various [coarse substances] such as earth, because, if it be such, these cannot be both the thing-to-be-phenomenalized and the conditions-which-phenomenalize. —And the [second] characteristic mark of air is that it is not covered [by anything more extensive]. If there were no air, the things not-limited-in-extent would be pressed together and could not be separated even by needles. And so as a result everything would be covered by everything. And it cannot be said that the not being covered [by anything] is merely because things-not-limited-in-extent are not present. For this negation implies a positive entity [for example, a thing-limited-in-extent]. And if this positive entity do not exist, there can be no negation of it. Nor can it be said that the

[1] Compare Vāiçeṣika-sūtra vii. 1. 22 together with the words of Çrīdhara, p. 61, ll. 19–21 (Vizian. ed.). See also Tarka-saṁgraha, § 14.

Energy of Intellect (*citiçakti*) could be the substrate for this[1] [free space not covered by anything]. For being immutable it cannot have [spatial] properties that precisely determine. And again it cannot be said that space (*diç*) and time are substances (*dravya*) over and above earth and the other [coarse elements]. Consequently that particular mutation [which is not covered by anything more extensive] belongs to air only. Thus all is cleared up.—When it is proved that the fact that nothing covers it is a characteristic mark of air,—so that wherever there is anything that has nothing covering it, there always air is,—then [all-] pervasiveness is also proved, as he says «Thus because a thing which is not-limited-in-extent.»—He gives the source-of-the-valid-idea to prove the real existence of the organ-of-hearing by saying «From the perception of sounds.» For [every] action is to be effected by an instrument, just as the action of chopping or the like is to be effected by the axe or something similar. So in this case also the act of perceiving sound must be accomplished by an instrument. And that which is the instrument is the organ-of-hearing. Now if it be asked why may not the eye or some other organ be the instrument of this [act], he replies «in the case of a deaf man and of a man not deaf.» This is determined by positive and negative arguments. And this is only an elliptical statement. For *mutatis mutandis* we must say that as a result of constraint upon the relation between the organ-of-touch and wind (*vāta*), between organ-of-sight and radiance, between the organ-of-taste and water, and between the organ-of-smell and earth, supernal touch and other [supernal sensations] would also arise.

42. Either as the result of constraint upon the relation between the body and the air (*ākāça*), or (*ca*) as the result of the balanced-state of lightness, such as that of the cotton-fibre, there follows the passing through air.

Wherever there is a body there is air, because it [air] gives space to the body. The relation [of the body] with this [air] is that of obtaining [pervasion]. By performing constraint upon this relation the yogin subjugates the relation with this [air]. And gaining the balanced-state of lightness such as that of the cotton-fibre, even to [that of] atoms [of cotton-fibre], he becomes light himself. And by reason of this lightness he walks with both feet upon water. Next after this, however, he walks upon nothing more than a spider's thread, and then upon sunbeams. Thereafter he courses through the air at will.

[1] Reading (with Poona text) *tad-āçrayā*.

42. . . . body . . . . passing through. By performing constraint upon the relation between the body and the air, or upon something light such as a cotton-fibre, [that is] by gaining the balanced-state [that is] the state of the mind which rests in the [thing] and in which it is tinged [i. 41] by it. He describes the sequence of the perfections by the words, «upon water.»

43. An outwardly un-adjusted fluctuation is the Great Discarnate; as a result of this the dwindling of the covering to the brightness.

The fluctuation assumed by the central-organ outside the body is the fixed-attention (*dhāraṇā*) called Discarnate. If it is only an outer[1] fluctuation of the central-organ which abides in the body, it is called adjusted (*kalpita*). But if it is an outer fluctuation of the central-organ, which is itself externalized, in that it [the fluctuation] disregards the body, it is of course called unadjusted. [The yogins] by means of the adjusted one among these two accomplish the unadjusted Great Discarnate, by means of which yogins enter the bodies of others. And as a result of this fixed-attention, the covering of the *sattva* of the thinking-substance, whose essence is brightness, which has the three-fold fruition from the hindrances and the karma, and whose root is *rajas* and *tamas*, dwindles away.

He describes yet another constraint which leads to the penetration of another's body and which leads to the dwindling of the hindrances and karma and fruitions. **43. An outwardly . . . . dwindling.** The discarnate he describes in the words «The fluctuation assumed.» In order to show the means to the Great Discarnate state which is unadjusted he first describes the discarnate in the words «If it is.» The words «only a fluctuation» mean thinking only in an imaginary way. He describes the Great Discarnate in the words «But if it is.» He shows that the adjusted and the unadjusted have the relation of means to end by saying «among these two.» Is it that one merely enters another's body as a result of this? Not so, he says in the words «And as a result of this.» «As a result of this fixed attention» means when the Great Discarnate activity of the central-organ has been perfected. It has its three-fold fruition, from the hindrances and from karma, in birth and length-of-life and kind-of-

[1] The outer adjustment would be in part a voluntary act. Compare the explanation in the Maṇiprabhā *me mano bahir astv ita kalpanayā*. But in the outwardly unadjusted state there is a renunciation of the self and of the sense of individuality as limited by a body *dehe 'hambhāvatyāgaḥ*.

experience [ii. 18]. And it is this that has its root in *rajas* and *tamas*. Since from mere *sattva* when freed from *rajas* and *tamas* there arises discriminative discernment only. Thus the three-fold fruition in so far as it is rooted in *rajas* and *tamas*, and because its essence is in them, obscures the *sattva* of the thinking-substance. And as soon as these have dwindled away, the mind-stuff of the yogin freed from its covering [by them] roves and discerns at will.

44. As a result of constraint upon the coarse (*sthūla*) and the essential-attribute (*svarūpa*) and the subtile *sūkṣma*) and the inherence (*anvaya*) and the purposiveness (*arthavattva*), there is a subjugation of the elements.

In this [system] i. the [five elements] beginning with earth [which in essence are a generic form and a particular] have [as particulars] sounds and other perceptible things; [these] particulars, together with their properties (*dharma*), shape and the rest [which are to be described], are technically called ‹coarse.› This is the first form of the elements.—ii. The second form is its generic-form. For example, limitation-in-extent (*mūrti*) is the [generic-form] of earth; liquidity, of water; heat, of fire; wind [is] mobile, for air goes everywhere. This second form is technically called ‹essential-attribute.› This generic-form has sounds and other [concrete perceptible things] as its particulars. And in this sense it has been[1] said, "All these [perceptible things] that are inseparably connected with one *genus praedicabile* are distinguished only by their properties." In this system a substance (*dravya*) is an aggregate[2] (*samudāya*) of the generic-form and of the particular. For a collection (*samūha*) is of two kinds, 1. that in which [the names of] its different component parts have disappeared, as for instance, a body, a tree, a herd, a forest[3]; and 2. that collection in which the different component parts are specified [each] by a term, as for instance 'of both kinds, gods-and-human-beings.'[4] One part of the collection is gods and the second part is human beings. Only by means of these two is it termed a collection. Furthermore, either

[1] Vijñāna Bhikṣu says *pūrvācārya-saṁvādam āha.*
[2] Compare Patañjali Mahābhāṣya I. 217[10]; I. 289[2f]; I. 377[11f]; III. 3[14f] (Kielhorn).
[3] Compare Tattva Bindu (Ben. ed.), p. 11[15].
[4] Compare Çatapathabrāhmaṇa ii. 2. 2.

the distinction or the identity may be emphasized. We may say 'a grove of mango-trees' [or] 'gathering of Brahmans' or we may say 'a mango-grove' [or] 'a Brahman-gathering.' Again the [collection] is two-fold, 1. that of which the parts exist separately; and 2. that of which the parts do not exist separately.[1] A grove [or] a gathering is a collection from which the parts are separable. A body or a tree or an atom is a whole[2] (*saṁghāta*) of which the parts are not separable. Patañjali says that a substance is a collection the different component parts of which do not exist separately. Thus it has been explained what the essential-attribute is.—iii. Now what is the subtile form, [of these elements]? [The answer is] it is subtile-substance, the cause of the elements. Of [any] one of these [elements] an atom is one part. Its essence is the generic-form and the particular and it is an aggregate consisting of different parts which cannot exist separately. Similarly with all the *tanmātras*. This is the third [form].—iv. Now the fourth form of the elements. The aspects with dispositions to discernment and to activity and to inertia and conforming to the nature of [their] effects are described by the word inherence.—v. Now the fifth form of these [elements] is purposiveness. The having of experience and of release as their purpose is inherent in the aspects (*guṇa*). And the aspects are [inseparably connected] with the elements and the products of the elements. Thus all has a purpose. By constraint upon these five elements of the present time in their five forms, the sight of the essential-attribute of this or that form and the subjugation of it come about. [The yogin] by mastering the five essential-attributes of the elements, masters the elements, [and] as a result of their subjugation, the evolving-causes of the [coarse] elements follow the commands of his will just as the cows follow their own calves.

44. . . . coarse . . . subjugation . . . . [The compound is to be analysed as] the coarse and the essential-attribute and the subtile and the inherence and the purposiveness. As a result of constraint upon these, the coarse and the essential-attribute and the subtile and the inherence and the purposiveness, there

[1] Compare Nyāya-sūtra ii. 1. 32.

[2] Compare Patañjali Mahābhāṣya I. 30[26]; I. 31[9]; I. 32[2]; I. 169[187]; III. 324[12] (Kielhorn).

is a subjugation of them. i. He describes the coarse[1] by saying «In this [system].» The sounds and touches and colours and tastes and smells, belonging [respectively] to the earthen and watery and fiery and windy and airy [classes or elements], have correspondingly the particulars, such as the first (*ṣaḍja*) or the third notes, or heat or cold, or blue or yellow, or astringent or sweet, or fragrant or other [particular instances]. For because these are different from each other in name and form and use they are the particulars. Of these particulars there are five in earth, four (counting out smell) are in water, three (counting out smell and taste) are in fire, two (counting out smell and taste and colour) are in wind (*nabhasvant*), sound alone is in the air. Particulars such as these, together with their properties (*dharma*), form and the rest, are technically called ‹coarse› in [this] system. 1. And in this [system], to begin with, the properties belonging to the earthen [element] are "Shape, weight, roughness, resistance, and stability; sustenance (*vṛtti*), divisibility, endurance, meagreness, hardness, and usefulness to all." 2. The properties of water, "Liquidity, subtilty, brilliance, whiteness, sinuosity (*mārdava*), weight, coolness, protectiveness, purification, cohesion are the qualities of water." 3. The fiery properties, "Tending-upwards, purifier, burner, cooker, without weight, resplendent, destructive, yielding strength,—this is fire having characteristics different from the two previous [elements]." 4. The windy properties, "Horizontal movement, purification, felling, impulsion, power, changeability, casting no shadow, aridity,—these are the various properties of wind." 5. The airy properties, "Pervasiveness, interpenetration, unobstructiveness are enumerated as three properties of air distinct in character from the previous properties." These are those properties, the shape and the following; [the particulars were said to be] together with these. And shape is a particular instance of generic nature, such as cow-ness. ii. He describes the second form [of the elements] by saying «The second form is its generic-form.» Limitation-in-extent means natural[2] density. Liquidity is [the generic-form of] water and it is the effective cause of cleanliness (*mṛja*) and plumpness and vigour. Heat is [the generic-form of] fire (*vahni*), since everywhere [heat], whether it be abdominal or solar or earthly, is inherent in fire (*tejas*). All this moreover is intended to show the identity of property and substance. Wind is motor. So he says "By the movement of grass and because it makes the body wander, motivity is inferred to be the generic-form of wind which goes everywhere. Going-everywhere is air, since it is clear that we apperceive sounds in all directions. For it has been previously [iii. 41] explained that one apperceives earthen and other sounds by means of the sound which is a [specific] quality of air the substance-in-which the organ-of-hearing inheres. This is what is

[1] Compare Bhāgavata Pur. xi. 24. 16.

[2] Whatever is natural (*sāṁsiddhika*) is distinct from the thing itself (*svabhāva*) and yet is not generated by a cause outside the substance. For example, liquidity is a natural property of water; but the solidity of snow is not natural, in that it is due to cause. On the other hand solidity is a natural property of ghee; whereas liquidity is not, in that it is an effect of something outside the substance.

described by the word essential-attribute. One such generic-form such as limitation-in-extent has the particular sounds and other perceptible things, such as the first note, such as heat, such as whiteness, such as astringency, such as fragrance, these constituting the particular instances of the generic-forms such as limitation-in-extent. That is to say, the generic-forms,[1] such as the limitations-in-extent, such as [the shapes of] lemons or bread-fruit or myrobolans, are also distinguished from each other by differences in taste and so on. So that these tastes and other qualities are particulars of these [generic-forms]. «And in this sense it has been said, "All that are inseparably connected with one *genus praedicabile*"» would refer to each of [the elements] such as earth. [Each of these] is inseparably connected with some one *genus praedicabile*, limitation-in-extent, for example, or liquidity. [These that are thus inseparably connected] are distinguished only by their properties,[2] such for example as the first note. Thus the generic-form such as limitation-in-extent has been described, and the particulars such as the sounds have been described.—And to those[3] who assert that substance (*dravya*) is a substrate (*āçraya*) for the generic-form and for the particular—[to them] he says, «of the generic-form.» In this system substance is an aggregate (*samudāya*) of the generic-form and of the particular. Those who take the point of view that substance is a substrate of these [two]—even they cannot deny that both are experienced as an aggregate. For if this experience be denied, the two cannot have a container-(*ādhāra*)-which-underlies them. Therefore let us suppose that this [aggregate] is itself the substance. But we do not apperceive any substance underlying them different from both and from the aggregate of the two [which might be supposed to contain-them-by-underlying them], just as the mountain-peak is a distinct thing and other than the stones or the aggregate of stones, and underlies them. Thus we say that substance is a collection [and not anything underlying]. From this point of view, to prevent the [error that substance is any kind of a collection and] to reach the position that substance is a special kind of collection, he describes various kinds of collections in the words, «For . . . of two kinds.» Since this is so, substance is not any kind of a collection. «Of two kinds» is a thing which exists in two ways. a. One of these kinds is given in the words «has disappeared.» These are so-called in whose case the difference between the parts has disappeared. One which has parts in whose case the differences have disappeared is of this kind. What he means to say is this. The idea of the collection raised by words like body, tree, herd, or forest does not bring into consciousness the difference between the several parts, since the words are not used to express this [difference]. So the collective [sense] only is brought to mind. There are four cases given as illustrations: 1. the case in which the parts can exist separately, 2. the case in which they cannot exist separately, 3. an animate thing, 4. an inanimate thing. That parts can exist separately or

[1] Reading *sāmānyāny api*.
[2] This would be equivalent to the particular (*viçeṣa*).
[3] The Vāiçeṣikas.

cannot exist separately will be stated later.—b. The second of the two kinds is described in the words, «2. that collection in which the different component parts are specified [each] by a term, as for instance 'of both kinds, gods-and-human-beings.'» Now by the expression «gods-and-human-beings» the two parts of the collection which are expressed by the words «of both kinds» have been specified as being separate. An objection is raised, 'the expression «of both kinds» does not bring the difference between the parts of that [collection] into consciousness. How then can we say that the [collection] in which the different component parts have been described has received [names]?' The reply is in the words «of these two.» And it is because of these very parts that the term collection can be imposed. By the words «of both kinds» which describe a thing as having two parts, the idea of the collection is expressed, since a sentence cannot but express the object-intended by the sentence. This is the point. Once more he describes a difference in qualities by saying «Furthermore.» Both the identity and the distinction are emphasized. He describes the emphasis laid upon the difference in the words, «'a grove of mango-trees' [or] 'a gathering of Brahmans.'» Because the genitive case is prescribed [1] to express a distinction, as for instance, 'a cow belonging to the Gargas.' He describes the emphasis laid upon the identity in the words [2] «'a mango-grove' [or] 'a Brahman-gathering.'» [The compound is to be analysed thus,] the mango-trees which themselves make up the grove. Inasmuch as he wishes to emphasize the identity between the collection and its parts, [the words] refer to the same subject. This is the meaning. He states another kind of collection by saying «Again [the collection] is two-fold.» A collection of which the parts exist separately, is one the parts of which have an independent existence, apart, with intervals between; for when the word 'herd' or 'grove' is spoken, the trees and the cows which are the parts of these [collections are thought to] have intervals between them. A tree, a cow, or an atom is a collection of which the parts do not exist separately, since neither the generic-form and the particular, which are the parts of these, have intervals between them, nor do the dewlap and the other [characteristic parts] of the cow have intervals between them. From among these same collections he selects that collection which constitutes a substance (*dravya*), saying «cannot be separated.» Having thus incidentally explained what a substance is, he sums up the topic in hand in the words «Thus it has been explained what the essential-attribute is.»—iii. With the intent to state the third form he asks «Now?» He gives the answer in the words «from which these [coarse elements] are made.» «Of [any one of] these [coarse elements]» one part, a single mutation, is an atom. The generic-form is the limitation-in-extent or the like. The sounds and other [perceptible things] are the particulars. [The atom] has its essence in these [two parts]. A collection corresponds to such instances [of things] as are in part a generic-form, and in

[1] Pāṇini ii. 3. 50. [2] According to Pāṇ. viii. 4. 5 the *n* should be changed to *ṇ*.

part a particular, wherein these parts cannot separately exist and yet have no intervals between them. And just as the atom is a subtile (*sūkṣma*) form, so all the fine elements (*tanmātra*) are a subtile form. He brings this to a close in the words «This is.»—«iv. Now the fourth form of the elements. The aspects with dispositions to discernment and to activity and to inertia and conforming to the nature of [their] effects» means those whose disposition it is to be inseparably connected with (*anu-gantum*), that is, to conform to (*anu-pat*) the nature of [their] effects. Hence they are described by the term inherence (*anv-aya*).—«v. Now the fifth form of these [elements] is purposiveness.» He elaborates the word purposiveness by saying «experience.» An objector asks 'Even if it be granted that the aspects have a purpose, how can you still say that their effects are purposive?' In reply to this he says «the aspects.» Products of the elements are such things as cows or water-jars.—Having thus described the object of the constraint, he describes the constraint itself and its results in the words «upon these.» «The evolving-causes of the [coarse] elements» are the elements themselves.

---

45. As a result of this, atomization (*aṇiman*) and the other [perfections] come about; [there is] perfection of body; and there is no obstruction by the properties of these [elements].

As to these[1] [eight perfections], 1. atomization occurs in case [the yogin] becomes atomic; 2. levitation occurs in case [the yogin] becomes light; 3. magnification (*mahiman*) occurs in case [the yogin] becomes magnified; 4. extension (*prāpti*) occurs in case [the yogin] touches the moon with a mere finger's tip; 5. efficacy, the non-obstruction of desire, occurs in case [the yogin] dives into the earth underground [and] emerges again, as if in water; 6. mastery (*vaçitva*) occurs in case [the yogin] masters elements and products of elements and is not mastered by others; 7. sovereignty occurs in case [the yogin] is sovereign over the production, absorption, and arrangement of these [elements and products]; 8. the capacity of determining things according to desire (*yatra-kāmāvasāyitva*) is the capacity to will actual facts so that the elements which are the evolving-causes remain as he wills. And although having power, he does not cause reversal of things. Why not? Because at the will of another [the Īçvara], who determines things according to desire, and who from the beginning is perfected, the elements have been so willed. These are the eight powers.—

[1] See Vācaspati in Sāṁkh. Tat. Kāum. on Kār. xxiii.

Perfection of body is described later. And its external-aspects are not obstructed. Earth with its limitation-in-extent [its essential-attribute] does not restrict the action of the body and [organs] of the yogin. For he penetrates even the rock. The water, liquid as it is, wets him not. The fire, hot as it is, burns him not. The wind, motor as it is, budges him not. And even in the air, whose essence is that nothing is covered [by it], his body is covered. Nay more, not even the Siddhas may behold him.

When the elements follow the commands of his will, what perfection is attained by the yogin? In reply he says **45. As a result of this . . . and . . . no obstruction.** From the mastery resulting from constraint upon the **a.** coarse [elements], four perfections follow, as he says «As to these.» 1. Atomization [that is] although great he becomes small. 2. Levitation [that is] although great, he becomes light and stays in the air like the tuft of a reed. 3. Magnification [that is] although small he becomes in dimension an elephant or a mountain or a town. 4. Extension [that is] all things become close at hand for the yogin. For instance, even while standing on the earth he touches the moon with the tip of his finger.—He describes the perfection resulting from the subjugation by constraint of b. the essential-attribute in the words «5. efficacy, the non-obstruction of desire.» His own form is not obstructed by the limitations-in-extent and other essential-attributes of the elements. He dives underground and emerges again as if in water. c. He now gives the perfection resulting from the subjugation by constraint of a subtile object by saying «6. mastery.» The elements are earth and the other [coarse elements]. The products-of-the-elements are such things as cows and water-jars. He becomes master of them, independent with regard to them, and not mastered by them. Since there is a mastery of the atoms of earth and of the other [coarse elements], and of the subtile elements which are the causes of these [elements and products], there follows a mastery of the effects of these. Therefore those particular elements or products of elements when put into a certain state remain in that state. d. He now gives the perfection which results from subjugation by constraint upon inherence (*anvaya*) as its object by saying «7. sovereignty.» Having subjugated the radical cause of these elements and products-of-elements, he becomes sovereign both over their growth [or] production, and over their decay [or] destruction, and over their arrangement or proper arrangement. e. He now describes the perfection which is the result of constraint upon purposiveness by saying «8. Fulfilment of whatever is desired is the volition which becomes effective.» Whenever a yogin who has been successful with regard to the purposiveness of the aspects wishes anything to serve a particular purpose, that thing serves him for that purpose. Making others eat poison,[1]

[1] Cf. Raghuvañça viii. 46, *srag iyaṁ yadi*, &c.; the stanza is missing in some ed.'s.

he wills that it have the effect of nectar and makes them live. An objector says 'This may be so. But why does he not make an interchange of things also, just as he makes a reversal of powers, so that he might make the moon into the sun, or make Kuhū into Sinīvālī?' The reply is «And although having the power, he does not.» For assuredly these whose desires are fulfilled do not venture to transgress the order of the Exalted Highest Içvara. But the powers (*çakti*) of things are not limited in their nature, in so far as they differ in species and place and time and intensity. So it is proper that these [powers] should follow the commands of this [yogin]. These are the eight powers (*āiçvarya*).—With regard to the words <and there is no obstruction by the properties of these [elements].> By the very mentioning that atomization and the other [perfections] come about, it is clear that there is no obstruction by the properties of these [elements]. But this is mentioned again to make known the fruitions resulting from the constraints upon all the objects mentioned in this sūtra. And the same holds good with reference to perfections of body. The rest is easy.

46. Beauty and grace and power and the compactedness of the thunderbolt,—[this is] perfection of body.

The perfect body is handsome and alluring and unexcelled in power and compact as the thunderbolt.

He describes the perfection of the body. **46. Beauty . . . perfection . . . .** A compactness as of the thunderbolt. Of such a kind that the arrangement of the parts is firm and solid.

47. As a result of constraint upon the process-of-knowing and the essential-attribute and the feeling-of-personality and the inherence and the purposiveness, [there follows] the subjugation of the organs.

The object-to-be-known is the sounds and other [perceptible objects] whose essence is both the generic-form and the particular. 1. The process-of-knowing is a fluctuation of the organs with reference to these [objects]. And this [process] has not the character (*ākāra*) of being a process-of-knowing their generic-form only. How, if the object as a particular were not seen by the organ, could it be determined by the central-organ? 2. But the essential-attribute[1]

[1] The self-luminous nature of cognition is set forth with most subtle discrimination by Mr. A. Venis in his note on the Siddhānta Muktāvalī (1898), pp. 131–134.

is a collection, inherent in the different parts which cannot exist separately, [a collection] of the generic form [for example, the audibility] and of the particular [for example, the sounds and so forth], [a collection] which belongs to the *sattva* of the thinking-substance whose essence is brightness. The organ is [itself such] a substance. 3. The third form of these [organs] is the personality-substance with the feeling-of-personality (*asmitā*) as its distinguishing-characteristic. Organs are particulars of this generic-form. 4. The fourth form is the aspects (*guṇa*) whose essence is determination[1] (*vyavasāya*) and whose disposition is to brightness and to activity and to inertia. Of which [aspects] the organs together with the personality-substance are a mutation. 5. The fifth form inseparably connected with the aspects is the purposiveness[2] of the Self.—Constraint is performed upon one after another of these five forms of the organs. As a result of the subjugation of the five forms of accomplishing the subjugation in each several one of them, there comes about for the yogin the subjugation of the organs.

After the yogin has subjugated the elements his means for subjugating the organs is described. **47. Process-of-knowing . . . subjugation.** As a result of constraint upon these, the process-of-knowing and the essential attribute and the feeling-of-personality and the inherence and the purposiveness. The process-of-knowing is an act-of-perception (*grhiti*). And this [process], for its description, requires the object-to-be-known. So he describes the object-to-be-known by saying «whose essence is both the generic-form and the particular.» Having described the object-to-be-known, he describes the process-of-knowing in the words «with reference to these.» The fluctuation is about the same as an external-sense-process (*alocana*), an act-of-mutating into the form of an object. In reply to those who say that the fluctuation of an organ has as its object only the generic-form he says «And this has not.» It is a process-of-knowing because [something] is known. And the process-of-knowing has not[3] for its object the generic-form only. For the central-organ, which depends upon the external organs, acts upon the external [and not upon the generic-form]. Otherwise we should have to admit that there are, for example, no blind or dumb persons. So then if the organ were not to have a particular as its object, then

[1] In accordance with Sāṁkhya-kārakā xxiii it is clear that this term denotes the *guṇas* in so far as they function as thinking-substance (*buddhi*).

[2] Compare ii. 23, p. 158[4] (Calc. ed.); also Sāṁkhya-kārikā xv and Sāṁkhya-sūtra i. 129.

[3] Reading *na sāmānyamātragocaram*.

that particular would not be externally-sensed by that [organ]. How then could particulars be determined by the central-organ? Therefore the perception of the organs has for its object both the generic-form and the particular. This then is the process-of-knowing which is the first form of the organs. 2. He describes the second form in the words «But the essential-attribute.» For the personality-substance out of a portion of its own *sattva* generated the organs. Hence that generic-form of the organs which belongs to all of them, and those particular features which are limited to some such object as colour,—both of these two kinds also have brightness as their essence. 3. By saying «The third form of these [organs]» he refers to the personality-substance as the cause of the organs. So wherever there are organs, there this [personality-substance] must be. Thus since it is common to all the organs, it is the generic-form of the organs. This is the meaning. 4. He speaks of «The fourth form» because the aspects (*guṇa*) have a double form, one whose essence is a determination, and another whose essence is to be the object of the determination. Of these [two forms], with reference to the fact that its essence is an object of determination [and] that it is an object of knowledge, the five fine elements and the elements and the products of the elements form themselves; but with reference to the fact that its essence is a determination and that it has the form of a process-of-knowing, the organs together with the personality-substance [form themselves]. This is the meaning. The rest is easy.

48. As a result of this [there follows] speed [great as that] of the central-organ, action of the instruments of [knowledge] disjunct [from the body], and the subjugation of the primary-cause.

Speed of the mind means that the body acquires motion comparable [to that] of the mind. Action of the instruments[1] of knowledge disjunct [from the body] is the acquisition by the discarnate organs of the fluctuation required for the place and time and object desired. Subjugation of the primary cause is the mastery over all evolving causes and evolved effects. These three perfections are called Honey-Faced (*madhupratīka*). And they are acquired as the result of the subjugation in five forms of instruments [of perception].

He describes the perfections which result from the subjugation, in five kinds, of the organs. **48. As a result of this . . . . and the subjugation.** The fact that the organs are instruments [of perception] even for the discarnate is described as being the action of the instruments [of perception] disjunct [from the body].

[1] Compare Çaṁkara on Brahma-sūtra ii. 1. 31.

The place is Kashmir or some other [place]. The time is the past or some other [time]. The object is subtile or other. As a result of the subjugation of the organ and of the inherence, [there follows] mastery of all evolving-causes and evolved-effects, a subjugation of the primary cause. These perfections are called Honey-Faced by those persons who are expert in the yoga system. An objector says 'This may be true. By subjugation of the organs, the organs together with their objects may be mastered. But what is gained [by subjugation] of the primary cause and the other causes of these [organs]?' In reply to this he says «And they.» The instruments [of perception] are the organs. The five forms are [the five] processes-of-knowing [iii. 47]. [The result follows] from the subjugation of these. What he means to say is this: These perfections are not a result of a subjugation of organs in general but of the five forms [of the processes-of-knowing]. And included in these [five] is the primary-cause and the rest.

---

49. He who has only the full discernment into the difference between the *sattva* and the Self is one who has authority over all states-of-existence and is one who knows all.

He who is grounded in only the full discernment into the difference between the *sattva* and the Self, and who is in the higher consciousness[1] of being master in the higher clearness, and who has the *sattva* of his thinking-substance cleansed from the defilement of *rajas* and *tamas* is one who has authority over all states-of-existence. The aspects (*guṇa*) which are the essence of all things, which have both the determinations and the objects-of-determinations as their essence, present themselves as being the essence of the object-for-sight in its totality to their Owner, the Soul (*kṣetrajña*). This is the meaning.—Being ‹one who knows all› refers to the [intuitive] knowledge, produced by discrimination and rising instantaneously [into consciousness], of the aspects (*guṇa*) which are the essence of all, whether they be [iii. 14] quiescent or uprisen or indeterminable. This is the meaning. It is this perfection that is termed [i. 36] the 'undistressed,' by attaining to which the yogin who knows all, whose hindrances and bondages have dwindled, takes his recreation as having mastery.

These same constraints, which whether mediately or immediately lead to powers in the form of knowledge and of activity, are for the sake of the discernment into the difference between the *sattva* and the Self by way of the confidence

[1] See also i. 15, pp. 41[6] and 42[8]; i. 35, p. 81[4]; i. 40, p. 84[6,9]; ii. 26, p. 164[11] (Calc. ed.).

produced by grasping the perfections in turn and binding them together. The supernormal powers subsidiary to this [discernment] are shown [in the sūtra]. **49.** *Sattva* . . . **and.** There is clearness in so far as the defilement by *rajas* and *tamas* has been washed away. As a result of this there is the higher consciousness of being master. It was inevitable that the *sattva* of the mind-stuff should be overwhelmed by the *rajas* and *tamas*. But when the latter subside, it is this [*sattva*] that is to be mastered by the yogin its master. When it is mastered, the yogin who is grounded in only the full discernment of the difference between the *sattva* and the Self, is one who has authority over all states-of-existence. This same he explains by the words «essence of all things.» «Both the determination and the object-of-determination» mean both the inert (*jaḍa*) and bright kind. In this way the power of action has been described. He describes the power of knowledge in the words «one who knows all.» With the intent to create passionlessness with regard even to this two-fold perfection he gives the technical name current among yogins in the words «that is termed the 'undistressed.'» One whose karmas, both hindrances [ii. 3] and bonds [i. 24], have dwindled away. He is of that kind.

---

50. As a result of passionlessness even with regard to these [perfections] there follows, after the dwindling of the seeds of the defects, Isolation.

When, after the dwindling of hindrances and of karma, [intuitive knowledge] comes to him thus, 'This presented-idea of discrimination is an external-aspect of the *sattva*. And *sattva* is to be reckoned with those things that are to be escaped. The Self moreover is immutable, undefiled (*çuddha*) [by the aspects], and other than the *sattva*,'—when he is thus unaffected [by the aspects], those seeds of the hindrances which, like burned [1] seeds of rice, are incapable of generation, go together with the central-organ to their rest,—and when, these being resolved into the primary cause, the Self does not again have the experience of the three pains (*tāpa*),—then these aspects, in that they are manifested in the central-organ as being karma and hindrances and fruitions, have fulfilled [2] their purpose, and invert-the-process-of-generation. Then there is the absolute absence of correlation of the Self with

[1] Compare *sūkṣmīkṛta dagdha-bīja-kalpa* ii. 2, 10, 11, pp. 107[4] and 120[2,7]; *dagdha-bījānām aprararoha* ii. 4, p. 110[4]; *dagdha-bījabhāva* ii. 4, 26, pp. 110[1], 165[2], and iii. 50, p. 264[8] and iv. 28, p. 312[7]; *dagdha-kleça-bīja* ii. 4, 13, pp. 109[6] and 124[1] and iii. 55, p. 273[9] (Calc. ed.).

[2] Compare *carita-adhikāra* ii. 10, p. 120[3]; ii. 24, p. 162[2]; ii. 27, p. 166[5]; iii. 55, 274[6].

the aspects, [which is] Isolation. Then the Self is nought else than the Energy of Intellect (*citi*) grounded in itself.

With the intent to show that constraint upon the discriminative discernment is the purpose of the Self, whereas other constraints result in what is a pseudo-purpose of the Self, he describes the result of discriminative discernment by means of the gain in the higher passionlessness. **50. As a result of passionlessness even with regard to these . . . Isolation.** When after the dwindling of hindrances and karmas the yogin has [intuitive] knowledge thus,—of what sort is this [knowledge]? In reply he says «'This presented-idea of discrimination is an external-aspect of the *sattva*.'» The rest has been explained in various places and is accordingly easy.

51. In case of invitations from those-in-high-places, these should arouse no attachment or pride, for undesired consequences recur.

Now there are four kinds of yogins,[1] 1. *Prathama-kalpika*, 2. *Madhubhūmika*, 3. *Prajñājyotis*, 4. *Atikrāntabhāvanīya*. Of these [four], 1. The first is the observant-of-practice (*abhyāsin*) for whom light is just beginning. 2. The second has the truth-bearing insight [i. 48]. 3. The third is he who has subjugated the elements and the organs, and who has provided means for keeping all that has been cultivated [such as super-reflective states] and is yet to be cultivated [such as the undistressed perfection: see i. 36], and who has the means-of-attainment and so forth for what has been done and is yet to be done. 4. But the fourth, who has passed beyond that which may be cultivated, has as his sole aim the resolving (*pratisarga*) of the mind-stuff [into its primary cause]. His is the seven-fold [ii. 27] insight advancing in stages to the highest [concentration].—The purity of the *sattva* in that Brahman among these [four] who has directly experienced the [second] Honeyed (*madhumatī*) Stage is observed by those-in-high-places, the gods. With their high-places they invite[2] him. 'Sir, will you sit here? Will you rest here? This pleasure might prove attractive. This maiden might prove attractive. This elixir checks old age and death. This chariot passes through air. Yonder are the Wishing Trees; the Stream-of-heaven (*mandākinī*) confers blessedness; the sages are perfected; the nymphs are

[1] Compare SBE. xxi, Kern, Saddharmapuṇḍarīka, p. 387. [2] Invite, seek to attract.

incomparable and not prudish. Eyes and ears [will become] supernal; the body like diamond. In consequence of your peculiar virtues, Venerable Sir, all these things have been won by you. Have entrance to this high-place which is unfading and ageless and deathless and dear to the gods.' Thus addressed let him ponder upon the defects of pleasure. 'Baked upon the horrible coals of the round-of-rebirths, and writhing[1] in the darkness of birth and of death, I have hardly found the lamp of yoga which makes an end to the obscurations of the hindrances. And of this [lamp] the lust-born gusts of sensual things are enemies. How then could it be that I who have seen its light could be led astray by these things of sense, a mere mirage, and make of myself fuel for that same fire of the round-of-rebirths as it flares up again? Fare ye well! Sensual things [deceitful] as dreams and to be craved by vile folk!' His purpose thus determined, let him cultivate concentration. Giving up attachment [for things of sense] let him not even take pride in thinking it is he that is thus urgently desired even by gods. Such a one, if in his pride he deem himself secure, will not feel as if he were one whom Death had gripped[2] by the hair. And so Heedlessness, on the lookout for his weak points and failures, and always carefully to be watched, will have found an opening and will arouse the hindrances. As a result of this undesired consequences recur. So then he who in this way does not become attached or take pride will attain permanently the purpose which he has cultivated within, and will find himself face to face with the purpose which he has yet to cultivate.

Now obstructions to the yogin who has started to acquire Isolation are possible. So he gives instruction as to the cause which leads to their dispulsion [in the sūtra]. 51. Those-in-high-places . . . undesired consequences recur. Those-in-high-places are those who, like the Great Indra, have high-places [in the Heaven-world]. The invitation is from them. No attachment to it or pride in it should be allowed to enter the mind, because ‹undesired consequences recur.› In order to select [from among the four classes] that yogin only whom the gods invite with offers of high-places, he mentions all possible kinds of yogins by saying «four kinds of yogins.» From among these [four] he describes the essential-attribute of the *Prathama-kalpika* by saying

[1] Writhing, or wandering.

[2] Compare the stanza *ajarāmaravat prājñaḥ*, &c., Hitopadeça, Introd., verse 3.

«Of these [four], 1. . . . the observant-of-practice.» One for whom light is just beginning, but is not yet mastered, one whose [intuitive] knowledge has such an object as the mind-stuff of another. 2. He describes the second by saying «truth-bearing insight.» In whose case this has been said [i. 48] "In this [concentrated mind-stuff] the insight is truth-bearing." For he is one whose wish is to subjugate the elements and the organs. 3. He describes the third class by saying «he who has subjugated the elements and the organs.» For by him the elements and the rest and the organs have been subjugated by constraint upon coarse elements and by constraint upon the process-of-knowing and the other [four constraints mentioned in iii. 47]. This same yogin is further described in the words «all that.» He is one who has provided means for keeping all that has been cultivated, [that is] acquired, such as [intuitive] knowledge and so on of another's mind-stuff and so on, as a result of the subjugation of the elements and the organs. Consequently he does not lapse from them. One who has unperfected means-of-attainment for what is yet to be cultivated, [that is] acquired, such as the undistressed [perfection], extending as far as to the higher passionlessness. For human effort, only when it operates upon the instrument-of-acquisition, leads to the acquisition of the end. 4. He describes the fourth [kind of yogin] in the words «the fourth.» For this Exalted [yogin], released yet alive in the body, whose present body is his last, has as his sole aim the resolving of the mind-stuff [into its primary cause]. So from among all these yogins he determines that one to whom the invitation is directed by saying «among these [four], the [second] Honeyed Stage.» As to the one in the *Prathama-kalpika* stage, there is not even a possibility of his receiving this [invitation] from the Great Indra and the other [gods]. The third also cannot be invited by them, since by mastery over the elements and the organs he has [already] obtained this [invitation]. And as to the fourth, because he has attained to the higher passionlessness, the possibility of an attachment is far-removed. Thus all that remains is the second, the truth-bearing insight. Thus, by elimination, only the second, the [yogin]-of-truth-bearing-insight, [remains] as a proper recipient (*viṣaya*) of this invitation.—«Passes through air» means roving through the air. «Unfading» is imperishable. «Unaging» is always new. He describes the defect due to the arousal of pride in the words «Such a one, if in his pride.» One who in his pride counts himself secure will not feel the impermanence [of things] and will not reflect upon this. The other part is easy.

---

52. As a result of constraint upon moments and their sequence [there arises the intuitive] knowledge proceeding from discrimination.

Just as the atom is the minimal limit of matter,[1] so the moment is

[1] Similarly the moment (*samaya*) in the Jain system, equivalent to the *kṣaṇa* of the yoga, is a *dravya*. And time is an endless succession of these moments. See Umāsvāti: Tattvārthādhigama-sūtra, iv. 15 and v. 38–39.

the minimal limit of time. Or, the time taken by an atom in motion in order to leave one point and reach the next point is a moment. But the continuous flow of these [moments] is a sequence. Moments and the sequences of these [moments] cannot be combined into a [perceptually] real (*vastu*). Hours-of-eight-and-forty-minutes, days-of-thirty-such-hours and so on are combinations by a mental-process (*buddhi*). Thus time, being of this nature, does not correspond to anything [perceptually] real, but is a structure by a mental-process and follows as a result of perceptions or of words. [Thus] to the ordinary thinking of the emergent mind it might appear as if it were [perceptually] real. But the moment does come within the [real] objects[1] and rests[2] upon the sequence. Furthermore the sequence has its essence in an uninterrupted succession of moments. This [sequence] is called time by experts in time. So the yogins use the term. For two moments cannot occur simultaneously. Because it is impossible that there be a sequence between two things that occur simultaneously. When a later moment succeeds an earlier without interruption, there is a sequence. Thus in the present there is a single moment and there are no earlier or later moments. Therefore there is no combination of them. But those moments which are past and future are to be explained as inherent in the mutations. Accordingly the whole world passes through a mutation in any single moment. So all those external-aspects of the world are relative to this present moment. By constraint upon moments and their sequence both are directly perceived. And as a result of this, the [intuitive] knowledge proceeding from discrimination comes about.

It has been stated in one place and another that as a result of constraint upon certain objects, knowledge of all follows. This [knowledge of all] is not a knowledge of everything whatsoever without remainder. But it only emphasizes what

[1] A moment belongs to the real objects; but there is no time outside the sequence of moments. Thus the theory of time is midway between that of the Buddhists and the Vaiçeṣika school; and resembles the Jain doctrine (Umāsvāti v. 39).

[2] Vācaspatimiçra says the opposite.—The form *avalambī* is wrong and popular. See W. Kirfel, Beiträge zur Gesch. d. Nominalkomposition, Bonn, 1908, pp. 78-79.

kind of knowledge it is, just as in the expression 'Eaten with all the condiments.' For in this [expression] the sense is that [the meal] was eaten with as many kinds of condiments as were [served], but not all condiments whatsoever without remainder. For all that, the word 'all' has in some cases the sense of 'without remainder,' in the sentence for instance, 'The glutton has eaten all the food that was brought to him.' For here it is understood as meaning 'without remainder.' So now here he describes the constraint which leads to [intuitive] knowledge proceeding from discrimination and characterized as being a knowledge of everything without remainder. **52. Moments . . . [intuitive] knowledge.** He describes the meaning of the word «moment» by means of an analogy and in the words «Just as.» When a clod of earth is being broken up, that bit of it wherein the gradations of smallness reach their minimal limit of smallness is the atom. So similarly the moment is the minimal limit of time. In other words it is a particle of time which has no prior and subsequent [within itself]. This same moment is illustrated in another way by the words «Or, the time taken.» The meaning is that [the atom] would traverse the distance measured by an atom.—He now describes the meaning of the word «sequence» by saying «the flow of these [moments].» The word «these» refers to the moments. And the sequence which is of this kind is not [perceptually] real; but it is abstractly [real]. Because, when so combined, it cannot possibly be thought of as perceptually real in the case of things which do not occur simultaneously. This has been said in the words «Moments and the sequences of these.» Since a sequence consists of moments which do not arise simultaneously, and since a combination of moments is not [perceptually] real, therefore also a combination of moments and of their sequences is not [perceptually] real. Ordinary persons who have neither [natural] excellence of the thinking-substance nor that resulting from disputation,[1] whose emergent way of thinking is every moment new, and who deem such time a [perceptual] reality, are in error, So then, is the moment [as contrasted with time perceptually,] unreal? Not so, as he says in the words «But the moment.» «Does come within the [perceptually] real» means that it is [perceptually] real. It is the basis (*avalambana*) for the sequence. It is the basis for it. It is supported by the sequence only in terms of predicate relations. This is the meaning. He gives the reason why the sequence should be the basis for the moment by saying «Furthermore the sequence.» He gives the reason for the [perceptual] unreality of the sequence in the words «For . . . not.» The word «for (*ca*)» expresses the idea of reason. To him who might suppose that they occur simultaneously since they belong to different classes he says «impossible between two things.» Why is this impossible? To this he replies «an earlier.» He brings the discussion to a close in the word «Thus.» So then,

[1] Where one contends without reasons for contending. See Nyāya-sūtra i. 2. 3 (= 44).

are the earlier and later moments merely hare's horns? Not so, as he says in the words «But . . . . which.» The words «inherent in» mean inseparably connected with the generic form. He sums up the discussion by saying «Accordingly.» Since it is the present only which has the capacity to fulfil the purposes proper to itself.

The particular that is the object of this [intuitive knowledge proceeding from discrimination] is brought[1] forward.

53. As a result of this there arises the deeper-knowledge of two equivalent things which cannot be distinctly qualified in species or characteristic-mark or point-of-space.

If two equivalent things resemble each other in point-of-space and in characteristic-mark, it is the difference in species which makes [us] distinguish between them, for instance, 'This is a cow; that is a mare.' If the place and the species be equivalent, it is the characteristic-mark that makes [us] distinguish between them, for instance, 'This cow has black eyes; that cow is lucky.'[2] Since two myrobolan-fruits resemble each other in species and in characteristic-mark, it is the difference as to point-of-space that makes [us] distinguish between them, for instance, 'This one is in front; this [other] is behind.' But when the myrobolan which was in front is put, while the attention of him who has the intuitive [knowledge] is elsewhere occupied, in the place of the one behind, then, if the places are equivalent so that one would think 'That is the one in front; that is the one behind,' a right classification (*pravibhāga*) is impossible. Since the right view of things (*tattva-jñāna*) must be free from doubt, it was said ‹As a result of this there arises the deeper-knowledge,› as a result [that is] of the [intuitive] knowledge proceeding from discrimination. How is this? The point-of-space coincident with the myrobolan in front is distinct from the point-of-space coincident with the myrobolan behind. And the two myrobolans are distinct in that they pass through the incidents peculiar to their own points-of-space. But it is this passing through the incident belonging to another point-of-space

[1] See Çaṁkara on ii. 1. 37.

[2] The Rahasyam says that cows with white eyes are lucky.

that is the cause of the distinction between the two. This example illustrates how the supreme yogin has the presented-idea (*pratyaya*) of the difference between two atoms as a result of his direct experience of the point-of-space coincident with the atom in front, which atom is equivalent [to the other] in species and characteristic-mark and point-of-space. The reason for this is that the [only] distinction is between the coincidents [with the points-of-space]; inasmuch as it is impossible that an atom which is behind can have the point-of-space of the one [in front], the passing of the atom behind through its own point-of-space is different [from the front atom's passing through its point-of-space]. Others [*Vāiçeṣikas*], however, describe [the same matter thus]: "These particulars (*viçeṣa*), which are ultimates, produce the idea of the difference." Even in this [opinion of theirs] the difference as to the point-of-space and as to the characteristic-mark and the difference as to limitation-in-extent and as to the intervening-space and as to species [might be a sufficient] cause of distinction. But it is the difference as to the incident that is accessible to the thinking-substance of the yogin only. Therefore it has been said,[1] "Since there is no difference as to limitation-in-extent or by reason of intervening-space or of species there is no distinction in the [primary] root [of things]." So says Vārshagaṇya.[2]

Although the knowledge proceeding from discrimination is to be described later as having for its objects all things without remainder, still, since this knowledge is exceedingly subtile, the particular that is the object of it is first of all brought forward [in the words of the sūtra]. **53. Species . . . deeper-knowledge.** To ordinary persons a distinction in the species [intelligibilis] is the means-of-knowing the difference between things. [But when] the species [intelligibilis], the common-nature-of-the-cow, is equivalent, [and when] the place, in front or elsewhere, is equivalent, the differentia (*param*) is the distinction in the characteristic-marks of the black-eyed and of the lucky [cows].

[1] Vijñānabhikṣu interprets the passage as referring to the teaching of the Vāiçeṣikas. He asserts that there is something such as limitation-in-extent which distinguishes permanent substances; but that there is no such entity as a *viçeṣa* the property of the substances. For there is no differentiating attribute over and above the differences in limitation or similar differences. The context alone can determine which interpretation is right.

[2] See Sāṁkhya Tattva Kāumudī xlvii for another quotation from Vārshagaṇya.

In the case of two myrobolans, the common-nature-of-the-myrobolan, the species [intelligibilis] is equivalent; the characteristic-mark, such as roundness, is equivalent. But the difference in point-of-space is the differentia. When, however, one wishes to test the yogin's knowledge, and, while the yogin who has the [intuitive] knowledge has his attention occupied elsewhere, puts the myrobolan which was in front behind, and removes or hides the one that was behind, then—inasmuch as the places are equivalent so that one would think, 'That [myrobolan] is the one in front, and that is the one behind'—a right classification is impossible for an ordinary person, [however] wise, who is conversant with the three sources-of-valid-ideas [only]. Whereas the right-view-of-things must be free from doubt. And in the case of the yogin who has [intuitive] knowledge proceeding from discrimination there cannot be the possibility of doubt. So the author of the sūtra says ‹As a result of this there arises the deeper-knowledge.› [The Comment] explains the words ‹As a result of this› by the words «as a result [that is] of the [intuitive] knowledge proceeding from discrimination.» A question is asked 'How can [intuitive] knowledge proceeding from constraint upon moments and upon their sequences discriminate one myrobolan from another having an equivalent species and characteristic-mark and point-of-space?' This he asks by the words «How is this?» The reply is given in the words «The point-of-space coincident with the myrobolan in front.» The point-of-space which characterizes the myrobolan in front is limited to one moment of the myrobolan in front. Or we may say that there is an incessant mutation [of the point-of-space as compared] with it [the moment]. And this is distinct from the incessant mutation of the myrobolan which is behind, distinct, that is, «from the point-of-space coincident with the myrobolan behind.» Very well then, let there be a distinction as to points-of-space. How does this bear upon the distinction between the myrobolans themselves? The answer is in the words «And the myrobolans are distinct in that they pass through the incidents peculiar to their own points-of-space.» The coincidence with its own point-of-space is that digit of time belonging to the myrobolan which, with respect to its own point-of-space, is characterized by a kind of mutation in terms of nearness or furtherness. That is its incident peculiar to its point-of-space. Its «passing through» is either its getting [to a point-of-space] or it is knowledge. The two myrobolans are different in so far as there is this [passing through]. When the two myrobolans had a moment of the mutation in terms of nearness and furtherness, in so far as the two points-of-space are in front or behind, then [the yogin] performing-constraint (*saṁyamin*) experiences the particularity of the incident of the mutation belonging to the two, in terms of nearness and furtherness with reference to another point-of-space. And he admits that they are quite different. Although at present [one of the myrobolans has such] a mutation that it is in the point-of-space of this [myrobolan], [still] up to the present it had the mutation with reference to a different point-of-space. So it is the moment of the mutation of this point-of-space which distinguishes it [from the other point-of-space]. And this moment it is which is directly perceived by constraint. So it was this that was said «But it is this passing through the moments belonging to another point-of-space that is the cause of the distinction between the two.» With the help of this example and by dialogues[1] between laymen and experts and others one comes to believe that the distinction between even such kinds of atoms is accessible to the thinking-substance of the yogin, as he says «This.» «Others [Vāiçeṣikas], however, describe» [that is] set forth [this] description by saying «which.» For the Vāiçesikas say that there are ultimate particulars functioning in permanent substances. So they say. To explain. Yogins, [when they consider] liberated beings who are equivalent in respect of species and of point-of-space and of time and who are also free from [particular] specifications, have a [deeper] knowledge of each person as he really is as different from other persons. Therefore, they say, there is some ultimate particular. And if so, this same [distinction] is one that serves to distinguish permanent substances such as atoms. This he controverts in the words «Even in this opinion of theirs.» Species and point-of-space and characteristic-mark have been illustrated. Limitation-in-extent is an arrangement-of-parts (*saṁsthāna*). In which case [of limitation-of-extent], after a thing whose arrangement of parts is flawless has been removed and after another thing whose combination of parts is defective has been put in its place, while the observer meanwhile is elsewhere occupied, then there is a presented idea of the difference in so far as there is a difference in the arrangement of parts of this [thing]. Or limitation-in-extent might be body. There is a distinction, between the persons-in-the-rounds-of-rebirths, whose souls (*ātman*) are bound to this or that [body], and between those whose souls are liberated [from the round-of-rebirth], based on the different relations with the elements of one kind or another. So in all cases the presented-idea of the difference is established on other grounds [than the existence of ultimate particulars]. [Consequently] there is no [need of an] assumption[2] of ultimate particulars.—Intervening-space[3] (*vyavadhi*) makes a difference between things, as in the case of the Lands[4] of Kuça and of Puṣkara, which are as such two points-of-space. Because differences in species and in point-of-space and in other respects are accessible by the ordinary thinking-substance, therefore it was said «But the difference as to the incident is accessible to the yogin only.» The word «*eva*» limits the words «difference as to the incident,» but not the words «accessible to the thinking-substance of the yogin.» It follows then that the distinction between liberated souls with respect to their relations with their

[1] See Çloka-Vārttika, p. 412 (Chaukambha S. Ser.), for *saṁvādapravṛtti*.

[2] The Vāiçeṣika doctrine is also rejected in i. 43 in the phrases *aṇu-pracaya-viçeṣa-ātmā* and *sa ca saṁsthāna viçeṣaḥ* pp. 89[6] and 90[1] (Calc. ed.).

[3] See also Vācaspati, p. 271[17].

[4] See iii. 26, p. 238[3] (Calc. ed.).

bodies that have been[1] is also accessible to the yogin. But in the case of one who has not got the above-mentioned grounds for distinction, there is no division in the primary-cause. So the Master has thought. For this reason it was said [ii. 22] "Though it has ceased [to be seen] in the case of one whose purpose is fulfilled, it has not ceased to be, since it is common to others beside him." This is expressed in the words «limitation-in-extent and intervening-space.» This statement is to be understood as partial and is to be extended to the different causes of difference already described [species, place, time, and so on]. The meaning is that in the primary-cause which is the root of the world there is no distinction, [that is] no difference.

54. The [intuitive] knowledge proceeding from discrimination is a deliverer, has all things as its object, and has all times for its object and is [an inclusive whole] without sequence.

The word ‹deliverer[2] (*tāraka*)› means that it arises out of its own vivid light without further suggestion. For it has all things for its object. This means that there is nothing that is not its object. It has all times for its object. This means that it has intuitive knowledge at all times of one whole (*sarvam*), past and future and present, with [the sum of] its states.[3] ‹[An inclusive whole] without sequence› means that it grasps one whole, striking upon [the thinking-substance] at one moment, with all its times. Such in its complete form is the [intuitive] knowledge proceeding from discrimination. Of this same the lamp of yoga is a part, beginning with the Honeyed[4] Stage until it reaches final perfection.

Having thus shown a part of the object of [intuitive] knowledge proceeding from discrimination, he gives the distinguishing-characteristic of the [intuitive] knowledge itself which proceeds from discrimination. **54. Deliverer . . . [intuitive] knowledge.** He points out [intuitive] knowledge proceeding from discrimination as the object of the statement; the rest is the characteristic-mark. It is called «the deliverer» because it delivers from the ocean of the round-of-rebirths. He distinguishes this from the Vividness which was previously [iii. 33] mentioned by saying «has all times for its object.» «With [the sum of] its states» means in all its subordinate particulars. Hence the [intuitive] knowledge proceeding from discrimination is complete. For there is nothing, in any place or in any way or in any time, which is not in its

[1] The force of the suffix *caraṇa* is explained in Pāṇ. v. 3. 53.

[2] See iii. 33, p. 243[5].

[3] Defined by Umāsvāti v. 43 as a group of *pariṇāma*.

[4] iii. 51, p. 266[4] (Calc. ed.).

sphere. Why speak of (*āstām*) of other kinds of knowledge? For even [concentration] conscious [of objects] is a part of this [completed intuitive knowledge]. So then there is nothing more complete than this as he says «Of this same the lamp of yoga is a part.» The lamp of yoga is [concentration] conscious [of an object]. How does that begin and how end? The reply is «the Honeyed.» The truth-bearing insight [i. 48] is itself the honey, because it gives a flavour, as has[1] been said [Comment on i. 47], "Having risen to the undisturbed calm of insight." Beginning with that which has this, with the Honeyed Stage, until it is finally perfected, [until] insight seven-fold in advancing stages [ii. 29] has reached the highest. Hence [intuitive] knowledge proceeding from discrimination becomes the Deliverer, since even a part of it, the lamp of yoga, is a deliverer.

In either case, whether one has attained to [intuitive] knowledge proceeding from discrimination or has not attained to [intuitive] knowledge proceeding from discrimination,

55. When the purity of the *sattva* and of the Self are equal [there is] Isolation.

When the *sattva* of the thinking-substance is freed from the defilement of the *rajas* and *tamas*, and when it has no task other than with the presented-idea of the difference of [the *sattva*] from the Self, and when the seeds of the hindrances within itself have been burned, then the *sattva* enters into a state of purity equal to that of the Self. When-this-is-so (*tadā*), purity is the cessation of the experience which is falsely attributed to the Self. In this state [of purity] Isolation follows for one-who-has-supremacy (*īçvara*) or for one-who-has-not-supremacy, for one who partakes of the [intuitive] knowledge proceeding from discrimination or for another. For if there be [intuitive] knowledge in the case of one whose hindrances have become burned seed, there is no further need of any [supernormal power]. As being the means of purifying the *sattva*, both the supremacy (*āiçvarya*) proceeding from concentration and the [intuitive] knowledge have been introduced-into-the-discussion. But strictly speaking the [intuitive] knowledge represses not-sight (*adarçana*). When this is repressed there are no more hindrances. Because there are no more hindrances there is no fruition of karma. In this state the aspects,

[1] See above, p. 98[6] (Calc. ed.).

their task done, do not again submit themselves as objects-for-sight to the Self. That is the Self's Isolation. Then the Self having its light within itself becomes undefiled and isolated.

Of the Exposition of the Comment on the Pātañjalan [Treatise], the Book on Supernormal Powers, the Third.

Having thus described the [various] constraints together with their supernormal powers, all of which indirectly prepare the way for Isolation, with the intent to show that the [intuitive] knowledge of the difference between the *sattva* and the Self leads directly to Isolation, he here introduces the sūtra by the words «whether one has attained.» Whether [intuitive] knowledge proceeding from discrimination has been attained or not, nevertheless the insight into the difference between the *sattva* and the Self always brings Isolation to pass. This is the meaning. **55. When the purity of the *sattva* and of the Self are equal [there is] Isolation.** [The last word] *iti* is meant to indicate the end of the sūtras [of this Book].—1. The words «one-who-has-supremacy» refer to one who has the powers of action and of [intuitive] knowledge by reason of the constraints previously described. 2. The words «or for one-who-has-not-supremacy» refer to one who partakes of the [intuitive] knowledge proceeding from discrimination by reason of the constraint described [ii. 52] immediately before. 3. The words «or for another» refer to one in whom this [intuitive] knowledge has not risen [into consciousness]. In these cases there is no need at all for supernormal powers. Therefore he says «For . . . no.» And if it should be objected that there is no need of supernormal powers in connexion with Isolation, and that therefore instruction in them is useless, the reply is «As being the means of purifying the *sattva*.» The instrumental case is used to indicate such a kind of a mark [Pāṇ. ii. 3. 21].—For the attainment of Isolation the supernormal powers are not absolutely useless, but they are not directly causes. This is the meaning. But it is the [intuitive] knowledge proceeding from discrimination that is the topic-under-discussion. And that which is a cause indirectly [the powers] is only figuratively a cause, not a principal cause. Strictly speaking, however, insight alone is the principal cause; [and not the discrimination]. This is the meaning. By the words «[intuitive] knowledge» he means the Elevation.

In this [Book] the indirect aids and the aids and the mutations have been treated at length, and the attainment of supernormal powers, and among these [powers] the [intuitive] knowledge proceeding from discrimination.

Such is the stanza which summarizes the contents of [this] Book.

Of the Explanation of the Comment on Patañjali's [Treatise, which Explanation is entitled] the Clarification of the Entities, composed by the Venerable Vācaspatimiçra, the Third Book, on Supernormal Powers, is finished.

BOOK FOURTH

ISOLATION

BOOK FOURTH

ISOLATION

1. Perfections proceed from birth or from drugs or from spells or from self-castigation or from concentration.

1. The power of having another body is the perfection by birth. 2. [Perfection] by drugs is by an elixir-of-life [1] [got] in the mansions of the demons, and by the like. 3. By spells, such as the acquisition of [the power of] passing through space and atomization [iii. 45]. 4. [Perfection] by self-castigation is the perfection [2] of the will, the faculty of taking on any form at will (*kāmarūpin*) [or] of going anywhere at will, and so on. 5. Perfections proceeding from concentration have been explained.

Thus, in the First and Second and Third Books, concentration and the means of this [concentration] and the supernormal powers [produced] by it have been especially discussed. And other [matter] incidental [3] or suggested-by-the-course-of-the-discussion has been discussed. Now Isolation as resulting from this [concentration] is to be expounded. And this Isolation cannot be expounded unless one have analysed the mind-stuff which is conducive to Isolation; and the world beyond; and the self which is to be in the world beyond and which is over and above the sum of mental-states (*vijñāna*) and which is the enjoyer, by means of the mind-stuff which is its instrument, of the sounds and other [things] whose essence is pleasure, [pain,] and so on; and the higher limit of Elevation (*prasaṁkhyāna*). So all these things are to be expounded in this Book, as also other matter incidental or suggested-by-the-course-of-the-discussion. Of these, with the intent first to determine-the-nature-of mind-stuff which is conducive to Isolation, in the case of persons whose mind-stuff is perfected, he states the five-fold perfections by the words [of the sūtra]. **1. Perfections proceed from birth or from drugs or from spells or from self-castigation or from concentration.** He explains [the sūtra] by saying «1. The power of having another body.» When karma, conducive to the enjoyment of heaven and performed by one of

[1] Treated at length in the Rasāyana-tantra, the seventh of the eight subdivisions of the Āyur-veda.

[2] Equivalent to *kāmāvasāyitva*, the eighth *siddhi*, iii. 45, p. 259[9] (Calc. ed.).

[3] Such as the agglomeration of atoms or the doctrine of momentariness. The distinctions between the fluctuations would be "suggested by the course of the discussion."

the human species, obtains its fruition from some cause or other, then a man, from the mere fact of being born into a certain group of gods, passes into another body, to the perfection which has atomization and other [supernormal powers]. 2. He describes the perfection which proceeds from drugs. A human being when for some cause or other he reaches the mansions of the demons (*asura*), and when he makes use of elixirs-of-life brought to him by the lovely damsels of the demons, attains to agelessness and to deathlessness and to other perfections. Or [this perfection may be had] by the use of an elixir-of-life in this very world. As for instance the sage Māṇḍavya,[1] who dwelt on the Vindhyas and who made use of potions. 3. He describes the perfections by spells in the words «by spells.» 4. He describes the perfection due to self-castigation in the words «from self-castigation.» He describes the perfection of the will in the words «taking on any form at will.» Whatever he desires, atomization for instance, precisely that he attains on the spot. In case he wishes to hear or think of anything, that very thing he hears and thinks. The words «and so on» include sight and the other senses. The perfections proceeding from concentration have been described [iii. 16–19, 21–36, 39–42, 51] in the previous (*adhastana*) Book.

As to these [perfections], with regard to those bodies and organs which enter into the mutation of another birth,—

2. The mutation into another birth is the result of the filling-in of the evolving-cause.

When the previous mutation has passed away, the rise of the subsequent mutation follows, since [this body and] these [organs] interpenetrate the new [arrangement] of parts. And the evolving-causes of the body and organs give aid to their own peculiar evolved-effects by filling-in in dependence upon such instrumental-causes[2] as merit.

Now in the case of those four perfections the means for which are the drugs and the other [three] means, the same body and organs must enter into the mutation of another birth. But this mutation does not follow from material-causes in general. For the same quantity of material-causes cannot belong to him when he attains to a supernal or to a not-supernal state-of-existence which is

[1] See Mārkaṇḍeya Pur. xvi. 27 and Bhāgavata Pur. iii. 5. 20. Compare MahāBh. I. 107-8. He keeps himself alive after robbers, who have entered his hermitage by mistake, have impaled him. He was famous for curses, which were so mighty as to blight even Yama. One man was cursed to die before sunrise. The wife of this person, however, refused to let the sun rise. Accordingly even Māṇḍavya Muni was obliged to beat a retreat.

[2] Compare Vācaspati on iii. 18, p. 230[6]. See also i. 44, p. 94[1] and iv. 10, p. 283[7] (Calc. ed.).

either more or less [than the present state]. For certainly a material cause which is to bring forth something not different is not sufficient to produce an effect of a different kind altogether. And so with a view to exclude the possibility of any accidental [difference between cause and effect] he supplies the following words, «As to these [perfections], with regard to those bodies and organs which enter into the mutation of another birth.» And then recites the sūtra **2. The mutation into another birth is the result of the filling-in of the evolving-cause.**

When the body and organs, which have entered into the mutation of a human birth, enter into a birth as god or animal, the mutation is the result of the filling-in of the evolving-cause. Now the evolving-cause of the body is earth and other [coarse] elements, and the evolving-cause of the organs is the personality-substance. The interpenetration into the parts of these is the filling-in. From this filling-in there results [this mutation],—as he says in the words «When the previous mutation.» An objection might be made to the effect that if this aid is to follow from mere filling-in, why is it not eternally so? To which the reply would be «such . . . as merit.» So we have explained[1] how the same body can attain to the different stages of childhood and boyhood and young manhood and age and so on, or how a *nyagrodha* seed can become a *nyagrodha* tree, or how a particle of fire when placed on a pile of grass can envelop the region of the sky by the flaring forth of thousands of flames.

3. The efficient cause gives no impulse to the evolving-causes; but [the mutation] follows when the barrier [to the evolving-causes] is cut, as happens with the peasant.

For an efficient cause such as merit gives no impulse to the evolving-causes (*prakṛti*), since a cause is not set into activity by an effect. In that case, how is this? [The answer is,] but in that case there is a cutting of the barrier, as happens with the peasant. Just as a peasant wishing to overflow[2] one meadow-plot, whether it be on the level or below or still lower, by filling-in with water from another meadow-plot, does not remove the waters with his hand, but cuts [the rim-of-turf which is] the barrier (*āvaraṇa*) of them. And after this is cut, the water itself overflows the other meadow-plot. So similarly merit cuts demerit, the barrier (*āvaraṇa*) of the evolving-causes; and after this is cut, the evolving-

[1] By stating that a mutation, from the *mahat* down, follows whenever particles of the evolving-cause enter or are removed, we have the explanation.

[2] See Sir Walter Lawrence: The Vale of Kashmir, p. 327.

causes themselves overflow each its own appropriate evolved-effect (*vikāra*). Or again, just as the same peasant, after the same [rim-of-turf] is cut, cannot force the watery or earthen essences to interpenetrate the roots of the different kinds of grain. In that case, what [can he do]? He removes from among them the pulse or maize or red rice or what not. And when they are thus removed, the essences interpenetrate of themselves the roots of the grain. Similarly merit is an efficient cause in the sense that it follows upon nothing more than the mere cessation of demerit, by reason of the absolute opposition between purity and impurity. But merit is not the cause which sets the evolving-causes into activity. Of this Nandīçvara and others may be cited as examples. And conversely demerit inhibits merit; and as a result of this there is a mutation of impurity. And of this Nahuṣa[1] [the king who was changed into] a serpent, and others may be cited as examples.

The statement was that this filling-in is by the evolving-causes. With regard to this a doubt arises. 'Is the filling-in by the evolving-causes natural or is it due to merit? Which seems plausible [to the objector]? It seems plausible that even when the evolving-causes are there, the filling-in is accidental; and since we are traditionally taught that merit [and demerit] are causes, [the filling-in] is due to these causes.' To this he replies [in the sūtra]. **3. The efficient cause gives no impulse to the evolving-causes; but [the mutation] follows when the barrier [to the evolving-causes] is cut, as happens with the peasant.** True—merit [and demerit] are efficient causes. But they are not impelling causes, since even these causes are the effects of the evolving-causes. And an effect does not impel a cause, forasmuch as this [effect]. (in so far as its coming into existence is dependent upon this [cause]) is dependent on a cause, and [forasmuch as] the function of impelling belongs to what is independent. For surely when the potter is not there, the clay and the rod and wheel and the water and so on are not impelled by the jar which is to be produced or which has been produced. But they are impelled by a potter who is independent of them. Nor again can it even be supposed that it is the purpose of the Self that sets all in motion. But the Içvara [sets all in motion] as being the final-end of this [purpose of the Self]. For the purpose of the Self is described as setting all in motion only as being the final end[2] (*uddeça*). While this purpose of the Self is

[1] By virtue of knowledge and asceticism and the power of yoga, Nahuṣa was equal to the task of ruling the Three Heavens. But he became blinded by pride and was degraded to the state of a serpent (Bhāg. Pur. vi. 13. 16; ix. 17. 1; and ix. 18. 1). Compare in this book, ii. 12, p. 122[6] (Calc. ed.).

[2] In the sense of being the object of desire. See Nyāya-Koça under *Uddeçatvam*, ग.

yet to be, it is right that the unphenomenalized matter should be the cause of the stability [of matter]. But it does not follow from this that merit [and demerit] are not efficient causes at all. Since it is quite consistent that they, like the peasant, should only remove obstructions. And in the case of the Içvara we must understand that his functional activity is limited to the removal of obstructions with a view to securing a basis for merit. All this, stated by the Comment, is clear upon a mere reading.

But [if it be asked], while the yogin creates many bodies for himself, do these [bodies] then have a single central-organ, or have they several central-organs? The answer is,

4. Created mind-stuffs may result from the sense-of-personality[1] and from this alone.

Assuming nothing more than the sense-of-personality as the cause of mind-stuff, [the yogin] makes created mind-stuffs. As a result of this, [the bodies] have [separate] mind-stuffs.

Having disposed-of-the-subject of perfections as taking place by the filling-in of evolving-causes, he now raises the question as to the oneness or the manyness of the mind-stuff resident in the various bodies produced by the perfections, by saying «But [if it be asked], while.» 'If this is so, there would be many central-organs. And because the intention varies according to each mind-stuff of the [various] bodies, there would be no conformity to one intention and also there would be no readjustment [of memory], quite as in the case of distinct persons. Therefore [there is] only one mind-stuff, [which,] inasmuch as, like a lamp, it has a diffusive nature, pervades even many created bodies.' To this view he replies,—**4. Created mind-stuffs may result from the sense-of-personality and from this alone.** Each body so long as it lives is evidently inseparably connected with an individual mind-stuff, such a body, for instance, as that of Chaitra or of Maitra. And the same holds good in the case of bodies [created by the yogin]. So it is established that each of these [bodies] has a separate central-organ of its own. With this in mind he says ‹from the sense-of-personality and from this alone.›

---

5. While there is a variety of actions, the mind-stuff which impels the many is one.

How can many mind-stuffs have their action provided with a purpose by a single mind-stuff? [The answer is], the yogin makes a single mind-stuff which impels all the mind-stuffs. From this [mind-stuff] the variety of actions is obtained.

[1] Compare Sāṁkhya-sūtra vi. 64.

As to the contention that, if there be many mind-stuffs, there cannot be conformity to one intention [of this yogin who has many bodies], nor can there be a readjustment of memory, the reply is in the next sūtra. **5. While there is a variety of actions, the mind-stuff which impels the many is one.** This would be a weakness in the argument, if one mind-stuff which is to guide the central-organ resident in the various bodies were not to be created. But when such a [mind-stuff] is created, there is no weakness in the argument. And it should not be said that [the yogin] having one [mind-stuff] needs no separate central-organ proper to each body; or that there is no need of the creation of a guide, because the yogin's own mind-stuff is the guide. Since what is established by proofs is not rightly-subject to command[1] or to question. On this point there is a Purāṇa passage[2] "By virtue of his authoritative power the Içvara, though one, becomes many. Then being many he becomes one. And from him also proceed all these variations of the central-organ. The Yogīçvara makes the bodies one-fold or two-fold or three-fold or manifold and again unmakes them. With some he may partake of objects, with others he may practise fierce austerities. All these again he may draw in, as the sun draws in the multitude of rays." With this same intention he says, «many mind-stuffs.»

6. Of these [five perfections] that which proceeds from contemplation leaves no latent-deposit.

The created[3] mind-stuff is of five kinds. For the perfections proceed from birth and from drugs and from spells and from self-castigation and from concentration. Of these five kinds only that mind-stuff which proceeds from contemplation leaves no latent-deposit. It alone has no latent-deposit which comes into action as a result of passion or similar [states]. It has accordingly no connexion with merit or evil, since the yogin's hindrances have dwindled away. For the others, however, there is a latent-deposit of karma.

Now of these five [iv. 1] perfected mind-stuffs which have arisen thus he selects that mind-stuff which is conducive to release. **6. Of these [five perfections] that which proceeds from contemplation leaves no latent-deposit.** Latent-

[1] Compare the use of these words by Vācaspati on i. 32, p. 73[17] (Calc. ed.[1]), p. 74[3] (Calc. ed.[2]).

[2] With some omissions this passage is found in the Vāyu Pur. lxvi. 143 and 152-3 [in the Calcutta edition ii. 5. 139]. See also Kūrma Pur. i. 4. 54-5. The phrase *tasmāc ca manaso bhedā jāyante* is found in Vāyu Pur. vi. 22. All this illustrates how various the readings of the Vāyu are and how much need there is of a critical edition.

[3] Compare i. 25, p. 62[1]; iv. 4, p. 278[10]; and the phrase *buddhi-nirmāṇaḥ* iii. 52, p. 268[6] (Calc. ed.).

deposits are things that lie latent, subconscious-impressions of karma and subconscious-impressions of hindrances. That mind-stuff in which these [subconscious-impressions] are not, is said to have no latent-deposit. In other words it is conducive to the liberation. Since it does not act with reference to passion or similar [states], it is therefore not connected with merit or evil. But why is there no activity generated by passion or similar [states]? The reply is in the words «since the yogin's hindrances have dwindled away.» With the intent to show that the central-organ, which is produced in contemplation, and in which there is no latent-deposit, is distinct from the others, he says that the others have latent-deposits, in the words «For the others, however.»

For—

7. The yogin's karma is neither-white-nor-black; [the karma] of others is of three kinds.

Karma as a class is, as every one knows, quadripartite (*catuṣpāt*), black and white-and-black and white and neither-white-nor-black. Of these [four], 1. the black is found in villains. 2. The white-and-black is attainable by outer means-of-attainment. The accumulation of the latent-deposit of karma in this [division] is by means of injury or of benefit to others. 3. The white belongs to those who castigate themselves and recite the sacred texts and practise contemplation. Because this kind of karma is confined to the central organ alone, it does not depend upon outer means and it does not grow as a result of injury to others. 4. The neither-white-nor-black[1] is found in the mendicant-saints (*sannyāsin*), whose hindrances have dwindled away, and whose [actual] bodies are their last. Of these four, the yogin alone has the not-white karma, since he has renounced (*sannyāsāt*) the fruition [even of good], and has not-black, since he will have nought of it. But the three kinds just mentioned are found in other living beings.

On this same point also he introduces by the word «For» a sūtra which gives the reason. **7. The yogin's karma is neither-white-nor-black; [the karma] of others is of three kinds.** A division (*pada*) is a topic. [The karma as a class which is] contained in four divisions is in-four-divisions (*catuṣpadā*).—2. Whatever karma is attainable by outer means-of-attainment always contains some injury to others. For even in an action in which rice-grains[2] or some-

[1] See E. W. Hopkins: Great Epic of India (1901), p. 180.

[2] Compare Çāstra Dīpikā (Ben. ed., 1885), p. 3, first lines.

thing similar are the means-of-attainment, one cannot say that there is no injury to others. Because one might possibly kill an ant while pounding [the grains]. And after all, by killing the seeds, one prevents the growth of stalks and so forth. On the other hand there is benefit in this action, in that the Brahmans and others receive their gifts. 3. The white belongs to those who castigate themselves and recite sacred texts and practise contemplation,[1] to those who are not mendicant-saints. He gives the reason for the whiteness in the words «Because this.» 4. The neither-white-nor-black is found in the mendicant-saints. He refers to the mendicant-saints when he says «have dwindled away.» Because persons who have renounced all karma, do not come into activity with reference to any karma which can be attained by outer means-of-attainment. And accordingly they have no latent-deposit of black karma. And because they have altogether offered up to the Içvara the fruition of the latent-deposit of karma, which is attainable by the following up of yoga, they have no latent-deposit of white karma. For that the fruit of which is indestructible, [that is, Isolation] is called white [karma]. The meaning is, one who has no fruit at all,[2]—how can he have that, the fruit of which is indestructible? Having thus described the four-fold kinds of karma, he determines which belongs to which by saying «Of these four . . . the not-white.»

8. As a result of this there follows the manifestation of those subconscious-impressions only which correspond to the fruition of their [karma].

‹As a result of this› means of the three kinds of karma. The words ‹of those only which correspond to the fruition of their [karma]› means that those subconscious-impressions which correspond to the fruition of that karma which is comparate with them, dwell upon the fruition of karma. The manifestation of these only follows. For when karma of the gods is in fruition it is not the efficient cause for the manifestation of hellish or of brutish or of human subconscious-impressions. It does, however, make manifest those subconscious-impressions only which correspond to it. And the reasoning is the same with regard to hellish or brutish or human [subconscious-impressions].

Having discussed in detail the latent-deposit of karma, he tells what the outcome of the latent-deposit of the hindrances will be. **8. As a result of this there follows the manifestation of those subconscious-impressions only which correspond to the fruition of their [karma].** [The subconscious-impressions]

[1] Compare ii. 1 and notice that *dhyāna* takes the place of *īçvarapraṇidhāna*.

[2] If they have no white karma, how can they have the fruit of white karma?

correspond to a particular fruition of karma, whether supernal or hellish birth or length-of-life or kind-of-experience, which belongs to a particular class, whether it be the class of merit or the class of demerit. These same [subconscious-impressions] are described in the words «subconscious-impressions which . . . dwell upon the fruition of karma.» They dwell[1] upon [or] imitate. For the subconscious-impressions which correspond to the fruition of supernal karma are generated by supernal enjoyments. Therefore subconscious-impressions correspond to their own fruition and are to be manifested by their own karma. This is the meaning of the Comment.

9. There is an uninterrupted [causal] relation [of sub-conscious-impressions], although remote in species and point-of-space and moment-of-time, by reason of the correspondence between memory and subliminal-impressions.

Although a hundred species or a distance in points-of-space or a hundred mundane periods intervene, if there is a manifestation of the phenomenal [form] by the operation of the conditions-which-phenomenalize (*vyañjaka*) a given thing (*sva*), namely, that from which the fruition [which results in a birth] as cat rises [into consciousness],—and if again just that phenomenal [form] by the operation of the conditions-which-phenomenalize that given thing should arise [into consciousness],—it would in an instant be phenomenalized, in association with the subconscious-impressions, subliminally existent, of the fruition, [which results in the birth as] cat, and which had been experienced in former time. Why is this? Because, although those [subconscious-impressions] are remote, the karma [which produces] the same [result] becomes their manifester, [that is] efficient-cause; and so there is an uninterrupted [causal] relation. And wherefore is this? The answer is ‹by reason of the correspondence between memory and subliminal-impressions.› Because subliminal-impressions are like experiences, and the latter correspond with the subconscious-impressions of karma, and because memory is like subconscious-impressions, [therefore] memory arises from subliminal-impressions, [although] species and points-of-space and moments-of-time intervene, and again, subliminal-impressions arise from memory. Thus it is that memory

[1] Compare ii. 7.

and subliminal-impressions are phenomenalized by virtue of the fact that the latent-deposit of karma assumes a fluctuation [of mind-stuff]. And consequently the uninterrupted-succession [of subconscious-impressions], although there be interventions, is provèd from the fact that the relation of the determination to the determined is not cut through.

An objector says, 'This may be true. But in the case of a man who immediately after his death passed into an existence as a cat, one would expect a manifestation of human subconscious-impressions, in that these came immediately before. For it cannot be that one should not remember what was experienced on the day immediately preceding, but should remember what was experienced in the days before the intervention.' In reply to this he says, 9. **There is an uninterrupted-[causal] relation [of subconscious-impressions], although remote in species and point-of-space and moment-of-time, by reason of the correspondence between memory and subliminal-impressions.** Although the subconscious impression of the cat pass through intervening births and so on, still there is an uninterrupted-succession of this subconscious-impression with respect to its fruit. For in consequence of the karma the fruition of which was [birth as] a cat, that particular subconscious-impression which corresponds to its fruition would become manifest, and the memory of that subconscious-impression would be produced, as he says «the rise [into consciousness] of the fruition [which results in a birth] as cat.» The rise [into consciousness] means that from which something rises into consciousness, [that is] the latent-deposit of karma. The words, «and if again just that phenomenal [form] by the operation of the conditions-which-phenomenalize that given thing should rise [into consciousness]» would mean that it would be manifested [that is] it would be brought near to the beginning of its fruition. This is the meaning. «Subliminally existent» means activities [of certain impressions]. «In association with»: it would be phenomenalized after having seized. The meaning is that if it is to be phenomenalized, it would be phenomenalized only after having seized the subliminal-impressions which correspond to its own fruition. Having explained that the result is in immediate succession with respect to the cause, he now explains the same with respect to the effect [memory] in the words «And wherefore is this? . . . memory.» There is similarity since both [memory and impression] correspond. This same thing he says by the word «like.» It is objected 'If the subliminal-impressions are of the nature of experience, then in that case, since experiences are transitory, so also should the subliminal-impressions be transitory. How can they be capable of producing an experience capable of lasting a long time?' In reply to this he says «And the latter correspond with the subconscious-impressions of karma.» Just as the invisible-influence (*apūrva*) [of the sacrifice] is stable, although caused by momentary sacrifice (*karma*), so a subliminal-impression is stable, although caused by momentary experience. Similarity is based upon some kind of difference. Otherwise if there were an identity in essence, similarity would be impossible. The rest is easy.

10. Furthermore these [subconscious-impressions] have no beginning [that we can set in time], since desire is permanent.

These subconscious-impressions, because of the permanence of desire, have no beginning. This well-known desire [ii. 9] for one's self, 'May I not cease to be! May I be!' which is found in every one, is not self-caused. Why [not]? [The answer is,] how could the fear of death, determined by the recollection of hatred and of pain, arise in an animal (*jantu*) just brought into life, in a condition wherein death has never been experienced? Furthermore a self-caused thing does not need an efficient cause. It is for these reasons that this mind-stuff, commingled with subconscious-impressions which have no beginning, by the efficient-cause lays hold of certain subconscious-impressions, and presents itself for the experience of the Self. Others have come to the conclusion that, like [the light of] a lamp which is contracted[1] [if in] a jar and diffused [if in] a palace, the mind-stuff has such a form [as corresponds to] the dimension of the body. And thus [they say] there is an intermediate state and there is ground for the round-of-rebirths.—It is only this all-pervasive [mind-stuff's] fluctuation which contracts and expands. So the Master says. This [mind-stuff] furthermore requires such efficient-causes as right-living. And this efficient-cause is of two kinds, that which is external and that which has to do with self. The external requires the body and other means, such as praises and almsgiving and salutations. That which like belief, for instance, has to do with self is subject to the mind-stuff only. And in this sense it has been said "As for friendliness and such [exalted states-of-mind], they are the diversions of contemplative [yogins]; they are in their essence unaided by outer means; they bring right-living to perfection." Of these two, [the inner and the outer means], that of the central-organ is the stronger.

[1] Compare Sāṁkhya Pravacana Bhāṣya (Garbe), i. 68 (HOS. 34[18]), v. 69 (132[34]), v. 91 (133[7]).

How is this? [The answer is, that intuitive] knowledge and passionlessness are unsurpassed by any other [force]. Who by bodily action and without the force of mind-stuff could empty[1] the Daṇḍaka Forest [of people], or like Agastya[2] drink up the sea?

An objector says, 'This may be true. But subconscious-impressions subliminally-impressed in the previous or in a preceding birth might become phenomenalized, provided there be any source-of-valid-ideas [to prove] the existence of a previous or a preceding birth. But this is just what there is not. And it should not be said that the mere experience of joy or of grief in an animal just born is the source-of-the-valid-idea [to prove the existence of the previous birth]. For this may be explained by saying that it is self-caused like the contraction and expansion of the lotus.' In reply to this he says **10. Furthermore these [subconscious-impressions] have no beginning [that we can set in time], since desire is permanent.** The beginninglessness of these subconscious-impressions furthermore, not their mere uninterrupted [causal] relation is meant by the word «Furthermore.» This is because desire is permanent, since desire for one's self never loses its permanent character, for the reason that subconscious-impressions have no [assignable] beginning. And if it be objected that the permanent character of desire is unproven, inasmuch as it could be explained as being self-caused, the reply is «This well-known desire.» A heterodox person asks «Why [not]?» The answer is «an animal just brought into life» and therefore in a condition wherein death has not been experienced in this birth. In other words, he is one who has not experienced the condition which is death. How can there be in the child, fallen forward from its mother's lap and trembling in consequence, a fear of death due to the memory of pain associated with aversion, as is inferred from the peculiar quivering of the child as it clasps very tightly in its hand the thread[3] marked with the disk and other auspicious objects, which hang around its mother's neck? And if again it is urged that this is self-caused, the reply is «Furthermore not.» Furthermore a self-caused thing does not need [that is] take an efficient cause in order that it itself should come into existence. What he means to say is this. The tremor that is seen in the little child is grounded in fear. Because it is a tremor of a particular kind just like our own. And the fear of the child is based on the memory of pain and aversion because it is a fear like any one of our own fears. And so the fear which is characterized by an expectancy of something disagreeable to come does not arise from the mere memory of pain. But having inferred that the thing of which he is afraid is the cause of something disagreeable,

[1] Uçanas by his curse burned the land to ashes and covered it with a shower of dust (Rāmāyaṇa vii. 81. 8-10).

[2] See MahāBh. iii. 105 (Bomb.) and Jacobi's article on Agastya (Hastings: Cycl. of Rel. and Ethics, vol. i, p. 180[b]).

[3] Compare Bāṇa: Kādambarī, p. 152[14] (ed. M. R. Kale) and p. 93[20] (ed. Peterson, BSS.).

[the child] now also is afraid of something disagreeable. So as a result of the memory of that kind of pain accompanied by aversion for that kind of cause of fear which has been previously experienced,—when that kind of cause of fear is now experienced,—he [the child] inferring that it would cause pain is afraid of it. And the child has not come to the conclusion at any other time in this birth that falling is the cause of pain. And he has not experienced that kind of pain. So that the only alternative that remains is an experience relating to previous births. All this can be logically formulated thus. The memory belonging to a child just born is based on a previous experience. Because it is a memory. Just like our own. Nor can it be said that the expansion and contraction of the lotus is self-caused. For what is self-caused cannot stand in need of another cause. Because if this were so, even the heat of fire would require another cause. Therefore what leads to the expansion of the lotus is merely an accidental cause, such as, for instance, contact with the rays of the early sun. And the cause of its closing is the subliminal-impression[1] which leads it to recover its original position. Similarly from laughter and other [physical acts] we must infer joy [and grief] in some previous life to be the causes [of the acts of the child]. So now let the topic rest. He brings the discussion to a close by saying «It is for these reasons.»—By the words «efficient cause» he means that karma has reached the time for its fruition. «Laying hold of» means manifestation. Incidentally, with the intent to do away with the diversity of opinions concerning the dimensions of the mind-stuff, he first of all describes the diversity in the words, «a water-jar . . . a palace.» [The Sāṁkhya view.] 'Since we see works performed only when [the mind-stuff] functions within the limits of the body,[2] there is no means-of-proving that mind-stuff exists outside the body. Nor is it of the dimension[3] of an atom. For then it would follow that at the time of eating and [handling] a long corn-cake,[4] the five-fold sensation by the organs simultaneously could not be produced. And there is no means-of-proof for the assumption of a sequence[5] [of sensations when] not actually in experience. Furthermore one atomic central-organ cannot simultaneously[6] come in contact with organs located in several regions [of the body]. The only remaining alternative [for the Sāṁkhya] is that the mind-stuff is of the dimension of the body. And in the body of an ant or of an elephant [as the case may be] it is liable to expansion or contraction, like a lamp placed in a [small] water-jar or in

[1] The word *saṁskāra* is defined in Tarka-saṁgraha, § 75.

[2] The Sāṁkhya school holds the theory of *madhyama-parimāṇa* (Sut. v. 69).

[3] This is directed against the argument in Nyāya-sūtra iii. 2. 62.

[4] This is a cake eaten at the Hindu New Year and on birthdays and on the feast of Dewali. In the west it is made of corn and ghee or oil with spices and salt and is called in Marathi *kodabole*. On the plains it is made of sugar and wheat with almonds, sugar, and bits of coco-nut in the middle and is boiled in ghee. In Hindi it is called *karanji*.

[5] Compare Nyāya-sūtra iii. 2. 61.

[6] See Nyāya-sūtra iii. 2. 59.

a [large] palace.' [So it is that] others have come to the conclusion that the form [of the mind-stuff] is the dimension of the body itself; it is that of which the dimension [is the body]. The [Sāṁkhya] objector continues. 'If this [atomic theory] were true (*evam*), how can this [mind-stuff] come into relation with the womb (*kṣetra*) or the seed? For surely without something-in-which-it-resides (*āçraya*), this [mind-stuff] cannot from the dead body enter the blood and seed resident in the body of the mother and the father. Since [this mind-stuff] is dependent. For certainly when posts and such things do not move, their shadows do not move; nor when the canvas is not moving does the picture which rests upon (*āçraya*) it move. And further according to this theory the round-of-rebirth would be impossible.' Therefore he says «And thus [they say] there is an intermediate state and there is ground for the round-of-rebirths.» The words «And thus» mean when [the mind-stuff] is of the dimension of the body, there is, in order to get into another body, both the leaving of the first body and the getting into the other body, by means of a correlation, while on the way[1] (*antarā*) with a migratory body.[2] For of course by this [correlation] he would pass[3] into another body as the Purāṇa passage[4] also says, "Yama by force drew forth a man the size of a thumb." This is what is meant by saying that there is an intermediate state and that consequently there would be ground for the round-of-rebirths.' Not tolerating this opinion, he gives his own by saying «the fluctuation.» It is only the all-pervasive mind-stuff's fluctuation which contracts and expands. So the Master, the Self-born,[5] set forth. His point [in rejecting the other theory] is this. If the mind-stuff without something-in-which-it-resides cannot get into a body, how does it [in the first place] find this something-in-which-it-resides in the migratory[6] body? And if we imagine another body in this case, that would involve an infinite regress. Further, it is not possible that this migratory body be drawn forth from the body, since it is only when drawn forth that the mind-stuff can come into correlation with [the migratory body]. Therefore let there be[7] a subtile body from the moment of creation and up to the time of the great [mundane] dissolution. It would be limited in its function to the six-sheathed body, which would be the locus of the mind-stuffs. For so the mind-stuff could pass about in one body after another up to the Truth-world and down to Avīci. And one could explain the drawing forth of this subtile body from the six-sheathed body. For in this case there is [no difficulty as to an] intermediate state of this [subtile body], because this [subtile body] is always necessarily there. Moreover there is no means-of-proof for the existence of this [subtile body] also, indeed it is not within the range of

[1] Adverbially, according to Pāṇini ii. 3. 4.

[2] Compare Çaṁkara on Vedānta-sūtra iii. 1. 1–6 and on iv. 2. 6–11.

[3] See Sāṁkhya-sūtra v. 103.

[4] Compare MBh. iii. 16763.

[5] The Vārttika says that the *Svayambhū* is Patañjali.

[6] This is of course the *sūkṣma-çarīra*. Compare Sāṁkhya-sūtra v. 103.

[7] So Çaṁkara on iii. 1. 1.

ocular [demonstration]. Nor can the round of rebirths be the means-of-inference for this [subtile body]. For [this round-of-rebirths] can be explained quite as well by the theory of the Master. While (*tu*) as for the Tradition (*āgama*), it speaks of drawing out a man (*puruṣa*). And a man is neither mind-stuff nor subtile body, but the Energy of Intellect which unites not with objects. And since a drawing out of this [Energy of Intellect] is impossible, we must understand [the quotation] as being merely metaphorical. And so [the explanation of the metaphor is] that the meaning of the drawing out is only the non-existence of a fluctuation, belonging to both the Intellect and to the mind-stuff, with reference to this [object] or that. As to what has been said in the Smṛti or in the Itihāsa or in Purāṇas with regard to [the mind-stuff] just after death getting into the body of a Preta and that through the agency of commemorative-feasts (*sapiṇḍīkaraṇa*)[1] and so on [the mind-stuff] is liberated from this body—all this we accede to. But what we cannot tolerate is that mind-stuff should be migratory. And there is no Tradition to support your theory. For the messengers of Yama carry him bound with fetters only as having a body [in general]. But it is not said that there is a migratory body. Hence since mind is an effect of the personality-substance; and since the personality-substance like the sphere of the atmosphere pervades the three worlds, the central-organ is also all-pervasive.[2] An objector says, 'If this be so, the fluctuation of this [mind-stuff] would also be [all-]pervasive, and there would be a universal omniscience.' The reply to this is «only this . . . . fluctuation.» The objector replies, 'This may be true. But how has this fluctuation, which depends on mind-stuff only, its contraction and expansion from time to time?' In reply to this he says «This [mind-stuff] furthermore.» And this mind-stuff for its fluctuation requires some such [efficient-cause] as right-living. He classifies [this efficient-cause] by saying «And this efficient-cause.» By the words «such . . . as» we are to understand energy and wealth and the like. By the words «like belief, for instance» we are to understand energy and mindfulness and such qualities [i. 20]. As to their being internal [means] he adduces the consensus of the Teachers by saying «And in this sense it has been said.» «Diversion» is functional activity. «Perfection» means whiteness. «Of these two» means among the inner and the outer. «[Intuitive] knowledge and passionlessness» mean the qualities engendered by them. By what quality of outer means-of-attainment are these [outer means] surpassed [or] overwhelmed? It is the qualities resulting from [intuitive] knowledge and passionlessness which overcome it, in that they remove it from the condition

[1] See Vishṇu Pur. iii. 13. 29.

[2] The Mīmāṅsā holds the ātman is permanent and omnipresent (Çloka-Vārttika v. 18). The Sāṁkhya-sūtras (v. 69–71) deny that the central-organ is all-pervasive; and assert that it is of a middle dimension (*madhyama-parimāṇa*). The Vāiçeṣika (viii. 1. 2) and the Nyāya conceive the ātman to be atomic. The Yoga teaches that mind-stuff is all-persuasive; its fluctuations, however, expand and contract.

of seed. This is the meaning. On this point he gives a well-known illustration n the words «the Daṇḍaka Forest.»

---

11. Since [subconscious-impressions] are associated with cause and motive and mental-substrate (*āçraya*) **and stimulus, if these cease to be, then those [subconscious-impressions] cease to be.**

1. As to cause. From right-living results pleasure; from wrong-living, pain; from pleasure, passion; from pain, aversion; and from this, struggle. Quivering in central-organ or in vocal-organ or in body with this [struggle], he either helps or injures another. From this again result right-living and wrong-living, pleasure and pain, passion and aversion. Thus revolves [1] the six-spoked wheel [2] of the round-of-rebirths. And as it ceaselessly revolves, undifferentiated-consciousness (*avidyā*), the root of all the hindrances, is its motive-power. Such is cause. 2. But motive is that [human purpose] with reference to which any condition (*yasya*) such as right-living becomes operative [in the present]. For it is not the rise of anything new. 3. The central-organ, however, while its task is yet unfulfilled, is the mental-substrate of subconscious-impressions. For when the task of the central-organ is fulfilled, the subconscious-impressions, now without mental-substrate, are not able to persist. 4. When a thing confronted [with some object] phenomenalizes any subconscious-impression [in itself], then [that object] is the stimulus of that [subconscious-impression]. Thus all subconscious-impressions are associated with these causes and motives and mental-substrates and stimuli. If they cease to be, the subconscious-impressions cohering with them also cease to be.

The question is raised, if these fluctuations of mind-stuff and the subconscious-impressions are without beginning, how can they be destroyed? For surely the Energy of Intellect (*citi*) which is without beginning cannot be destroyed. In reply to this he says, **11. Since [subconscious-impressions] are associated with cause and motive and mental-substrate** (*āçraya*) **and stimulus,**

[1] Compare i. 5, p. 20[2] (Calc. ed.).

[2] A six-spoked wheel occurs in the Rig-veda i. 164[12], and in the Divyāvadāna p. 180[22] and 281[29] we find *pañcagaṇḍakaṁ saṁsāracakram*. Professor Jacobi calls my attention to the passage in Samaraicca Kahā p. 338[10].

if these cease to be, then those [subconscious-impressions] cease to be. Even a beginningless thing evidently perishes, for instance, the fact that a thing is yet to be (*unāgatatva*). [This is *prāg-abhāva.*] So it is not [a proper] middle-term (*sādhana*) because it is too wide. As to the Energy of Intellect, on the other hand, since there is no cause which could make it perish, it does not perish. But the reason for this is not that it has no beginning. And it has been stated in the sūtra that there is a cause which brings about the destruction of subconscious-impressions, although they are from time without beginning. Helping and injuring are partial expressions for the efficient-cause of right-living and wrong-living and so on. Under this expression the drinking of spirits and similar acts are also included. The motive-power (*netṛ*) is that which keeps [the wheel] moving (*nāyikā*). He gives the reason for this in the words «the root.» Becoming operative is presentness; but it does not mean that right-living as such is made to grow. Of this very point the reason is given in the words «For it is not.» That thing to which one is confronted would be such as contact with a maiden. So the meaning of the sūtra is that where the more extensive is not, there the less extensive also is not.

Since there is no production of that which is non-existent nor destruction of that which is existent, how will subconscious-impressions, by reason of their existence as things, cease to exist?

12. Past and future as such exist; [therefore subconscious-impressions do not cease to be]. For the different time-forms belong to the external-aspects.

The future is that the phenomenalization of which is yet to come. The past is that the [individual] phenomenalized [form] of which has been experienced. The present is that which has entered into its functional activity. And this three-fold thing is the object for the [intuitive] knowledge [of the yogin]. And if they did not exist as such, this [intuitive] knowledge, not having any object, would not emerge[1] [in the mind-stuff]. Therefore past and future as such exist. Moreover if the result of the karma, either that which is conducive to experience or that which is conducive to liberation, when it is yet to emerge, were without-any-describable-existence, then the actions of the wise, directed towards this [or] for the purpose of this, would have no ground. And a cause is capable of making an already existent result present, but not of producing[2]

[1] With *udapatsyata* (rare: Whitney, § 941), compare *niramāsyata*, above 279[3].

[2] For the word *upajanana* compare iii. 11, p. 201. For the word *upajana* see ii. 19, p. 150[7]; iv. 2 and 11, pp. 276[6] and 288[4]. For the verb see i. 33, p. 78[1] (Calc. ed.).

something [altogether] new. The efficient cause when fully established gives aid to the particularized [form] of the effect, but it does not cause anything [quite] new to come into existence. A substance, moreover, consists of a number of external-aspects. And by variation of this [substance's] time-forms the external-aspects are in successive states. The past or the future does not, like the present, exist as a material thing, in that it has been changed into a particularized phenomenal form. How then is it? The future has its peculiar existence as a thing yet to be phenomenalized. The past has its peculiar existence as having an [individual] phenomenalized [form] already experienced. The [individual] phenomenalized [form] of the thing itself belongs to the present time-form only. This cannot be for the past and the future time-forms. And while one time-form is present, the two [other] time-forms are of course inherent in the substance. Hence the three time-forms do not come into a state-of-existence after having-been-in-a-state-of-non-existence.

With the intent to introduce the next sūtra he raises a doubt by saying «there is no.» The words «of that which is non-existent» have been introduced either incidentally or by way of illustration. **12. Past and future as such exist; [therefore subconscious-impressions do not cease to be]. For the different time-forms belong to the external-aspects.** There is no production of things non-existent, nor destruction of things existent. But emergence and remergence (*udaya-vyayāu*) are nothing but a mutation of the different time-forms of external-aspects which are existent. This is the meaning of the sūtra. «Experienced» is that by which one gets to the [individual] phenomenal [form]. The meaning is that at present its [individual] phenomenal [form] is not. And so the external-aspect [is] existent in all three times, as he says «And if.» For what is non-existent does not become an object of knowledge, because it is without-any-describable existence. For a mental act is nothing but a shining-forth of the object. And it cannot occur where there is no object. Whereas the mental-act of yogins has the three worlds for its object. The mental-act of such as we are also would not arise if there were no object. And this is [quite] consistent. Therefore the past and the future exist as connected-inseparably with their generic-forms. So the [intuitive] knowledge of one who has experience of this kind is called the cause of the existence of the object. Because the future exists as something stateable, it also exists as an object, as he says in the words «Moreover . . . conducive to experience.» «The wise» is the clever man. And as to any acts to be performed, when one thing is the cause of another, it can bring its particular function into play only when the effect is [already] existing, for instance, the chapters of the Veda referring to the [cutting of] sacrificial-reeds (*kāṇḍalāva*). For certainly these cuttings of reeds do not bring into existence what is not existing. But they cause modifications[1] or they bring near a thing which is existing. Similarly the potter and the [efficient causes] lead to the present existence of a water-jar which already exists as he says «an already existent.» But if the past and future are to be supposed as being non-existent simply because they are not in the present, then, whew! Sir! the present also would be non-existent, because it is not in the past and future. But as to existence irrespective of its relation to time-form or to substance, it equally holds for all three, as he says «A substance, moreover.» The words «are in successive states» mean belonging to each state one by one. The expression «as a material thing» means in a substance which is a material thing. The termination *-tas* is used for all case-endings. If the past and the future are, only so far as they are past and future, then at the present they are not, because at this time they are not past or future, as he says «And while one.» He brings the discussion to a close in the words «state-of-existence after having-been-in-a-state-of-non-existence.»

---

13. These [external-aspects with the three time-forms] are phenomenalized [individuals] or subtile [generic forms and] their essence is the aspects (*guṇa*).

‹These› are of course those external-aspects with the three time-forms: those which are [phenomenalized] are the present; those which are subtile are the past and the future, the six[2] non-particulars. Since this whole world is nothing more than a particular collocation of aspects (*guṇa*), it has in the strict sense the aspects as its essence. And in this sense the Exposition[3] of the System has said,

"The aspects from their utmost height
Come not within the range of sight.
But all within the range of sight
A phantom seems and empty quite."

[1] For the compound *prāptivikārāu* see Pāṇ. ii. 2. 32.

[2] ii. 19, p. 147⁷ (Calc. ed.).

[3] The quotation is attributed to *Vārṣagaṇya* by Vācaspatimiçra in his Bhāmatī on Vedānta-sūtra ii. 1. 2. 3 in the following words *ata eva yogaçāstraṁ vyutpādayitā-āha sma Bhagavān Vārṣagaṇyaḥ "guṇānām* (Nirṇayasāgara, first edition, p. 352). Compare Vijñāna Bhikṣu in his Vijñānāmṛta (Benares ed. 1901), p. 101.

An objector says, 'This may be true. But this manifold amplification (*prapañca*) of the varied forms of the universe (*viçva*), having as its essence the kinds of mutation which are the states of the substance and its external-aspects, cannot properly come out of one primary substance. For from a cause which has no diversity, diversities of effect cannot come to pass.' In reply to this he says **13. These [external-aspects with the three time-forms] are phenomenalized [individuals] or subtile [generic forms and] their essence is the aspects** (*guṇa*). These external-aspects with the three time-forms, both the phenomenalized and the subtile, have the aspects as their essence. For they have no other cause than the three-fold aspects. But as to their diversity, it follows from the diversity attending upon the beginningless subconscious-impressions from hindrances produced by these [aspects (*guṇa*)]. In which sense it has been said in the Vāyu[1] Purāṇa, "Because the primary cause has manifold forms, there is a marvellous mutation." Of the earth and the other phenomenalized [individuals], and of the eleven organs, which are present forms, there are past and future [forms], which are the six non-particularized [forms; and these] arise according to their capacity.—Making now a distinction between the permanent and the impermanent forms of the universe, he gives first its permanent form in the words «this whole world.» «This» [that is] the visible [world]. «A collocation» means a mutation with a particular arrangement of parts. On this point there is a specific mention of the Shaṣṭitantra[2] text. It is like a phantom (*māyā*), but not quite a phantom. «Empty quite» means perishable. For just as a phantom in no time assumes different shapes, so those evolved-effects whose external-aspects become visible and invisible, change from moment to moment. Whereas primary-matter is permanent, and thus not homogeneous with a phantom, and is accordingly an ultimate reality.

But if all things are aspects (*guṇa*), how is it that there is a single sound and a single organ [of sense]?

14. The that-ness of a thing is due to a singleness of mutation.

When the aspects disposed to vividness and to activity and to inertia have as their essence processes-of-knowing, in so far as they are instruments [of perception], there is a single mutation, for instance, the organ-of-hearing. When their essence is objects-for-

[1] xlix. 182, Anandāçrama ed., p. 153, and liii. 20, Anandāçrama ed., p. 175. See also Sāṁkhya Tattva Kāumudī xlii [Garbe's translation, p. 86].

[2] See Garbe: Mondschein der Sāṁkhya Wahrheit, p. 111, note 3; and Garbe's Translation of the Sāṁkhya Pravacana Bhāṣya, vi. 3, p. 147.

knowledge, in so far as they are sounds, there is a single mutation, a sound, an object of sense. The sounds and other [perceptible objects], belonging to the general class of limitation-in-extent,[1] have a single mutation, an atom of earth, a part of a fine-substance (*tanmātra*). And these [atoms] have a single mutation, the earth, a cow, a tree, a mountain, for examples. By adding [to each of] the other [coarse] elements [successively] liquidity and heat and motivity and the making of a space, a generic-form, the beginning of a single evolved-effect, would be formed.—They who from the following point of view deny the existence of a thing as such by saying, 'There is no intended-object dissociated from a mental act, but percepts are dissociated from intended-objects and imagined as in dreams and similar states,' and they who say 'a thing is only a readjustment of percepts, like the objects of a dream, and not a thing in the full sense of the word,'—these, when the thing is presented by its own authority as it is (*tathā*) [according as it is seen] to be there (*idam*), since they throw overboard the thing as such by an abstract (*vikalpa*) thinking without force of proof,—how in the very act of prattling it away can their own words be worthy of belief?

It may be granted that the three-fold aspects (*guṇa*) have such a diversity of mutation. But whence comes a single mutation, so that one says 'This is earth' or 'This is water'? By raising this objection, since there is a contradiction between the three essences and the singleness, he introduces the sūtra. **14. The that-ness of a thing is due to a singleness of mutation.** We see a single mutation belonging to many, for instance, when a cow or a horse or a buffalo or an elephant is huddled together in a brackish[2] [land], each has a single mutation characterized by the common nature of salt. And [similarly] a wick and oil and fire form a lamp. In the same way the aspects (*guṇa*), though many, have a single mutation. As a result of this, each of the fine elements (*tanmātra*) and of the elements and of the products-of-the-elements has a that-ness, that is a singleness. [When their] essence is objects-for-knowledge, in so far as *sattva* is predominant, their essence is vividness. And

[1] Compare iii. 44, p. 254[2] (Calc. ed.).

[2] The Maṇiprabhā says *rumāsthale*. And the Pātañjala Rahasyam says, 'If cows and other animals are huddled together in that brackish spot (*rumālavaṇa-bhūmi*), then all of them together will have the brackish flavour attaching to their bodies.' Colonel Jacob adduces evidence to show that *rumā* is the name of a particular salt-lake or mine (Second Handful of Popular Maxims, 2nd edition, 1909, p. 69).

being subsidiary-products of the personality-substance they have a single mutation in the form of instruments [of perception], [for instance], the organ-of-hearing. In so far as the *tamas* of these same [aspects] is predominant, inasmuch as they are insensate (*jaḍa*) and thus have objects-for-knowledge as their essence, there is a single mutation as being the fine element sound, an object of sense. By the words «a sound» he indicates the fine element sound; by the words «object of sense» he indicates that it is insensate. But the fine element cannot possibly be the object of the organ-of-hearing. The rest is easy.—He now raises up a Destructionist (*vāināçika*), who holds the Theory of Ideas (*vijñānavādin*), by saying «'There is no intended-object dissociated from a mental-act.'» 'For if there be elements and products of elements distinct from mental-acts, then we might suppose a productive cause of them such as the primary cause. But in the strict sense they are not anything different from ideas. How is it then that a primary cause is presupposed? And how is it that processes-of-knowing, the organs-of-sense, which are evolved-effects of the personality-substance, are presupposed? To explain. Since an insensate intended-object cannot be vivid of itself, there is no intended-object dissociated from some mental-act. [Association is] coexistence [that is] a relation. The absence of this is dissociation. The prefix *vi-* is used in the sense of absence. The meaning is that there is nothing unrelated to some idea; [in other words] something which might properly be described as non-existing. On the other hand mental-acts do exist dissociated from intended-objects. For in so far as this mental-act is vivid in itself, it does not require an insensate intended-object in order to make a statement as to its own existence.' So then the holder of the Theory of Ideas (*vijñānavādin*) has indicated two requisites, 1. the fact[1] that it is perceived (*vedyatva*), and 2. the fact that it is apperceived along with something else (*sahopalambha*). 'These two points can further be brought out in a syllogism thus. Whatever is perceived by whatever process-of-perception, that [intended-object] is not distinct from that [process-of-perception]. Just as the soul in the case of knowledge. And the elements and the products-of-the-elements are perceived. So this apperception [of elements] is pervaded by the contrary proposition, [that is, it refutes the absence of distinction between the process and the object]. So the fact-that-it-is-perceived, which is less-extensive as compared with what-is-the-opposite of the distinction which-we-wish-to-deny, [as soon as this fact] is known, posits the absence-of-distinction, which is more extensive with regard to itself [the perception]. And when we see this, [the fact that they are seen as different], which is just the contrary of this, is denied. Accordingly, when any thing is invariably seen with another thing, then the one is not different from the other, just as the second moon which is always perceived with the [actual] moon. And it is the case that the object is always invariably perceived with

[1] Similar discussion by Çaṁkara on ii. 2. 28. See also Sarva-darçana-saṁgraha (Anand. ed.), pp. 9–10 and 13.

the thought. Thus this perception contradicts the more extensive [term]; the invariable relation contradicts the variable relation which is more extensive than the distinction, which we must deny. Removing thus the variable relation, it rejects the distinction, which is less extensive than this [relation].[1] Let this be assumed. And if the intended-object is not different from the thought, then how is it that they seem to be different?' In reply to this [the Vijñānavādin] says '«imagined.» As the Destructionists[2] say "Because there is invariably an apperception of [the object] blue and of the percept of this [blue] at the same time, there is no difference [between them]. And the difference that may be seen between them results from illusions of mental-acts just as a pair of moons may be seen when there is one only without a second." [The Vijñānavādin] makes clear the imaginary [difference] in the words «only a readjustment of percepts.'» [The author of the Comment] refutes this by saying «these.» The construction of the sentence is, how can their own words be worthy of credence?—«Presented» means brought before them at the time of each perception. How [is it presented]? He replies «as it is.» In the different ways that [a thing] shines forth as being [the thing] that is pointed to as this and this, in that very way *eo ipso* (*svayam*) it is presented; but not as being reduced to an object of a mental-act [or] as being a figment of the imagination. The words «by its own authority» point out that the intended-object acts as cause with reference to the mental-act, because the intended-object has given rise to the mental-act by virtue of its own power as an object-for-knowledge. It is on account of this that the mental-act is the perceiver of the intended-object. Now how could a thing, which is of such a kind, [be thrown away] by reason of an [empty] abstract thinking having no force of proving? For since an [empty] conception is no means-of-proof, therefore what is based upon it and what is in essence that [empty abstraction] is no means-of-proof. In this way throwing overboard the thing as such, [that is] setting it afloat.—An occasional reading is 'holding it under.' In this case too the meaning is the same. Prattling away this object in this way, [how] can their own words be worthy of belief? This is what is intended. The two middle terms given, the invariable apperception at one time and the fact of being perceived, are non-conclusive. Because the negative statement is open to doubt. To explain. The coarseness and externality appear [in consciousness] in the case of elements and products of elements which [as you say] have the form of thought [only], but these two [qualities] are not possible in the case of thought [only]. To explain. Coarseness means pervading several points-of-space. Externality means related to separated points-of-space. And it is impossible that a single mental-act should pervade several points-of-space and also

[1] If there is *bheda*, there is *a-niyatasahopalambha*; but there is none of this latter; therefore there is no *bheda*.

[2] Quoted Sarva Darç. Saṁg. p. 16 (Anandāç. ed.) and de la Vallée Poussin's note in Le Bouddhisme (Muséon, 1902), p. 84.

41 [H.O.S. 17]

[occupy] separated points-of-space. For it is impossible to have in a single thing the confusion of contrary qualities such as occupying this point-of-space and not occupying this point-of-space. Else if this were possible, one would have to admit that all three worlds are a single thing. If it be said that for this very reason we should admit that there is a difference in the mental-acts [as to coarseness and externality, in that there are as many thoughts as there are forms of the thing], then the reply would be, Then! Sir! in the case of the ideas which can grasp even the extremely subtile objects [finer than coarseness and externality], and which take no notice of each other's behaviour, and which are awake only to that [one atomic object] which comes within their range—how could there be the appearance of coarseness? And you cannot talk [of what is perceived by the later-distinct-impression (*vikalpa*) in language] which refers to the later-distinct-impression. Because there is no confusion of [the content of this impression with anything else], and [on the other hand] there is a clear appearance [of coarseness]. Nor can it be said that coarseness is externally sensed (*ālocitam*) [by the first-indistinct-impression], and so the clearness of the knowledge (*savikalpa*) which follows this, and which is conditioned by this [*avikalpa*] could be explained. Further this later-distinct-impression is not, like the first-indistinct-impression, limited to its form (*ākāra*) and to nothing else. For since this [later-indistinct-impression] is not itself a coarse [thing], it cannot make the coarse [manifest] as its object. Therefore if an idea is to be outer, since, as we have shown it, it cannot be coarse or outer, then these coarse and outer [impressions] may be counted, if you will, as altogether false. And you cannot say that such a false impression is just the same as a mental-act. For then you would have to admit that the mental-act is as empty as this [false impression].—So to resume the argument (*tathā ca*). In so far as the fact of being perceived is not less extensive than the absence of difference between [the idea and the object], how can the fact of its being perceived refute the fact of the difference?—And as to being invariably together. Just as in the case of the mental-act and of the coarseness, the one existent and the other non-existent, so likewise in the case of two existing things [the being perceived invariably together] may be explained on the ground of the nature of things or on the ground of some kind of an obstruction [in the thinking apparatus]. Accordingly those two fallacious middle terms [put forth by the opponent], because they are non-conclusive, only give rise to an [empty] abstraction (*vikalpa*), if there be no external [thing]. And the authority of a perception is not to be gainsaid by a mere [empty] abstraction. So the point was well taken when he said «by an abstract (*vikalpa*) thinking without force of proof.» By this [discussion we must understand that also the view which attempts to prove that objects] are ideas, urged as a ground that ideas have no external-basis, as illustrated by the ideas of a dream, is also overthrown. And the alternatives (*vikalpa*) regarding the object-of-the-illation have been offered-in-rebuttal by stating that the relation is that between whole

and [part]. For details the Nyāya Kaṇikā[1] is to be consulted. So there is no need of details here.

Why is this incorrect?

15. Because, while the [physical] thing remains the same, the mind-stuffs are different, [therefore the two are upon] distinct levels-of-existence.

A single [physical] thing is the common [physical] basis for many mind-stuffs. It is not, of course, figured forth by a single mind-stuff, nor yet is it figured forth by many mind-stuffs. It is rather grounded in itself. Why is this? Because, while the [physical] thing remains the same, the mind-stuffs are different. When the mind-stuff is in relation with right-conduct, the mind-stuff has thoughts of pleasure, the [physical] thing remaining the same. When in relation with wrong-living, from the same [physical thing] it has thoughts of pain. When in relation with undifferentiated-consciousness, from the same [physical thing] it has thoughts of infatuation. When in relation with complete insight, from the same thing it has thoughts of detachment.[2] If this is so, by whose mind-stuff would this thing be formed? Nor would it be sound to say that one person's mind-stuff is affected when brought into relation with an object formed by the mind-stuff of another person. Consequently the [physical] thing and the thought distinct because of dissimilarity, in that the thing is the object-for-knowledge and the thought is the process-of-knowing, [are upon] distinct levels-of-existence. There is not even a trace [3] of a blending of the two. But from the point-of-view of the Sāṁkhya, since a thing has three aspects (*guṇa*) and since the changes of the aspects[4] are unstable, it comes into relation with the mind-stuffs [of men], dependent [for its existence in this case or the other] upon such determinants as right-living [or wrong living or undifferentiated consciousness or complete insight], it becomes the cause, in one form

[1] Reference is made to this work by Vācaspatimiçra at i. 32, p. 75[1] (Calc. ed.), and also in the Tattva Bindu (Benares, 1892), p. 23[12].—The *Nirālambanavāda* is discussed in the Çāstra-dīpikā, p. 32; in the Nyāya kaṇikā, p. 261; and in the Bhāmatī on Vedānta-sūtra ii. 2. 25 (Nirṇaya-sāgara ed.), p. 462.

[2] Compare ii. 28.

[3] Compare Pāṇ. i. 2. 15.

[4] Compare ii. 15, p. 135[11]; iii. 9 and 13, pp. 199[3] and 204[4] (Calc. ed.).

or another, of presented-ideas, as they rise [into consciousness], corresponding [in quality] to the [determining] efficient-cause.

So having in this manner, independently of the sūtra, given the reason for setting up [the physical thing] as something over and above the mental-act, the author of the Comment introduces the reason as given in the sūtra itself by the words «Why is this?» **15. Because, while the [physical] thing remains the same, the mind-stuffs are different, [therefore the two are upon] distinct levels-of-existence.** Whatever units are in the manifold these differ absolutely from the manifold. For instance, a single thought in Chāitra or in Māitra is distinct from the presented-ideas in Devadatta and in Vishṇumitra, which are dissimilar. And since the intended-object is not different, even when the thoughts about it are manifold, it is other than the mental-acts. And further the identity of the intended-object, although the thoughts of those who know it validly are different, is determined by the connexion of one [thought] with another [in memory]. For in the case of a single woman who is presented-to-the-minds of several persons, enamoured or ill-disposed or infatuated or detached, we see a reciprocal connexion so that one thinks 'She who is seen by you is seen by me also.' Consequently while the [physical] thing remains the same, because the mind-stuffs are different, because there is a difference of thoughts, [therefore] the two, the intended-object and the thought, [are upon] distinct levels-of-existence [that is] [distinct] means of distinguishing the essential attributes. In the lover, a thought of pleasure with reference to the woman loved; in rival mistresses, a thought of pain; but in Chāitra who has not obtained her, a thought of infatuation, a depression. 'This may be so,' the objector says, 'but that intended-object with the distinguishing characteristic of being loved is figured forth by a mind-stuff of one person. And this same [intended-object] affects the mind-stuff of the others also. So [this mind-stuff] might be supposed to be common.' In reply to this he says «nor would it be . . . another.» For if that were so, when one person has the thought of blue, all would have the thought of blue. A further objection would be this 'Even according to the view which maintains the distinct existence of objects (*arthavāda*), how can one and the same object be the cause of mental-acts differing according to the difference in pleasure and the other [experiences]? For from a cause which is not different in its distinguishing characteristics there should be no difference in effects.' In reply to this he says «from the point-of-view of the Sāṁkhya.» It is quite consistent to say that the same external thing which is a mutation of the three aspects (*guṇa*) has three forms. The objector says 'Even if it be so, then all without distinction would have a mental-act of pleasure and of pain and of infatuation.' In reply to this he says «dependent [for its existence] upon such determinants as right-living.» The *sattva* accompanied by the *rajas* and determined by right-living produces the sensation of happiness. But this same *sattva* when determined by knowledge (*vidyā*), after the *rajas* has been removed, gives rise to a sensation of detachment. And right-living and the other [experiences]

are not all in all persons. Some of it is in some persons. So this arrangement [of pleasures and of pains] is quite consistent.

There are some who say that a thing is coextensive with its thought, in so far as like pleasure and the other [experiences] it is experienced. · In this way when they thus reject the quality of being common [to several mind-stuffs], they deny the existence of the thing in both its earlier and its later moments.

16. And a thing is not dependent upon a single mind-stuff, [for then in certain cases] it could not be proved [by that mind-stuff], [and] then what would it be?

If a thing were dependent[1] upon a single mind-stuff, then if the mind-stuff be distracted or restricted, it itself would be untouched by that mind-stuff. And not coming within the range of that [mind-stuff], and not being proved [by that mind-stuff], and unperceived in its nature by any one, would it then be at all?[2] And how could it be produced again in relation to the mind-stuff? It would not possess those parts of it which are not apparent. So that if one says the back does not exist, neither could the belly be known. Consequently an intended-object is independent [of mind-stuff] and common to all the Selves. And again independent mind-stuffs function differently for each Self. As a result of a relation between these two [the intended-object and the mind-stuff] there follows an apperception, an experience of the Self.

On this point there are some disputatious persons who say that the object is coexistential with the idea. Because it is the object of experience, like pleasure. What he means to say is this. The intended-object might be admitted to be distinct from knowledge, still since it is insensate (*jaḍa*), it cannot be perceived in the absence of knowledge, but must be illumined by the knowledge. Accordingly [the object] is only at the time of the idea, and not at other times. Since there is no evidence that it exists at other times. This the author of the Comment confutes independently of the sūtra in the words «In this way when they.» For a [physical] thing (*vastu*) is experienced by ordinary observers[3] as common to all mind-stuffs and as persisting[4] in the succession of various moments and as consisting of a mutation. Now if the thing is coexistential with the mental-act, then it would be of this sort [that its appearance and

[1] As the Vijñānavāda maintains.

[2] Compare de la Vallée Poussin: La Négation de l'Âme (Journal Asiatique, 9e serie, tome xx, 1902, pp. 248 and 254).

[3] This would be the point of view of the Sarvāstivādin.

[4] Compare Nyāya-sūtra i. 1. 40.

disappearance would be coexistential with the appearance and disappearance of the idea]. If so, how can one act up to (*anurodha*) this objective-factor (*idamañça*) so that one shall not at the same time deny it? This is the meaning. Or we may suppose that there is not a denial of this objective-factor. Let the intended-object be coexistential with the knowledge. To this also the reply is in the sūtra. **16. And a thing is not dependent upon a single mind-stuff, [for then in certain cases] it could not be proved [by that mind-stuff], [and] then what would it be?** For the same mind-stuff which perceives a water-jar, when distracted by another substance such as a piece of cloth, does not remain upon the water-jar; or when the mind-stuff which has discrimination as its object, attains at that very time to restriction;—at these times, since there is no knowledge of the water-jar or of the discrimination, the water-jar and the discrimination, being dependent for their existence upon one particular knowledge only, would surely cease when this [knowledge] ceases. This he says in the words «dependent upon a single mind-stuff.» The words «how could it be» mean that it could not be. How does it happen that the mind-stuff is in relation to this thing whether it be a water-jar or discrimination? For the effects invariably are where the cause is, and invariably are not where the cause is not. Without regard to their own peculiar cause they cannot be produced by another cause. And if they are supposed to be causeless, then one would have to deny [such] an inconsistency as the accidental existence of them [the effects]. And there is no ground for saying that whatever causes the knowledge of the thing also causes the thing. For then it would follow that the taste and the sensific power and the digestion and so on would be the same whether one makes use of an actual sweetmeat or of a sweetmeat[1] of hope. Therefore the point is well taken when he says «And how could it be produced again in relation to the mind-stuff?» Furthermore the front part of anything is implied by the middle and hind part. But if the existence [of the thing] were to depend upon the knowledge, then the upper and middle parts would not exist, since this [idea of them] is not in experience. And accordingly since the pervader [the upper and middle parts] are not, the lower part, which is pervaded, would also not be. And thus if the whole object be absent, how could it be urged that the intended-object is coexistential with the knowledge, as he says «It would not possess those parts.» The words «are not apparent» mean are not perceived. He brings the discussion to a close by saying «Consequently.» The rest is easy.

This is an allusion to the stanza in Çrīharṣa's Khaṇḍanakhaṇḍakhādya
"*Āçāmodakatṛptā ye, ye copārjitamodakāḥ* |
Rasavīryavipākādi tulyaṁ teṣām prasajyate."
(Lazarus and Co's edition, Medical Hall Press, Benares, p. 37; Chaukhamba Sanskrit Series, fascicle I, p. 66.) This stanza is given as a quotation in Çrīharṣa's work also. There is another book of the same title on astronomy. See also de la Vallée Poussin, Le Boudhisme (Muséon, 1902), p. 35, and Hoernle's translation of the Suçruta, p. 12.

17. A thing is known or not known by virtue of its affecting [or not affecting] the mind-stuff.

Objects-of-sense like magnets, bind to themselves the mind-stuff, as if it had qualities of iron, and affect it. The object whereby the mind-stuff is affected is known. But [the Self], who is other than this, is not known. The mind-stuff enters into mutations because the nature of the thing is now known[1] and now not known.

This might[2] be conceded. 'But,' as the objector says, 'if the object is to be independent, in that it is insensate, it can never throw out light, or if it does throw out light, then its insensate character would vanish. And so (*iti*) it would cease also to be. For surely a thing cannot exist after casting off its own nature. Moreover it cannot be urged that throwing out light is a property of the intended-object which is really insensate by nature, and that this [property] is put into it by the organs. For if throwing out light were to be a property of the intended-object, it would be, like blueness, common to all persons. Thus if a single person knows the meaning of the [philosophical] systems, then all would be scholars and there would be no incompetent persons. Nor is it correct to say that a present external-aspect should exist in the past or in the future. Therefore that an intended-object exists independently as an object of apperception is nothing but a wish.' In reply to this he recites the sūtra 17. **A thing is known or not known by virtue of its affecting [or not affecting] the mind-stuff.**

Although the intended-object is by nature insensate, still by the channel of the organs it affects the mind-stuff. The Energy of Intellect (*citi-çakti*), whose reflection enters into the mirror of the mind-stuff which is in such a state [of being affected] as has been just described, enlivening (*cetayamānā*) the mind-stuff which is affected by the intended-object, experiences the intended-object. But it does not impart to the object anything like visibility. Neither [is the Energy of Intellect] out of relation with the mind-stuff. For we have said that its reflection unites with the mind. And although both the mind-stuff, because it is omnipresent, and the organ which is made of the personality-substance, are not in relation[3] with the object-of-sense, still that mind-stuff which has its fluctuation in any particular body is in relation with objects-of-sense. Thus it is that objects are said to be like a magnet. Since the mind-stuff is like the iron in its properties, the objects, having by the channel of the organs brought it into relation, affect it. And hence mind-stuff is capable of mutations, as he says «Of the thing.»

[1] ii. 20, p. 152[3] (Calc.). [2] The purpose of this sūtra is to demolish idealism.
[3] Reading *viṣaye nāsti*.

But as for [the Self] for whom this same mind-stuff is an object-of-sense—

18. Unintermittently the Master of that [mind-stuff] knows the fluctuations of mind-stuff [and thus] the Self undergoes-no-mutations.

If, like the mind-stuff, the Master also, that is, the Self, should undergo mutation, then fluctuations of mind-stuff which are its objects would be, like objects-of-sense, the sounds and other [perceptible things], sometimes known and sometimes not known. The fact, however, that the central organ is unintermittently known by its Master, the Self, leads us to infer that [the Self] is an entity that undergoes-no-mutations.

Thus then he has established the existence of the intended-object as distinct from mind-stuffs. Now with the intent of showing that the Self is distinct from these [mind-stuffs] whose nature is to enter into mutation, he asserts its [the Self's] immutability, the quality which differentiates it from these [mind-stuffs]. This he does by supplying some words and by reciting the sūtra. «But as for [the Self] for whom this same mind-stuff is an object-of-sense.» **19. Unintermittently the Master of that [mind-stuff] knows the fluctuations of mind-stuff [and thus] the Self undergoes-no-mutations.** The mind-stuff, whether it be restless or infatuated or distracted or in a state of focusedness, is always up to the time of restriction, experienced by the Self as in mutation. Why is this so? Because the Self does not undergo mutation. If he entered into mutations, then the Self also, like the mind-stuffs, would sometimes know objects-of-sense and sometimes not. Whereas objects-of-sense are only known [and never unknown] to him. Therefore he does not undergo mutation. And as a result he is something distinct from things that are in mutation. The same he says in the words «If like the mind-stuff.» It is the central-organ, when in fluctuation, that he unintermittently knows. Of this he is the Master [and] Owner, in other words, the Experiencer. Of this Master, the Self, [the above fact] leads us to infer the immutability. To explain: The point is that this Self which does not enter into mutation is distinct from the mind-stuff which enters into mutation.

Should the doubt arise whether the mind-stuff like fire illumines itself and at the same time illumines objects—

19. It does not illumine itself, since it is an object-for-sight.

Just as the organs-of-sense and the sounds and other perceptible [things] do not illumine themselves, since they are objects for sight, so the central-organ is also to be represented. And accordingly, fire as an example could not apply to it. For fire does not throw light upon its own self which [before was something] without light. And here light is thrown [only] when there is a relation of the light-giver with something [which is yet] to be lighted. Furthermore such a relation [of a thing] does not occur with the thing itself. Besides, the meaning of the words ‹the mind-stuff illumines itself› is that it is not an object-for-knowledge for any one. Just as the words 'Air is grounded in itself' mean that it is not grounded in something else. For the reason that creatures are conscious-by-reflection of the processes of their own thinking-substances, when they say 'I am angry, I am afraid, I feel a passion for that person, I am angry with that person,' there is purposive action. This is impossible unless there be a knowledge of one's own thinking-substance.

With the words «Should the doubt arise» he sets up a Destructionist (*vāināçika*) as an opponent, who argues as follows: 'All this may be so, provided mind-stuff be the object of the Self. But this it is not. On the contrary, this [mind-stuff] throws light upon itself [and] illumines the objects [and] originates in-dependence-upon previous mind-stuff. How then can the Self always have the objects perceived? And still more how can it be distinct from the mind-stuff which enters-into-mutation?' **19. It does not illumine itself, since it is an object-for-sight.** It might be so [self-illumining], providing mind-stuff had consciousness of itself. This, however, it does not have. It is, like the colour blue, [an object] capable of being included in experience in so far as it undergoes mutation. And whatever is capable of being included in experience cannot throw light upon itself. For it cannot be a fluctuation with regard to itself [and not to mind-stuff]. Since the same thing cannot be the act, the object of the act, and [one of] the relations[1] of the act. For the act of cooking is not cooked; nor is the act of chopping chopped. On the other hand, the Self does not undergo mutation and is not an object of experience. Therefore with reference to him self-enlightenment is not inexplicable. For his self-enlightenment is nothing but an enlightenment[2] which is not dependent on any other; and it is not his being an object of experience. Therefore because it is an object-for-sight, the mind-stuff which is the object of the seeing does not illumine in itself. The objects of the fluctuations of that mind-stuff only which has the reflections of the light of the self (*ātman*) throw light. This is the point. An objector says, 'But don't you see that fire is an object-for-sight and yet has

[1] These relations are those expressed by the cases other than the nominative and possessive.

[2] Reading *prakāçatā hy asya . . . nānubhavakarmatā.*

enlightenment in itself. It is not with a fire as it is with water-jars and so on, which may be made manifest by [the light of a] fire; for a fire is not [made manifest] by another fire.' In reply to this he says «And so, fire as an example.» Why? «For fire does not.» The meaning is that fire does not require any other fire to throw light upon it, but has light thrown upon it by a mental-act. So it does not throw light upon itself. Thus [fire] is not an exception-to-general-principle [stated in the sūtra]. This is the meaning. The word «here» in the expression «And here light is thrown» distinguishes [fire] from the light which is the nature of the Self, in other words, the light which is of an active kind. What he means to say is this: Wherever there is an action, it is in all cases seen to exist as related to an agent and to an instrument-of-action and to an object. Just as we see the act of cooking as related to Chāitra and to the fire and to the rice. Similarly throwing-light is an action. And this [action] too must be in the same [threefold] relation. Now a relation must be based upon a difference. It is impossible where there is no difference. This is the meaning. When it is said «Besides, the meaning of the words ‹the mind-stuff illumines itself› is that it is not an object-for-knowledge for any one,» the objector grants, 'This may be so. But let it not be said that the mind-stuff is an object-for-knowledge. For when the process-of-knowing, which is neither the cause nor the pervader [of the mind-stuff] is repressed, it does not follow that the mind-stuff must be repressed.' To this he replies, «of their own thinking-substance.» The «thinking substance» means the mind-stuff.[1] «Movements» mean functional-activities. «Beings» mean living beings. The different fluctuations of mind-stuff, anger or greed for instance, are, together with their basis the mind-stuff and with their objects, experienced by each individual; and refute that statement that the mind-stuff is not an object-for-knowledge. He makes clear this same perception of the movements of one's own thinking-substance by the words «I am angry.»

20. And there cannot be a cognition of both [thinking-substance and thing] at the same time.

And it is impossible in a single moment to cognize one's own form and another's as well. It is a supposition[2] of the Momentarists that whatever exists is both action and the means-related-to-an-action.

20. And there cannot be a cognition of both [thinking-substance and thing] at the same time. He who says that mind-stuff illumines itself and illumines objects-of-sense cannot at least say that mind-stuff cognizes itself by the same functional-activity as that by which it cognizes objects. For a

[1] That the *buddhi* is equivalent to *citta*; that in I. 2, p. 6[18], it is equivalent to *antaḥkaraṇam*; and that at the end of iv. 19 Vācaspati uses it as equivalent to *manas*;—these are indications of a wide divergence from the Sāṁkhya.

[2] Compare Çaṁkara on ii. 2. 20.

functional-activity which has not a different distinguishing-characteristic is not adequate to producing a difference in effect. Therefore a difference in functional-activity has to be presupposed. In the opinion of the Destructionists there is no functional-activity over and above the various originations. And from the same act of origination which is without different distinguishing-characteristics, there cannot possibly come effects which have distinguishing-characteristics. For then this difference would be quite accidental. Neither [as in the last alternative] can it be urged that one and the same thing can have two originations. Therefore at one moment of time (*samaya*) the mind-stuff cannot determine the objects and also its own kind of thought; [it cannot illumine itself]. The Comment states this in the words «And it is impossible in a single moment.» And in this sense it has been said[1] by the Destructionists, "Whatever is the being of a thing that is itself the action and the means-related-to-action." Therefore this fact that mind-stuff is an object-for-sight, which is eternal, takes from it its character of illumining itself and points to a seer, and to the fact that the seer does-not-enter-into-mutations.

If there be the opinion that a mind-stuff naturally[2] restricted is [yet] known by another mind-stuff immediately contiguous to it, [the answer is,]

21. If [one mind-stuff] were the object-for-sight for another, there would be an infinite regress from one thinking-substance to another thinking-substance, as well as confusion of memory.

If one mind-stuff were perceived by another mind-stuff, by whom would the thinking-substance of the thinking-substance be perceived? Because this would be perceived by still another, and that by yet one more, there would be an infinite regress. And there would be a ‹confusion of memory.› As many memories would obtain as there would be, on the part of the thinking-substances, experiences. And as a result of the confusion of these [memories] there would be no limit to the memory of one [thinking-substance]. Thus everything is put into disorder by the Destructionists' prattling away of the Self who is conscious by reflecting the thinking-substance. But those who assume that the experiencer as such [experiences] anywhere soever do not conform to the rules [of logic]. There are some who assume an existence as such, and that it is this existence which casts off those five divisions-of-existence (*skandha*) of theirs and puts others together again. But

[1] Compare Vācaspatimiçra's Bhāmatī on ii. 2. 4. 20. (Nir. Sāg. ed., p. 456, last line.)
[2] Compare ii. 9.

these are afraid of this very [existence]. Thus in the very act of saying, 'That I may feel the passionlessness of the Great Disgust for the divisions-of-existence and that they may arise no more and altogether cease, I will lead the student's life[1] in the presence of my spiritual guide,' they deny after all the existence of the existence. But the systems with the Sāṁkhya and Yoga at their head denote[2] by the word 'self' the Self, the Owner, the experiencer of the mind-stuff.

Again he sets up a Destructionist as opponent with the words «If there be the opinion.» 'It may be granted that because [mind-stuff is] an object-for-sight it is not conscious of itself. But this does not necessitate the existence of a self (*ātman*). For any later moment of mind-stuff belonging to the same continuous-series (*santāna*) can perceive the moment of the mind-stuff which gave it birth and which became naturally restricted.' This is the meaning. [This latter moment of mind-stuff is called] immediately contiguous (*samanantara*) because it is alike (*sama*) in point of knowledge, and immediate (*anantara*) in point of not being separated. **21. If [one mind-stuff] were the object-for-sight for another, there would be an infinite regress from one thinking-substance to another thinking-substance, as well as confusion of memory.** The word «thinking-substance» means mind-stuff. When the succeeding thinking-substance is not itself known, it is not able to know the previous thinking-substance. And a previous thinking-substance as long as it is unrelated with the thinking-substance cannot be supposed to be perceived. For certainly a man who does not know what a staff is cannot know what it means to speak of a man with a staff. Therefore there would be an infinite regress. The [divisions of existence are the five] groups[3] (*skandha*), consciousness and sensations and perceptions and forms and predispositions. When he says «But the systems with the Sāṁkhya and Yoga at their head» he means to say that the Sāṁkhya and Yoga are at the head of such systems as the Vāiçeṣika. The rest is easy.

How [is this]?

22. The Intellect (*citi*) which unites not [with objects] is conscious of its own thinking-substance when [the mind-stuff] takes the form of that [thinking-substance by reflecting it].

"For, the Energy of the experiencer,[4] which is immutable and

[1] Similar discussion in Caraka-Saṁhitā, fifth *adhyāya*.

[2] The word *sva* as applied to the mind-stuff implies a contrast to the owner (*svāmin*). The reference is to the beginning of the Comment on iv. 19.

[3] The order varies from the Buddhist order. See H. C. Warren's Buddhism in Translations, Appendix, p. 487.

[4] This is Pañcaçikha's ninth fragment (according to Garbe), quoted a second time (see ii. 20), and misprinted both times (*pratisaṁkrāteva*).

which unites not with objects, seeming to unite with something mutable [the thinking-substance], takes the form of the fluctuations which that [thinking-substance] undergoes. And [this Energy] being identified with a fluctuation of the thinking-substance in so far as it is nothing but an imitation of a fluctuation of the thinking-substance that has come under the influence of the intelligence (*cāitanya*), it is termed a fluctuation of the thinking-substance." And in this sense it has been said "That hiding-place in which the everlasting Brahman lies concealed is not an under-world nor mountain-chasm nor the darkness nor caverns of the sea, but is the working of the mind when not distinguished [from Himself]. So the sages tell."

The objector says, 'This might be conceded. But if mind-stuff does not illumine itself and is not knowable by another mind-stuff, how then will even the self (*ātman*) experience the mind-stuff? For surely the Self, even if it have light in itself, cannot have any activity, and in the absence of any activity he cannot be an agent. And while the self is unrelated with the mind-stuff, the object-of-the-action, it cannot be the experiencer of this [mind-stuff]. For this would prove too much.' With this in view he asks «How [is this]?» The reply is given in the sūtra. **22. The Intellect (*citi*) which unites not [with objects] is conscious of its own thinking-substance when [the mind-stuff] takes the form [by reflecting it].** What was said before [i. 4] of that [thinking-substance] "At other times it takes the same form as the fluctuations [of mind-stuff]" is based on this. The Intellect's consciousness of its own thinking-substance takes place when the thinking-substance, in so far as it is a receptacle for the reflection of the Intellect, passes into the form of that [Intellect], [that is], passes into a resemblance (*rūpāta*) of the Intellect (*citi*). For just as even without activity of the moon the clear water, into which the reflection of the moon has passed over, makes the moon seem to be quivering, although the moon itself is not quivering, so similarly, even in the absence of any operation of the Intellect, the mind-stuff with which the reflection of the Intellect has become united, makes by its own activity the Energy of Intellect seem to have activity, makes it seem to have attachment even when it is without attachment. The transforming of itself into an object of experience makes this [Energy of Intellect] an experiencer. This is the meaning of the sūtra. This is also the meaning of the Comment. And since it has been explained more than once in various places, it is not explained here.—To show that the fluctuation of thought (*jñāna*) is not distinguished from the fluctuation of the thinking-substance, he quotes the Sacred Word (*āgama*), saying «And in this sense it has been said "... not an under-world."» Just the mental activity of the eternal Çiva, [that is] Brahman, whose nature is undefiled, which changes into an image of Intellect, [and which,] inasmuch as it changes into an image of Intellect, is not distinguished from Intellect even, [the sages] explain as a "hiding-place" (*guhām*). In that same hiding-place is that hidden Brahman; but when that hiding-place is done away with (*apanaye*), [then] Brahman, self-illumined, unobscured, unobstructed, flashes forth for the Exalted [yogin] who has reached his last bodily existence.

And for this reason we reach this result:

23. Mind-stuff affected by the Seer and by the object-for-sight [leads to the perception of] all intended-objects.

For the central-organ is affected by the object-for-meditation, and is itself on account of its objectivity connected by one of its own fluctuations with the subject, with the Self also. Thus the same mind-stuff is affected by the Seer and by the object-for-sight and is seemingly both object and subject. Assuming a form both intelligent and unintelligent, appearing (although really an object) as that which is not object, while unintelligent it appears to be intelligent, [and] like a crystal, is described as [perceiving] all intended-objects. Accordingly there are some, deceived by this resemblance to mind-stuff, who say that [mind-stuff] itself is intelligent. There are others who say that this whole universe is nothing more than mind-stuff, and that this world of things, cows and water-jars and other things, together with their causes, does not exist. They are to be pitied. Why so? Because their mind-stuff, shining forth [in consciousness] in all kinds of forms is the source of error.—Consequently in concentrated insight the object-for-the-insight when once reflected is other than [the mind-stuff] because this [Self] is that upon which [the insight] rests. If this object were the mind-stuff and nothing more than that, how could the insight by itself ascertain its form as being insight? Accordingly when in the insight an object is reflected it is the Self who determines [the object]. Thus, by dividing mind-stuff as such into knower and process-of-knowing and object-for-knowledge, they classify it according to its kinds [i. 41] as a triad also. These are men of complete insight. By them the Self has been reached.

So then since mind-stuff is an object-for-sight and enters-into-mutation, the Self who has the property of immutability has been proved to be over and above the mind-stuff. Now he makes even ordinary perception a means of validating this [transcendence of the Self] in the words «And for this reason we reach this result.» He means to say [we] necessarily [reach] this [result]. **23. Mind-stuff affected by the Seer and by the object-for-sight [leads to the perception of] all intended-objects.** For just as when affected by blue or other [colour], the mind-stuff makes a blue or other object stand before us by direct perception, so the mind-stuff affected by the Seer, in that it has changed into an image of the Seer, makes the Seer also stand before us, by direct perception. For knowledge has two[1] kinds of forms 'I am aware of—the blue.' So although the knower also, like the object known, can be established by direct perception, still special pains were not taken to give a distinct proof of it. Just as the statement 'the image of the moon is in the water' does not mean that the image cannot be directly perceived. And further if you say that this [image] which has entered the water does-not-validate (*apramāṇa*) this [moon], you have no right to say that the [actual] form also of the moon is-not-validated. Consequently the fluctuation of the mind-stuff, in so far as the mind-stuff reflects the [Intelligence], has Intelligence as an object. Still we are able to say that [the fluctuation of the mind-stuff] does not contain Intelligence as an object. This is what is meant by saying that mind-stuff [leads to the perception] of all objects. This same is expressed by the words «For the central-organ.» The central-organ is affected not only by the [external] object-for-meditation, by assuming the form of the intended-object, but as he says «itself . . . also.» The word «also» comes in the wrong place and should be after «the Self.» The fluctuation of the Self is [this] change so that it is reflected in this [mind-stuff]. And this identity of the mind-stuff with the reflection of the Intelligence must have been assumed by the Destructionists (*vāinaçika*). How otherwise could these have attributed Intelligence to mind-stuff—as he says «Accordingly»? The word «some» refers to those Destructionists who hold the theory that there are external things. The word «others» refers to those who hold the theory that there are mental-acts (*vijñāna*) and nothing more. An objector says 'If the mind-stuff only is experienced as having the form of the Seer and the form of the object-for-sight, then surely the Seer and the object-for-sight must be not different from the mind-stuff, as they say, "For although the soul (*ātman*) is not different from the thinking-substance, [still] by wrong-headed persons it is characterized as if it were possessing-a-difference [brought about by] the recognition (*saṁvitti*) of the object-for-knowledge and the knower (*grāhaka*)." So then how is it that these Destructionists deserve our pity?' In reply to this he says «in concentrated insight.» Because in accordance with the arguments already stated they should be led to assume that the Self is something different from the mind-stuff. And by instruction in yoga with

[1] The Bikāner MS. and other texts read *tryākāra*. This would refer to *grahītṛ*, *grahaṇa*, and *grāhya*. Possibly the reference would be to iii. 18, p. 231[11] (Calc. ed.). The double form would apparently be the *viṣaya* and *viṣayin*. The *cittam* is the common medium.

its eight aids which would introduce them to concentrated insight the object of which is the self they should be awakened. To explain: In the concentrated insight the object-for-the-insight, the self, is other [than the mind-stuff] when [the self] is reflected. Why so? Because the self becomes that upon which that [mind-stuff] rests. And if, although instructed by this argument, the opponent perversely should say, 'Why should not that upon which it rests be the mind-stuff itself,' he replies «If this object.» If this object, which is the self (*ātman*), be merely the mind-stuff and not something over and above this [mind-stuff], then how could the insight by itself ascertain its form as being insight? For there cannot be a fluctuation of a thing with reference to itself. He brings the discussion to a close by saying «Accordingly.» One shows them pity by giving them the proper instruction, as he says «Thus.» «According to its kinds» means according to its nature.

And for what reason is this?

24. This [mind-stuff], although diversified by countless subconscious-impressions, exists for the sake of another, because its nature is to produce [things as] combinations.

Although diversified by absolutely countless subconscious-impressions, this same mind-stuff exists for the sake of another, for the sake of the experience and the release of another; not for its own sake. Because like a house[1] its nature is to work as a combination. The mind-stuff must act as a combiner [for the Self] and not for its own sake. Pleasurable mind-stuff is not for the pleasure [of the mind-stuff]. The mind-stuff of thought is not for the thought [of the mind-stuff]. But both of these two kinds exist for the sake of another. And that very Self which has its purpose in the two purposes of experience and liberation is this ‹other›, not any other in general. Any indefinite other as such which the Destructionists set forth in general terms, would all still exist for the sake of some other, since [after all] they [too] act [only] to produce things to be combined. But that particular other which is the Self does not act as a combination.

He introduces another reason for the existence of the self (*ātman*) over and above the mind-stuff by asking, «And for what reason is this?» **24. This [mind-stuff], although diversified by countless subconscious-impressions, exists for the sake of another, because its nature is to produce [things as] combinations.**

[1] See Sāṁkhya-kār. xvii.

Although countless subconscious-impressions of karma and subconscious-impressions of hindrances remain attached to (*adhiçerate*) the mind-stuff only, but not to the Self,—and although, accordingly, the fruitions which depend upon subconscious-impressions, in so far as they are contained in the mind-stuff, would lead one to suppose that mind-stuff is the experiencer,—and although, because all objects-of-experience are for the experiencer, everything would be supposed to be for the mind-stuff,—still the mind-stuff diversified as it is by countless subconscious-impressions must be supposed to exist for the sake of another. Why? Because it acts as a combination. This is the meaning of the sūtra. He explains [the sūtra] by saying «this same.» An objector asks, 'This may be true. But what contradiction is there in supposing that the mind-stuff acts in combination and yet still for its own sake?' If some one were to urge this, he replies «since it acts in combination.» The words «Pleasurable mind-stuff» are a partial expression for experience [in general]. Painful mind-stuff also is to be understood as expressed by these [words]. And when he says «thought» he means release. What he means to say is this. Pleasure and pain may be in essence both counteractive and coactive with reference to the mind-stuff, but cannot be so with reference to themselves. For there cannot be a fluctuation with reference to itself. Neither is there any other thing acting as a combination and itself giving rise, directly or indirectly, to pain and pleasure, for which the pain and the pleasure can be counteractive or coactive. Therefore he who is in no wise concerned either directly or indirectly with pleasure or pain, can be brought into a state of counteraction to them or of coactivity with them; and that one is the permanently detached Self. Similarly that thought (*jñāna*) which leads to liberation, in so far as it also depends upon objects-of-knowledge, and because a fluctuation cannot exist with reference to itself, is not for thought itself. And it cannot be that release would arise when this thought has reference to another. For this would make release impossible in the case of the discarnate and of those whose [bodies] are resolved into primary matter. Therefore [intuitive] thought also is for the sake of the Self only; and it is not for its own sake; neither for any other whatsoever. And if it were for the sake of any other who acted as a combination, the result would be an infinite regress. So it is settled that thought is for another who does not act as a combination.

25. For him who sees the distinction, the pondering upon his own states-of-being ceases.

Because a blade of grass sprouts during the rains we infer the existence of seed. Just so in the case of him who betrays thrills of joy and falling tears in hearing of the way of release, we may likewise infer that there is in him [good] karma rooted in the knowledge of the difference [between the *sattva* and the Self], conducive to liberation, and brought to completion [in the past]. In him, the pondering upon his own states-of-being which is natural[1] to him comes into activity.—When there is none of this (*yasya*) [good karma], this has been said "For [those] who, after having renounced their own nature [of pondering upon themselves], there is by reason of lack [of good karma], a liking (*ruci*) for the opposing view and no liking for the ascertainment of truth—, [for them there is no sight of the distinction and no cessation of the pondering]."—Now-as-to-this-point (*tatra*), the pondering upon his own states-of-being [ii. 39] is in this fashion, 'Who was I? How was I? What is this [birth]? How is this [birth]? What shall we become? or how shall we become?' But this pondering ceases for one who sees the distinction [between the *sattva* and the Self]. For what reason is this? Since it is this mind-stuff[2] which undergoes this diversified mutation. But when there is no longer undifferentiated-consciousness (*avidyā*), the Self is purified and untouched by the conditions of the mind-stuff. For this reason this skilful person ceases pondering upon his own states-of-being.

Having thus enunciated the doctrine about the Self, as based upon reasonings, which is the primary source of Isolation, he discriminates the man who is competent for this teaching from the other man who is not competent. **25. For him who sees the distinction, the pondering upon his own states-of-being ceases.** For one who ponders upon the existence of the Self,—for him, after his instruction in the eight aids to yoga, if he follow [the instruction] up [and] practise yoga, as a result of that [following and practice and] after he sees the difference between the Self and the *sattva* of the mind-stuff, there comes a cessation of pondering upon the being of the self. For one who does not ponder at all upon the existence of the self, the heretic,—for him, incompetent [to receive] the instruction, and failing to make out the existence of the self in this or the other world, [there is] no instruction, no seeing of the distinction, no cessation of pondering upon the existence of the self. Such is the meaning of the sūtra. An objector asks 'How may we conclude that there is in the mind-stuff a pondering upon the states of the self?' In reply to this he says «in the rains . . . just so.» It is inferred that there has been performed in a previous existence a karma which was the following up of the eight aids to yoga, or of a part of them, which is the seed of the sight of the thing-as-it-is (*tattva*) and which is conducive to release. In such a person, unavoidably, the pondering upon the states of the self naturally goes on, even when there is no practice[3] [in concentration] upon the thing. He shows who these persons are who, according to the statements of

[1] Compare the expressions at iv. 10, p. 283[6,7]. [2] Reading *cittasyāivāiṣa*.

[3] Compare the Bhāṣya on iii. 51, p. 265[8] (Calc. ed.).

the traditionalists, are not competent, by saying «When there is none of this (*yasya*) [good karma], this.» The opposing view is that there is no fruition of karma because there is no one in any other world, since no other world exists. There are those who have a liking for this [doctrine] and no liking for the demonstrated truth of the five-and-twenty entities. The pondering upon one's own states-of-being has already [ii. 39] been explained. He refers to the man who sees the distinction by saying «since it is this mind-stuff.» For him who is skilful in the sight of the distinction, pondering upon his own states-of-being ceases.

---

26. Then the mind-stuff is borne down to discrimination, onward towards Isolation.

That mind-stuff of his which formerly was borne onward towards objects-of-sense, down to non-thinking, becomes changed for him. It is borne onward towards Isolation, down to the thinking which comes from discrimination.[1]

Now to the question 'What kind of mind-stuff has the man who sees the distinction?' he replies: **26. Then the mind-stuff is borne down to discrimination, onward towards Isolation.** [This is] explained by merely reading.

27. In the intervals of this [mind-stuff] there are other presented-ideas [coming] from subliminal-impressions.

The mind-stuff which is [borne] down towards discrimination of the presented-idea and the flow of which is towards nothing but discernment of the difference between the *sattva* and the Self, has in its intervals other presented-ideas, either 'It is I' or 'It is mine' or 'I think' or 'I do not think.' From what source? From the dwindling seeds, from previous subliminal-impressions.

An objector says 'This may be so. But if the sight of the distinction has as its final goal (*niṣṭhā*) the discrimination, then the mind-stuff would at no time be emergent. Whereas we see that [the mind-stuff] of one who goes the rounds for alms is emergent.' To which the reply is this. **27. In the intervals of this [mind-stuff] there are other presented-ideas [coming] from subliminal-impressions.** A presented-idea is that by which a thing is presented [to the Self]. It is the *sattva* of the mind-stuff. From this [*sattva*] the Intelligence is discriminated. By this it is [borne] down to [discrimination]. By the words 'I think' liberation is plainly indicated as distinct [from infatuation]. By the words 'I do not think' infatuation is [plainly shown]. By the words 'It is I' or the words 'It is mine', the sense-of-personality (*ahaṁkāra*) and the sense-of-property (*mamakāra*), which are the sources of infatuation, are indicated.—

[1] Compare i. 12.

The compound (*kṣīyamāṇabīja*) is to be analysed [as meaning] seeds which are dwindling. The words «from previous subliminal-impressions» means from subliminal-impressions of emergence.

28. The escape from these [subliminal-impressions] is described as being like [the escape from] the hindrances.[1]

The hindrances when in the condition of burned seed are unfit[2] for generation. Just so a previous subliminal-impression, when in the condition of seed burned by the fire of [intuitive] thinking, does not generate presented-ideas. But because the subliminal-impressions of [intuitive] knowledge are dormant[3] until the task of the mind-stuff is completed, they are not considered here.

'This might be granted,' the objector says; 'but even if there be discriminative thinking, supposing the subliminal-impressions of emergence generate other presented-ideas,—what means is there then for escaping them to the end that they in turn shall not generate other presented-ideas?' In reply to this he says **28. The escape from these [subliminal-impressions] is described as being like [the escape from] the hindrances.** In the case of one whose discriminative thinking is not thoroughly mature, the subliminal-impressions of emergence not having dwindled away generate other presented-ideas. Whereas in the case of one in whom discriminative thinking is mature, the subliminal-impressions have dwindled and are not capable of generating other presented-ideas, just as the hindrances, although arising in the intervals of the discrimination, do not generate other subliminal-impressions. Why is this so? Because in that case these hindrances are in the condition of seeds burned by the fire of discriminative thinking. Similarly also the subliminal-impressions of emergence. —Now these subliminal-impressions of emergence must be restricted by the subliminal-impressions of discriminative thinking, and the subliminal-impressions of discrimination by the subliminal-impressions of restriction. But as for the subliminal-impressions of restriction, we have shown that they are outwardly objectless. The means of restriction must in all cases be considered, [but not the subliminal-impressions[4] of intuitive knowledge], as he says «of intuitive knowledge.» He refers to the subliminal-impressions of the higher passionlessness.

29. For one who is not usurious even in respect of Elevation, there follows in every case, as a result of discriminative discernment, the concentration [called] Rain-cloud of [knowable] things.

This Brahman even in respect of Elevation, is not usurious, [that

[1] See ii. 10–12.
[2] Compare ii. 4 and 13.
[3] See ii. 7.
[4] Because these cease of themselves.

is to say] is not looking for anything [as a reward] even from that (*tato 'pi*); [and] if, even in respect of that, he be passionless, in every case nothing-less-than-the discriminative discernment becomes his. In this way, when, because the seeds of the subliminal-impressions have perished, there do not spring up for him any more presented-ideas,—then the concentration called Rain-cloud [1] of [knowable] things becomes his.

So the author of the sūtras, after describing the Elevation (*prasaṁkhyāna*) as the means for the restriction of emergence, gives the means for the restriction of the Elevation itself. **29. For one who is not usurious even in respect of Elevation, there follows in every case, as a result of discriminative discernment, the concentration [called] Rain-cloud of [knowable] things.** [This Brahman] looks for nothing, for example, dominion over all things. «Even from that» means even from Elevation. [When] on the contrary, he is hindered even in respect of that, and is disaffected towards it, because he sees the defects of mutability, in every case nothing less than discriminative discernment becomes his. This same he explains in the words «even in respect of that.» Whenever presented-ideas of emergence may arise, then this Brahman has not attained to discriminative discernment at all times. After he has no other presented-ideas, he has at all times attained to discriminative discernment. Then the concentration called the Rain-cloud of [knowable] things becomes his. What he means to say is this: When he becomes disaffected towards Elevation and longs for its restriction, he should devote himself to the concentration [called] the Rain-cloud of [knowable] things. And by thus devoting himself to the Rain-cloud of [knowable] things he attains to discriminative discernment at all times. And thus he is capable of making it restricted.

30. Then follows the cessation of the hindrances and of karma. After the attainment of this [Rain-cloud of knowable things], undifferentiated-consciousness (*avidyā*) and the other hindrances are extirpated root and [branch]. And the latent-deposits of karma, good and bad, are destroyed with their roots. Upon the cessation of the hindrances and of karma, the wise man, even while yet alive, is released. Why is this? Because misconception is the cause of the world (*bhavasya*). For surely no one has ever seen the birth of any one whose misconceptions have dwindled away.

And he tells what the purpose of this is. **30. Then follows the cessation of the hindrances and of karma.** But why does he become liberated even while living? The answer is in the word «Because.» For verily the latent-deposit

[1] See i. 2, p. 11[4], and iv. 32, p. 315[5] (Calc. ed.).

of karma kindled by subconscious-impressions of hindrances and of karma is the source of birth and of other [fruitions]. And when there is no source, there can be nothing following from the source, as on this point the Exalted Akṣapāda[1] says "Because we see that persons free from passion have no birth."

31. Then, because of the endlessness of knowledge from which all obscuring deflements have passed away, what is yet to be known amounts to little.

The knowledge which is freed from all obscurations by hindrances and by karma becomes endless. The *sattva* of the obscured knowledge overwhelmed by the *tamas* which obscures it, and kept in motion here and there only by the *rajas*, is set free [from the *tamas*] and becomes fit for the process-of-knowing. In this case when it has become rid of defilement by any of the defilements of the covering, it becomes endless. In consequence of the endlessness of knowledge what is yet to be known amounts to little, to no more than a firefly in the sky. On which point this has been said[2] "A blind man pierced a jewel; one without fingers strung it on a cord; one without a neck put it on; a dumb man paid honour to it."

Now what kind of mind-stuff is there, when thus there is the Rain-cloud of [knowable] things? The reply is this. **31. Then, because of the endlessness of knowledge from which all obscuring deflements have passed away, what is yet to be known amounts to little.** The obscurations are those things by which the *sattva* of the mind-stuff is obscured. The defilements are the hindrances and the karma. The compound is to be analysed into ‹all› and ‹obscuring-defilements.› All these obscuring defilements have passed away from the *sattva* of the mind-stuff. Knowledge is that by which we know—this is the derivation. Because of the endlessness, by reason of its immeasurability, what is yet to be known amounts to very little. For just as in the autumn when the rays of the moon are freed from a dense veil [of cloud], and when they are brilliant in all directions, the light is so endless that water-jars and other things which are to be lightened up [amount to very] little,—similarly owing to the endlessness of light from the *sattva* of the mind-stuff from which all *rajas* and *tamas* have passed away, the things to be lightened up [amount to] little. This same he says in the words «from all.» He makes this clear from the negative side by the words, «overwhelmed by the *tamas* which obscures it.» Kept in motion by the *rajas*, whose disposition is to activity, and hence set free, [because] the *tamas* is removed from the spot. This is the meaning. Hence because by its

[1] Nyāya-sūtras iii. 1. 25. [2] Tāitt. Āraṇyaka i. 11[5].

light it rains [that is] pours down all kinds of knowable things, it is called the Rain-cloud of [knowable] things. The objector says 'We may admit the existence of this Rain-cloud of [knowable] things, the concentration, which is the cause of the subsidence of the hindrances with their subconscious-impressions and of the latent-deposit of karma. But even when this [concentration] exists, why should a creature not be a reborn?' In reply to this he says «On which point this has been said.» If an effect is to take place even when the cause is totally uprooted, then whew! Sir! piercing of jewels by blind men and similar performances would take place before our eyes. And so this proverb popular with reference to any inexplicable thing would be explicable. A blind man pierced a jewel. He strung it, that is, put it on a thread. He put it on, that is, fastened it on. He paid honour to it, that is, spoke in praise of it.

32. When as a result of this the aspects (*guṇa*) have fulfilled their purpose, they attain to the limit of the sequence of mutations.

As a result of the rise [into consciousness] of the Rain-cloud of [knowable] things, when the aspects have fulfilled their purpose, they end the sequence of their mutations. For [the aspects] having completed their experience and their liberation, and having attained the limit of their sequence, are incapable of lingering even for a moment.

The objector says 'The last limit of the Rain-cloud of [knowable] things, the undisturbed calm of thought, the higher passionlessness, may remove to their very roots the subliminal-impressions of emergent concentration, the latent-deposits of hindrances and of karma. Still since the aspects of themselves are disposed to form evolved-effects, why do they not, even in case of such a Self, produce a body and organs and the rest?' The reply is this. **32. When as a result of this the aspects (*guṇa*) have fulfilled their purpose, they attain to the limit of the sequence of mutations.** The disposition of the aspects is such that when they have fulfilled their purpose with reference to any [Self] they do not continue active with reference to that [Self]. This is the point.

What now is this so-called sequence?

33. The positive correlate to the moment, recognized as such at the final limit of the mutation, is a sequence.

A sequence has as its essence a continuous series of moments and is cognized as such at the final limit [or] termination of the mutation. For when a new garment has come to the end [of its newness], there is no oldness, unless [the oldness] has passed through the moments of the sequence. In permanent things also it is evident that there is a sequence. There are moreover two kinds of permanences, the absolutely unchanging permanence and the permanence in mutation. Of these two the Self's permanence is the absolutely unchanging, and the aspects' permanence is in mutation. A thing is permanent when its essence is not destroyed while it is passing through mutations. Both of these two kinds have a [certain] permanence, because the essential nature of them is not destroyed. Of these two: with regard to the external-aspects of the aspects (*guṇa*), the thinking-substance and the others for example, the sequence, having reached its end, is recognizable at the final limit of the mutation; with regard to permanent substances [that is] the aspects (*guṇa*), the end has not been reached; with regard to the absolutely unchanging permanent, the liberated Selves grounded in themselves and in nothing else, the being in themselves is experienced, to be sure, as a sequence, yet it has not reached its end [and is not recognizable at the final limit]. [The sequence is] abstracted from the act of existence and is based upon words [only].—Now has this round-of-rebirths as it exists in the aspects (*guṇa*), either in [actual] motion or in [potential] equilibrium, a final consummation of the sequence or not? This is incapable of answer. How then? A question capable of answer is this, 'Will every one who is born die?' 'Yes, sir.' There is [however] a question capable of alternative answers, 'Will every one after he has died be born again?' The skilful man upon whom discernment has dawned[1] and whose craving has dwindled will not be born again; but any other will be born again. Likewise in case this question should be raised 'Will the human race be more fortunate or not?' A partial answer to this question is this 'It will be more fortunate in comparison with animals; it will not be more fortunate in comparison with gods and sages.' On the other hand a question incapable of answer is this 'Will this round-of-rebirths have an end or will it be endless?' [But] in case there be a limitation [of the question] in either one of two ways, so that there be a consummation of the series of the

[1] Compare i. 16, p. 45[1]; ii. 27, p. 165[5] (Calc. ed.).

round-of-rebirth for the good man, but not for any other, then there is no defect [in the question]. Consequently the only [way] is that this question be analysed.

Meanwhile he asks what a sequence of mutations is by saying «What now is this?» **33. The positive correlate to the moment, recognized as such at the final limit of the mutation, is a sequence.** The sequence of the mutation is that which has the moment as its positive correlate; it is that to which the moments are related. It is that in which the accumulation of moments inheres. This is the meaning. And a sequence can never be explained unless there be that which the sequence contains. Neither can there be a sequence of only a single moment. Therefore the remaining alternative is that in which the accumulation of moments inheres. As he says in the words, «a continuous series of moments.» He gives the source-of-the-valid-idea for the sequence of the mutation by saying «of the mutation.» The final limit or termination of the mutation is the observed fact that even a new garment, although kept with care, after a time looks old. So then there is a sequence of the mutation. And before this point is reached the successive stages of oldness, the slightest, very slight, slight, noticeable, more noticeable, most noticeable, are inferred [already to exist]. This same he sets forth by a negative argument in the words «For when.» The words «unless . . . has passed through» refers to [an oldness] in which a [particular] moment in the sequence has not been reached. The objector says 'Such a sequence is impossible in the case of primary matter since that is permanent.' In reply to this he says «In permanent things also.» By the use of the plural he asserts that the sequence is to be found among all permanent things. As to this he shows first what the different kinds of permanent things are, and then explains how the sequence is found among permanent things in the words «two kinds.» The objector says 'The absolutely unchanging, because it does not swerve from its own nature, may be conceded to be permanent. But how can that which is in mutation, which unceasingly swerves from its own nature, be permanent?' In reply to this he says «When.» External-aspects and time-variations and intensities, of these it is the nature to rise and fall. But for a substance there is no dislodging it from its essential nature. And to the question whether all the sequences are cognizable at the final limit of mutation, he says No. «Of these two: with regard to the external-aspects of the aspects (*guṇa*), the thinking-substance and the others for example.» Since it has reached the end because of the destruction of the properties, [therefore the sequence is cognizable at the end of the mutation]. In the case of the primary cause, however, the sequence of mutations does not reach an end.—The objector says 'Since the original substance undergoes mutation in the form of external aspects, it may have a sequence of mutation. But how can the Self who does not enter into mutation have a sequence of mutation?' In reply he says «with regard to the absolutely unchanging permanent.» Persons who are in bondage, because they assume that they are not over and above mind-stuff, have the mutations of this [mind-stuff] attributed to them. And in the case of the liberated a mutation based upon the [mere] act of existence and having no material existence is wrongly predicated. Since it is a word only, [if we say that the liberated exist,] which comes first, the predicate-relation which follows is based on the act of existence [only and on nothing more], when he says «from the act of existence.» As to the aspects (*guṇa*) it has been said that their sequence of mutation reaches no end.—Not enduring this some one asks «Now?» The words «in equilibrium» mean in the condition of a great mundane dissolution; «in motion» means at the time of creation. What he means to say is this: 'If owing to endlessness, there is no end of the mutations of the round-of-existence, why, then! Sir! how at the time of a great mundane dissolution could it suddenly, for all selves, cease? And how at the time of the beginning of a creation, could the round-of-existence suddenly be produced? Accordingly in a sequence of liberations of the selves, one by one, because all of them would be set free, in a sequence of rounds-of-rebirths all [of these rounds-of-rebirths] would be destroyed, [that is] would reach a final consummation of the mutations of the primary cause. And if this be so, the primary cause itself would prove to be impermanent. Inasmuch also as you are not willing [to admit] that quite a new principle should come forth, you cannot say that [the mutations] are endless. For if that be so, beginninglessness would be contradicted and one would be involved in a breaking of all the statements of the books (*çāstra*).' This is the point. He gives the reply in the words «This is incapable of answer.» This contention does not deserve a reply. In order to show that it is absolutely incapable of answer, he shows that there is a question absolutely capable of answer by saying «A question . . . is.» The question is «'Will every one who is born die?'» He gives the answer by saying «'Yes, sir.'» In other words, 'Assuredly, sir.' Having asked a question which admits of only one answer, he asks a question which admits of alternative answers in the words «'Will every one?'» He shows how it is that this admits of several answers in the words «alternative answers.» He gives another question which also admits of alternative answers and which makes the meaning clear in the words «Likewise . . . the human race.» But this is incapable of an absolute answer. For it is not possible to say absolutely and in general whether the round-of-rebirth of fortunate and unfortunate persons has an end or not. Just as we cannot ascertain absolutely the blissfulness or the lack of blissfulness in the case of all living beings. [This cannot be asserted] with the same absolute certainty as the certainty that all who are born will die. But the question is capable of answer in alternative ways as he says «for the fortunate being.» What he intends is this. The inference is that when there is a series of liberations, all would be liberated and the round-of-rebirths would be cut short. Now this [inference] is based on the liberation established by the Sacred

Tradition (*āgama*). So how can the fact of the validity of the Sacred Tradition that establishes the liberation which we assume, invalidate the same Sacred Tradition with reference to the permanence of the evolved-effects of the primary cause? Therefore this inference, the object of which runs counter to the Sacred Tradition is not the source-of-a-valid-idea. For it is taught in the Sacred Word and the Tradition and the Legends and the Purāṇas that the succession of creations and resolutions (*pratisarga*) is without beginning and without end. And so first of all in the case of all the selves (*ātman*) a simultaneous destruction of the round-of-rebirths is not possible. For even learned men are not grounded in discriminative discernment, although it is to be acquired by the toils of study in a succession of many births. How much less, then, all living creatures in general, both animate and inanimate and so on on, suddenly at one time! For if causes are not simultaneous, effects should not be simultaneous. But discriminative discernment occurs in a sequence, and when numberless beings are liberated in a sequence, there is no destruction of the round-of-rebirth. For living beings are endless [in number], because they are countless. Thus all is cleared up.

Isolation is said to follow after the sequence of the task of the aspects (*guṇa*) has been completed. The nature of this is defined.

34. Isolation is the inverse generation of the aspects, no longer provided with a purpose by the Self, or it is the Energy of Intellect grounded in itself.

When the aspects (*guṇa*), whose essence is causes and effects, are inversely generated,—now that experience and liberation have been accomplished [for the Self] and now that a purpose is no longer provided by the Self,—this is Isolation. The Self's Energy of Thought becomes isolated, since it is grounded in itself and is not again related to the *sattva* of the thinking-substance. Its continuance thus for evermore is Isolation.

In the Pātañjalan authoritative book on yoga, the Exposition of the Sāṁkhya, the Book on Isolation, the Fourth.

The subordinate connexions of the sūtra, whose purpose is to determine the nature of Isolation, [with other topics] he gives in the words «task of the aspects.» **34. Isolation is the inverse generation of the aspects, no longer provided with a purpose by the Self, or it is the Energy of Intellect grounded in itself.** In so far as their work is done, the aspects, no longer provided with a purpose by the Self, are inversely generated. They are resolved into their cause which is the primary-cause (*pradhāna*). Of the aspects, whose essence is causes and effects, the subliminal-impressions of the restriction of emergent concentration are resolved into the central-organ; and the central-organ into the personality-substance; and the personality-substance into resoluble [primary matter]; and resoluble [primary matter] into unresoluble [primary matter]. This resolution (*pratisarga*) of the aspects (*guṇa*), whose essence is causes and effects, is Isolation, the release of some Self from the primary cause.—Or release is the Self grounded in itself, as he says «grounded in itself.» For the Energy of Thought even in a great mundane dissolution is grounded in itself. But that is not release. So he says «again.» The word *iti* in the sūtra signifies the completion of the [authoritative] work.

In this Book he has described first the mind-stuff fit for release, then the perfections of the other world, and of the external objects and of the knower (*jña*), the Cloud of [knowable] things, concentration and the two kinds of release, and incidentally other things. There has also been a description of the source of anguishes, and anguishes [themselves] have been recounted. Here also the two kinds of yoga with the eight aids to yoga have been set forth. The path of release, the distinction between the aspects and the Self, has also been made more clear. Isolation has been discriminated and the Intellect (*citi*) has been made free from the anguishes.

In the Explanation of the Comment on Patañjali's [Yoga-treatise], [which Explanation is entitled] Clarification of the Entities (*Tattva-vāiçāradī*), and which was composed by the Venerable Vācaspatimiçra, the Book on Isolation, the Fourth, is finished.

APPENDIXES

APPENDIX 1

BIBLIOGRAPHY OF WORKS REFERRED TO IN THIS VOLUME

1834–39. **Mahābhārata.** 4 vols. and index, Calcutta.

1837. **Turnour, George.** The Mahāwanso in Roman characters, with the translation subjoined, and an introductory essay, Cotta, Church Mission Press, Ceylon.

1856. **Hall, Fitz-Edward.** Sānkhya-Pravacana-Bhāshya with the editor's Preface, Bibliotheca Indica, Calcutta.

1859. **Çatapatha Brāhmaṇa.** Edited by Albrecht Weber, Berlin.

1861. **Çāṇḍilya.** Aphorisms with the commentary by Swapneśwara, edited by J. R. Ballantyne, Bibliotheca Indica, new series, Calcutta.

1864. **Cowell, E. B.** The Kusumāñjali, Calcutta.

1869. **Rig-Veda-Prātiçākhya.** Edited with a German translation by Max Müller, Leipzig.

1869–74. **Tāṇḍya-Mahābrāhmaṇa** or **Pañcaviñça-Brāhmaṇa.** Bibliotheca Indica, vol. 62.

1873–87. **Jāiminī.** The Aphorisms of the Mímáńsá with the Commentary of Śavara-svámin, edited by Maheśachandra Nyáyaratna, Bibliotheca Indica, Calcutta.

1874. **Āryabhaṭa.** Āryabhaṭīya, edited with commentary by H. Kern, Leyden.

1875. **Jacobi, Hermann,** Ueber tejas, vāyu, ākāça, speciell in der Vāiçeṣika-Philosophie, ZDMG., Bd. 29, p. 241.

1877–88. **Mahābhārata,** oblong folio, Gaṇapata-Kṛṣṇājī Press, Bombay.

1877. **Kālidāsa.** Çakuntalā, the Bengali recension; with critical notes, edited by Richard Pischel, Kiel.

1878–88. **Vāyu-Purāṇa,** edited by Rājendralāla Mitra, Bibliotheca Indica, vol. 85, Calcutta.

1878. **Çāṇḍilya.** Aphorisms with the Commentary of Swapneśwara, or, the Hindu Doctrine of Faith, edited by E. B. Cowell, M.A., Asiatic Society of Bengal, Calcutta.

1880–1906. **Patañjali.** The Vyākaraṇa-Mahābhāshya, edited by F. Kielhorn, Ph.D., three volumes, Bombay Sanskrit Series, xix–xxii, xxvi, xxviii–xxx.

1880. **Mitra, Rājendralāla.** Catalogue of the Sanskrit Manuscripts in the Library of His Highness the Mahārāja of Bikāner, Calcutta.

1880–85. **Vāyu-Purāṇa.** Edited by Rājendralāla Mitra, Bibliotheca Indica. Calcutta.

1883. **Bāṇa.** Kādambarī, edited by Peter Peterson, Bombay Sanskrit Series, xxiv.

1883. **Īçvarakṛṣṇa.** Sāṁkhya-Kārikā, with an Exposition called Chandrikā, by Nārāyaṇa Tīrtha, and Gāuḍapādāchārya's Commentary, Benares Sanskrit Series, No. 9.

1883. **Bhojarājā.** Rājamarttaṇḍa, edited by Rājendralāla Mitra. [See Patañjali: Yoga Aphorisms.]

1883. **Patañjali.** Yoga Aphorisms with the commentary of Bhoja Rājá and an English translation by Rājendralāla Mitra, Asiatic Society of Bengal, Calcutta.

1884. **Morris, Richard.** Notes and Queries, Journal of the Pāli Text Society, London.

1884. **Vijñānabhikṣu.** Yoga-vārttika, edited by Rāmakṛṣṇa Shāstrī and Keshava Shāstrī, Medical Hall Press, Benares.

1885. **Telang, K. T.** A Note on Bādarāyaṇa, the Author of the Brahma Sūtras, Journal of the Bombay Branch of the Royal Asiatic Society, vol. xvi, p. 190.

1885. **Sutta-Nipāta.** Edited by V. Fausböll, and published for the Pāli Text Society, London.

1885. **Dhammasangaṇi,** edited by Edward Müller, Pāli Text Society, London.

1885. **Pārthasārathimiçra.** Çāstra-Dīpikā, reprinted from the Pandit, Benares.

1885. **Grierson, George A.** Behār Peasant Life, Calcutta.

1885. **Bhāravi.** Kirātārjunīya, edited with Mallinātha's comment, Nirṇaya-Sāgara Press, Bombay.

1886. **Divyāvadāna,** A Collection of Early Buddhist Legends, edited by E. B. Cowell and R. A. Neil, Cambridge University Press.

1887. **Āpastambīya-Gṛhya-Sūtra.** Edited by M. Winternitz, Vienna.

1887. **Pāṇini.** Grammatik, herausgegeben, übersetzt, erläutert von Otto Böhtlingk, Leipzig.

1887. **Nārāyaṇa.** Hitopadeça: edited by P. Peterson, Bombay Sanskrit Series, xxxiii.

1887–. **Bhartṛihari.** Vākyapadīya, A Treatise on the Philosophy of Sanskrit Grammar, with a commentary by Puṇyarāja, Benares Sanskrit Series, Nos. 11, 19, and 24 [uncompleted].

1888. **Lanman, Charles Rockwell.** A Sanskrit Reader, with vocabulary and Notes, Boston.

1889. **Garbe, Richard.** Sāṁkhya-Pravacana-Bhāshya, Vijñānabhikṣu's Commentar zu den Sāṁkhyasūtras, Abhandlungen für die Kunde des Morgenlandes, IX. Band, No. 3, Leipzig.

1889. **Vishṇu-Purāṇa.** With ṭīkā, Oriental Press, Bombay.

1889–1911. **Dīgha Nikāya.** Vol. i (1889) and vol. ii (1903) edited by T. W. Rhys Davids and J. Estlin Carpenter, vol. iii (1911) edited by J. Estlin Carpenter, Pāli Text Society, London.

1889. **Jacobi, Hermann.** On Bhāravi and Māgha, Vienna Oriental Journal, vol. iii, No. 2, p. 121.

1889. **Vācaspatimiçra.** Sāṁkhya-Tattva-Kāumudī, edited by Çrībhāratī, the pupil of Bodhāyana, Jāinaprabhākara Press, Benares.

1889. **Dharmottarāchārya.** Nyāya-Bindu-ṭīkā, to which is added the Nyāya-Bindu. Edited by Peter Peterson, published in the Bibliotheca Indica, Calcutta.

1889. **Varāha Mihira.** Pañcasiddhāntikā, edited by G. Thibaut and L. Dvivedī, Benares.

1889. **Whitney, W. D.** A Sanskrit Grammar, Bibliothek Indogermanischer Grammatiken, Band ii, Leipzig.

1890. **Yoga-darçana.** Bhagavan-Mahāmuni-Patañjali-praṇītam, with the Bhāṣya, and the Tattva-Vāiçāradī of Vācaspatimiçra, and a ṭippaṇa by Bālarāma, Calcutta, Saṁvat 1947 [reprinted with unchanged pagination at Benares in 1908 A. D.].

1891. **Kālidāsa.** Abhijñāna-Çakuntalā, edited by Goḍabole and Parab, Third revised edition, Nirṇaya-Sāgara Press, Bombay.

1891. **Ānandavardhanācārya.** Dhvanyāloka with the Commentary of Abhinavagupta, edited by Paṇḍit Durgāprasād and K. P. Parab, Nirṇaya-Sāgara Press, Bombay.

1891. **Garbe, Richard.** Mondschein der Sāṁkhya-Wahrheit, aus den Abhandlungen der k. bayer. Akademie der Wiss., I Cl., xix Bd., iii Abth., München.

1891. **Pathak, K. B.** Dharmakīrti and Shankarācārya, Journal of the Bombay Branch of the Royal Asiatic Society, vol. xxviii, No. 48.

1892. **Vācaspatimiçra,** Tattvabindu, edited by Çrī Gañgādhara Shāstrī Tāilanga, reprinted from the Pandit, Benares.

1892. **Yājñavalkya-Smṛti.** With the Mitākṣarā, edited by Bapu Shastri Moghe, third edition, published by Janārdan Mahādev Gurjar, Ramwadi, Bombay.

1892. **Pātañjala-sūtrāṇi.** With the Scholium of Vyāsa and the Commentary of Vācaspati, edited by Rājārām Shāstrī Bodas, Bombay Sanskrit Series xlvi.

1893. **Garbe, Richard.** Pañcaçikha und seine Fragmente, in Festgruss an Roth, Stuttgart, p. 75.

1893. **Barth, A.** Bulletin des Religions de l'Inde, Paris.

1893. **Açvaghoṣa.** Buddhacarita, edited by E. B. Cowell (Anecdota Oxoniensia, Aryan Series, i. 7), Oxford.

1893. **Bhīmācārya Jhaḷakīkar.** Nyāyakośa, Second edition, Bombay Sanskrit Series, No. xlix.

1893. **Svātmārāma.** Haṭhayogapradīpikā, aus dem Sanskrit übersetzt und als Inaugural-dissertation der philosophischen Fakultät, Section I, der Universität München, vorgelegt von Hermann Walter, F. Straub, München.

1893. **Ruyyaka.** Alaṁkārasarvasva (Kāvymālā 35), edited by Durgāprasād and Parab, Nirṇaya-Sāgara Press, Bombay.

1894. **Stein, M. A.** Catalogue of the Sanskrit Manuscripts in the Raghunātha Temple Library of His Highness the Mahārāja of Jammu and Kashmir, Bombay.

1894. **Sadānanda.** Vedāntasāra, edited by Colonel George A. Jacob, Nirṇaya-Sāgara Press, Bombay.

1894. **Garbe, Richard.** Die Sāṃkhya-Philosophie, Leipzig.

1895. **Vāiçeṣika-sūtras** with the Bhāṣya of Praçastapāda together with the Nyāyakandalī of Çrīdhara, edited by Vindhyeshvarī-prasāda Dvivedin, Vizianagaram Sanskrit Series, vol. iv, Benares.

1895. **Lawrence, Walter R.,** The Vale of Kashmir, London.

1895. **Thirty-two Upanishads.** With Dīpikās, edited by Pandits at the Ānandāçrama. Ānandāçrama Sanskrit Series, No. 29, Poona.

1895. **Patañjalicarita.** Edited by Paṇḍit Śivadatt Rāmabhadradīkṣita and K. P. Parab, Kāvyamālā, vol. li, Bombay.

1896. **Gāutama.** Nyāya-sūtras with Vātsyāyana's Bhāṣya, edited by Çrī Gaṅgādhara Shāstrī Tāilanga, Vizianagaram Sanskrit Series, vol. ix, Benares.

1896. **Warren, Henry C.** Buddhism in Translations, Harvard Oriental Series, vol. iii, Cambridge.

1896. **Bāṇa.** Kādambarī, edited with full Sanskrit commentary and copious notes in English by M. R. Kale, Bombay.

1896. **Yogāvāsiṣṭha.** Mahārāmāyaṇam with ṭīkā, published by Gopālanārāyaṇa, Bombay.

1897. **Kālidāsa.** Ṛtusaṁhāra with notes and English translation by Sitārām Āyangar, Bombay.

1897–8. **Tāittirīya-Āraṇyaka.** Edited by Pandit Baba Shāstrī Phadke, Anandāçrama Sanskrit Series, No. 36, in two parts, Poona.

1897. **Annambhaṭṭa.** Tarka-Sangraha, edited by Yaśavanta Vāsudev Athalye and Mahādev Rājārām Boḍas, Bombay Sanskrit Series, No. 55.

1897. **Suçruta-Saṁhitā.** Translated by A. F. R. Hoernle, Bibliotheca Indica, new series, 911, Calcutta.

1897. **Caraka-Saṁhitā.** Edited by K. Debendra Nath Sen and K. Upendra Nath Sen, Calcutta.

1897. **Kālidāsa.** Raghuvaṅça, edited by G. R. Nandargikar, third edition, published by R. A. Sagoon, Kalkadevi, Bombay.

1898. **Vācaspatimiçra.** Nyāyavārttika-tātparyaṭīkā, edited by Çrī Gaṅgādhara Shāstrī Tailanga, Vizianagaram Sanskrit Series, vol. xiii, Benares.

1898. **Prakāśānanda.** Siddhānta-Muktāvalī, with English translation and notes by Arthur Venis, Benares.

1898. **Kumārila-bhaṭṭa,** Çlokavārttika, edited by Rāma Śāstrī Tailanga, Chowkamba Sanskrit Series, Benares.

1898. La Vallée Poussin, L. de. Le Bouddhisme, Études et Matériaux, London, Luzac & Co.

1900. Macdonell, A. A. A History of Sanskrit Literature, London.

1901. Vijñānabhikṣu. Vijñānāmṛtam, a Commentary on Bādarāyaṇa's Brahmasūtras, Chowkamba Sanskrit Series, No. 40, Benares.

1901. Jolly, Julius. Medicin, in Grundriss der Indo-Arischen Philologie und Alterthumskunde, iii Band, 10 Heft, Strassburg.

1901. Hopkins, E. W. The Great Epic of India, New York.

1901. Hopkins, E. W. Yoga-technique in the Great Epic, in Journal of the American Oriental Society, vol. xxii, part 2, p. 333.

1901. Mammaṭa, Kâvyaprakâśa. Edited, with his own Commentary, the Bâlabodhinî, by Bhaṭṭa Vâmanâcârya, Second edition, Nirṇaya-Sāgara Press, Bombay.

1902. Leuba, J. H. Hallucinations of Light, Revue Philosophique, vol. liv, p. 447, Paris.

1902. Vālmīki. Rāmāyaṇa with the Commentary of Rāma, edited by K. P. Parab, Second edition, Nirṇaya-Sāgara Press, Bombay.

1902. Çūdraka. Mṛcchakaṭika, with the commentary of Pṛithvīdhara, Nirṇaya-Sāgara Press, Bombay.

1902. Manusmṛti. Edited by Vāsudeva Çarman, with the commentary of Kullūka, Nirṇaya-Sāgara Press, Bombay.

1902. La Vallée Poussin, L. de. La Négation de l'âme, Journal Asiatique, 9e série, tome xx, p. 248, Paris.

1903. Rāmānanda Yati. Maṇiprabhā, Benares Sanskrit Series, No. 75.

1903. Rādhakānta Deva. Çabdakalpadruma, third edition, edited by Kṛṣṇagopāla Bhakta, Calcutta.

1903. Bhâskarodayā. A Commentary on Nīlakaṇṭhabhaṭṭa's Tarka-sangraha-dīpikā-prakāsha, edited by Mukunda Jhā, Nirṇaya-Sāgara Press, Bombay.

1903–. Nāgārjuna. Mūlamadhyamaka-kārikās, avec la Prasannapadā, Commentaire de Candrakīrti, publié par Louis de la Vallée Poussin, Bibliotheca Buddhica, iv.

1903. Umāsvāti. Tattvārthādhigamasūtram, Bibliotheca Indica, Calcutta.

1903. Appayadīkṣita. Kuvalayānanda with the Candrāloka, Nirṇaya-Sāgara Press, Bombay.

1904. Bhaṭṭoji Dīkṣita. Siddhānta Kāumudī, edited by Dinkar Keśava Shâstrī Gâdgil and Vâsudev Lakshman Shâstrî Paṇśikar, Nirṇaya-Sāgara Press, Bombay.

1904. Çrīharṣa. Khaṇḍanakhaṇḍakhādya, fascicles 1–9 (1909), Medical Hall Press, Benares.

1904. Takakusu, Junjiro. La Sāṁkhya-Kārikā étudiée à la lumière de sa version chinoise, Bulletin de l'École Française d'Extrême-Orient, tome iv, p. 1, Hanoi.

1904. **Haraprasâd Shâstrī.** Notices of Sanskrit MSS., Second Series, volume ii, Calcutta. [The introduction is bound with volume ii, part ii.]

1904. **Pātañjala-yoga-sūtrāṇi.** With Vācaspatimiçra's ṭīkā and Vyāsa's Bhāṣya together with Bhojadeva's Vṛtti and with Indices, Ānandāçrama Sanskrit Series No. 47, Poona.

1904. **Râmânuja.** Vedânta-Sûtras with the Commentary, translated by George Thibaut, Sacred Books of the East, vol. xlviii, London.

1904. **Brahmasūtra-Shankarabhâṣyam.** With the commentaries Ratnaprabhā, Bhâmati, and Nyâyanirṇaya of Shrīgovindânanda, Vācaspatimiçra, and Ânandagiri, Nirṇaya-Sāgara Press, Bombay.

1905. **Kūrma-Purāṇa.** Published at the Shrī-Venkateshwar Steam Press, Bombay.

1905. **Subhāṣitaratna-bhāṇḍāgaram.** Selected and arranged by K. P. Parab, fourth edition, Nirṇaya-Sāgara Press, Bombay.

1905. **Vāyu-Purāna.** Ānandāçrama Sanskrit Series No. 49, Poona.

1905. **Bhāgavata-Puraṇa.** Edited by Vāsudevaçarman, Nirṇaya-Sāgara Press, Bombay.

1905. **Nāradīya-Mahāpurāṇa.** Shrī-Venkateshwar Press, Bombay.

1905. **Mâgha.** Śiśupâlavadha, edited by Durgâprasâd and Śivadatta, Fourth edition, Nirṇaya-Sāgara Press, Bombay.

1906. **Kielhorn, Franz.** Epigraphic Notes. Nachrichten von der Königlichen Gesellschaft der Wissenschaften zu Göttingen, Philologisch-historische Klasse, Heft 2, S. 143, Berlin.

1906. **Āpodeva.** Mīmāṅsā-nyāya-prakāça, reprinted from the Pandit, Benares.

1906. **Gāruḍa-Purāṇa.** With ṭīkā, Shrī-Venkateshwar Steam Press, Bombay.

1906. **Mādhavācārya.** Sarva-Darçana-Sangraha with the Prasthānabheda, edited by H. N. Apte, Ānandāçrama Sanskrit Series No. 51, Poona.

1906. **Caland, W., and Henry, V.** L'Agniṣṭoma, 2 vols., Paris.

1906. **Jacobi, Hermann.** Eine Jaina-Dogmatik, Umāsvāti's Tattvārthādhigama-sūtra übersetzt und erläutert (Sonderabdruck aus Band LX der Zeitschrift der Deutschen Morgenländischen Gesellschaft), Leipzig.

1906. **Liṅga-Purāṇa.** With ṭīkā, published by Khemraj Shrikrishnadas at the Shrī-Venkateshwar Steam Press, Bombay.

1907. **Udayana.** Atma-Tattva-Viveka, edited by Vindhyeśvaraprasāda-dvivedin, Bibliotheca Indica, new series, No. 1165, Calcutta.

1907. **Udyotakāra.** Nyāya-vārttika together with Vācaspatimiçra's Nyāyasūcī-nibandha, Bibliotheca Indica, Calcutta.

1907. **Içvarakṛṣṇa.** Sāṁkhya-kārikā, with the Sāṁkhya-Tattva-Kāumudī and a ṭippaṇa by Bālarāmodāsīna, published by Jyeṣṭhārāmamukunda, Bombay.

1907. **Jacob, George A.** A [first] Handful of Popular Maxims, Second edition, Nirṇaya-Sāgara Press, Bombay.

1907. Chakravarti, Nilmani. Chronology of India, Journal of the Asiatic Society of Bengal, vol. iii, Calcutta.

1907. Maṇḍanamiçra. Vidhiviveka together with the Nyāyakaṇikā by Vācaspatimiçra, reprinted from the Pandit, Benares.

1907. Kaye, G. R. Notes on Indian Mathematics, Journal of the Asiatic Society of Bengal, vol. iii, No. 7, p. 474, Calcutta.

1907. Asaṅga. Mahāyāna-Sūtrālaṁkāra, Exposé de la Doctrine du Grand Véhicule, par Sylvain Lévi, tome i, Texte, Champion, Paris.

1908. Mahāvaṁsa. Edited by Wilhelm Geiger, Pali Text Society, London.

1908. Pathak, K. B. Bhāmaha's Attacks on the Buddhist Grammarian Jinendrabuddhi, Journal of the Bombay Branch of the Royal Asiatic Society, vol. xxiii, No. 63, p. 18.

1908. Deussen, Paul. Allgemeine Geschichte der Philosophie, Erster Band, Dritte Abtheilung, Die Nachvedische Philosophie, pp. 507–578, Leipzig.

1908. Kālidāsa. Kumārasaṁbhava with the Commentary of Mallinātha (1–8) and of Sītārām (8–17), edited by Vāsudev Lakshmaṇ Shāstrī Paṇsīkar, Fifth edition, Nirṇaya-Sāgara Press, Bombay.

1908. Kirfel, Willibald. Beiträge zur Geschichte der Nominalkomposition in den Upanishads und im Epos, Bonn.

1908. Wogihara, Unrai. Asanga's Bodhisattvabhūmi, Ein dogmatischer Text der Nordbuddhisten, Kreysing, Leipzig.

1909. Jacob, George A. A Second Handful of Popular Maxims, Second edition, Nirṇaya-Sāgara Press, Bombay.

1909. Kane, P. V. Bhāmaha, the Nyāsa and Māgha, Journal of the Bombay Branch of the Royal Asiatic Society, vol. xxiii, No. 64, p. 91.

1910. Jacobi, Hermann. Agastya, Encyclopaedia of Religion and Ethics, edited by James Hastings, vol. i, p. 181.

1910. Jacobi, Hermann. Ābhāsvaras, Encyclopaedia of Religion and Ethics, vol. i, p. 202.

1910. Jacobi, Hermann. Atomic Theory (Indian), Encyclopaedia of Religion and Ethics, vol. ii, p. 199[a].

1910. Jacobi, Hermann. Abode of the Blest, Encyclopaedia of Religion and Ethics, vol. ii, p. 698.

1910. Jacobi, Hermann. The Date of the Philosophical Sūtras of the Brahmans, Journal of the American Oriental Society, thirty-first volume, Part I, pp. 1–29.

1910. Hopkins, E. W. Mythological Aspects of Trees and Mountains in the Great Epic, Journal of the American Oriental Society, thirtieth volume, Part IV, p. 347.

1910. Kaye, G. R. The Sources of Hindu Mathematics, Journal of the Royal Asiatic Society, July, p. 749.

1910. Andersen, Dines. A Pali Reader, Part I, Second edition: Part II, First edition (1907), Copenhagen.

1910. Six Buddhist Nyāya Tracts, edited by Mahāmahopadhyāya Haraprasād Shāstrī, Bibliotheca Indica (New Series), No. 1226, Calcutta.

1911. Dharmakīrti. Nyāyabindu and Nyāyabinduṭīkā, edited by Th. I. Stcherbatskoi, Bibliotheca Buddhica, vol. vii. [This book is in the press; but the proofs have been in my hands.]

1911. Jacobi, Hermann. Zur Frühgeschichte der indischen Philosophie, Sitzungsbericht der königlich Preussischen Akademie der Wissenschaften, 22 Juli, Berlin.

1911. Asaṅga. Mahāyāna-Sūtrālamkāra, Exposé de la Doctrine du Grand Véhicule selon le Système Yogācāra, édité et traduit par Sylvain Lévi, tome ii, Paris.

1911. Jacobi, Hermann. Kultur-, Sprach- und Literarhistorisches aus dem Kāuṭilīya, Sitzungsbericht der königlich Preussischen Akademie der Wissenschaften, Phil.-hist. Klasse, 2 November, Berlin.

1911. Shastri, Haraprasad. Notes on the newly-found Manuscript Catuḥśataka by Āryadeva, from the Journal and Proceedings, Asiatic Society of Bengal (New Series), vol. vii, No. 7, p. 431.

1911. Peri, Noël. À Propos de la Date de Vasubandhu, Bulletin de l'École Française d'Extrême-Orient, tome xi, p. 339, Hanoi.

1912. Shüwo, Benkyo. Doctor Takukusu and Monsieur Peri on the date of Vasubandhu, Tetsugaku Zasshi, vol. xxvii, November–December, Tokyo.

APPENDIX 2

INDEX OF QUOTATIONS IN THE COMMENT

Following the order in which they are cited in the text of the Bhāṣya or Comment, and with indication of their sources.

Synopsis of the sources, with indication of Abbreviations used.

		Anadhikāriṇa Āgaminah.
		Āgama.
		Āmnāya.
Chānd. Up.	=	Chāndogya Upaniṣad.
Tāitt. Ār.	=	Tāittirīya Āraṇyaka.
		Pañcaçikha.
Bṛh.	=	Bṛhadāraṇyaka Upaniṣad.
MBh.	=	Mahābhārata.
		Vātsyāyana Bhāṣya.
Vā P.	=	Vāyu Purāṇa.
		Vārṣagaṇya.
VP.	=	Viṣṇu Purāṇa.
		Vāiyāsikī Gathā.
		Çravaṇa.
		Çruti.
		Saṁgraha Kārikā.

The numbers on the left refer to the page and line of the Calcutta edition of 1890 reprinted in 1908 in Benares without change of pagination, but with slight differences in the lines. Quotations which are not verbally accurate are marked with an asterisk. An interrogation-point, placed after the sign of equality, means that the source of the quotation concerned has not been discovered.

207[7] = Pañcaçikha 11.
213[3] = ?
217[3] = Saṁgrahakārikā.
236[5] = Saṁgrahaçloka.
243[9] = Chānd. Up. viii. 1. 1.
245[4] = Bṛh. ii. 4. 14; iv. 5. 15.
249[7] = Pañcaçikha 12.
255[1] = Pūrvācārya.
272[2] = Vārṣagaṇya.
287[1] = Pūrvācārya.
291[5] = Vārṣagaṇya.
306[4] = Pañcaçikha 9.
306[7] = Āgama.
311[1] = Anadhikāriṇa Āgaminaḥ.
315[1] = Taittirīya Āraṇyaka, i. 11[5].

APPENDIX 3

INDEX OF QUOTATIONS IN THE COMMENT, GROUPED ACCORDING TO THEIR SOURCES

The explanations prefixed to Appendix 2 apply to this Appendix also.

46 [H.O.S. 17]

APPENDIX 4

INDEX OF QUOTATIONS IN THE TATTVA-VĀIÇARADĪ

Following the order in which they are cited in the text of Vācaspatimiçra's Vyākhyā, entitled Tattva-Vāiçaradī, and with indication of their sources.

Synopsis of the sources, with indication of the Abbreviations used.

		Kātyāyana.
Tāṇḍ.	=	Tāṇḍya Mahābrāhmaṇa.
		Nyāya-Kaṇikā.
NS.	=	Nyāya-Sūtra.
Pat. MBhāṣ.	=	Patañjali Mahābhāṣya.
Pāṇ.	=	Pāṇini.
		Purāṇa.
Bṛh.	=	Bṛhadāraṇyaka Upaniṣad.
		Brahma Tattva Samīkṣā.
Bhag.	=	Bhagavad-Gītā.
		Manu.
Māṇḍ.	=	Māṇḍūkya Upanisad.
		Moksa Dharma.
Yogiyāj.	=	Yogiyājñavalkya Smṛti.
VāP.	=	Vāyu Purāṇa.
VP.	=	Viṣṇu Purāṇa.
		Vāinaçika.
		Vāiyākarana.
		Çikṣā.
Çrīhar.	=	Çrīharṣa Khaṇḍana-khaṇḍakhādya.
Çvet.	=	Çvetāçvatara Upaniṣad.
		Saṁgraha Çloka.
Sāṁkh. Kār.	=	Sāṁkhya Kārikā.
		Smṛti.

The numbers on the left refer to the page and to the line of Vācaspati's text in the Calcutta edition. The pages in the Benares reprint agree with those of the Calcutta edition; the lines vary a little. Quotations which are not verbally accurate are marked with an asterisk. An interrogation-point placed after the sign of equality, means that the source of the quotation concerned has not been discovered.

3^{4} = Tāṇḍ. xix. 2. 1.
3^{6} = Bṛh. iv. 4. 23.
4^{9} = Yogiyāj.
20^{5} = Pāṇ. v. 2. 42.
20^{7} = Pāṇ. ii. 2. 29.
27^{7} = *Pat. MBhāṣ. i. 2. 45.
27^{8} = ?
27^{9} = Manu ii. 7.
31^{5} = Sāṁkh. Kār. xlviii.
33^{11} = Māṇḍ. 5 and 11.
44^{10} = Sāṁkh. Kār. xlv.
50^{8} = VāP. ?
51^{4} = VāP. ?
75^{2} = Nyāyakaṇikā ?
75^{9} = Brahma-Tattva-Samīkṣā ?
102^{2} = ?
104^{14} = Saṁgraha Çloka.
106^{1} = VP. vi. 7. 33.

106^{11} = Smṛti ?
106^{18} = Bhag. ii. 47.
112^{4} = Saṁgraha Çloka.
126^{6} = Pāṇ. ii. 1. 49.
129^{3} = ?
132^{10} = ?
132^{12} = Manu iii. 68.
133^{5} = Bhag. xviii. 38.
134^{4} = VP. iv. 10. 9.
137^{5} = ?
142^{1} = Çvet. iv. 5.
143^{8} = Pāṇ. i. 4. 22.
156^{6} = Çvet. iv. 5.
159^{12} = Manu iv. 37.
162^{11} = VāP. lxix. 2.
176^{9} = VP. vi. 7. 36–37.
180^{4} = Pāṇ. ii. 4. 9.
183^{2} = VP. iv. 10. 12.
186^{10} = VP. vi. 7. 39.
190^{4} = Pāṇ. iii. 4. 68.
190^{11} = Manu vi. 72.
190^{12} = VP. vi. 7. 40–41.
191^{11} = VP. vi. 7. 43.
192^{1} = VP. vi. 7. 44.
194^{10} = VP. vi. 7. 45.
195^{11} = VP. vi. 7. 89.
196^{4} = VP. vi. 7. 90.
196^{6} = VP. vi. 7. 92.
197^{6} = VP. vi. 7. 86–88.
210^{7} = MBh. xii. 318. 102.
218^{8} = Çikṣā 13.
225^{7} = Vāiyākaraṇa.
227^{4} = Kātyāyana.
240^{11} = VāP. ci. 85.
248^{4} = Sāṁkh. Kār. xxix.
248^{10} = Bṛh. iv. 4. 3.
254^{1} = ?
279^{6} = VāP. lxvi. 143.
285^{11} = Purāṇa ?
294^{2} = ?
299^{8} = Çrīhar.
304^{4} = Vāināçika ?
308^{2} = ?
314^{4} = NS. iii. 1. 25.

APPENDIX 5

INDEX OF QUOTATIONS IN THE TATTVA-VÂIÇARADI GROUPED ACCORDING TO THEIR SOURCES

The explanations prefixed to Appendix 4 apply to this Appendix also

APPENDIX 6

QUOTATIONS IN THE TATTVA-VĀIÇĀRADĪ NOT YET TRACED TO THEIR SOURCES

APPENDIX 7

INDEX OF WORDS IN THE SŪTRAS

An alphabetic index of the Sūtras themselves is given in the edition of the Bombay Sanskrit Series, and in that of the Ānandāçrama Series of Poona.—This index is designed to include all the words of the text of the Sūtras, and no others. The text is that of the Calcutta edition of Saṁvat 1947 (Baptist Mission Press, A.D. 1891); and accordingly *pañca*, for example, is included. The numbers refer to pāda and sūtra.

The Sūtras contain almost no finite verb-forms (*asti, syāt, kṣiyate, jāyante*), and I have therefore put the participles, not under the verbal roots, but in their proper alphabetic place: so *atīta, apeta, udita, vīta* under *a-, u-, v-*, not under root *i*; similarly *abhijāta, āsanna, utpanna, ukta* (not under *vac*), *a-labdha* (under *al-*); and so the other negatives beginning with *an-* or *a-*. On the other hand, the pronominal forms are assembled in the usual way: *tat, tasya, tāḥ, sa*, under *tad*; *asya, eṣām*, under *idam*; *etena* under *etad*.

abhibhava, abhibhavaprādurbhavāu iii. 9.

abhimata, yathābhimatam i. 38.

abhivyakti, abhivyaktir vāsanānām iv. 8.

abhyantara, ii. 50, 51.

abhyāsa, tatra sthitāu yatno 'bhyāsaḥ i. 13; abhyāsa-vāirāgyābhyām i. 12; ekatattva‿abhyāsa, i. 32; virāma-pratyaya‿abhyāsa i. 18.

ariṣṭa, ariṣṭebhyo vā iii. 22.

artha, çabda‿artha-jñāna i. 42; çabda‿artha-pratyaya iii. 17; cittaṁ sarva‿arthaṁ iv. 23; sva‿artha iii. 35; cittam api para‿artham iv. 24; puruṣa‿artha iv. 34; tad-artha eva dṛçyasya‿ātmā ii. 21; artha-mātra i. 43 and iii. 3; kṛta‿artha ii. 22 and iv. 32; tad-artha-bhāvanam i. 28; bhāvana‿artha, ii. 2; tanūkaraṇa‿artha ii. 2; apavarga‿artham ii. 18; tat-pratiṣedha‿artham i. 32.

arthatā, sarva‿arthatā iii. 11.

arthatva, viçeṣa‿arthatva i. 49; para‿arthatva, iii. 35.

arthavattva, anvaya‿arthavattva iii. 44; arthavattva-saṁyamāt iii. 47.

alabdha, alabdha-bhūmikatva i. 30.

aliñga, liñgamātra‿aliñgāni ii. 19; aliñga-paryavasānam i. 45.

alpa, jñeyam alpam iv. 31.

avadhāraṇa, an-avadhāraṇam, iv. 20.

avasthā, dharma-lakṣaṇa‿avasthā iii. 13.

avasthāna, draṣṭuḥ svarūpe 'vasthānam i. 3.

avidyā, avidyā‿asmitā- ii. 3; anitya‿açuci-duḥkha‿anātmasu nitya-çuci-sukha‿ātma-khyātir avidyā ii. 5; avidyā kṣetram uttareṣām ii. 4; tasya hetur avidyā ii. 24.

aviplava, viveka-khyātir aviplavā ii. 26.

avirati, ālasya‿avirati, i. 30.

aviçeṣa, *1. unparticularized,* viçeṣa‿aviçeṣa ii. 19. *2. failing to distinguish,* pratyaya‿aviçeṣo bhogaḥ iii. 35.

aviṣayībhūtatva, iii. 20.

avyapadeçya, çānta‿udita‿avyapadeçya iii. 14.

açukla, açukla‿akṛṣṇa iv. 7.

açuci, anitya-açuci ii. 5.

açuddhi, açuddhi-kṣayāt ii. 43.

aṣṭāu, aṣṭāv añgāni ii. 29.

asaṁkīrṇa, atyanta‿asaṁkīrṇayoḥ iii. 35.

asaṁkhyeya, asaṁkhyeya-vāsanābhiḥ iv. 24.

asañga, kaṇṭaka‿ādiṣu asañga iii. 39.

asaṁpramoṣa, anubhūta-viṣaya‿asaṁpramoṣaḥ i. 11.

asaṁprayoga, cakṣuḥ prakāça‿asaṁprayoge iii. 2; viṣaya‿asaṁprayoge ii. 54.

asaṁsarga, parāir asaṁsargaḥ ii. 40.

asti, svarūpato 'sty adhvabhedāt iv. 12; tadā kiṁ syāt iv. 16.

asteya, satya‿asteya ii. 30; asteya-pratiṣṭhāyām ii. 37.

asmitā, avidyā‿asmitā- ii. 3; dṛg-darçana-çaktyor-ekātmatā‿iva‿asmitā ii. 6; vitarka-vicāra‿ānanda‿asmitā i. 17; asmitā‿anvaya‿arthavattva iii. 47; nirmāṇa-cittāny asmitāmātrāt iv. 4.

asya, asya vaçīkāraḥ i. 40.

ahiṅsā, ahiṅsā-satya- ii. 30; ahiṅsā-pratiṣṭhāyām ii. 35.

ā, ā vivekakhyāteḥ ii. 28.

ākāça, çrotra‿ākāçayoḥ saṁbandha iii. 41; kāya‿ākāçayoḥ saṁbandha . . . ākāça-gamanam iii. 42.

ākṣepin, viṣaya‿ākṣepī ii. 51.

āgama, anumāna‿āgamāḥ i. 7.

ubhaya, ubhaya‿anavadhāraṇam iv. 20.

ṛtambhara, ṛtambharā tatra prajñā i. 48.

---

eka, prayojakaṁ cittam ekam iv. 5; eka-citta-tantram iv. 16; eka‿ātmatā ii. 6; eka-rūpatvāt iv. 9; eka-tattva‿abhyāsaḥ i. 32; eka-samaye iv. 20.
ekatānatā, pratyaya‿ekatānatā iii. 2.
ekatra, trayam ekatra saṁyamaḥ iii. 4.
ekatva, pariṇāma‿ekatvāt iv. 14.
ekāgratā, cittasya‿ekāgratā iii. 12; sarvārthatā‿ekāgratā iii. 11.
ekāgrya, sāumanasya‿ekāgrya‿indriya-jaya ii. 41.
etad, etayāiva savicārā i. 44; etena bhūtendriyeṣu iii. 13.
eva, i. 44, i. 46, ii. 6, ii. 15, ii. 21, iii. 3, iv. 8.

---

oṣadhi, janma‿oṣadhi-mantra iv. 1.

---

ka, tadā kiṁ syāt iv. 16.
kaṇṭaka, jala-pañka-kaṇṭaka iii. 39.
kaṇṭha, kaṇṭha-kūpe iii. 30.
kathaṁtā, janma-kathaṁtā-saṁbodha ii. 39.
karaṇa, sākṣāt-karaṇāt iii. 18.
karuṇā, māitrī-karuṇā-muditā‿upekṣā i. 33.
karman, kleça-karma-vipāka i. 24; kleça-karma-nivṛttiḥ iv. 30; karma‿āçaya ii. 12; nirupakramaṁ ca karma iii. 22; karma‿açukla‿akṛṣṇam iv. 7.
kalpitā, bahir-akalpitā iii. 43.
kāya, kāya‿indriya-siddhiḥ ii. 43; kāya-rūpa-saṁyamāt iii. 21; kāya-vyūha-jñānam iii. 29; kāya-saṁpat iii. 45, 46; kāya‿ākāçayoḥ saṁbandha iii. 42.
kāraṇa, bandha-kāraṇa-çāithilyāt iii. 38.
kārita, kṛta-kārita‿anumodita ii. 34.
kāritva, iv. 24.
kāla, deça-kāla ii. 31, ii. 50, iv. 9; dīrgha-kāla-nāirantarya i. 14; kālena‿anavacchedāt i. 26.
kim, tadā kiṁ syāt iv. 16.
kūpa, kaṇṭha-kūpe iii. 30.
kūrma, kūrma-nāḍyām iii. 31.
kṛta, kṛta‿artha ii. 22, iv. 32.
kāivalya, saṁyogābhāvo hānaṁ tad-dṛçeḥ kāivalyam ii. 25; sattva-purusayoḥ çuddhi-sāmye kāivalyam iii. 55; doṣa-bīja-kṣaye kāivalyam iii. 50; guṇānām pratiprasavaḥ kāivalyam iv. 34; kāivalya-prāgbhāraṁ cittam iv. 26.
krama, kṣaṇa-pratiyogī pariṇāma‿aparānta-nirgrāhyaḥ kramaḥ iv. 33; pariṇāma-krama iv. 32; kṣaṇa-tat-kramayoḥ iii. 52; krama‿anyatvam iii. 15.
kriyā, kriyā-yogaḥ ii. 1; kriyā-phala ii. 36; prakāça-kriyā ii. 18.
krodha, lobha-krodha-moha ii. 34.
kliṣṭa, vṛttayaḥ pañcatayyaḥ kliṣṭa‿akliṣṭāḥ i. 5.
kleça, pañca kleçāḥ ii. 3; kleça-mūla-karmāçaya iii. 12; kleça-karma-vipāka i. 24; kleça-karma-nivṛttiḥ iv. 30; kleça-tanūkaraṇa ii. 2; hānam eṣāṁ kleça-vad uktam iv. 28.
kṣaṇa, kṣaṇa-pratiyogī . . . kramaḥ iv. 33; kṣaṇa-tat-kramayoḥ saṁyamāt iii. 52; nirodha-kṣaṇa iii. 9.
kṣaya, kṣaya-udayāu iii. 11; prakāça‿āvaraṇa-kṣaya iii. 43; doṣa-bīja-kṣaya iii. 50; açuddhi-kṣaya ii. 28, 43.
kṣi, tataḥ kṣīyate prakāça‿āvaraṇam ii. 52; kṣīṇa-vṛtteḥ i. 41.
kṣudh, kṣut-pipāsā iii. 30.

nitya, nitya-çuci-sukha‿ātma-khyāti ii. 5.
nityatva, āçiṣo nityatvāt iv. 10.
nidrā, abhāva-pratyaya‿ālambanā vṛttir nidrā i. 10; nidrā-smṛtayaḥ i. 6; svapna-nidrā-jñāna‿ālambanam i. 38.
nibandhanin, sthiti-nibandhanī i. 35.
nimitta, nimittam aprayojakam iv. 3.
nimna, viveka-nimnam iv. 26.
niyama, yama-niyama- ii. 29; çāuca-saṁtoṣa-tapaḥ-svādhyāya-īçvarapraṇidhānāni niyamāḥ ii. 32.
niratiçaya, niratiçayaṁ sarvajñabījam i. 25.
nirupakrama, sopakramaṁ nirupakramaṁ ca karma iii. 22.
nirodha, yogaç citta-vṛtti-nirodhaḥ i. 2; abhyāsa-vāirāgyābhyāṁ tan‿nirodhaḥ i. 12; tasya‿api nirodhe sarva-nirodhān nirbījaḥ samādhiḥ i. 51; vyutthāna-nirodha-saṁskārayorabhibhava-prādurbhāvāu nirodha-kṣaṇa-citta‿anvayo nirodhapariṇāmaḥ iii. 9.
nirgrāhyā, aparānta-nirgrāhyaḥ kramaḥ iv. 33.
nirbīja, sarva-nirodhān nirbījaḥ samādhiḥ i. 51; tad api bahirañgaṁ nirbījasya iii. 8.
nirbhāsa, artha-mātra-nirbhāsam i. 43, iii. 3.
nirmāṇa, nirmāṇa-cittāni iv. 4.
nirvicāra, savicārā nirvicārā ca sūkṣma-viṣayā i. 44; nirvicāra-vāiçāradye 'dhyātmaprasādaḥ i. 47.
nirvitarka, smṛti-pariçuddhāu svarūpa-çūnyā‿iva‿arthamātra-nirbhāsā nirvitarkā i. 43.
nivṛtti, pipāsā-nivṛtti iii. 30; kleça-karma-nivṛttiḥ iv. 30; ātma-bhāva-bhāvanā-nivṛttiḥ iv. 25.
nāirantarya, dīrghakāla-nāirantarya- i. 14.
nyāsa, āloka-nyāsāt iii. 25.

---

pañka, jala-pañka-kaṇṭaka iii. 39.
pañca, pañca kleçāḥ ii. 3.
pañcataya, vṛttayaḥ pañcatayyaḥ i. 5.
panthan, vibhaktaḥ panthāḥ iv. 15.
para, 1. *other,* cittam api para‿artham iv. 24; bhogaḥ para‿arthatvāt iii. 35; para-çarīra‿āveçaḥ iii. 38; para-citta-jñānam iii. 19; parāir asaṁsargaḥ ii. 40;
2. *higher,* tat paraṁ [vāirāgyam] i. 16.
parama, paramā vaçyatā ii. 55; parama-mahattva‿anta i. 40.
paramāṇu, paramāṇu-paramamahattva i. 40.
pariṇāma, dharma-lakṣaṇa‿avasthā-pariṇāma iii. 13; pariṇāma-traya iii. 16; pariṇāma-krama iv. 32; krama‿anyatvaṁ pariṇāma‿anyatve hetuḥ iii. 15; pariṇāma‿aparānta iv. 33; pariṇāma-tāpa-saṁskārāiḥ ii. 15; jāty-antara-pariṇāma iv. 2; pariṇāma‿ekatvād vastu-tattvam iv. 14; cittasya‿ekāgratā-pariṇāmaḥ iii. 12; nirodha-pariṇāma iii. 9; samādhi-pariṇāma iii. 11.
paritāpa, hlāda-paritāpa ii. 14.
paridṛṣṭa, saṁkhyābhiḥ paridṛṣṭa ii. 50.
pariçuddhi, smṛti-pariçuddhi i. 43.
paryavasāna, aliñga-paryavasānam i. 45.
parvan, guṇa-parvāṇi ii. 19.
pipāsā, kṣut-pipāsā iii. 30.
puṇya, puṇya‿apuṇya i. 33, ii. 14.
punar, tataḥ punaḥ çāntoditāu iii. 12; punar aniṣṭaprasañgāt iii. 51.
puruṣa, sattva-puruṣayor atyanta-saṁkīrṇayoḥ iii. 35; tat-prabhoḥ puruṣasya iv. 18; sattva-puruṣa‿anyatā-khyātimātra iii. 49; puruṣa-khyāter guṇa-vāitṛṣṇyam i. 16; sva‿artha-saṁyamāt puruṣa-jñānam iii. 35; puruṣa‿artha-çūnyam iv. 34;

vitarka, 1. *deliberation* [*upon coarse objects*], vitarka-vicāra‿ānanda- i. 17. 2. *perverse consideration,* vitarkā hiṅsādayaḥ kṛta-kārita‿anumoditāḥ ii. 34; vitarka-bādhane pratipakṣa-bhāvanam ii. 33.

vitṛṣṇa, viṣaya-vitṛṣṇasya i. 15.

Videha, Videha-Prakṛtilayānām i. 19; bahir-akalpitā vṛttir mahāvidehā iii. 43.

vidvāṅs, viduṣo 'pi ii. 9.

vidhāraṇa, pracchardana-vidhāraṇābhyāṁ i. 34.

viniyoga, bhūmiṣu viniyogaḥ iii. 6.

vinivṛtti, bhāvanā-vinivṛttih iv. 25.

viparyaya, pramāṇa-viparyaya-vikalpa- i. 6; viparyayo mithyājñānam atadrūpapratiṣṭham i. 8.

vipāka, kleça-karma-vipāka‿aparāmṛṣṭaḥ i. 24; sati mūle tad-vipāko jāty-āyur-bhogāḥ ii. 13; vipāka‿anuguṇānām . . . vāsanānām iv. 8.

viprakṛṣṭa, viprakṛṣṭa-jñānam iii. 25.

vibhakta, vibhaktaḥ panthāḥ iv. 15.

virāma, virāma-pratyaya‿abhyāsa-pūrvaḥ i. 18.

virodha, guṇa-vṛtti-virodhāc ca ii. 15.

viveka, viveka-nimnaṁ kāivalya-prāg-bhāraṁ cittam iv. 26; viveka-khyāti ii. 26, ii. 28, iv. 29; viveka-jaṁ jñānam iii. 54; viveka-jaṁ dhyānam iii. 52.

vivekin, duḥkham eva sarvaṁ vivekinaḥ ii. 15.

viçeṣa, 1. *the particular,* puruṣa-viçeṣa i. 24; viçeṣa‿arthatvāt i. 49; viçeṣa‿aviçeṣa ii. 19. 2. *the distinction,* tato 'pi viçeṣah i. 22; viçeṣa-darçinaḥ iv. 25.

viçoka, viçokā vā jyotiṣmatī i. 36.

viṣaya, anubhūta-viṣaya i. 11; viṣaya-vitṛṣṇasya i. 15; sva-viṣaya‿asaṁprayoge cittasya ii. 54; tārakaṁ sarva-viṣayaṁ sarvathā-viṣayam akramaṁ ceti vivekajaṁ jñānam iii. 54; prajñābhyām anya-viṣayā i. 49; savicārā nirvicārā ca sūkṣma-viṣayā i. 44; apuṇya-viṣayāṇām i. 33; bāhya‿abhyantara-viṣaya ii. 51; vītarāga-viṣayam i. 37.

viṣayatva, sūkṣma-viṣayatvaṁ ca‿aliṅga-paryavasānam i. 45.

viṣayavant, viṣayavatī vā pravṛttiḥ i. 35.

vīta, vītarāga-viṣayam i. 37.

vīrya, çraddhā-vīrya-smṛti-samādhi-prajñā i. 20; brahmacarya-pratiṣṭhāyāṁ vīrya-lābhaḥ ii. 38.

vṛtti, yogaç citta-vṛtti-nirodhaḥ i. 2; vṛttayaḥ pañcatayyaḥ kliṣṭa‿akliṣṭāḥ i. 5 [*the list forms the next sūtra*]; vṛttir nidrā i. 10; sadā jñātāç citta-vṛttayas tat-prabhoḥ puruṣasya‿apariṇāmitvāt iv. 18; vṛtti-sārūpyam i. 4; guṇa-vṛtti-virodhāc ca ii. 15; bāhya‿abhyantara-stambha-vṛttiḥ ii. 50; dhyāna-heyās tad-vṛttayaḥ ii. 11; kṣīṇa-vṛtteḥ i. 41; bahir-akalpitā vṛttiḥ iii. 43.

vedana, vedana‿ādarça‿āsvāda- iii. 36.

vedanīya, janma-vedanīyaḥ ii. 12.

vāitṛṣṇya, guṇa-vāitṛṣṇyam i. 16.

vāira, vāira-tyāgaḥ ii. 35.

vāirāgya, dṛṣṭa‿ānuçravika-viṣaya-vitṛṣṇasya vaçīkārasaṁjñā vāirāgyam i. 15; abhyāsa-vāirāgyābhyām i. 12; tad-vāirāgyād api doṣa-bīja-kṣaye kāivalyam iii. 50.

vāiçāradya, nirvicāra-vāiçāradye i. 47.

vyakta, vyakta-sūkṣmāḥ iv. 13.

vyapadeçya, a-vyapadeçya iii. 14.

vyavahita, kāla-vyavahita iv. 9; sūkṣma-vyavahita iii. 25.

vyākhyāta, pariṇāmā vyākhyātāḥ iii. 13; sūkṣma-viṣayā vyākhyātā i. 44.

satkāra, nāirantarya-satkāra‿āsevita i. 14.

sattva, sattva-çuddhi ii. 41; sattva-puruṣayoḥ çuddhi-sāmye kāivalyam iii. 55; sattva-puruṣa-anyatā-khyāti-mātra iii. 49; sattva-puruṣayor atyanta-saṁkīrṇayoḥ iii. 35.

satya, ahiṅsā-satya ii. 30; satya-pratiṣṭhāyām ii. 36.

sadā, sadā jñātāç citta-vṛttayaḥ iv. 18.

sant, sati: *see* sati.

saṁtoṣa, çāuca-saṁtoṣa-tapaḥ- ii. 32; saṁtoṣād anuttamaḥ sukhalābhaḥ ii. 42.

saṁnidhi, tt-saṁnidhāu vāira-tyāgaḥ ii. 35.

saptadhā, tasyasaptadhā prāntabhūmiḥ prajñā ii. 27.

sabīja, sabījaḥ samādhiḥ i. 46.

samaya, jāti-deça-kāla-samaya ii. 31; eka-samaye ca‿ubhaya‿anavadhāraṇam iv. 20.

samādhi, tad eva‿arthamātranirbhāsaṁ svarūpaçūnyam iva samādhiḥ iii. 3; sabījaḥ samādhiḥ i. 46; nirbījaḥ samādhiḥ i. 51; dhāraṇā-dhyāna-samādhayaḥ ii. 29; çraddhā-vīrya-smṛti-samādhi-prajñā i. 20; samādhi-siddhi ii. 45, iv. 1; samādhi-pariṇāma iii. 11; samādhi-bhāvana‿arthaḥ ii. 2; te samādhāv upasargāḥ iii. 37; dharma-meghaḥ samādhiḥ iv. 29.

samāna, samāna-jayāt iii. 40.

samāpatti, tatstha-tadañjanatā samāpattiḥ i. 41; laghu-tūla-samāpatteḥ iii. 42; savitarkā samāpattiḥ, i. 42; Ananta-samāpattibhyām ii. 47.

samāpti, pariṇāma-krama-samāptiḥ iv. 32.

saṁpad, kāya-saṁpat iii. 45, 46.

saṁprajñāta, vitarka . . . saṁprajñātaḥ i. 17.

saṁbandha, saṁbandha-saṁyamāt iii. 41, 42.

saṁbodha, janma-kathaṁtā-saṁbodha ii. 39.

sarva, sarva-jña i. 25; sarva-jñātṛtvam iii. 49; sarva-viṣayam iii. 54; cittaṁ sarva‿artham iv. 13; sarva‿arthatā iii. 11; sarva-bhāva iii. 49; duḥkham eva sarvam ii. 15; sarva‿āvaraṇa-mala iv. 31; sarva-nirodhāt i. 51; prātibhād vā sarvam iii. 33; sarva-ratna‿upasthānam ii. 37; sarva-bhūta-ruta iii. 17.

sarvathā, sarva‿viṣayaṁ sarvathā viṣayam akramam iii. 54; sarvathā viveka-khyāteḥ iv. 29.

savicāra, savicārā . . . sūkṣmaviṣayā i. 44.

savitarka, savitarkā samāpattiḥ i. 42.

sahabhū, vikṣepa-sahabhuvaḥ i. 31.

sākṣāt, saṁskāra-s° iii. 18.

sādhāraṇatva, tad-anya-sādh° ii. 22.

sāmya, çuddhi-sāmye kāivalyam iii. 55; vastu-sāmye iv. 15.

sārūpya, vṛtti-sārupyam i. 4.

sārvabhāuma, sārvabhāumā mahāvratam ii. 31.

sālambana, tat sālambanam iii. 20.

siddha, siddha-darçanam iii. 32.

siddhi, kāya‿indriya-siddhiḥ ii. 43; vyutthāne siddhiḥ iii. 37; samādhi-siddhiḥ ii. 45; samādhi-jāḥ siddhayaḥ iv. 1.

sukha, sukha‿anuçayī rāgaḥ ii. 7; nitya-çuci-sukha-ātma-khyātiḥ ii. 5; sthira-sukham āsanam ii. 46; sukha-duḥkha-puṇya-apuṇya-viṣayāṇām i. 33; anuttamaḥ sukha-lābhaḥ ii. 42.

sūkṣma, vyakta-sūkṣmā guṇātmānaḥ iv. 13; sūkṣma-vyavahita- iii. 25; dīrgha-sūkṣmaḥ ii. 50; pratiprasava-heyāḥ sūkṣmāḥ ii. 10; sūkṣmaviṣayā

HARVARD ORIENTAL SERIES

Founded in 1891 by Charles Rockwell Lanman and Henry Clarke Warren.

Edited, with the coöperation of various scholars, by Charles Rockwell Lanman, A.B. and LL.D. (Yale), LL.D. (Aberdeen), Professor of Sanskrit (since 1880: Wales Professor since 1903) at Harvard University (founded, 1636).

Member of the American Philosophical Society (founded, 1727); Fellow of the American Academy of Arts and Sciences (1780); President (for 1889–1890) of the American Philological Association (1869); President (for 1907–1908 and 1919–1920) of the American Oriental Society (1842).

Honorary Fellow of the Asiatic Society of Bengal (Calcutta, 1784); Honorary Member of the Société Asiatique (Paris, 1822); the Royal Asiatic Society (London, 1823), and the Deutsche Morgenländische Gesellschaft (Leipzig, 1845).

Honorary Member of the North-China Branch of the Royal Asiatic Society (Shanghai), the Finnish-Ugrian Society (Helsingfors), the India Society (London); Honorary Correspondent of the Archæological Department of the Government of India; Foreign Member of the Bohemian Society of Sciences (Prague, 1759); Member of the Colonial Society of Massachusetts; Corresponding Member of the Academy of Sciences of the Institute of Bologna (1712), of the Society of Sciences at Göttingen (1751), of the Russian Academy of Sciences (Petrograd, 1725), and of the Académie des Inscriptions et Belles-Lettres (1663) of the Institute of France.

Published by the Harvard University Press, Cambridge, Massachusetts, U.S. of America. The home office of the Press is at Randall Hall, Cambridge. The Agent of the Press in Great Britain is Humphrey Milford, Oxford University Press, Amen Corner. London, E.C., England.

Direct application for books of this Series may be made, with remittance, to the Harvard University Press at Cambridge, Massachusetts. The volumes will then be sent by mail or parcel-post direct to the buyer.

The list-prices are subject to a trade-discount. No extra charge is made for postage. This list is here revised up to date of December, 1925. Prices of previous revisions are cancelled.

Descriptive List. A substantial pamphlet, containing a list of the volumes, and a brief memorial of Henry Clarke Warren, joint-founder, will be sent free upon application to the Harvard University Press, Cambridge, Massachusetts. — The List tells the general nature and contents of each work of the Series, and the uses which that work is designed to serve.

Externals of the volumes. The books of this Series as a whole are printed on paper of a quality and tensile strength far above the average. They are all bound durably in full buckram. The edges are cut, but the margins are ample; and the tops are gilded, not for ornament, but to make cleaning easy. The backs are properly lettered. No work is issued until it is complete. Volume 10 is royal quarto (32 cm.); volumes 7 and 8 are super-royal octavo (28 cm.); the rest are royal octavo (26 cm.).

For sale or public inspection. A complete stock of the publications of the Harvard University Press is carried by the Oxford University Press in London. Copies of this Series may be seen also at Randall Hall, Cambridge, and at the New York Public Library.

LIST OF THE HARVARD ORIENTAL SERIES

REVISED TO DECEMBER, 1925

Volume 1. Jātaka-Mālā. Stories of Buddha's former incarnations, by Ārya Çūra. Edited in Sanskrit [Nāgarī letters] by Professor Hendrik Kern, University of Leiden, Netherlands. 1891. Second issue, 1914. Pages, 270. Royal 8°. Price, $5.

A masterpiece, as to language and style and metrical form, of Buddhist literature of the Northern Canon. By the Honorable (ārya) Çūra. Stories used as homilies in old Buddhist monasteries. Editio princeps. Kern (1833-1917), long the honored Dean of the Dutch Orientalists, thought that Çūra flourished not far from 600 A.D., or earlier. English translation by Speyer, London, 1895, Frowde.

Volume 2. Sānkhya-Pravachana-Bhāshya, or Commentary on the Exposition of the Sānkhya philosophy. By Vijñāna-Bhikshu. Edited in Sanskrit [Roman letters] by Professor Richard Garbe, University of Tübingen, Germany. 1895. Pages, 210. Royal 8°. Price, $5.

Sānkhya is dualistic. It recognizes souls and primeval matter, but not God. Vijñāna, however, is a pronounced theist. But in spite of his distortions of the original system, his Commentary (about 1550 A.D.) is the fullest source that we have for a knowledge of the Sānkhya system, and one of the most important (Garbe's Preface). Garbe studied the whole work with Bhāgavata Āchārya in Benares. German translation by Garbe, Leipzig, 1889, Brockhaus. Partial English version in J. R. Ballantyne's The Sānkhya Aphorisms of Kapila, London, 1885, Trübner.

Volume 3. Buddhism in Translations. Passages selected from the Buddhist sacred books, and translated from the original Pāli into English, by Henry Clarke Warren, late of Cambridge, Massachusetts. 1896. Eighth issue, 1922. Pages, 522. Royal 8°. Price, $3. Prefixed is a beautiful photogravure of a Gandhāra Buddha.

The seventh issue, 1922, is an abridged one, a reprint of the first part, the legendary life of Buddha. With photogravure. Pamphlet. Pages, 136. Price, $1.

Buddhism portrayed in the words of the Buddhists themselves. The life of Buddha (a beautiful narrative), his teachings, and his monastic order form the substance of this work. The Pāli passages, done into vigorous English and accurately rendered, are chosen with such broad and learned circumspection that they make a systematically complete presentation of their difficult subject. Warren's material is drawn straight from the fountain-head. It is this fact that has given to his work an abiding importance and value. It has been highly praised by competent judges. Moreover, it has enjoyed a very wide circulation in America and Europe and the Orient. And nearly half of the work was included by President Eliot in *The Harvard Classics* (New York, P. F. Collier and Son), of which a quarter of a million sets and more have been sold. The usefulness of Warren's work has thus been incalculably enhanced.

The life of Henry Warren as a scholar is memorable in the annals of American learning. A brief memorial of his life and public services is appended to volume 30 of this Series, of which he was joint-founder. It is also issued with the Descriptive List of this Series (see above, page 1). The List may be had, free, upon application to the Harvard University Press.

Volume 4. Karpūra-Mañjarī. A drama by the Indian poet Rāja-çekhara (900 A.D.). Critically edited in the original Prākrit [Nāgarī letters], with a glossarial index, and an essay on the life and writings of the poet, by Sten Konow, Professor of Indic Philology at the University of Christiania, Norway, and Epigraphist to the Government of India.

— And translated into English with introduction and notes, by C. R. LANMAN. 1901. Pages, 318. Royal 8°. Price, $5.

A play of court-intrigue, and the only extant drama written entirely in Prākrit. It presents interesting parallels with the Braggart Soldier of Plautus.

Volumes 5 and 6. Brhad-Devatā (attributed to Çāunaka), a summary of the deities and myths of the Rig-Veda. Critically edited in the original Sanskrit [Nāgarī letters], with an introduction and seven appendices [volume 5], and translated into English with critical and illustrative notes [volume 6], by Professor ARTHUR ANTHONY MACDONELL, University of Oxford. 1904. Pages, 234 + 350 = 584. Royal 8°. Not sold separately. Price, $7.50

The Great-Deity (-book), "hardly later than 400 B.C.," is one of the oldest books ancillary to the Rig-Veda. It includes very ancient epic material: so the story of Urvaçī, the nymph that loved a mortal (whence Kālidāsa's great drama, Urvaçī). The text is edited in a way that meets the most rigorous demands of exact philological criticism. The typographic presentation of text, version, and notes (critical and expository) is a model of convenience.

Volumes 7 and 8. Atharva-Veda. Translated, with a critical and exegetical commentary, by WILLIAM DWIGHT WHITNEY, late Professor of Sanskrit in Yale University, Editor-in-Chief of *The Century Dictionary*, an Encyclopedic Lexicon of the English Language. — Revised and brought nearer to completion and edited by C. R. LANMAN. 1905. Pages, 1212. Super-royal 8°. Not sold separately. Price, $15.

The Atharva-Veda is, next after the Rig-Veda, the most important of the oldest texts of India. Whitney (1827–1894) was the most eminent American philologist of his century, and these monumental volumes form the crowning achievement of his life-long labors as an Indianist. For his translation, he expressly disclaims finality; but his austere self-restraint, resisting all allurements of fanciful interpretation, makes of his version, when taken with his critical and exegetical commentary, the sure point of departure for future study of this Veda and for its final comprehension.

The text-critical notes form the most important single item of the work. These give the various readings of the "authorities." The term "authorities" includes not only manuscripts (of Europe, India, Kashmir), but also living reciters (the Hindu equivalents, and in some respects the superiors, of manuscripts); and, in addition, the corresponding (and often variant) passages of the other Vedas. Whitney gives also the data of the scholiast as to authorship and divinity and meter of each stanza; extracts from the ancillary literature concerning ritual and exegesis; and a literal translation. Version and Comment proceed *pari passu*. Prefixed is an elaborate historical and critical introduction, and a sketch of Whitney's life, with a noble medallion portrait. A leaf of the birch-bark ms. from Kashmir is beautifully reproduced in color. The typography is strikingly clear.

Few texts of antiquity have been issued with appurtenant critical material of so large scope. And never before or since has the material for the critical study of an extensive Vedic text been so comprehensively and systematically gathered from so multifarious sources, and presented with masterly accuracy in so well-digested form.

Volume 9. The Little Clay Cart (Mrc-chakaṭika). A Hindu drama attributed to King **Shūdraka.** Translated from the original Sanskrit and Prākrits into English prose and verse by ARTHUR WILLIAM RYDER, Instructor in Sanskrit in Harvard University. 1905. Pages, 207. Royal 8°. Price, $3.

A play of such variety, humor, and swift-moving action, that it has often been produced on the modern stage. Version, true and spirited. "The champagne has been decanted, and has not lost its fizz." Noble typography (Merrymount Press). Most books of this Series are technical. This one, like Warren's *Buddhism*, may be happily chosen as a gift-book.

Volume 10. Vedic Concordance: being an alphabetic index to every line of every stanza of the published Vedic literature and to the liturgical formulas thereof, that is, an index [in Roman letters] to the Vedic mantras, together with an account of their variations in the different Vedic books. By Professor MAURICE BLOOMFIELD, of the Johns Hopkins University, Baltimore. 1906. Pages, 1102. Royal 4°. Price, $25.

The Vedas are, in general, the oldest extant records of the antiquity of India, and indeed of Indo-European antiquity. They are the sacred books of the oldest religion of the Hindus. They represent parts of a mass of traditional material, current in the various schools of Vedic learning, and handed down from teacher to pupil by word of mouth. What was originally one and the same stanza, appears in the texts of the various schools in more or less varying forms. The variations are often such as appear in the varying forms of popular ballads or of church hymns. Thus it happens that the texts of these different Vedic schools are often virtually related to each other and to their presumable original, as are the several kindred manuscripts of (let us say) a Greek play to each other and to the archetype from which they are descended. The comparison of these variant forms of a given text is often indispensable for ascertaining its original form and true meaning. This comparison is just what the Concordance enables us easily to effect. It is a tool of the very first importance for future editors and revisers and translators of Vedic texts.

The Concordance covers nearly all the important published texts, and is in one single alphabetic arrangement and one single volume. It is a royal quarto of over 1100 pages, of double columns, containing 125,000 lines or more. For the lines of the Rig-Veda alone, about 40,000 entries are required. The lines of the Atharva-Veda by themselves would require over 18,000 entries, but are often merged with those of their Rig-Veda correspondents. No less than 119 texts have been drawn upon for contributions to the work.

The book was printed (in the early years of the century) in a limited edition of 1000 copies, now half exhausted; and was printed, not from electrotype plates, but from type. The expense in money alone, to say nothing of scholarly labor, was about seven thousand dollars. It is not likely that any publisher or scholar will soon undertake a new edition. For many decades, doubtless, the work will maintain its value unimpaired, an enduring monument to the industry and learning and resolute will of Professor Bloomfield.

Volume 11. The Pañcha-tantra: a collection of ancient Hindu tales, in the recension (called Pañchākhyānaka, and dated 1199 A.D.) of the Jaina monk, **Pūrna-bhadra,** critically edited in the original Sanskrit [in Nāgarī letters; and, for the sake of beginners, with word-division] by Dr. JOHANNES HERTEL, Professor am königlichen Realgymnasium, Doebeln, Saxony. 1908. Pages, 344. Royal 8°. Price, $4.

Volume 12. The Pañchatantra-text of Pūrnabhadra: critical introduction and list of variants. By Professor HERTEL. 1912. Pages, 246. Royal 8°. Price, $2.

Volume 13. The Pañchatantra-text of Pūrnabhadra, and its relation to texts of allied recensions, as shown in **Parallel Specimens.** By Professor HERTEL. 1912. Pages, 10: and 19 sheets, mounted on guards and issued in atlas-form. Royal 8°. Price, $1.

Volume 14. The Pañchatantra: a collection of ancient Hindu tales, in its oldest recension, the Kashmirian, entitled **Tantrākhyāyika.** The original Sanskrit text [in Nāgarī letters], editio minor, reprinted from the critical editio major which was made for the Königliche Gesellschaft der Wissenschaften zu Göttingen, by Professor HERTEL. 1915. Pages, 160. Royal 8°. Price, $4.

For two thousand years and more, the tales of the Panchatantra have instructed and delighted the Hindus. The Panchatantra has exercised a greater influence than any other work of India upon the literature of the world. It was the Panchatantra that formed the basis of the studies of the immortal pioneer in the field of comparative literature, Theodor Benfey. His Pantschatantra laid the foundation of the scientific treatment of the history of the fable. From the Panchatantra there came the lost Pahlavi translation, among whose effluxes are some of the most famous books of south-western Asia and of Europe, the Arabic Kalilah and Dimnah, the Directorium of John of Capua (1270), the Buch der Beispiele (1483) in German of great vigor and beauty, — and so on, down to that gem of racy Tudor English, Sir Thomas North's translation of Doni (1570), reprinted by Joseph Jacobs, London, 1888.

Hertel gives us here one recension of known authorship and date (1199), and another, the Kashmirian, many centuries older. To volume 11, Lanman adds an essay on The Externals of Indian Books. Of the Kashmirian recension, Hertel made a German version (Berlin, 1909, Teubner). The typography of both editions is clear and beautiful. The confusing emboxments of the stories (a second in the first, a third in the second, and so on) are disentangled in a most ingenious and simple way.

Volume 15. Bhāravi's poem Kirātārjunīya, or Arjuna's combat with the Kirāta. Translated from the original Sanskrit into German, and explained, by CARL CAPPELLER, Professor at the University of Jena. 1912. Pages, 232. Royal 8°. Price, $3.50.

The subject-matter is taken from the great epic of India, the Mahā-Bhārata. Like the Ajax of Sophocles as compared with the Ajax of Homer, this poem is an instructive example for the student of literary evolution or literary genetics. For centuries it has been acknowledged in India as one of the six Mahā-kāvyas or most distinguished specimens of artificial poetry, a masterpiece of its kind.

Volume 16. Çakuntalā, a Hindu drama by Kālidāsa: the Bengālī recension, critically edited in the original Sanskrit and Prākrits by RICHARD PISCHEL, late Professor of Sanskrit at the University of Berlin. Pages, 280. Royal 8°. Price, $5.

As descendants of Bhārata, the Hindus are called Bhāratans. Their " continent " is called Bhārata-varsha, and their great epic is called the Great Bhāratan (Story or Fight), Mahā-Bhārata. Çakuntalā is the mother of Bhārata, and the beautiful story of her birth and life is told in the Great Epic. This play is a dramatization of that story, and is the masterpiece of the literature of India.

In 1898, Pischel wrote: " Es ist der sehnlichste Wunsch meines Lebens eine korrekte Ausgabe zu machen." His Prākrit Grammar was off his hands in 1900. In 1902 he was called to the Berlin professorship. The six years of his tenancy were crowded with toil (finds from Chinese Turkestan, etc.). Then came the call to Calcutta, and, in 1908, his death at the threshold of India. Under many difficulties, the book (all but a couple of sheets) was printed at Stuttgart (Kohlhammer). Then came the world-conflagration. . . . The printed sheets reached America November 28, 1923.

Volume 17. The Yoga-system of Patañjali, or the ancient Hindu doctrine of concentration of mind. Embracing the Mnemonic Rules, called Yoga-sūtras, of Patañjali; and the Comment, called Yoga-bhāshya, attributed to Veda-Vyāsa; and the Explanation, called Tattva-vāiçāradī, of Vāchaspati-Miçra. Translated from the original Sanskrit by JAMES HAUGHTON WOODS, Professor of Philosophy in Harvard University. 1914. Pages, 422. Royal 8°. Price $5.

Three works in one pair of covers. The Rules are a set of mental pegs on which to hang the principles and precepts of a system which you must learn from the living teacher of your "school." The Comment is a reinvestiture of the skeleton of the Rules with the flesh and blood of comprehensible details. And the Explanation is of course a commentary on the Comment. The Comment is the oldest written systematic exposition of Yoga-doctrine in Sanskrit that we possess.

Of the Hindu philosophies, by far the most important are the ancient dualism called Sānkhya, the monism of the Vedānta, and the Yoga-system. Kāuṭilya, prime-minister of Chandragupta (300 B.C.), mentions Sānkhya and Yoga as current in his day. But the elements of Yoga, rigorous austerities and control of the senses, are indefinitely antique, and are one of the oldest and most striking products of the Hindu mind and character.

When one considers the floods of pseudo-scientific writing with which the propagandists of Indian "isms" in America have deluged us, one is the better prepared to appreciate the self-restraint of Dr. Woods in keeping all that pertains to miracle-mongering and sensationalism in the background, and in devoting himself to the exposition of the spiritual and intellectual aspects of Yoga. His work "continues the tradition of austere scholarship" which has, from the beginning, characterized the Harvard Oriental Series.

Volumes 18 and 19. The Veda of the Black Yajus School, entitled Tāittirīya Samhitā. Translated from the original Sanskrit prose and verse, with a running commentary. By Arthur Berriedale Keith, D.C.L. (Oxford), of the Inner Temple, Barrister-at-law, and of His Majesty's Colonial Office, sometime Acting Professor of Sanskrit at the University of Oxford, Author of 'Responsible Government in the Dominions.' Volume 18, kāṇḍas I–III; volume 19, kāṇḍas IV–VII. 1914. Pages, 464 + 374 = 838. Royal 8°. Price, $10. Not sold separately.

The Rig-Veda holds unquestioned primacy in the sacred literature of the Hindus; but their greatest mediæval scholiast on the Vedas, Sāyaṇa, did not write his commentary on the Rig-Veda until after his commentary on the Yajur-Veda, because (as he expressly tells us) of the transcendent importance of the Yajur-Veda for the sacrifice. The Yajur-Veda is the Veda of sacrificial formulas. An accurate edition of the Tāittirīya-Samhitā was published in 1871–2 by Weber. It waited nigh fifty years for a translator.

For the difficult task of translation, no English or American Sanskritist was so well qualified by previous studies as Keith. To it he has brought his wide and varied learning, and with such effectiveness as to produce a work, which, in spite of its large extent, is notable for its well-rounded completeness. The entire text is translated. The commentary runs *pari passu* with the version, embodies the gist of Sāyaṇa's scholia, and is presented with the utmost typographical perspicuity. An elaborate introduction is given, treating of the relation of this text to kindred texts, its contents, language, style, and date ('about 600 B.C.'), and the religious ritual of ancient India.

Volumes 20 and 24. Rig-Veda Repetitions. The repeated verses and distichs and stanzas of the Rig-Veda in systematic presentation and with critical discussion. By Maurice Bloomfield, Professor of Sanskrit and Comparative Philology in the Johns Hopkins University, Baltimore. 1916. Pages, 508 + 206 = 714. Royal 8°. Not sold separately. Price, $10.

Volume 20 contains Part 1: The repeated passages of the Rig-Veda, systematically presented in the order of the Rig-Veda, with critical comments and notes. Volume 24 contains Part 2: Comments and classifications from metrical and lexical and grammatical points of view, and from the point of view of the themes and divinities of the repeated passages. Also Part 3: Lists and indexes.

The aim of this work is to help us to understand the oldest religious document of Indo-European antiquity. The arrangement of Part 1 enables the student to bring under his eye at one time all the passages that he needs to compare, and to do so with utmost ease and speed. The material of this work was, from a typographical point of view, exceedingly intractable. The result as a whole is a marvel of clarity and convenience.

This work is the first of three natural sequels to Bloomfield's great Vedic Concordance: 1. The Rig-Veda Repetitions; 2. The Reverse Concordance; 3. The Vedic Variants. A draft of the second has been actually prepared by Bloomfield. And he and Edgerton have in hand the first draft of the third, a systematic presentation and critical discussion of the variant readings of the Vedic texts.

Volumes 21 and 22 and 23. Râma's Later History, or Uttara-Râma-Charita, an ancient Hindu drama by Bhavabhūti. Critically edited in the original Sanskrit and Prākrit, with an introduction and English translation and notes and variants, etc. By Shripad Krishna Belvalkar, Graduate Student of Harvard University. (Now, 1920, Professor of Sanskrit at Deccan College, Poona, India.)

Dr. Belvalkar, when returning to India in 1914 from his studies at Harvard, shipped his manuscript-collations and other papers and his books by the German freighter, Fangturm. In August, 1914, the Fangturm was interned at the port of Palma, Balearic Islands. In 1919, she was released. In May, 1920, Dr. Belvalkar recovered his papers.

Volume 21 was issued in 1915, complete.

Of volume 22, the first 92 pages, containing the text of the whole play, have been in print since January, 1915, awaiting for nigh five and one-half years the recovery of the material for the rest of the book.

Of volume 23, the material included collation-sheets giving the readings of manuscripts from widely-separated parts of India, from Nepal to Madras, from Calcutta to Bombay. In spite of the generous assistance of His Majesty's Secretary of State for India in Council, the work of getting the loan of these mss. was so great that it seemed best not to try to do it again, but to await the release of the Fangturm. — There is hope now that volumes 22 and 23 may be issued.

Volume 21. Râma's Later History. Part 1. Introduction and translation. (Prefixed is a convenient synoptic analysis of the play. The introduction treats of Bhavabhūti's life and date and works, and includes a summary of the Rāma-story as given by the Rāmāyaṇa. Lanman adds an essay entitled 'A method for citing Sanskrit dramas.' The method is very simple and practical.) 1915. Royal 8°. Pages 190. Price, $3.

Volume 22. Râma's Later History. Part 2. The text, with index, glossaries, etc. (This was printed at Bombay, with the exquisitely beautiful type, newly cast for this work, of Jāvajī's Nirṇaya Sāgara Press, and upon paper made expressly for this edition at the Wolvercote Mill of Oxford. Each Prākrit speech is followed by the Sanskrit version in immediate sequence.) See above.

Volume 23. Râma's Later History. Part 3. Explanatory and critical epilogue. (Critical account of the manuscripts. Running expository comment. The variant readings of the mss. The typographical 'make-up' of Comment and Variants into pages is such that they go *pari passu*. These epilegomena close with an essay on the two text-traditions of the play, a time-analysis, a note on the Hindu stage, etc.) See above.

Volume 24. Rig-Veda Repetitions. Parts 2 and 3. By Professor Bloomfield. Described above, with volume 20.

Volume 25. Rig-Veda Brāhmaṇas: The Aitareya and Kauṣītaki Brāhmaṇas of the Rig-Veda. Translated from the original Sanskrit. By ARTHUR BERRIEDALE KEITH, D.C.L., D.Litt., of the Inner Temple, Barrister-at-law, Regius Professor of Sanskrit and Comparative Philology at the University of Edinburgh. 1920. Pages, 567. Royal 8°. Price $7.50.

In August, 1915, this work was ready for printing. In August, 1916, it was delivered to the Controller of the Oxford University Press. In 1918, the Press had nigh 350 men at the war. Of the older men who were left, many were busy with urgent war-work, such as a Report on Trench-fever for the American Expeditionary Force. And when, after the armistice, the printing was resumed, the author was engrossed in the work of Lord Crewe's Committee on the Home Administration of Indian Affairs.

The Vedic literature falls into three clearly sundered groups: the Vedic hymns or Mantras; the Brāhmaṇas, 'the priestlies' or 'priestly (discourses)'; and the Sūtras. Keith thinks that the Aitareya is not later than 600 B.C. The plan of the work is like that of volumes 18–19: elaborate introduction; translation; running comment on the same page. The skill of the priestly story-tellers is at its best in the splendid legend of Çunaḥçepa (threatened sacrifice of son by father: cf. Isaac, Iphigeneia, Phrixos). Despite the pseudo-profundity and puerility of the Brāhmaṇas, they are of genuine significance to the student of Hindu antiquity, social and religious. And they are in fact the oldest Indo-European prose extant.

Volumes 26 and 27. Vikrama's Adventures, or The Thirty-two Tales of the Throne. A collection of stories about King Vikrama, as told by the Thirty-two Statuettes that supported his throne. Edited in four different recensions of the Sanskrit original (Vikrama-charita or Sinhāsana-dvātrinçakā) and translated into English with an introduction, by FRANKLIN EDGERTON. Professor of Sanskrit at the University of Pennsylvania. 1926. Pages, 372 + 384 = 756. Royal 8°. Not sold separately. Price, $10.

Vikrama's Adventures is one of the most famous story-books of mediæval India. Vikrama is one of the most noted quasi-historical heroes of his times. His magic throne, hidden upon his death, is discovered by a later king, Bhoja. Each of the thirty-two (dvā-trinçat) statuettes that support his throne (sinhāsana) tells one story to Bhoja. Hence the alternative title. The theme of the tales is Vikrama, who is meant to serve as a kind of Hindu King Arthur, an example for real kings.

Edgerton hopes that his work may prove suggestive as a model for students of comparative literature. The text of each of the recensions (Southern, Metrical, Brief, Jain) is printed in horizontally parallel arrangement, so that the stories which correspond to each other in substance are given, each story in all four recensions, in immediate juxtapositon. And the translation is treated in like manner. Comparisons are thus facilitated to a degree never before attained in a work of this kind.

From all this, Edgerton reconstructs, with some detail, and with reasonable certainty, the original work from which the current versions are derived. This he presents in the form of a Composite Outline, the concrete solution of a problem in literary genetics.

Volumes 28 and 29 and 30. Buddhist Legends. Translated from the original Pāli text of the Dhammapada Commentary, by EUGENE WATSON BURLINGAME, Fellow of the American Academy of Arts and Sciences, sometime Harrison Fellow for Research at the University of Pennsylvania, and Johnston Scholar in Sanskrit at the Johns Hopkins University, and Lecturer on Pāli in Yale University. 1921. Pages, 366 + 370 + 378 = 1114. Royal 8°. Not sold separately. Price $20.

Dhámma-pada, or Way of Righteousness, is the name of one of the canonical books of the Buddhist Sacred Scriptures. It consists of 423 stanzas. These are reputed to be the very words of the Buddha himself. The Dhammapada Commentary, composed by an unknown author in Ceylon about 450 A.D., purports to tell the circumstances under which Buddha uttered each one of these stanzas. In telling them, it narrates 299 stories or legends. These stories are the preponderating element of the Commentary, and it is these which are here translated.

In style and substance the tales resemble those of the famous Jātaka Book, the Buddhist Acta Sanctorum, a counterpart of the Legends of the Christian Saints. And they present many parallels to well-known stories of mediæval literature, Oriental and European. For the comparative study of such parallels, Dr. Burlingame's Synopses, clear and brief, will prove a very great convenience. His vigorous diction suggests familiarity with such " wells of English undefyled " as the Bible and the Book of Common Prayer. The work gives a vivid picture of the every-day life of the ancient Buddhists — monks, nuns, lay disciples. It is thus, incidentally, an admirable preparative for the study of the more difficult Buddhist books in the original. As especially attractive stories may be cited: Lean Gotamī seeks mustard-seed to cure her dead child; Murder of Great Moggallāna; Buddha falsely accused by Chinchā; Visākhā; the Hell-pot. A critical and historical introduction is prefixed. At the end is an *intelligent* index, modeled after that of George Foot Moore's *History of Religions*.

In September, 1909, Mr. Burlingame came to Harvard University to pursue his studies with Mr. Lanman. It was at the suggestion of the latter that Mr. Burlingame undertook the task of translating into English the Dhammapada Commentary. He first made a table of contents of the work, giving the title of each story and the place of its occurrence in the Burmese text and also in the Cingalese text. He added an index to the titles, and an extremely good analysis of Books 1 to 4. This most useful preliminary work was formally presented to the American Academy of Arts and Sciences on December 8, 1909, by Mr. Lanman. The manuscript of the article was delivered February 5, 1910, and published soon after as pages 467–550 of volume 45 of the Proceedings of the Academy. The admirably elaborated manuscript of the entire translation of the Dhammapada Commentary was delivered by its author on January 10, 1917, just before the War.

Volumes 31 and 32. The Religion and Philosophy of the Veda and Upanishads. By ARTHUR BERRIEDALE KEITH, D.C.L., D.Litt., Of the Inner Temple, Barrister-at-Law, and of the Scottish Bar; Regius Professor of Sanskrit at the University of Edinburgh. 1925. Pages, 384 + 332 = 716. Royal 8°. Not sold separately. Price, $10.

This work, which owes its inception to the suggestion of Professor Charles R. Lanman of Harvard University, endeavors to present to the student of religion a comprehensive but concise account of the whole of the religion and philosophy of the Vedic period in India (1500–500 B.C.). The author has made full use of recent research into the origin and development of religion, and, while dealing clearly and fully with Vedic Mythology, has devoted special attention to such vital questions as the relation of the worshippers to their gods, and the existence of higher and lower strata of religious thought and action. The description of the ritual is the most elaborate yet attempted in English, and due care has been taken to detach what is essential from the vast mass of details given in the original sources. Of special interest at the present time, when public attention is again being attracted to the modern Theosophy which claims Indian inspiration ,is the account of the beginnings of Indian Philosophy in the hymns of the Rigveda and of its development in the Upanishads. The author writes, critically but with great appreciation, of the remarkable intellectual efforts of these early seekers after truth, who would, it may be asserted, have learned with equal surprise and regret of the strange transmutations which their profound doctrines have undergone at alien hands.

THE HARVARD UNIVERSITY PRESS

publishes other works relating to India, as follows:

Sanskrit Reader: Text and Vocabulary and Notes. By CHARLES ROCKWELL LANMAN, Wales Professor of Sanskrit at Harvard University. Seventh issue, 1920. Royal 8°. Pages, 430. Price, $3.

The Reader furnishes the text for 60 or 80 lessons, and with it the needed lexicon and notes. The notes make constant reference to Whitney's Sanskrit Grammar: see below. These two volumes supply all that is strictly indispensable for the beginner. The text is in the Oriental (Nāgarī) letters; but a transliteration of the first four pages in Roman letters is added. The Reader is designed especially to meet the needs of those who have not the aid of a teacher.

The text is chosen: 1. from Classical Sanskrit works (Nala-story, fables of Hitopadeça, "Manu's Laws"); and 2. from the Vedic literature (Rig-Veda hymns, Brāhmaṇas, Sūtras for wedding and burial). A literary-historical introduction is given for each kind of text. The vocabulary is in Roman letters, and is elaborated with the utmost care. Special heed is given to the development of the meanings (semantics: pāda, foot, leg, leg of lamb, quarter, quarter of a four-lined stanza, line, line of a three-lined stanza), and also to the etymological cognates in English, Greek, and so on (ta-d, τό, ðæ-t tha-t, is-tu-d).

Parts of Nala and Hitopadesha in English letters. Prepared by C. R. LANMAN. 1889. Royal 8°. Pages, 50. Price, 50 cents.

A reprint of the first 44 pages of the Reader (see above), transliterated from the Oriental characters into English letters. It corresponds page for page and line for line with its original, so that the references of the Vocabulary and Notes of the Reader apply exactly to this reprint. With the Grammar and Reader and this reprint, the student is enabled to acquire a knowledge of the structure of the Sanskrit and to do some reading, without first learning the Oriental letters.

Sanskrit Grammar: including both the Classical language, and the older dialects of Veda and Brāhmaṇa. By WILLIAM DWIGHT WHITNEY, late Professor of Sanskrit at Yale University. Fifth issue, 1923, of second edition, 1889. 8°. Pages, 578. Price, $4.50.

The greatest extant repository of the grammatical facts concerning the Sanskrit language. A masterpiece of orderly arrangement. Prefixed is a brief account of the literature of India.

Vedanta Philosophy. Outline of the Vedanta system of philosophy according to Shankara. By PAUL DEUSSEN. Translated by JAMES H. WOODS, Professor of Philosophy at Harvard University, and CATHARINE B. RUNKLE of Cambridge, Massachusetts. Second edition. 1915. 8°. Pages, 56. Price, $1.

This book, a translation of the summary given by Deussen at the end of his monumental work, Das System des Vedanta, was first published in 1906. Since then, thanks to the learning and enthusiasm of Charles Johnston, the whole great work has been made accessible in an English version (Chicago, 1912, The Open Court Publishing Company). Nevertheless, the small book was so inexpensive and practical that a new edition was made in 1915. The summary, although brief and compact, is yet so lucid and adequate, — in short, so altogether admirable, that it is not likely soon to be superseded by a better exposition of what has been to untold millions at once a philosophy and a religion.